alles klar?

Beginning German in a Global Context

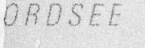

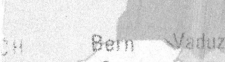
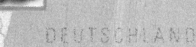

Karl F. Otto, Jr.
University of Pennsylvania

Keri L. Bryant
Murray State University

Wolff von Schmidt
University of Utah

p. 6p 7 ß8 ♂89
199

Prentice Hall Upper Saddle River, NJ 07458

Executive Editor: Laura McKenna
Director of Development: Marian Wassner
Assistant Editor: María F. García
Editorial Assistant: Karen George

Senior Managing Editor: Debbie Brennan
Project Editor: Jacqueline Bush
Graphic Project Coordinator: Ximena de la Piedra
Illustrator: Andrew Lange
Realia Design: Siren Design
Page Layout: Siren Design
Interior Design: Hothouse, Ximena de la Piedra
Manufacturing Buyer: Tricia Kenny, Nick Sklitsis

Printed in the United States of America
10   9   8   7   6   5   4   3   2   1

ISBN   0-13-249905-3

Prentice Hall International (UK) Limited, *London*
Prentice Hall of Australia Pty. Limited, *Sydney*
Prentice Hall Canada Inc., *Toronto*
Prentice Hall Hispanoamericana, S. A., *México*
Prentice Hall of India Private Limited, *New Delhi*
Prentice Hall of Japan, Inc., *Tokyo*
Simon & Schuster Asia Pte. Ltd., *Singapore*
Editora Prentice Hall do Brasil, Ltda., *Rio de Janeiro*

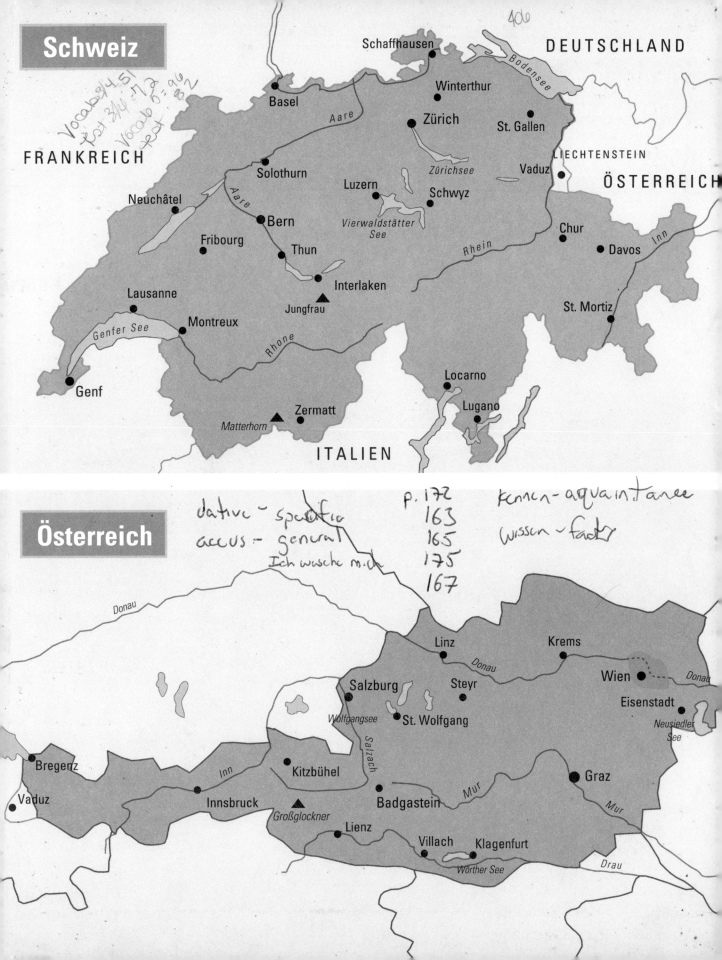

Schweiz

DEUTSCHLAND

Schaffhausen
Winterthur
Basel
Zürich
St. Gallen
Bodensee
Aare
FRANKREICH
LIECHTENSTEIN
Solothurn
Vaduz
ÖSTERREICH
Luzern
Schwyz
Zürichsee
Neuchâtel
Aare
Bern
Vierwaldstätter See
Fribourg
Chur
Thun
Davos
Rhein
Inn
Interlaken
Jungfrau
Lausanne
St. Moritz
Montreux
Genfer See
Rhone
Genf
Locarno
Zermatt
Lugano
Matterhorn
ITALIEN

Vocab 4.51
Test 3/4 :17.2
Vocab b = 96
Test 82
400

Österreich

dative – specific
accus – general
Ich wasche mich

p. 172
163
165
175
167

kennen – aquaintance
wissen – fact

Donau
Linz
Krems
Salzburg
Steyr
Wien
Donau
Donau
Eisenstadt
Wolfgangsee
St. Wolfgang
Neusiedler See
Bregenz
Salzach
Kitzbühel
Inn
Mur
Graz
Vaduz
Innsbruck
Großglockner
Badgastein
Mur
Lienz
Villach
Klagenfurt
Drau
Wörther See

Table of Contents

Kapitel 6: Ich bin gesund! 155

Kapitel 7: Laß uns zusammen etwas unternehmen! 187

Kapitel 8: Ja, gerne, aber... 221

Kapitel 9: Guten Appetit! 251

Kapitel 10: Unterwegs 281

Die ersten Schritte

Na, los!

Die ersten Schritte

Na, los!

Scope and Sequence

Die ersten Schritte

Na, los!

Preface

Alles klar? is a new beginning German program that presents the essentials of grammar and offers a four-skills approach to the language and culture of the German-speaking countries. Informed by a variety of pedagogical approaches and techniques and supported by carefully integrated supplementary materials, the program is the result of years of market research, development, class-testing, and revision.

Alles klar? is eclectic in its design and approach. The text's flexible format, reduced grammatical syllabus, and innovative ancillary package offer instructors and students a range of choices to suit individual goals, curricula, interests, and methodological preferences.

Highlights of the Program

Emphasis on communicative competency. *Alles klar?* is a versatile program that can be adapted to many teaching styles. At the same time it aims to meet the increasing demand for a communicatively-oriented, rather than a grammar-based, curriculum. To that end, grammatical structures are not introduced and practiced in isolated sentences. Instead, they are presented within cultural themes and language functions. Numerous group- and pair-activities provide students with ample opportunity to build and increase their communication skills. These skills are further reinforced in the information gap activities (*Zu zweit*) and the role-play activities (*Situationen*) at the end of every chapter.

Broadened cultural discussions. The authors of *Alles klar?* recognize that although beginning students may be limited in their ability to discuss issues and questions associated with multiculturalism, they are capable of making observations about the diverse nature of culture(s) in photographs, dialogues, and reading texts. In this way, the German-speaking countries are represented throughout *Alles klar?* as multicultural and multiracial societies. Emphasis has been placed on presenting a true picture of the diverse composition of contemporary German-speaking countries and on fostering opportunities for students to explore new and sometimes controversial materials. Additionally, the use of German as an international language of business, research, and other endeavors is featured in *Alles klar?*, especially in the *Überall spricht man Deutsch* sections.

Reduced grammatical syllabus. One of the most innovative features of *Alles klar?* is its streamlined grammatical syllabus. Nationwide surveys indicate that instructors and students have become frustrated by the pace at which they must move if they are to cover all of German grammar in one year. The authors of *Alles klar?* believe that first-year students need focus only on those frequently-used structures over which they will need to gain control. Hence, while the *Alles klar?* program covers the grammatical structures needed to converse about basic topics and concerns, it introduces fewer structures than many other beginning German texts.

Balanced grammatical sequence. *Alles klar?* provides a balanced presentation of grammatical topics throughout the text. Important structures are presented early; a student completing only one semester of the program should be able to create sentences in the present and conversational past tenses, use the modals successfully, and demonstrate a working understanding of German case (nominative, dative, and accusative). An even pace is maintained during the second semester, when other programs traditionally address the bulk of important grammar.

Systematic recycling and review. An additional innovative feature of *Alles klar?* is its method of built-in review. Several chapters in the second half of the book systematically recycle and expand upon essential but somewhat complex grammar topics that were introduced in earlier chapters. This approach ensures that students gain greater control over the material and engenders in them a greater feeling of competence as they use these structures naturally in a variety of communicative contexts.

A four-skills approach. Both the complete *Alles klar?* program and the student text itself offer ample coverage of all four skills, plus culture:

- Listening opportunities are provided through the many *Gespräche* that are not only printed in the book, but recorded on cassettes as well. For each one, annotations in the **Annotated Instructor's Edition** provide suggestions for listening comprehension activities. Additional listening practice is also offered in the **Lab Manual** and accompanying cassette program.

- Speaking and communication are practiced extensively in *Alles klar?*, in the numerous activities that are intended for pair- or group-work and in the culminating *Zu zweit* (information gap) and *Situationen* activities.

- Reading opportunities abound in the *Lesestücke* that appear in most chapters. In the second half of the book, a number of them consist of authentic texts. In addition, *Alles klar?* contains two short stories, several poems, and plentiful realia.

- Writing skills are reinforced in the *Zusammenfassung* section that concludes each chapter. They are further practiced in the accompanying **Workbook**.

- Cultural information permeates *Alles klar?*. Cultural contrasts are presented not only in the *Kulturnotiz* boxes that appear in every chapter, but are also more subtly reinforced through dialogues, reading passages, realia, and photos.

Chapter Organization and Pedagogy

Alles klar? contains fifteen *Kapitel*, each based on a theme that encourages communication and develops insight into German language and culture. These themes are both practical and informative; they include topics such as housing, health and physical fitness, making plans and using the telephone, the media, and interpersonal relationships in contemporary life.

Each *Kapitel* is divided into a series of *Schritte* that contain conversations, reading, realia, and other language samples. All *Kapitel* maintain the following consistent structure:

Lernziele. Objectives are divided into functional goals, structural goals, and a summary of the cultural material presented in the chapter.

Die ersten Schritte. Na los! Each chapter opens with a series of lively vocabulary presentations, promptly reinforced by brief activities that set the stage for immediate communication. Some activities in this section serve as a vehicle for previewing structures lexically prior to their formal grammatical presentation. Other activities reenter vocabulary, grammar, and culture from preceding chapters. In *Kapitel* 1-10, this section also includes a rhyme, tongue twister or other text that focuses on a particular sound or aspect of German pronunciation (*Versuch's mal!*).

Die weiteren Schritte. Alles klar? In this section, grammar explanations, followed by immediate practice, are preceded by dialogues (*Gespräche*) and readings (*Lesestücke*) that serve as language samples. The *Gespräche* may be used for either listening comprehension or reading practice. The *Lesestücke* are preceded by a brief pre-reading section that prepares students for the material to come. Both the dialogues and the readings are accompanied by comprehension questions and other follow-up activities.

After the language sample, grammar explanations contrast English and German with clear examples and abundant charts. The **Alles klar?** exercise sets include a wide variety of contextualized drills, guided practice, and personalized and communicative activities. Direction lines are in English in *Kapitel* 1-5, in both German and English in *Kapitel* 6-8, and in German in *Kapitel* 9-15.

Throughout both *Die ersten Schritte* and *Die weiteren Schritte*, key cultural similarities and contrasts are highlighted in the *Kulturnotizen*, which are often accompanied by annotations that provide thought-provoking questions as points of departure for classroom discussion.

Die letzten Schritte. Wer macht mit? The contents of each chapter come together in this section. To provide a balance to the numerous oral activities in *Die ersten Schritte* and *Die weiteren Schritte*, the *Zusammenfassung* activities allow students to practice their writing skills. These activities prompt students to recombine vocabulary, structures, and cultural topics via a series of communicative contexts that include guided and open-ended formats. Next, information-gap activities in the *Zu zweit* section provide stimulating material for pair work. Finally, the *Situationen* include role-plays and others situation-based activities. An array of illustrations, photos, realia, and readings inspire students to put their German to active use in personalized settings.

Themenwortschatz and Weiterer Wortschatz. New active vocabulary words in each chapter are listed in either the *Themenwortschatz* or the *Weiterer Wortschatz*. As its title indicates, vocabulary in the *Themenwortschatz* is directly related to the chapter theme and has usually been first presented in *Die ersten Schritte*. These words and expressions are grouped thematically and functionally for easy mastery. The *Weiterer Wortschatz*, also organized by linguistic category, consists of other high-frequency vocabulary that occurs naturally throughout the chapter and is essential for any first-year student, regardless of theme or context. Scattered throughout the chapter, a series of *Redewendung* boxes highlight flavoring particles and other useful or idiomatic phrases that have a distinct conversational focus. These expressions are included in one of the two end-of-chapter lists. In addition, at the back of the book, a *Zusätzlicher Themenwortschatz* provides additional, theme-related vocabulary that enables students to develop a personalized lexicon.

Überall spricht man deutsch! This special section, which follows alternate chapters, highlights the use of German worldwide as a language of business, trade, scientific or scholarly research, and other areas of endeavor. It offers students a glimpse of some of the doors that a knowledge of German will open for them.

Netzboxen. A first in the history of foreign language textbooks, *Alles klar?*'s innovative *Netzboxen* provide a wealth of Internet resources of interest to students and instructors of German. Designed to be interdisciplinary and to build on chapter themes, *Netzboxen* motivate students to use German to read authentic documents, read and respond to bulletin board postings, and send and receive e-mail messages. Related activities and address updates for the *Netzboxen* are available to adopters and their students on the Prentice Hall home page (http://www.prenhall.com/~german).

Jetzt lesen wir! *Kapitel* 10 and 15 each conclude with an authentic short story: *Fahrkarte bitte*, by Helga Novak, and *Aspirin*, by Wolf Wondratschek, both with by pre-reading information and follow-up questions.

Components of the *Alles klar?* Program

Alles klar? Die deutsche Grammatik klar gemacht

This handbook provides a comprehensive review of all points of German grammar and is also suitable for use as a reference text at the intermediate level. Students will receive a complimentary copy of Die deutsche Grammatik klar gemacht when they purchase *Alles klar?*

Annotated Instructor's Edition

Marginal annotations in the **Annotated Instructor's Edition** include warm-up and expansion exercises and activities, and teaching tips.

Lab Manual/Workbook and Cassettes

The organization of the combined *Lab Manual/Workbook* parallels that of the main text. The *Lab Manual* and audio program contain additional pronunciation practice, drills that reinforce the chapter structures, scripted and semi-authentic recordings that challenge students to move beyond the in-text *Gespräche*. A wealth of written exercises and activities in the *Workbook* support those in the main text.

Instructor's Manual with Tests

The *Instructor's Manual* contains sample syllabi, the Tapescript of the audio program, and tests. There are two tests for every chapter, four final examinations (two each after chapters 7 and 15), and suggested questions for oral interviews at various stages. In addition, there is a communicative testing program for each chapter.

Acknowledgements

The publication of *Alles klar?* culminates years of planning and interacting with instructors and students to arrive at a mix of pedagogical techniques and activities that will ensure an inspiring and successful second-language learning experience. *Alles klar?* is the result of the efforts and collaboration of numerous friends and colleagues, many of whom took time from busy schedules and other commitments to assist us with comments and suggestions over the course of the development of the program. We extend our deepest thanks and appreciation to Renate Schulz, University of Arizona, for her insight and guidance during the concept stage, and to the many colleagues around the nation who reviewed and help shape *Alles klar?* during its various stages of development. We gratefully acknowledge their participation and candor:

Robert Acker, *University of Montana*

Reinhard Andress, *Alfred University*

Claudia Becker, *University of Illinois, Chicago*

John M. Brawner, *University of California, Irvine*

James Davidheiser, *University of the South*

Leon J. Gilbert, *California State University, Fullerton*

Beverly Harris-Schenz, *University of Pittsburgh*

Wilhelmine Hartnack, *College of the Redwoods*

Robert G. Hoeing, *University of Buffalo*

Dieter Jedan, *Southeast Missouri State University*

Peggy Nickson, *Blue Ridge Community College*

Anthony J. Niesz, *Yale University*

Judith Ricker-Abderhalden, *University of Arkansas*

Volker Schmeissner, *Northern Virginia Community College*

Michael Schultz, *New York University*

Debra L. Stoudt, *University of Toledo*

Jan van Valkenburg, *University of Michigan*

At Prentice Hall, we received the support and guidance of many individuals. We would like to thank especially Phil Miller, President, Humanities and Social Sciences; Steve Debow, Editor-in-Chief; Laura McKenna, Executive Editor; Marian Wassner, Director of Development; María F. García, Assistant Editor; Karen George, Editorial Assistant; Debbie Brennan, Senior Managing Editor; Jacqueline Bush, Project Editor; Ximena de la Piedra, Designer, Leslie Osher, Creative Director; Carol Anson, Cover Designer.

We are especially indebted to Joan Schoellner, the developmental editor for this volume, and to Eva-Maria Bates, University of Utah, the author of many of the ancillary items. The untiring efforts of both these individuals have helped make the *Alles klar?* package truly innovative. In addition, we would like to thank Reyes I. Fidalgo, Bowling Green State University, for authoring the communicative testing program and for her general methodological advice.

A special note of thanks is due to the many teaching assistants and lecturers in the Department of Germanic Languages and Literatures at the University of Pennsylvania, who spent time talking with us about various components of this program and who were always ready and willing to try out specific exercises, explanations, and chapters in their respective classes. Each of the three authors, finally, is indebted to colleagues, friends, and family members for their patience and understanding.

Grüß dich!
Ich heiße...

Kapitel 1

Schritt 1: Wie heißt du? Ich heiße...

Below are some greetings you can use with fellow students.

ANY TIME:	**Grüß dich!**
	Hallo!
	(Guten) Tag!
IN THE MORNING:	**(Guten) Morgen!**
IN THE EVENING:	**(Guten) Abend!**

To find out another student's name, you would ask:

Wie heißt du?   *Wie heisen Sie = Formal*

To tell your name, say:

Ich heiße [+ name].

The appropriate response after meeting someone new is:

Es freut mich.   *Pleased to meet you.*

((((📼)))) Gespräche

In the exchanges below, students are greeting each other on the first day of class at a German university. Repeat their conversations after your instructor or the tape.

– Grüß dich! Ich heiße Peter.
– Ich heiße Rudi, Rudi Hansen.

– Hallo. Wie heißt du?
– Ich heiße Erika Müller. Und du?
– Ich heiße Jutta Fischer.
– Es freut mich sehr.

Redewendung

Und du?   *And you?*

Kulturnotiz: Shaking hands with friends and acquaintances

A handshake is a routine part of greeting and leave-taking in German-speaking countries. People shake hands not only when they are introduced, but also when they greet each other and say good-bye. Young people as well as adults may shake hands with friends and acquaintances several times a day. Usually the handshake is accompanied by a nod of the head.

ALLES KLAR?

A. Wie heißt du? Form a circle of approximately ten students. Your instructor will hand one of you a ball.

■ The person with the ball says, **Ich heiße** [+ name]. **Wie heißt du?** and tosses the ball to a second student.

■ The student who catches the ball replies, **Ich heiße** [+ name]. **Wie heißt du?**, tossing the ball to a third person.

■ The game continues until everyone has had a turn to catch and throw the ball at least once.

You may then vary the game by tossing the ball to someone and saying, "**Du heißt** [+ name]." If the name is correct, that person continues by tossing the ball to a third person and saying his/her name. If the name is incorrect, that person says "**Nein** (*no*), **ich heiße** [+ name]" and then continues tossing the ball. The faster the game, the more fun!

B. Grüß dich! Now that you know your classmates' names, walk around the room and greet at least three other students. For the first time, pretend that it is early morning; for the second time, midday; and for the third, evening. The person you greet should respond appropriately.

Schritt 2: Woher kommst du? Ich komme aus…

To find out where another student is from, you would ask:

[handwritten: From wher]

Woher kommst du?

[handwritten: wohin = to where]

To tell where you're from, say:

Ich komme aus [+ place].   OR: **Ich bin aus** [+ place].

(((🔊))) Gespräche

In the following conversations, two students greet each other, then ask each other's names and places of origin. Repeat the conversations after your instructor or the tape.

— Tag! Wie heißt du?
— Ich heiße Ulrike Bender. Und du?
— Ich heiße Inge Schneider. Woher kommst du?
— Ich komme aus Berlin. Und du?
— Ich komme aus Salzburg.

— Guten Abend. Ich heiße Dieter Kamm. Und du?
— Ich heiße Karin Zimmermann.
— Woher kommst du, Karin?
— Ich bin aus Zürich.
— Ach was! Ich auch.
— Tatsächlich!

Redewendung

Ach was!	*Oh, wow!*
Ich auch!	*Me too.*
Tatsächlich!	*Really!*

To say *good-bye*, you can use either of the following phrases:

Tschüs!
(Auf) Wiedersehen!

Alles klar?

 A. Ein kurzes Gespräch (*a brief conversation*). With a partner, complete and practice the following conversation, exchanging roles.

— Guten _____! (*It is 10:00 A.M.*) *morgen*
— ~~tax~~ !
— Ich heiße ~~TJS~~ Wie heißt du?
— Ich heiße __X__. Woher kommst du?
— Aus _lok_. Und du?
— Ich bin aus _Columbia_

B. Bekanntschaft machen (*making acquaintances*). Find and greet a new partner. That person will greet you in return and ask you your name. You will answer and find out that student's name. Then each of you inquires where the other is from. To close, look at your watch and say good-bye.

Schritt 3: **Wie geht's? Es geht mir...**

To ask how someone is, say:

> **Wie geht es dir?**   OR:
> **Wie geht's?**

Possible responses include:

Es geht mir...	*I'm...*
...**[sehr] gut.**	*[very] well.*
...**nicht so gut.**	*not so well.*
...**[sehr] schlecht.**	*...[very] bad.*
Ich bin müde.	*I'm tired.*
Ich bin krank.	*I'm sick.*

To inquire about the other person, add the phrase **Und dir?**

Es geht mir gut. Und dir?
I'm fine. And you?   *Wie geht es ihnen*

If the other person is not doing well, you express sympathy by saying:

Es tut mir leid.
I'm sorry.

Das tut mir leid.
I'm sorry about that.

leiden = suffer

In the following conversations, two students greet each other and ask how the other is doing. Repeat the conversations after your instructor or the tape.

—Tag, Ulrike!
—Hallo, Inge. Wie geht's?
—Sehr gut! Und dir?
—Es geht mir nicht so gut. Ich bin müde.

—Grüß dich, Dieter!
—Tag, Karin! Wie geht es dir?
—Es geht mir sehr schlecht. Ich bin krank.
—Das tut mir leid.

ALLES KLAR?

Wie geht's? Respond to your partner's inquiry using the pictures as cues.

BEISPIEL: —Wie geht's?
   —Nicht so gut.

Schritt 4: **Wie schreibt man das?**

((🔊)) Das Alphabet

The German alphabet contains the same twenty-six letters as the English alphabet. Note how they are pronounced.

a (ah)	g (geh)	m (emm)	s (ess)	y (üppsilon)
b (beh)	h (hah)	n (enn)	t (teh)	z (tsett)
c (tseh)	i (ih)	o (oh)	u (uh)	
d (deh)	j (jot)	p (peh)	v (fau)	
e (eh)	k (kah)	q (kuh)	w (veh)	
f (eff)	l (ell)	r (err)	x (iks)	

It also includes these four additional letters.

ß (ess-tsett)   ä (äh)   ö (öh)   ü (üh)

To find out how something is spelled, you would ask:

Wie schreibt man [+ word or name]?
Wie schreibt man das?   } *How do you spell (write) that?*

Tip!

Man is used frequently in German; it corresponds to English *one*, *they*, *people*, *you*, etc.

ALLES KLAR?

A. Abkürzungen (*abbreviations*). Below is a list of abbreviations in German. Some of them are well-known in this country; others are the names of German political parties. With a partner, take turns saying them aloud. Can you think of others?

BMW	**FDP** (Freie Demokratische Partei)
USA	**CDU** (Christlich-Demokratische Union)
VW	**SPD** (Sozialdemokratische Partei Deutschlands)
IBM	
BASF (Bayerische Anilin- und Soda Fabrik)	

Kulturnotiz: *du* or *Sie*?

Languages have different ways of showing whether a situation is formal or informal. For example, speakers of German do not use first names as freely as Americans; in addition, they differentiate between a formal and an informal you. The informal **du** (sing.) or **ihr** (plur.) is the form you have used thus far: **Wie heißt du? Woher kommst du?** This form is normally used within the family, among children and younger people (including students), among good friends, for pets, and when addressing God; otherwise, Germans use **Sie**. If you have any doubt about which form to use, say **Sie** to anyone over fourteen unless the **du**-form is offered; e.g., **Sagen Sie du zu mir; Bitte, sagen wir du zueinander** (*to each other*); or **Wollen wir uns duzen?**

B. Namen (*names*). Write a list of five names—first and last—of students in the class. Then spell the names to a partner, who will write them down. Do not say the names before you spell them. Then you write the five names that your partner spells. Finally, exchange lists to check your accuracy.

Schritt 5: Wie heißen Sie?

In a more formal situation you would use the following greetings.

- any time:
  Guten Tag!

- in the morning:
  Guten Morgen!

- in the evening:
  Guten Abend!

- to say good-bye:
  Auf Wiedersehen!

- the formal way to ask someone's name:
  Wie heißen Sie?

- the formal way to find out where someone is from:
  Woher kommen Sie?

- and how someone is:
  Wie geht es Ihnen?

- when speaking with people in formal situations:
  Frau Müller (*Ms.* or *Mrs. Müller*)
  Herr Müller (*Mr. Müller*)

Kulturnotiz: *Frau* or *Fräulein*?

Unlike *Mr.* or **Herr**, traditional forms of address for women specify marital status. A recent survey shows that the term **Frau** is becoming more widely used, regardless of the actual marital status of the woman addressed. Of those interviewed, 40% used **Frau** even if they knew the woman was single, compared to 26% in 1980. Only 15% still use **Fräulein**, compared to 29% in 1980. 45% varied their use of the terms, according to the age of the woman. There are also regional variances in the use of **Frau** for unmarried women, with Bavaria being least receptive to the trend. Members of the more liberal Green Party also use **Frau** more often than the more conservative **Republikaner**.

"The Week In Germany"
Published by the German Information Center

 **Gespräche**

Barbara Vernon has an appointment at an office in Düsseldorf. She announces herself, but the secretary can't catch her name.

Redewendung

bitte
please; you're welcome

danke sehr
thank you very much

ja / nein
yes/no

Nehmen Sie Platz!
Have a seat.

Wie, bitte?
(I beg your) Pardon?

Wo wohnen Sie?
Where do you live?

Ich wohne in...
I live in...

SEKRETÄRIN:	Guten Morgen! Wie heißen Sie, bitte?
BARBARA:	Ich heiße Barbara Vernon.
SEKRETÄRIN:	Wie, bitte?
BARBARA:	Barbara Vernon.
SEKRETÄRIN:	Wie schreibt man «Vernon»? Mit w (weh)?
BARBARA:	Nein, mit v (fau): fau - eh - err - enn - oh - enn.
SEKRETÄRIN:	Und wo wohnen Sie, Frau Vernon?
BARBARA:	Ich wohne hier in Düsseldorf.
SEKRETÄRIN:	Danke sehr. Bitte, nehmen Sie Platz!

Student Dieter Thielmann meets his new history teacher, Professor Lieselotte Hoffmann.

PROF. HOFFMANN:	Guten Tag! Wie heißen Sie?
DIETER:	Guten Tag. Ich heiße Thielmann, Dieter Thielmann.
PROF. HOFFMANN:	Thielmann - wie schreibt man das?
DIETER:	Teh - hah - ih - eh - ell - emm - ah - enn - enn.
PROF. HOFMANN:	Ach so, danke, und woher kommen Sie?
DIETER:	Ich komme aus Bremen.
PROF. HOFFMANN:	Ach was! Ich auch.
DIETER:	Tatsächlich!

ALLES KLAR?

 A. Wer sind Sie? (*Who are you?*). You and your partner are well-known personalities. Interview each other.

BEISPIEL: — Ich heiße Elizabeth Taylor.
— Und ich heiße _____.
— Wo wohnen Sie?
— Ich wohne in Hollywood. Und Sie?
— Ich wohne in _____.

MÖGLICHKEITEN [*possibilities*]

Hillary Clinton, Jimmy Carter, Prinz Charles, Boris Yeltsin.

B. Neue Nachbarn (*New neighbors*). Enact the following situation.

STUDENT 1
You have just moved into an apartment next to an elderly neighbor, and you want to introduce yourself. Decide what time of day it is, and greet that neighbor. Use the formal questions to find out his/her name and place of origin; if either reply is unusual, ask how the word is spelled. Then say good-bye. Be sure to address your neighbor as **Frau** or **Herr** using only the last name.

STUDENT 2
You are an elderly person and a student has just moved into the apartment next to you. The student knocks on the door and wants to get to know you. Respond appropriately to the greeting and questions.

Schritt 6: Eins, zwei, drei,…

0 null	10 zehn	20 zwanzig
1 eins	11 elf	21 einundzwanzig
2 zwei	12 zwölf	22 zweiundzwanzig
		…*what comes next?*
3 drei	13 dreizehn	30 dreißig
4 vier	14 vierzehn	31 einunddreißig
		…*what comes next?*
5 fünf	15 fünfzehn	40 vierzig
6 sechs	16 sechzehn	50 fünfzig
7 sieben	17 siebzehn	60 sechzig
8 acht	18 achtzehn	70 siebzig
9 neun	19 neunzehn	80 achtzig
		90 neunzig

100	(ein)hundert	1 000 000	eine Million
101	(ein)hunderteins	2 000 000	zwei Millionen
200	zweihundert	1 000 000 000	eine Milliarde
1 000	(ein)tausend	2 000 000 000	zwei Milliarden
1 001	eintausendeins		

ALLES KLAR?

 A. Nummern (*numbers*). With a partner, practice the numbers you see shown below.

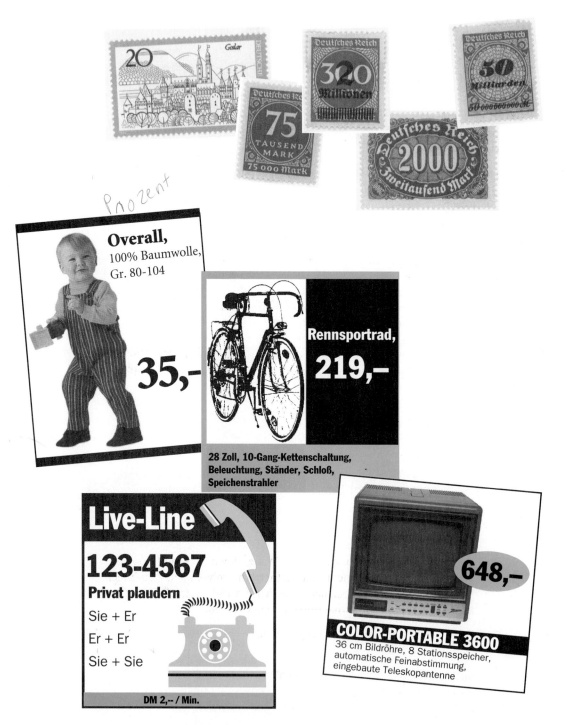

Prozent

Overall,
100% Baumwolle,
Gr. 80-104

35,–

Rennsportrad,

219,–

28 Zoll, 10-Gang-Kettenschaltung,
Beleuchtung, Ständer, Schloß,
Speichenstrahler

Live-Line

123-4567

Privat plaudern

Sie + Er

Er + Er

Sie + Sie

DM 2,-- / Min.

648,–

COLOR-PORTABLE 3600
36 cm Bildröhre, 8 Stationsspeicher,
automatische Feinabstimmung,
eingebaute Teleskopantenne

B. Zählen Sie schnell! (*Count quickly!*). With a partner, practice counting in the following ways.

1. Alternate counting

   BEISPIEL: — eins
   — zwei
   …

2. Alternate counting in pairs of numbers

   BEISPIEL: — eins zwei
   — drei vier
   …

3. Alternate counting by twos (even numbers)

   BEISPIEL: — zwei
   — vier
   …

4. Alternate counting by twos (uneven numbers)

   BEISPIEL: — eins
   — drei
   …

5. Alternate counting by fives

   BEISPIEL: — fünf
   — zehn
   …

C. Ein Spiel (*a game*). Form small groups and count aloud, going around the circle. For every multiple of 3 (4, 5…), substitute a German word or phrase such as **Guten Tag**. Whoever forgets and says the number is out.

   BEISPIEL: STUDENT 1: eins
   STUDENT 2: zwei
   STUDENT 3: Guten Tag!
   STUDENT 4: vier
   STUDENT 5: fünf
   STUDENT 6: Guten Tag!
   STUDENT 7: sieben
   …

D. Wieviel ist…? (*How much is…?*). Write down five addition and subtraction problems. Read them to a partner, who solves them aloud; then you solve the problems given by your partner. Note that the arithmetical + (plus) and - (minus) signs are pronounced somewhat differently in German.

   BEISPIELE: — Wieviel ist 2 + 3? (zwei plus drei)
   — 2 + 3 ist 5.

   — Wieviel ist 25 - 11? (fünfundzwanzig minus elf)
   — 25 - 11 ist 14.

E. Die Telefonnummer. Ask five classmates for their telephone numbers.

BEISPIEL: — Wie ist deine Telefonnummer?
— Meine Telefonnummer ist drei sieben zwei vier vier sechs neun.

OR: Meine Telefonnummer ist drei sieben zwei, vierund-
vierzig, neunundsechzig.
— Drei sechs zwei vier fünf sechs neun?
— Nein, drei sieben zwei vier vier sechs neun.
…

F. Wie alt bist du? (*How old are you?*). Ask various classmates how old
they are.

BEISPIEL: — Wie alt bist du?
— Ich bin… Jahre alt.

Schritt 7: **Wer ist das?**

Until now you have only talked about yourself or asked questions of others. Here are
some expressions you would use to talk about a third person.

Wer ist das?	*Who is that?*
Das ist…	*That's…*
Woher kommt er/sie?	*Where is he/she from?*
Er/Sie kommt aus…	*He/She is from…*
Er/Sie ist aus…	*He/She is from…*
Wo wohnt er/sie?	*Where does he/she live?*
Er/Sie wohnt in…	*He/She lives in…*
Wie ist seine/ihre Telefonnummer?	*What is his/her telephone number?*
Seine/Ihre Telefonnummer ist…	*His/her telephone number is…*
Wie alt ist er/sie?	*How old is he/she?*
Er/Sie ist… Jahre alt.	*He/She is… years old.*

((◉)) **Gespräche**

Johanna thinks she recognizes a new student
at the university in Konstanz. She asks her
friend Reinhard about her.

borget
HERRENAUSSTATTUNG

Bachmann Emma Dr. jur.	3 62 90	Baeutsch
Steubenstr. 52		Baeutsch
Bachmann Hans Frankenstr. 63	2 83 88	Lärcher
Bachmann Karl An der Kirche 7	2 79 79	Bagatell
Bachmann M. Hubertusweg 32	2 90 63	Sch
Bachmann Manfred	2 76 34	B—
Hauptstr. 142		
Bahmann Maria Hubertusweg 3	3 48 74	
Bachmann Martha Alterprgerin	3 74 79	
(Ste) Bachhausweg 8a		
Bachmann R.	2 65 3?	
Bachmann Reinhard (Ste.)		
Kirchstr. 27		
Bachmann Roland G. 3 1		
Lindenstr. 51		
Bachmann Rolf		
Unter dem Rotdom		
Bachmann Rudol'		
Backes Klara F		
Bader A—t		

JOHANNA: Wer ist das?
REINHARD: Das ist Maria, Maria Bachmann.
JOHANNA: Woher kommt sie?
REINHARD: Sie kommt aus Bayern. Sie ist aus
München.
JOHANNA: Und wo wohnt sie?
REINHARD: Sie wohnt hier in Konstanz.
JOHANNA: Wie ist ihre Telefonnummer?
REINHARD: Warte mal. Hier ist das Telefonbuch.
JOHANNA: Danke. Bachmann. B - a - c - h - m - a - n - n… Ach, hier ist ihre
Telefonnummer – 3 48 74.

A. Wer ist das? Think of someone you know—a friend or family member. With that person in mind, complete the following conversation with a partner. Then exchange roles.

STUDENT 1: Wer ist das?
STUDENT 2: Das ist _____.
STUDENT 1: Woher kommt [sie/er]?
STUDENT 2: [Sie/Er] kommt aus _____.
STUDENT 1: Und wo wohnt [sie/er] jetzt ?
STUDENT 2: [Sie/Er] wohnt in _____ [*name of dorm or state*].
STUDENT 1: Wie alt ist [sie/er]?
STUDENT 2: [Sie/Er] ist _____ Jahre alt.

B. Der Schwimmausweis. Below is a swimming pass for a German teenager. See how much you can tell about its owner.

1. Wie heißt sie?
2. Wie alt ist sie?
3. Wo wohnt sie?

C. Interview. Now interview another student in your class; find out his/her name, age, place of origin, residence, and phone number. Take notes if necessary. Then report to the class.

BEISPIEL: Erika ist zwanzig Jahre alt.
Sie kommt aus New Mexiko.
…

Schritt 8: **Ausdrücke für die Deutschstunde**

1. Language practice

Langsamer, bitte!	*More slowly, please.*
Lauter, bitte!	*Louder, please.*
Noch einmal, bitte!	*Once more, please.*
Schreiben Sie, bitte!	*Please write.*
Wiederholen Sie, bitte!	*Please repeat.*

2. Clarification

Verstehen Sie das? (formal)	*Do you understand that?*
Verstehst du das? (informal)	
Das verstehe ich nicht.	*I don't understand that.*
Haben Sie eine Frage? (formal)	*Do you have a question?*
Hast du eine Frage? (informal)	
Ich habe eine Frage.	*I have a question.*
Wie sagt man… auf deutsch?	*How does one say… in German?*

3. Feedback

Sehr gut!	*Very good!*
Ausgezeichnet!	*Excellent!*
Das ist richtig.	*That's right.*
Richtig!	*Right!*
Das ist falsch.	*That's wrong.*
Falsch!	*Wrong!*
Ruhe, bitte!	*Quiet, please.*
Schnell, bitte!	*Quickly, please.*

▶ *Versuch's mal!* Die *ie-/ei-* Laute

Eins, zwei, drei, vier, fünf, sechs, sieben
Fritz hat mir drei Brief' geschrieben
einen für mich, einen für dich,
einen für Vetter Heinerich.

Lieselotte Schmetterlein
und Rosmaria Elfenbein
streiten um den bess'ren Wein.
"Der Riesling ist der beste Wein!"
"Nein, nein," schiebt Lieselotte ein.
"Mir viel zu süß ist dieser Wein.
Er sollte lieber sauer sein.
Dann freute sich das Herze mein."

Aus: Ruth Dirx (Hrsg.), KINDERREIME By Ravensburger Buchverlag,
Ravensburg (Germany) 1987

Schritt 9: **Subject pronouns**

Subject pronouns answer the question *who?* (**wer?**); they perform the action of the sentence. The subject pronouns in German are:

SINGULAR		PLURAL	
ich	*I*	**wir**	*we*
du	*you* (informal)	**ihr**	*you* (informal)
er/sie/es	*he/she/it*	**sie**	*they*
Sie	*you* (formal)	**Sie**	*you* (formal)

Note that **sie** and **Sie** sound alike in speech; context or the following verb form generally makes the meaning clear. In writing, **Sie** meaning *you* is always capitalized; however, unlike English, the personal pronoun **ich** is not capitalized unless it appears at the beginning of a sentence.

ALLES KLAR?

A. *Du* **oder** *Sie?* Pretend you are speaking to those listed below; which pronoun would you use?

1. several children
2. your dog
3. your dentist
4. several of your parents' friends

B. *Er* **oder** *sie* **oder…?** Now you are talking about the people shown. Which pronoun would you use?

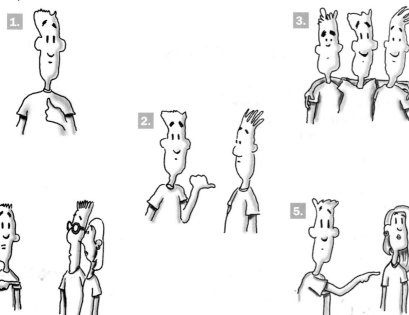

The infinitive

Verbs are listed in the vocabulary and in dictionaries in their basic form, i.e., in the infinitive form. While in English the infinitive of a verb consists of *to* plus the verb, in German the infinitive ends in **-en**, as in **heißen**, or in **-n**, as in **sein**.

heißen	*to be called*
kommen	*to come*
sein	*to be*
wohnen	*to live*

The verb *sein*

Like its English equivalent, the verb **sein** (*to be*) is irregular.

sein *to be*					
ich	**bin**	*I am*	wir	**sind**	*we are*
du	**bist**	*you are*	ihr	**seid**	*you are*
er/sie/es	**ist**	*he/she/it is*	sie	**sind**	*they are*
		Sie **sind**	*you are*		

Basic forms for regular verbs

The other verbs you have used thus far—**heißen, kommen**, and **wohnen**—are examples of verbs that are regular in the present tense; that is, they follow a set pattern.

The present tense of regular German verbs is formed by dropping the infinitive ending **-en** or **-n** and adding personal endings to the remaining stem.

INFINITIVE	STEM	STEM + ENDING
kommen	komm-	(ich) komme
wohnen	wohn-	(du) wohnst

The personal endings are:

ich	-e		wir	-en
du	-st		ihr	-t
er/sie/es	-t		sie	-en
		Sie	-en	

kommen	*to come*				
ich	**komme**	*I come*	wir	**kommen**	*we come*
du	**kommst**	*you come*	ihr	**kommt**	*you come*
er/sie/es	**kommt**	*he/she/it comes*	sie	**kommen**	*they come*
	Sie	**kommen**	*you come*		

wohnen	*to live, to dwell*				
ich	**wohne**	*I live*	wir	**wohnen**	*we live*
du	**wohnst**	*you live*	ihr	**wohnt**	*you live*
er/sie/es	**wohnt**	*he/she/it lives*	sie	**wohnen**	*they live*
	Sie	**wohnen**	*you live*		

When the verb stem ends in **-s, -ss, -ß,** or **-z,** only a **t** (not **st**) is added in the **du**-form.

heißen	*to be called, to be named*				
ich	**heiße**	*I am called*	wir	**heißen**	*we are called*
du	**heißt**	*you are called*	ihr	**heißt**	*you are called*
er/sie/es	**heißt**	*he/she/it is called*	sie	**heißen**	*they are called*
	Sie	**heißen**	*you are called*		

When the verb stem ends in **-d** or **-t,** an extra **-e-** is inserted in the **du-, er/sie/es-** and **ihr**-form endings, to facilitate pronunciation.

arbeiten	*to work*				
ich	**arbeite**	*I work*	wir	**arbeiten**	*we work*
du	**arbeitest**	*you work*	ihr	**arbeitet**	*you work*
er/sie/es	**arbeitet**	*he/she/it works*	sie	**arbeiten**	*they work*
	Sie	**arbeiten**	*you work*		

The German present tense is used to express all three forms of the English present tense.

ich wohne {
I live (present)
I am living (progressive)
I do live (emphatic)

The present tense is also frequently used, usually with specific expressions of future time, to express future action.

Sie kommen morgen.	*They are coming tomorrow.*
Sie kommt nicht.	*She isn't coming.*
OR:	*She isn't going to come.*

ALLES KLAR?

A. Wir sind aus… Say where the following people are from. Follow the model.

> **BEISPIEL:** Rebecca / New York
> Rebecca ist aus New York.

1. ich / Mexiko
2. ihr / Italien
3. er / Ägypten
4. sie (pl.) / Dänemark
5. wir / Indien
6. du / Spanien
7. sie (sg.) / England
8. Sie / Liechtenstein

sind

B. Ich komme aus Amerika. Refer to *Activity A* and use the verb **kommen** to say where each person is from.

> **BEISPIEL:** Rebecca kommt aus New York.

C. Wohnen. Peter and Lukas are discussing in which dorm their friends are living this year. Complete their conversation with the correct forms of the verb **wohnen**.

PETER: Ich _____ in Matthews Hall. Wo _____ du?

LUKAS: Ich *wohne* in Bryant Hall, und Ted und Michael *wohnen* auch da (*there*).

PETER: Aber Simon *wohnt* in Davis Hall.

 D. Woher kommt ihr? Walk around the room and ask various students where they are from. Record their answers. Then discuss your findings with a partner.

> **BEISPIELE:** Margit und ich kommen aus…
> Hans kommt aus…
> Zehn Studenten kommen aus…

Schritt 11: Nicht wahr?

In English as well as in German, speakers frequently seek confirmation of their statements. In English this is done by adding on one of many possible tag questions like *isn't he?*, *aren't they?*, *won't you?*, *haven't we?*, etc.

The German equivalent of all such questions is **nicht wahr?**, regardless of person, number, etc.

> Sie heißen Jutta Wagner, **nicht wahr?**
> *Your name is Jutta Wagner, **isn't it?***

> Herr Meyer wohnt in Hamburg, **nicht wahr?**
> *Mr. Meyer lives in Hamburg, **doesn't he?***

ALLES KLAR?

Nicht wahr? Introduce yourself to a classmate, then talk with him/her. See whether you both know everyone in the class yet.

BEISPIEL: — Ich bin Karin Klein.
    Du bist Peter Busch, nicht wahr?
  — Ja, ich bin Peter Busch.
    Du kommst aus Kalifornien, nicht wahr?
  — Nein, ich komme aus Nevada.
  — Das ist Kurt Kleinau, nicht wahr?
  — Ja/Nein, das ist…

Die letzten Schritte

Wer macht mit?

Zusammenfassung

A. Frau Hart und Herr Weich. Complete the following conversations by filling in the blanks.

1. **HERR WEICH:** Guten _Tag_ !
    FRAU HART: _guten_ Tag! _wie_ geht es Ihnen?
    HERR WEICH: Danke, es _geht_ mir gut. Und _ihnen_?
    FRAU HART: Danke, auch _gut_ .

2. **HERR WEICH:** Guten _Tag_ !
    FRAU HART: _Guten_ Tag! Wie _heißen_ Sie?
    HERR WEICH: Ich _heiße_ Weich. Und Sie?
    FRAU HART: Ich _____ Hart.
    HERR WEICH: Woher _com_ Sie?
    FRAU HART: Ich _komme_ aus Leipzig. Und Sie?
    HERR WEICH: Ich _bin_ aus Frankfurt.

3. **FRAU HART:** Wer _ist_ das?
    HERR WEICH: Das _ist_ Fritz Lichtenberg, nicht _____ ? Wo wohnt er?
    FRAU HART: _er_ wohnt in Ithaca.
    HERR WEICH: Wie bitte? Das verstehe _ich_ nicht. Wie schreibt _____ das?
    FRAU HART: I-T-H-A-C-A .
    HERR WEICH: Ach so. Jetzt verstehe _ich_. In Ithaca.
    FRAU HART: Richtig!
    HERR WEICH: Tschüs!
    FRAU HART: _Auf_ Wiedersehen!

B. Fragen und Antworten. Form sentences from the following words. If they are questions, make up answers for them as well.

> BEISPIEL: wie/heißen/du
> Wie heißt du?
> Ich heiße Peter.

1. woher/kommen/du *Wo woher Kommst du*
2. wie/alt/sein/sie (*pl.*) *wie alt seinst sie*
3. wie/sein/deine/Telefonnummer *wie main et ist sein deine plus*
4. ich/sein/aus/Berlin *ich bin aus Berlin*
5. er/kommen/aus/New York *er Komt aus*
6. wie/heißen/du *wie heiβt du*
7. wie/schreiben/man/das *wie schreibt man das*
8. wo/wohnen/du *wo wohnst du*
9. wie/gehen/dir *wie geht est dir*

C. Interviews. Interview three classmates about their backgrounds. Ask for their names, their ages, where they are from, and their telephone numbers. Enter the information in a chart like the one shown below, then write several statements about each classmate you interviewed.

> BEISPIEL: Sie heißt Barbara Winder und ist neunzehn Jahre alt. Barbara kommt aus Kansas City und ihre Telefonnummer ist 5 34 79 83.

NAME	ALTER (AGE)	STADT (CITY)	TELEFONNUMMER
Barbara Winder	19	Kansas City	5 34 79 83
...			

D. Persönlichkeiten. Look at the following chart and answer the questions in complete sentences.

1. Wie alt ist Arnold Schwarzenegger? *56*
2. Wo wohnt die Königin Elisabeth? *B. Pal.*
3. Woher kommt Katarina Witt?
4. Wie alt ist Ronald Reagan?
5. Wo wohnt Arnold Schwarzenegger?

NAME	WIE ALT IST ER/SIE?	WOHER KOMMT ER/SIE?	WO WOHNT ER/SIE?
Arnold Schwarzenegger	geb. 1947	Österreich	Hollywood
Ronald Reagan	geb. 1911	Amerika	Kalifornien
Königin Elisabeth	geb. 1926	England	Buckingham Palace
Katarina Witt	geb. 1965	Deutschland	Berlin

Zu zweit: **Student 1**

In this section you and your partner will be working on different pages—one of you on this page, one on the other side.

A. Woher kommt…? Match each person with her/his residence and tell your partner where these famous people live. Then ask your partner where they are from.

> **BEISPIEL:** —Königin Elisabeth wohnt in London. Woher kommt sie?
> —Sie kommt aus England.

Steven King	Massachusetts
Bill Clinton	Moskau
Steffi Graf	Washington
Edward Kennedy	Maine
Boris Yeltsin	Brühl

Your partner will now tell you where some other famous people live. Using the place names below, tell your partner where these people are from.

> **BEISPIEL:** —Ross Perot wohnt in Texas. Woher kommt er?
> —Er kommt aus Amerika.

Albanien   Südafrika   Kuba   Italien   Amerika

Now match your names and those of your partner with their current or past professions.

___ der Präsident von Rußland	___ der Präsident von Kuba
___ ein Autor	___ der Premierminister von Israel
___ eine Tennisspielerin	___ ein Senator
___ eine Nonne in Indien	___ der Präsident von Südafrika
___ ein Opernsänger	___ ein Pastor und Politiker

B. Städte und Personen (*cities and people*). Spell the names of these six German cities to your partner.

Frankfurt	Rostock	Heidelberg
Leipzig	Dresden	Nürnberg

Now listen as your partner spells the names of six famous people from the German-speaking world. Write down what you hear.

1. _____
2. _____
3. _____
4. _____
5. _____
6. _____

Now, working together, match the names of the people with their professions.

___ a. Nobel prize winner in physics	___ d. politician and statesman
___ b. psychiatrist	___ e. Olympic skater
___ c. actress	___ f. artist

Zu zweit: Student 2

In these sections you and your partner will be working on different pages—one of you on this page, one on the other side.

A. Woher kommt…? Your partner will tell you where some famous people live. When asked, tell her/him where they are from, using the cues provided.

> **BEISPIEL:** —Königin Elisabeth wohnt in London. Woher kommt sie?
> —Sie kommt aus England.

| Amerika | Deutschland | Rußland | Israel |

Now match the people in the following list with their residences and tell your partner where these people live. Ask where they are from.

> **BEISPIEL:** —Ross Perot wohnt in Texas. Woher kommt er?
> —Er kommt aus Amerika.

Luciano Pavarotti	Kapstadt
Nelson Mandela	Südkarolina
Fidel Castro	Kalkutta
Jesse Jackson	Modena
Mutter Teresa	Havana

Now match your names and those of your partner with their current or past professions.

___ der Präsident von Rußland	___ der Präsident von Kuba
___ ein Autor	___ der Premierminister von Israel
___ eine Tennisspielerin	___ ein Senator
___ eine Nonne in Indien	___ der Präsident von Südafrika
___ ein Opernsänger	___ ein Pastor und Politiker

B. Städte und Personen (*cities and people*). Listen as your partner spells the names of six German cities. Write down what you hear.

1. _____
2. _____
3. _____
4. _____
5. _____
6. _____

Now spell the names of these six famous people from the German-speaking world. Your partner will write them down as you spell.

1. Albrecht Dürer	4. Katarina Witt
2. Willi Brandt	5. Sigmund Freud
3. Albert Einstein	6. Marlene Dietrich

Now, working together, match the names of the people in the list with their professions.

___ a. Nobel prize winner in physics	___ d. politician and statesman
___ b. psychiatrist	___ e. Olympic skater
___ c. actress	___ f. artist

Situationen

Ich wohne in . . .

Wie alt bist du?

Wie ist deine Telefonnummer?

Wie heißt du?

Ich heiße . . .

Woher kommst du?

Meine Telefonnummer ist . . .   Wo wohnst du?

A. Wieviel ist...? With a partner, take turns asking and answering the following questions. Add any others you can think of. You'll be surprised how much you have already learned!

1. Wieviel ist sieben plus fünf? Wieviel ist drei minus zwei? Wieviel ist zwölf minus eins? Wieviel ist acht plus sechzehn?...
   zwölf.   *einz*   *elf*
2. Wie alt bist du?   *19*
3. Wie ist deine Telefonnummer?   *544-1090*
4. Woher kommst du?   *New Jersey*   *vier*
5. Wie schreibt man...?   *David*
6. Wer ist das?   *David*
7. Wo wohnst du?   *Columbia*
...

zehn = teen
zig = ty
30 = dreißiz

B. Wie heißen Sie? You are meeting a professor for the first time. Introduce yourselves to each other and exchange personal information.

C. Wie heißt du? You are meeting another student for the first time. Introduce yourselves to each other and exchange personal information.

D. Richtig oder falsch? (*Right or wrong?*) In small groups, select a person to be the "emcee" of a game show. The "emcee" will ask you to spell words (**Wie schreibt man...?**), solve arithmetic problems (**Wieviel ist/plus/minus?**), and to recall people's names (**Wie heißt sie/er?**), places of origin (**Woher kommt er/sie?**) or places of residence (**Wo wohnt er/sie?**). Participants receive one point per correct answer. The first person to accumulate five points takes over as "emcee."

E. Ich habe eine Frage. Form teams of three. Prepare a set of four questions with **wer**, **wie**, **wieviel**, and **wo**. The rest of the class attempts to answer each team's questions.

German as a First Language

out that some people

*A*s you begin to study German, you should know who speaks this language, how many people speak it, and how easy it will be for you to communicate with them.

German is the primary language in four countries in Europe: Germany, Austria, Switzerland, and Liechtenstein. There are about 91,000,000 native speakers of German residing in these countries. What is particularly interesting about these people is that while they all understand High German (**Hochdeutsch**), many of them speak a dialect whenever possible. Dialectical differences might be noticeable in areas such as vocabulary, grammar, intonation, and pronunciation.

No one understands all dialects; two native Germans, speaking their different native dialects, may not even be able to understand each other! For example, many Germans would have difficulty translating and understanding the brief newspaper item printed here, although this is only a transcription of a sentence in Viennese dialect. Generally, however, the official language of these countries is High German, the language that you are going to learn. (In Switzerland, however, the Swiss dialect is preferred to High German.)

„weana schbrüch"

Di wiina luft muas
scho sea guad sei
weu sunst schdrafad
ned di gmoa bei de
schanigeatn so füü
dafia ei.

Ernst KEIN

Because High German is the official language, newspapers, magazines, radio, and television all use it, except for unusual situations where a dialect is called for. In addition, most literature is also written in High German, although some noted writers have produced masterpieces in dialect.

The Goethe Institute, a world-wide organization dedicated to the promotion of the German language abroad, estimates that about 18 million people around the world are learning High German. How will you and other non-native speakers get along in German-speaking countries? Probably just fine — they'll almost always understand you, but occasionally you may have to get used to their way of speaking. As the Germans say, **Wir drücken Ihnen den Daumen!** (*We're crossing our fingers for you!*)

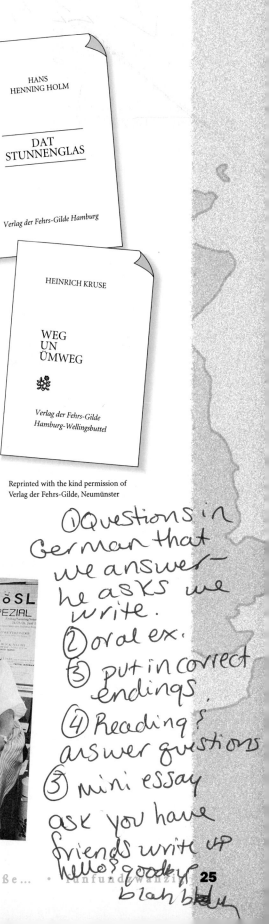

HANS
HENNING HOLM

DAT
STUNNENGLAS

Verlag der Fehrs-Gilde Hamburg

HEINRICH KRUSE

WEG
UN
ÜMWEG

❀

*Verlag der Fehrs-Gilde
Hamburg-Wellingsbuttel*

Reprinted with the kind permission of
Verlag der Fehrs-Gilde, Neumünster

BÄCKER, *zu den Umstehenden, ohne seine Stimme zu dämpfen.* Das is a schäbiges. Trinkgeld, weiter nischt. Da soll eens treten vom friehen Morg'n bis in die sinkende Nacht. Und wenn man achtz'n Tage ieberm Stuhle geleg'n hat, Abend fer Abend wie ausgewund'n, halb drehnig vor Staub und Gluthitze, da hat man sich glicklich dreiz'ntehalb. Beehmen erschind't.
PFEIFER Hier wird nich gemault!
BÄCKER Vo Ihn laß ich mersch Maul noch lange nich verbiet'n.
PFEIFER *springt mit dem Ausruf.* Das mecht ich doch amal sehn! *nach der Glastür und ruft ins Kontor.* Herr Dreißicher, Herr Dreißicher, mechten Sie amal so freundlich sein!
DREISSIGER *kommnt. Junger Vierziger. Fettleibig, asthmatisch. Mit strenger Miene.* Was gibt's denn, Pfeifer?
PFEIFER, *glubsch.* Bäcker will sich's Maul nich verbieten lassen.
DREISSIGER *gibt sich Haltung, wirft den Kopf zurück, fixiert Bäcker mit zuckenden Nasenflügeln.* Ach so - Bäcker! *Zu Pfeifer.* Is das der? *Die Beamten nicken.*
BÄCKER, *frech.* Ja, ja, Herr Dreißiger! *Auf sich zeigend.* Das is der - *auf Dreißiger zeigend.* und das is der.
DREISSIGER, *indigniert.* Was erlaubt sich denn der Mensch!?
PFEIFER, Dem geht's zu gutt! Der geht aso lange aufs Eis tanzen, bis a's amal versehen hat.

① Questions in German that we answer - he asks we write.
② oral ex.
③ put in correct endings.
④ Reading & answer questions
⑤ mini essay
ask you have friends write up hello? goodby blah blah

✓ LEARN ✓

Themenwortschatz

Substantive	Nouns	Adjektive/Adverbien	Adjectives/Adverbs
die Frau	Mrs.; Ms.; woman; wife	gut	good
das Fräulein	Miss, Ms; unmarried woman	nicht so gut	not so good
		schlecht	bad
der Herr	Mr.; man	krank	sick
die Telefonnummer	telephone number	müde	tired
		nicht	not
		sehr	very

Verben	Verbs
heißen	to be called, named
kommen	to come
sein	to be
wohnen	to live, reside

Grüße — Greetings

Grüße	Greetings
Grüß dich!	Hello! Hi!
Guten Abend!	Good evening.
Guten Morgen!	Good morning.
Guten Tag!	Hello. (lit. Good day.)
Hallo!	Hello!
Tag! (informal)	Hi!

Personalpronomen	Personal pronouns
ich	I
du	you (sg. familiar)
er	~~he~~ he or it
sie	she
es	it
wir	we
ihr	you (pl. familiar)
sie	they ~~scribble~~
Sie	you (sg. and pl. formal)
man	one

der mann = man

Gesprächsthemen — Conversational topics

Gesprächsthemen	Conversational topics
Wer ist das?	Who is that?
Das ist…	That is…
Wie alt bist du? (…sind Sie?)	How old are you?
Ich bin… Jahre alt.	I am… years old.
Wie geht es Ihnen? (formal)	How are you?
Wie geht es dir?/ Wie geht's? (informal)	
Es geht mir…	I am…
Es /Das tut mir leid.	I'm sorry (about that).
Wie heißt du/? heißen Sie?	What is your name?
Ich heiße…	My name is…
Es freut mich.	Pleased to meet you.
Wie ist deine (Ihre) Telefonnummer?	What is your telephone number?
Woher kommst du (kommen Sie)?	Where do you come from?
Ich komme/bin aus…	I come/am from…

Fragewörter	Question Words
was?	what?
wer?	who?
wie?	how?
wieviel?	how much?
wo?	where?
woher?	where from?

↓ LEARN ↓

Verabschiedungen	Good-byes
Auf Wiedersehen	Good-bye.
Tschüs! (informal)	So long, bye.

Ausdrücke für die Deutschstunde / *Expressions for German class*

Langsamer, bitte!	More slowly, please.
Lauter, bitte!	Louder, please.
Noch einmal, bitte!	Once more, please.
Schreiben Sie, bitte!	Please write.
Wiederholen Sie, bitte!	Please repeat.
Verstehen Sie das? (formal)	Do you understand that?
Verstehst du das? (informal)	
Das verstehe ich nicht.	I don't understand that.

Haben Sie eine Frage? (formal)	Do you have a question?
Hast du eine Frage? (informal)	
Ich habe eine Frage.	I have a question.
Wie sagt man… auf deutsch?	How do you say… in German?
Sehr gut!	Very good!
Ausgezeichnet!	Excellent!
Das ist richtig.	That's right.
Richtig!	Right!
Das ist falsch.	That's wrong.
Falsch!	Wrong!
Ruhe, bitte!	Quiet, please.
Schnell, bitte!	Quickly, please. Hurry up!

Ausdrücke	Expressions
Danke sehr.	Thank you very much
Ich auch.	I (me) too.
Nehmen Sie Platz!	Please sit down!
nicht wahr?	isn't that so?
Warte mal! (informal)	Wait!
Wie bitte?	What, please? What did you say?
Wie schreibt man…?	How do you spell (lit. write)…?
Wieviel ist…?	How much is…?

Verben	Verbs
arbeiten	to work
schreiben	to write
warten	to wait
verstehen	to understand

Adjektive/Adverbien / *Adjectives/Adverbs*

auch	also, too
hier	here
jetzt	now
morgen	tomorrow

Andere Wörter / *Other words*

aber	but
ach	oh, ah
bitte	please; you're welcome
danke	thank you, thanks
ja	yes
nein	no
minus	minus, less
plus	plus
tatsächlich	really, truly, surely
und	and

Willkommen zum Internet!

Welcome to the Internet!

These **Netzboxen** link you to virtual study sites on the German World Wide Web. In browsing through them, you can learn more about the theme and cultural content of the chapters in which they appear. For related activities and address updates, see the Prentice Hall home page at http://www.prenhall.com/~german.

Here is some German cyberspace vocabulary with which you should be familiar. Notice the strong influence of English!

das Internet
das World Wide Web
das Bookmark
das Thema (*topic, theme*)
die Leitseite (home page)

der Browser
der Link
der Site
der URL (*Universal Resource Locator*)
die E-Mail

These URL addresses lead to interesting home pages on the culture and geography of various German-speaking countries:

1. **Deutschland: Länder und Leute**
   Interactive home page for Germany: its geography and people.
   http://www.chemie.fu-berlin.de/adressen/bl/bundeslaender.html

2. **Österreich: Geographie**
   Austrian home page with superb links to cities and sights.
   http://austria-info.at/dindex.html

3. **Schweizer Leitseiten**
   Swiss web page with fast gateways to cities and regions.
   http://www.swisshome.ch/swisshome/subdirl/german.html

4. **Liechtenstein im Netz**
   Best online information for Liechtenstein and its culture.
   http://www.LOL.li/LOL/

5. **Sprache und Landeskunde: Links**
   Extensive list of German language and culture trails on the Internet.
   http://www.uncg.edu/~lixlpurc/german_www/lang_culture2/language_and_culture.html

6. **Deutsche Internet Chronik: Geographie**
   Geography of the German-speaking countries, with web exercises.
   http://www.uncg.edu/~lixlpurc/GIP/german_units/Geography.html

Meine Familie und meine Freunde

Kapitel 2

Na, los!

Schritt 1: Das ist meine Familie

Look at the words below. Most are cognates—that is, words that are similar in German and in English. You may already know more German than you think!

DIE FAMILIE

Oma die Großmutter	die Mutter	die Tochter	die Schwester
Opa der Großvater	der Vater	der Sohn	der Bruder
der Onkel	die Tante	die Kusine	der Vetter (*male cousin*)

ALLES KLAR?

A. Mein Stammbaum (*my family tree*).

1. Draw your family tree. Add labels, using words from the above list. Then explain it to a partner.

   BEISPIEL: Das ist meine Mutter. Sie heißt Helga. Sie ist 49 Jahre alt.

2. Now have your partner describe your family tree. Correct him/her if necessary.

   BEISPIELE: — Das ist dein Vater (deine Mutter).
   — Nein, das ist nicht mein Vater, das ist mein Onkel.
   — Meine Mutter heißt nicht Klara. Sie heißt Sabine.

3. Ask your partner questions about her/his family members.

   BEISPIELE: Wie heißt deine Schwester?
   Wie alt ist dein Bruder?
   Wo wohnt dein Onkel?

B. Woher kommen sie?

1. Now discuss with a partner where various relatives are from. Some country names are listed below; ask your instructor, or refer to the Supplementary Vocabulary in the Appendix, for names of any others that you need.

   BEISPIEL: — Woher kommt deine Tante?
   — Sie kommt aus Italien.

Deutschland (*Germany*)	Afrika
England	Asien
Frankreich (*France*)	Australien
Italien	Südamerika
Portugal	Nordamerika
Spanien	

Tip!

In this and the following exercises, use **meine** (*my*) or **deine** (*your*) in conjunction with females, and **mein** or **dein** in conjunction with males. With all plural nouns use **meine** or **deine**. This structure will be explained in detail in this chapter in **Schritt 5**.

2. As a class, compile a list of where the grandparents of each class member are from. Practice asking and answering questions about their origins.

BEISPIEL: — Woher kommt Gabis Großmutter?
              — Sie kommt aus Kalifornien.

Schritt 2: **Ist dein Bruder ledig?**

Below are six words that will allow you to ask and answer more questions about members of your family.

ledig	*single, unmarried*
verlobt	*engaged*
verheiratet	*married*
getrennt	*separated*
geschieden	*divorced*
tot	*deceased*

WIR GEBEN UNSERE VERLOBUNG BEKANNT

Peer Kolb und *Sylke Hauser*

1. Juli 1995
Brüder-Grimm-Straße

Wir heiraten am 19. August 1996

Gabriele Schmidt
Andreas Franck

Bokholt
Kirchliche Trauung um 16 Uhr in
der Marienkirche

The following words refer to people. Some of them are cognates and therefore easy to guess.

der Herr	der Partner
die Frau	die Partnerin
der Mann	der Student
der Freund	die Studentin
die Freundin	
der Professor	
die Professorin	

Sing. Plural
in=innen

ALLES KLAR?

A. Fragen (*questions*). With a partner, take turns asking and answering questions about each other's families. Form questions from the word groups below.

> **BEISPIEL:** — Wie heißt deine Schwester?
> — Sie heißt Petra.
> — Ist sie ledig?
> — Nein, sie ist geschieden.

Wie	heißt	deine Eltern	verlobt
Wie alt	ist	deine Mutter/dein Vater	getrennt
	sind	deine Freundin/dein Freund	ledig
Ist		deine Partnerin/dein Partner	verheiratet
Sind			tot
			geschieden

B. Freunde und Bekannte (*friends and acquaintances*). In small groups, take turns making statements about people you know (a professor, friend, classmate, relative, etc.)

> **BEISPIEL:** Meine Schwester heißt Antje. Sie ist 25 Jahre alt. Sie ist verheiratet.

Kulturnotiz: *Freunde* vs. *Bekannte*

As opposed to the English term *friend*, which can indicate either a close friend or a more casual acquaintance, the German words **Freund** and **Freundin** imply a close or intimate relationship. German speakers also use **Freund** or **Freundin** when referring to *boyfriend*, *girlfriend*, or *best friend*. Casual friends are referred to as **Bekannte**.

Schritt 3: Was macht deine Schwester?

BERUFE (*OCCUPATIONS*)

der Arzt/die Ärztin	*male/female physician*
der Computerprogrammierer/ die Computerprogrammiererin	*male/female computer programmer*
der Fabrikarbeiter/die Fabrikarbeiterin	*male/female factory worker*
der Ingenieur/die Ingenieurin	*male/female engineer*
der Kellner/die Kellnerin	*waiter/waitress*
der Lehrer/die Lehrerin	*male/female teacher*
der Rechtsanwalt/die Rechtsanwältin	*male/female lawyer*
der Sekretär/die Sekretärin	*male/female secretary*
der Soldat/die Soldatin	*male/female soldier*
der Verkäufer/die Verkäuferin	*salesman/saleswoman*

ALLES KLAR?

A. Was sind sie von Beruf (*by profession*)? With a partner, discuss what the following people do for a living.

BEISPIEL: Sie ist Ärztin.

Kaufen = to buy
Ver Kaufer = to sell

1.

2.

3.

4.

B. Was macht dein(e)...? In small groups, tell what your relatives do for a living.

BEISPIELE: —Meine Mutter ist Ärztin.
—Mein Vater ist Lehrer.

Freundliche
Verkäuferin
für sofort gesucht
Vorstellung Freitag
von 9 bis 11 Uhr.
Süßwaren - Topf
Stadtmitte

Das Hotel zur Sonne ★★★★
sucht für die Zentralverwaltung dringend eine
SEKRETÄRIN
für den Marketingleiter.
Gerne erwarten wir Ihre Bewerbung!
Das Hotel zur Sonne
Zentralverwaltung
Goslarer Platz 27
10589 Berlin
030/4 56 67 78 (Herr Hinderling)

Tip!

When stating someone's profession or nationality, don't use *a* or *an* in German.

Meine Großmutter ist Lehrerin.
My grandmother is a teacher.

Mein Onkel ist Bolivianer.
My uncle is a Bolivian.

Schritt 4: **Was machst du gern?**

Was macht Karsten gern? Er spielt gern Gitarre.
Was machen der Vater und die Mutter gern? Sie spielen gern Karten.

Er/Sie spielt gern
  Tennis

Sie spielen gern
  Basketball
  Karten
  Monopoly
  Gitarre

<table>
<tr><td>

Redewendung

To say that you like to do an activity, use a verb plus **gern**. To say that you do not like to do it, use **nicht gern**.

Karsten spielt gern Gitarre, aber er kocht nicht gern.
Karsten likes to play the guitar, but he doesn't like to cook.

</td></tr>
</table>

ALLES KLAR?

A. Wer macht was gern? Tell what these people like to do.

tanzen

kochen

wandern

schreiben

B. Was macht deine Familie gern? Tell what some members of your family like to do. Form sentences from the word groups below.

Meine	Mutter	tanzt	gern.
Mein	Freundin	singt	
…	Vater	kocht	
	Bruder	wandert	
	…	schreibt	
		studiert	
		campt	
		schwimmt	
		…	

> *Versuch's mal!*   Der *ch*-Laut
>
> Herr und Frau Schmacht, aus Lambach, besuchen heute Familie Tiech in Bad Nachtheim. "Grüß dich!" sagt Frau Tiech. "Habt ihr Hunger? Ja?" "Ich auch!" sagt Herr Tiech. Nach dem Nachtisch lachen und sprechen sie bis spät in die Nacht. Dann sagt Herr Tiech: "Es ist immer schön, alte Nachbarn in Bad Nachtheim zu besuchen, nicht wahr?" Herr Schmacht antwortet: "Ach, das müssen wir nochmal machen!"

Die weiteren Schritte

Alles klar?

Schritt 5: Erikas Familie

Gespräch

Worum geht es hier? Reading a text in a foreign language is more challenging than reading in one's native language. When approaching any German text, first look it over for clues as to what it may be about: pictures, charts, maps. etc. Then, in this book, you may wish to study the questions following each passage. These will help you focus on the most important information. Next, skim the text, looking for the answers as you read. For example, **Wer ist Herr Hiebert?**, **Was macht Erika?**, **Wer kommt später zu Besuch?**, etc.

Then read the passage again more carefully, paying particular attention to parts you may not have understood the first time. Even though you may not know every word, you may be able to guess the meaning from context. Looking for cognates—words that are similar in both German and English—will also help. For example, can you guess the meaning of **natürlich**? **das Wetter**? **besser**? **um sechs Uhr**? Here, and in all other reading texts in this book, any key words that cannot be easily guessed are glossed below the text.

ERIKA:	Guten Tag, Großvater!
HERR HIEBERT:	Guten Tag, Erika. Wie schön, du kommst zu Besuch!
ERIKA:	Wie geht es dir heute? Bist du wirklich wieder gesund?
HERR HIEBERT:	Danke, es geht mir jetzt viel besser[1]. Ich bin nicht mehr krank. Wie geht es dir, und woher kommst du denn?
ERIKA:	Danke, mir geht es sehr gut. Ich komme gerade von[2] zu Hause.
HERR HIEBERT:	Das Wetter[3] ist heute schön, nicht wahr? Es ist so warm. Ich gehe morgen einmal in die Stadt[4].
ERIKA:	Natürlich. Jetzt bist du ja wieder gesund.
HERR HIEBERT:	Und wie geht es deinem Bruder? Kommt Peter auch bald?
ERIKA:	Der kommt später[5]. Er spielt noch Tennis mit Susie. Susie ist Peters Freundin. Er kommt heute abend um sechs Uhr[6] mit Mutter.

[1]*much better* [3]*weather* [5]*later*
[2]*right from* [4]*into town* [6]*at six o'clock*

ALLES KLAR?

Haben Sie verstanden? (*Did you understand?*)

1. Wer ist Herr Hiebert? Herr Hiebert ist Erikas...
2. Was macht Erika?
3. Was macht Herr Hiebert morgen?
4. Wer ist Peter? Peter ist Erikas...
5. Wer ist Susie?
6. Ist Herr Hiebert gesund oder krank?
7. Was macht Peter? Was macht Susie?
8. Wer kommt später?

Nouns

Nouns and gender

German nouns are always capitalized, no matter where they appear in a sentence.

Meine Telefonnummer ist 369 5483.
Erika ist Studentin in München.

In both English and German, nouns have gender; that is, they are masculine, feminine, or neuter. English uses a system of natural gender: *man = he, woman = she, weather = it*. German often uses natural gender as well: **Mann** is masculine, **Frau** is feminine. In German, however, not only words for living beings, but all nouns have gender; for example, **Besuch** (*visit*) is masculine, **Stadt** (*city*) is feminine, and **Wetter** (*weather*) is neuter.

It is the definite article—English *the*—that shows the gender of a noun. German has three definite articles, one for each gender. **Der** indicates a masculine noun, **die** a feminine noun, and **das** a neuter noun.

MASCULINE	FEMININE	NEUTER
der Vater	die Mutter	das Kind
der Besuch	die Stadt	das Wetter

Since gender is so important to the structure of the German language, you must memorize the definite article that goes with each noun you learn.

English and German also use different pronouns to indicate gender. In English, *he, she,* and *it* refer to masculine, feminine, and neuter nouns respectively. As you learned in **Kapitel 1**, the equivalent German pronouns are **er, sie, es**. Always use **er** to refer to a masculine noun, **sie** to a feminine noun, and **es** to a neuter noun. Note that **er** and **sie** can mean *it* as well as *he* and *she*.

Der Besuch war sehr schön.
The visit was very nice.

Er war sehr schön.
It was very nice.

Die Stadt ist nicht groß.
The city is not large.

Sie ist nicht groß.
It is not large.

Das Wetter ist zu warm.
The weather is too warm.

Es ist zu warm.
It is too warm.

In the plural, the definite article is **die** and the pronoun **sie** for all genders.

Die Tage sind schön und warm.
The days are nice and warm.

Sie sind schön und warm.
They are nice and warm.

Below are the names for some common classroom objects. Be sure to learn the article along with the noun. (Their plural endings are shown as well; you'll learn about those in the next section.)

1. der Bleistift, -e
2. der Kugelschreiber, -
   (der Kuli, -s)
3. der Stuhl, ⁻e
4. der Tisch, -e
5. die Kreide
6. die Landkarte, -n
7. die Tafel, -n
8. die Wand, ⁻e
9. das Bild, -er
10. das Buch, ⁻er
11. das Fenster, -
12. das Heft, -e
13. das Papier, -e

ALLES KLAR?

A. Im Klassenzimmer. Replace the noun with the pronoun.

> **BEISPIEL:** Der Student ist aus Österreich.
> Er ist aus Österreich.

1. Die Bleistifte sind nicht hier.
2. Die Landkarte hängt an der Wand.
3. Das Buch ist sehr alt.
4. Der Kugelschreiber fehlt (*is missing*).
5. Die Bilder sind nicht schön.
6. Der Stuhl ist kaputt.
7. Die Fenster sind offen.
8. Die Tafel ist grün.
9. Wo ist das Heft?
10. Der Tisch ist neu.

B. In unserem Klassenzimmer. Using the antonyms provided, ask and answer questions about the objects in your classroom. In your answer, replace the noun with the appropriate pronoun.

groß/klein   altmodisch/modern
alt/neu   billig/teuer (*cheap/expensive*)

> **BEISPIELE:** —Ist das Buch teuer?
> —Ja, es ist teuer.
>
> —Sind die Stühle neu?
> —Nein, sie sind alt.

1. Sind die Schreibtische…?
2. Ist die Tafel…?

…

Plurals

Whereas almost all English nouns take the plural ending -**s**, German has many different plural endings. Look at the nouns in the preceding section and in the **Themenwortschatz** to see these various endings. As with gender, there is often no way to determine what the plural form is to be, and therefore you must memorize the plural of German nouns as well. You will find the plural forms indicated with every noun in the **Themenwortschatz** as well as in the end vocabulary; they are indicated in the following way:

VOCABULARY LISTING		PLURAL FORM
der Besuch, -e	*visit*	**die Besuche**
das Kind, -er	*child*	**die Kinder**
die Mutter, ⸚	*mother*	**die Mütter**
die Stadt, ⸚e	*city*	**die Städte**
der Lehrer, -	*teacher*	**die Lehrer**

A. Im Schreibwarengeschäft. You are the salesperson in a stationery store. Answer the customer's questions, using the plural. Look back at the listing of classroom objects on the previous page for help with the plurals of these nouns.

> BEISPIEL: Wieviel kostet das Heft? (3,- DM)
> Die Hefte kosten drei Mark.

1. Wieviel kostet der Bleistift? (50 Pfennig)
2. Wieviel kostet das Buch? (5,- DM)
3. Wieviel kostet die Postkarte? (80 Pfennig)
4. Wieviel kostet der Kuli? (2,- DM)
5. Wieviel kostet die Landkarte? (9,- DM)

B. Was macht die Familie? Change the sentences to the singular.

1. Die Brüder kommen zu Besuch.
2. Die Kinder spielen Karten.
3. Die Söhne sind nicht zu Hause.
4. Die Tanten wohnen in Berlin.
5. Die Kusinen arbeiten um 8 Uhr.

Nominative case

To show how nouns function within a sentence, English uses word order: for example, in an English sentence the subject precedes the verb.

> *My grandfather is retired.*
> *Tomorrow my cousin is coming to visit.*

Rather than relying on word position, German uses what is called a case system. It has four cases: **nominative**, **accusative** (direct object), **dative** (indirect object), and **genitive** (possessive). In this chapter you will learn about the nominative.

The nominative case is used for the subject of a sentence:

SUBJECT

Der Großvater ist krank.
Erika kommt zu Besuch.
Wie heißen **Sie**?

and for the predicate nominative. (Reminder: the predicate nominative is a noun that is the same as the sentence subject. It follows the verbs **sein**, **heißen**, or **werden** [*to become*].)

SUBJECT		PREDICATE NOMINATIVE
Das	ist	meine Schwester.
Der Professor	ist	mein Vater.
Der Amerikaner	heißt	George.

Definite and indefinite articles

As you learned in the preceding section, German has three words for the definite article (*the*): **der**, **die**, **das**. These are their nominative forms; the other cases have different forms, which you will study in later chapters.

Like English, German also has an indefinite article meaning *a*. Its nominative forms are **ein**, **eine**, **ein**.

	DEFINITE ARTICLE	INDEFINITE ARTICLE
MASCULINE	der Herr	ein Herr
FEMININE	die Frau	eine Frau
NEUTER	das Kind	ein Kind
PLURAL	die Kinder	(no plural)

Kein

Kein is the negative form of **ein**, i.e., the equivalent to English *not a*, *not any*, or *no*. Its plural form is **keine**.

	SINGULAR	PLURAL
MASCULINE	kein Herr	keine Herren
FEMININE	keine Frau	keine Frauen
NEUTER	kein Kind	keine Kinder

Kein can be used to form the negative of any noun phrase with an indefinite article. Compare its use to that of **nicht** (see p. 49).

Ein Soldat wohnt hier.
A soldier lives here.

Kein Soldat wohnt hier.
No soldier lives here.

ALLES KLAR?

A. Was sind sie von Beruf? Ask about the professions of the people you see. Follow the model.

BEISPIEL: —Ist das ein Arzt?
—Nein, das ist kein Arzt, das ist eine Ärztin.

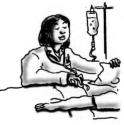

ein Arzt

1. eine Computerprogrammiererin

2. ein Soldat

3. ein Ingenieur

4. eine Lehrerin

5. eine Sekretärin

B. Was sind deine Verwandten von Beruf? With your partner, take turns asking and answering questions about the professions of your relatives.

> **BEISPIEL:** Ist deine Mutter Ingenieurin?
> Nein, sie ist keine Ingenieurin.

1. Ist dein Onkel Arzt?
2. Ist deine Schwester Kellnerin?
3. Ist/war (*was*) dein Großvater Lehrer?
4. Ist deine Tante Verkäuferin?
5. Ist dein Vater Rechtsanwalt?
6. Ist deine Mutter Computerprogrammiererin?
7. Ist dein Bruder Sekretär?

Possessive adjectives

Possessive adjectives indicate ownership and are expressed in English by *my, your, our, their,* etc.

> **Unsere Mutter** spielt gut Tennis.
> ***Our mother*** plays tennis well.

> Ist das **euer Bruder?**
> Is that ***your brother?***

The following chart shows the possessive adjectives in German.

SINGULAR			PLURAL		
ich	**mein**	*my*	wir	**unser**	*our*
du	**dein** (informal)	*your*	ihr	**euer** (informal)	*your*
er	**sein** (masc.)	*his; its*	sie	**ihr**	*their*
sie	**ihr** (fem.)	*her; its*			
es	**sein** (neut.)	*its*			
Sie	**Ihr** (formal)	*your*	Sie	**Ihr** (formal)	*your*

Note that the formal possessive adjective, **Ihr** (*your*), is always capitalized, as is the formal personal pronoun **Sie.**

Possessive adjectives take the same endings as **ein** and **kein.** That is, in the nominative case, the feminine singular and the plural end in -**e**:

MASCULINE:	**Mein Bruder** kocht gern.
FEMININE:	**Meine Schwester** wohnt in New York.
NEUTER:	**Mein Kind** singt nicht gut.
PLURAL:	**Meine Großeltern** sind geschieden.

When **euer** takes an ending, it drops the -**e**- in front of -**r**:

> eu**er** Freund → e**ure** Freundin

ALLES KLAR?

A. Sie auch? Respond to each statement by saying that it also applies to the other person.

> **BEISPIEL:** Seine Freundin singt sehr schön. (*my*)
> Meine Freundin singt auch sehr schön.

1. Unser Großvater kommt zu Besuch. (*her*)
2. Dein Kind ist noch [*still*] klein. (*their*)
3. Deine Mutter arbeitet schwer. (*his*)
4. Dein Vetter spielt gern Monopoly. (*your*, informal pl.)
5. Ihre Tante verkauft Bücher. (*our*)
6. Sein Sohn ist zu Hause. (*my*)
7. Seine Geschwister (*siblings*) sind nicht hier. (*your*, formal sing.)

B. Eine moderne Familie.

 1. Discuss the family relationships shown below, using possessive adjectives (The broken line indicates the people are divorced.)

> **BEISPIEL:** Stefan
>
> Stefans Eltern sind geschieden. Seine Mutter heißt Susanne. Sein Vater heißt Peter. Seine Schwester heißt Brigitte. Brigitte ist 12 Jahre alt. Stefan und Brigitte wohnen in Berlin.

1. Susanne
2. Christiane
3. Uwe
4. Peter

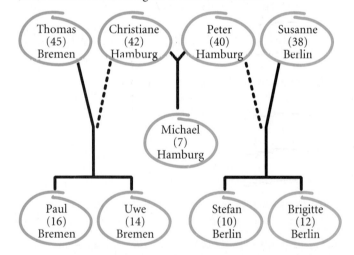

 2. Now assume the role of one of the members of the family shown in Part 1. Your partner will ask questions, trying to guess which person you are.

> **BEISPIEL:** —Sind deine Eltern geschieden?
> —Nein, sie sind nicht geschieden.
> —Heißt deine Mutter Christiane?
> —Ja, meine Mutter heißt Christiane.
> —Jetzt ist alles klar! Du bist ___.

 3. Tell a third person about your partner's assumed character. Use the possessive adjectives.

> **BEISPIEL:** Michaels Eltern sind nicht geschieden.
> Seine Mutter heißt Christiane.

Demonstrative pronouns

German frequently uses the definite articles **der**, **die**, and **das** as demonstrative pronouns, without a following noun. They refer to a specific person or thing, often with emphasis. They usually occur at the beginning of the sentence.

—Kommt Peter auch bald?	*Is Peter also coming soon?*
—**Der** kommt später.	*He's coming later.*
—Wo wohnen deine Eltern?	*Where do your parents live?*
—**Die** wohnen in Bremen.	*They live in Bremen.*

ALLES KLAR?

Weiter mit der Familie. Refer back to the family tree on p. 44. With a partner, ask and answer questions about the family members.

BEISPIEL: —Ist Susanne geschieden?
—Ja, die ist geschieden.
—Heißt Pauls Vater auch Paul?
—Nein, der...

Schritt 6: Meine Familie kommt aus Deutschland und Österreich

Lesestück

Worum geht es hier? This text briefly discusses one family's origins and their life in America. First read the questions that follow it, then skim the passage, looking for key words—the names of cities, countries, professions, and fill in the following chart. Then read the text more carefully a second time.

	KOMMEN AUS?		WOHNEN JETZT IN?	BERUF?
	STADT	LAND		
GROSSMUTTER				
GROSSVATER				

Meine Großeltern kommen aus Deutschland und Österreich. Meine Großmutter kommt aus Hamburg — das ist in Norddeutschland. Mein Großvater kommt nicht aus Deutschland, er kommt aus Linz in Österreich. Jetzt wohnen meine Großeltern schon zweiundzwanzig Jahre in Amerika, in Frankfort, Kentucky. Mein Großvater und meine Großmutter sind schon viele Jahre Amerikaner. Meine Großmutter ist Lehrerin von Beruf. Mein Großvater ist kein Lehrer. Er ist Verkäufer, er verkauft Möbel[1]—Lampen, Tische, Stühle. Manchmal besuchen meine Großeltern Deutschland und Österreich. Ihr Deutsch ist natürlich noch[2] sehr gut. Ihr Englisch ist aber auch gut, es ist sogar[3] sehr gut.

---

[1]*furniture*   [2]*still*   [3]*even*

Redewendung

Another common flavoring particle is aber. In addition to its primary meaning of *but*, it can be used to add emphasis to a statement, or sometimes to indicate surprise.

Ihr Englisch ist aber auch gut.
Their English is really good, too.

Das ist aber schön!
That's really pretty!

ALLES KLAR?

A. Haben Sie verstanden?

1. Woher kommen die Großeltern?
2. Woher in Deutschland kommt die Großmutter?
3. Wo wohnen die Großeltern?
4. Wie lange wohnen die Großeltern schon in Amerika?
5. Was ist die Großmutter von Beruf?
6. Was ist der Großvater von Beruf?

B. Persönliche (*personal*) Fragen.

1. Woher kommt Ihre Familie?
2. Woher kommt Ihr Großvater/Ihre Großmutter?
3. Wo wohnen Ihre Großeltern?
4. Was ist/war (*was*) Ihr Großvater/Ihre Großmutter von Beruf?
5. Wie lange wohnt Ihre Familie schon in Amerika?

Kulturnotiz: German immigrants in America

The immigration of German-speaking people has been one of the major elements in the development of the American population. In the 18th century, the German language rivaled English in importance in the colonies. As late as 1850, German-speakers still made up 70% of all immigrants. Over 6,000,000 Germans immigrated to the United States between 1700 and 1962.

The reasons for German immigration vary. Certain groups, such as the Amish and Mennonites, came seeking religious freedom. Some of these communities use a German dialect at home (such as Pennsylvania Dutch), and standard German in church even today. Other German-speakers came as a result of political upheavals, such as the revolutions of 1848, or to avoid persecution after the rise of Hitler, in 1933. A desire for economic opportunity and freedom from social restrictions was also a powerful motivation to immigrate to the U.S.

German was widely spoken in many parts of the US. For instance, in 1900 Wisconsin had about 100 German language newspapers. In Milwaukee, the German language dailies had almost twice the circulation of the English language press. As late as 1946, churches in Perry County, Missouri still used German as a means of communication.

3 Perry County, Missouri

Heeszel Alfred Rt 1 Perry 5957......... 824-
Heinbokel Dan Frohna 824-
Hellwege N Frohna 824-
Herman Lou Frohna 67................... 824-
Hoehn Fran Farrar 63746 824-
Hoffmann Carol Altenburg 824-

I

Immanuel L Altenburg 824-

J

Jablonski Roy Wittenberg.............. 82-
Joint Utilities Gas Dept Box 22 63 82-

K

Kaempfe Ann Altenburg 824-
Kaempfe B Rt 1 Frohna 824-
Kassel Ed Rt 1 824-
Kasten George HCR Box 6890........... 824-
Katt E Rt 1............................ 824-
Kaufmann B Perry County 824-

Können Sie die deutschen Namen finden?

Although the use of spoken German has declined in the US, the vestiges of the enormous German immigration are visible everywhere. Many Americans have German surnames, and many more have German-speaking ancestors. German food stores and restaurants can be found in countless North American cities and towns, and place names such as Germantown, Pennsylvania; Berlin, Wisconsin; Hamburg, Arkansas; Dresden, Ontario; Hanover, New Hampshire; and Frankfort, Kentucky attest to German settlement. Are there traces of German immigration in your town? Where might you find them?

Word order

Statements and questions

1. German has several rules of word order, three of which you have already been using in **Kapitel 1** and in this chapter. They are very much like English word order.

   In so-called normal word order, the subject is in the first position, followed by the verb.

SUBJECT	VERB			
Sie	tanzt		gern.	*She likes to dance.*
Peter	kommt	aus	Deutschland.	*Peter is from Germany.*

   In questions that require a yes or no answer, the verb is in the first position, i.e., the sentence is in inverted word order.

VERB	SUBJECT		
Kommt	sie	morgen?	*Will she come tomorrow?*
Ist	Klaus	verheiratet?	*Is Klaus married?*

   In specific questions, specific information is sought. They begin with an interrogative word like **was, wer, wie, wo, wann**, etc. The interrogative word is followed by the verb.

INTERROGATIVE	VERB	SUBJECT	
Wo	wohnst	du?	*Where do you live?*
Wie	ist	deine Telefonnummer?	*What is your telephone number?*

2. Unlike English, German also uses inverted word order in statements. This is because, in German statements, the verb is *always* in second position, regardless of whether it is preceded by the subject or by some other word element—an adverb, prepositional phrase, etc. Compare the following sentences:

1   **2**

NORMAL WORD ORDER: Meine Großeltern **wohnen** jetzt in Amerika.

1   **2**

INVERTED WORD ORDER: Jetzt **wohnen** meine Großeltern in Amerika.

In the second sentence, the adverb **jetzt** is in first position; the verb **wohnen** must remain in second position; and the subject **Großeltern** therefore follows the verb. Note that the first element can consist of several words or phrases.

1   **2**

Heute abend um sechs Uhr spielt er Tennis.

ALLES KLAR?

A. Tante Rosa ist ein bißchen schwerhörig. Aunt Rosa is hard of hearing and has to ask questions about what has been said. Form questions from the statements below. Follow the model.

> **BEISPIEL:**   Mein Bruder kommt heute abend.
>   Kommt dein Bruder heute abend?

1. Ihre Großeltern kommen aus der Schweiz.
2. Sein Sohn ist Arzt.
3. Meine Schwester ist geschieden.
4. Unser Großvater verkauft Möbel. *Cal*
5. Ich bin schon achtzehn Jahre alt.

B. Tante Rosa hört nicht alles. Aunt Rosa misses the part of the sentence in italics. Ask a question beginning with an interrogative that corresponds to the missing information.

> **BEISPIEL:**   Ich wohne jetzt *in Frankfurt.*
>   Wo wohnst du jetzt?

1. Helena kommt *aus Österreich.*
2. *Peter* ist sieben Jahre alt.
3. Es geht mir *gut.*
4. Sabine fährt *heute* nach Hause.
5. Wir wohnen jetzt *in Freiburg.*
6. Das Haus kostet *200.000 DM.*
7. Herr Schmidt verkauft *Bücher.*

C. Die Antworten auf Tante Rosas Fragen. Answer Aunt Rosa's questions; emphasize the phrase in parentheses by placing it first in the sentence.

> **BEISPIEL:**   Wann arbeitet deine Mutter? (morgens)
>   Morgens arbeitet meine Mutter.

Im Januar Kommen deine

1. Wann kommen deine Eltern zu Besuch? (im Januar)
2. Wie lange wohnt dein Bruder in Amerika? (schon zwei Jahre)
3. Wann spielen wir Karten? (um acht Uhr)
4. Wann kommen die Kinder? (morgen)
5. Wo wohnt deine Schwester? (in Innsbruck)
6. Wann spielen die Kusinen Tennis? (jetzt)

The position of *nicht*

The position of **nicht** (*not*) within a sentence can vary considerably.

1. **Nicht** generally precedes the word or phrase it negates. It precedes:

   - **PREDICATE ADJECTIVES**
     Meine Schwester ist nicht verlobt.   *My sister isn't engaged.*

   - **PREDICATE NOUNS**
     Der Mann dort ist nicht mein Vater.   *That man there is not my father.*

   - **ADVERBS**
     Sein Bruder tanzt nicht gern.   *His brother doesn't like to dance.*

   - **PREPOSITIONAL PHRASES**
     Meine Eltern kommen nicht aus   *My parents don't come from Germany.*
     Deutschland.

   - **ANY ELEMENT THAT IS EMPHASIZED**
     Mein Großvater kommt nicht aus   *My grandfather doesn't come from*
     Deutschland, er kommt aus Linz   *Germany, he comes from Linz,*
     in Österreich.   *in Austria.*

2. If the entire sentence is negated, **nicht** often appears at the end of the sentence.

   Der Großvater kommt heute nicht.   *Grandfather is not coming today.*
   Kommst du morgen nicht?   *Aren't you coming tomorrow?*
   Ich verstehe das nicht.   *I don't understand that.*

ALLES KLAR?

Alles falsch! Correct Peter by negating the sentences. Pay careful attention to the position of **nicht**.

1. **PETER:** "Rolf ist/verheiratet."
2. **PETER:** "Er tanzt/gern."
3. **PETER:** "Seine Eltern kommen/aus Österreich."
4. **PETER:** "Das ist/sein Vater."
5. **PETER:** "Sein Vater spielt Karten/gern."
6. **PETER:** "Rolfs Schwester ist/verlobt."
7. **PETER:** "Sie kommt/morgen."
8. **PETER:** "Was ich sage (*say*) ist/richtig!"

nicht vs. *kein*

If a noun is preceded by the indefinite article **ein** or by no article at all, use **kein** to negate it. Otherwise use **nicht**.

Ist das ein Bleistift?   Nein, das ist **kein** Bleistift.
Ist dein Großvater Lehrer?   Nein, mein Großvater ist **kein** Lehrer.
Ist das sein Bruder?   Nein, das ist **nicht** sein Bruder.

ALLES KLAR?

A. Richtig oder falsch? Read each sentence. Correct the sentences that are not true for you by adding **nicht** or **kein**.

1. Meine Großeltern kommen aus England.
2. Mein Bruder ist ledig.
3. Meine Tante heißt Helene.
4. Mein Bruder hat eine Freundin.
5. Mein Vater schreibt oft.
6. Ich bin Amerikaner/Amerikanerin.
7. Ich verstehe meine Eltern.
8. Meine Familie und ich kommen aus Berlin.
9. Mein Großvater ist gesund.
10. Ich bin Kellner/Kellnerin.

 **B. Negativ!** Take turns telling what your family and friends are *not* doing and do *not* like to do. Use both **nicht** and **kein**.

> **BEISPIEL:**   Mein Vater ist kein Ingenieur.
> Er kocht nicht gern.

Vater/Mutter	Fabrikarbeiter(in)	arbeiten
Bruder/Schwester	Sekretär(in)	campen
Großmutter/Großvater	Lehrer(in)	kochen
Onken/Tante	Soldat(in)	schreiben
Kusine/Vetter	Professor(in)	wohnen in…
Freund/Freundin	Kellner(in)	wandern
Professor/Professorin	Ingenieur(in)	tanzen

Schritt 7: **Die Familie Krenz**

 Lesestück

Worum geht es hier? Before reading the paragraph on the next page, look at the picture below. Can you guess the relationships between these people?

Die Familie wohnt in Stuttgart und hat sechs Familienmitglieder. In dem Bild sind von links nach rechts[1] Großvater Krenz; Peter; Hanna; die Mutter, Frau Hildegard Krenz; der Vater, Herr Paul Krenz; und Peter und Hannas Onkel Heinz. Aber wo ist die Großmutter? Die Großmutter ist leider schon tot. Hat[2] Onkel Heinz eine Frau? Nein, Onkel Heinz ist nicht verheiratet, er ist geschieden. Wie alt sind Hanna und Peter? Hanna ist neunzehn, und Peter ist dreiundzwanzig. Sind Hanna und Peter verheiratet? Nein, sie sind Geschwister. Sie sind noch Studenten und sind ledig. Aber Peter hat eine Freundin. Wie heißt Peters Freundin? Sie heißt Monika, und sie ist Rechtsanwältin.

---

[1]*from left to right*
[2]*Does…have*

ALLES KLAR?

Wer ist wer? With a partner, identify the people in the picture.

BEISPIEL: Das ist der Onkel. Er heißt Heinz.

Proper names showing possession

In German, proper names showing possession or a close relationship add an **-s** just as in English, but without an apostrophe:

Peters Freundin
Hannas Onkel

If the name ends in an **-s**, no additional **s** is added but an apostrophe is used:

Klaus' Bruder
Paris' Wetter

ALLES KLAR?

Auf einem Familientag (*at a family gathering*). Show the relationship of one relative to another by using the name in parentheses.

BEISPIEL: Wessen (*whose*) Mutter ist auf Rente? (Karin)
                 Karins Mutter ist auf Rente.

1. Wessen Familie kommt aus Deutschland? (Frau Müller)
2. Wessen Tochter ist Ärztin? (Helmut)
3. Wessen Bruder ist Kellner? (Monika)
4. Wessen Freundin ist Professorin? (Hans)
5. Wessen Schwester ist nicht hier? (Birgit)

Die letzten Schritte

Wer macht mit?

Zusammenfassung

A. Ingrid und ihre Familie. Fill in the blanks.

Ingrids Familie kommt aus Deutschland, aber sie _wohnt_ jetzt in Amerika. _Ihr_ Vater, Herr Helm, ist _aus_ Stuttgart. Stuttgart _ist_ in Süddeutschland. _Ihre_ Mutter, Frau Helm, ist _aus_ Hamburg. Hamburg _ist_ in Norddeutschland. Natürlich _sind_ die Eltern schon Amerikaner. Ihr Englisch _ist_ auch gut. _Ihre_ Großeltern _sind_ leider schon tot. Ingrid und _ihr_ Mann, Ernst, fahren (*travel*) manchmal zu Besuch nach Deutschland. Ihr Deutsch _ist_ sehr gut. _Sie_ besuchen natürlich Hamburg und Stuttgart. Ingrids Eltern, _Frau_ und _Herr_ Helm, _sind_ schon sehr alt.

B. Meine Familie. Rewrite the exercise above, changing the information so that it describes your own family.

C. Wer ist das? Look at the photo below and speculate in writing about who she is. Consider the following questions:

Wie heißt sie?
Woher kommt sie?
Was macht sie (nicht) gern?
Was ist sie von Beruf?
Ist sie ledig? verheiratet? geschieden?
Hat sie (*does she have*) Kinder?

D. An meinen Brieffreund/An meine Brieffreundin. You have a new German pen-pal. Write a letter to your pen-pal describing your family. Ask about your pen-pal's family.

BEISPIEL:

Chicago, den 25.10.96

Liebe Katarina,

ich heiße Michael, und meine Familie ist groß. Wie heißt Deine Mutter?

Meine Mutter _____

Bis bald,
Michael

Tip!

In letters, all forms of the second-person are capitalized (**Du**, **Dich**, **Dein**, **Ihr**, **Euer**, etc.).

52 zweiundfünfzig • Kapitel 2

In this section, you and your partner will be working on different pages—one of you on this page, one on the other side.

A. Inventar. Compare your inventory list on this page with that of your partner to find out what you have in common. (Do not look at each other's pages!) Make a list of the items of which you and your partner have the same amount. To say what you have, use the phrase **Ich habe...**

> **BEISPIEL:** [2] Heft
> —Ich habe zwei Hefte.
> —Ich auch. (Ich nicht.)

[10] Buch   [6] Professor
[3] Tisch   [3] Stuhl
[1] Landkarte   [2] Bild
[20] Bleistift   [2] Kugelschreiber

B. Eine berühmte (*famous*) **Familie.** With a partner, complete this partial genealogy of Maria Theresa, Empress of Austria.

> **BEISPIELE:** Wie heißt Maria Theresias Mutter?
> Wie heißt Maria Theresias Mann?

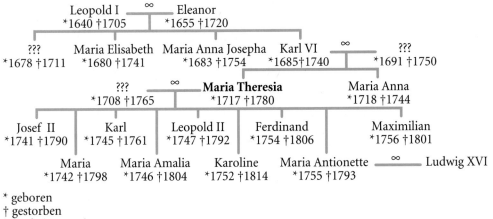

* geboren
† gestorben
∞ verheiratet mit

Now write about the relationships.

> **BEISPIEL:** [X] ist Maria Theresias Großvater. Seine Frau heißt ...

In this section, you and your partner will be working on different pages—one of you on this page, one on the other side.

A. Inventar. Compare your inventory list on this page with that of your partner to find out what you have in common. (Do not look at each other's pages!) Make a list of the items of which you and your partner have the same amount. To say what you have, use the phrase **Ich habe...**

> **BEISPIEL:** [2] Heft
> —Ich habe zwei Hefte.
> —Ich auch. (Ich nicht.)

[2] Bild   [1] Landkarte
[4] Kugelschreiber   [2] Stuhl
[6] Professor in   [8] Buch
[18] Bleistift   [2] Tisch

B. Eine berühmte (*famous*) **Familie.** With a partner, complete the genealogy of Maria Theresa, Empress of Austria.

> **BEISPIELE:** Wie heißt Maria Theresas Vater?
> Wie heißt Leopolds Frau?

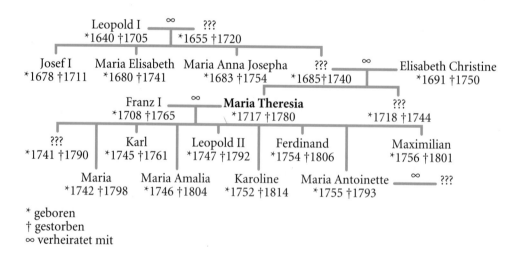

```
           Leopold I  ∞  ???
           *1640 †1705  *1655 †1720

Josef I      Maria Elisabeth   Maria Anna Josepha   ???      ∞   Elisabeth Christine
*1678 †1711   *1680 †1741     *1683 †1754     *1685 †1740      *1691 †1750

           Franz I  ∞  Maria Theresia        ???
           *1708 †1765  *1717 †1780      *1718 †1744

???      Karl     Leopold II   Ferdinand        Maximilian
*1741 †1790  *1745 †1761  *1747 †1792  *1754 †1806      *1756 †1801

   Maria     Maria Amalia   Karoline   Maria Antoinette  ∞  ???
   *1742 †1798  *1746 †1804  *1752 †1814  *1755 †1793
```

* geboren
† gestorben
∞ verheiratet mit

Now write about the relationships.

> **BEISPIEL:** [X] ist Maria Theresias Großmutter. Ihr Mann heißt ...

Situationen

A. Beschreiben Sie (*describe*) **Ihre Familie!** Bring in pictures of your own family and describe who is who to members of the class.

BEISPIEL: Links ist meine Mutter. Sie heißt Anne. Sie ist Lehrerin.
Das ist mein Bruder…

B. Familie X. Pretend that you are a member of a family you know well, or an imaginary family. Your partner will interview you and take notes. Then switch roles. Report back to the class.

SUGGESTED QUESTIONS
Woher kommt deine Familie?
Wie heißt dein Vater?/deine Mutter?
Wie heißen deine Geschwister?
Wo wohnst du?
Wie alt ist deine Mutter/Großmutter, dein Vater/Großvater?
Woher kommen deine Großeltern?
Wo wohnen deine Großeltern?
Was ist dein Vater/Großvater, deine Mutter/Großmutter von Beruf?

C. Die Volkszählung (*census*). You are a census-taker interviewing your partner. Ask about members of the family — their ages, their occupations, and their marital status. Remember to use the formal address: **Sie.**

YOU MIGHT BEGIN: —Wie viele Leute wohnen hier?
—Fünf Leute wohnen hier. Mein Vater…

Themenwortschatz

Familie/Freunde — *Family/Friends*

der Amerikaner, -	*[male] American citizen*
die Amerikanerin, -nen	*[female] American citizen*
der Bekannte, -n	*[male] acquaintance*
die Bekannte, -n	*[female] acquaintance*
der Bruder, ⁻	*brother*
die Eltern (pl.)	*parents*
die Familie, -n	*family*
das Familienmitglied, -er	*family member*
die Frau, -en	*woman; wife*
der Freund, -e	*[male] friend*
die Freundin, -nen	*[female] friend*
die Geschwister (pl.)	*siblings*
die Großeltern (pl.)	*grandparents*
die Großmutter, ⁻	*grandmother*
der Großvater, ⁻	*grandfather*
der Junge, -n	*boy*
das Kind, -er	*child*
die Kusine, -n	*[female] cousin*
die Leute (pl.)	*people*
das Mädchen, -	*girl*
der Mann, ⁻er	*man; husband*
die Mutter, ⁻	*mother*
der Onkel, -	*uncle*
der Partner, -	*[male] partner*
die Partnerin, -nen	*[female] partner*
die Schwester, -n	*sister*
der Sohn, ⁻e	*son*
der Student, -en	*[male] student (university level)*
die Studentin, -nen	*[female] student (university level)*
die Tante, -n	*aunt*
die Tochter, ⁻	*daughter*
der Vater, ⁻	*father*
der Vetter, -n	*[male] cousin*

Berufe — *Occupations*

der Arzt, ⁻e	*[male] physician*
die Ärztin, -nen	*[female] physician*
der Beruf, -e	*occupation*
der Computerprogrammierer, -	*[male] computer programmer*
die Computerprogrammiererin, -nen	*[female] computer programmer*
der Fabrikarbeiter, -	*[male] factory worker*
die Fabrikarbeiterin, -nen	*[female] factory worker*
der Ingenieur, -e	*[male] engineer*
die Ingenieurin, -nen	*[female] engineer*
der Kellner, -	*waiter*
die Kellnerin, -nen	*waitress*
der Lehrer, -	*[male] teacher*
die Lehrerin, -nen	*[female] teacher*
der Professor, -en	*[male] professor*
die Professorin, -nen	*[female] professor*
der Rechtsanwalt, ⁻e	*[male] lawyer*
die Rechtsanwältin, -nen	*[female] lawyer*
der Sekretär, -e	*[male] secretary*
die Sekretärin, -nen	*[female] secretary*
der Soldat, -en	*[male] soldier*
die Soldatin, -nen	*[female] soldier*
der Verkäufer, -	*salesman*
die Verkäuferin, -nen	*saleswoman*

Verben — *Verbs*

campen	*to camp, go camping*
kochen	*to cook*
machen	*to do*
schwimmen	*to swim*
singen	*to sing*
spielen	*to play*
studieren	*to study*
tanzen	*to dance*
wandern	*to hike*

Adjektive/Adverbien — *Adjectives/Adverbs*

geschieden	*divorced*
gesund	*healthy*
getrennt	*separated*
kurz	*short*
ledig	*single, unmarried*
tot	*dead*
verheiratet	*married*
verliebt	*in love*
verlobt	*engaged*

Andere Wörter — *Other Words*

gerade	*just*
gern	*gladly, with pleasure, readily*
kein	*not a, not any*
schon	*already*

Ausdrücke — *Expressions*

auf Rente sein	*to be retired*
Basketball (Gitarre, Karten, Tennis, Monopoly) spielen	*to play basketball (the guitar, cards, tennis, Monopoly)*
von Beruf	*by occupation, by profession, by trade*
zu Hause	*at home*
zu Besuch kommen	*to come to visit*

Weiterer Wortschatz

Gegenstände im Klassenzimmer	Objects in the Classroom
das Bild, -er	picture
der Bleistift, -e	pencil
das Buch, ¨er	book
das Fenster, -	window
das Heft, -e	notebook
die Kreide	chalk
der Kugelschreiber, - (der Kuli, -s)	ballpoint pen
die Landkarte, -en	map
das Papier, -e	paper
der Schreibtisch, -e	desk
der Stuhl, ¨e	chair
die Tafel, -n	blackboard
der Tisch, -e	table
die Wand, ¨e	wall

Andere Substantive	Other Nouns
(das) Amerika	America
(das) Deutschland	Germany
(das) Österreich	Austria
die Schweiz	Switzerland
die Stadt, ¨e	city
der Tag, -e	day
das Wetter	weather

Verben	Verbs
besuchen	to visit
gehen	to go, to walk
verkaufen	to sell
werden	to become

Adjektive/Adverbien	Adjectives/Adverbs
bald	soon
groß	big, great, large; tall
heute	today
klein	small; short
manchmal	sometimes
schön	nice; beautiful
warm	warm
wirklich	honestly, really, truly

Andere Wörter	Other Words
aber	really, certainly (flavoring particle)
ja	after all, of course (flavoring particle)
wann	when
wieder	again

to become - werden ≠ bekommen - to get something

Werden

ich werde   wir werden
du wirst   ihr werdet
sie, er, es wird   sie werden

Meine Sachen, deine Sachen...

Kommunikation

- Mentioning personal characteristics
- Discussing and describing personal possessions
- Talking about colors
- Describing your personal living space
- Discussing what you must, can, or want to do
- Stating what you would like to have

Strukturen

- The verb **haben**
- Accusative case
  Definite and indefinite articles
  Possessive adjectives
  Es gibt
  Personal pronouns
  Interrogative pronouns
  Prepositions with the accusative
- The modals **können**, **müssen**, and **wollen**
- The verb form **möchte**
- Verbs with stem vowel changes

Kultur

- Student housing

Kapitel 3

Na, los!

Schritt 1: Wie ist...?

In **Kapitel 2** you learned some cognates for the names of family members — e.g. **Vater** (*father*), **Onkel** (*uncle*), etc. Here are some additional words the meaning of which should be easy to guess.

alt/jung *or* **neu**	**(un)freundlich**
intelligent/doof	**(un)interessant**
fit	

A few more useful adjectives are:

fleißig/faul	*industrious/lazy*
froh/traurig	*happy/sad*
schön/häßlich	*pretty, nice/ugly*
böse	*angry, mad*
nett	*nice*
neugierig	*curious*
zufrieden	*content, satisfied*

ALLES KLAR?

A. Wie sind diese Leute? Describe the people in the drawings.

> **BEISPIEL:** Sie ist fit.

B. Wie ist deine Familie? Wie sind deine Freunde? Now describe your friends and family members to a partner. You may want to modify your descriptions by adding **nicht, sehr, nicht sehr,** or **manchmal.**

BEISPIELE: Mein Freund Hans ist sehr intelligent.
Meine Großmutter ist nicht sehr alt.

C. Wie ist es? Which of the words you just learned can you use to describe objects? Review the following vocabulary for classroom objects.

die Tafel *board*	die Tür	das Fenster *window*
der Schreibtisch *desk*	die Kreide *chalk*	der Stuhl *seat*
der Tisch *table*	das Bild *picture*	die Landkarte *map*

With a partner, describe the objects in your classroom.

BEISPIEL: Der Schreibtisch ist alt.

Schritt 2: Was haben Sie da?

"Daniels Zimmer"

1. der Computer	6. der Papierkorb	10. der Spiegel *– Time/Newsweek*
2. das Bett	7. das Poster *das plakat*	11. der Sessel *– easy chair*
3. das Bücherregal	8. das Radio	12. der Kühlschrank *– ice box, fridge*
4. der CD-Spieler	9. der Schrank	13. das Telefon
5. die Lampe		

Tip!

When discussing what someone has, use **einen** or **keinen** for masculine objects. You will learn more about this topic in **Schritt 4**.

ALLES KLAR?

 Was hast du? With a partner, discuss what belongings Daniel has that you either also own or that you do not own. Use the phrases **Daniel hat...** and **Ich habe....**

BEISPIELE: —Daniel hat einen Computer. Ich habe auch einen Computer.
—Daniel hat ein Poster. Ich habe kein Poster.

Schritt 3: Welche Farbe hat...?

drunk blau   *blue*   purpur   *purple*
braun   *brown*   rosa   *pink*
gelb   *yellow*   rot   *red*
grün   *green*   schwarz   *black*
orange   *orange*   weiß   *white*

To ask what color something is, say: **Welche Farbe hat [der Tisch]?** To answer, use the verb **sein**: **[Der Tisch] ist [braun]**.

ALLES KLAR?

A. Welche Farbe hat...? With a partner, take turns pointing to various objects and asking about their color.

BEISPIELE: —Welche Farbe hat der Bleistift?
—Er ist gelb.

—Welche Farbe hat Martins Buch?
—Es ist blau.

B. Meine Sachen. In **Schritt 2** you mentioned some of your belongings. Now describe them in more detail. Use at least two adjectives.

BEISPIEL: Ich habe eine Lampe. Meine Lampe ist groß und weiß.

▶ *Versuch's mal!*   Der *w*-Laut

ZUNGENBRECHER (*tongue-twister*)

—Wollen wir weiter durch den Wald wandern?
—Ja, aber wie wandern wir weiter, wenn wir nicht wissen, wohin wir wandern?
—Warte mal! Weißt du wirklich nicht, wohin wir wandern?
—Nein, das weiß ich wirklich nicht. Aber ich weiß, daß wir weiter wandern wollen, bis wir unsere warme Wohnung wiedersehen.

Schritt 4: Studenten in Tübingen

(((■))) Gespräch

Worum geht es hier? Hans, a student at the university in Tübingen, meets Wolfgang, a friend from his hometown. Skim the passage to find out what sort of living accommodations each has, then mark in the following chart who has (or has access to) what object.

HANS:	Wolfgang! Was machst denn du hier?
WOLFGANG:	Ach, Tag, Hans. Na, ich bin jetzt auch Student.
HANS:	So, das ist ja was[1]! Wohnst du hier in Tübingen?
WOLFGANG:	Nein, ich wohne in Bebenhausen. Das ist ein Vorort[2] von Tübingen. Und du?
HANS:	Na, ich wohne in Tübingen. Ich habe ein Zimmer bei einer Familie. Es ist sehr klein, aber es ist nicht teuer. Mietest[3] du ein Zimmer dort?
WOLFGANG:	Ja, ich habe auch nur ein Zimmer. Mein Zimmer ist jedoch groß. Ich habe einen Schreibtisch, einen Fernseher, einen Schrank und natürlich ein Bett. Ich habe sogar Platz genug für Bücherregale. Ich habe auch ein Waschbecken und eine Toilette. Die Dusche ist nebenan!
HANS:	Ach, ich habe nur ein Bett, einen Schreibtisch und einen Schrank. Ich habe keinen Fernseher, aber ich habe einen Walkman! Waschbecken und Toilette sind nebenan; ich habe überhaupt keine[4] Dusche!
WOLFGANG:	Wie? Was machst du denn?
HANS:	Ganz einfach[5]! Ich besuche dich sehr oft!

[1]**das...** *that's really something!*   [4]**überhaupt...** *not even a*
[2]*suburb*   [5]**ganz...** *easy*
[3]*rent*

(handwritten note: Chez)
(handwritten note: visit)

WER HAT WAS?

SACHEN	HANS	WOLFGANG	KEINER (neither)
eine Wohnung	___	___	___
ein Zimmer	✓	✓	___
einen Tisch	___	✓	___
einen Fernseher	___	✓	___
einen Walkman	✓	___	___
eine Dusche	___	___	___
einen Kühlschrank	___	___	___
eine Toilette	___	___	___
einen Schreibtisch	✓	___	___
ein Bett	✓	✓	___
einen Schrank	✓	✓	___
Bücherregale	___	✓	___
ein Waschbecken	___	✓	___
viel Platz	___	✓	___

(handwritten note: Versuchen — to attempt to do something)

Alles klar?

Vergleichen Sie! Work with a partner. One of you says what Hans has, the other says what Wolfgang has; do so by completing the following sentences and then add sentences of your own, based on the preceding conversation.

Hans wohnt in…, aber Wolfgang wohnt in… .
Hans' Zimmer ist… , aber Wolfgangs Zimmer ist… .
Hans hat…, aber Wolfgang hat… .
…

Kulturnotiz: Student housing

In the USA and Canada, most undergraduate students live either on campus in dormitories or in off-campus university housing; a few live at home and commute every day to classes. In Europe, especially in Germany, student housing is somewhat different. Very few universities offer dormitory quarters, and those that do have only a very limited number of beds available. Fraternities are not as common as they are in North America, and sororities do not exist in Europe. It is a rare European student who has a car at the university. Therefore, students generally choose one of two housing options: 1) a single room (often called **eine Bude** or **eine Studentenbude**) in a private home in the university area, or at least within easy reach of public transportation, or 2) a student co-op or communal living situation (**eine Wohngemeinschaft** or **WG**), again near the university or public transportation. Look at the classifieds below and see which of them are for which type of housing. Do students always seek their own rooms?

> **Zimmer, ca.** 20m², in WG, an Student/in, zum 1.11.90 frei ☎0145/677368

> **Beamter sucht für seine** Tochter (Pädag.-Studentin) Wohnung oder Zimmer (ab sofort oder später). ☎ 05575/9735

> **Ich,** 22, männl., Gartenbau-student, suche Zimmer in Osnabrück oder Umgebung ☎0452/ 75754 oder 05225/ 5886

> **Studentin** (20), Nichtraucherin, sucht Zimmer bis 300 DM im Stadtbusbereich☎0451/75801 ab 20 Uhr

The verb *haben*

The verb **haben** is irregular in the **du** and the **er/sie/es** forms.

HABEN (*to have*)					
ich	**habe**	*I have*	wir	**haben**	*we have*
du	**hast**	*you have*	ihr	**habt**	*you have*
er/sie/es	**hat**	*he, she, it has*	sie	**haben**	*they have*
			Sie	**haben**	*you have*

Hast du Geschwister und Freunde? Fill in the blanks with the appropriate forms of **haben**.

MONIKA: (1) _____*hast*_____ du eine Schwester?
CLAUDIA: Nein, ich (2) _____*habe*_____ keine Schwester.
MONIKA: (3) _____*hast*_____ du einen Bruder?
CLAUDIA: Ja, ich (4) _____*habe*_____ zwei Brüder.
MONIKA: (5) _____*Hat*_____ deine Brüder Freundinnen?
CLAUDIA: Karl (6) _____*hat*_____ eine Freundin, aber Peter (7) _____*hat*_____ keine.
MONIKA: (8) _____*Habt*_____ ihr auch Tanten und Onkel?
CLAUDIA: Ja, wir (9) _____*haben*_____ einen Onkel und eine Tante. Unsere Tante heißt auch Monika, wie du!

The accusative case

In **Kapitel 2** you learned that the nominative case is used for the subject of a sentence. The primary use of the second case you will study, the accusative case, is as the direct object of a sentence. For example, in English, when you say *I see the book*, then *book* is the direct object; it is what you see.

The thing that goes with the verb = nominitive

The thing that acts on the verb - transitive -

Wo ist das Objekt? Read the following English passage and underline the direct objects.

Peter rents a room with a family. His room is big and contains a desk, a TV, a wardrobe and, of course, a bed. He even has room for bookshelves, but he still has to buy some. He also has a sink and a toilet. The shower is next door.

Definite and indefinite articles

In German, case is often signaled by changes in the definite (**der**, **die**, **das**) or indefinite (**ein**, **eine**, **ein**) articles or their negative forms (**kein**, **keine**, **kein**). However, the forms of the nominative and accusative cases are identical, except for masculine singular. Nominative **der** becomes accusative **den**, and nominative **ein** or **kein** becomes accusative **einen** or **keinen**.

NOMINATIVE CASE (*Subject*)	ACCUSATIVE CASE (*Direct Object*)
Der Mann ist hier.	Ich sehe **den Mann**.
Ein Mann ist hier.	Ich sehe **einen Mann**.
Die Frau ist hier.	Ich sehe **die Frau**.
Eine Frau ist hier.	Ich sehe **eine Frau**.
Das Buch ist hier.	Ich sehe **das Buch**.
Ein Buch ist hier.	Ich sehe **ein Buch**.
Die Männer/Frauen/Bücher sind hier.	Ich sehe **die Männer/Frauen/Bücher**.
Keine Männer/Frauen/Bücher sind hier.	Ich sehe **keine Männer/Frauen/Bücher**.

Possessive adjectives

As in the nominative, the accusative case of the possessive adjectives (**mein**, **dein**, etc.) takes the same ending as **ein** and **kein** (see **Kapitel 1**, **Schritt 5**). Look at the following examples:

MASCULINE:	Ich habe mein**en** Walkman.
FEMININE:	Ich habe dein**e** Decke.
NEUTER:	Ich habe ihr Radio.
PLURAL:	Ich habe unser**e** Bilder.

ALLES KLAR?

A. Was brauchst du noch? You and a partner are shopping for furnishings for your room. Say that you need some or all of the following items; your partner will ask whether you plan to buy them.

BEISPIEL: der Schreibtisch
—Ich brauche einen Schreibtisch.
—Kaufst du den Schreibtisch?
—Ja, ich kaufe den Schreibtisch.

Use words from the ad to the right or use any of the following.

1. das Handtuch
2. der Spiegel
3. der Sessel
4. die Bettwäsche
5. das Telefon
6. das Bild
7. die Decke
8. der Fernseher

(handwritten annotations next to items: ihr, meinen, einen, eine, ihr, ihr, eine, einen)

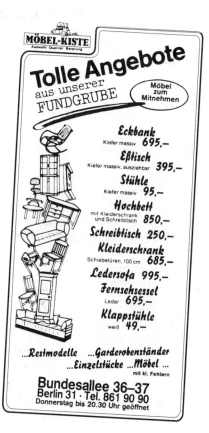

MÖBEL-KISTE
Auswahl Qualität Beratung

Tolle Angebote
aus unserer
FUNDGRUBE

Möbel zum Mitnehmen

Eckbank
Kiefer massiv **695,–**

Eßtisch
Kiefer massiv, ausziehbar **395,–**

Stühle
Kiefer massiv **95,–**

Hochbett
mit Kleiderschrank und Schreibtisch **850,–**

Schreibtisch **250,–**

Kleiderschrank
Schiebetüren, 100 cm **685,–**

Ledersofa **995,–**

Fernsehsessel
Leder **695,–**

Klappstühle
weiß **49,–**

...Restmodelle ...Garderobenständer
...Einzelstücke ...Möbel ...
mit kl. Fehlern

Bundesallee 36–37
Berlin 31 · Tel. 861 90 90
Donnerstag bis 20.30 Uhr geöffnet

B. Wo ist die Brille (*eye glasses*)? Fill in the blanks with appropriate possessive adjectives.

HARALD: Wer hat (1) _meine_ Brille? Thomas, hast du sie?

THOMAS: Nein, ich habe sie nicht. Hanna, hast du Haralds Brille?

HANNA: Nein. Harald, warum verlierst du immer wieder (*again and again*) (2) _deine_ Brille?

HARALD: Ich weiß nicht. Ihr habt ja (3) _eure_ Brillen, aber ich habe (4) _meine_ nicht. Ihr müßt aber meine, bitte, suchen!

THOMAS: Wir suchen sie ja schon. Ach, ich sehe (5) _meine_ Brille.

HARALD: Wo ist sie denn?

THOMAS: Du bist aber doof! Du hast sie auf der Nase (*nose*)!

C. Wer hat meinen Schläger (*racquet*)? Fill in the blanks with an appropriate possesive adjective or **kein**.

HANS: Ich kann nicht spielen. Ich habe (1) _keinen_ Schläger.

UWE: Wo ist (2) _dein_ Schläger?

HANS: Ich kann (3) _____ Schläger nicht finden. Ich sehe nur Papas Schläger hier.

UWE: Hat (4) _deine_ Mutter nicht auch einen Schläger? Kannst du (5) _ihren_ Schläger benutzen?

HANS: Sie hat schon einen Schläger, aber ich kann (6) _ihren_ Schläger nicht benutzen. Er ist zu klein. *to use*

UWE: Hat nicht auch Stefan einen Schläger? Vielleicht kannst du (7) _seinen_ Schläger benutzen.

HANS: Ja, aber er ist nicht zu Hause (*at home*). Ach, da kommt mein Papa. Papa, hast du vielleicht meinen Schläger?

PAPA: Ach, ja, es tut mir leid, ich habe (8) _deinen_ Schläger. Hast du vielleicht meinen?

HANS: Jawohl. So, jetzt können wir spielen!

The phrase *es gibt*

The phrase **es gibt** means *there is* or *there are*. It is always followed by an accusative object.

Es gibt keine Dusche. — *No sing/plural*
***There is** no shower.* — *Just GIBT*

Es gibt ein Bett, einen Schreibtisch und einen Schrank.
***There are** a bed, a desk, and a closet.*

ALLES KLAR?

Es gibt... Describe your room to your partner, using **es gibt**. Your partner should ask about things you might have forgotten to mention.

BEISPIEL: —Es gibt ein Telefon und zwei Poster.
—Gibt es denn keinen CD-Spieler?
—Nein, es gibt keinen.
—Gibt es denn keine Dusche?
—Doch, es gibt eine.

Redewendung

Doch is used at the beginning of a positive response to a negative question or statement.

Gibt es denn keine Dusche?
—**Doch, es gibt eine.**
Oh yes, there is one.

Dein Bruder ist nicht sehr fleißig.
—**Doch, er ist fleißig.**
But yes, he is.

Note the contrast in the use of **ja/nein** as responses to positive questions or statements.

—**Gibt es eine Dusche?**
Is there a shower?

—**Ja, es gibt eine Dusche.**
Yes, there is a shower.

—**Nein, es gibt keine Dusche.**
No, there is no shower.

—**Dein Bruder ist sehr fleißig.**
Your brother is very industrious.

—**Ja, er ist fleißig.**
Yes, he is.

—**Nein, er ist nicht fleißig.**
No, he isn't.

Personal pronouns

As in English, some personal pronouns in German have special forms when used as direct objects, that is, in the accusative case.

NOMINATIVE	ACCUSATIVE		
ich	**mich**	*me*	Helga besucht **mich**.
du	**dich**	*you*	Ich sehe **dich**.
er	**ihn**	*him*	Siehst du **ihn**?
sie	**sie**	*her*	Ich sehe **sie** nicht.
es	**es**	*it*	Brauchst du **es**?
wir	**uns**	*us*	Brauchst du **uns** bald?
ihr	**euch**	*you*	Wir sehen **euch** morgen.
sie	**sie**	*them*	Ich verstehe **sie** nicht.
Sie	**Sie**	*you*	Ich sehe **Sie**.

Remember that personal pronouns in German must agree in gender and number with the noun to which they refer.

Siehst du **den Tisch**?
Ja, ich sehe **ihn**.

Hast du **meine Kaffeemaschine**?
Ja, ich habe **sie**.

ALLES KLAR?

A. Generationskonflikt? Fill in the blanks with the appropriate personal pronoun.

PAUL: Linda, hast du auch Probleme mit deiner Familie? Ich verstehe meine Familie nicht!

LINDA: Wie? Meinst (*mean*) du deine Eltern?

PAUL: Ja, ich verstehe (1) _sie_ (*them*) nicht. Aber auch meinen Onkel. Ich verstehe (2) _ihn_ (*him*) auch nicht!

LINDA: Und deine Tante? Verstehst du (3) _sie_ (*her*)?

PAUL: Ja, aber ich sehe (4) _sie_ (*her*) nicht oft.

LINDA: Und deine Großeltern?

PAUL: (5) _sie_ (*them*) sehe ich oft, und ich verstehe (6) _sie_ (*them*) auch nicht!

LINDA: Ist das nur ein Problem mit älteren (*older*) Leuten? Verstehst du deinen kleinen Bruder?

PAUL: Nein, ich verstehe (7) _ihn_ (*him*) auch nicht. Aber meine kleine Schwester verstehe ich. Das Problem ist, sie versteht (8) _mich_ (*me*) nicht. Sie ist erst (*only*) zwei Jahre alt.

LINDA: Ich glaube (*believe*), das ist kein Generationsproblem. Du bist doch das Problem. Du verstehst nur dich selbst (*yourself*)!

B. Brauchst du…? With a partner, take turns asking and answering questions about the items listed below. Use the appropriate personal pronoun.

BEISPIEL: —Brauchst du die Kreide?
—Ja, ich brauche sie.
OR: —Nein, ich brauche sie nicht.

Brauchst du (*do you need*)…   der Stuhl
Siehst du (*do you see*)…   der Spiegel
Hast du…   der CD-Spieler
                                   der Computer
                                   das Bild
                                   die Lampe
                                   die Bücher
                                   das Poster

Interrogative pronouns

Interrogative pronouns introduce questions. In German, there are two interrogative pronouns.

wer   *who*   **was**   *what*

Only **wer** changes its form in the accusative.

NOMINATIVE: **Wer** kommt?   *Who is coming?*
ACCUSATIVE: **Wen** suchst du?   *Whom are you looking for?*
NOMINATIVE: **Was** ist das?   *What is that?*
ACCUSATIVE: **Was** suchst du?   *What are you looking for?*

ALLES KLAR?

A. Tante Rosa versteht immer noch nicht. Aunt Rosa still doesn't understand what is being said. Ask questions, based on the following statements.

BEISPIELE: Ich brauche *einen Tisch.*
—Was brauchst du?
Ich besuche *meine Mutter.*
—Wen besuchst du?

1. *Wir* kaufen einen CD-Spieler.
2. Ich brauche *eine Wohnung.*
3. Mein Bruder verkauft *sein Auto.*
4. Wir sehen *unseren Großvater* heute.
5. *Peter* hat viel Platz.
6. Ich habe *keine Dusche.*
7. *Sie* wohnt hier in Tübingen.
8. Ich besuche *dich* oft.

B. Wen suchst du? In small groups, one student thinks of a person in the group or an object in the room. Other students ask questions in order to guess the correct answer. Whoever guesses correctly then leads the game.

BEISPIELE: —Wen suchst du? Hans?
—Nein, ich suche ihn nicht.
—Was suchst du? den Tisch?
—Nein, ich suche ihn nicht.

Tip!

In spoken German, the prepositions **durch**, **für**, and **um** are frequently contracted with **das**:

durch das = **durchs**
      durchs Zimmer

für das = **fürs**
      fürs Kind

um das = **ums**
      ums Haus

Prepositions with the accusative

Certain prepositions always require the accusative case in German. Below you will find the basic meanings of the most common ones.

durch	*through*	Sie läuft **durch** mein Zimmer. *She is running through my room.*
für	*for*	Ich habe Platz genug **für** meinen CD-Spieler. *I have enough room for my CD player.*
gegen	*against*	Ich habe nichts **gegen** eine Schreibmaschine, aber ein Computer ist besser. *I have nothing against a typewriter, but a computer is better.*
ohne	*without*	Können wir das **ohne** einen Computer machen? *Can we do that without a computer?*
um	*around*	Er läuft jeden Tag **um** den Park. *He runs around the park every day.*
um	*at, about*	Er kommt **um** sechs Uhr. *He's coming at six o'clock.*

(handwritten: around = time)

(handwritten: Vm)

ALLES KLAR?

A. Unfreundlich? Ask whether your partner has anything against certain people.

BEISPIEL: —Hast du etwas **gegen** meinen Freund Bill?
—Nein, ich habe nichts **gegen** ihn.

(handwritten annotations: meinen, mein, mein, mein / mein, meine, meinen, mein)

meinen Vater
mein Freund(in)
mein das Kind
mein Rechtsanwälte

mein Mutter
meine Professor(in)
meinen Ärzte/Ärztinnen
mein Soldaten

B. ...oder freundlich? Now ask whether your partner can do something for another person, a friend or family member. Use the verb **tun**.

BEISPIEL: —Kannst du **für** meine Schwester etwas tun?
—Natürlich, **für** sie tue ich ja alles.

C. Onkel Max und sein Auto. Fill in the blanks with the appropriate accusative preposition, according to the context of the sentence.

(1) _Um_ zwölf Uhr kommt Onkel Max mit seinem Auto. Er hat jetzt einen Mercedes und er verkauft seinen VW. Er hat nichts (2) _gegen_ einen Volkswagen, aber ein Mercedes ist schneller (*faster*). Wir wollen alle in die Stadt fahren. Aber Onkel Max hat nicht genug Platz (3) _gegen für_ meine ganze (*whole*) Familie, und wir müssen (4) _ohne_ meinen Bruder fahren.

Wir fahren (5) _durch_ einen Tunnel, und auf der anderen Seite (*on the other side*) läuft ein Kind in die Straße. Onkel Max reagiert (*reacts*) schnell. Er fährt (6) _um_ das Kind aber (7) _gegen_ eine Mauer (*wall*). Sein Mercedes ist jetzt total kaputt! Wir sind alle unverletzt (*uninjured*), aber Onkel Max weint (*cries*). Er kann (8) _ohne_ seinen Mercedes nicht leben (*live*)!

Schritt 5: **Mußt du, oder willst du nur?**

((🔊)) **Gespräch**

Worum geht es hier? What is Erika's problem? What solution does she suggest?

HANS: Tag, Erika. Wie geht's?
ERIKA: Tag. Danke, es geht, aber ich habe ein Problem.
HANS: So? Was ist los? Schon wieder dein Zimmer?
ERIKA: Nein, nicht mein Zimmer. Ich habe keinen Computer, und ich will einen.
HANS: Ach, so. Wo ist denn das Problem? Mußt du einen Computer haben? Oder willst du nur einen haben?
ERIKA: Ich muß keinen haben, aber ich will einen. Das Problem ist, alle Computer sind so teuer, und ich kann nicht viel bezahlen[1].
HANS: Weißt du, es gibt auch Computer für wenig Geld.
ERIKA: Ja, aber sie sind so langsam! Mein Computer muß schnell und billig sein. Ich weiß! Du hast doch viel Geld[2]. Du fährst jetzt in die Stadt, oder? Du nimmst mich mit[3] und du kannst für mich einen Computer kaufen!

---

[1]*pay*
[2]*money*

[3]**nimmst...** *take me with you*

ALLES KLAR?

A. Was ist richtig? Decide whether the sentences are true or false. If they are false, correct them.

1. Erika muß einen Computer haben.
2. Erika will einen Computer haben.
3. Das Problem ist, alle Computer sind teuer.
4. Billige Computer sind schnell.
5. Erika hat viel Geld.

B. Du willst neue Sachen. You want something new. Describe to your partner what you are looking for.

BEISPIEL:　—Ich will einen Schreibtisch. Er muß groß und billig sein.

das Bett	interessant	braun
die Kaffeemaschine	neu	blau
der Kühlschrank	alt	grün
der Papierkorb	teuer	weiß
das Radio	billig	rot
der Sessel	groß	schnell
der Walkman	klein	langsam
das Stereo	schwarz	…

(handwritten notes in margin: Sie, eine / er, einen / es, eine / sein)

Modal verbs

The modal verbs tell us something about the subject's *attitude* toward an action rather than the action itself. That action is usually expressed in a dependent infinitive that appears at the end of the sentence or clause. Compare the following English and German sentences:

Ich **muß** morgen meine Tante **besuchen.**
I have to visit my aunt tomorrow.

Du **kannst** für mich einen Computer **kaufen.**
You can buy a computer for me.

There are six modal verbs in German; three of them are presented here: **können** (*can, to be able to*), **müssen** (*must, to have to*), and **wollen** (*to want to*).

Tip!

Do not confuse **ich will** or **er/sie/es will** with English *will*. You will learn the German future tense in **Kapitel 13**.

	KÖNNEN	MÜSSEN	WOLLEN
ich	kann	muß	will
du	kannst	mußt	willst
er/sie/es	kann	muß	will
wir	können	müssen	wollen
ihr	könnt	müßt	wollt
sie	können	müssen	wollen
Sie	können	müssen	wollen

können generally expresses the ability to do something. It implies ability rather than permission.

Kannst du gut kochen?	*Can you cook well?*
Ich **kann** nicht viel bezahlen.	*I'm not able to pay very much.*

müssen connotes necessity.

Mußt du einen Computer haben?	*Do you have to have a computer?*

wollen expresses intention or desire.

Ich **will** einen Computer haben.	*I want to have a computer.*

As you have seen, modal verbs generally have a dependent infinitive. However, the infinitive may be omitted if the meaning of the sentence is clear without it.

Ich **muß** nach Hause.
Ich **muß** nach Hause fahren.　　} *I have to go home.*

ALLES KLAR?

 A. Kannst du…? Discuss with your partner what both of you can or cannot do.

> **BEISPIEL:** —Kannst du Tennis spielen?
> —Ja, ich kann Tennis spielen.

gut kochen	im Winter schwimmen	Apfelstrudel backen
Gitarre spielen	deine Eltern verstehen	Spanisch sprechen
schnell laufen	gut singen	deine Familie bald besuchen

Then report to a new partner and tell him/her what you and your first partner can or cannot do.

> **BEISPIEL:** —Jörg und ich können Tennis spielen.
> OR: —Jörg kann Tennis spielen, aber ich kann nicht.

 B. Auf dem Bahnhof. You have just arrived at the train station. Tell a partner what is or is not permitted at the following locations.

> **BEISPIEL:** —Hier kann man Fragen stellen (*ask questions*).

die Sachen abgeben

NÜTZLICHE (*useful*) WÖRTER

die Fahrkarten - *tickets*	**warten** - *to wait*
das Wasser - *water*	**trinken** - *to drink*
die Reservationen - *reservations*	**telefonieren** - *to call on the telephone*
rauchen - *to smoke*	**essen** - *to eat*

 warten

1. essen 2. Fahrkarten 3. ? 4. rauchen

6. trinken 7. trinken 8. die Reservationen 9. rauchen 10. telefonieren

 **C. Was mußt du heute machen?** With a partner, discuss what you both have to do today.

> **BEISPIEL:** Ich muß heute viel lesen.

arbeiten	deine Großmutter besuchen
kochen	Hausaufgaben (*homework*) machen
…	

D. Was macht er am Samstag? Klaus has plans for Saturday, but his mother has other ideas. Tell what he has to do as opposed to what he wants to do.

> **BEISPIEL:** Klaus will Musik hören, aber er muß arbeiten.

WOLLEN	MÜSSEN
einen CD-Spieler kaufen	lernen
nach München fahren	seine Hausaufgaben machen
seine Freundin anrufen	seine Großmutter besuchen
einen Film sehen	sein Heft finden
Musik hören	sein Zimmer putzen (*clean*)

 E. Was machst du am Wochenende? Now ask your partner about what he/she wants to do on the weekend, but must do instead.

> **BEISPIEL:** —Was willst du am Wochenende machen?
> —Ich will zu einer Party gehen.
> —Was mußt du aber machen?
> —Ich muß ein Buch lesen.

The verb form *möchte(n)*

The verb form **möchte(n)** means *would like to*. It is derived from the verb **mögen**.(**Mögen** means *to like*; it will be presented in **Kapitel 5**.) **Möchten** is frequently used to express a polite request.

> Was **möchten** Sie?
> *What would you like?*

Like the modals, **möchte(n)** is often accompanied by another verb that is placed at the end of the sentence in its infinitive form.

> Was **möchten** Sie morgen tun?
> *What would you like to do tomorrow?*
>
> Ich **möchte** einen CD-Spieler kaufen.
> *I would like to buy a CD player.*

Again, when the meaning of the second verb is understood, it may be omitted, just as in English.

> Ich **möchte** eine Wohnung.
> Ich **möchte** eine Wohnung haben. } *I would like to have an apartment.*

The **er/sie/es**- ending of **möchte** is different from that of the regular verbs. (See Present tense, **Kapitel 1**.)

MÖCHTEN (would like to)			
ich	möchte	wir	möchten
du	möchtest	ihr	möchtet
er/sie/es	möchte	sie	möchten
	Sie	möchten	

ALLES KLAR?

A. Im Möbelgeschäft. Frank goes to a furniture store to try to buy an easy chair. Fill in the appropriate forms of **möchte(n)** and the modals.

FRANK: Entschuldigung (*excuse me*). Ich brauche Hilfe (*help*). Ich (1) _möchte_ diesen (*this*) Sessel kaufen.

VERKÄUFERIN: Es tut mir leid. Aber diese Frau (2) _möchte_ auch den Sessel kaufen. (3) _Mochten_ Sie vielleicht einen anderen Sessel?

DIE FRAU: Ich weiß nicht. Der Sessel ist für meine Kinder. Uli und Birgit, (4) _möchtet_ ihr einen anderen Sessel?

DIE KINDER: Nein, wir (5) _möchten_ diesen Sessel!

DIE FRAU: Ja, hören Sie, sie (6) _möchten_ unbedingt (*absolutely*) diesen Sessel.

FRANK: Gut, dann (7) _möchte_ ich diese Lampe hier.

DIE FRAU: Nein, die Lampe (8) _möchte_ wir auch! Sie paßt zu (*matches*) dem Sessel.

FRANK: Ja, sind Sie sicher (*sure*)? Sie (9) _möchten_ auch die Lampe? Dann (10) _möchte_ ich meine Sachen irgendwo anders (*somewhere else*) kaufen!

B. Was möchtest du? Think about things you would like to have or do. Discuss your ideas with a partner.

BEISPIELE: —Ich möchte Tennis spielen. Was möchtest du?
—Ich möchte Karten spielen.
—Ich möchte einen Kühlschrank. Und du?

ein Bier
Tennis spielen
einen Fernseher
meine Großmutter besuchen
eine Kaffeemaschine
tanzen

Verbs with stem vowel changes

Many verbs in German have a vowel change in both the second person singular (the **du** form) and the third person singular (the **er/sie/es** form) present tense. Note, for example, the conjugation of the verb **sehen** (*to see*).

SEHEN (*to see*)			
ich	**sehe**	wir	**sehen**
du	**siehst**	ihr	**seht**
er/sie/es	**sieht**	sie	**sehen**
	Sie	**sehen**	

There are two main types of changes: **e** to **i** or **ie**, and **a/au** to **ä/äu**. Here are some common verbs with changes.

essen	*to eat*	du **ißt**, er/sie/es **ißt**
fahren	*to go, to drive*	du **fährst**, er/sie/es **fährt**
laufen	*to run*	du **läufst**, er/sie/es **läuft**
lesen	*to read*	du **liest**, er/sie/es **liest**
nehmen	*to take*	du **nimmst**, er/sie/es **nimmt**
sehen	*to see*	du **siehst**, er/sie/es **sieht**
sprechen	*to speak*	du **sprichst**, er/sie/es **spricht**
wissen	*to know* (something)	du **weißt**, er/sie/es **weiß**

geben => (handwritten annotation)

modal auxilary (handwritten annotation)

The stem-vowel change of such verbs is noted in both the chapter vocabulary and in the vocabulary at the end of the book. It is important that you learn each of these verbs together with its vowel change

ALLES KLAR?

A. Josef übertreibt. Josef is exaggerating and Martha corrects him. Change the singular sentences to plural and the plural sentences to singular. Follow the examples.

> BEISPIELE: —Alle meine Professoren sprechen zu schnell!
> —Nein, nur ein Professor spricht zu schnell.
> —Nur ein Student liest die Zeitung!
> —Nein, viele Studenten lesen die Zeitung.

1. Alle meine Freunde fahren bald nach Hause!
2. Nur eine Person weiß die Antwort!
3. Alle meine Zimmerkameraden lesen zu viel!
4. Nur ein Student nimmt seine Seminare ernst (*seriously*)!
5. Alle meine Freunde essen nur Pizza!
6. Nur ein Film läuft jetzt!
7. Alle meine Nachbarn sehen immer nur Filme!
8. Nur eine Professorin liest meine Hausaufgabe!

 B. Was hast du gern? Find out what your partner likes to read and to eat. Use the following suggestions, or add your own ideas.

> BEISPIEL: —Liest du gern *Newsweek*?
> —Ja (Nein), ich lese es (nicht) gern.
> —Ißt du gern Pommes frites (*French fries*)?
> —Ja, ich esse Pommes frites gern.

Comic-Hefte	Pizza
Time Magazin	Pommes frites
die Zeitung	Steak
Science-fiction	Bananen
Steven King	Eis (*ice cream*)
	Salat

Die letzten Schritte

Wer macht mit?

Zusammenfassung

A. Ein Brief an Barbaras Eltern. Barbara, an exchange student in Regensburg for the year, is writing her first letter home to her parents. Fill in the blanks with appropriate forms of the words below.

schön	es gibt	Museum (nt.)
können	alt	Bett
Schrank	unser	klein
haben		

Liebe Mama, lieber Papa,

so, jetzt bin ich in Regensburg. Es ist sehr (1) __schön__ hier, aber mein Zimmer ist (2) __klein__. Ich habe natürlich ein (3) __Bett__, aber ich (4) __kann__ nicht sehr gut schlafen (*sleep*). Es gibt natürlich auch einen (5) __Schrank__. Es gibt __es gibt__ keine Dusche. Die Dusche ist ganz unten (*below*). Aber trotzdem (*nevertheless*) (7) __haber__ ich es hier gern.

Die Stadt ist auch sehr schön. Regensburg ist sehr (8) __alt__. Es gibt ein (9) __Museum__ und viele Kirchen (*churches*). Hier in Deutschland gibt es überall viele Kirchen!

Ach, da kommt schon Anna. Sie ist meine erste deutsche Freundin. Wir müssen Bücher kaufen, für (10) __unser__ Deutschstunde (f.). Das Semester beginnt schon morgen.

Jetzt muß ich gehen, aber ich schreibe Euch bald wieder.

Bis bald,
Eure
Barbara

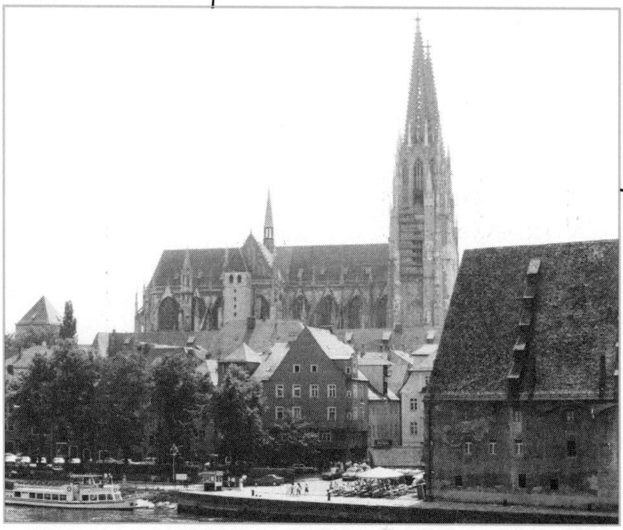

B. Was brauche ich? Write out the dialogue by using the phrases below.

BEISPIEL: was/müssen/du/für/dein/Wohnung/kaufen?
Was mußt du für deine Wohnung kaufen?

STUDENT 1: was/brauchen/du/für/Zimmer?
STUDENT 2: ich/brauchen/Sessel/Lampe
ich/möcht-/haben/auch gern/zwei Poster
und/ich/haben/auch/kein/Computer
haben/du/schon (*already*)/Computer?
STUDENT 1: natürlich!/ohne/mein/Computer/können/ich/nicht leben (*live*)

C. Fragen und Antworten. Express the following brief exchanges in German.

Do you want to buy the walkman?
Yes, I would like to buy it. *ihn*

Whom do you see there (**dort**)?
I see my brother.

nennen

Aren't there any telephones here?
Yes, I see them.

Would you like to go hiking?
No, I am too (**zu**) tired.

Do you read the newspaper?
Yes, I read it often (**oft**).

I always lose my books.
Then you have to look for them.

D. Ein Brief an meine Eltern. Reread the letter in Activity A; then write (in German) to your parents about your living quarters and the city where you are living as a student. Keep your letter simple. In describing the city, use the following phrases:

Es gibt viele/keine…

Kirchen (*churches*)
Museen (*museums*)
Theater
Restaurants
Geschäfte (*stores*)

Sie sind…

alt
neu
(un)interessant
groß
modern
häßlich
schön
…

A. Was gibt's? Was gibt es nicht? Working with a classmate, find at least five differences between the drawing below and your partner's drawing. Do not look at each other's drawings.

> BEISPIEL: —Es gibt eine Professorin.
>   —Ja, es gibt eine Professorin. (Nein, es gibt keine Professorin.
>   Es gibt einen Professor.)

B. Was möchtest du? Interview your partner.

> BEISPIEL: —Möchtest du einen CD-Spieler oder ein Stereo?
>   —Ich möchte _____ .

VERBS	PHRASES
wollen	Macintosh Computer
möchte(n)	auf dem Campus wohnen
können	Tennis spielen
müssen	viele Referate (*papers*) schreiben
	IBM Computer
	in einer Wohnung wohnen
	Karten spielen
	viel lesen

_____will _____

Sie/Er möchte _____

Sie/Er kann _____

Sie/Er muß _____

A. Was gibt's? Was gibt es nicht? Working with a classmate, find at least five differences between the drawing below and your partner's drawing. Do not look at each other's drawings.

BEISPIEL:　—Es gibt viele Bücher.
　　　　　　—Ja, es gibt viele Bücher. (Nein, es gibt keine Bücher.)

B. Was möchtest du? Interview your partner.

BEISPIEL:　—Möchtest du einen CD-Spieler oder ein Stereo?
　　　　　　—Ich möchte _____ .

VERBS	PHRASES
möchte(n)	Japanisch lernen
können	kochen
müssen	viele Textbücher kaufen
wollen	Stereo
	Spanisch lernen
	gut tanzen
	viele Möbel kaufen
	CD-Spieler

_____ will _____

Sie/Er möchte _____

Sie/Er kann _____

Sie/Er muß _____

Situationen

 A. Ein Student ist unzufrieden. Form small groups of four or five. One student takes the role of a disgruntled student who does not like anything about his/her surroundings. Others try to convince this student that things are not so bad.

BEISPIEL:

DISGRUNTLED STUDENT:	Ich habe mein Zimmer nicht gern.
OTHER(S):	Aber du hast viel Platz!
DISGRUNTLED STUDENT:	Ich habe meinen Schrank nicht gern.
OTHER(S):	Aber der Schrank ist groß und die Farbe ist auch schön!
	…

B. In meinem Zimmer. Find a student in your class whom you do not know well. Together discuss your rooms: What do they contain? What do you like? What do you dislike? What do you still need, or what would you like to buy?

C. Im Kaufhaus (*in the department store*).

STUDENT 1

At the beginning of the semester, you need to furnish your room. Describe to the salesperson in a department store what you want to buy. (Remember to use **Sie** with the salesperson.)

STUDENT 2

You are the salesperson in a department store. Since you have just had a sale and your inventory is low, you don't have many of the items your customer is looking for, but try to help him/her as best you can. (Remember to use **Sie** with the customer.)

BEISPIEL: —Guten Tag!
—Guten Tag! Was möchten Sie?
—Ich brauche einen Sessel. Er muß billig sein, und ich möchte den Sessel in braun.
—In braun haben wir nichts (*nothing*), aber der Sessel hier ist…

Überall spricht man Deutsch

German in Business and Research

As you learned in **Kapitel 1**, German is the first language of millions of people around the globe, especially in Europe. Its use is by no means limited to these native speakers, however; many others use it as a lingua franca, or trade language, and even more as a language of research and investigation.

By the end of the nineteenth and early twentieth centuries, Germany had established colonies and outposts around the world, for example, in Samoa, Togo, Southwest Africa, Turkey, Morocco, the Marshall Islands, and elsewhere.

Today, German remains widely used as a trade language because of the industrial importance of the Federal Republic. Especially in Eastern and Southern Europe, German is the preferred language of communication among trading partners, surpassing even English by a considerable degree. This situation is especially true for countries that were formerly under the influence of the Austro-Hungarian empire — Hungary, Rumania, etc. Your knowledge of German might open many doors to you in international commerce; your school may well offer a course in German for Business.

FORSCHUNG

HANDEL

TECHNOLOGIE

German is also of considerable importance in the area of research. For many years students in the US who were majoring in the sciences were required to take German as their preferred foreign language. Outstanding contributions continue to be written in German in all scientific areas. Today, while some important articles are translated into English, this is not universally the case. In addition, there are major, indeed essential, reference works in disciplines in both the humanities and social sciences (classics, art history, history of religion, archaeology, music history, and psychology, to name just a few) that have not been translated. Furthermore, the works of many German philosophers and theologians continue to be more readily understandable when read in the original. Do you anticipate using German as a research tool in your field? Do you know of any German reference works or any German scholars working in your area of interest?

Whether in business or research, you'll be surprised at how handy your knowledge of German will be. **Also, an die Arbeit!** (*So, let's get busy!*)

Major Reference Works Published in German

Pauly-Wissowa. *Real-Encyclopädie der classischen Altertumswissenschaft*

Encyklopädie des Islam. Geographisches, ethnographisches und biographisches Wörterbuch der muhammedianischen Völker. Hrsg. v. M.T. Houtsma. 4 Bde. + Erg-Bde.

Thieme-Becker. *Allgemeines Lexikon der bildenden Künstler von der Antike bis zur Gegenwart.* 37 Bde.

Büchmann's *Geflügelte Worte*

Reallexikon der germanischen Altertumskunde. Hrsg. v. Johannes Hoops

Themenwortschatz

Substantive — Nouns

Im Zimmer — **In the room**

das Bad, ¨er	bathroom
das Bett, -en	bed
die Bettwäsche (sg.)	bed linen
das Bücherregal, -e	bookcase
der CD-Spieler, - ✓	CD-player
der Computer, - ✓	computer
die Couch, -es	couch
die Decke, -n	blanket
die Dusche, -n	shower
der Fernseher, -	television set
das Handtuch, ¨er	towel
die Kaffeemaschine, -n	coffeemaker
der Kühlschrank, ¨e ✗	refrigerator
die Lampe, -n ✓	lamp
die Möbel (pl.)	furniture
der Papierkorb, ¨e	wastebasket
das Poster, -	poster
das Radio, -s	radio
die Sache, -n	thing, object
der Schrank, ¨e	wardrobe, closet
die Schreibmaschine, -n	typewriter
der Sessel, -	easy chair
der Spiegel, -	mirror
das Stereo, -s	stereo
das Telefon, -e	telephone
die Toilette, -n	toilet
die Tür, -en	door
der Walkman, -s	walkman
das Waschbecken, -	sink
das Zimmer, -	room

Verben — Verbs

benutzen	to use
brauchen	to need
haben (hat)	to have
können (kann)	to be able to; can
möchte(n)	would like
müssen (muß)	to have to; must
wollen (will)	to want

Adjektive/Adverbien — Adjectives/Adverbs

böse	angry
doof	dumb, stupid (slang)
fit	fit
(un)freundlich	(un)friendly
(un)intelligent	(un)intelligent
(un)interessant	(un)interesting
jung	young
nett	nice
neu	new
neugierig	curious
viel	much
(un)zufrieden	(dis)content, (dis)satisfied

Gegensätze — Opposites

faul/fleißig	lazy/industrious
froh/traurig	happy/sad
häßlich/schön	ugly/beautiful, pretty
langsam/schnell	slow/fast
teuer/billig	expensive/inexpensive

Präpositionen mit Akkusativ — Prepositions with the Accusative

durch	through
für	for
gegen	against
ohne	without
um	around; at

Farben — Colors

die Farbe, -n	color
blau	blue
braun	brown
gelb	yellow
grün	green
orange	orange
purpur	purple
rosa	pink
rot	red
schwarz	black
weiß	white

Ausdrücke — Expressions

es gibt	there is, there are
Welche Farbe hat…?	What color is…?
Ich habe… gern	I like….

Weiterer Wortschatz

Substantive / *Nouns*

Substantive	Nouns
das Auto, -s	*car*
der Platz, ̈e	*place, room*
die Wohnung, -en	*apartment*
die Zeitung, -en	*newspaper*

Verben / *Verbs*

Verben	Verbs
essen (ißt)	*to eat*
fahren (fährt)	*to drive, to go*
finden	*to find*
kaufen	*to buy*
laufen (läuft)	*to run*
lernen	*to learn; to study (as for an exam)*
lesen (liest)	*to read*
nehmen (nimmt)	*to take*
sehen (sieht)	*to see*
sprechen (spricht)	*to speak*
suchen	*to search for*
trinken	*to drink*
tun	*to do*
verlieren	*to lose*
wissen (weiß)	*to know something*

Adjektive/Adverbien / *Adjectives/Adverbs*

Adjektive/Adverbien	Adjectives/Adverbs
fast	*almost*
genug	*enough*
immer	*always*
nebenan	*next door*
nur	*only*
oft	*often*
weit	*far*

Andere Wörter / *Other Words*

Andere Wörter	Other Words
denn	*because*
doch	*(positive response to a negative question); after all, certainly (flavoring particle)*
oder	*or*
warum	*why*

Ausdrücke / *Expressions*

Ausdrücke	Expressions
Hausaufgaben machen	*to do homework*
Was ist los?	*What's going on? What's wrong?*

Wirtschaft und Forschung im Internet

Business and Research on the Internet

The following URL addresses will guide you to German home pages that focus on scientific and business themes. See the Prentice Hall home page for related activities and address updates (htt://www.prenhall.com/~german).

1. **Wirtschaft, Markt und Handel: Deutschland und Europa**
   Best German home page for information on European business and market affairs.
   http://www.gwdg.de/~ifbg/go13.html

2. **Firmen in Deutschland: Internet Leitseiten**
   Comprehensive list of European and German companies on the Internet.
   http://www.venture.net/venture/outerspace/comm-www.shtm

3. **Messen in Deutschland: Ausstellungen und Expos**
   Excellent links to German business fairs and exhibitions.
   http://www.wiso.gwdg.de/ifbg/go13e.htm

4. **Forschung und Wissenschaft: Links**
   Collection of research links to scientific sites on the Internet.
   http://www.uncg.edu/~lixlpurc/german_WWW/science_and_technology.html

5. **Wissenschaft und Forschung: Virtual Library**
   Complete index to German science and technology sites on the web.
   http://www.rz.uni-karlsruhe.de/Outerspace/VirtualLibrary/index.de.html

6. **Ministerium für Wissenschaft und Forschung: Bonn**
   Site of the German government's Department for Science and Research.
   http://www.dfn.de/bmbf/home.html

Tagaus, tagein

Kommunikation

- Referring to days, months, and seasons
- Giving temperature readings in Celsius
- Describing weather conditions
- Discussing giving gifts and lending items
- Telling time both informally and officially
- Talking about your daily routine
- Stating where or how you were at a past time

Strukturen

- Dative case
  Articles and possessive adjectives
  Personal pronouns
  Interrogative pronouns
  Word order with two objects
  Dative verbs
  Prepositions with the dative
- Time expressions
  Time of day
  Time expressions with the dative
  Time expressions with the accusative
- Coordinating conjunctions
- **aber** vs. **sondern**
- Simple past tense of **sein**

Kultur

- Birthday customs
- German vacations

Kapitel 4

Die Tage, die Monate, die Jahreszeiten

Seasons

Die Tage

The days of the week are masculine.

der Montag	*Monday*
der Dienstag	*Tuesday*
der Mittwoch	*Wednesday*
der Donnerstag	*Thursday*
der Freitag	*Friday*
der Samstag OR	*Saturday*
der Sonnabend	
der Sonntag	*Sunday*

To ask what day it is, you would say: **Welcher Tag ist heute?**

MAI						
Montag	**Dienstag**	**Mittwoch**	**Donnerstag**	**Freitag**	**Samstag**	**Sonntag**
		1	2	3	4	5
6	7	8	9	10	11	12
13	14	15	16	17	18	19
20	21	22	23	24	25	26
27	28	29	30	31		

Die Monate

The names of the months in German are very similar to their English counterparts. All month names in German are masculine.

der Januar	der Juli
der Februar	der August
der März	der September
der April	der Oktober
der Mai	der November
der Juni	der Dezember

Die Jahreszeiten

All four season names are also masculine.

der Frühling[1]

der Sommer

der Herbst

der Winter

ALLES KLAR?

 A. Heute ist … With a partner, take turns pretending it is a certain day of the week and ask what tomorrow will be.

BEISPIEL: —Heute ist Mittwoch. Was ist morgen?
—Morgen ist Donnerstag.

 B. Wann hast du Geburtstag? Survey your classmates to find out the month when most people have birthdays. Follow the model.

BEISPIEL: —Wann hast du Geburtstag?
—Ich habe im Juni Geburtstag.

---

[1]Another word for *spring* is: **das Frühjahr.**

Schritt 2: Die Temperatur und das Wetter

Temperature

Tip!

To change Fahrenheit to Celsius, subtract thirty-two and multiply the result by five ninths. To change Celsius to Fahrenheit, multiply the Celsius reading by nine fifths and add thirty-two to the result.

In the US, we use the Fahrenheit scale to measure temperature, while most other countries use the Celsius or centigrade system. The German word for *degree* is **Grad**; hence, **fünfzehn Grad** means *fifteen degrees Celsius* to a speaker of German. Look at the thermometer to find some common equivalents.

Descriptive terms for the weather

You already know or can guess the meanings of the following adjectives:

gut	**schlecht**	**warm**	**kühl**
kalt	**heiß**	**schön**	

A few others are:

wolkig	*cloudy*	**windig**	*windy*
sonnig	*sunny*	**bedeckt**	*overcast*
heiter	*bright, clear*		

Here are some other words frequently used to talk about the weather:

regnen	Es regnet.	*It's raining.*
schneien	Es schneit.	*It's snowing.*
scheinen	Die Sonne scheint.	*The sun is shining.*
der Regen		*rain*
der Schnee		*snow*

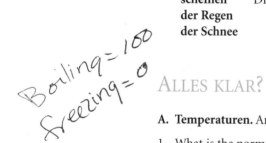

ALLES KLAR?

A. Temperaturen. Answer the following questions, using the centigrade scale.

1. What is the normal body temperature?
2. At what temperature do you have a fever?
3. What is a comfortable room temperature?
4. At what temperature would you go swimming? turn on the air conditioner? put on a winter coat?

90 neunzig · Kapitel 4

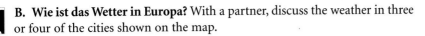

B. Wie ist das Wetter in Europa? With a partner, discuss the weather in three or four of the cities shown on the map.

BEISPIEL: —Wie ist das Wetter in Moskau?
—In Moskau ist es 19 Grad und wolkig.

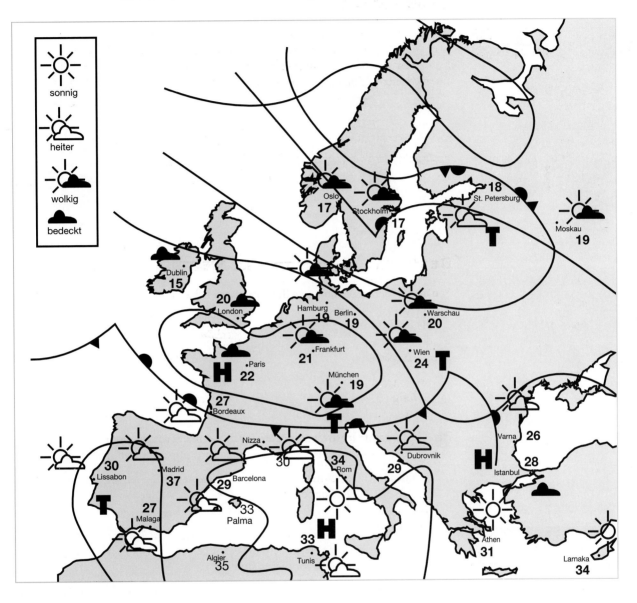

C. Wie ist das Wetter hier? Now discuss the weather in your town in various seasons of the year.

BEISPIELE: —Wie ist das Wetter im Herbst?
—Im Herbst ist es...

—Wie ist das Wetter heute?

Schritt 3: **Geschenke**

Look at the items in the picture below.

1. der Tennisschläger
2. die Kassette
3. die Kamera
4. die Turnschuhe

5. das Fahrrad
6. die Rollschuhe
7. der Badeanzug
8. die Badehose

Alles klar?

 A. Zum Geburtstag möchte ich… In small groups, discuss what you would like for your next birthday. Use the expression **zum Geburtstag**.

BEISPIEL: —Zum Geburtstag möchte ich ein Fahrrad. Was möchtest du?
—Ich möchte ein…

B. Ich schenke… Say what you would like to give various friends or relatives so that they can engage in their favorite activities. On the left is a list of activities, on the right is a list of appropriate gifts for these activities.

BEISPIEL: Meine Mutter spielt gern Tennis. Sie braucht einen Tennisschläger. Ich schenke ihr einen Tennisschläger.

Tennis spielen	Buch
fotographieren	Badeanzug/Badehose
lesen	Kugelschreiber
turnen (*to do gymnastics*)	Kassette
schreiben	Kamera
Musik hören (*to listen to*)	CD
schwimmen	Turnschuhe
	Tennisschläger

Tip!

In this activity, use **ihr** for *her* and **ihm** for *him*. You will learn more about this structure in **Schritt 4**.

Birthday customs in the German-speaking countries frequently differ from those in North America. Perhaps the major contrast is that different birthdays are considered important. In Germany, the eighteenth and the fiftieth are the most significant: the eighteenth, because Germans become adults at that time; the fiftieth, because the honoree has reached the half-century mark. When Germans become adults, they can vote, drink, and serve in the armed forces; but more importantly, they can obtain a driver's license. Most Americans need three birthdays to enjoy the same rights and privileges: the sixteenth, the eighteenth, and the twenty-first (16, 18, 21). Until Germans reach their eighteenth birthday, their celebrations are usually family-oriented and often include a birthday cake with candles (**Geburtstagskuchen**). As Germans get older, they give larger parties, for which they generally assume all costs. The fiftieth birthday is usually cause for the largest party one will give, although centenarians also celebrate in a major way. Often family or friends place announcements in newspapers, honoring the individual who is having a birthday. This custom is particularly common for the eighteenth and the fiftieth birthdays, and for all ten-year celebrations thereafter (60, 70, 80, 90, and 100). The most common way of wishing someone a "happy birthday" is to say **Herzlichen Glückwunsch zum Geburtstag!**

Meine liebe Frau,
unsere Mutti und Oma
Elfriede Hintz
wird heute

75

Es gratulieren recht herzlich
Dein Max
Kinder und Enkelkinder

Hallo, Nadine
Alles Liebe
zum Geburtstag
wünscht Dir
Deine Familie
18 18 18 18

Guten Morgen, lieber Papa!
Zum 50. Geburtstag wünschen
wir Dir alles Gute and Liebe

Karin, Michaela
und Thomas

▶ *Versuch's mal!*   Der *r*-Laut

Die Geschenkliste

Schwester werd' ich Turnschuh' schenken,
Vater kriegt eine Kamera,
Bruder muß doch Rollschuh' haben
aus den USA.

Rita soll eine Uhr bekommen
Mutter — einen Rock
Vetter Rolf — ein neues Fahrrad
Fritz — ein' Spazierstock.

Das will dieser, dies' will jener,
"Mutti, dieses möcht' ich sehr!"
Alle sind so wohl zufrieden,
Meine Taschen aber — leer!

Schritt 4: **Was machst du am Wochenende?**

Gespräch

Worum geht es hier? Heinz and Andreas are talking about their plans for the weekend. With a partner, make a list of all the activities you think they might do. Then read the dialogue. What does Andreas decide? Do you think his decision is final?

> **HEINZ:** So, Andreas, was machst du am Wochenende?
> **ANDREAS:** Ich weiß es noch nicht. Vielleicht bleibe ich einfach hier. Ich habe sehr viel Arbeit. Ich bin mit dem Referat[1] noch nicht fertig. Und du, Heinz?
> **HEINZ:** Ich fahre nach Hause. Meine Freundin hat am Samstag Geburtstag. Wir haben bestimmt viel Spaß. Möchtest du nicht mitkommen?
> **ANDREAS:** Das klingt[2] interessant, aber ich muß am Samstag und am Sonntag in der Bibliothek arbeiten. Was macht ihr denn?
> **HEINZ:** Das wissen wir noch nicht. Vielleicht Schlittschuh laufen oder Ski laufen…
> **ANDREAS:** Ach, weißt du, vielleicht…, nein, ich kann es wirklich nicht. Außerdem habe ich keine Schlittschuhe.
> **HEINZ:** Kein Problem. Mein Bruder hat Schlittschuhe, er braucht sie am Samstag und Sonntag nicht. Er kann dir seine Schlittschuhe leihen. So, du kommst? Die Arbeit ist am Montag auch noch da.
> **ANDREAS:** Das ist ja das Problem!

---

[1]*paper, report*   [2]*sounds*

Redewendung

Ich fahre **nach Hause**.
I'm going home.

Ich bin **zu Hause**.
I'm at home.

ALLES KLAR?

A. Heinz und Andreas. Fill in the blanks with the appropriate word to summarize the story.

Heinz fährt am (1)_____ nach Hause, denn seine Freundin hat (2)_____ . Andreas (3)_____ mitkommen, aber er hat viel (4)_____ . Heinz und seine Freundin möchten vielleicht (5)_____ oder (6)_____ und Heinz' Bruder kann Andreas (7)_____ leihen, wenn er sie braucht.

B. Wohin möchtest du? Tell a partner where you would like to go this weekend or during your next vacation. Use **nach** to say which city or country you would like to visit (or in the phrase **nach Hause**).

> **BEISPIEL:** —Ich möchte nach Dallas fahren. Und du?
> —Ich möchte nach…

C. Kannst du mir... leihen? You have certain activities planned for the afternoon. Find people in your class who can lend you the necessary items. Read the **Tip!** and follow the model.

> BEISPIEL: —Ich gehe Schlittschuh laufen. Kannst du mir deine Schlittschuhe leihen?
>
> —Ja, gerne.
>
> OR: —Nein, es tut mir leid, aber ich brauche meine Schlittschuhe.

You are going to... .

1. play tennis
2. go skiing
3. go swimming

The dative case

The dative case in German is generally used to indicate a person or an object *to whom* or *for whom* something is done. This person or object is referred to as the *indirect object*. Look at the following English examples:

> She gave a gift *to the man*.
> She gave *the man* a gift.

In both sentences, the man is the person to whom the gift is given; *man* is therefore the indirect object. In German *man* would be in the dative case.

The dative case is also used after certain verbs and prepositions and with some expressions of time.

Articles and possessive adjectives

Like the accusative case, the dative case is indicated by a change in the definite and indefinite articles. **Dem** (**einem**) is used for masculine and neuter singular nouns, **der** (**einer**) for feminine singular nouns, and **den** (**keinen**) for all plural nouns. In the plural, nouns themselves also add an -**n** unless they already end in -**n** (dative: **den Lampen**) or end in -**s** (dative: **den Stereos**).

> Sie gibt **dem Mann** ein Geschenk.
> *She gives **the man** a present.*
>
> Sie gibt **der Frau** ein Geschenk.
> *She gives **the woman** a present.*
>
> Sie gibt **dem Kind** ein Geschenk.
> *She gives **the child** a present.*
>
> Sie gibt **den Kindern** ein Geschenk.
> *She gives **the children** a present.*

Note that where English sometimes uses the preposition *to* or *for*, German never does; the dative case is used instead.

As with the accusative, the possessive adjectives take the same endings as the definite and indefinite articles.

Tip!

To say that you are going to do an activity, use the verb **gehen** plus an infinitive. The infinitive is placed at the end of the sentence.

Ich **gehe** heute abend **tanzen.**
I'm going (to go) dancing tonight.

If there are two infinitives, they both appear at the end of the sentence. **Gehen** is last.

Ich **möchte** heute abend **tanzen gehen**
I would like to go dancing tonight.

	MASCULINE	FEMININE	NEUTER	PLURAL
NOMINATIVE	der Mann ein mein	die Frau eine meine	das Kind ein mein	die Kinder keine meine
ACCUSATIVE	den Mann einen meinen	die Frau eine meine	das Kind ein mein	die Kinder keine meine
DATIVE	**dem** Mann ein**em** mein**em**	**der** Frau ein**er** mein**er**	**dem** Kind ein**em** mein**em**	**den** Kindern kein**en** mein**en**

ALLES KLAR?

A. Wo ist der Dativ? Underline the indirect objects in the following passage.

—Was schenkst du deinem Bruder zum Geburtstag? *zum = to the*

—Meinem Bruder schenke ich eine Kamera und meiner Mutter dieses Buch, denn sie hat nächsten Monat Geburtstag.

—Gibst du es deiner Mutter jetzt, oder wartest du?

—Sie hat meinem Vater gesagt, sie möchte das Buch selbst (*herself*) kaufen. Ich muß es ihr jetzt geben, sonst (*otherwise*) hat sie zwei davon (*of them*).

zum + der = sver   von + dem = vom

B. Wem gibst du das Buch? You have just bought a book to give as a gift. Say that it is for the following people.

> **BEISPIEL:** mein Onkel
> —Ich gebe meinem Onkel das Buch.

1. mein Vater *meinem*
2. das Kind *meiner*
3. seine Nichte *seiner*
4. deine Kinder *deinen Kindern*
5. die Lehrerin *meinen*
6. der Kellner *meinem dem*
7. die Ingenieure *meiner der*
8. Ihre Kusine *meiner*
9. unser Sohn *unserm*
10. die Männer *den Männern*

96 sechsundneunzig • Kapitel 4

— = i.o
☐ = d.o

C. Was schenkst du diesen Leuten? Discuss with a partner which of the following items you might give someone as a present. On the left is a list of recipients; on the right is a list of possible presents.

BEISPIEL:
—Was schenkst du deinem Bruder?
—Ich schenke meinem Bruder eine Badehose, und du?
—Ich habe keinen Bruder. Aber ich schenke meiner Schwester Rollschuhe.

Freund/Freundin
Bruder/Schwester
Tante/Onkel
Großeltern
Kusine/Vetter
Mutter/Vater
Professor/Professorin

Kuli
Poster
Computer-Spiel (nt.)
Walkman
Kamera
Tennisschläger
Landkarte
der Ball
Skier (pl.)
…

Personal pronouns

The personal pronouns also have dative forms.

NOMINATIVE	ACCUSATIVE	DATIVE
ich	mich	**mir** (*to, for me*)
du	dich	**dir** (*to, for you*)
er	ihn	**ihm** (*to, for him*)
sie	sie	**ihr** (*to, for her*)
es	es	**ihm** (*to, for it*)
wir	uns	**uns** (*to, for us*)
ihr	euch	**euch** (*to, for you*)
sie	sie	**ihnen** (*to, for them*)
Sie	Sie	**Ihnen** (*to, for you*)

Note that two accusative and dative forms are identical, **euch** and **uns**. Context will help you to determine which is meant.

The formal dative (**Ihnen**) is always capitalized, as are the formal nominative and accusative (**Sie**). In writing, this feature distinguishes these forms from those that are otherwise identical (**sie**, **ihnen**).

Interrogative pronouns

The interrogative pronoun **wer** also has its own dative form.

NOMINATIVE	ACCUSATIVE	DATIVE
wer	wen	**wem** (*to whom*)

Wem gibt sie eine Kassette?   *To whom does she give a cassette tape?*

There is no dative form for **was**.

ALLES KLAR?

A. Fritz hält (*holds*) **die Familie zusammen.** Fill in the blank with the appropriate dative pronoun.

THOMAS: Fritz, ich kann meinen Walkman nicht finden; leihst du (1)_ *mir* (*me*) deinen?

FRITZ: Ja, natürlich. Mutti, gehört (2) *dir* (*you*) diese Brille (*eyeglasses*)?

MUTTER: Ja, sie gehört (3) *mir* (*me*). Danke, Fritz.

KLAUS: Fritz, wir suchen Mariannes Kamera. Hast du sie gesehen (*seen*)?

FRITZ: Nein, aber ich leihe (4) *euch* (*you*, pl. familiar) meine.

MARIANNE: Vielen Dank. Und wenn du in die Stadt fährst, kaufst du (5) *uns* (*us*) auch einen Film?

FRITZ: Ich fahre heute nicht. Aber ich glaube, Vati fährt. Ich sage (6)_____ (*him*), daß (*that*) ihr einen Film braucht. Vati, die Kinder brauchen einen Film für die Kamera. Kaufst du (7) *ihnen* (*them*) einen?

VATER: Ja, und sagst du der Mutter, daß ich jetzt gehe?

FRITZ: Ja, ich sage es (8) *ihr* (*her*).

VATER: Fritz, du hältst die Familie wirklich zusammen! Ich weiß nicht wie wir leben können, wenn du mal nicht mehr zu Hause bist!

B. Wem gehört…? Form small groups, and put several objects into a pile in the center, e.g., a book, shoe, ring, notebook, etc. One student takes an object from the pile and asks to whom it belongs by saying:

—Wem gehört…?

Someone who is not the owner replies:

—…gehört mir.

The real owner then speaks up:

—Das gehört dir/ihr/ihm nicht; das gehört mir.

He/she then picks another object; the game continues until all objects have been returned to their owners.

Word order with two objects

Many sentences have two objects — an indirect object (indicating *to/for whom*) and a direct object (indicating *what*). When there are two objects within one sentence, the direct object precedes the indirect object when— and only when— the direct object is a personal pronoun. Otherwise the indirect object comes first. Look at the following examples:

	INDIR. OBJ.	DIR. OBJ.		DIR. OBJ.	INDIR. OBJ.
Ich gebe	meinem Bruder	das Poster.	Ich gebe	es	meinem Bruder.
Ich gebe	ihm	das Poster	Ich gebe	es	ihm.

ALLES KLAR?

A. Weihnachtsgeschenke. Mrs. Dette is giving gifts to several people this holiday season. On the left is a list of recipients, on the right a list of the presents she has in mind. With a partner, decide who gets which gift. Make complete sentences and be sure to use either **geben** or **schenken** as your main verb.

ihn = it

BEISPIEL: Sie schenkt ihrem Mann einen Ring.

ihm = him
ihr = her
ihrem = to him
ihnen = them

ihre Mann   *einen*   Kuli
Tobias (ein Sohn)   *einen*   Tennisschläger
Gabriel (ein Sohn)   Badehose
Onkel Siegfried   Kamera
Tante Elfriede   *einen*   Fernseher
Erika (eine Freundin)   Stereo
die Großmutter   Kassette
ihre Chefin (*boss*)   Buch

to him ru giving what!

B. Wem gibst du was? A friend asks you about your plans. Answer the questions, replacing the boldfaced words with a pronoun and changing the word order if necessary.

ihnen = you Formal

BEISPIELE: —Gibst du der Lehrerin **den Bleistift?**
—Ja, ich gebe ihn der Lehrerin.

—Verkaufst du **deinem Freund den Computer?**
—Ja, ich verkaufe ihn ihm.

1. Schenkst du **deiner Mutter** die Kassetten? *Ja ich schenke ihr die Kassetten.*
2. Gibst du dem Lehrer **die Geschenke?** *Ja ich gebe sie dem Lehrer*
3. Gibst du **dem Kind den Ball?** *Ja, ich gebe ihm ihn.*
4. Kaufst du deinem Bruder **das Fahrrad?** *Ja ich kaufe es für meinem Bruder*
5. Willst du deiner Schwester **ein Videospiel** geben? *Ja ich will es meiner Schwest*
6. Gibst du **dem Professor** die Antwort? *Ja ich gebe ihm die Antwort*

C. Möbel im Sonderangebot (*on sale*)! You are finishing your studies and selling all your furnishings. Tell your partner what you are selling to each person or group of persons.

BEISPIELE: —Verkaufst du Robert deine Lampe?
—Ja, ich verkaufe sie ihm.

—Wem verkaufst du deine Bücher?
—Ich verkaufe sie meiner Freundin Ute.

—Was verkaufst du Monika?
—Ich verkaufe ihr das Bett.

Dative verbs

There are several commonly used German verbs that cannot take an accusative object but that are frequently followed by an object in the dative. Such dative objects usually refer to people.

antworten	*to answer* Warum antwortest du mir nicht? *Why don't you answer me?*
danken	*to thank* Er dankt meiner Schwester. *He thanks my sister.*
folgen	*to follow* Warum folgst du mir nicht? *Why don't you follow me?*
gefallen	*to please* Dein Zimmer gefällt mir sehr. *I like your room very much.*
gehören	*to belong to* Gehört dir dieses Buch? *Does this book belong to you?*
helfen	*to help* Warum hilfst du deinem Vater nicht? *Why don't you help your father?*
schmecken	*to taste* Das Essen schmeckt ihm gut. *He likes the meal.* (Literally, *The meal tastes good to him.*)

[handwritten margin notes: gefält; Die lampe gefält mis.]

The verb **glauben** (*to believe*) takes a dative object when referring to a person but the accusative when referring to a story or other statement.

Sie glaubt **mir** nicht. (dative)
*She doesn't believe **me**.*

Ich glaube **die Geschichte** nicht. (accusative)
*I don't believe **the story**.*

Das glaube ich nicht. (accusative)
*I don't believe **that**.*

Alles klar?

A. Wem…? Answer the following questions about the picture below, using the cues.

> **BEISPIEL:** Wem antwortet der Kellner? (die Kunden [*customers*])
> Der Kellner antwortet den Kunden.

1. Wem hilft die Kellnerin? (die Studentin)
2. Wem danken die Touristen? (der Koch)
3. Wem antwortet das Kind?
   (seine Mutter)
4. Wem gefällt das Restaurant?
   (die Kunden)
5. Wem folgt der Großvater?
   (der Kellner)
6. Wem schmeckt die Pizza nicht?
   (das Kind)
7. Wem gehören die Rucksäcke?
   (die Studenten)

[Handwritten annotations: "der = Nom / den = ACC. / Dem = Dative"; "Sie hilft der Studentin"; "Die Touristen danken dem Koch"; "Es antwortet seiner Mutter"; "Den Kunden gefällt das Restaurant"; "Er folgt dem Kellner"]

B. Wem gefällt…? Go around the classroom, surveying your classmates as to what they like. Write down the names of those who like the following items. Follow the model.

> **BEISPIELE:** —Gefällt dir das Buch?
> —Ja, das Buch gefällt mir.
>
> —Gefallen dir Komödien (*comedies*)?
> —Ja, Komödien gefallen mir.

[Handwritten: "gefallen / gefält / gefälst"]

die Oper (*opera*)   Regenwetter
klassische Musik   Talk-Shows
Horror-Filme   Jazz
dein Zimmer   das Theater
deine Kurse (*courses*)   deine Universität

Now, report your findings to the class.

> **BEISPIELE:** Dave sagt, das Buch gefällt ihm (nicht).
> Laurie sagt, Komödien gefallen ihr (nicht).
> Tom und Peter sagen, der Horror-Film gefällt ihnen (nicht).

Tip!

There are also four contractions of prepositions with the dative article:

bei dem	=	beim
von dem	=	vom
zu dem	=	zum
zu der	=	zur

These contracted forms are used very frequently in both spoken and written German.

Redewendung

meiner Meinung nach
in my opinion

zum Geburtstag
for one's birthday

zu Fuß
on foot

Prepositions with the dative

Just as some prepositions always take an accusative object (**durch, für, gegen, ohne, um**), others always take a dative object. The most common of these are:

aus	*out of, from*	Das Kind läuft **aus** dem Zimmer. *The child is running **out of** the room.*
		Sie kommen **aus** der Schweiz. *They come **from** Switzerland.*
außer	*except for*	**Außer** ihm will niemand arbeiten. ***Except for** him, no one wants to work.*
bei	*near, at the home of*	Der Tisch ist **bei** dem Fenster. *The table is **near** the window.*
		Er wohnt **bei** seinem Onkel. *He lives **at** his uncle's.*
mit	*with, by means of (transportation)*	Ich wohne **mit** meinem Bruder zusammen. *My brother and I are living together.*
		Ich bin **mit** meinem Referat nicht fertig. *I am not done **with** my paper.*
		Er kommt **mit** dem Fahrrad nach Hause. *He is coming home **by** bike.*
nach	*after, to (with cities and countries)*	Erst **nach** dem Mittagessen ist der Arzt da. *The doctor is not in until **after** lunch.*
		Wir wollen **nach** Deutschland fahren. *We want to go **to** Germany.*
seit	*since*	Schon **seit** ihrem Geburtstag ist sie krank. *She has been sick ever **since** her birthday.*
von	*of, from, by*	Das ist aber wirklich nett **von** Ihnen! *That is really nice **of** you!*
		Er kommt **vom** Bahnhof. *He's coming **from** the train station.*
		Das ist ein Buch **von** Christa Wolf. *That is a book **by** Christa Wolf.*
zu	*to*	Wir fahren morgen **zu** meiner Großmutter. *We're going **to** my grandmother's tomorrow.*

Memorize these prepositions and remember to use a dative object with them.

ALLES KLAR?

A. Was macht deine Familie? Answer the question in the negative, saying instead that the word in parentheses applies.

> BEISPIEL: Fährst du oft zu deiner Tante? (Onkel)
> Nein, ich fahre oft zu meinem Onkel.

1. Wohnt deine Schwester jetzt mit ihrer Freundin? (Freund) *Nein, oft meine Schwester wohne mit ihren*
2. Kommen deine Großeltern nach dem Mittagessen? (Frühstück [breakfast]) *Nein, meine Großeltern Freud. kommen*
3. Haben jetzt alle außer deinem Bruder ein Auto? (meine Schwester)
4. Muß deine Großmutter Montag zum Arzt gehen? (Ärztin)
5. Wohnt dein Bruder jetzt bei deiner Mutter? (meine Großeltern)
6. Kommt deine Familie aus Deutschland? (die Schweiz)
7. Sind deine Kusinen seit einer Woche hier? (ein Tag)
8. Gehst du heute abend zu deinem Freund? (meine Familie)

B. Mein Leben in Heidelberg. Complete the paragraph with the appropriate prepositions.

Ich komme (1) _____aus_____ (from) Liechtenstein. (2) ___Seit___ (since) Juli wohne ich in Heidelberg (3) ___bei___ (at the home of) meiner Tante. Oft gehe ich (4) ___mit___ (with) ihr in die Stadt; normalerweise fahren wir (5) ___mit___ (by) dem Bus. Morgen fahren wir (6) ___zu___ (to) meiner Großmutter; sie hat Geburtstag. (7) ___Nach___ (After) dem Besuch essen wir in einem Restaurant. Aber (8) ___außer___ (except for) Pizza esse ich nicht gern italienisch; ich esse lieber (rather) chinesisch. Erst am Freitag beginnt mein Studium an der Universität.

C. Wie kommst du dahin? With a partner, discuss how you each get to the following destinations. Use the verb **gehen** with the phrase **zu Fuß**, and the verb **fahren** with all other expressions. Follow the model.

> BEISPIEL: —Ich fahre mit dem Flugzeug nach Hause. Und du?
> —Ich fahre mit dem Bus.

mit dem Bus	nach Hause
mit dem Flugzeug	zur Universität
mit der Straßenbahn	nach Kanada
mit dem Zug	nach Deutschland
mit dem Auto	zu meinen Großeltern
mit dem Schiff	zum Museum
zu Fuß	zum Supermarkt
	…

Tip!

State the means of transportation before the destination:

Ich gehe **zu Fuß** zu meinen Großeltern.

You will learn the reason for this in **Kapitel 8**.

Time expressions

Time of day

Wieviel Uhr ist es? }
Wie spät ist es? }   *What time is it?*

In German, as in English, there are various ways to indicate the time of day. For example, in English you could say either *three-fifteen* or *quarter past three*. In German, you would state the time in the following ways. Note that the word **Uhr** is the equivalent of the English *o'clock*.

Es ist drei Uhr.

Es ist ein Uhr.
Es ist eins.

Es ist halb zwei.
Es ist ein Uhr dreißig.

Es ist Viertel nach zwei.
Es ist zwei Uhr fünfzehn.
Es ist Viertel drei.

Es ist zwölf Uhr zehn.
Es ist zehn nach zwölf.

Es ist Viertel vor sechs.
Es ist fünf Uhr fünfundvierzig.
Es ist drei Viertel sechs.

Es ist zwanzig vor vier.
Es ist drei Uhr vierzig.

Es ist sieben Uhr zwanzig.
Es ist zwanzig nach sieben.

To say at what time something will occur, use **um**:

Ich spiele **um** zwei Uhr Tennis.

For official schedules (transportation, radio, movies, or television) the German-speaking countries, as well as many other countries of the world, use a twenty-four hour system, somewhat comparable to our "military" system of time. Hours after 12 noon are counted as 13:00, 14:00, etc. up to 24:00. To specify 6:30 p.m., for example, you would say **achtzehn Uhr dreißig**.

ALLES KLAR?

 A. Wie spät ist es? With a partner, practice the times shown below. Say each time several ways, if possible.

> BEISPIEL: 5:20
> —Wie spät ist es?
> —Es ist fünf Uhr zwanzig.
> OR: Es ist zwanzig nach fünf.

1. 4:00 *vier uhr*
2. 8:15 *acht uhr fünfzehn*
3. 6:37
4. 12:45
5. 10:30
6. 3:18
7. 2:20
8. 11:50

Kurz nach - shortly after

zehn uhr dresig

 B. Der Zug fährt am Abend. Now assume the times in Activity A refer to a train departure and are in the evening. Repeat the activity, converting the times to the 24-hour system. Follow the model.

> BEISPIEL: 5:20
> —Wann fährt der Zug?
> —Der Zug fährt um siebzehn Uhr zwanzig.

C. Schilder. Look at the following signs. Then, work with a partner to find the correct answers to the questions below.

Öffnungszeiten:

Montag	9.00 – 13.00
Mittwoch	14.00 – 16.00
Freitag	
Dienstag	9.00 – 13.00
Donnerstag	14.00 – 18.00

SB-Bankgeschäfte Tag + Nacht

CIRCUS
M.-Roncalliplatz

Heute Premiere: 19.30 Uhr!

Ab morgen täglich zwei Vorstellungen
16.00 + 19.30 Uhr

sonntags 15.00 + 18.00 Uhr

TELEFON: 0 89/3 27 04 69

Karten am Roncalliplatz

**Sie erreichen den Roncalliplatz
mit Tram 18 und U 8**

**Schüler-Sonderpreise
(bis 16 J.) Parkett DM 12.--**

CINEMA PARIS

DIENSTAG UND MITTWOCH KINOTAGE

BETTY
MARIE TRINTIGNANT

15.30   18.00   20.30 FR SA MI 2245

SONNTAG MATINEE 11.30
GUSTAF GRÜNDGENS **FAUST** WILL QUADFLIEG

Luise

Berlin - Dahlem - Königin-Luise-Str. 40
Telefon 8 32 84 87
Öffnungszeiten von 10.00 bis 1.00 Uhr
Frühstück von 10-15 Uhr
Warme Küche von 12.00 bis 24.00 Uhr

1. Es ist zwei Uhr nachmittags (*in the afternoon*); können Sie noch in der "Luise" Frühstück (*breakfast*) essen?
2. Heute is Freitag. Wie spät (*how late*) können Sie "Betty" sehen? Was können Sie Sonntag um 11.30 im Kino sehen?
3. Morgen möchten Sie zum Circus gehen. Um wieviel Uhr können Sie gehen?
4. Heute ist Freitag, und Sie brauchen Geld (*money*); wann können Sie zur Bank gehen? (—Ich kann von _____ bis _____ zur Bank gehen.)

D. Die Routine. In groups of three, find out when each of you does the following activities. Write down the times so that you can compare schedules.

	Ich	Student(in) 1	Student(in) 2
1.Wann beginnt für dich der Tag?			
2.Um wieviel Uhr frühstückst du?			
3.Um wieviel Uhr gehst du zur Uni?			
4.Um wieviel Uhr ißt du zu Mittag?			
5.Um wieviel Uhr kommst du nach Hause?			
6.Um wieviel Uhr ißt du Abendbrot?			
7.Um wieviel Uhr gehst du zu Bett?			

Time expressions with the dative

In referring to specific days or parts of the day, German-speakers use the word **am**:

Ich arbeite **am Montag.**   *I work **on Monday.***
Er kommt **am Abend.**   *He is coming **in the evening.***
So, was machst du **am Wochenende**? *So, what are you doing **on the weekend?***

Am is a contraction of **an** and **dem**, which shows that it is also a form of the dative case. In referring to months and seasons, however, German uses **im**:

Im Juni ist es warm.   ***In June** it is warm.*
Im Winter laufen wir oft Ski.   ***In the winter** we often go skiing.*
Im September beginnt die Schule. *School begins **in September.***

Im is a combination of **in** and **dem**, indicating that this, too, is a dative form.

Time expressions with the accusative

To say exactly when, for how long, or how often something will occur, German-speakers use the accusative.

Meine Großmutter kommt   *My grandmother is coming*
  nächste Woche.   ***next week.***
Sie bleibt **drei Tage.**   *She's staying **for three days.***
Sie kommt **jeden Monat** zu Besuch. *She comes to visit **every month.***

ALLES KLAR?

A. Diese Woche. With a partner, discuss your plans for the week.

Am Montag	gehe ich	Tennis spielen
Am Dienstag	mache ich	schlafen
Jeden Tag	spiele ich	nach Hause
…	muß ich	zur Deutschstunde
	möchte ich	schwimmen
	…	nichts tun
		Hausaufgaben
		…

B. Genau wann? Now be even more specific and tell your partner at what time you will do the activities you named.

BEISPIELE: —Ich spiele am Montag um 8 Uhr Tennis.
                —Ich mache am Mittwoch um 8 Uhr meine Hausaufgaben.

C. Meine Lieblingsaktivitäten. With a new partner, discuss what you like to do during different months or seasons of the year.

Im Januar	gehe ich	Schlittschuh laufen
Im Sommer	spiele ich	Tennis
Im…		

Schritt 5: **Die Herbstzeit in Deutschland**

Lesestück

Worum geht es hier? The title of this passage tells you what it is about — fall in Germany. Here you can use your background knowledge — your own impressions of fall — to help you understand the text. Depending on where you live, you should find many similarities — and some differences as well.

As you skim the text the first time, look for key words that help you understand the gist. You should be able to guess the meanings of some new words — **Äpfel**, **reif**, **Schule** — without resorting to the side glosses or to the end vocabulary. Then read the passage more carefully, looking for the answers to these two questions:

1. Wie ist das Wetter im Herbst?
2. Warum gefällt vielen Menschen die Herbstzeit?

Wie[1] in Amerika gibt es in Deutschland vier Jahreszeiten - den Frühling, den Sommer, den Herbst und den Winter. Nach dem langen Winter ist der Frühling immer schön. Der Sommer ist heiß, aber nicht so heiß wie in vielen Teilen[2] Amerikas, denn Deutschland liegt[3] weiter nördlich als[4] Amerika. Im Winter machen viele Deutsche einen Skiurlaub, oder sie fahren nach Italien oder Spanien, in die Sonne! Aber der Herbst ist für viele Leute die beste Jahreszeit.

Im Herbst ist das Wetter immer noch schön. Es ist nicht so warm wie im Sommer und nicht so kalt wie im Winter. Die Durchschnittstemperatur[5] liegt um etwa 12 Grad, aber manchmal steigt[6] die Temperatur bis zu 20 Grad oder sogar bis zu 25 Grad. Das Obst[7] wird reif[8], zum Beispiel, die Äpfel und die Birnen[9]. Das Laub[10] wird sehr bunt: rot, gelb, orange. Oft regnet es im Herbst, und manchmal gibt es Gewitter[11]. Schnee gibt es noch nicht — außer vielleicht in den Alpen.

Anfang[12] September kommen viele Familien vom Urlaub wieder nach Hause. Schüler und Schülerinnen gehen wieder in die Schule und Studenten und Studentinnen gehen im Oktober wieder zur Universität. Alle müssen arbeiten, und niemand[13] kann den ganzen Tag spielen oder einfach faulenzen[14]. Aber der Herbst ist trotzdem[15] schön.

[1]as	[6]climbs	[12]beginning
[2]parts	[7]fruit	[13]no one
[3]lies	[8]ripe	[14]lie around, be lazy
[4]**weiter ...** farther north than	[9]pears	[15]nevertheless
[5]average	[10]foliage	
	[11]thunderstorm(s)	

ALLES KLAR?

A. Richtig oder falsch? Decide whether each statement is true or false. If it is false, correct it.

1. In Deutschland gibt es drei Jahreszeiten.
2. Die Jahreszeiten sind Frühling, Sommer und Winter.
3. Der Herbst ist für viele die Lieblingsjahreszeit (*favorite season*).

4. Im Herbst liegt die Durchschnittstemperatur um 25 Grad.
5. Im Herbst werden Äpfel und Birnen reif.
6. Im Herbst sind die Blätter (*leaves*) alle grün.
7. Das Wetter im Herbst ist schön, aber oft regnet es.
8. Viele Familien fahren im Sommer weg; sie machen Urlaub.
9. Im Herbst müssen Schüler und Schülerinnen wieder zur Schule.
10. Die Universitäten in Deutschland beginnen erst im Oktober.

B. Persönliche Fragen.

1. Wie ist die Herbstzeit bei Ihnen zu Hause?
2. Wie ist die Durchschnittstemperatur im Herbst?
3. Was für (*what kind of*) Obst gibt es im Herbst?
4. Was machen Sie im Sommer?
5. Wann beginnt Ihre Universität?

Kulturnotiz: German vacations

Summer vacations in Europe are usually family vacations. School is out for a shorter time than in the US and Canada, and children do not usually go to summer camp while their parents work. Rather, the entire family drives (along with hundreds of thousands of other Germans) in the family car, to the vacation spot. Places where the Germans spend most of their vacation "marks" can be seen in the accompanying chart. Typical Americans would envy their German counterparts because of the thirteenth month of pay most Germans receive in order to be able to pay for their vacation. In addition, almost all Germans are contractually guaranteed a minimum of five weeks of vacation; most receive at least six.

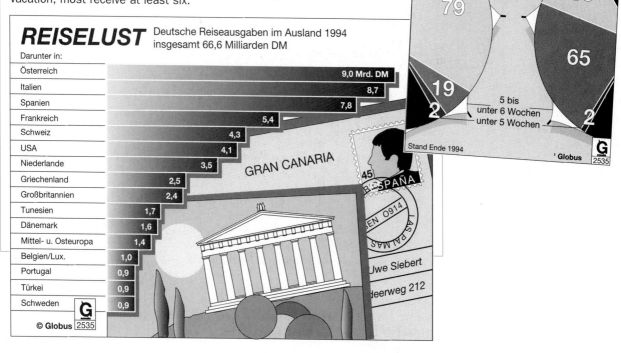

Coordinating conjunctions

Conjunctions are words that connect words, phrases, or entire sentences. German has two kinds of conjunctions, coordinating and subordinating. You will learn about subordinating conjunctions in **Kapitel 8**.

Coordinating conjunctions link words or phrases, or they join two independent clauses, each of which can stand alone as a complete sentence. They do not affect the word order of either clause.

> Alle müssen arbeiten. Niemand kann faulenzen.
> Alle müssen arbeiten, und niemand kann faulenzen.

The most common coordinating conjunctions in German are:

aber	*but*
denn	*for, because*
oder	*or*
sondern	*but, but rather*
und	*and*

Coordinating conjunctions are preceded by a comma when both clauses contain a subject and a verb. If either the subject or the verb of the second clause is omitted, there is no comma.

> Im Winter machen viele Deutsche einen Skiurlaub, oder sie fahren in die Sonne.
> Im Winter machen viele Deutsche einen Skiurlaub oder fahren in die Sonne.

aber vs. *sondern*

Although **aber** and **sondern** both mean *but*, they are used differently. **Sondern** is used when the first clause is negative; it expresses two mutually exclusive ideas.

NOT MUTUALLY EXCLUSIVE:	Der Herbst ist warm, aber manchmal regnet es. *Fall is warm, but sometimes it rains.*
MUTUALLY EXCLUSIVE:	Der Herbst ist nicht warm, sondern kühl. *Fall is not warm, but cool.*

ALLES KLAR?

A. Was machst du bei[1] diesem Wetter? Join the two sentences with a coordinating conjunction that fits the context.

1. Im Sommer ist es warm. Im Sommer regnet es oft.
2. Bei Gewitter gehen wir nicht spazieren. Bei Gewitter bleiben wir zu Hause.
3. Wir möchten heute schwimmen. Es ist zu kalt.
4. Möchtest du Ski laufen? Möchtest du Schlittschuh laufen?
5. Heute fahren wir an den Strand (*to the beach*). Die Sonne scheint und es ist warm.

---

[1]**bei** can also be used with weather to mean *in*, or *when:* **bei diesem Wetter** - *in this weather;* **bei gutem Wetter** - *in good weather;* **bei Gewitter** - *in a thunderstorm, when it thunders;* **bei Regen** - *when it rains.*

B. Der Wetterbericht (*weather report*). Fill in the blanks with **aber** or **sondern**, as appropriate.

1. Gestern war es nicht heiter, _Sondern_ bedeckt.
2. Heute scheint die Sonne, _aber_ es ist kalt.
3. Es ist nicht 15 Grad wie gestern, _Sondern_ 10.
4. Der Wind kommt nicht aus dem Süden (*south*), _Sondern_ aus dem Norden (*north*).
5. Morgen liegt die Temperatur um 15 Grad, _aber_ es ist wolkig.
6. Am Morgen regnet es, _aber_ am Nachmittag scheint die Sonne.

Simple past tense of *sein*

The past tense of the verb **sein** (*to be*) is irregular in German:

SEIN (to be)			
ich **war**	*I was*	wir **waren**	*we were*
du **warst**	*you were*	ihr **wart**	*you were*
er/sie/es **war**	*he/she/it/was*	sie **waren**	*they were*
		Sie **waren**	*you were*

ALLES KLAR?

A. Wo war Anna?

THOMAS: Anna, wo (1) _warst_ du gestern?
ANNA: Ich (2) _war_ in Köln.
THOMAS: (3) _Warst_ du allein in Köln?
ANNA: Nein, meine Mutter (4) _war_ auch da. Wir (5) _waren_ im Museum.
THOMAS: Wie bitte? Wo (6) _wart_ ihr?
ANNA: In einem Museum. Da (7) _waren_ sehr viele Leute.

B. Wo warst du gestern? Work in small groups and find out where your classmates were yesterday at various times.

Wo warst du um halb fünf?   Um (Uhrzeit) war ich…   zu Hause
Wo warst du um zehn Uhr?   bei meiner Tante
…   bei meinem Freund
                                              in meinem Zimmer
                                              bei meiner Freundin
                                              bei einer Vorlesung
                                              im Bett
                                              in der Bibliothek
                                              …

C. Wie warst du als (*as a*) **Kind?** With a partner, discuss what you were both like as children. Refer to the characteristics in the **Themenwortschatz** of **Kapitel 3**, or use some of the new words below. If you wish, you may express an opinion about your partner's statement.

BEISPIEL: —Wie warst du als Kind?
—Als Kind war ich glücklich und gesund. Wie warst du?
—Ich war auch glücklich, aber nicht sehr gesund.
—Das glaube ich dir (nicht).
…

aggressiv

albern ✓
silly, content

ängstlich ✓
Afraid

eifersüchtig –
Jealous

gelangweilt –
bored

glücklich –
happy

nachdenklich ✓
thoughtful

schüchtern ✓
shy

Zusammenfassung

A. Der Sommer in Deutschland. Complete the following paragraph with words chosen from the list below. (You may use some words more than once.)

zur	den	~~sondern~~	haben	~~aber~~	warm
nach	dem	schön	~~August~~	~~Wochen~~	arbeiten

Der Sommer beginnt Ende Juni. Der Juli und der _____ gehören auch noch zum Sommer. Im Sommer ist es _____ und _____ , _____ manchmal ist es auch kalt. Im Sommer machen viele Leute Urlaub; sie bleiben zwei oder drei _____ weg (*away*). Schüler und Schülerinnen, Studenten und Studentinnen müssen natürlich nicht _____ Schule oder _____ Universität, _____ sie haben natürlich auch Urlaub. Die Leute aus dem Süden fahren _____ dem Norden auf Urlaub; die Leute aus _____ Norden fahren nach _____ Süden auf Urlaub. Im Sommer _____ wir nicht, _____ wir faulenzen!

B. Mein Freitag. Complete the following paragraph with words chosen from the list below. (You may use some words more than once.)

um	Freundinnen	muß	zu	bei
mit	meinem	nach	ich	halb	mir

Am Freitag habe ich sehr viel zu tun. _____ 9.00 Uhr habe ich eine Vorlesung. Ich gehe mit _____ Freund zur Vorlesung. _____ der Vorlesung trinken (*drink*) wir einen Kaffee. Um 11.00 Uhr _____ ich im Labor sein; da arbeite _____ bis 1.00 Uhr. Dann esse ich _____ meinen _____ in der Mensa (*student cafeteria*). Die Mensa gefällt _____ nicht und das Essen schmeckt _____ auch nicht, aber ich habe nicht viel Geld. Ich gehe um 3.00 Uhr schwimmen. Ich schwimme nur eine Stunde (*hour*). Um _____ fünf habe ich wieder eine Vorlesung. Meine Freundin kommt immer am Abend _____ mir. Wir essen zusammen. Sie fährt dann _____ Hause. Der Tag ist für mich eigentlich zu kurz.

C. Die Tante hat Geburtstag. Choose the correct answer to complete each sentence.

_____ Großeltern kommen aus Zürich, aber _____ Großvater

a. Mein
b. Meine
c. Meinen

a. mein
b. meinen
c. meinem

wohnt jetzt in Tübingen. Ich wohne bei _____ . Morgen hat _____ Tante

a. ihr
b. ihm
c. ihn

a. mein
b. meinen
c. meine

Geburtstag. Ich schenke _____ Blumen und mein Großvater schenkt _____

a. ihm
b. sie
c. ihr

a. seiner
b. seine
c. sein

Tochter ein Buch. Dieses Buch gefällt _____ , und ich bin sicher (*certain*),

a. mich
b. ich
c. mir

es gefällt _____ auch.

a. sie
b. ihr
c. ihm

D. Peters Stundenplan (*schedule*). Peter, a university student, has the following schedule this week. Write a brief paragraph in which you describe what he does. Remember to mention the day before the time.

	MONTAG	DIENSTAG	MITTWOCH	DONNERSTAG	FREITAG	SAMSTAG	SONNTAG
9.00	Golf spielen	schlafen				zum Supermarkt gehen	nichts tun
11.00	im Labor sein						
1.00	Mittagessen						
3.00	Vorlesung	schwimmen	in der Bibliothek arbeiten	Vorlesung	mit Freunden	Fußball spielen	
5.00	Vorlesung			Vorlesung			
7.00	Abendbrot, am Sonntag mit Freunden, sonst allein						
9.00	in der Bibliothek arbeiten	ins Kino gehen			bei seiner Freundin	tanzen gehen	zu Hause lesen

E. Meine Heimat. Write a brief paragraph (8-10 sentences) describing your hometown — how the climate is there, what you like to do, whom you see there. You might include the following phrases:

Ich komme aus…
Im Winter/Sommer…
Meine Freunde sind auch/nicht im Sommer zu Hause.
Meine Geschwister/Großeltern wohnen noch (*still*) da…

or write a paragraph describing fall in your hometown:

Herbst in…

 Zu zweit: **Student 1**

A. Karins Stundenplan. Work with a partner to complete Karin's class schedule.

> BEISPIELE: Um wieviel Uhr hat Karin am Montag Sport?
> Was hat Karin um _____ ?
> Wer ist der Lehrer oder die Lehrerin?

	Montag	Dienstag	Mittwoch	Donnerstag	Freitag
8.00–8.45	Deutsch FRAU GRUBMEYER	Religion	 FRAU WEHMÜLLER	Deutsch FRAU GRUBMEYER	HERR LEIMBACH
8.50–9.35	Französisch HERR LAMBOIS	Geschichte FRAU KEIS	Mathematik FRAU SEILMANN	Deutsch FRAU GRUBMEYER	HERR LEIMBACH
9.35–9.50			Pause		
9.55–10.40	Sport	 FRAU WALTHER	Biologie HERR WOLENSKI	Französisch HERR LAMBOIS	Geschichte FRAU KEIS
10.45–11.30	Sport	Mathematik FRAU SEILMANN	Biologie HERR WOLENSKI	Religion	Geschichte FRAU WALTHER
11.30–11.45					
11.45–12.30	Latein HERR SCHURMANN	Französisch	Physik	Englisch FRAU WALTHER	Musik FRAU SCHWARZENTRUBER
12.35–13.20	Latein HERR SCHURMANN	 HERR SCHMIDT	Physik	Mathematik	Musik FRAU SCHWARZENTRUBER
	Politik				

B. Mit dem Zug. You are on the phone with a friend who has a train schedule. You need to go from Berlin-Hauptbahnhof (*main station*) to Frankfurt an der Oder (O). You have a meeting in Berlin until 3:00 p.m. Find out from your partner when you can leave, when you will arrive, and other pertinent information. What happens if you miss this train? Possible statements and questions include:

> Ich möchte von _____ nach _____ fahren.
> Ich kann erst (*only*) nach _____ Uhr fahren.
> Wann komme ich in _____ an?
>   (an…kommen = *to arrive*)
> Wie ist die Zugnummer?
> Kann man auch erste Klasse fahren?
> Dieser Zug ist zu früh (*early*). Gibt es einen späteren
>   (*later*) Zug?
> Kann man im Zug essen?

Now switch roles. You have the train schedule below. Answer your partner's questions to help him/her plan the trip.

Zeit	**Zug Nr Klasse**	**Abgangsbahnhof**	**Bahn-steig/ Gleis**	**nach**
18.44	D 526	Bln-Lichtenberg	D	(Oranienburg ab 19.18) - Neustrelitz Hbf 20.05 - Waren 20.32 - Güstrow 21.11 - Rostock Hbf 21.42 verk. nicht am 31. XII.
18.46 19.05 19.24 19.56	D 137	Berlin Hbf Bln-Friedrichstraße Bln-Zoolog Garten Bln-Wannsee	3 A 4 C	"Spree-Alpen-Expreß" Schlaf - und Liegewagenzug auch mit Autobeförderung, Reservierung erforderlich München Ost 6.23 nach Innsbruck, an 9.40 nach Villach Hbf, an 12.31 verk. nur 5/6 und nur bis 5./6. X., vom 4./5. I. bis 5./6. IV. und ab 10./11. V., auch am 21./22., 22./23. XII. und 28./29. III., jedoch nicht am 29./30. II., am 13./14. VII., 3/4., 24./25. VIII.
19.20 19.29 20.08	3929 D 135	Berlin Hbf Bln-Karlshorst Berlin Hbf	1 A 3	Fürstenwalde (Spree) 19.57 - Frankfurt (O) 20.27 S-Bahn-Fahrkarten haben keine Gültigkeit. Karlsruhe Durlach 6.23 - Lörrach 8.48 Zug verk. nur 21./22.XII., 22./23. II.
20.27 20.43 21.19		Bln-Friedrichstraße Bln-Zoolog Garten Bln-Wannsee	A 4 C	Schlaf- und Liegewagenzug, auch mit Autobeförderung, Reservierung erforderlich
20.14	D 314	Bln-Lichtenberg	C	(Bernau ab 20.42) - Szczecin Gumience 22.10 - Szczecin G 23.10 - Gdynia 4.45 "Gedania"
21.00 21.15 21.34 21.49	D 301	Berlin Hbf Bln-Friedrichstraße Bln-Zoolog Garten Bln-Wannsee	2 A 4 C	Halle (Saale) 0.05 - Ludwigstadt 3.17 - Nürnberg Hbf 5.08 -München Hbf 7.27 Stuttgart Hbf 8.05
21.16	D 395	Berlin Hbf	3	Frankfurt (O) 22.15 - Poznan 1.40 - Warszawa Wsch 7.14

Eisenbahn / Abfahrt

Zu zweit: **Student 2**

A. Karins Stundenplan. Work with a partner to complete Karin's class schedule.

BEISPIELE: Um wieviel Uhr hat Karin am Montag Sport?
Was hat Karin um _____ ?
Wer ist der Lehrer oder die Lehrerin?

	Montag	Dienstag	Mittwoch	Donnerstag	Freitag
8.00–8.45	Deutsch FRAU GRUBMEYER	Religion HERR MÜLLER	Politik FRAU WEHMÜLLER	FRAU GRUBMEYER	Chemie HERR LEIMBACH
8.50–9.35	Französisch HERR LAMBOIS	Geschichte FRAU KEIS	FRAU SEILMANN	FRAU GRUBMEYER	Chemie HERR LEIMBACH
		Pause			
9.55–10.40		Englisch HERR SCHMIDT	Biologie FRAU WALTHER	Französisch HERR WOLENSKI	Geschichte FRAU KIES
10.45–11.30		HERR SCHMIDT	FRAU SEILMANN	Religion HERR WOLENSKI HERR MÜLLER	FRAU WALTHER
11.30–11.45		Pause			
11.45–12.30	HERR SCHURMANN	Französisch HERR LAMBOIS	Physik FRAU SCHULZ	FRAU WALTHER	Musik
12.35–13.20	HERR SCHURMANN	Sport HERR SCHMIDT	Physik FRAU SCHULZ	Mathematik FRAU SEILMANN	Musik
13.25–14.10	Politik FRAU WEHMÜLLER				

B. Mit dem Zug. You are on the phone with a friend who wants to take a train trip. However, your friend doesn't have a train schedule and you do. Answer your friend's questions, using the train schedule below, to help him/her plan the trip.

Now switch roles. You are in Berlin-Wannsee and want to go to München. You can leave anytime after 6:00 p.m., but would prefer not to get to München much before 9:00 a.m., since your meeting isn't until 9:30. Find out from your partner when you can leave, when you will arrive and other pertinent information. Possible statements and questions include:

Ich möchte von _____ nach _____ fahren.
Ich kann nach _____ Uhr fahren.
Wann komme ich in _____ an? (an...kommen = *to arrive*)
Wie ist die Zugnummer?
Hat dieser Zug einen Namen?
Kann man auch erste Klasse fahren?
Dieser Zug ist zu früh (*early*). Gibt es einen späteren (*later*) Zug?
Kann man im Zug essen?

Eisenbahn / Abfahrt

Zeit	Zug Nr Klasse	Abgangsbahnhof	Bahn-steig/ Gleis	nach
14.03	D 393	Berlin Hbf	3	Frankfurt (O) 15.38 - Poznan G 18.25
14.20	E 685	Bln-Lichtenberg	C	(Königs-Wusterhausen ab 14.50) - Lübbenau 15.33 - Cottbus 16.00 - Weißwasser 16.49 - Görlitz 17.33 - Zittau 18.52
15.01	D 616	Berlin Hbf	3	(Oranienburg ab 15.53) - Neustrelitz Hbf 16.39 nach Neubrandenburg 17.23 auch am 22. und 29. XII.
15.09 15.25	D 555	Bln-Schöneweide Flgh Bln-Schönefeld	C D	Lutherst. Wittenberg 16.36 - Bitterfeld 17.06 - Halle Hbf 17.26 - Weimar 18.31 - Erfurt Hbf 18.51 verk nur 7, auch am 26. XII., 1. I., 30. XII., 31. II. und 19. V.
15.25	Ex 24	Berlin Hbf	2	Frankfurt (O) 16.18 - Poznan G 19.15 - Warszawa 23.04 (von Paris Nord als D 243) "Berolina"
16.03 16.38	D 814	Flgh Bln-Schönefeld Bln-Lichtenberg	C B	(Oranienburg ab 17.12) - Neustrelitz Hbf 18.03 - Demmin19.31 - Stralsund 20.15 verk. nicht 25. XII. (von Leipzig)
16.26	D 514	Bln-Lichtenberg	D	(Bernau ab 16.55) - Angermünde 17.32 - Prenzlau 18.02 - Pasewalk 18.24 - Greifswald 19.19 - Stralsund 19.46
16.50 17.00	392	Berlin Hbf Bln-Karlshorst	1 A	Fürstenwalde (Spree) 17.29 - Frankfurt (O) 18.02 - Eisenhüttenstadt 18.41 - Guben 19.10 S-Bahn-Fahrkarten haben keine Gültigkeit
16.51 17.07	D 507	Bln-Schöneweide Flgh Bln-Schönefeld	C D	Halle (S) Hbf 18.55 - Jena Saalbf 20.25 - Rudolstadt (Thür) 21.05 - Saalfeld (S) 21.20

Situationen

 A. Im Reisebüro (*travel agency*). Enact the following situation, then exchange roles.

STUDENT 1

Your point of departure is Nürnberg. Choose a destination from the plane schedules below. Talk with a travel agent (your partner) about the flight possibilities for the trip there and back, asking questions such as:

Ich möchte nach _____ . Kann ich am Montag fliegen?
Um wieviel Uhr kann ich fliegen?
Wann bin ich in _____?
Wie ist die Flugnummer (*flight number*)?
Um wieviel Uhr kann ich zurückkommen (*come back*)?

Be sure to thank the agent for her/his help (**Ich danke Ihnen**), then say good-bye.

STUDENT 2

You are a travel agent. Answer your customer's questions about various flights, using the schedule below.

Sommmerflugplan 1996   **Linienverkehr**

Nürnberg Abflug	Flug.-Nr.	Verkehrstage	Ankunft	Zielort	Abflug	Verkehrstage	Flug.-Nr.	Nürnberg Ankunft
6.30	LH 1215	Mo-Fr	7.25	Düsseldorf	6.20	Mo-Fr	LH 1214	7.20
8.30	LH 4026	täglich	9.30		6.50	Mo-Fr	LH 1226	7.55
10.35	NS 094	Freitag	11.55		13.50	Sonntag	LH 5361	15.10
11.15	NS 094	Mo-Do	12.30		14.30	Mo-Do	NS 093	15.45
15.40	LH 5362	Sonntag	17.00		14.45	Freitag	NS 093	16.00
15.45	LH 1221	Mo-Fr	16.40		15.40	tägl.a.So	LH 1210	16.40
18.10	LH 1223	Mo-Fr	19.10		17.35	Samstag	LH 5361	18.55
19.25	LH 5362	Samstag	20.45		18.00	tägl.a.Sa	LH 1212	19.00
7.00	LH 361	täglich	7.50	Frankfurt	9.35	täglich	LH 362	10.20
10.55	LH 367	täglich	11.45		12.30	Mo-Fr	NS 153	13.20
14.35	LH 369	täglich	15.25		13.15	täglich	LH 366	14.00
15.45	NS 154	Mo-Fr	16.35		16.55	täglich	LH 368	17.40
19.30	LH 377	täglich	20.20		21.40	täglich	LH 368	22.25
7.00	LH 1453	Mo-Fr	8.10	Hamburg	6.30	Mo-Fr	LH 1462	7.35
9.25	LH 5050	Samstag	10.55		7.25	Samstag	LH 5051	8.55
12.05	LH 5052	tägl.a.Sa.	13.35		14.35	tägl.a.Sa.	LH 5053	16.05
17.10	LH 1455	Mo-Fr	18.20		17.25	Mo-Fr	LH 1464	18.30
6.35	NS 190	Mo-Fr	8.10	Hannover	6.35	Mo-Fr	NS 191	7.40
12.15	NS 194	Mo-Fr	13.25		13.50	Mo-Fr	NS 193	15.00
18.10	NS 196	Mo-Fr	19.15		19.45	Mo-Fr	NS 195	20.55
11.30	TK 506	Mo+Do	15.15	Istanbul	8.50	Mo+Do	TK 505	10.40
15.50	TK 504	Samstag	19.35		13.00	Samstag	TK 503	14.50
17.50	TK 502	Sonntag	21.35		15.00	Sonntag	TK 501	16.50
20.50	TK 536	Freitag	0.35		18.00	Freitag	TK 535	19.50

B. Meine Lieblingsjahreszeit. With a partner, discuss your favorite season.

Im Sommer ist das Wetter fast immer… Ich kann…

C. Geburtstagspläne.

STUDENT 1

You are talking on the phone with a friend (your partner). Discuss what you might buy as a gift for a family member or a friend. Tell whose birthday it is, when it is, what the person needs, and mention some ideas (**vielleicht kaufe ich ihm/ihr…**). Some items might be too expensive (**zu teuer**). You appreciate any suggestions (**Gute Idee!**)

STUDENT 2

Your friend is talking with you about plans to buy a birthday present for a friend or relative. You react with interest (**Wann hat er/sie Geburtstag?**) and suggestions (**Warum kaufst du ihm/ihr nicht… ?**)

D. Wir suchen… Organize a scavenger hunt. Work in small groups to draw up a list of fifteen items you might be able to find in the classroom. Then exchange your list with another group. Ask around the room until you find someone who can give you (or lend you) the item(s). The group that accumulates all fifteen items first wins. Ideas: **Chemiebuch**, **Bleistift**, **Kuli**, **Rucksack**, etc.

Alle Guten Wünsche zum Geburtstag

S. KOCHAN

Themenwortschatz

Substantive	Nouns
Jahreszeiten, Monate, Tage	***Seasons, months, days***
die Jahreszeit, -en	*season*
der Frühling	*spring*
der Sommer	*summer*
der Herbst	*autumn, fall*
der Winter	*winter*
der Monat, -e	*month*
der Januar	*January*
der Februar	*February*
der März	*March*
der April	*April*
der Mai	*May*
der Juni	*June*
der Juli	*July*
der August	*August*
der September	*September*
der Oktober	*October*
der November	*November*
der Dezember	*December*
der Wochentag, -e	*weekday*
der Montag	*Monday*
der Dienstag	*Tuesday*
der Mittwoch	*Wednesday*
der Donnerstag	*Thursday*
der Freitag	*Friday*
der Samstag/Sonnabend	*Saturday*
der Sonntag	*Sunday*

Wetter	***Weather***
der Grad, -e	*degree*
der Regen	*rain*
der Schnee	*snow*
die Sonne, -n	*sun*

Urlaub	***Vacation***
der Badeanzug, ¨e	*bathing suit*
die Badehose, -n	*swimming trunks*
der Schlittschuh, -e	*ice skate*
der Ski, -er	*ski*
der Urlaub	*vacation*

Zum Geburtstag	***For one's birthday***
der Ball, ¨e	*ball*
das Fahrrad, ¨er	*bicycle*
~~der~~ die CD, -s	*CD*

das Computerspiel, -e	*computer game*
der Geburtstag, -e	*birthday*
das Geschenk, -e	*present*
die Kamera, -s	*camera*
die Kassette, -n	*cassette tape*
der Rollschuh, -e	*roller skate*
der Tennisschläger, -	*tennis racquet*
der Turnschuh, -e	*gym shoe*

Verben	Verbs
fotografieren	*to photograph, take pictures*
Musik hören	*to listen to music*
regnen	*to rain*
scheinen	*to shine*
Schlittschuh laufen (läuft Schlittschuh)	*to ice skate*
schneien	*to snow*
Ski laufen (läuft Ski)	*to ski*

Verben mit Dativ	Verbs with dative
antworten	*to answer*
danken	*to thank*
folgen	*to follow*
geben (gibt)	*to give*
gefallen (gefällt)	*to please*
gehören	*to belong to*
glauben	*to believe*
helfen (hilft)	*to help*
leihen	*to lend*
schenken	*to give as a present*
schmecken	*to taste*

Adjektive/Adverbien	Adjectives/Adverbs
bedeckt	*overcast*
heiß	*hot*
heiter	*bright, clear*
kalt	*cold*
kühl	*cool*
sonnig	*sunny*
windig	*windy*
wolkig	*cloudy*

Präpositionen mit Dativ	Prepositions with the Dative	Ausdrücke	Expressions
aus	out of, from	am Morgen/Abend	in the morning/evening
außer	except for	am Wochenende	on the weekend
bei	near, at the home of	Es ist halb sieben (Uhr).	It is 6:30 (o'clock).
mit	with, by means of	Es ist Viertel vor/nach zehn (elf, …)	It is a quarter of/past ten (eleven …)
nach	after, to	Spaß haben	to have fun
seit	since	tagaus, tagein	day after day; day in, day out
von	of, from; by	um (zwei) Uhr	at (two) o'clock
zu	to	Wann hast du (haben Sie) Geburtstag?	When is your birthday?
		Welcher Tag ist heute?	What day is today?
		Wie spät ist es? Wieviel Uhr ist es?	} What time is it?

Weiterer Wortschatz

Substantive	Nouns	Adjektive/Adverbien	Adjectives/Adverbs
Verkehrsmittel	**Means of transportation**	fertig	finished, done
das Auto, -s	car	gestern	yesterday
der Bus, -se	bus	halb	half
das Flugzeug, -e	airplane	letzt-	last
das Schiff, -e	ship	nächst-	next
die Straßenbahn, -en	streetcar, trolley	viel, viele	much, many
der Zug, ¨e	train	vielleicht	perhaps, maybe
		zusammen	together

Andere Substantive	Other Nouns	Beiordnende Konjunktionen	Coordinating Conjunctions
das Abendbrot	evening meal, supper	aber	but
die Arbeit, -en	work	denn	because, for
die Bibliothek, -en	library	oder	or
das Kino, -s	movie theater	sondern	but, but rather
die Menschen (pl.)	people	und	and
die Schule, -n	school		
die Uhr, -en	clock	Der-Wörter	Der-Words
die Universität, -en	university	dies-	this, that
das Viertel, -	quarter	jed-	each, every
die Vorlesung, -en	lecture	welch-	which

Verben	Verbs	Ausdrücke	Expressions
beginnen	to begin	ins Kino gehen	to go to the movies
bleiben	to stay, remain	meiner Meinung nach	in my opinion
frühstücken	to eat breakfast	mit dem Bus (Zug, Auto, …)	by bus (train, car, …)
schlafen (schläft)	to sleep	nach Hause gehen	to go home
		noch nicht	not yet
		zu Fuß	on foot

Wie und wo wohnen wir?

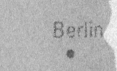

Kommunikation
- Describing your daily activities (past time frame)
- Talking about living arrangements and housing situations
- Describing your furnishings
- Discussing what you may or should do
- Telling what you like and dislike

Strukturen
- Present perfect tense
- Separable and inseparable prefix verbs
- Modal verbs **dürfen**, **sollen**, **mögen**, and summary of all modals

Kultur
- Housing terminology
- Housing possibilities
- Living space

Kapitel 5

Schritt 1: **Ich wohne...**

The following words will be useful in discussing your living situation on or off campus.

allein	*alone*
zusammen	*together*
mieten	*to rent*
teilen	*to share*
das Studentenwohnheim, -e	*student dormitory*
die Wohngemeinschaft , -en (WG)	*student co-op/communal living situation*
die Wohnung, -en	
das Zimmer, -	
der Zimmerkamerad, -en/	*roommate*
die Zimmerkameradin, -nen	

ALLES KLAR?

 Ich wohne... With a partner, discuss your living situation and your roommate(s).

MÖGLICHE FRAGEN

Mit wem wohnst du zusammen?
Wie ist er/sie?
Was macht er/sie gern?
Was macht ihr zusammen?
Wer putzt (*cleans*) das Zimmer?
Seid ihr gute Freunde/Freundinnen?

MÖGLICHE ANTWORTEN

Ich habe... Zimmerkameraden /
  Kameradinnen.
Ich wohne mit... zusammen.
Wir mieten/teilen/wohnen...
Er/sie ist sehr (intelligent/fleißig/
  nett usw.).
Er/sie spielt gern...
Zusammen...
Ich wohne allein in einem/einer...

Kulturnotiz: Housing terminology

In German, the number of rooms in an apartment is expressed by a compound noun; for example, **Dreizimmerwohnung**[1] means *a three-room apartment*. The count of three rooms excludes the kitchen and bathroom.

Various floors or levels are referred to as **Stockwerke**. Again, counting is different than in English: the first floor is called **das Erdgeschoß** (*ground floor*), the second floor **der erste Stock**, the third floor **der zweite Stock**, etc.

---

[1]You will also see the word hyphenated: **Drei-Zimmer-Wohnung**. Both forms are correct.

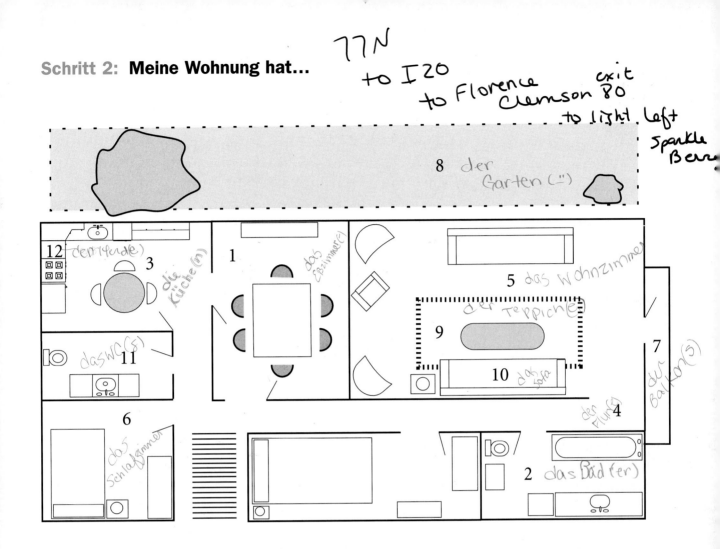

1. das Eßzimmer, -
2. das Bad, ¨er / das Badezimmer
3. die Küche, -n
4. der Flur, -e
5. das Wohnzimmer, -
6. das Schlafzimmer, -
7. der Balkon, -s
8. der Garten, ¨
9. der Teppich, -e
10. das Sofa, -s
11. das WC, -s
12. der Herd, -e

ALLES KLAR?

A. Die Wohnung. Describe the apartment shown above, using both the new vocabulary and the vocabulary you already know.

> BEISPIEL: Das ist eine Vierzimmerwohnung. Sie hat eine Küche, ein
> Wohnzimmer,…
> Im Wohnzimmer gibt es…
> Im Schlafzimmer sind…

B. Wo machst du…? Ask a fellow student where she or he does the following activities.

> BEISPIEL: —Wo liest du gern?
> —Im Garten.

lernen
lesen
singen
Musik hören

zu Mittag essen
Briefe schreiben
Karten spielen

 C. Zu Hause. Describe to a new partner the house or apartment where your family lives.

> BEISPIEL: Unser Haus hat zwei Stockwerke. Mein Zimmer ist im ersten Stock.
> Das Wohnzimmer ist klein, aber es hat viele Bücherregale…

Your partner may ask questions: **Ist euer Haus alt oder modern? Welche Farbe hat dein Schlafzimmer? Habt ihr ein Eßzimmer, oder eßt ihr in der Küche?…**

Tip!

To discuss on what floor something is located, use the phrases **im Erdgeschoß**, **im ersten Stock**, **im zweiten Stock**, **im dritten Stock**, etc.

Tip!

As in English, the prefix **un-** can make the meaning of many adjectives negative:

unbequem = *uncomfortable*
unfreundlich = *unfriendly*
unmöbliert = *unfurnished*
but **unruhig** = *restless*.

Schritt 3: Meine Wohnung ist…

The following words will help you describe not only what your room or apartment contains, but what it is like. Use **zu** (*too*) to denote excess: **zu laut** = *too loud*, etc.

(un)bequem	*(un)comfortable*
billig	*cheap*
teuer	*expensive*
laut	*loud, noisy*
ruhig	*quiet*
hell	*light*
dunkel	*dark*
(un)möbliert	*(un)furnished*

ALLES KLAR?

 A. Wo ich wohne. Draw a picture of your room or of a room in the apartment or house where you are presently living. As you sketch each object, your partner will ask a question about it.

> BEISPIEL: —Hier ist mein Bett.
> —Ist dein Bett bequem?
> —Ja, es ist bequem.
> ODER: —Nein, es ist nicht bequem, sondern sehr unbequem.

B. Meine Wohnsituation. In small groups, discuss your current living situation, either on campus or at home. Be sure to ask each other questions.

BEISPIEL: —Unsere Wohnung ist sehr klein; sie hat nur ein
Schlafzimmer, und die Küche ist alt.
—Ist eure Wohnung teuer?
—Nein, sie ist nicht teuer, sondern billig. Sie ist auch sehr ruhig.

Bett	alt	teuer
Sofa	neu	billig
Computer	modern	(un)bequem
Teppich	schön	
Schrank	häßlich	*schmutzig*
Sessel	groß	
Lampe	klein	*miete*
Schreibtisch	laut	
Fernseher	ruhig	
Kühlschrank		
Telefon		

C. Ich möchte diese Wohnung. With a partner, discuss which of the following apartments you would prefer to rent.

BEISPIEL: Ich möchte Wohnung A mieten, denn sie ist ruhig.

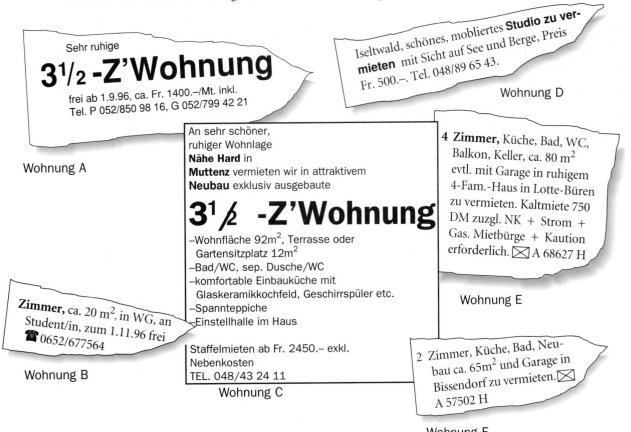

Sehr ruhige

3¹⁄₂ -Z'Wohnung

frei ab 1.9.96, ca. Fr. 1400.–/Mt. inkl.
Tel. P 052/850 98 16, G 052/799 42 21

Wohnung A

Iseltwald, schönes, möbliertes **Studio zu vermieten** mit Sicht auf See und Berge, Preis Fr. 500.–. Tel. 048/89 65 43.

Wohnung D

An sehr schöner, ruhiger Wohnlage **Nähe Hard** in **Muttenz** vermieten wir in attraktivem **Neubau** exklusiv ausgebaute

3¹⁄₂ -Z'Wohnung

–Wohnfläche 92m², Terrasse oder Gartensitzplatz 12m²
–Bad/WC, sep. Dusche/WC
–komfortable Einbauküche mit Glaskeramikkochfeld, Geschirrspüler etc.
–Spannteppiche
–Einstellhalle im Haus

Staffelmieten ab Fr. 2450.– exkl. Nebenkosten
TEL. 048/43 24 11

Wohnung C

4 Zimmer, Küche, Bad, WC, Balkon, Keller, ca. 80 m² evtl. mit Garage in ruhigem 4-Fam.-Haus in Lotte-Büren zu vermieten. Kaltmiete 750 DM zuzgl. NK + Strom + Gas. Mietbürge + Kaution erforderlich. ✉ A 68627 H

Wohnung E

Zimmer, ca. 20 m², in WG, an Student/in, zum 1.11.96 frei ☎ 0652/677564

Wohnung B

2 Zimmer, Küche, Bad, Neubau ca. 65m² und Garage in Bissendorf zu vermieten.✉ A 57502 H

Wohnung F

The range of housing possibilities in Germany is as varied as in North America. Typical arrangements might include single and multiple family houses, Wohngemeinschaften (**WG**), apartments, condominiums (**Eigentumswohungen**), and housing developments for people who live as singles, couples, or families. In addition, Germany has its share of squatters and homeless people. In contrast to the United States and Canada, there is a distinct shortage of housing facilities all over the Federal Republic of Germany, in part because of the recent influx of immigrants from eastern Europe.

Versuch's mal!   Der z-Laut

Zesi und ihre Zimmerkameradin, Zarathustra, sind in eine Fünfzimmerwohnung eingezogen. Die Wohnung ist im zweiten Stock und hat zwei Schlafzimmer, ein Eßzimmer, ein Wohnzimmer und ein Arbeitszimmer. Die Heizung müssen sie selbst bezahlen.

Zarathustra hat auch eine Katze, Zickzack. Zesi, Zarathustra und Zickzack wohnen seit zwei Jahren zusammen. Zesi ist Zahnärztin und Zarathustra arbeitet im Zoo. Zickzack faulenzt den ganzen Tag und zerstört ab und zu Zesis Pflanzen. Dann sagt ihr Zarathustra: "Zickzack, wenn du den ganzen Tag zu Hause faulenzt, sollst du wenigstens etwas nützliches machen — vielleicht putzen oder mindestens die Zeitung lesen, aber Zesis Pflanzen zu zerstören — das ist nicht zulässig!"

Schritt 4: Wer bekommt das Zimmer?

📖 Lesestück

Worum geht es hier? The Martin family has just moved into a new apartment, but Bobby isn't happy. Skim the text and complete the following table. Then read the passage a second time and answer the questions in Activity A.

	WIE IST ES? (ADJEKTIVE)	WAS IST IN DEM ZIMMER? (SACHEN)
STEVES ZIMMER		
BOBBYS ZIMMER		

Die Familie Martin hat seit zwei Wochen eine Wohnung. Es ist noch alles neu. Jetzt hat jeder endlich genug Platz. Bisher[1] haben Steve und Bobby, die zwei Söhne, ein Zimmer geteilt.

Das Zimmer von Steve, neunzehn Jahre alt, ist groß und hell, mit zwei Fenstern. Steve hat es schon sehr schön eingerichtet; seine Freundin Barbara hat ihm geholfen. Die Stereoanlage gehört nicht ihm, er hat sie von seiner Freundin bekommen. In seinem Zimmer ist ein Bett, ein Sessel, ein Schrank und natürlich ein Schreibtisch mit einem Stuhl und einer Lampe. Die Wand ist schon voll mit Postern und Bildern. Besonders[2] die Poster gefallen ihm sehr gut. Aber er arbeitet schon und ist nicht oft zu Hause.

Bobby, sechzehn Jahre alt, hat sein Zimmer nicht ganz eingerichtet, denn er braucht viel Platz und sein Zimmer ist etwas klein. Es ist auch dunkel, denn es gibt nur ein kleines Fenster. Bobby ist Musikfanatiker und hat einen teuren CD-Spieler und zweihundert CDs. Er hört gern Musik und bleibt oft zu Hause.

Zusammen mit der Mutter haben Steve und Bobby eine Küche, ein Bad, eine Toilette und ein Wohnzimmer. Das Wohnzimmer ist groß und hell mit einem Sofa und davor[3] steht ein Fernseher. Besonders abends sehen die Martins gerne fern. Natürlich hat die Mutter auch ein Schlafzimmer, aber sie hat es noch nicht eingerichtet, denn sie hat keine Zeit gehabt. Steve und Bobby wollen ihr helfen, denn Frau Martin arbeitet von acht Uhr morgens bis fünf Uhr nachmittags. Dann kommt sie nach Hause und ist meistens sehr müde.

Es ist jetzt sechs Uhr abends, und Frau Martin kommt nach Hause. Ihr Tag war lang, und sie ist müde. Ihre zwei Söhne haben Streit[4]. Bobby will das Zimmer von Steve haben.

---

[1]*until now*
[2]*especially*
[3]*in front of*
[4]*argument, fight*

ALLES KLAR?

A. Haben Sie das verstanden?

1. Was hat die Familie Martin seit zwei Wochen?
2. Hat Steve das Zimmer allein eingerichtet? Erklären Sie (*explain*)!
3. Von wem hat Steve die Stereoanlage bekommen?
4. Hat Bobby sein Zimmer schon ganz eingerichtet? Warum (nicht)?
5. Beschreiben Sie die Zimmer von Steve und Bobby.
6. Wie ist das Wohnzimmer?
7. Was machen die Martins gern abends?
8. Warum haben Steve und Bobby Streit?

B. Der Streit. What should the Martin family do? In small groups, discuss the following possible solutions.

- Steve soll das Zimmer behalten (*keep*). Er ist älter (*older*) und er hat es schon eingerichtet.
- Bobby soll das Zimmer bekommen. Er bleibt oft zu Hause.
- Frau Martin soll ihr Zimmer mit Bobby tauschen (*exchange*).
- Bobby und Steve müssen jedes Jahr die Zimmer tauschen.

C. Verb am Ende. With a partner, write out or underline all sentences from the **Lesestück** in which the main verb appears at the end of the sentence—but not in its infinitive form. Then group the verbs according to their similarities. What are these similarities? What are the differences between groups? (You will learn the reasons for these similarities and differences in the following pages.)

> **BEISPIEL:** Bisher haben Steve und Bobby… ein Zimmer geteilt.

Kulturnotiz: Living space

Germans use their private living space differently than do Americans. For example, most homes or apartments have separate entry halls, and Germans generally keep the doors to all rooms closed.

Since space is at a premium, privacy is carefully protected, often by gardens, which are more coveted than in North America. They are cultivated more frequently, are usually fenced in, and are often painstakingly decorated. Even small apartments often have flower pots on a balcony or window boxes in the windows.

In the kitchen, appliances like refrigerators and built-in stoves are smaller, and there are fewer gadgets. The most common small appliances include coffee grinders and bread slicers. Elsewhere in the home, built-in closets are rare; large wooden wardrobes or armoires are used instead. Larger German homes are frequently equipped with a guest bathroom, which is separate from the family bathroom; this contains only a toilet and a sink and is generally referred to as the **WC** (*water closet*). Most homes or apartments have a cellar and an attic for storage.

The present perfect tense

German has two verb forms to express events that happened in the past. One is the simple past; in **Kapitel 4** you learned the simple past tense of **sein**. With most verbs, however, the other form is more common. It is called the present perfect tense and is used frequently in conversation.

The present perfect tense is called a compound tense because it consists of two parts: the auxiliary verb, i.e., the present tense of either **haben** or **sein**, plus the past participle of the main verb. The past participle appears at the end of the sentence.

	AUXILIARY		PAST PARTICIPLE	
Wir	**haben**	eine Wohnung	**gefunden.**	*We found an apartment.*
			OR:	*We have found an apartment.*
Mein Sohn	**ist**	von Rostock	**gekommen.**	*My son came from Rostock.*
			OR:	*My son has come from Rostock.*

The auxiliary verb

Haben is used as the auxiliary with most verbs in the present perfect. **Sein** is used with verbs that:

(1) express a change in location or in condition and
(2) do not have a direct object

werden:	Meine Zimmerkameradin **ist** Ärztin **geworden.** (change of condition)
fahren:	Wir **sind** nach Halle **gefahren.** (change of location)
passieren:	Wie **ist** denn das **passiert**? (change of condition)
einziehen:	Letzten August **bin** ich **eingezogen.** (change of location)

Exceptions to the "change of location or condition rule" are **sein** and **bleiben**, which also take the auxiliary **sein**.

Ich **bin** beim Studentenwohnheim nebenan **gewesen.**.
Bist du gestern abend zu Hause **geblieben**?

[handwritten note: Vor = ago]

ALLES KLAR?

A. Die Wohnungssuche.
Complete the following sentences, using the appropriate auxiliary.

[handwritten note: no object →]

Lieber Scott,

Du (1) _hast_ gefragt, wo wir als Studenten in Deutschland wohnen. Vor zwei Monaten (2) _bin_ ich beim Studentenwohnheim gewesen und (3) _habe_ ein Zimmer beantragt. Ich (4) _habe_ sehr lange gewartet. Es (5) _hat_ einfach nichts gegeben. Dann (6) _haben_ mein Freund Peter und _hat_ ich vor drei Wochen eine Wohnung gefunden. Es (7) _hat_ nicht einfach gewesen. Wir (8) _haben_ viele Inserate (ads) in der Zeitung gelesen. Endlich (9) _haben_ wir eine Drei-Zimmer-Wohnung gefunden. Sie (10) _ist_ auch nicht sehr teuer gewesen. Dann (11) _sind_ wir eingezogen. Mein Zimmer (12) _habe_ ich schon eingerichtet, denn Laurie (13) _hat_ mir geholfen. Peter (14)_____ sein Zimmer noch nicht eingerichtet, denn er (15)_____ noch keine Zeit gehabt.

Dein John

B. Was hast du gestern gemacht? Discuss with a partner what you did yesterday. Use the list below as a starting point. Use the correct auxiliary with each phrase.

… Stunden gelernt	Fußball gespielt
zur Uni gegangen	in die Stadt gefahren
geputzt	im Restaurant/in der Mensa (*student cafeteria*) gegessen
Musik gehört	
das Bett gemacht	gelesen
Hausaufgaben gemacht	Briefe geschrieben
ferngesehen	

The past participle of the main verb

German verbs fall into three main categories, depending on how their past participle is formed.

1. **Regular verbs.** The past participle of regular (so-called "weak") verbs is formed by adding the prefix **ge-** and the suffix **-(e)t** to the unchanged stem of the verb.

INFINITIVE	PREFIX + STEM + SUFFIX	PRESENT PERFECT TENSE
brauchen	ge + brauch + t	hat gebraucht
haben	ge + hab + t	hat gehabt
meinen	ge + mein + t	hat gemeint

Sie **haben** eine Wohnung **gebraucht**.
They needed an apartment.

Ihre Mutter **hat** keine Zeit **gehabt**.
Their mother had no time.

Hat sie das wirklich **gemeint**?
Did she really mean that?

If the stem of a verb ends in **-d** or **-t** (**arbeiten**) or in **-m** or **-n** preceded by a consonant other than **l** or **r** (**öffnen**), an **-e-** is inserted to facilitate pronunciation.

INFINITIVE	PREFIX + STEM + SUFFIX	PRESENT PERFECT TENSE
arbeiten	ge + arbeit + et	hat gearbeitet
kosten	ge + kost + et	hat gekostet
öffnen	ge + öffn + et	hat geöffnet

Sie **hat** bis fünf Uhr **gearbeitet**.
She worked until five o'clock.

Was **hat** der CD-Spieler **gekostet**?
What did the CD player cost?

Ich **habe** das Fenster **geöffnet**.
I opened the window.

Verbs ending in **-ieren** are also regular verbs. However, they do not add the prefix **ge-**, but only the suffix **-t**.

INFINITIVE	STEM + SUFFIX	PRESENT PERFECT TENSE
studieren	studier + t	hat studiert
probieren	probier + t	hat probiert

Wo **hast** du **studiert**?
Where did you study?

Habt ihr den Nachtisch **probiert**?
Did you try the dessert?

ALLES KLAR?

A. Wie hast du gewohnt? With a partner, take turns asking and answering the following questions about looking for a room or apartment at the beginning of the year.

1. Hast du letztes Jahr ein Zimmer (eine Wohnung) geteilt oder hast du allein gewohnt?
2. Hast du letztes Jahr ein Zimmer im Studentenheim oder eine Wohnung gemietet?
3. Hast du dieses Jahr eine Wohnung (ein Zimmer) gesucht?
4. Hast du ein großes Zimmer (eine große Wohnung) gebraucht? Warum (nicht)?
5. Hast du Glück (*luck*) gehabt?

B. Austauschstudent. Mark was an exchange student last year in Austria. Fill in the blanks with the appropriate auxiliary and past participle of the verbs in the list.

arbeiten   kosten   studieren
probieren   reisen (*to travel*)   putzen
lernen   haben

Letzes Jahr (1) _____ Mark in Wien (2) _____. Er ist am fünfzehnten September nach München geflogen (*flew*) und (3) _____ mit dem Zug von München nach Wien (4) _____. Er (5) _____ ein Zimmer bei einer Familie (6) _____. Es (7) _____ nicht viel (8) _____ — nur öS 2600,-[1] im Monat — aber es gab (*there was*) auch keine Putzfrau (*cleaning lady*); deshalb (9) _____ er selbst (10) _____.

An einem normalen Tag (11) _____ Mark viel (12) _____, denn seine Kurse waren nicht leicht (*easy*). Er (13) _____ nicht (14) _____, denn als Ausländer (*foreigner*) kann man nicht arbeiten. Jeden Tag (15) _____ er eine andere Wiener Spezialität (16) _____ : Sachertorte, Kaffee oder Wiener Schnitzel.

---

[1]«öS» stands for **österreichischer Schilling**, the currency in Austria.

Wie und wo wohnen wir? • hunderteinunddreißig **131**

2. **Irregular verbs.** The past participle of irregular (or "strong") verbs is formed with the prefix **ge-** and the suffix **-en**. In addition, the stem of the verb often undergoes a vowel change, and sometimes a consonant change as well. You must therefore memorize the past participle of each irregular verb you learn.

INFINITIVE	PREFIX + STEM + SUFFIX	PRESENT PERFECT TENSE
gehen	**ge** + gang + **en**	**ist ge**gang**en**
heißen	**ge** + heiß + **en**	**hat ge**heiß**en**
kommen	**ge** + komm + **en**	**ist ge**komm**en**
schreiben	**ge** +schrieb + **en**	**hat ge**schrieb**en**
sein	**ge** + wes + **en**	**ist ge**wes**en**
werden	**ge** + word + **en**	**ist ge**word**en**

Ich **habe** ihr **geschrieben**.
I wrote to her.

Sie **sind** nicht hier **gewesen**.
They weren't here.

Er **ist** leider krank **geworden**.
Unfortunately he became ill.

Here is a list of the irregular verbs you have learned in **Kapitel 1-4**:

INFINITIVE	STEM-VOWEL CHANGE	PAST PARTICIPLE	MEANING
bleiben		ist geblieben	*to stay*
essen	ißt	gegessen	*to eat*
fahren	fährt	ist gefahren	*to drive, go*
geben	gibt	gegeben	*to give*
gefallen	gefällt	gefallen	*to be pleasing to*
gehen		ist gegangen	*to go*
heißen		geheißen	*to be called*
helfen	hilft	geholfen	*to help*
kommen		ist gekommen	*to come*
laufen	läuft	ist gelaufen	*to run*
leihen		geliehen	*to loan*
lesen	liest	gelesen	*to read*
nehmen	nimmt	genommen	*to take*
scheinen		geschienen	*to shine*
schreiben		geschrieben	*to write*
schwimmen		ist geschwommen	*to swim*
sehen	sieht	gesehen	*to see*
sein	ist	ist gewesen	*to be*
singen		gesungen	*to sing*
sprechen	spricht	gesprochen	*to speak*
trinken		getrunken	*to drink*
tun		getan	*to do, make*
verlieren		verloren[1]	*to lose*
verstehen		verstanden[1]	*to understand*
werden	wird	ist geworden	*to become*

[1]See the following section on separable and inseparable prefixes.

ALLES KLAR?

 A. Auf einer Reise. With a partner, take turns asking and answering questions about a trip you took. Use complete sentences.

1. Wohin bist du gefahren? (Ich bin nach…)
2. Hat es dir gefallen? Warum (nicht)?
3. Was hast du alles gesehen?
4. Bist du jeden Tag ins Restaurant gegangen, oder hast du auch manchmal ein Picknick gemacht?
5. Hast du deinen Freunden / deiner Familie oft Postkarten geschrieben?
6. Bist du jeden Abend müde gewesen?

B. Was hat Mark alles in Wien gemacht? Fill in the blanks with the appropriate auxiliary and past participle of the verbs in the list.

gehen	sein	werden
essen	fahren	lesen
sehen	trinken	

Im ersten Monat (1)_____ Mark ein Buch über Wien (2)_____. Am nächsten Wochenende (3)_____ er das Opernhaus (4)_____; dann (5)_____ er mit der Straßenbahn um die Ringstraße (6)_____. Er (7)_____ nicht zu Fuß (8)_____, denn er (9)_____ zu faul (10)_____ . Am Ende des Jahres (*of the year*) (11)_____ Mark ein bißchen dicker (*fatter*) (12)_____, denn er (13)_____ in Wien sehr gut (14)_____ und (15)_____.

3. **Mixed verbs.** There are only a few mixed (or "irregular weak") verbs. They are called "mixed verbs" because their past participle is formed by placing **ge-** and **-t** around the verb stem, as with regular verbs, but there is often a stem change as well.

INFINITIVE	PREFIX+STEM+SUFFIX	PRESENT PERFECT TENSE
denken	**ge** + dach + **t**	**hat ge**dacht
kennen	**ge** + kann + **t**	**hat ge**kannt
wissen	**ge** + wuß + **t**	**hat ge**wußt

Ich **habe** an sie **gedacht**.
I thought of her.

Wir **haben** ihn damals nicht **gekannt**.
We didn't know him then.

Das **habe** ich nicht **gewußt**.
I didn't know that.

The past participles of all irregular and mixed verbs will be listed in the **Themenwortschatz** and end vocabulary. In addition, there is a separate list of Irregular and Mixed Verbs in the appendix. Verbs requiring the auxiliary **sein** in the perfect tenses are also indicated in the verb lists.

ALLES KLAR?

A. Wie findest du sie? Restate the following exchange in the present perfect tense.

—Wie findest du Sandy?
—Ich kenne sie nicht, aber ich weiß, sie ist eine intelligente Frau.
—Ja, das finde ich auch.

B. Verben im Perfekt. Look at the following verbs and complete the chart.

INFINITIVE	AUXILIARY	PAST PARTICIPLE
finden	*haben*	*gefunden*
_____		gedacht
helfen	*haben*	*~~mit~~geholfen*
schwimmin	*ist*	geschwommen
meinen	*haben*	*gemeint*
bleiben	*sein*	geblieben
öffnen		*geöffnit*
Verlüren	*haben*	verloren
sagen	*habe*	*gesagt*
nehmen	*habe*	genommen
kennen	*habe*	*gekennt*
Kommen	*sein*	gekommen

C. Sätze schreiben. Now prepare at least four questions, using the verbs from Activity B in the present perfect tense. Use some regular verbs and some irregular or mixed verbs. Your partner will answer the questions, also using the present perfect.

> **BEISPIELE:** Bist du gestern abend zu Hause geblieben?
> —Nein, ich bin nicht zu Hause geblieben.
>
> Hast du gestern etwas verloren? Hast du es gefunden?
> —Ja, ich habe…
>
> Hast du das Fenster geöffnet?
> — Nein, ich habe…

D. Gestern habe ich Probleme gehabt. Talk to your partner about problems you had yesterday.

ich	krank	gewesen
meine Familie	nicht freundlich	gehabt
mein Zimmerkamerad	laut	gewartet
ihr	keine Zeit	gefunden
meine Bücher	zu teuer	gekostet
mein Zimmer	lange	gearbeitet
du	nichts	getan
meine Professoren	zu viel	
es	zu warm/kalt	

Separable and inseparable prefix verbs

Many German verbs take prefixes that change their meaning, sometimes in a substantial way. These prefixes fall into two categories: separable prefixes, which separate from the verb in certain types of sentences, and inseparable prefixes, which always remain attached to the verb.

take sein: Changing place, condition

Verbs with separable prefixes

German, like English, has many two-part verbs.

ausprobieren	*to try out*
einziehen	*to move in*
vorbeikommen	*to come by*

In German, the separable prefix is usually an adverb (**vorbeikommen**) or a preposition (**ausprobieren**), or sometimes another verb (**kennenlernen**, *to get to know*). If you know the meaning of both the verb and its prefix, you can frequently guess the meaning of the combined verb: for example, **zurück** (*back*) + **kommen** (*to come*) = **zurückkommen** (*to come back*). In other cases, the prefix alters the meaning of the verb in less predictable ways: **fern** (*far*) + **sehen** (*to see*) = **fernsehen** (*to watch television*).

In pronunciation, the separable prefix is always stressed. Separable-prefix verbs are conventionally indicated in vocabulary lists by a raised dot: **an•hören**, **aus•ziehen**. This dot, however, is not part of the spelling; it is simply meant as an aid in recognition.

1. **Present tense.** In the present tense, separable prefixes are separated from the main verb and placed at the end of the sentence or clause. Therefore, in order to be sure that you understand a sentence correctly, look at the end and check whether there is a separable prefix.

   Morgen richtet Bobby sein Zimmer ein.
   Tomorrow Bobby will furnish his room.

   Michelle und Tom probieren das Sofa aus.
   Michelle and Tom are trying out the sofa.

   Die Martins sehen abends gerne fern.
   The Martins like to watch TV in the evenings.

   Stimmt ihr jetzt überein?
   Do you agree now?

2. **Present perfect tense.** The past participle of separable-prefix verbs is formed by inserting the -**ge**- between the separable prefix and the verb stem with its regular past participle ending.

> Steve hat sein Zimmer schon eingerichtet.
> *Steve already furnished his room.*

> Die Martins haben abends gerne ferngesehen.
> *The Martins liked to watch TV in the evenings.*

> Habt ihr nicht übereingestimmt?
> *Didn't you agree?*

As always, verbs ending in -**ieren** do not take a -**ge**-.

> Michelle und Tom haben das Sofa ausprobiert.
> *Michelle and Tom tried out the sofa.*

ALLES KLAR?

A. Die neue Wohnung. Tom and Michelle are talking about their new apartment, and Michelle has some questions. Form complete sentences in the present tense.

> BEISPIEL: wann / einrichten / wir/ die Wohnung?
> Wann richten wir die Wohnung ein?

1. wann / ausprobieren / du / die Heizung?
2. wie / das Sofa von deinen Eltern / aussehen?
3. wann / einziehen / wir ?
4. warum / übereinstimmen / wir / nie?
5. wann / kennenlernen / wir / die Nachbarn?
6. wann / zurückgeben / wir / der Schlüssel zur alten Wohnung?

B. Die Wohnung ist nicht mehr neu. A year later, Michelle and Tom are reminiscing. Put Michelle's questions in Activity A into the present perfect tense.

> BEISPIEL: Wann haben wir die Wohnung eingerichtet?

C. Betty ist ahnungslos (*clueless*). Betty has been away on vacation and doesn't know what has been going on with your friends and family. Answer the following questions affirmatively, saying that the following events already occurred.

> BEISPIEL: Kommt dein Bruder wieder zurück?
> Er ist schon zurückgekommen.

1. Geht Sarah mit Ernie aus?
2. Zieht Brenda in eine neue Wohnung ein?
3. Geht Lisa nach Kalifornien zurück?
4. Zieht Robert von zu Hause aus?
5. Gibt Linda ihrem Freund den Ring zurück?

D. Jill will einkaufen. Fill in the blanks by using the correct form of the verbs from the list below. Some verbs will be used more than once.

fernsehen _ferngesehen_   aussehen *(to look, appear)* _ist ausgesehen_
mitkommen _ist mitgekommen_   aussuchen _ausgesucht_
gehen _ist gegangen_   einziehen _ist eingezogen_

JILL: Ich möchte heute mal in ein Möbelgeschäft _gean_ .

DIRK: Was willst du denn da machen?

JILL: Möbel ansehen, natürlich. Du hast deinen Fernseher, und du _fernsiehst_
immer _fern_ , aber wir haben keine Möbel! Wir sind vor vier Wochen
hier _eingezogen_, und die Wohnung ist noch leer. Sie _aussehen ist_
schrecklich _aus_.

DIRK: Aber ich möchte auch heute gern _fernsehen._ Das Tennisspiel soll sehr gut
sein.

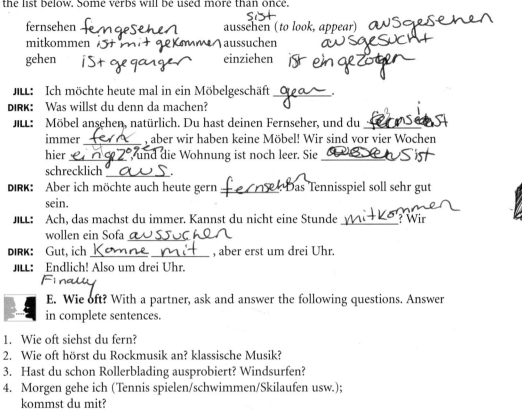

JILL: Ach, das machst du immer. Kannst du nicht eine Stunde _mitko_ ? Wir
wollen ein Sofa _aussuchen_

DIRK: Gut, ich _komme mit_ , aber erst um drei Uhr.

JILL: Endlich! Also um drei Uhr.
Finally

E. Wie oft? With a partner, ask and answer the following questions. Answer
in complete sentences.

1. Wie oft siehst du fern?
2. Wie oft hörst du Rockmusik an? klassische Musik?
3. Hast du schon Rollerblading ausprobiert? Windsurfen?
4. Morgen gehe ich (Tennis spielen/schwimmen/Skilaufen usw.);
   kommst du mit?
5. Hast du dein Zimmer sehr schön eingerichtet?
6. Stimmst du oft mit deinem Zimmerkameraden/mit deiner
   Zimmerkameradin überein?
7. Gehst du immer am Wochenende aus?

Verbs with inseparable prefixes

Inseparable prefixes are never separated from the verb and are always unstressed. Some
common inseparable prefixes are **be-**, **emp-**, **ent-**, **er-**, **ge-**, **ver-**, and **zer-**. Unlike the
separable prefixes, these inseparable prefixes have no distinct meaning in themselves.
Examples of words with these prefixes are:

bezahlen	*to pay for*
empfehlen	*to recommend*
entdecken	*to discover*
erzählen	*to tell*
gefallen	*to be pleasing to*
verlassen	*to leave _+ take D.O_*
wiederholen	*to repeat*
zerstören	*to destroy*

The past participle of inseparable prefix verbs is formed by adding the suffixes -**t** or -**en** to the stem, depending on whether the verb is regular or irregular. They do not take a **ge-** prefix.

REGULAR VERB: bezahl- + t   bezahlt
IRREGULAR VERB: begonn- + en   begonnen

Wir **haben** die Miete gestern **bezahlt**.
Er **hat** eine lange Wohnungssuche **begonnen**.

ALLES KLAR?

A. Trennbar oder nicht? Check whether each of the following verbs is separable or inseparable.

	SEPARABLE-PREFIX VERB	INSEPARABLE-PREFIX VERB
zurückgehen	✓	
ansehen	✓	
beantworten		✓
wiederholen	✓	
ausgehen	✓	
verkaufen		✓
entdecken		✓
beginnen	✓	✓
bekommen	✓	✓
übereinstimmen	✓	
empfehlen		✓
benutzen		✓
mitkommen	✓	

B. Sätze im Präsens und Perfekt schreiben. Select five of the verbs in Activity A with inseparable prefixes, or use other inseparable-prefix verbs of your choice. Create two sentences for each verb: one sentence in the present tense and one in the present perfect.

BEISPIEL: bezahlen
Ich bezahle monatlich sechshundert Mark für Miete.
Michelle hat das Sofa bezahlt.

C. **Paul kommt nach Hause.** With a partner, tell the following story in complete sentences, using separable or inseparable prefix verbs. You may wish to use verbs like **fernsehen, ausprobieren, zerstören, verlassen….**

1.

2.

Paul kommt nach Hause

3.

Paul will wisen

4.

5.

6.

Nein ich will den Sessel nicht ausprobieren

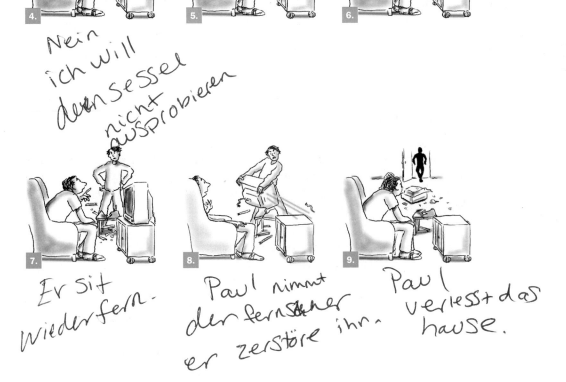

7. *Er sit wieder fern.*

8. *Paul nimmt den fernsher er zerstöre ihn.*

9. *Paul verlesst das hause.*

Schritt 5: **Michelle und Tom kaufen zusammen ein**

(((□))) Gespräch

Worum geht es hier? Michelle and Tom have just moved into a new housing co-op in Karlsruhe; now they are looking for a sofa. Do they agree on a purchase? Skim the passage to find out; then read it more carefully and answer the questions in Activity A.

Before you begin, think about what you would consider when buying a piece of furniture: price, comfort, color, etc. Make a list and look for these key factors as you read the conversation.

VERKÄUFERIN: Guten Tag! Kann ich Ihnen helfen?

MICHELLE: Ja, guten Tag! Ich habe gestern hier ein Sofa gesehen. Ich bin mit meinem Freund zurückgekommen. Wir wollen es zusammen anschauen.

VERKÄUFERIN: Welches Sofa meinen Sie?

MICHELLE: Dieses hier.

VERKÄUFERIN: Es ist wirklich sehr preiswert.[1]

TOM: Du, das Sofa gefällt mir; es sieht bequem aus, und es ist tatsächlich nicht zu teuer. Dürfen wir es ausprobieren?

VERKÄUFERIN: Natürlich.

(Michelle und Tom probieren es aus.)

MICHELLE: Du hast recht, es ist eigentlich sehr bequem.

VERKÄUFERIN: Wir haben schon viele von diesen Sofas verkauft; sie sind sehr beliebt,[2] denn sie sind preiswert und stabil.

TOM: Aber gibt es das nur in braun? Das finde ich etwas langweilig.[3]

VERKÄUFERIN: Nein, dieses Sofa können Sie auch in schwarz, rot und beige bekommen. Sehen Sie, dort ist es in beige.

TOM: Zu unserem Teppich paßt[4] rot sehr schön. Was meinst du, Michelle?

MICHELLE: Ja, rot oder beige. Mir gefällt beige besser.

TOM: Meinst du? Das Sofa muß gut zu unserem Tisch, den Sesseln und dem Bücherregal passen. Du hast recht, beige ist besser. Das ist genau richtig für unser Wohnzimmer.

(Michelle fragt die Verkäuferin.)

MICHELLE: Kostet das Sofa in beige auch fünfhundertzehn Mark?

VERKÄUFERIN: Ja, das ist diese Woche im Sonderangebot.[5] Normalerweise[6] kostet es fünfhundertfünfundneunzig Mark.

TOM: Was meinst du, Michelle, sollen wir es kaufen?

(Michelle fragt die Verkäuferin.)

MICHELLE: Ist das inklusive Lieferung?[7]

VERKÄUFERIN: Natürlich ist das inklusive Lieferpreis, und wir können schon morgen liefern.

(Tom zu Michelle)

TOM: Also, stimmen wir überein?

MICHELLE: Ja, schon.

Redewendung

Also does not mean *also*, but rather *well, so, therefore.*

Also, stimmen wir überein?
Well, do we agree?

Schon is another flavoring word. It usually strengthens or confirms a statement.

Ja, wir stimmen schon überein.
Yes, we do agree.

The word **finden** means not only *to find*; it is also used to express an opinion

Braun finde ich etwas langweilig.
I think brown is kind of boring.

---

[1] *a good value*
[2] *popular*
[3] *boring, uninteresting*
[4] *matches*
[5] *on sale*
[6] *normally*
[7] *delivery*

ALLES KLAR?

A. Haben Sie verstanden?

1. Was möchten Michelle und Tom kaufen?
2. Was hat Michelle gesehen?
3. Warum hat sie das Sofa nicht gleich (*immediately*) gekauft?
4. Wie sieht das Sofa aus?
5. Was tun Michelle und Tom?
6. Warum hat das Geschäft schon viele von diesen Sofas verkauft?
7. In welchen Farben gibt es das Sofa?
8. Ist das Sofa teuer? Was kostet es?
9. Ist der Preis inklusive Lieferung (*delivery*)?
10. Wann kann das Möbelgeschäft das Sofa liefern?
11. Stimmen Michelle und Tom überein? Warum (nicht)?

B. Was sagen Sie dazu? Tell your partner about a recent shopping trip, using the following questions as guidelines.

1. Was haben Sie gekauft ? (Stereoanlage, Fernseher, Möbel,…)
2. Wer hat eingekauft ?(Sie, Ihre Schwester, Ihr Freund, Ihre Eltern,…)
3. Wo haben Sie eingekauft? (im Geschäft, im Bücherladen [*bookstore*], im Möbelgeschäft, im Kaufhaus [*department store*]…)
4. Was haben Sie im Geschäft gemacht ? (etwas ausprobiert, viel gefragt, nichts gefunden,…)?
5. Wieviel hat er/sie/es gekostet?

C. Wie soll es sein? You have just earned enough money to buy a sofa. In small groups, discuss what you would like.

- Das Sofa soll… sein. (groß, bequem, schwarz, aus Leder…)
- Soll es zu etwas passen? (zu einem Tisch, zu einem Bücherregal…)
- Welche Farbe soll es sein?
- Welches von diesen Sofas gefällt Ihnen? Warum?

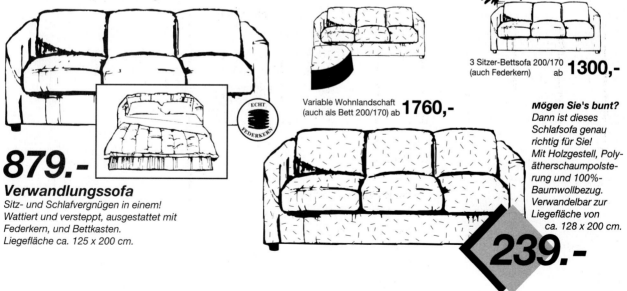

879.-

Verwandlungssofa
Sitz- und Schlafvergnügen in einem!
Wattiert und versteppt, ausgestattet mit
Federkern, und Bettkasten.
Liegefläche ca. 125 x 200 cm.

ECHT FEDERKERN

Variable Wohnlandschaft
(auch als Bett 200/170) ab **1760,-**

3 Sitzer-Bettsofa 200/170
(auch Federkern)   ab **1300,-**

Mögen Sie's bunt?
Dann ist dieses
Schlafsofa genau
richtig für Sie!
Mit Holzgestell, Poly-
ätherschaumpolste-
rung und 100%-
Baumwollbezug.
Verwandelbar zur
Liegefläche von
ca. 128 x 200 cm.

239.-

Modal verbs *dürfen*, *sollen*, *mögen*, and summary of all modals

As you learned in **Kapitel 3**, modal verbs tell something about the attitude a speaker has toward an action. You are already familiar with the modal verbs **können** (*can, to be able to*), **müssen** (*must, to have to*), and **wollen** (*to want to*). The remaining three modals are: **dürfen** (*may, to be permitted to*), **sollen** (*should, to be supposed to*), and **mögen** (*to like*).

	DÜRFEN	SOLLEN	MÖGEN
ich	darf	soll	mag
du	darfst	sollst	magst
er/sie/es	darf	soll	mag
wir	dürfen	sollen	mögen
ihr	dürft	sollt	mögt
sie	dürfen	sollen	mögen
Sie	dürfen	sollen	mögen

(handwritten above table headers: May — Should — to like)

dürfen generally implies that one has permission to do something.

> **Dürfen** wir das Sofa **ausprobieren**?
> *May we try out the sofa?*

> **Darf** ich Ihnen **helfen**?
> *May I help you?*

Note how **dürfen** is used in the negative, meaning *must not*.

> Die Kinder **dürfen nicht** in diesem Garten **spielen.**
> *The children must not/may not play in this garden.*

sollen generally conveys the idea that one *should, ought to*, or *is supposed to* do something.

> Was meinst du? **Sollen** wir **es kaufen**?
> *What do you think? Should we buy it?*

> Wir **sollen** heute **einziehen**.
> *We are supposed to move in today.*

Reminder: Although sentences with modal verbs usually include a dependent infinitive, it may be omitted when it is understood.

> Jetzt **soll** ich nach Hause.
> *I should go home now.*

mögen expresses the idea of liking someone or something. It is most often used in questions or in negative statements.

> Ich **mag** dieses Sofa nicht.
> *I don't like this couch.*

> **Magst** du dein Zimmer?
> *Do you like your room?*

Redewendung

You have now learned three ways of expressing a liking for something or someone.

1. **Ich mag diesen Garten.**
2. **Dieser Garten gefällt mir.**
3. **Ich habe diesen Mann gern.**

I like this garden/man.

The least common of these phrases is mögen; gern haben and gefallen are used much more frequently. Of these three, mögen and gefallen are used for people and things; gern haben is usually used for people.

mögen is the one modal that is usually used without a dependent infinitive. Remember that it's subjunctive form, **möchte**, is used with another verb to mean *would like to*. Compare the differences in meaning:

Magst du dieses Poster?
Do you like this poster?

Möchtest du dieses Poster?
Would you like this poster?

ALLES KLAR?

A. Was dürfen/sollen Alex und Jessica nicht machen? Tell what Alex and Jessica shouldn't do or are not allowed to do in their housing situation.

erlaubt	allowed
nie	never
rauchen	to smoke
der Hund	dog

BEISPIEL: Sie dürfen nicht rauchen.

B. Was dürfen / sollen wir machen? In small groups, discuss what you should do or may (not) do around the house—either your own home during the holidays, or where you live now.

BEISPIELE: Zu Hause darf ich nicht zuviel fernsehen.
Ich soll heute putzen.

C. Wieviel Grad soll es sein? Skim the following short article to find out what temperatures the Bureau of Consumer Affairs recommends for each room. Don't worry if you don't understand every word. Then with a partner, answer the following questions.

1. Wieviel Grad soll es im Winter in der Küche sein?
   im Schlafzimmer?
   im Wohnzimmer?
   im Bad?

2. Wieviel Grad ist das in Fahrenheit?

3. Stimmen Sie mit diesen Empfehlungen (*recommendations*) überein?

Heizung: 20 Grad sind genug

Energie sparen und trotzdem nicht frieren. Die Verbraucherzentrale Frankfurt empfiehlt: Küche und Schlafzimmer sollen im Winter nicht mehr als 17 bis 18 Grad, Wohn-, Eß- und Kinderzimmer um 20 Grad haben, das Bad ist mit 23 Grad richtig beheizt. Übrigens: Wer nachts die Temperatur auf 15 Grad senkt, spart rund zwölf Prozent Energie.

D. Magst du…? Ask other students whether they like the things in the following list. In this activity, use **mögen**.

	NAME	MAG	MAG NICHT
dieses Zimmer	_____	__	__
dieses Buch	Jason	__	✓
den Präsidenten der USA	Kyle	__	✓
das Wetter hier	_____	__	__
Deutsch	_____	__	__
die Farbe gelb	Kyle	__	✓
New York	_____	__	__
diese Gegend	_____	__	__
den Winter	_____	__	__
Tennis	_____	__	__
das Studentenwohnheim	_____	__	__
diese Universität	_____	__	__

Summary of the modal verbs

(handwritten annotations above columns: May, Kann, Like, must, Should, will)

	DÜRFEN	KÖNNEN	MÖGEN	MÜSSEN	SOLLEN	WOLLEN
ich, er/sie/es	darf	kann	mag	muß	soll	will
du	darfst	kannst	magst	mußt	sollst	willst
wir, sie, Sie	dürfen	können	mögen	müssen	sollen	wollen
ihr	dürft	könnt	mögt	müßt	sollt	wollt

ALLES KLAR?

A. Willst du ins Kino? Read the story and decide which modal verb best fits the context of the sentence. Don't forget to conjugate it appropriately.

Karen (1) _will_ heute abend ins Kino gehen, aber sie (2) _darf_ nicht zu spät nach Hause kommen, denn sie (3) _soll_ am nächsten Morgen früh arbeiten. Sie telefoniert mit ihrem Freund Jeff: «Jeff, ich (4) _will_ ins Kino. (5) _willst_ du mitkommen?» «Ja, aber ich (6) _muß_ zuerst (*first*) meine Hausaufgaben machen. (7) _Können_ wir um 10.00 Uhr gehen?» Karen antwortet: «Nein, das (8) _kann_ ich nicht. Ich (9) _muß_ morgen früh aufstehen (*get up*). (10) _willst_ du jetzt gehen und später lernen?» «Schön, Karen! (11) _Können_ wir dann den neuen Film von Sylvester Stallone sehen?» «Prima, Jeff, den (12) _will_ ich auch sehen.»

B. Wie soll das Zimmer aussehen? With a partner, draw the outline of a room—a bedroom, living room, etc. Then, using the modal verbs, discuss how you will furnish it, drawing in the items as you go. Some useful phrases are:

links	*to the left*
rechts	*to the right*
neben + dative	*next to*

BEISPIEL: —Wir müssen ein Sofa kaufen.
—Das Sofa darf aber nicht grün sein.
—Ich möchte das Sofa dort rechts haben, neben dem Fenster.
—Nein, ich will es links neben dem Tisch.
…

C. Die Familie sucht ein Haus. Working in small groups, each person assumes the role of a different family member. Decide who you are, what your names are, how old you are, what you do. Then discuss what kind of a house you are looking for. According to your role, you might want to mention size, cost, individual room preferences, location, etc. Use modal verbs in your discussion. You may want to refer to the list of adjectives in Schritt 3, Activity A.

BEISPIELE: Ich möchte…
Mein Zimmer muß… sein.
Das Haus darf/soll nicht… sein.
Die Gegend/Nachbarschaft soll… sein.
…

Zusammenfassung

A. Ein Brief an meine Eltern. In German, write a letter to your parents in which you describe your room or your apartment and your roommate(s). You may wish to include the following topics:

> Wie ist die Wohnung / das Zimmer? (hell/dunkel, laut/ruhig, teuer/billig, [un]möbliert,…)
> Wieviele Zimmer gibt es? (Es ist eine [Zweizimmerwohnung] mit…)
> Welche Möbel haben Sie / brauchen Sie noch?
> Wie sind die Möbel? ([un]bequem, alt/neu/modern, die Farbe,…)
> Wie ist Ihr Zimmerkamerad / Ihre Zimmerkameradin?
> Wie ist die Gegend? (schön, gefährlich, laut…)
> Was dürfen Sie (nicht) tun?
> Wie ist Ihre Telefonnummer?

BEGINNEN SIE: Liebe Eltern!/Liebe Mutter!/Lieber Vater!

ENDEN SIE: Herzliche Grüße,
   ODER: Euer / Dein [John]
         Eure / Deine [Susan]

B. Ich bin gerade eingezogen. You have just moved into a new room or apartment. What have you already done? What still needs to be done? Write a short paragraph.

NÜTZLICHE (*USEFUL*) VERBEN

putzen	kaufen	einrichten
suchen	finden	ausprobieren
öffnen	helfen	leihen
tun	arbeiten	brauchen
haben	…	

C. Was haben Sie gestern zu Hause gemacht? Write a short paragraph.

NÜTZLICHE AUSDRÜCKE

putzen	das Bett machen	Karten spielen
fernsehen	zu Mittag essen	lesen
etwas verlieren / finden	Hausaufgaben machen	im Garten arbeiten
allein sein (use **war**)	Briefe / Referate (*reports*) schreiben	frühstücken
Musik hören	mit… am Telefon sprechen	fernsehen

D. Was sind die Wohnmöglichkeiten? A German friend is coming to study for a year at your university and has asked you about housing possibilities. Reply in writing, providing all the information you can.

E. Steve und Bobby haben Streit. Reread "Wer bekommt das Zimmer?" in **Schritt 4**, then write a short dialogue in which Steve and Bobby argue about their rooms.

Zu zweit: **Student 1**

A. Was habt ihr gemacht? Ask your partner what happened in the following contexts. Write her/his answers in the appropriate column opposite the context.

> **BEISPIEL:** —Was habt ihr gestern gemacht?
> —Wir haben im Restaurant Sauerbraten gegessen.

Now your partner will ask you what happened in various other contexts; choose an appropriate reply in the right-hand column and write the context in the box next to it.

KONTEXT	AKTIVITÄT
in McDonald's	
	der Professor / alles wiederholen
zu Hause	
	wir / schlafen
im Restaurant	

B. Meine Wohnung oder deine? Compare the floorplan of your apartment with that of your partner. Note the differences.

> **BEISPIEL:** —Meine Wohnung hat…, aber deine hat kein-…

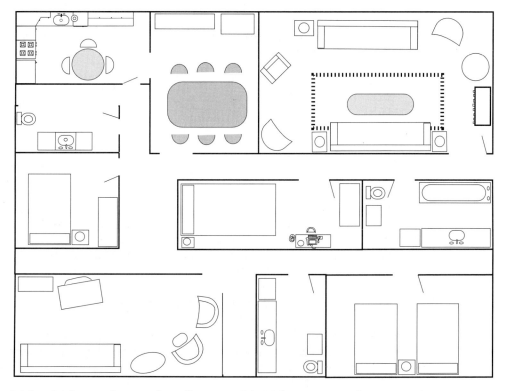

Meine Wohnung hat…, aber die von meiner Partnerin/von meinem Partner hat kein-

Die Wohnung von meiner Partnerin/von meinem Partner hat…, aber meine Wohnung hat kein-

Zu zweit: **Student 2**

A. Was habt ihr gemacht? Your partner will ask you what happened in various contexts. Answer by choosing the most appropriate reply from the right-hand column. Then write the location in the appropriate box next to your reply.

> **BEISPIEL:** —Was habt ihr gestern gemacht?
> —Wir haben im Restaurant Sauerbraten gegessen.

KONTEXT	AKTIVITÄT
	wir / ein Steak teilen
im Winter	
	mit meiner Schwester / nicht übereinstimmen
in der Deutschstunde	
	Pommes frites (*french fries*) essen

Now ask your partner questions about the contexts in the left-hand column. Write his/her answers to the right.

B. Meine Wohnung oder deine? Compare the floorplan of your apartment with that of your partner. Note the differences.

> **BEISPIEL:** —Meine Wohnung hat…, aber deine hat kein-…

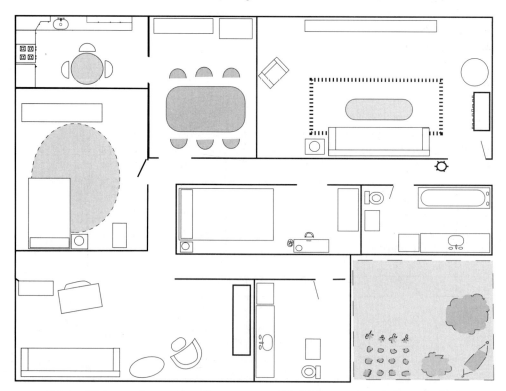

Meine Wohnung hat…, aber die von meiner Partnerin / von meinem Partner hat kein-

Die Wohnung von meiner Partnerin / von meinem Partner hat…, aber meine Wohnung hat kein-

Situationen

A. Auf der Wohnungssuche. You are back home after having gone to look for an apartment near the university. You run into a friend who was apartment-hunting as well. Ask about your friend's success and respond to questions about yours.

BEISPIELE: Hast du lange gesucht?
Hast du etwas gefunden?
Wie sieht sie aus?
Was kostet die Wohnung monatlich?

B. Ein langer Tag. You and your roommate have different summer activities: one of you is taking classes, the other has a job. Both of you have had a bad day. Tell each other about it. (If you use the verb **sein**, say **war[en]**.)

STUDENT 1

den ganzen Tag zu Hause bleiben
Heizung / kaputt•gehen (*to break*) / kalt
    sein
Notizen verlieren
Mittagessen / schlecht sein
keine Ideen für das Referat (*paper*) haben
Nachbar / zu laut sein / nicht mit ihm
    übereinstimmen
mit der Nachbarin Streit haben
nicht fernsehen
nur Textbücher lesen
Tante / zu Besuch kommen
müde sein
putzen
schwer arbeiten

STUDENT 2

der Kollege Sallinger / krank sein
die Kollegin Johnson / unfreundlich sein
der Kollege Turner / nur 2 Stunden
    arbeiten, dann nach Hause gehen
Computer / kaputtgehen
viele Briefe mit der Hand schreiben
keine Zeit zum Essen haben
keine Pause haben
der Rechtsanwalt / telefonieren / lange
    sprechen

C. Mieter und Vermieter. You are a landlord/landlady with a Dreizimmerwohnung for rent. Read the following "Mietsuche" ads. Which tenant(s) would you prefer? Call that person and discuss the situation. You describe your apartment, and the person who placed the ad—your partner—will also tell you what is being sought. See whether or not you can reach an agreement.

Junges Paar (gesichertes Einkommen) sucht 3-Zimmer-Wohnung mit Balkon 1.3.96 oder später ☎ 06509/096

2-bis 4-Zimmer-Wohnung dringend gesucht, Mithilfe in Haus und Garten oder sonstiges wird gern übernommen. ✉A 68884 H.

Alleinstehende Dame sucht sofort, spätestens zum 1.9.96, 3-Zimmer-Wohnung gerne mit Balkon, in Schledehausen o. nähere Umgebung. ☎ 05442/ 98543 (Rückruf)

Mutter mit 2 Kindern sucht 3 Zimmer, Küche, Bad ☎ 0652/87234

German in North America

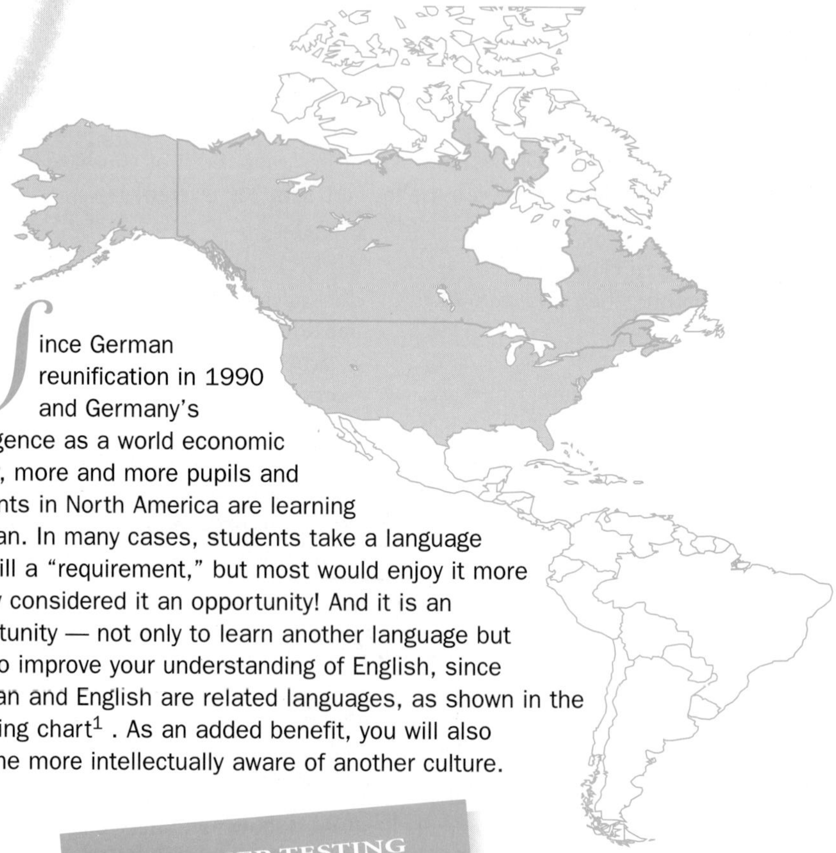

Since German reunification in 1990 and Germany's emergence as a world economic power, more and more pupils and students in North America are learning German. In many cases, students take a language to fulfill a "requirement," but most would enjoy it more if they considered it an opportunity! And it is an opportunity — not only to learn another language but also to improve your understanding of English, since German and English are related languages, as shown in the following chart[1] . As an added benefit, you will also become more intellectually aware of another culture.

MANAGER TESTING

Looking for qualified person to manage the testing operations of a multinational company which manufactures and supplies batching and mixing machinery. Responsiblities include managing applications lab, scheduling lab activities, testing equipment, sales support, and training sales reps. Equipment used includes Ribbon Blenders, High-Energy Mixers, and Mix-Pelletizers.
Must have a B.A. or M.A. in Ceramic or Chemical Engineering.
Must have 3–5 years in similar position; German language a plus.
Position requires extensive training in Germany and Canada
Send resume to:
Elrich Machine
3815 Gra

You are not alone in studying or knowing German. The
basic professional organization for teachers of German
in the USA (The American Association of Teachers of
German) currently has approximately 7500 members.
The Modern Language Association (New York),
composed mainly of college/university teachers, has some
2300 members who are German teachers. These numbers
represent only the tip of the proverbial iceberg. In addition,
thousands of businesspeople have learned German as a
second language (especially in New York, Chicago, San
Francisco, and South Carolina) and thousands more bi-lingual women and men
work in offices, banks, airline companies and in other fields where a second
language is a positive ancillary skill.

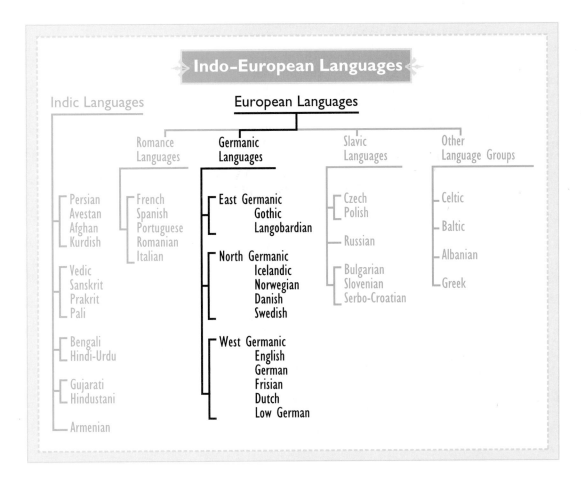

[1]This is only a simplified chart
and does not include all the
Indo-European languages.

Themenwortschatz

Substantive / Nouns

Wohnraum

der Balkon, -s	balcony
das Eßzimmer, -	dining room
der Flur	hall, entryway
der Garten, ⸚	yard, garden
die Gegend, -en	area
der Geschirrspüler, -	dishwasher
die Heizung, -en	heating radiator
der Herd, -e	range, stovetop
die Küche, -n	kitchen
die Nachbarschaft, -en	neighborhood
der Ofen, ⸚	oven
das Schlafzimmer, -	bedroom
das Sofa, -s	sofa
das Studentenwohnheim, -e	student dorm
der Teppich, -e	carpet
das WC, -s	toilet
die Wohngemeinschaft, -en (WG)	group of people sharing an apartment or house
das Wohnzimmer, -	living room
der Zimmerkamerad, -en/die Zimmerkameradin, -nen	roommate

der mitbewohner (—)
mitbewoherin (nen)

Verben / Verbs

aus•ziehen[1], ist ausgezogen	to move out
bekommen, hat bekommen	to receive
ein•richten *eingerichtet*	to furnish
ein•ziehen, ist eingezogen	to move in
kosten *hat gekostet*	to cost
mieten *gemietet*	to rent
öffnen *geöffnet*	to open
putzen *geputzt*	to clean, polish
teilen *geteilt*	to share
vermieten	to rent (accommodations to someone)

Modalverben / Modal verbs

dürfen (darf), gedurft	to be permitted to; may
können (kann), gekonnt	to be able to; can
mögen (mag), gemocht	to like
müssen (muß), gemußt	to have to; must
sollen, gesollt	to be supposed to; should
wollen (will), gewollt	to want to

Adjektive/Adverbien / Adjectives/Adverbs

allein	alone
(un)bequem	(un)comfortable
dunkel	dark
gefährlich	dangerous
hell	light
laut	loud, noisy
(un)möbliert	(un)furnished
preiswert	worth the money, of good value
ruhig	quiet
schrecklich	awful
zu	too

Ausdrücke / Expressions

Geschirr spülen	to do the dishes
im ersten, zweiten, dritten,… Stock	on the second, third, fourth… floor
Wie findest du…?	What do you think of…?

Wäsche wäschen

---

[1]The raised dot indicates separable prefix verbs.

Weiterer Wortschatz

Substantive	Nouns
der Brief, –e	letter
das Geschäft, -e	store, shop
das Problem, -e	problem
die Zeit, -en	time

Verben	Verbs
aus•gehen, ist ausgegangen	to go out
aus•probieren *(hose)* *hat probiert*	to try out
aus•suchen	to pick out
beantworten *hat beantwortet*	to answer
bezahlen *bezahlt* *hat*	to pay
denken, gedacht	to think, believe
empfehlen (empfiehlt), *(erzählst)* empfohlen *hat*	to recommend
entdecken *hat entdeckt*	to discover
erzählen *hat erzählt*	to tell
fern•sehen (sieht fern), ferngesehen *hat*	to watch TV
kennen, gekannt *hat*	to know (someone)
kennen•lernen	to become acquainted with, meet
meinen *gemient*	to mean; to think
mit•kommen, ist mitgekommen	to come along
passieren, ist passiert	to happen
probieren *hat probiert*	to try
sagen *hat gesagt*	to say
überein•stimmen	to agree
verlassen (verläßt), verlassen *hat*	to leave
vorbei•kommen, ist vorbeigekommen	to come by
wiederholen *hat wiederholt*	to repeat
zerstören *zerstört* *hat*	to destroy
zurück•gehen, ist zurückgegangen	to go back
zurück•kommen, ist zurückgekommen	to return

Adjektive/Adverbien	Adjectives/Adverbs
also	well, so, therefore
früh	early
schon	(flavoring word)
spät	late
wirklich	really
zurück	back

Andere Wörter	Other Words
zu	too

Ausdrücke	Expressions
recht haben	to be right

[handwritten notes:]

* All verbs that take Direct object use haben

Ich habe mein neues Auto nach Chan. gefaren

* NO D.O plus the verb expresses motion to a point
I drove to charleston
Ich bin nach Ch. gfarhen

Change of physical condition
freez thaw
Plus verb express Change of state
Ich bin eingeschlafen

Germanistik in Nordamerika

German Studies Resources in North America

The URL addresses in this **Netzbox** lead to American Internet sites for Germanistik, the study of German language, culture and literature. See the Prentice Hall home page for related activities and address updates (http://www.prenhall.com/~german).

1. **Austria Culture Net: Wiener Institut in New York**
   Extensive guide to Austrian culture sites on the web.
   http://www.austriaculture.net/outindex.html

2. **Deutsches Goethe Institut: Sprache und Kultur, Links**
   Well-known German language and culture institute, offering courses, exhibits and events.
   http://www.goethe.de/dindex.htm

3. **Germanistik in Nordamerika und Übersee**
   Comprehensive list of German Studies home pages and resources worldwide.
   http://polyglot.lss.wisc.edu/german/links.html

4. **Virtuelle Germanistik**
   Excellent list of resources for German Studies on the net.
   http://weber.u.washington.edu/~uwgerman/research.html

5. **German Studies Trails on the Internet**
   Large collection of links to the German-speaking Internet.
   http://www.uncg.edu/~lixlpurc/german.html

6. **Deutsch in Amerika für Studenten und Lehrer**
   German Studies in North America: Links for Students and Teachers.
   http://www.ualberta.ca/~german/professi.htm

Ich bin gesund!

Kommunikation

- Describing your daily routine
- Discussing physical characteristics in greater detail
- Talking about minor aches and pains
- Discussing your health and well-being

Strukturen

- **wissen/kennen/können**
- Reflexive verbs
  Reflexive pronouns in the accusative case
  Reflexive pronouns in the dative case
  Word order with reflexives
  Reflexive pronouns with parts of the body
    and clothing
- Adjective endings
  Adjective endings after **der**-words
  Adjective endings after **ein**-words
  Additional points

Kultur

- Health and Fitness in Germany
- Die Krankenkasse

Kapitel 6

Na, los!

Schritt 1: **Wie oft?**

To express how often you do something, use the following expressions:

täglich	*daily*
jede Woche	*every week*
jedes Jahr	*every year*
zweimal täglich	*twice a day*
dreimal pro Woche	*three times a week*

ALLES KLAR?

A. Manchmal, oft oder nie? Schauen Sie sich den Wochenplan an, und sagen Sie, wie oft Sebastian die verschiedenen Dinge (*things*) macht. (*Look at the weekly calendar and say how often Sebastian does the various activities.*)

Montag	1	8	15	22	29
Dienstag	2	9	16	23	30
Mittwoch	3	10	17	24	
Donnerstag	4	11	18	25	
Freitag	5	12	19	26	
Samstag	6	13	20	27	
Sonntag	7	14	21	28	

seine Freundin anrufen
putzen

Kaffee trinken
Tennis spielen

B. Wie oft machst du das?

1. **Kreuzen Sie an.** (*Check how often you do the following activities.*)

	TÄGLICH	2MAL PRO WOCHE	4MAL PRO WOCHE	JEDES JAHR	OFT	NIE
Vitamintabletten nehmen	____	____	____	____	____	____
acht Stunden pro Nacht schlafen	____	____	____	____	____	____
Mineralwasser trinken	____	____	____	____	____	____
Alkohol trinken	____	____	____	____	____	____
Gemüse- oder Obstsaft trinken (*vegetable or fruit juice*)	____	____	____	____	____	____
mehr als acht Stunden pro Tag arbeiten	____	____	____	____	____	____
Sport treiben	____	____	____	____	____	____
krank sein	____	____	____	____	____	____
viel Fisch essen	____	____	____	____	____	____
Obst oder Gemüse essen	____	____	____	____	____	____
Schokolade essen	____	____	____	____	____	____
rauchen (*smoke*)	____	____	____	____	____	____
zum Arzt gehen	____	____	____	____	____	____
zum Zahnarzt (*dentist*) gehen	____	____	____	____	____	____

C. Jetzt besprechen Sie es. (*Now discuss your answers with a partner. You may want to comment on each other's habits.*)

BEISPIEL: —Wie oft treibst du Sport?
—Ich treibe täglich Sport. Und du?
—Ich treibe zweimal pro Woche Sport.
—Das ist nicht sehr oft.

MÖGLICHE REAKTIONEN
Das ist (nicht) sehr oft.
Das finde ich toll!
Das ist (nicht) sehr gesund.
Mußt du wirklich so oft zum Zahnarzt gehen?
Du sollst nicht so viel trinken!
Du sollst mehr schlafen.
Darfst du auch zu Hause Alkohol trinken?

D. Berichten Sie über Ihren Partner/Ihre Partnerin. (*Now report your partner's answers to a third person.*)

BEISPIEL: —Martina treibt täglich Sport.

Germans have long been concerned with health and fitness — despite the fact that they continue to smoke much more and to drink more alcohol

(usually beer or wine) than do North Americans. Their interest in fitness is perhaps best exemplified by the traditional Sunday afternoon walk, in which the entire family participates, small children and teenagers included; it usually lasts two to three hours and is taken every Sunday, no matter what the weather.

Germans have long been devotees of gymnastics; its founding father is **Turnvater Jahn**. In addition, there are many health food stores, commonly called **Reformhäuser** or **Bioläden**. The current American health and fitness craze is reflected in the dominance of anglicized words in German, e.g., **Fitneß**, **Streß** or even **joggen**, used as a verb.

School or university sports teams are virtually unknown in the German-speaking countries; instead young and old alike join a local **Sportverein** (sports club) for the particular sport in which they are interested. Almost every sport has its own club (there are currently some 80,000 clubs with over 23.7 million members), and rules and tournaments are strictly regulated by the **Verein**. It is, for example, quite difficult to find public tennis courts in Germany; they all belong to the local **Tennisverein**. Even table tennis is commonly played only at the local sports club.

Schritt 2: **Das Gesicht**

1. das Haar, -e
2. ~~das Gesicht, -er~~
3. das Auge, -n
4. das Ohr, -en
5. der Mund, ⸚er
6. der Zahn, ⸚e
7. die Zunge, -n
8. der Hals, ⸚e

You can often describe your appearance by using colors: **Mein Haar ist braun, meine Augen sind blau**, etc. Some additional words that add more detail are:

lockig	*curly*	**oval**
glatt	*straight, smooth*	**round**
kurz	*short*	**blond**
breit	*wide*	**lang**
dick	*fat*	
dünn	*thin, skinny*	

ALLES KLAR?

 A. Wie sehen wir aus?

1. **Beschreiben Sie sich.** (*Describe yourself briefly to a partner, then listen as your partner describes herself or himself to you.*)

> BEISPIEL: —Mein Haar ist kurz, lockig und braun. Meine Augen sind blau, und meine Nase ist klein. Mein Gesicht ist nicht rund, sondern oval.

2. **Berichten Sie über Ihre Partnerin/Ihren Partner.** (*Now turn to another person in your class and describe your previous partner.*)

> BEISPIEL: —Meine Partnerin war Hanna. Ihr Haar ist lang, blond und glatt. Ihre Zähne sind schön.

B. Ratespiel (*Guessing game*). Schreiben Sie auf eine Karte, wie Sie aussehen. Dann sammeln Sie die Karten Ihrer Gruppe. Wählen Sie eine Karte und lesen Sie sie laut. Raten Sie, wer das ist. (*Each member of the group writes a description of himself or herself on an index card and puts the card into a box. Take turns choosing cards and reading them aloud to see whether your classmates can guess who wrote each description.*)

Schritt 3: Der Körper

1. **der Kopf, ̈-e**
2. **die Schulter, -n**
3. **die Brust, ̈-e**
4. **der Arm, -e**
5. **die Hand, ̈-e**
6. **der Finger, -** — Nagel
7. **der Rücken, -**

8. **der Bauch, ̈-e**
9. **der Magen, ̈-**
10. **das Bein, -e**
11. **das Knie, -**
12. **der Fuß, ̈-e**
13. **der Zeh, -en**

ALSO:

der Körperteil, -e *part of the body*
das Herz, -en *heart*

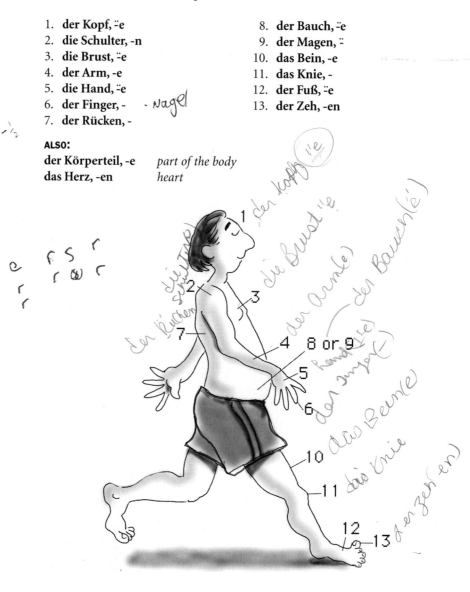

ALLES KLAR?

Simon sagt… "Simon" gibt Ihnen Befehle. Wenn Sie die Worte **Simon sagt** hören, zeigen Sie auf die genannten Körperteile. Wenn Sie **Simon sagt** nicht hören, machen Sie nichts. (*Play a German version of Simon says. One student is Simon. He or she begins:* **Simon sagt, zeigt auf…** (*+ accusative ending*). *When the other students hear* **Simon sagt**, *they point to the part of the body that has just been mentioned. Whoever points to the wrong part or points without the words* **Simon sagt** *having been said is out of the game.*)

BEISPIELE: (Simon sagt,) zeigt auf den Kopf.
die Nase.
die Füße.

…

Schritt 4: Aua! Es tut mir hier weh!

In **Kapitel 1** you learned the most basic way of telling how you feel: **Es geht mir gut/schlecht**, etc. You can use the following words and phrases to discuss your health in greater detail.

To inquire what is wrong with someone, you could ask:

Wo tut es Ihnen/dir weh?
Was tut Ihnen/dir weh?
Was ist los?

or, more casually:

Tut's weh?

The answer might include the following possibilities:

Der Rücken tut mir weh.	*My back hurts.*	
Die Ohren tun mir weh.	*My ears hurt.*	
Ich habe	**Magenschmerzen.**	*I have a*	*stomachache.*
	Kopfschmerzen.		*headache.*
	Halsschmerzen.		*sore throat.*
	Zahnschmerzen.		*toothache.*
Ich habe mir	**das Bein gebrochen.**	*I broke*	*my leg.*
	den Arm gebrochen.		*my arm.*

To say that you hope someone feels better soon, you would say: **Gute Besserung!**

[handwritten notes in margin: Der fuss tut mir weh / der Augenarzt / Die füsse tun weh / schmerzen]

ALLES KLAR?

A. Wo tut es weh? Was fehlt (*is wrong with*) diesen Leuten?

> **BEISPIEL:** Der Kopf tut ihr weh.
> **ODER:** Sie hat Kopfschmerzen.

[handwritten: Schmerzen]

[handwritten: schmerzen]

B. Wo tut es Ihnen weh? Beschreiben Sie Ihre Schmerzen. (*Talk with your partner about the aches and pains you have—or do not have, using the words in the following lists as a guide.*)

BEISPIEL: —Manchmal tut mir der Rücken weh. Dir auch?
—Ich habe fast nie Rückenschmerzen. Aber ich spiele oft Handball, und manchmal tut mir die Hand weh.

manchmal	der Kopf
oft	der Magen
selten	der Hals
nie	der Zahn
immer	das Knie
	der Rücken
	der Fuß
	die Schulter

C. Was sollen Sie tun? Heute geht es Ihnen schlecht. Sagen Sie einer Partnerin/einem Partner, was los ist. Sie/er wird Ihnen raten, was Sie tun sollen. (*You are not feeling well today. Tell your partner what is wrong. He/she will tell you what you should do.*)

BEISPIEL: —Ich habe Kopfschmerzen.
—Du sollst Aspirin nehmen.

MÖGLICHER RAT
ins Bett gehen
zum Arzt gehen
den Arzt anrufen
Aspirin nehmen
viel Orangensaft trinken
nichts essen
nichts tun

Kulturnotiz: Die Krankenkasse

Health insurance in Germany, which is quite comparable to that in many other European countries, differs vastly from that in the United States. Practically every single resident of Germany has health insurance, including both salaried and non-salaried employees as well as all the unemployed, pensioners, and younger individuals who are in an apprenticeship program. Most are covered by a national, socialized insurance, but private health insurers also provide either basic or supplemental coverage.

Most routine services are covered, including services for sickness, pregnancy, death-related costs, and family assistance. Both medical and dental costs are covered, as are prescriptions and glasses (although some prescriptions for dentures may not be covered). Preventive check-ups are not only covered but required.

In almost all cases, there is no paperwork for the patient; everything is taken care of by the doctor, who simply submits the appropriate forms.

Versuch's mal!   Der **s** + Konsonant Laut

Steffi Schleiermacher spricht mit ihrem Arzt, Stefan Sprengermann. Sie sprechen über Steffis Streß und Schmerz. Steffi entspannt sich nie, treibt keinen Sport und schläft wenig. Sie hat Kopfschmerzen, Magenschmerzen und Schmerzen in der Brust. Der Arzt sagt ihr, sie soll früh aufstehen und jeden Morgen eine Stunde Sport treiben. Abends soll sie sich entspannen: mit Freunden sprechen oder Karten spielen. Er gibt ihr Schlaftabletten, damit sie besser schlafen kann. Steffi soll sofort zurückkommen, wenn der Streß und Schmerz schlimmer wird.

Die weiteren Schritte

Alles klar?

Schritt 5: **Ein Besuch bei der Ärztin**

)))) Gespräch

Worum geht es hier? Edith ist Studentin; sie fühlt sich gar nicht wohl und geht zur Ärztin. Sie erzählt ihrer Ärztin ihre Probleme. Was ist nur mit Edith los?

Bevor Sie lesen, diskutieren Sie die folgenden Fragen: Wie fühlen Sie sich, wenn Sie viel Streß haben? Schlafen Sie weniger? Entspannen Sie sich? Werden Sie krank?

Während des Lesens[1] finden Sie die neuen Wörter, die Sie in den ersten Schritten gelernt haben, z.B. Rückenschmerzen, usw.

ÄRZTIN: Guten Tag, Frau Chen. Wie ich sehe, fühlen Sie sich heute nicht ganz wohl? Können Sie mir sagen, wo es Ihnen weh tut?

EDITH: Ja, mir geht es heute gar nicht gut; der Hals und der Rücken tun mir weh, und ich habe auch Kopfschmerzen. Ich habe mich aber nicht erkältet....

ÄRZTIN: So, Rücken- und Kopfschmerzen. Wie lange schlafen Sie denn pro Nacht? Haben Sie ein bequemes Bett?

EDITH: Ich schlafe nicht sehr lange — vier oder fünf Stunden pro Nacht. Meine Zimmerkameradin hat einen Freund. Er ist immer da — sie spielen ihre Musik sehr laut. Ein bequemes Bett? Nein, leider nicht. Die Betten hier, also im Studentenwohnheim, sind nicht sehr bequem, Sie wissen doch.

ÄRZTIN: Nun, Sie leiden wohl unter viel Streß. Was essen Sie denn?

EDITH: Ja, viel Streß; nur das typische Mensaessen[2]. Das Essen schmeckt mir nicht. Außerdem habe ich keine Zeit. Ich muß zu viel arbeiten, zu viel pauken[3].

ÄRZTIN: Sie müssen sich aber auch entspannen.

Redewendung

The word **wohl** means *good, well,* as in the phrase **Ich fühle mich (nicht) wohl**. In addition, however, it is also used as a flavoring particle, conveying a sense of probability or certainty.

Sie leiden wohl unter viel Streß.
You're probably under a lot of stress.

---

[1] *während . . .while reading*   [2] *cafeteria food*   [3] *cram*

EDITH: Nein, das kann ich nicht. Gute Noten[4] sind für mich viel zu wichtig. Ich will einmal Medizin studieren.

ÄRZTIN: Medizin studieren? Also anderen Menschen helfen? Dann ist es wirklich wichtig — Sie müssen sich entspannen, Sie müssen gesund leben.

EDITH: Was heißt denn das? Gesund leben?

ÄRZTIN: Das heißt: viel Gemüse[5], Geflügel[6] und Fisch essen, mindestens[7] sieben oder acht Stunden schlafen, regelmäßig Sport treiben und sich entspannen, vielleicht Yoga oder Meditation. Ein Leben ohne Streß—das ist für Sie sehr wichtig.

EDITH: Na—Yoga oder Meditation— Nein, ich will doch kein Swami werden. Ich brauche nur Schlaftabletten.

ÄRZTIN: Nein, Schlaftabletten gebe ich Ihnen nicht. Sie müssen sich zuerst entspannen. Dann vielleicht.

---

[4] *grades*   [5] *vegetables*   [6] *poultry*   [7] *at least*

ALLES KLAR?

A. Welche Probleme hat Edith? Mit einer Partnerin/einem Partner schreiben Sie Ediths Probleme auf. (*Working with a partner, do an associative activity. Put* **Ediths Probleme** *in the center and jot down Edith's problems around it.*)

BEISPIEL:

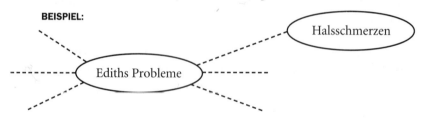

B. Was soll Edith tun? Schreiben Sie die Empfehlungen der Ärztin auf. Ihr Partner/Ihre Partnerin und Sie sollen dann die Listen vergleichen. (*Jot down the doctor's recommendations, then compare your list with that of a partner. If there are any discrepancies, listen to the tape or read the passage again.*)

C. Was soll das alles? Was ist die Hauptidee der Konversation? Was bedeutet **sich entspannen**? Diskutieren Sie mit einer zweiten Person die Frage: Wie entspannst du dich? (*What is the central idea of this whole conversation? What does* **sich entspannen** *mean? Discuss briefly with a partner:* **Wie entspannst du dich?**)

BEISPIEL: —Wie entspannst du dich?
              —Ich höre Musik.

Musik hören	Sport treiben
wandern	mit einem Freund/einer Freundin sprechen
lesen	meine Goldfische ansehen
im Garten arbeiten	fernsehen
nichts tun	in der Sonne liegen (*lie*)

wissen/kennen/können

In German, there are three ways to indicate that you *know* something. Study the following examples:

Was **weißt** du über Geschlechtskrankheiten?
What do you know about sexually transmitted diseases?

Kennst du diesen Arzt?
Do you know this doctor?

Ich glaube, wir **kennen** uns schon seit zehn Jahren.
I think we've known each other for ten years already.

Er **kennt** die Symptome dieser Krankheit.
He knows the symptoms of this disease.

Ich **kann** meine Symptome nicht beschreiben.
I don't know how to describe my symptoms.

wissen is used to indicate that *one knows facts or specific things*. **kennen** means *to be acquainted with* or *familiar with* someone or something. **Kennen** always appears with a direct object (accusative case). **können** is used to indicate that one *knows how to* or *is able to do something*, e.g., *to swim, to speak German.*

The conjugation of **wissen** is irregular.

WISSEN	to know		
ich	**weiß**	wir	**wissen**
du	**weißt**	ihr	**wißt**
er/sie/es	**weiß**	sie	**wissen**
	Sie	**wissen**	

Remember that **können** is a modal verb.

Kennen is a mixed verb; its past participle is **gekannt**. **Kennen** can also function as a separable prefix in the verb **kennen•lernen**, (*to become acquainted with someone*).Its past participle is **kennengelernt**.

ALLES KLAR?

A. Ein Besuch beim Arzt. Ergänzen Sie mit **wissen**, **kennen** oder **können**. (*Fill in the blanks with the correct form of* **wissen**, **kennen**, *or* **können**.)

DR. UNRUH: Na, guten Tag!

HERR SCHNEIDER: Guten Tag! Ich __1__, daß Sie mich nicht __2__, aber Sie __3__ meinen Freund, Herrn Schmidt; er hat Sie mir empfohlen.

DR. UNRUH: Ach ja, den Schmidt __4__ ich gut. So, was fehlt Ihnen denn? __5__ Sie mir Ihre Symptome beschreiben?

HERR SCHNEIDER: Ja, ich bin immer müde, __6__ Sie, und nicht nur bei der Arbeit.

DR. UNRUH: So. Ich untersuche (*examine*) Sie jetzt. ... Na, es ist alles in Ordnung, aber ich gebe Ihnen etwas. Nehmen Sie diese Tabletten, dreimal täglich. Sie sind dann nicht so müde. Sie _____ mich morgen oder übermorgen anrufen.

HERR SCHNEIDER: Danke schön, Herr Doktor! Auf Wiedersehen!

Handwritten margin notes:

Ich kenne / wir kennen
du kennst / ihr kennt
er/sie kennt / Sie kennen

Kennen = PERSON
Skill – Kann
fact = wissen
Cause ↗

Weisst
Kennen
~~weiss~~ kenne
weisst
weiss
weiss
~~Können~~ kann
kennst
kann
kannst
6-1 kennst
6-11 weiss
✗ kann
6-18

B. Wen kennst du? Was kannst du? Fragen Sie, ob verschiedene Klassenkameraden eine bestimmte Person kennen und ob sie verschiedene Aktivitäten auch so gut machen können. (*Ask various members of your class whether they know a given person. Then say what that person does and find out whether your classmate can do that activity as well.*)

BEISPIEL: —Kennst du Jackie Joyner-Kersee?
—Nein, ich kenne sie nicht.

ODER: —Ja, ich kenne sie.
—Sie kann sehr schnell laufen. Kannst du auch schnell laufen?
—Nein, ich kann nicht schnell laufen.

ODER: —Ja, ich kann auch schnell laufen.

Kennst du → Martina Navratilova Tennis spielen
Michael Jordan *Ich kenne ihn* Basketball spielen
Mark Spitz schwimmen
Julia Child kochen
Carl Lewis laufen
Mohammed Ali boxen
Pelé Fußball spielen

Reflexive verbs

In most sentences the subject and the object of the sentence are two different people or things:

SUBJECT		OBJECT
Der Student	wäscht	sein Auto.
Er	wäscht	es.

Sometimes, however, the subject and object are the same person or thing:

SUBJECT		OBJECT	
Der Student	wäscht	sich.	*The student is washing himself.*

Verbs that have the same subject and object are called **reflexive verbs**. Reflexive verbs are more frequent in German than in English. Many of them refer to personal grooming activities.

sich anziehen	*to get dressed*
sich ausziehen	*to get undressed*
sich umziehen	*to change (one's clothes)*
sich waschen	*to wash up*
sich die Haare waschen	*to wash one's hair*
sich die Hände waschen	*to wash one's hands*
sich die Haare kämmen	*to comb one's hair*
sich die Zähne putzen	*to brush one's teeth*
sich rasieren	*to shave*
sich schminken	*to put on make up*

mir! dir

In a reflexive construction, the object pronoun that refers back to the subject is called the **reflexive pronoun**. Depending on the verb, the reflexive pronoun may be either dative or accusative. It is equivalent to the English pronouns that end in -*self* or -*selves*: *myself, ourselves*, etc. Most German reflexive pronouns are the same as the corresponding dative or accusative object pronouns, except for the **er/sie/es, sie** (*they*), and **Sie** (*you*) forms. With these forms the reflexive pronoun is **sich**.

The chart below summarizes the reflexive pronouns:

NOMINATIVE	ACCUSATIVE	DATIVE
ich	mich	mir
du	dich	dir
er/sie/es	**sich**	**sich**
wir	uns	uns
ihr	euch	euch
sie	**sich**	**sich**
Sie	**sich**	**sich**

Note that only for **ich** and **du** are there different pronouns for the dative and the accusative.

Reflexive pronouns in the accusative case

Verbs that take direct objects can often be used reflexively. As always, the direct object pronoun is in the accusative case.

NON-REFLEXIVE:	Ich ziehe das Kind an.
	I dress the child.
REFLEXIVE:	Ich ziehe **mich** an.
	I get dressed.
NON-REFLEXIVE:	Du sollst das Kleid waschen.
	You are supposed to wash the dress.
REFLEXIVE:	Du sollst **dich** waschen.
	You are supposed to wash yourself.
NON-REFLEXIVE:	Er wiederholt den Satz.
	He is repeating the sentence.
REFLEXIVE:	Er wiederholt **sich**.
	He is repeating himself.

(handwritten margin notes: anziehen, ausziehen, anziehen, ausziehen, umziehen)

With certain meanings, some German verbs always take an accusative reflexive pronoun, even though they are not reflexive in English.

| **sich erkälten** | *to catch a cold* |
| **Ich erkälte mich jedes Jahr.** | *I catch a cold every year.* |

(handwritten margin note: rasieren)

| **sich (wohl/ schlecht) fühlen** | *to feel (good/bad)* |
| **Fühlst du dich nicht wohl?** | *Don't you feel well?* |

ALLES KLAR?

A. Die Kinder können es jetzt selbst. Brigitte erzählt ihrer Mutter, was die Kinder jetzt alles selbst machen können. Ergänzen Sie. (*Fill in the blanks with the appropriate reflexive pronoun.*)

Liebe Mutti,

Du hast gefragt, wie es den Kindern geht. Sie werden jetzt groß! Jetzt können Eva und Fritz ___1___ selbst anziehen, aber Fritz vergißt immer, daß er ___2___ warm anziehen muß und er erkältet ___3___ oft. Martina ist jetzt 14 und sie glaubt, sie ist eine Frau. Sie will ___4___ immer schminken, denn ihre Freundinnen schminken ___5___. Ich fühle ___6___ ein bißchen altmodisch, aber ich finde, dafür (for that) ist sie noch viel zu jung! Und Heinrich ist jetzt 17 und muß _____ jeden Morgen rasieren! Und ich? Mit den vier Kindern habe ich wenig Zeit. Nachmittags lege ich ___8___ ein bißchen hin und entspanne ___9___ . Und Freitag abends haben Marcus und ich Zeit für uns allein. Wir ziehen ___10___ um und gehen ins Restaurant oder ins Konzert. Und Du und Vati? Haltet Ihr ___11___ fit?

Deine
Brigitte

B. Persönliche Fragen. Besprechen Sie die Fragen mit Ihrer Partnerin/Ihrem Partner. Dann berichten Sie den Klassenkameraden und -kameradinnen über die Antworten. (*Discuss the questions with your partner, and then report their answers to the class.*)

1. Für Männer: Rasierst du dich jeden Tag?
   Für Frauen: Schminkst du dich jeden Tag?
2. Erkältest du dich leicht? *wenn ich eine Prüfung habe*
3. Wann fühlst du dich nicht wohl?
4. ___ spannst du dich?
5. Wie hältst du dich fit?

Trimm Dich durch Sport

Tanz mal wieder

Reflexive pronouns in the dative case

When the sentence already contains an accusative (direct) object, the reflexive pronoun must be in the dative case.

Ich wasche mich.	*I'm getting washed up./I'm washing myself.*
Ich wasche **mir** die Hände.	*I'm washing my hands.*
Wie oft rasierst du dich?	*How often do you shave?*
Wie oft rasierst du **dir** die Beine?	*How often do you shave your legs?*

A dative reflexive pronoun is also used when the subject of the sentence is the same as the indirect object. In some cases, as in the following example, the indirect object is optional and may be omitted from the sentence.

NON-REFLEXIVE:	Ich habe **dir** ein Buch gekauft.	*I bought a book for you.*
REFLEXIVE:	Ich habe (**mir**) ein Buch gekauft.	*I bought (myself) a book.*

Some verbs always take a dative reflexive pronoun in German, even though they are not reflexive in English.

sich (etwas) **ansehen**	*to look at something*
Ich habe mir die Wohnung angesehen.	*I took a look at the apartment.*
sich (etwas) **leisten**	*to afford something*
Kannst du dir eine Reise leisten?	*Can you afford a trip?*

ALLES KLAR?

A. Hast du dir auch…? Ergänzen Sie die Gespräche mit dem Reflexivpronomen. (*Complete the conversations with the appropriate dative reflexive pronouns.*)

1. Mutti, ich habe __mir__ die Hände gewaschen.
   Hast du __dir__ auch die Haare gekämmt?
2. Wir sehen __uns__ jedes Wochenende neue Wohnungen an.
   Könnt ihr __euch__ eine neue Wohnung leisten?
3. Ich habe __mir__ ein neues Motorrad (*motorcycle*) gekauft.
   Dann hast du __dir__ den Arm gebrochen, oder?

B. Die Party. Carola und ihre Freundinnen bereiten sich auf eine Party vor. Bilden Sie Sätze oder Fragen mit dem neuen Subjekt. (*Carola and her friends are getting ready for a party. Create sentences or questions with the new subject.*)

> **BEISPIEL:** Violetta wäscht sich zuerst die Haare. (ich)
> —Ich wasche mir auch die Haare.

1. Wir putzen uns jetzt die Zähne. (Sophie) *Sophie putzt sich jetzt auch die Zähne*
2. Carola hat sich ein neues Kleid gekauft. (ich) *Ich habe mir auch neues*
3. Kämmt sich Lotte die Haare? (du) *Kämmst du dir auch die Ha.*
4. Hast du dir die Beine rasiert? (Lotte) *Lotte rasiert die Bein rasiert*
5. Ich ziehe mir jetzt die Schuhe an. (Katharina und Sophie) *Zieht sich du*

Word order with reflexives

Reflexive pronouns follow the same word order rules as all the other pronouns.

Ich wasche **mir** die Hände.	(an indirect object pronoun precedes a direct object noun)
Ich wasche sie **mir**.	(a direct object pronoun precedes an indirect object)
Sie müssen **sich** aber auch **entspannen**.	(with a modal verb, the infinitive moves to the end of the sentence or clause)
Ich habe **mich** aber nicht **erkältet**.	(the past participle appears at the end of the sentence or clause)

Reflexive pronouns with parts of the body and clothing

Unlike English, German does not use a possessive adjective (**mein**, **dein**, etc.) with actions involving parts of the body or articles of clothing. Instead, it uses a definite article and the dative reflexive.

Ich habe mir die Hände gewaschen.
I washed my hands.

Der Skiläufer hat sich das Bein gebrochen.
The skier broke his leg.

Das Kind hat sich die Schuhe angezogen.
The child put on its shoes.

ALLES KLAR?

A. Jeden Morgen! Beschreiben Sie, was die Familie Hartmann jeden Morgen macht. (*Look at the following scene and describe what the Hartmann family does to get ready for school and work each morning.*)

Die Familie Hartmann besteht aus (*consists of*):

Herrn Hartmann	Dieter, 14 Jahre
Frau Hartmann	Angela, 12 Jahre
der Großmutter	Rudi, 4 Jahre

BEISPIEL: Die Kinder stehen um 6.45 Uhr auf.

B. Dasselbe ist gestern geschehen. Beschreiben Sie, was gestern geschah. (*Now describe the same scene as if it had taken place the previous day, using the present perfect tense.*)

C. Wie oft? Fragen Sie Ihren Partner/Ihre Partnerin, wie oft er/sie verschiedene Aktivitäten macht. (*Ask your partner how often he or she does various activities using the following phrases.*)

> BEISPIEL: —Wie oft putzt du dir die Zähne?
> —Ich putze mir zweimal täglich die Zähne.

täglich	sich die Zähne putzen	sich die Haare kämmen
pro Woche	sich die Haare waschen	sich umziehen
pro Monat	sich erkälten	sich entspannen
pro Jahr	sich schminken	sich einen Film ansehen
nie	sich wiederholen	sich nicht wohl fühlen
	sich nachmittags hinlegen	sich besonders schick anziehen
	sich duschen	...

D. Ein Wochenende in den Bergen. Sie sind in einem Dorf hoch in den Bergen weit weg von der Zivilisation. Was machen Sie da nicht oder nicht so oft? (*Imagine that you are on a weekend get-away in a mountain village that is almost untouched by civilization. Tell a new partner what regular activities you would not do or would do less frequently. Use the list in Aufgabe C, or add new ideas.*)

> BEISPIEL: —Ich putze mir nur einmal täglich die Zähne.

Schritt 6: Quittung[1] fürs Rauchen

📓 Lesestück

Worum geht es hier? Schon lange hat man von dem Zusammenhang[2] zwischen Rauchen und Lungenkrebs[3] gesprochen. Trotzdem rauchen die Leute weiter. Kann man diesen Menschen helfen, sie heilen? Wie viele sterben[4]? Rauchen die Leute immer noch so viel wie früher[5]?

Bevor Sie lesen: Besprechen Sie mit einem Partner/einer Partnerin: was wissen Sie über die Gefahren[6] vom Rauchen? Was sagen die Ärzte? Gibt es neue Information in der Kontroverse?

Während des Lesens: 1) In einem technischen Artikel gibt es viele Wörter, die dem Englisch en ähnlich sind, z.B. die Patienten, die Operation. Suchen Sie diese Wörter im Text. 2) Suchen Sie auch Wörter im Text, die[7] mit anderen Wörtern verwandt[8] sind, die Sie schon kennen, z.B. kennen (*to know*)—bekannt (*well-known*); gefährlich (*dangerous*)—die Gefahr (*danger*). 3) Suchen Sie in jedem Absatz die Hauptidee. Fassen Sie jeden Absatz zusammen[9].

Redewendung

Weit means *far*; **weiter** means *farther*. It can also be used as a separable prefix to express the continuation of an action.

Der Mann will nicht weiterrauchen.
The man does not want to continue smoking.

Willst du weiterfahren?
Do you want to keep on driving?

Quittung fürs Rauchen
Prof. Dr. Hans Harald Bräutigam

Ein britischer Arzt und seine Kollegen haben jetzt gezeigt[10], daß Zigaretten sehr gefährlich sind. Der Zusammenhang zwischen Lungenkrebs und Rauchen ist schon bekannt. Aber dieser Arzt zeigt, daß Rauchen auch Herzkrankheiten und Kreislaufstörungen[11] verursacht[12]. In den alten Bundesländern[13] allein starben 1995 zwei Millionen Menschen; warum? Sie haben geraucht!

Aber die Menschen hören nicht auf; sie rauchen weiter. 1991 sind etwa 143.000 Amerikaner an Lungenkrebs gestorben. Aber die American Cancer Society hat auch gute Nachrichten[14], jedoch nur für Männer: die amerikanischen Männer rauchen nicht mehr so viel. Die amerikanischen Frauen rauchen aber jetzt mehr als früher. In den letzten Jahren in den USA raucht man nicht mehr so oft in öffentlichen Gebäuden[15], in öffentlichen Verkehrsmitteln[16] und in Hotels. Aber in anderen Ländern raucht man weiter und oft auch mehr.

Nur bei 20% [zwanzig Prozent] der Krebspatienten weiß man, daß eine Operation erfolgreich[17] ist. Bei den meisten sieht man die Symptome erst, wenn es zu spät ist. Später muß man die Patienten mit einer Kombination von Strahlen[18] und Chemotherapie behandeln. Aber manchmal hilft das auch nicht mehr. Chemotherapie ist nicht ohne Gefahr. Ärzte loben[19] heute nicht mehr so oft den medizinisch-technischen Fortschritt[20], denn oft kommen mit dem Fortschritt nur neue Probleme und Gefahren.

Adapted from *Die Zeit*/Hamburg

[1] result	[8] related	[15] public buildings
[2] connection	[9] summarize	[16] transportation
[3] lung cancer	[10] shown	[17] successful
[4] die	[11] circulatory problems	[18] radiation
[5] before	[12] caused	[19] praise
[6] dangers	[13] former West Germany	[20] progress
[7] which	[14] news	

ALLES KLAR?

A. Richtig oder falsch? Verbessern Sie die falschen Sätze. (*If the sentences are false, correct them.*)

1. Der Zusammenhang zwischen Lungenkrebs und Rauchen ist neu.
2. Ein englischer Arzt hat einen Zusammenhang zwischen Herzkrankheiten und Rauchen festgestellt (*determined*).
3. 1995 starben mehr als zwei Millionen Menschen in ganz Deutschland, denn sie haben geraucht.
4. In den USA rauchen nicht viele Frauen.
5. Heutzutage rauchen viele Amerikaner und Amerikanerinnen in öffentlichen Verkehrsmitteln.
6. Eine Operation heilt viele Menschen mit Lungenkrebs.
7. Strahlen- und Chemotherapie sind immer erfolgreich.
8. Ärzte loben den technischen Fortschritt.

B. Was soll das alles? Was bedeutet der Titel dieses Artikels? (*What does the title of this article mean? How does it fit in with the content of the reading passage?*)

C. Was sind deine Rauchgewohnheiten? Diskutieren Sie mit einer Partnerin/einem Partner. (*Discuss the following questions with a partner.*)

1. Rauchst du? Warum (nicht)?
2. Hast du das Rauchen probiert? Wenn ja, wann hast du zum letzten Mal (*the last time*) geraucht? Und warum?
3. Wenn du rauchst: Willst du mit dem Rauchen aufhören?
4. Rauchen deine Freunde und Freundinnen? Wann, wie viele Zigaretten pro Tag?
5. Rauchen deine Geschwister oder deine Eltern? Wann, wie viele Zigaretten pro Tag?
6. Was sind die Gefahren von dem Rauchen?

Adjective endings

In both German and English, adjectives may appear in either of two positions in a sentence: after a linking verb (i.e., **sein**, **werden**, **bleiben**), or directly before the noun it modifies.

> Meine Nase ist **lang**.
> *My nose is long.*
>
> Ich habe eine **lange** Nase.
> *I have a long nose.*

In the first example above, **lang** is called a *predicate adjective*, since it appears in the predicate of the sentence. Predicate adjectives do not have endings. **Lange** is called an *attributive* adjective. In German, attributive adjectives always have endings.

Adjective endings after *der*-words

Adjectives that follow **der**-words always have the ending -**e** or -**en**. The **der**-words are the definite articles (**der**, **die**, **das**) and **dies**-, **jed**-, and **welch**-.

	MASCULINE	FEMININE	NEUTER	PLURAL
NOM.	der gute Mann	die alte Frau	das kleine Kind	die neuen Bücher
ACC.	den guten Mann	die alte Frau	das kleine Kind	die neuen Bücher
DAT.	dem guten Mann	der alten Frau	dem kleinen Kind	den neuen Büchern

Notice that the -**e** ending appears in the following situations:

NOMINATIVE SINGULAR: masculine, feminine, neuter
ACCUSATIVE SINGULAR: feminine, neuter

In all other cases—including all plurals—the ending is -**en**.

Welcher alt**e** Mann hat sich das Bein gebrochen?
Das ganz**e** Essen hat mir geschmeckt.
Ich kenne diese fleißig**e** Studentin nicht.

Siehst du den groß**en** Basketballspieler?
Bei dem kalt**en** Wetter bleiben wir zu Hause.
Die amerikanisch**en** Männer rauchen nicht so viel.

ALLES KLAR?

A. Wir kaufen ein.

1. **Nominativ**

   —Gefällt dir dies_e_ billig_e_ Lampe, de_r_ teuer_e_ Schrank oder d_as_ schwarz_e_ Bett?

   —D_er_ weiß_e_ Schrank gefällt mir, aber d_ie_ Lampe ist nicht schön. Nicht d_as_ schwarz_e_ Bett gefällt mir, sondern d_as_ braun_e_ Bett.

2. **Akkusativ**

   —Was hast du alles gekauft?

   —Ich habe d_as_ neu_en_ Sofa, d_en_ weiß_en_ Sessel, d_ie_ schön_en_, rot_en_ Lampen und auch d_ie_ toll_en_ Plakate (poster, n.) gekauft.

3. **Dativ**

   —Das Sofa paßt (goes with) gut zu d_en_ ander_en_ Möbel_n_. Es paßt zu d_em_ neu_en_ weiß_en_ Sessel und d_en_ neu_en_, schön_en_ Lampen, aber auch zu d_em_ alt_en_ Kaffeetisch und d_er_ alt_en_, schwarz_en_ Lampe.

B. Der Einkaufsbummel. Lesen Sie den Dialog. Dann lesen Sie den Dialog noch einmal und ersetzen Sie das Wort **Hemd** mit **Bluse**. Dann mit **Mantel**, und dann mit **Schuhe** (pl.). (*Read the dialog aloud. Then reread it substituting the word* **Bluse** *for* **Hemd**. *Then substitute* **Mantel**, *and then* **Schuhe** (pl.).)

das Hemd	*shirt*
die Bluse	*blouse*
der Mantel	*coat*
die Schuhe	*shoes*

KUNDIN:	Entschuldigen Sie, bitte (excuse me)! Wieviel kostet das rote Hemd da?
VERKÄUFERIN:	Welches rote Hemd meinen Sie?
KUNDIN:	Dieses hier finde ich schön.
VERKÄUFERIN:	Tja, dieses Hemd ist sehr schön, und es kostet nur DM 50,—.
KUNDIN:	Und das andere da?
VERKÄUFERIN:	Das blaue kostet DM 45,—. Und Ihre Hose paßt sehr schön zu dem blauen Hemd! Möchten Sie das blaue anprobieren?
KUNDIN:	Ja, bitte.

Adjective endings after *ein*-words

Remembering adjective endings after **ein**-words is not difficult once the principle behind adjective endings is clear: that is, some word preceding the noun must convey information about its number, gender, and case. **Der**-words do convey this information; therefore the adjectives following them don't have to. Some **ein**-words, however, do not provide this information—in which case the adjective must supply it instead. Study the chart for the adjective endings following **ein**-words.

	MASCULINE	FEMININE	NEUTER	PLURAL
NOM.	ein guter Mann	eine alte Frau	ein kleines Kind	meine neuen Bücher
ACC.	einen guten Mann	eine alte Frau	ein kleines Kind	meine neuen Bücher
DAT.	einem guten Mann	einer alten Frau	einem kleinen Kind	meinen neuen Büchern

[handwritten note: Er, ES = missing ending]

Notice that the endings are the same as for adjectives after **der**-words, except when the **ein**-word has no ending. This occurs in the following situations:

NOMINATIVE SINGULAR:	masculine, neuter
ACCUSATIVE SINGULAR:	neuter

Once again, all plural adjective endings are -**en**.

Ein britisch**er** Arzt hat Lungenkrebs studiert.
Siehst du mein krank**es** Kind?

Die Zahnärztin hat ihrer jung**en** Schwester geholfen.
Dieser Patient hat keine neu**en** Symptome.

A. Wie viele verschiedene Endungen? Sehen Sie die Tabellen an. Wie viele **-en** Endungen gibt es? Wie viele **-e** Endungen? usw. (*Look at the preceding tables for adjective endings. Write down how many instances of an **-en** ending you find on the adjective itself [not on the **der** or **ein** word]. How many **-e** endings? How many others?*)

-en = _____
-e = _____

OTHER
____ = _____
____ = _____

B. Substantive. Geben Sie mit einem Partner/einer Partnerin den richtigen Artikel der folgenden Wörter an. Manche sind in der Pluralform. (*With a partner, review the gender of the following nouns. Some are given in the plural.*)

das Bett   das Schlafzimmer   der Professor
der Schreibtisch   die Sachen   die Frau
die Zeitung   die Küche   die Familie
der Tennisschläger   das Fahrrad   die Brüder
die Wohnung   der Computer   die Schwester
das Sofa   die Lampen   der Onkel
die Möbel   das Geschenk   die Freunde
    die Kusine
    die Kinder

Here are some adjectives to go with them.

neu	alt	schön	rot	blau
rot	schwarz	weiß	klein	groß
schnell	langsam	ganz	jung	doof
kalt	fleißig	intelligent	laut	verheiratet
modern	glücklich	neugierig	traurig	bunt

1. **Bilden Sie Sätze im Nominativ.** Folgen Sie dem Beispiel. (*Take turns forming sentences with these nouns and adjectives, based on the model.*)

   BEISPIEL: Dein- ___ ___ gefällt mir (nicht).
   Dein **alter Schreibtisch** gefällt mir nicht.

2. **Bilden Sie Sätze im Akkusativ.** (*Now form new sentences in the accusative.*)

   BEISPIEL: Ich möchte ein- ___ ___ haben.
   Ich möchte eine **neue Wohnung** haben.

   ODER: Ich möchte kein- ___ ___ haben.
   Ich möchte keine **modernen Möbel** haben.

3. **Bilden Sie Sätze im Dativ.** (*Now form sentences in the dative.*)

   BEISPIEL: Diese Sachen gehören ___ ___ ___.
   Diese Sachen gehören unserem netten Arzt.

C. Meine Familie. Beschreiben Sie Ihre Familie. (*Describe various members of your family to the class. Before you start, jot down the specific features you wish to mention.*)

BEISPIEL:

Vater	*Mutter*
Gesicht - rund	Nase - lang
Ohren - groß	
Haare - rot, lockig	

Mein Vater hat ein rundes Gesicht. Seine Ohren sind groß; seine Haare sind rot und lockig... Die Mutter hat eine lange Nase. ...

das Gesicht	schön/häßlich
das Haar	dick/dünn
die Nase	blond
der Hals	braun
die Ohren	glatt/lockig
die Zähne	lang/kurz
der Mund	groß/klein
die Augen	oval/rund
der Kopf	breit

Additional points:

1. All attributive adjectives in a sequence take the same ending.

   Sie hat ein klein**es**, rund**es** Gesicht.
   Die meist**en** amerikanisch**en** Männer rauchen nicht.

2. The adjective **hoch** (*high*) becomes **hoh-** when used attributively.

   Das ist ein **hohes** Haus.

3. Adjectives ending in -**el** (**dunkel**) or -**er** (**teuer**) drop the final **e** when endings are added.

   Der Student hat ein **dunkles** Zimmer.
   Hast du die **teuren** Schlaftabletten gekauft?

4. As in English, a noun can be omitted when the meaning is clear. The adjective takes the same ending as if the noun were still present.

   Siehst du die Badeanzüge? Ich mag **den** roten.

A. Uwe und Gunther sprechen über… Üben Sie die Dialoge mit einer Partnerin/einem Partner. (*Practice these dialogues with a partner.*)

1. **der Wagen**

   UWE: Siehst du d_en_ schön_en_ Wagen da?

   GUNTHER: Meinst du d_en_ schwarz_en_ oder d_en_ braun_en_?

   UWE: Eigentlich habe ich d_en_ klein_en_ weiß_en_ gemeint. So ein_en_ schön_en_ Wagen möchte ich auch haben.

   GUNTHER: Ja, aber mir ist ei_n_ groß_er_ schwarz_er_ Wagen eigentlich lieber!

2. Sie sprechen jetzt von **einem Auto**. (*Substitute the word **Auto** for **Wagen** in the above dialogue.*)

3. Sie sprechen jetzt von **einer Katze** (cat, f.). (*Substitute the word **Katze** for **Wagen** in the above dialogue.*)

4. Jetzt ergänzen Sie die Endungen in einem Dialog über **Schuhe**. (*Now fill in the endings for a similar dialog about shoes.*)

   UWE: Siehst du d_ie_ schön_en_ Schuhe da?

   GUNTHER: Meinst du d_ie_ schwarz_en_ oder d_ie_ braun_en_?

   UWE: Eigentlich habe ich d_ie_ weiß_en_ gemeint. Solche schön_en_ Schuhe möchte ich auch haben.

   GUNTHER: Ja, aber mir sind d_ie_ schwarz_en_ Schuhe eigentlich lieber!

(handwritten margin note: neuter = es, masc = er)

Zusammenfassung

Die letzten Schritte

Wer macht mit?

A. Mein Onkel Friedrich. Ergänzen Sie mit Reflexivpronomen oder Adjektivendungen. (*Fill in the blank with the correct adjective endings or reflexive pronouns.*)

Ich habe ein ___en___ alt ___en___ Onkel. Er heißt Friedrich. Er ist mein einzig ___er___ ledig ___er___ Onkel. Seine dunkelbraun ___en___ Augen sind nie traurig. Er lacht immer, und man sieht, er ist glücklich. Er hält ___sich___ fit. Er steht früh auf, wäscht ___sich___, kämmt ___sich___ und putzt ___sich___ die Zähne. Er ist sehr oft unterwegs. Er besucht sein ___e___ Schwestern oder sein ___e___ Brüder und auch die Kinder von dies ___en___ Geschwistern. Manchmal kommt er zu uns. Er bringt immer etwas mit, und dies ___e___ klein ___en___ Geschenke machen uns viel Spaß. Wir möchten ihm auch etwas geben, aber was kann man ein ___em___ froh ___en___, alt ___en___, ledig ___er___ Mann denn geben? Kannst du mir einen Rat geben?

(handwritten margin notes: Sind Verben Heiße Bleiben allway nom; Dative; der)

B. Meine Tante Berta. Schreiben Sie die Geschichte jetzt über die Tante Berta. (*Rewrite the above paragraph, substituting Aunt Berta for Uncle Friedrich, making all the endings correspond.*)

C. Wer ist das? Beschreiben Sie jemanden in Ihrer Familie. (*Describe someone in your family. Use as many adjectives as possible.*)

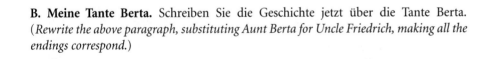

D. Ich bin schlank (*slender*) **und groß.** Schreiben Sie eine Personalanzeige für die Zeitung. (*Your social life needs some improvement. Place an ad in the personal column of the newspaper, describing yourself.*)

BEISPIELE:

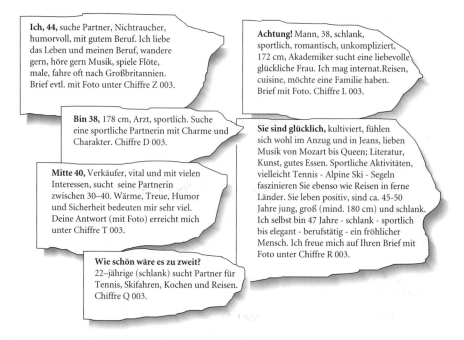

Ich, 44, suche Partner, Nichtraucher, humorvoll, mit gutem Beruf. Ich liebe das Leben und meinen Beruf, wandere gern, höre gern Musik, spiele Flöte, male, fahre oft nach Großbritannien. Brief evtl. mit Foto unter Chiffre Z 003.

Achtung! Mann, 38, schlank, sportlich, romantisch, unkompliziert, 172 cm, Akademiker sucht eine liebevolle glückliche Frau. Ich mag internat.Reisen, cuisine, möchte eine Familie haben. Brief mit Foto. Chiffre L 003.

Bin 38, 178 cm, Arzt, sportlich. Suche eine sportliche Partnerin mit Charme und Charakter. Chiffre D 003.

Sie sind glücklich, kultiviert, fühlen sich wohl im Anzug und in Jeans, lieben Musik von Mozart bis Queen; Literatur, Kunst, gutes Essen. Sportliche Aktivitäten, vielleicht Tennis - Alpine Ski - Segeln faszinieren Sie ebenso wie Reisen in ferne Länder. Sie leben positiv, sind ca. 45-50 Jahre jung, groß (mind. 180 cm) und schlank. Ich selbst bin 47 Jahre - schlank - sportlich bis elegant - berufstätig - ein fröhlicher Mensch. Ich freue mich auf Ihren Brief mit Foto unter Chiffre R 003.

Mitte 40, Verkäufer, vital und mit vielen Interessen, sucht seine Partnerin zwischen 30–40. Wärme, Treue, Humor und Sicherheit bedeuten mir sehr viel. Deine Antwort (mit Foto) erreicht mich unter Chiffre T 003.

Wie schön wäre es zu zweit? 22–jährige (schlank) sucht Partner für Tennis, Skifahren, Kochen und Reisen. Chiffre Q 003.

E. Eine Geschichte. Benutzen Sie die folgenden Anweisungen (*suggestions*) und ergänzen Sie die Geschichte. Geben Sie die richtigen Adjektivendungen. (*Using the following suggestions, complete the story by supplying an appropriate word when requested and changing the adjective endings as needed.*)

Eines Tages habe ich ein- [Adjektiv] [Person #1] gesehen. [Pronomen] hatte ein- [Adjektiv] [Körperteil] und trug (*wore*) ein- [Adjektiv] [Kleiderstück]. [Pronomen] hatte mit ein— [Adjektiv] [Person #2] eine Auseinandersetzung (*argument*). D- [Adjektiv] [Person #1] hat gesagt: "Sie sind ein- [Adjektiv] [Tier]!" D- [Adjektiv] [Person #2] hat gesagt: "Und Ihre Mutter ist ein [Adjektiv] [Tier]!" Dann hat d- [Adjektiv] [Person #1] d- [Adjektiv] [Person #2] geschlagen (*hit*) und ist weggelaufen.

ADJEKTIVE:	klein, groß, schön, häßlich, jung, alt, lang, kurz, rund, schwarz, weiß...
PERSONEN:	Frau, Mann, Kind, Arzt, Politiker, Spion (*spy*, m.), Clown (m.)...
KÖRPERTEILE:	Kopf, Arm, Nase, Gesicht, Bein, Fuß, Mund, ...
KLEIDERSTÜCKE:	die Bluse, das Hemd, die Hose (*pants*), der Mantel, die Jacke, der Hut (*hat*)...
TIERE (*animals*):	der Hund, die Katze, das Schwein, der Tiger, die Ziege (*she-goat*), der Bock (*billygoat*), die Kuh (*cow*), ...

Zu zweit: **Student 1**

A. Die Körperteile. Working with a partner, complete the following chart.

DER KÖRPERTEIL	WAS KANN/MUSS MAN DAMIT (*with it*) MACHEN?
die Hand	
	Man kann damit laufen.
die Ohren	
	Man kann damit essen.
die Arme	
	Man kann damit riechen (*smell*).
die Finger	
	Man kann damit sehen.
der Kopf	
	Man muß sie sich zwei Mal täglich putzen.
die Haare	
	Man kann damit den Ball schießen (*kick*).

B. Ein Raub (*robbery*). You have just witnessed a robbery committed by a person in your class. Answer the police officer's questions about the person's appearance.

> **BEISPIELE:** War es eine Frau oder ein Mann?
> Ich habe einen Mann gesehen.
> Welche Farbe haben seine Augen?
> Sie sind braun.
> Welche anderen Merkmale (*other characteristics*) hat er?
> Er hat ein rundes Gesicht und eine lange Nase.

Now switch roles. You are the police officer trying to get a description of the robber. Ask questions to fill out the chart:

Mann oder Frau?	
Wie groß?	
Haare: Farbe, lang oder kurz	
Augen: Farbe	
Gewicht (*weight*): dick oder dünn?	
Andere Merkmale (*other characteristics*) (ein rundes Gesicht/eine lange Nase?)	

MÖGLICHE FRAGEN
—War es eine Frau oder ein Mann?
—Welche Farbe hatte sein-/ihr- _____ ?
—War er/sie dick/dünn?
—Hatte er/sie ein…

Can you tell from the description which person in your class is the "robber"?

Zu zweit: **Student 2**

A. Die Körperteile. Working with a partner, complete the following chart.

DER KÖRPERTEIL	WAS KANN/MUSS MAN DAMIT (*with it*) MACHEN?
	Man kann damit hören.
die Nase	
	Man kann damit Gitarre spielen.
die Beine	
	Man kann damit Briefe schreiben.
die Zähne	
	Man kann damit denken (*think*).
die Augen	
	Man muß sie sich kämmen.
der Fuß	
	Man kann damit den Freund/die Freundin umarmen (*hug*).
der Mund	

B. Ein Raub (*robbery*). You are the police officer interviewing a witness to try and get a description of the robber. Ask questions to fill out the chart:

Mann oder Frau?	
Wie groß?	
Haare: Farbe, lang oder kurz	
Augen: Farbe	
Gewicht (*weight*): dick oder dünn?	
Andere Merkmale (*other characteristics*) ein rundes Gesicht/eine lange Nase?	

> **MÖGLICHE FRAGEN**
> —War es eine Frau oder ein Mann?
> —Welche Farbe hatte sein-/ihr- _____ ?
> —War er dick/dünn?
> —Hatte er ein…

Can you tell from the description which person in your class is the "robber"?

Now switch roles. You have just witnessed a robbery committed by a person in your class. Answer the police officer's questions about the person's appearance.

> BEISPIELE: —War es eine Frau oder ein Mann?
> —Ich habe einen Mann gesehen.
> —Welche Farbe haben seine Augen?
> —Sie sind braun.
> —Welche anderen Merkmale hat er?
> —Er hat ein rundes Gesicht und eine lange Nase.

Situationen

A. Meine Schmerzen… With a partner, enact one of the following situations.

1. You are not really sick, but have many minor aches and pains. Tell your doctor about them. She or he will respond with advice.

2. You are an elderly person talking with a friend. Tell your friend about your aches and pains and mention the health of others in your family as well. Your friend commiserates (**Das tut mir leid. Das ist aber furchtbar. Da haben Sie Pech gehabt!** [*What bad luck!*]) and offers advice.

MÖGLICHE PROBLEME

deprimiert (*depressed*) sein
nicht gut schlafen
immer müde sein
keinen Appetit haben
sich oft erkälten
Augen/müde sein
manchmal Kopf-/Magenschmerzen
Rücken/weh tun
sich den Arm brechen

MÖGLICHER RAT (*ADVICE*)

sich entspannen
sich fit halten
regelmäßig Sport treiben
keinen Alkohol/keinen Kaffee trinken
viel Wasser trinken
nicht mehr rauchen
viel Obst und Gemüse essen
Yoga machen
sich nachmittags hinlegen
Vitamintabletten nehmen
regelmäßig um 7 Uhr aufstehen und
    um 11 Uhr ins Bett gehen

Er kämmt sich Haare

i Adam hat die Blonden Haare

Seine blauen Augen

B. Was ich heute gemacht habe. Discuss with a partner everything you have done today, beginning with when you got up. Mention minor as well as major activities. Then tell a third person everything your partner did.

C. Die Traumfrau/Der Traummann. You are trying to set your friend up on a blind date. Describe the person you have in mind. Your friend reacts according to his/her tastes.

BEISPIELE: —Ich kenne den perfekten Mann für dich! Seine Haare sind
braun und er hat...
—Aber ich möchte einen blonden Mann!
—Und seine Augen sind dunkelblau.
—Und hat er eine große Nase? Eine große Nase mag ich nicht.

Themenwortschatz

Substantive — *Nouns*

Körperteile — *Bodyparts*

der Arm, -e	*arm*
das Auge, -n	*eye*
der Bauch, ̈e	*belly; stomach*
das Bein, -e	*leg*
die Brust, ̈e	*chest; breast*
der Finger, -	*finger*
der Fuß, ̈e	*foot*
das Gesicht, -er	*face*
das Haar, -e	*hair*
der Hals, ̈e	*neck*
die Hand, ̈e	*hand*
das Herz, -en	*heart*
das Knie, -	*knee*
der Kopf, ̈e	*head*
der Körper, -	*body*
der Körperteil, -e	*part of the body*
der Magen, ~~̈~~ (–)	*stomach* [handwritten: smiley face crossed out, "Wrong"]
der Mund, ̈er	*mouth*
die Nase, -n	*nose*
das Ohr, -en	*ear*
der Rücken, -	*back*
die Schulter, -n	*shoulder*
der Zahn, ̈e	*tooth*
der Zeh, -en	*toe*
die Zunge, -n	*tongue*

Meine Gesundheit — *My health*

das Aspirin	*aspirin*
die Erkältung, -en	*cold*
die Gesundheit	*health*
die Halsschmerzen (pl.)	*sore throat*
die Kopfschmerzen (pl.)	*headache*
die Krankheit, -en	*sickness, illness; disease*
die Magenschmerzen (pl.)	*stomachache*
die Medizin	*medicine*
die Schlaftablette, -n	*sleeping pill*
der Schmerz, -en	*pain*
der Streß	*stress*
die Vitamintablette, -n	*vitamin pill*
die Zahnschmerzen (pl.)	*toothache*

Verben — *Verbs*

leben	*to live*
leiden, gelitten	*to suffer*
rauchen	*to smoke*
weh tun, getan (+ dat.)	*to hurt, ache*

Reflexive Verben — *Reflexive Verbs*

sich etwas an•sehen (sieht an), angesehen	*to look at something*
sich an•ziehen, angezogen	*to get dressed*
sich aus•ziehen, ausgezogen	*to get undressed*
sich etwas brechen (bricht), gebrochen	*to break something*
sich duschen	*to take a shower*
sich entspannen	*to relax*
sich erkälten	*to catch a cold*
sich fit halten (hält)	*to keep fit, stay in shape*
sich die Haare kämmen	*to comb one's hair*
sich die Hände waschen (wäscht), gewaschen	*to wash one's hands*
sich (etwas) leisten	*to afford (something)*
sich rasieren	*to shave*
sich schminken	*to put on make-up*
sich waschen (wäscht), gewaschen	*to wash up, get washed*
sich (nicht) wohl fühlen	*to (not) feel well*
sich um•ziehen, umgezogen	*to change (one's clothing)*
sich die Zähne putzen	*to brush one's teeth*

Adjektive/Adverbien — *Adjectives/Adverbs*

blond	*blonde, fair*
breit	*broad; wide*
dick	*thick; heavy*
dünn	*skinny, thin*
ganz	*completely*
glatt	*straight, smooth*
hoch	*high*
lang	*long*
lockig	*curly*
nie	*never*
regelmäßig	*regular, regularly*
rund	*round*
selten	*rarely, seldom*
täglich	*daily*
wohl	*good, well; also used as flavoring particle*

Ausdrücke — *Expressions*

Gute Besserung!	*I hope you feel better soon!*
Sport treiben, getrieben	*to engage in sports*
unter Streß leiden, gelitten	*to suffer from stress*
Was tut Ihnen/dir weh?	*What hurts?*
zweimal pro Woche	*twice a week*

Weiterer Wortschatz

Substantive	Nouns
der Wagen, -¨	car, vehicle
der Zahnarzt, ¨e	[male] dentist
die Zahnärztin, -nen	[female] dentist

Verben	Verbs
an•rufen, angerufen	to call (on the phone)
auf•hören	to stop
auf•stehen, ist aufgestanden	to get up
beschreiben, beschrieben	to describe
sich hin•legen	to lie down
spülen	to rinse (dishes)

das Geschirr

Adjektive/Adverbien	Adjectives/Adverbs
glücklich	happy
mehr	more
oval	oval
toll!	great!
wenig	little
wichtig	important
zuerst	at first

Ich habe das Glas Kapputtgemacht — Something

Laß uns etwas zusammen unternehmen!

Kapitel 7

Schritt 1: In der Stadt

In the preceding chapters you came across words for various buildings. Here is a more complete list of what you might find in a typical European city.

1. **das Kino, -s**   *movie theater*
2. **die Metzgerei, -en**   *butcher shop*
3. **das Café, -s**   *café*
4. **der Blumenladen, ¨**   *flower shop*
5. **das Restaurant, -s**   *restaurant*
6. **die Brücke, -n**   *bridge*
7. **die Kirche, -n**   *church*
8. **die Bäckerei, -en**   *bakery*
9. **das Lebensmittelgeschäft, -e**   *grocery store*
10. **die Bibliothek, -en**   *library*

11. **das Kaufhaus, ̈er**	*department store*
12. **die Disco, -s**	*disco, dance club*
13. **das Hotel, -s**	*hotel*
14. **der Bahnhof, ̈e**	*train station*
15. **die Post**	*post office*
16. **das Museum (die Museen)**	*museum*

ALLES KLAR?

 Meine Heimatstadt. Beschreiben Sie Ihre Heimatstadt. (*With a partner, discuss what your hometown is like.*)

Beispiel: — Ich komme aus ___. Es ist eine sehr kleine Stadt. Es gibt nur ein kleines Kino.

— Ich komme aus ___. Das ist sehr groß. Wir haben viele Kinos. Wir haben auch eine tolle Disco. Es gibt viele Restaurants und ein teures Hotel. Ein sehr interessantes Museum ist auch da.

NÜTZLICHE ADJEKTIVE

klein/groß	interessant	alt/neu/modern
schön/häßlich	toll	gut/schlecht
teuer/billig		

Tip!

When giving directions to someone you address with **Sie**, invert the subject and the verb to form a command.

Gehen Sie geradeaus.
Biegen Sie links **ab**.

You will learn more about command forms in **Schritt 5** of this chapter.

Schritt 2: **Wie komme ich...?**

In **Kapitel 4** you learned different phrases for various means of transportation: **mit dem Auto, mit dem Bus, zu Fuß**, etc. To request directions to some place, you would ask:

Entschuldigen Sie, bitte. (*Excuse me, please.*) **Wie komme ich zum/zur ___ ?**

For a reply, you might need some of the following words or phrases:

ab•biegen (**ist abgebogen**)	*to turn off (as in a car or on a road)*
ein•steigen (**ist eingestiegen**)	*to get in, board*
aus•steigen (**ist ausgestiegen**)	*to get out or off*
um•steigen (**ist umgestiegen**)	*to transfer, change (trains, busses)*

hinten	*in back*	**(nicht) weit**	*(not) far*
vorne	*in front*	**bis zu**	*up to, until*
gegenüber	*opposite*	**die Kreuzung, -en**	*intersection*
(nach) links	*(to the) left*	**die Ampel, -n**	*traffic light*
(nach) rechts	*(to the) right*	**die Bushaltestelle, -n**	*bus stop*
geradeaus	*straight ahead*	**die Straße, -n**	*street*
um die Ecke	*around the corner*	**in der Nähe**	*nearby, in the vicinity*

ALLES KLAR?

A. Wie komme ich dahin? Sie möchten sich die Stadt ansehen, aber Sie kennen die Stadt nicht. Fragen Sie eine Person auf der Straße. Benutzen Sie die "**Sie**"-form und die Zeichnung (*drawing*) auf der nächsten Seite. Sehen Sie sich den Tip an. (*You want to visit certain locations, but you aren't familiar with the city. Ask someone you see on the street for directions from and to the following places. Use the "Sie"-form and the map on the following page. Read the* Tip! *before you begin.*)

> **Beispiel:** vom Bahnhof zur Bibliothek
> —Entschuldigen Sie, bitte, können Sie mir helfen?
> —Vielleicht; was möchten Sie?
> —Wie komme ich zur Bibliothek?
> —Das ist nicht weit; Sie können zu Fuß gehen. Gehen Sie geradeaus bis zur ersten Kreuzung. Biegen Sie links ab. Das ist die Hauptstraße. Gehen Sie drei Straßen weiter. Links sehen Sie den Stadtpark. Die Bibliothek ist gegenüber, auch links, in der Sebastianstraße.
> —Danke schön! Auf Wiedersehen.

1. vom Museum zur Bäckerei
2. vom Hotel zum Café
3. von der Brücke zur Kirche
4. vom Kaufhaus zum Museum
5. vom Café zum Kino
6. von der Disco zur Post

B. Wie komme ich mit dem Bus dahin? Sie möchten sich die Stadt ansehen, aber Sie kennen die Stadt nicht, und Sie können nicht zu Fuß gehen — Sie haben sich das Bein gebrochen. Fragen Sie eine Person auf der Straße. Benutzen Sie die "**Sie**"-form. (*You want to see the city, but you aren't familiar with it and you can't walk — you have broken your leg. Ask someone you see on the street how to get to and from the following locations by bus. Use the "**Sie**"-form.*)

Beispiel: von der Brücke zum Museum
—Entschuldigen Sie, bitte, können Sie mir helfen?
—Vielleicht; was möchten Sie denn?
—Wie komme ich mit dem Bus zum Museum?
—Die Bushaltestelle ist hier links. Sie müssen die Nummer 4 nehmen bis zur Charlottenstraße. Da müssen Sie umsteigen. Steigen Sie in die Nummer 8 ein. Wenn Sie den Stadtpark links sehen und ein Cafe rechts, steigen Sie aus. Das Museum ist an der Ecke.

1. von der Brücke zur Kirche
2. vom Hotel zur Disco
3. vom Blumenladen zur Bibliothek
4. von der Kirche zur Post
5. vom Hotel zum Café
6. von der Disco zum Kino

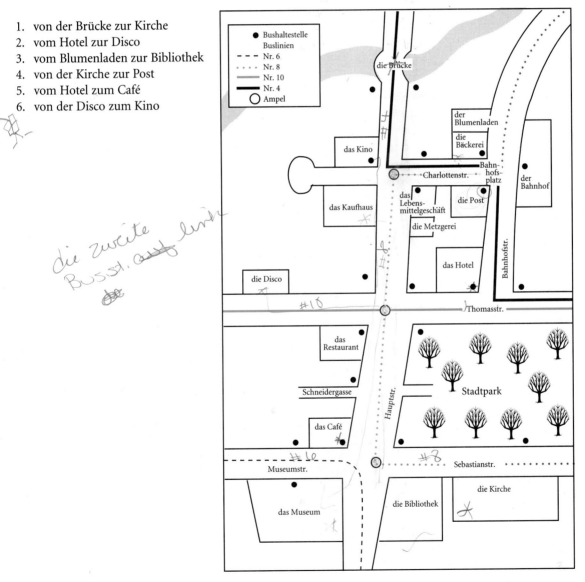

▶ *Versuch's mal!* Der *ä*-Laut

Bäckereien, Blumenläden
Supermärkte und Geschäfte,
In den Städten aller Länder
Sind zu finden Gegenstände.

Suchst du Äpfel oder Plätzchen
oder mal ein kleines Kätzchen?
Bälle und ein'n Tennisschläger?
alte Bände, neu' Fahrräder?

In der Stadt ist viel zu kaufen
täglich für dich ausgewählt.
Im Geschäft und auf der Straße
Alles, was dem Herz' gefällt.

Kulturnotiz : Public transportation in the German-speaking countries

The public transportation system in Europe is better than in America. Every large German-speaking city has a bus system and usually some form of subway or surface rail system — **U-Bahn** (Untergrund-Bahn) or **S-Bahn** (Stadt-Bahn). Lines intersect at many major points in the city. Public transportation in the German-speaking countries is not always cheap, but it is usually comfortable, reliable and punctual. Most people take subways, trains, busses or streetcars every day to work or to go shopping because it is both convenient and good for the environment. If public transportation doesn't go where you want to go, you can always take a taxi. Taxis are usually rather expensive; however, many Americans consider them worth the ride, since German taxis are often Mercedes. In Germany, single passengers often sit in front with the driver, rather than in back. Of course, if two or more people are travelling, passengers also sit in the back.

- Park & Rail
  Parkplätze in der Nähe des
  Bahnhofes – zu ermäßigten
  Preisen
  Buchung an der
  Fahrkartenausgabe
  Telefonische Vorbestellung
  unter (0 30) 29 76 11 26

Schritt 3: Machen wir etwas zusammen?

(((🔊))) Gespräch

Worum geht es hier? Monique ist Studentin in Göttingen. Sie ist im ersten Semester an der Universität und sehr oft in der Bibliothek. Sie sieht ihre Freundin Graciela auf der Straße. Wo arbeitet Monique? Was macht sie mit Graciela zusammen? Wann?

Während des Lesens suchen Sie die verschiedenen Gebäude: Bibliothek, Post, Restaurant, usw. auf der Karte auf Seite 194.

MONIQUE: Graciela, grüß dich!

GRACIELA: Tag, Monique! Schon lange nicht gesehen. Was machst du denn?

MONIQUE: Es ist schrecklich. Ich gehe immer in die Bibliothek, dann gehe ich zu meinen Vorlesungen und dann gehe ich ins Restaurant, wo ich arbeite.

GRACIELA: Das ist ja schlimm. Wie entspannst du dich denn?

MONIQUE: Ich würde mich gerne entspannen, aber ich habe keine Zeit dazu.

GRACIELA: Du, ich habe einen Vorschlag[1]. Kommst du heute abend mit mir ins Kino?

MONIQUE: Weißt du, ich muß arbeiten im Restaurant.

GRACIELA: So, schade. Aber morgen, so um 3.00 Uhr. Wir treffen uns vor dem Café *Zur Ruhe*[2] und trinken einen Kaffee.

MONIQUE: Wo? Ich weiß gar nicht, wo das Café ist.

GRACIELA: Wie, bitte? Das weißt du doch! Von der Bibliothek gehst du geradeaus bis zur dritten Kreuzung. Da ist die Post. Es ist gleich neben der Post, also zwischen der Post und dem Kaufhaus.

MONIQUE: Ach so — ich gehe da jeden Tag vorbei, aber ich habe es nie gesehen.

GRACIELA: Siehst du, du mußt dich entspannen. Machen wir doch mehr zusammen!

---

[1] *suggestion*   [2] **die Ruhe** = *rest, tranquility*

ALLES KLAR?

A. Haben Sie verstanden?

1. Was macht Monique?
2. Wann entspannt sich Monique?
3. Welchen Vorschlag macht Graciela?
4. Warum kann Monique nicht mit ins Kino?
5. Wo ist das Café *Zur Ruhe*?
6. Wieso weiß Monique nicht, wo das Café ist?
7. Wann treffen sich Graciela und Monique morgen?
8. Welchen zweiten Vorschlag macht Graciela?

B. Präpositionen. Lesen Sie das Gespräch ein zweites Mal durch. Unterstreichen Sie alle Präpositionen. Welchen Fall nimmt jede Präposition? Warum? Wenn Sie es nicht wissen, raten Sie mal. (*Read through the conversation again. Underline all of the words in the conversation that you think are prepositions. Which case follows each of these prepositions? Why? If you don't know, try to guess.*)

C. Moniques Leben in Göttingen. Schauen Sie sich die Karte von Göttingen an. Erklären Sie, wie Monique irgendwohin (*somewhere*) kommt. (*Look at the map of Monique's world. With a partner, explain how she reaches the following places.*)

How does Monique get…

1. from her room to the restaurant
2. from the restaurant to the lecture hall
3. from the lecture hall to the library
4. from the library to the restaurant
5. from the restaurant to her room

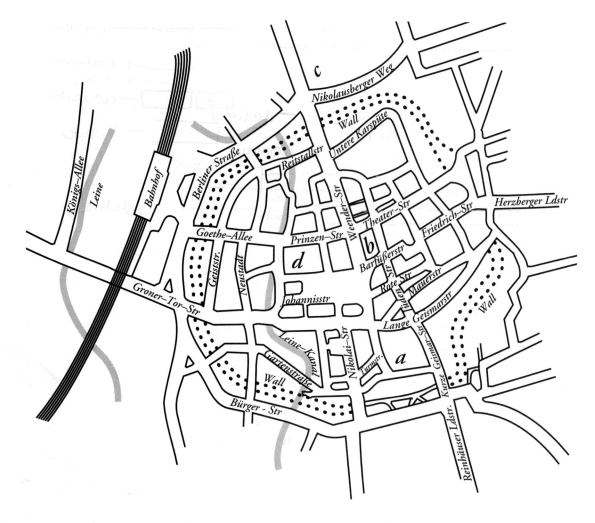

a. Moniques Zimmer
b. das Restaurant
c. der Vorlesungssaal
d. die Bibliothek

D. Machen wir etwas zusammen? Mit einem Partner/einer Partnerin planen Sie, etwas zusammen zu machen. Dann erzählen Sie einer dritten Person von Ihren Plänen. (*Talk with your partner and plan to do something together. Then tell a third person about your plans.*)

Beispiel: —Kommst du heute mit mir ins Museum?
—Nein, ich muß lernen.
—Gehen wir dann morgen?
—Nein, morgen habe ich auch keine Zeit.
—Gehst du dann nächste Woche mit mir schwimmen?
—Ja, das kann ich.

Kulturnotiz: Libraries in German-speaking countries

In the country that saw the invention of the printing press, books continue to play an important role in national culture. There are several contrasts, however, between German libraries and their American counterparts. While most American university libraries and even a good portion of local libraries now have computerized catalogs, European libraries lag behind in this respect. In many of the most important research libraries in German-speaking countries, readers must still rely on card catalogs and reference librarians; sometimes the catalogs are hand-written rather than typed. In contrast to most American libraries, German libraries do not generally have open stacks where readers can browse through shelves of books. Instead, the reader puts in a request at the circulation desk, and, if lucky, receives the requested books a few hours later; otherwise, it may take days.

One aspect of the German libraries that may intrigue American or Canadian students is the actual library building. Many large German collections are housed in buildings that are gems of architecture themselves. For example, the Herzog August Bibliothek in Wolfenbüttel, which specializes in works from the early modern era, is worth a trip just to view the painted ceilings and thousands of volumes bound in white leather or parchment and arranged symmetrically.

On the opposite end of the architectural spectrum is the Stadt -und Universitätsbibliothek in Frankfurt-am-Main. The main library has moved 250,000 of its 3.4 million volumes into the subway station at Bockenheimer Warte. Borrowers can go directly from the public transportation system and pick up their books.

Ordinal numbers and dates

Ordinal numbers

Ordinal numbers indicate the order of an object or a person in a sequence.

> Heute ist der 15. [fünfzehnte] Januar.
> *Today is the fifteenth of January.*

> Sie feiert morgen ihren 20. [zwanzigsten] Geburtstag.
> *She is celebrating her twentieth birthday tomorrow.*

> Sie ist die 1. [erste] Präsidentin der USA.
> *She is the first female president of the US.*

In English, the ending for ordinal numerals is usually -*th* (e.g., *fifth, fiftieth, hundredth,* etc). In German, the ending **-t** is added to numbers one to nineteen, **-st** to numbers twenty and above. Note the three exceptions.

erst-	neunt-
zweit-	zehnt-
dritt-	elft-
viert-	zwölft-
fünft-	dreizehnt-
sechst-	zwanzigst-
siebt-	hundertst-
acht-	tausendst-

Ordinal numbers take the usual adjective endings.

> Von der Bibliothek gehst du geradeaus bis zur drit**ten** Kreuzung.
> *From the library you go straight until the third intersection.*

> Ein zwei**tes** Auto brauchen wir eigentlich nicht.
> *We really don't need a second car.*

Note that a written number followed by a period indicates an ordinal number. These ordinal numbers always have adjective endings when spoken or written.

> der **13.** Januar = der **dreizehnte** Januar

Dates

Ordinal numbers are used with dates:

> —Den wievielten haben wir heute?
> —Der wievielte ist heute?   *What is today's date?*

> —Heute haben wir den 5. (fünften) Januar.
> —Heute ist der 5. (fünfte) Januar.   *Today's the fifth of January.*

In letters, the date is expressed as follows: **den** + [ordinal for *day*] + [ordinal for *month*] + [year].

den 2. 1. 1996

This refers to January 2nd; it is read aloud as:

den zweiten ersten (*or* zweiten Januar) neunzehnhundertsechsundneunzig.

To indicate that something will occur or has occurred on a specific day, German-speakers use the word **am** plus the date: **am 1. Oktober**.

Sie hat **am 3. Oktober** Geburtstag.
Her birthday is on October third.

To say that something occurred in a certain year, they use **im Jahr[e] 1996** or the year by itself: **1996**.

ALLES KLAR?

A. Die Zahlen. Schreiben Sie die Nummern. (*Write out the following numbers, paying attention to the ending on the numbers.*)

1. der 4. Juli
2. am 31. Oktober   am (dative) →en
3. der 3. Dezember

4. am 1. Mai
5. vor ihrem 70. Geburtstag

B. Wann ist...? Beantworten Sie die Fragen mit einem Partner/einer Partnerin. (*With a partner, take turns answering the following questions.*)

Beispiel: —Wann ist der Urlaub?
           —Der Urlaub ist vom zwanzigsten Juli bis zum dritten August.

1. Wann ist Sommer-Schluß-Verkauf?

Urlaubsperre von 20. 7. – 3. 8

SSV
Sommer-Schluß-Verkauf
vom 27. Juli bis 8. August

↳sten   ↳ achten

2. Wann können Kinder
   "Das doppelte Lottchen"
   sehen?

Kinderkino BRÜCKE
Sonnabend 14.10.1995
Holstenbrücke 8–10   91415

10.30 UHR

Das doppelte Lottchen
BRD 1950

Zwillingsschwestern, nach der Schei-
dung der Eltern getrennt, treffen einander durch Zufall in einem Ferien-
heim und bereiten raffiniert die Wie-
dervereinigung der Originalfamilie vor.
Ein Klassiker der Jugendbuchverfilmung —
nach Erich Kästner.

— **Ohne Altersbeschränkung** —

im Sweiter

3. Wo ist das Bistro?

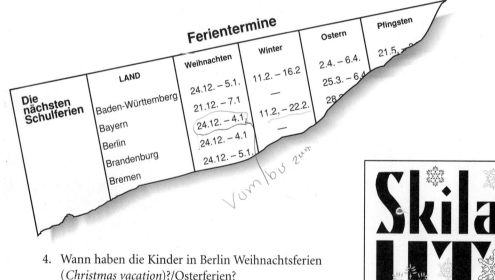

Ferientermine

Die nächsten Schulferien	LAND	Weihnachten	Winter	Ostern	Pfingsten
	Baden-Württemberg	24.12. – 5.1.	11.2. – 16.2	2.4. – 6.4.	21.5.
	Bayern	21.12. – 7.1	—	25.3. – 6.4	
	Berlin	24.12. – 4.1.	11.2. – 22.2.	28.	
	Brandenburg	24.12. – 4.1	—		
	Bremen	24.12. – 5.1.			

Vom bis zum

4. Wann haben die Kinder in Berlin Weihnachtsferien
   (*Christmas vacation*)?/Osterferien?

Skilaufen
UTAH
28.2 bis 7.3   DM 2.995,-

5. Wann kann man in Utah Skilaufen?

C. Wann...? Beantworten Sie die folgenden Fragen mit einer Partnerin/einem Partner.

1. Wann hast du Geburtstag?
2. Wann hat deine Mutter/dein Vater /dein Freund/ usw. Geburtstag?
3. In welchem Jahr bist du geboren (*born*)?
4. Wann ist dieses Jahr dein letzter Vorlesungstag?
5. Wann fängt das Semester im Herbst wieder an?
6. Den wievielten haben wir heute?

Movement versus location

Two-way prepositions

In **Kapitel 3** and **Kapitel 4** you learned about several prepositions that require objects either in the accusative:

durch   **ohne**
für   **um**
gegen

or in the dative:

aus   **nach**
außer   **seit**
bei   **von**
mit   **zu**

There are also several prepositions that can take either the accusative or the dative, depending on the context. The following prepositions belong to this group; here are their basic meanings:

an	*at, at the side of* (with dative) *to, toward* (with accusative)
auf	*on top of, on, onto*
hinter	*behind, in back of*
in	*in, into*
neben	*next to, beside*
über	*over, above*
unter	*under, beneath*
vor	*in front of*
zwischen	*between*

Tip!

The following contractions are very common:

an das	ans
an dem	am
auf das	aufs
in das	ins
in dem	im.

To understand how these prepositions are used in the dative and the accusative, study the differences between these pairs of sentences.

	ACCUSATIVE	DATIVE
an	Er geht **an das** Fenster.	Er steht **an dem** Fenster.
	He is going to the window.	*He is standing at the window.*
auf	Legen Sie die Bücher **auf den** Tisch.	Die Bücher liegen **auf dem** Tisch.
	Put the books on the table.	*The books are lying on the table.*
hinter	Fahr den Wagen **hinter das** Haus!	Der Wagen steht **hinter dem** Haus.
	Drive the car behind the house.	*The car is behind the house.*
in	Sie geht jetzt **ins** Restaurant.	Sie arbeitet jetzt **im** Restaurant.
	She is going into the restaurant now.	*She is working in the restaurant now.*
neben	Ich setze mich in der Vorlesung **neben dich** (hin).	Ich sitze in der Vorlesung immer **neben dir**.
	I'll sit down next to you in the lecture.	*I always sit next to you in the lecture.*
über	Sie hat ein Schild **über die** Tür gehängt.	Ein Schild hängt **über der** Tür.
	She hung a sign above the door.	*A sign hangs above the door.*
unter	Der Zug fährt **unter die** Brücke.	Der Zug hält nicht **unter der** Brücke.
	The train goes under the bridge.	*The train does not stop under the bridge.*
vor	Der Student fährt den Wagen **vor das** Haus.	Der Wagen steht **vor dem** Haus.
	The student is driving the car to the front of the house.	*The car is in front of the house.*
zwischen	Ich stelle den Nachttisch **zwischen die** Betten.	Der Nachttisch steht **zwischen den** Betten.
	I'm putting the night table between the beds.	*The night table is standing between the beds.*

As you have probably noticed, both sentences provide an answer to the English question: *where?* In German, there are two ways of asking *where*:

■ **wo** asks where something is located; it implies that the person or thing is stationary.

■ **wohin** asks in which direction something is going; it implies that the person or thing is moving.

Responses to **wohin?** require the accusative case.

Responses to **wo?** require the dative case.

ALLES KLAR?

A. Wo ist…? Schauen Sie sich die Zeichnung (*drawing*) in **Schritt 1** wieder an. Beschreiben Sie, wo die Gebäude sind. (*Look again at the scenes in* **Schritt 1**. *Work with your partner to describe where the buildings are located.*)

BEISPIELE: Das Hotel ist neben der Post.
Die Bibliothek liegt zwischen dem Museum und der Kirche.

B. Wohin gehen sie? Besprechen Sie mit einer Partnerin/einem Partner, wohin diese Leute gehen wollen. Benutzen Sie wieder die Zeichnung von **Schritt 1**. Benutzen Sie die Präposition "in" für diese Orte. (*Now discuss with a new partner where the following people would want to go. Again, use the drawing from* Schritt 1. *Use the preposition* **in** *for these destinations.*)

BEISPIEL: Frau Marcher hat Hunger (*is hungry*).
Sie geht **ins** Restaurant.

1. Josette will ein Buch lesen.
2. Herr von Berg will sich entspannen.
3. Graciela und ihre Freundinnen wollen tanzen gehen.
4. Frau Svenson muß neues Geschirr kaufen.
5. Herr Svenson kauft Brötchen (*rolls*) fürs Frühstück (*breakfast*).
6. Elise will mit ihrer Mutter Kaffee trinken.

C. Wo oder wohin? Lesen Sie den Satz. Ihre Partnerin/Ihr Partner stellt die Frage. (*With a partner, take turns reading the statement and forming the corresponding question.*)

BEISPIEL: —Gestern war ich im Kino.   —Wo warst du?
—Morgen fahre ich nach Hause.   —Wohin fährst du?

1. Ich bin gestern zum Bahnhof gefahren.
2. Wir gehen heute abend in die Disco.
3. Meine Mutter arbeitet bei einer Metzgerei.
4. Wir haben gestern einen Spaziergang im Stadtpark gemacht.
5. Ich gehe heute abend ins Kino.
6. Wir sind über die Brücke gegangen.

D. Zwei Detektive. Ergänzen Sie die Konversation. Normalerweise brauchen Sie eine Präposition und den folgenden Artikel. Manchmal paßt eine Kontraktion. (*With a partner, fill in the blanks in the following paragraph. In most instances you will need both a preposition [accusative, dative, or two-way] and the following article. Sometimes a contraction will be appropriate.*)

Zwei Detektive suchen einen Dieb (*thief*); sie glauben, sie haben ihn jetzt gefunden.

SVEN: Du, siehst du ihn? Da, im blauen Mantel (*coat*)!

RALF: Ach ja, er geht gerade ___in___ ___das___ große Geschäft da ___an___ ___der___ Ecke. Jetzt müssen wir wieder warten. Später muß er ja wieder ___aus___ ___dem___ Geschäft herauskommen.

SVEN: Da ist er! Aber er hat es sehr eilig. Da läuft er ___in___ ___die___ zwei Häuser. Sollen wir ihm folgen?

RALF: Nein, er kommt wieder heraus. Da, er ist jetzt ___in___ ~~dem~~ weißen Haus. Jetzt geht er langsam.

SVEN: Er geht nun ___in___ ___das___ Restaurant. Siehst du ihn?

RALF: Ja, er setzt sich ___an___ ___das___ Fenster. Da kommt die Kellnerin und er bestellt (*orders*) etwas. Jetzt geht sie ___in___ ___die___ Küche. Da ist sie wieder. Er hat sie wohl etwas gefragt. Sie spricht jetzt ___mit___ der anderen Kellnerin.

[...]

RALF: So, nun bekommt er das Essen.

RALF: Jetzt will er zahlen. Er sucht aber etwas unter ___dem___ Tisch. Vielleicht hat er da das Geld?

SVEN: Nein, das hat er in ___der___ Tasche(*pocket*). Vielleicht hat er einen Koffer (*suitcase*) ___unter___ ___dem___ Tisch.

RALF: Jetzt will er ___aus___ ___dem___ Restaurant, er steht ___vor___ ___der___ Tür. Da sucht er nach etwas ___in___ ___der___ Tasche. Was ist das? Spricht er ___mit___ einem Kollegen?

SVEN: Wahrscheinlich! Komm, dieses Mal entgeht (*escapes*) er uns nicht.

RALF: Denkst du! Er ist schon wieder weg. Ich sehe ihn ja gar nicht mehr. Du?

SVEN: Nein, er ist da ___in___ ___das___ Restaurant gelaufen und ist dann ___in___ ___den___ Wagen hineingesprungen (*jumped into*). Schade!

E. Was möchtest du machen? Diskutieren Sie, was Sie machen möchten. Benutzen Sie Präpositionen in der Antwort. (*With a partner, discuss what you would like to do. Use prepositions in your answer.*)

BEISPIEL: —Was möchtest du heute machen?
—Ich möchte in die Stadt fahren.
—Und am Wochenende?
—Am Wochenede will ich...

ins Kino gehen

im Restaurant essen

zu meiner Tante fahren

in der Bibliothek arbeiten

in einer Disco tanzen

an den Strand (*beach*) fahren

mit meiner Freundin ausgehen

auf dem Sofa schlafen

mit dem Fahrrad durch die Stadt fahren

...

hin/her

Hin and **her** are prefixes that indicate direction:

Hin generally indicates movement **away from** the speaker or the point of origin.

Her generally indicates movement **toward** the speaker or the point of origin.

Look at the following illustrations:

Hin and **her** often combine with other separable prefixes or with verbs of motion. Some additional examples are:

hineingehen	*to go in*
herauskommen	*to come out*
hinaufgehen	*to go up*
herunterkommen	*to come down*
hinfahren	*to go (to someplace)*
herkommen	*to come (from someplace)*

ALLES KLAR?

A. Hilft sie ihm oder nicht? Ergänzen Sie mit **hin-** oder **her**-Kombinationen.
(*Complete the following dialogue, using* **hin-** *and* **her-** *combinations.*)

JEAN-CLAUDE:	Ich bin hier unten. Kommst du bitte mal _herunter_? ~herunter~
MICHELLE:	Wo soll ich denn _herunter_? ~hinunter~
JEAN-CLAUDE:	Du sollst zu mir _herunter_ ~kommen~ kommen!
MICHELLE:	Ich kann im Moment nicht zu dir _herab_ kommen!
JEAN-CLAUDE:	Komm mal bitte _herunter_! Du mußt mir einfach ein bißchen helfen.

Redewendung

Herein and **heraus** can stand alone in the following commands:

Herein!   *Come in!*
Heraus!   *Get out!*

As you already know, **hin** and **her** can also combine with **wo** to form questions:

wohin?   *to where?*
woher?   *from where?*

Wohin gehst du?
—*Ich gehe ins Lebensmittelgeschäft.*

Woher kommen Sie?
—*Ich komme aus Zürich.*

Hin and **her** can also separate from **wo** and stand at the end of the sentence:

Wo gehst du hin?
Wo kommen Sie her?

There is no difference in meaning between these two forms:

Wohin gehst du?
Wo gehst du hin?
Where are you going?

Woher kommen Sie?
Wo kommen Sie her?
Where do you come from?

B. Wo gehst du am Samstag abend hin? Fragen Sie fünf Klassenkameraden, was sie für Samstag abend vorhaben. Notieren Sie die Antworten und berichten Sie Ihren Klassenkameraden darüber. (*Ask five of your classmates where they plan to go Saturday evening. Note their answers, and be prepared to report back to the class on where each of them is headed.*)

Kulturnotiz: Wolf Biermanns "Kleinstadtsonntag"

Wolf Biermann (1936-   ) is a well-known poet and songwriter. The son of a Jewish communist who died at Auschwitz, Biermann was born in Hamburg and lived there until 1953. At age sixteen he emigrated to the former German Democratic Republic. There, as a theater director, political poet, and songwriter (**Liedermacher**), his works so antagonized the Communist Party that they were banned, although they were still published and widely circulated in the West. In 1976 he was expelled from East Germany. He returned to Hamburg, where he still lives and works when he is not on tour. Today his work deals with social conditions and the ever-present moral and social rift between Germans from the former East and West.

As you read the poem, note the informal language: **gehn** for **gehen**, **heut** for **heute**, **rein** for **herein**, etc. What does **"Kleinstadtsonntag"** mean? What is this poem about?

Kleinstadtsonntag

Gehn wir mal hin?
Ja, wir gehn mal hin.
Ist hier was los?
Nein, es ist nichts los.
Herr Ober, ein Bier!
Leer[1] ist es hier.
Der Sommer ist kalt.
Man wird auch alt.
Bei Rose gabs Kalb[2].
Jetzt isses[3] schon halb.
Jetzt gehn wir mal hin.
Ja, wir gehn mal hin.
Ist er schon drin[4]?
Er ist schon drin.
Gehn wir mal rein[5]?
Na gehn wir mal rein.
Siehst du heut fern?
Ja, ich sehe heut fern.
Spielen sie was[6]?
Ja, sie spielen was.
Hast du noch Geld?
Ja, ich habe noch Geld.
Trinken wir ein'?
Ja, einen klein'.
Gehn wir mal hin?
Ja, gehn wir mal hin.
Siehst du heut fern?

Ja   ich   sehe   heut   fern.

---

[1]*empty*
[2]*veal*
[3]**ist es**
[4]**darin**=*inside, in there*
[5]**herein** (*used colloquially here*)
[6]**etwas**

The *würde* construction

The verb form **würden**[1] is used for *unreal or hypothetical situations, wishes, and polite requests*. Like the modals, it is always used with an infinitive. The English equivalent is *would*.

WÜRDEN			
ich	**würde**	wir	**würden**
du	**würdest**	ihr	**würdet**
er/sie/es	**würde**	sie	**würden**
	Sie	würden	

Ich **würde** das nicht tun.
I wouldn't do that.

Ich **würde** mich gern entspannen.
I would like to relax.

Würden Sie mir bitte helfen?
Would you please help me?

ALLES KLAR?

Würdest du bitte...? Sie fühlen sich heute nicht wohl. Fragen Sie Ihren Zimmerkameraden/Ihre Zimmerkameradin, ob er/sie Ihnen helfen würde. (*You are not feeling well today and you want your roommate to do the following things for you. Ask politely, using* **würde**.)

> **BEISPIEL:** meine Bücher kaufen
> —Würdest du bitte meine Bücher kaufen?

1. mir eine Suppe (*soup*) kochen *Würdest du bitte mir eine Suppe kochen*
2. nicht so laut sein
3. ein Buch in der Bibliothek suchen
4. meinen Freund anrufen
5. meine Hausaufgaben machen
6. das Zimmer putzen

---

[1]**Würden** and **möchten** are both subjunctive forms (**würden** from **werden** and **möchten** from **mögen**). You will learn about the subjunctive in **Kapitel 15**.

Schritt 4: **Kommen Sie nach Bad Herschheim!**

 **Lesestück**

Worum geht es hier? Was für ein Artikel ist das? Wer hat ihn geschrieben? Was können Erwachsene (*adults*) in Bad Herschheim machen? Was können Kinder machen? Würden Sie nach Bad Herschheim reisen? Was würden Sie da machen?

BAD HERSCHHEIM

LIEBE LESER:

Fühlen Sie sich in Ihrer Stadt eng¹? Kommen Sie dann zu uns! In Bad Herschheim fühlt man sich nie eng! Probieren Sie unsere Gastfreundlichkeit², unsere erstklassigen Restaurants, Hotels und Sportmöglichkeiten aus. Sie haben alle Vorteile³ von der Zivilisation, aber auch eine wunderbare Landschaft, wo Sie den ganzen Tag wandern können, ohne Autos, Hochhäuser oder Personen zu sehen. Wir leben hoch in den Alpen, wo man:

- **die Natur aktiv oder passiv genießen⁴ kann**
- **bergsteigen⁵ kann**
- **einfach auf dem Balkon sitzen kann**
- **oder sich die Berge ansehen kann.**

Genießen Sie im Sommer unsere Wanderwege, im Winter die Skiwege, am Morgen die ruhigen Wälder⁶ und am Abend die musikvollen Discos!

Und für kleine Gäste gibt's auch 'was! Unser Dorf⁷ ist besonders kinderfreundlich:

- **schwimmt im Schwimmbad**
- **spielt im Wald oder im Schnee**
- **reitet ein Pony**
- **oder fahrt mit einem Rodel⁸.**

Bei uns haben alle Spaß! Nun bringen Sie Ihre ganze Familie und besuchen Sie uns. Entspannen wir uns zusammen!

¹*crowded*
²*hospitality*
³*advantages*
⁴*enjoy*

⁵*mountain climbing*
⁶*forests*
⁷*village*
⁸*sled*

Command forms (the imperative)

The imperative is used to give commands. There are four different forms:

Formal singular and plural **Sie**-forms
The **wir**-form
Familiar plural **ihr**-form
Familiar singular **du**-form

The *Sie*-form command

This form, used for persons you would address with **Sie**, is identical to the present tense form, but the verb and subject pronoun change positions.

STATEMENT	COMMAND
Sie bezahlen.	Bezahlen Sie! (*Pay!*)
Sie sprechen nicht.	Sprechen Sie nicht! (*Do not speak!*)
Sie lesen jetzt.	Lesen Sie jetzt! (*Read now!*)

The *wir*-form command

This form is equivalent to English *let's*. As with the **Sie**-form, the subject and verb simply switch positions.

STATEMENT	COMMAND
Wir bezahlen.	Bezahlen wir! (*Let's pay.*)
Wir sprechen nicht.	Sprechen wir nicht! (*Let's not talk.*)
Wir lesen jetzt.	Lesen wir jetzt! (*Let's read now.*)

ALLES KLAR?

A. Soll ich jetzt...? Ein Tourist bittet Sie um Hilfe. Beantworten Sie die Fragen mit einer Imperativ-Form. (*A tourist asks you for directions/opinions. Answer the questions, using a command with* **Sie**.)

> BEISPIEL: Soll ich den Bus nehmen?
> —Ja, nehmen Sie den Bus.

1. Soll ich das Museum besuchen?
2. Soll ich zu Fuß gehen?
3. Soll ich hier links abbiegen?
4. Soll ich im chinesischen Restaurant essen?
5. Soll ich im Stadtpark spazierengehen?

B. Was sollen wir? Besprechen Sie mit einer Freundin, was Sie alles in der Stadt machen sollen. Beantworten Sie die Fragen mit dem **wir**-Imperativ. (*Discuss with a friend what you should do in the city. Following are some possibilities. Answer your friend's questions with a **wir**-imperative.*)

> **BEISPIEL:** im Café einen Kaffee trinken
> —Sollen wir im Café einen Kaffee trinken?
> —Ja, trinken wir im Café einen Kaffee!

1. im Blumenladen Rosen kaufen
2. ins Kino gehen
3. die Kirche besuchen
4. in der Bäckerei Brot kaufen
5. bei der Post Briefmarken (*stamps*) kaufen
6. im Kaufhaus einkaufen.

The *ihr*-form command

Used when speaking to more than one person whom you know well, this form is identical to the **ihr**-form in the present tense, but the pronoun is omitted.

STATEMENT	COMMAND
Ihr bezahlt.	Bezahlt! (*Pay!*)
Ihr sprecht nicht.	Sprecht nicht! (*Don't speak!*)
Ihr lest jetzt.	Lest jetzt! (*Read now!*)

The *du*-form command

This form is used when speaking to one person whom you would address with **du**. It consists of the stem of the **du**-form in the present tense without the -**st** ending. As with **ihr**-, the pronoun is omitted. When a verb has a stem-vowel change, that change is retained in the imperative.

STATEMENT	COMMAND
Du bezahlst.	Bezahl! (*Pay!*)
Du sprichst nicht.	Sprich nicht! (*Don't speak!*)
Du liest.	Lies jetzt! (*Read now!*)

iß mich täglich!

frisch aus deutschen Landen

CMDA Bonn

On the other hand, verbs that add an umlaut in the present tense **du**-forms do *not* make this change in the imperative:

STATEMENT	COMMAND
Du fährst.	Fahr(e)!
Du läufst.	Lauf!

In the **du**-form command, a final **-e** may be added to most verbs[1], but it is obligatory when the verb stem ends in **-t** or **-d**.

STATEMENT	COMMAND
Du arbeitest.	Arbeite!
Du sendest.	Sende!
Du gehst.	Geh(e)!

Frequently, **du**-form commands are found in proverbs and colloquial sayings. Below are a few such proverbs and phrases:

Sag, was wahr ist; iß, was gar ist; trink, was klar ist!
Say what is true, eat what is cooked, drink what is pure.

Lerne was, so kannst du was!
Learn something and you'll be able to do something!

sein

The verb **sein** has the following irregular forms:

Seien Sie doch bitte vorsichtig! ⎫
Seid doch bitte vorsichtig! ⎬ *Please be careful!*
Sei doch bitte vorsichtig! ⎭

Seien wir vorsichtig! *Let's be careful!*

ALLES KLAR?

A. Die Verwandten sind zu Besuch. Sagen Sie Ihren Verwandten, was sie alles machen sollen. (*Using the following suggestions, tell your visiting relatives what they should do.*)

> BEISPIEL: Vielleicht fahren wir nach München.
> —Ja, fahrt nach München!

1. Vielleicht gehen wir ins Museum.
2. Vielleicht sehen wir uns die Kirche an.
3. Vielleicht essen wir im französischen Restaurant.
4. Vielleicht gehen wir im See (*lake*) schwimmen.
5. Vielleicht tanzen wir heute abend in der Disco.

---

[1]This final **-e** is never added to verbs with stem vowel changes: **Lies! Sprich!** With other verbs (except those that end it **-t** or **-d**) it is uncommon, and you will rarely hear it in conversation.

B. Gib' mir einen Rat! Sagen Sie Ihrem Partner/Ihrer Partnerin, was er/sie machen soll. Dann tauschen Sie die Rollen. (*Give your partner advice for some problems. Then switch roles and ask for advice.*)

PROBLEM	RAT (*advice*)
1. Ich bin sehr müde.	lang schlafen
Ich kann nicht schlafen.	ein Buch lesen
Ich habe kein Buch.	in die Bibliothek gehen
Die Bibliothek ist zu weit.	mit dem Bus fahren!
2. Ich habe Heimweh (*am homesick*).	nach Hause fahren
Ich habe kein Geld.	einen Job finden
Ich kann nichts machen.	etwas lernen
Ich habe keine Zeit.	nicht so viel machen!

C. Sei nicht so! Sagen Sie den folgenden Leuten, Sie sollen nicht so sein! Benutzen Sie die richtige Imperativform. (*Tell the following people not to be that way. Use the correct imperative form.*)

> **BEISPIEL:** Frau Karamakis, ungeduldig (impatient)
> —Seien Sie nicht so ungeduldig, Frau Karamakis!

1. Tomaso und Angelo, aggressiv
2. Herr von Meter, faul
3. Rosita, pessimistisch
4. wir, immer skeptisch
5. Jacques, dumm
6. Herr und Frau Tanyel, langsam

Zusammenfassung

A. Der Weg zum Kunstmuseum. Ergänzen Sie mit den Wörtern in der Liste. (*Fill in the blanks in the following passage. The basic forms of the words you need are given below.*)

gehen	umsteigen	nehmen
direkt	Haltestelle ⟵busstop	rechts
aus	zu	gegenüber
bis	mit	ein
einsteigen	aussteigen get off	

HERR: So, jetzt weiß ich nicht, wo das Kunstmuseum ist. Vielleicht frage ich mal. Entschuldigen Sie!

FRAU: Ja, bitte?

HERR: Wie komme ich _mit_ dem Bus _zum_ Kunstmuseum?

FRAU: Warten Sie mal… Sie _gehen_ hier vorne die Nummer 5 _bis_ zum Bahnhof. Steigen Sie dann _aus_ und _gehen_ Sie links in die Ludwigstraße. Dann sehen Sie die _bushaltestelle_ für die Nummer 3. Steigen Sie _ein_, und fahren Sie, bis Sie auf der rechten Seite eine Kirche sehen. Steigen Sie _aus_ und das Kunstmuseum ist _gegenüber_.

HERR: Ich weiß nicht, ob ich das alles verstanden habe. Also, hier vorne die Nummer 5 nehmen, dann am Bahnhof _umsteigen_. Mit der Nummer 3 fahre ich, bis ich _rechts_ eine Kirche sehe und das Kunstmuseum ist _direkt_ gegenüber.

FRAU: Toll! Sie haben alles verstanden. Gute Fahrt!

B. Wie ihr hierher kommt. Wählen Sie eine Situation und schreiben Sie einen kurzen Brief. (*Choose one situation and write a short letter.*)

1. Explain to a friend how he would get from the train station to your campus. Would he have to take the bus or could he walk?
2. Explain to your parents how they would get from the library to your dorm.
3. Explain to your sister how she would get from your dorm to the gym.

C. Kommen Sie zu uns! Schreiben Sie eine Anzeige für Ihre Stadt, wie in **Schritt 4**. Erklären Sie den Touristen, was sie da alles machen können. (*Write an advertisement for your hometown, like the one in* Schritt 4. *Explain to your prospective tourists what they can do and see there.*)

BEISPIEL: Kennen Sie Philadelphia noch nicht? Kommen Sie zu uns und lernen Sie etwas über die amerikanische Geschichte. Besuchen Sie die Freiheitsglocke[1], das Haus von Betsy Ross….

[1]*Liberty Bell*

A. Bitte, wo ist...? Ihr Partner/Ihre Partnerin ist auf dem Campus zu Besuch. Erklären Sie den Weg. Der Partner/die Partnerin zeichnet den Weg auf die Karte. (*Your partner will play the role of someone visiting the campus. Tell this person how to get where she/he wants to go, mentioning street names and other landmarks. See the Supplementary Vocabulary in the back of the book for names of more campus buildings. Your partner will draw the route on her/his map. Then check whether your partner understood your directions.*)

BEISPIEL: —Bitte, wie komme ich zur Mensa (*cafeteria*)?
—Gehen Sie die 64. Straße geradeaus. Biegen Sie in die Walnußstraße. Die Mensa ist links, neben der Bibliothek.
—Vielen Dank!

X
Sie sind hier.

Now you are the campus visitor and need to get from the dorm to the post office. Ask your partner how to go there and draw the route on the map above, writing in the street names and other landmarks. Then check with your partner whether you have correctly understood the directions.

B. Die neuen Möbel. Sagen Sie Ihrem Partner/Ihrer Partnerin mit Hilfe des Bildes unten, wo die Möbel hingehören. Benutzen Sie die **du**-Form. (*Tell your partner how to arrange his/her house, according to the diagram below. Use familiar commands.*)

BEISPIEL: —Stell den Schreibtisch ins erste Schlafzimmer!
—Neben das Bett?
—Nein, vor das Fenster.

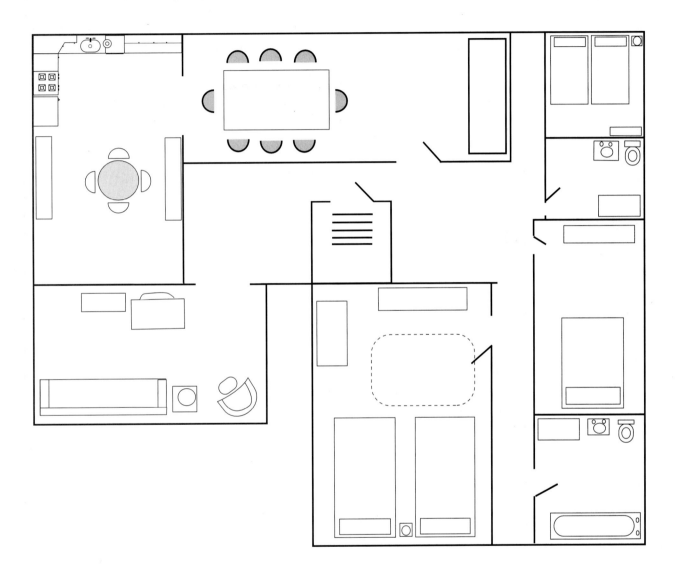

A. Wo ist... ? Sie sind auf dem Campus zu Besuch. Sie sind im Studentenwohnheim und Sie möchten die neue Bibiliothek sehen. Fragen Sie Ihre Partnerin/Ihren Partner, wie Sie dorthin kommen. Zeichnen Sie den Weg — mit Straßen und Gebäuden — auf die Karte. (*You are playing the role of a campus visitor. You are in the dorm and would like to see the new library. Ask your partner how to get there. He/she will give you directions; mark the route on the map below, writing in street names and other landmarks. Then check with your partner to be sure you have understood correctly.*)

BEISPIEL: —Bitte, wie komme ich zur Mensa (*cafeteria*)?
—Gehen Sie die 64. Straße geradeaus. Biegen Sie in die Walnußstraße. Die Mensa ist links, neben der Bibliothek.
—Vielen Dank!

X
Sie sind hier.

Now your partner is the campus visitor. Tell him/her how to get where he/she wants to go, mentioning street names and other landmarks. Your partner will draw the route on the map provided, then check with you to see whether he/she correctly understood the directions.

B. Die neuen Möbel. Ihre Partnerin/Ihr Partner sagt Ihnen, wo die Möbel hingehören. Zeichnen Sie sie auf den Plan. (*Furnish your house according to your partner's instructions; draw in the appropriate items.*)

BEISPIEL: —Stell den Schreibtisch ins erste Schlafzimmer!
—Neben das Bett?
—Nein, vor das Fenster.

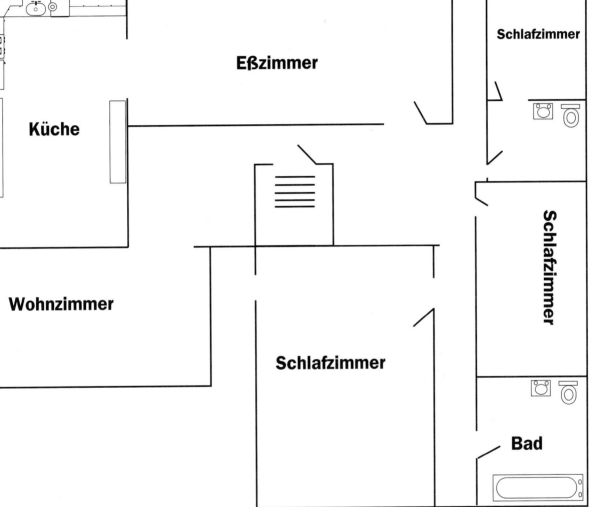

Situationen

 A. Die Einladung. Invite your partner to have lunch with you after class, then tell him/her how to get from the classroom to your dorm (or wherever you plan to eat). Your partner will reciprocate by suggesting that you study together at his/her place and will tell you how to get there from your dorm.

B. Gehen wir zum Rathaus! You and your roommate want to register to vote. Discuss together how you can get from your campus to the city hall (**Rathaus**) in your town. Can you walk there? Will you go by bus? by car?

C. In Osnabrück. Die folgende Karte zeigt die Stadt Osnabrück.

1. Sie und Ihre Partnerin/Ihr Partner wohnen in der Martinistraße. Vor dem Rathaus gibt es ein großes Straßenfest; Sie wollen beide hingehen. Besprechen Sie zusammen, wie Sie zum Fest kommen.

2. In den Städtischen Bühnen spielt Dürrenmatts "Besuch der alten Dame". Sie müssen arbeiten, aber Ihr Partner/Ihre Partnerin möchte sich das Spiel gern ansehen. Er/sie wohnt in der Bismarckstraße. Erzählen Sie, wie er/sie zum Theater kommt.

3. Ein bekannter, ausländischer Professor hält einen Vortrag (*lecture*) in der Universitätsbibliothek. Ihr Freund und sein Zimmerkamerad wollen hingehen. Erklären Sie den beiden, wie sie zur Universitätsbibliothek kommen.

4. Sie und drei Freunde/Freundinnen haben in dem Hotel Kulmbacher Hof übernachtet. Sie wollen jetzt zum Hotel Hohenzollern, zu einem Bierfest. Wer kommt mit? Wie kommen Sie dort hin? Besprechen Sie zusammen.

5. Ihre Eltern sind in Osnabrück zu Besuch, und jetzt müssen sie wieder nach Hause. Erklären Sie ihnen, wie sie von der Universität bis zum Hauptbahnhof kommen.

6. Sie sind am Rosenplatz, und ein Tourist/eine Touristin fragt Sie, wie er/sie zum Dom kommt. Sagen Sie es ihm/ihr.

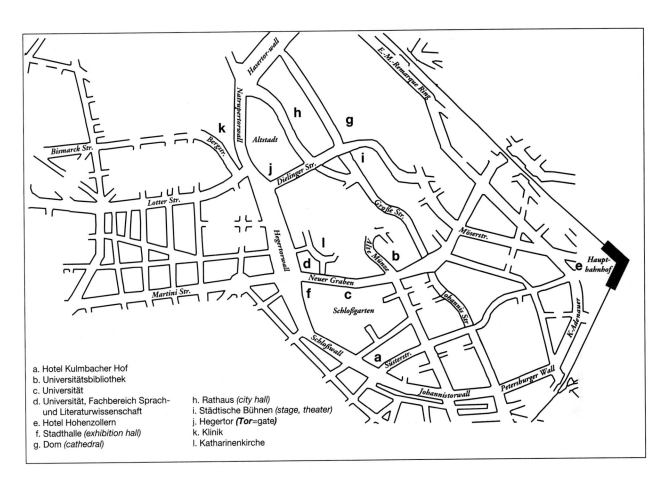

a. Hotel Kulmbacher Hof
b. Universitätsbibliothek
c. Universität
d. Universität, Fachbereich Sprach-
   und Literaturwissenschaft
e. Hotel Hohenzollern
f. Stadthalle (exhibition hall)
g. Dom (cathedral)

h. Rathaus (city hall)
i. Städtische Bühnen (stage, theater)
j. Hegertor (Tor=gate)
k. Klinik
l. Katharinenkirche

Reisen, Tourismus und Transport

Travel, Tourism and Transportation

The German addresses in this **Netzbox** offer a wealth of helpful information about traveling around Europe.
See the Prentice Hall home page for related activities and address updates
(http;//www.prenhall.com/~german).

1. Berliner U-Bahn und S-Bahn
Virtual tours around Berlin's subway and public transportation systems.
http://www.informatik.hu-berlin.de/BIW/d_oenv.html

2. Reisen mit Zug und Bahn: Fahrkarten, Eurail Passes
Information about special offers, trips and tickets for travel on German railroads.
http://www.bahn.de/

3. Tourismus in Bayern
Tourism links to Bavaria and its cities.
http://www.bayern.de/Tourismus/

German in Western Europe

*G*erman is alive and well in western Europe! Clearly, history, geography and commerce contribute substantially to that situation. During the major German economic boom (the 1950s and 1960s), many "guest workers" were imported from other European countries. These people learned German and

often took it back with them to their native countries — Italy, Greece, and Turkey among others. The lingering influence of this phenomenon can be seen today in the fact that fully 30% of the elementary schools in Turkey require pupils to learn German. Conversely, only three western European countries do not offer German in high school: Andorra, Monaco, and Vatican City!

In other European countries, German is in a close race with English as the first foreign language. In Denmark and Sweden, some secondary schools offer German as the first foreign language. In elementary schools in Denmark, as many as 90% of all pupils learn German; it is available in 94% of the schools there. In the Netherlands, German is a required subject in 80% of all elementary schools, as well as in 60% of the junior high schools, and in 53% of the high schools. In England, a Center for German Studies, the first of its kind in Great Britain, recently opened at the University of Birmingham.

Overall, the number of years of German study is important for acquiring fluency. A quick look at some western European countries shows why pupils from these countries are fluent in German. Pre-university students often study German for many years: ten years (Finland and Italy), nine years (France), or six to eight years (Denmark, Great Britain, Ireland, the Netherlands, Portugal, Sweden, Turkey, and others).

Just imagine the level of your own skills in German had you begun at the age of seven, eight, or even ten!

Themenwortschatz

Substantive / *Nouns*

Verkehr / *Traffic*

die Ampel, -n	*traffic light*
die Bahn, -en	*train*
der Bahnhof, ̈-e	*train station*
die Brücke, -n	*bridge*
die Bushaltestelle, -n	*bus stop*
die Fahrkarte, -n	*ticket [for travelling]*
der Flughafen, ̈-	*airport*
die Kreuzung, -en	*crossing, intersection*
die S-Bahn, -en	*local [elevated] train*
das Schild, -er	*sign*
der Stadtplan, ̈-e	*city map*
die Straße, -n	*street*
das Taxi, -s	*taxi*
die U-Bahn, -en	*underground train, subway*
der Verkehr	*traffic*

Orte / *Places*

die Bäckerei, -en	*bakery*
der Blumenladen, ̈-	*flower shop*
das Café, -s	*café*
die Disco, -s	*disco*
das Hotel, -s	*hotel*
das Kaufhaus, ̈-er	*department store*
die Kirche, -n	*church*
der Laden, ̈-	*store*
das Lebensmittel- geschäft, -e	*grocery store*
die Metzgerei, -en	*meat market, butcher shop*
das Museum, die Museen	*museum*
die Post	*post office*
das Restaurant, -s	*restaurant*

Verben / *Verbs*

biegen, ist gebogen	*to turn*
fragen	*to ask*
unternehmen (unternimmt), unternommen	*to do, undertake*

Verben der Bewegung / *Verbs of Motion*

ab•biegen, ist abgebogen	*to turn off (as a car on a road)*
ab•fahren (fährt), ist abgefahren	*to drive off, leave*
aus•steigen, ist ausgestiegen	*to get off or out*
ein•steigen, ist eingestiegen	*to get in, board*
heraus•kommen, ist herausgekommen	*to come out*
her•kommen, ist hergekommen	*to come (from someplace)*
herunter•kommen, ist heruntergekommen	*to come down*
hinauf•gehen, ist hinaufgegangen	*to go up*
hinein•gehen, ist hineingegangen	*to go in*
um•steigen, ist umgestiegen	*to transfer*

Adjektive/Adverbien / *Adjectives/Adverbs*

bis zu	*up to, until*
gegenüber	*across*
geradeaus	*straight ahead*
hinten	*in back*
(nach) links	*(to the) left*
(nach) rechts	*(to the) right*
vorne	*up front, in front*
wahrscheinlich	*probably*
weg	*away*
wohin	*where to*

Wechselpräpositionen / *Two-way Prepositions*

an	*at, at the side of (with dative)*
	to, toward (with accusative)
auf	*on, on top of, onto*
hinter	*behind, in back of*
in	*in, into*
neben	*beside, next to*
über	*above, over*
unter	*beneath, under*
vor	*in front of*
zwischen	*between*

Den wievielten haben wir heute?	*What is today's date?*	**in der Nähe**	*nearby, in the vicinity*
Heute haben wir den [5. (fünften) Januar].	*Today is [January fifth].*	**laß uns…**	*let us…*
Entschuldigen Sie, bitte.	*Excuse me please.*	**um die Ecke**	*around the corner*
es eilig haben	*to be in a hurry.*	**Wie komme ich zum/zur…?**	*How do I get to…?*
Heraus!	*Get out!*		
Herein!	*Come in!*		
Ich würde…	*I would…*		

Zum = Zu dem
Zur = Zu der

Weiterer Wortschatz

Substantive	*Nouns*	**Adjektive/Adverbien**	*Adjectives/Adverbs*
das Geld, -er	*money*	**beliebt**	*well-liked, popular*
der Vorlesungssaal, -säle	*lecture hall*	**genau**	*exactly*
		schade	*too bad*
Verben	*Verbs*	**schlimm**	*terrible, bad*
		vorsichtig	*careful*
auf·passen	*to watch out, pay attention*		
bezahlen/zahlen	*to pay*	**Ausdrücke**	*Expressions*
denken, gedacht	*to think*		
halten (hält), gehalten	*to hold, to stop*	**(keine) Zeit haben**	*to have (no) time*
hängen, gehangen	*to hang (+dat.)*		
hängen, gehängt	*to hang (+acc.)*		
legen	*to lay*		
liegen, gelegen	*to lie, repose*		
setzen	*to set (down)*		
sich setzen	*to sit down*		
sitzen, gesessen	*to sit*		
stehen, gestanden	*to stand*		
stellen	*to place, set*		
sich treffen, getroffen	*to meet*		

Im hanying the picture

Ja gerne, aber...

Kommunikation

- Purchasing items in a drugstore
- Shopping for and discussing clothing
- Placing and receiving telephone calls
- Making plans
- Giving reasons and excuses

Strukturen

- Subordinating conjunctions
- Question words as subordinating conjunctions
  weil vs. **denn**
  als/wann/wenn
- Compound nouns
- Word order: time, manner, place
- General time and specific time
- **der–** and **ein–**words: Review and expansion

Kultur

- Shopping in Germany
- The German telephone system

Kapitel 8

Schritt 1: In der Apotheke

In **Kapitel 7** you learned the names of some different kinds of stores: **die Bäckerei, die Metzgerei**, etc. Two other kinds of shops are **die Apotheke** (*pharmacy*) and **die Drogerie** (*drugstore*). In the German-speaking countries there is a greater difference between the two than in North America; an **Apotheke** sells prescription and non-prescription drugs, while a **Drogerie** generally carries toiletries. For example, you would go to a **Drogerie** for the following items:

das Deo, - (**das Deodorant**)	*deodorant*
der Kamm, ⁻e	*comb*
die Seife, -n	*soap*
das Shampoo, -s	*shampoo*
die Zahnbürste, -n	*toothbrush*
die Zahnpasta	*toothpaste*

In an **Apotheke**, among other medications you would find:

Vitamintabletten	**Schlaftabletten**
Aspirin	

ALLES KLAR?

 A. Ich mache eine Reise. Spielen Sie nach dem Beispiel. (*Play the game "I'm going on a trip." Follow the model.*)

BEISPIEL: —Ich mache eine Reise und nehme die Zahnbürste mit.
—Ich mache eine Reise und nehme die Zahnbürste und den Kamm mit.
…

B. Wo kaufst du…? Ihr Partner/Ihre Partnerin fragt, wo man etwas kaufen kann. Antworten Sie nach dem Beispiel. (*Your partner will ask where you can buy certain things. Answer according to the model.*)

BEISPIEL: Zahnpasta

ODER: —Wo kaufst du Zahnpasta?
—Wo kann man Zahnpasta kaufen?

ODER: —Zahnpasta kaufe ich in der Drogerie.
—Zahnpasta kann man in der Drogerie kaufen.

Rosen	Brot
Butter	Seife
Aspirin	einen Kaffee
Schokolade	Fahrkarte
Briefmarken (*stamps*)	

People living in the United States or Canada are often used to being able to shop for anything at any time, on any day, including Sundays and holidays. The situation is quite different in Germany. By law, all stores (including open-air farmers' markets) close in the evenings and on Saturday at 1:00 pm, or in some cities at 2:00 pm. They remain closed until 8:00 am Monday.

This has been the case for many years; however, a few years ago, the notion of **langer Samstag** was introduced in the Federal Republic. This means that, on the first Saturday of every month, stores may stay open until 4:00 pm, at which time they then close for the remainder of the weekend. Even more recently, some stores initiated "**langer Donnerstag**" once a month, when stores might stay open until around 8:00 pm. Even pharmacies must abide by these hours, although in large towns one pharmacy will have **Dienstbereitschaft** on the weekend and in the evenings; persons needing prescriptions can go to the one pharmacy open that night. In addition, many stores of all kinds will close for the midday lunch hour. The concept of twenty-four-hour convenience stores, to which we have grown so accustomed, is unknown in German-speaking countries.

NOTFÄLLE		
Ärzte **Zahnärzte** **Apotheken**	**Notruf 251 61 61**	
Tierärzte	**Notruf 250 78 50**	
Apotheken-Notfalldienst vom 18. bis 24. Juli 1996		
ganze **Nacht:**	Greifen-Apotheke Kasernenstrasse 36	611 61 82
	Breite-Apotheke Zürcherstrasse 97	379 11 61
bis **22 Uhr:**	Spalen-Apotheke Spalenvorstadt 19	350 72 61
Sanitäts-Notruf nur Notfall-Transporte	**222**	

Schritt 2: **Kleider machen Leute**

1. der Hut, ⸚e
2. die Mütze, -n
3. die Bluse, -n
4. das Hemd, -en
5. das T-Shirt, -s
6. das Sweatshirt, -s
7. der Pullover, - (der Pulli, -s)
8. die Jacke, -n
9. der Anzug, ⸚e
10. der Mantel, ⸚
11. das Kleid, -er
12. die Handtasche, -n
13. der Rock, ⸚e
14. die Hose, -n
15. die Jeans (pl.)
16. der Schuh, -e
17. die Socke, -n

The following verbs will be useful when shopping for clothing. You already know a few of them:

an•ziehen, angezogen	*to put on*
sich an•ziehen	*to get dressed*
aus•ziehen, ausgezogen	*to take off*
sich aus•ziehen	*to get undressed*
sich um•ziehen, umgezogen	*to change clothes*
an•probieren	*to try on*
ein•kaufen	*to shop*
kosten	*to cost*
tragen (trägt), getragen	*to wear*

ALLES KLAR?

A. Was trägt man wo? Füllen Sie die Tabelle aus. (*Fill in the table with the appropriate pieces of clothing.*)

WO? WANN?	WAS TRÄGT MAN?
auf dem Kopf	
wenn das Wetter kalt ist	
wenn das Wetter warm ist	
wenn man kalte Hände hat	
wenn man kalte Beine hat	
wenn man kalte Füße hat	
bei der Arbeit	
in der Freizeit	

B. Detektiv. Eine Person (der Detektiv) verläßt das Zimmer. Die Klasse entscheidet, wer "der Verbrecher" ist. Sie merken sich die Kleidung von dem Verbrecher. Der Detektiv kommt wieder herein und stellt Ja/nein-Fragen über die Kleidung. (*One person [the detective] leaves the room. The class decides who will be the "criminal" and memorizes his/her clothing. The detective returns and asks yes/no questions to determine who is the criminal.*)

BEISPIEL: —Ist die Hose blau?
—Nein.
…
—Ist der Verbrecherin Debbie?

C. Der Geschenkgutschein. Sie haben einen Geschenkgutschein für DM 200,- bei einem Kaufhaus bekommen und Sie wollen Kleider kaufen. Schauen Sie sich die Preise im Schaufenster oben (in **Schritt 2**) an. Was kaufen Sie alles? Die Verkäuferin/der Verkäufer (Ihre Partnerin/Ihr Partner) schreibt alles auf. (*You received a gift certificate for 200 Marks at a department store and want to buy clothes. Look at the prices in the store window in **Schritt 2**. What will you buy? The salesperson (your partner) will write everything down.*)

BEISPIEL: —Was möchten Sie?
—Ich möchte zwei T-Shirts; die ~~sind~~ kosten 15 Mark.
—Zwei mal 15 sind 30. Sonst noch etwas?
…
—Was ist die Gesamtsumme (*total*) jetzt?
—DM 150,-. Sie haben noch 50 Mark.
—Dann nehme ich…

Tip!

German currency is the **Deutsche Mark**, or **DM**. Each **Mark** contains 100 **Pfennige**. A price such as DM 15, 95 means that the item costs 15 marks and 95 pfennigs; it is read aloud as follows: **fünfzehn Mark fünfundneunzig**.

WIEVIELE?	WAS?	WAS KOSTET ES?
2	T-Shirts	2 x DM 15,- = DM 30,-
1	anzug / Schue	
4	J-s	1000 DM
		Gesamtsumme =

(handwritten: Vorwahl USA – 011-49 – 30)

Schritt 3: **Becker, guten Tag!**

Making phone calls in German-speaking countries is easy, once you know a few phrases—and the phone number! Read or listen to the following two dialogues in which Christoph tries to get in touch with someone he has just met. Note the terms that are particularly related to making calls; can you guess their meanings from the context?

die Auskunft	**falsch verbunden**
die Vorwahl	**wählen**

Auskunft, bitte!

CHRISTOPH: Guten Tag. Ich möchte gern eine Nummer in Berlin.
AUSKUNFT: Wie ist der Name, bitte?
CHRISTOPH: Becker, Barbara Becker. Becker mit «eh.»
AUSKUNFT: Es gibt dreimal Barbara Becker. Wissen Sie die Adresse?
CHRISTOPH: Ach…nein, ich bin nicht sicher. Wohnt eine in der Bleibtreustraße?
AUSKUNFT: Nein. Soll ich Ihnen alle drei Nummern geben?
CHRISTOPH: Ja, wenn das geht.
AUSKUNFT: Die erste Nummer ist 3 62 97 14; die zweite ist 3 29 68 54; und die dritte ist 4 12 98 61.
CHRISTOPH: Haben Sie recht herzlichen Dank! Und noch eine kleine Frage, bitte. Wie ist die Vorwahl für Berlin?
AUSKUNFT: Die Vorwahl ist 30. Sonst noch etwas?
CHRISTOPH: Nein, danke. Auf Wiederhören!
AUSKUNFT: Auf Wiederhören!

ALLES KLAR?

Ich möchte eine Telefonnummer. Wählen Sie einen Namen aus dem Telefonbuch und führen Sie das Gespräch. Die Vorwahl für diese Stadt ist 6441. (*Look at the following excerpt from a German telephone directory and select one of the names. Then, with a partner, conduct a conversation similar to the one in "**Auskunft, bitte.**" Take turns playing the roles of the operator and the person seeking the number. The area code for this town is 6441.*)

Rösch Otto Bachstr.7	7 23 26
Rösch Marita Volpertshäuser Str.5	7 27 23
Röseler Herbert Weingartenstr.15	5 22 22
Rösser Alfred Junkersgrund 10	5 47 95
Rösser Oskar Schwalbengraben 7	5 13 62
Röskamp Klaus Friedenstr. 12	5 39 88
Rösler Alfred Redakteur Neubomer Str. 166	9 57 32
Rösner Anna Am Sturzkopf 5	9 14 70
Rössler Anna Untergasse 35	
Rössler Mathias Germanenweg 69	3 14 70
Rössler Gerhard Albertstr.18	8 23 08
Röth Mathias Am Altbecker 2	5 29 51
Röth Eva Frommerstr.22	3 52 46
Rötig Frank u. Elisabeth Lampengraben 2	7 77 34
Rogge Marianne Röntgenstr.21	5 02 05
Rogge Rudolf Dipl. Ing. Am Sturzkopf 27e	7 92 34
Rogge Anton Westerwaldstr. 27	7 09 13
Roggendorf V. Jacobistr. 22	7 91 30
	6 86 73

Tip!

German phone numbers are not all the same length: in small towns they may only be four digits; in larger cities, up to 8 digits. They are grouped in two's (except the first if there is an odd number), and are normally read as a series of two digit numbers:
3 62 97 14 is read
drei, zweiundsechzig, siebenundneunzig, vierzehn
although some prefer a series of individual numbers: **drei, sechs, zwei, neun,** etc.

Redewendung

Note that when speaking on the telephone, German-speakers use the phrase **Auf Wiederhören** to say *good-bye.*

Die falsche Nummer

FRAU BENDER:	Bender, guten Tag.
CHRISTOPH:	Hier ist Christoph Schultz. Darf ich mal mit Barbara sprechen?
FRAU BENDER:	Barbara? Hier wohnt keine Barbara. Ich glaube, Sie sind falsch verbunden.
CHRISTOPH:	Ist das die Nummer 3 62 97 40?
FRAU BENDER:	Das schon; Sie haben vielleicht die falsche Vorwahl gewählt.
CHRISTOPH:	Na, das kann sein. Ist das nicht Vorwahl 30? Ist das nicht richtig?
FRAU BENDER:	Doch, dies ist 30, also Berlin, aber hier wohnt keine Barbara.
CHRISTOPH:	Entschuldigen Sie, bitte, die Störung[1]!
FRAU BENDER:	Keine Ursache[2]! Auf Wiederhören.
CHRISTOPH:	Auf Wiederhören!

[1] *interruption*
[2] *Don't mention it!*

ALLES KLAR?

A. Was soll Christoph machen? Besprechen Sie mit einem Partner/einer Partnerin, was Christoph falsch gemacht hat. Was soll er jetzt machen? (*Discuss with a partner what Christoph did wrong. What should he do now?*)

Soll er die anderen Nummern versuchen? Soll er im Telefonbuch nachschauen (*look*)? Soll er die Auskunft noch einmal anrufen? Soll er den Anruf noch machen?

B. Brauchst du oft das Telefon? Besprechen Sie die Fragen. (*With a partner, discuss the following questions.*)

1. Wie oft telefonierst du?
2. Wie oft rufst du deine Eltern an?
3. Wie oft rufen dich deine Eltern an?
4. Wie lange dauern deine Telefongespräche?
5. Mit wem telefonierst du oft?
6. Wie lange dauern die Telefongespräche von deinem ~~Zimmer~~kameraden oder deiner ~~Zimmerkameradin~~? Ist das ein Problem?

[handwritten: mitbewohnern]
[handwritten: Mit bewohner]

[handwritten: Es kommt darauf an, mit wem ich spreche]

In Germany, the telephone system is a government monopoly tied to the postal system. Despite recent efforts to terminate this linkage, at present the Bundespost still has complete responsibility for the phone system. For this reason the post office is the place to go if you have to make a call and you don't have access to a private phone or change to call from a telephone booth. To alleviate this problem, many Germans now purchase **Telefonkarten**, which are good for a certain amount and can be used at booths with the Kartentelefon sign. Charges for all calls are based on units (**Einheiten**); each unit costs a certain amount of money.

Overall, telephone service is more expensive in Germany than in North America; this applies to installation charges as well as to both local and long distance calls. Calls made from home cost more per call (or unit) than they do when made from a telephone booth. Installation is not only more expensive than in North America, but there is sometimes a considerable delay before a new line can be connected. For this reason cellular phones have greatly increased in popularity throughout Germany and the rest of Europe.

There are also other differences between Germany and North America regarding the use of a telephone. For example, German-speakers don't say "Hello" when answering the phone; rather, they give their name, as did Frau Bender in the preceding dialogue. Only afterward does one say **Guten Tag**.

Versuch's mal! Der *ü*-Laut

Below is a list of nouns and adjectives that you have learned so far that contain **ü** or **u**. Combine adjectives and nouns to finish the ad for **Kaufhaus Süßmuth**. Create five household items and five personal items. Practice reading your ad aloud to your partner. Make sure you emphasize the difference between the **u** and **ü**.

Bei Kaufhaus Süßmuth finden Sie alles!

—**fürs Haus:** gute Geschirrspülmaschinen...

—**für Sie:** dunkle Anzüge...

Haarbürste	dünn
Hüte	früh
Haustür	kühl
Handtücher	kürzer
Geschirrspülmaschine	müde
Gemüse (*vegetables*)	verrückt
Füße	geblümt (*flowered*)
Züge	glücklich
Tür	grün
Stühle	zusätzlich (*additional*)
Münder	russisch
Müll (*garbage*)	gesund
Kühlschrank	jung
Bücherregal	genug
Bücher	gut
Badeanzüge	bunt
Telefonbücher	dunkel
Kostüme (*women's suits*)	kurz
Mützen	
Anzüge	
Zahnbürste	

Der *ö*-Laut

Zungenbrecher:

Können Sie die schönen höheren Töne der Flöte hören?
Die bösen Söhne zerstören die größten Möbel — ist das nötig?
Gibt es Öl in Österreich?

Die weiteren Schritte

Alles klar?

Redewendung

Another flavoring particle is **nun**; it generally means something like *well, well now, well then.*

Das würde ich nun wirklich gerne machen.
Well, I would really like to do that.

Schritt 4: Ein erfolgreiches Gespräch

Gespräch

Worum geht es hier? Christoph versucht schon lange, mit Barbara Becker zu sprechen. Er hat zuerst bei der Auskunft angerufen, dann hat er falsch gewählt, jetzt versucht er noch einmal. Was schlägt Christoph jeden Tag vor? Was hat Barbara jeden Tag vor?

BARBARA: Barbara Becker, guten Tag.

CHRISTOPH: Christoph Schultz hier. Wir haben gestern im Zug gesprochen. Erinnerst du dich an mich? Wie geht's?

BARBARA: Ach, ja, Christoph, danke, es geht. Was gibt's denn?

CHRISTOPH: Möchtest du heute abend mit mir ins Kino gehen?

BARBARA: Leider geht das nicht, weil ich heute abend lesen muß. Obwohl "Der Tod in Venedig" das Thema für unser Seminar morgen ist, habe ich die Novelle noch nicht gelesen.

CHRISTOPH: Na, schade, aber, sag mal. Möchtest du morgen mit mir in die Disco?

BARBARA: Das klingt schön, aber ich kann nicht, weil ich mich mit einer Freundin treffe.

CHRISTOPH: So. Naja, am Samstag? Oder am Sonntag? Möchtest du mit mir einen Spaziergang machen? Im Stadtwald.

BARBARA: Also, das würde ich nun wirklich gerne machen. Nur am Wochenende fahre ich nach Hause. Können wir den Spaziergang vielleicht auf Montag verschieben, wenn ich wieder da bin?

CHRISTOPH: Gern. So um fünf Uhr? Wollen wir uns vor der Bibliothek treffen?

BARBARA: Jawohl. Bis dann, und schönen Dank für die Einladung. Tschüs!

CHRISTOPH: Tschüs!

ALLES KLAR?

A. Haben Sie verstanden?

1. Warum hat Christoph am Anfang keinen Erfolg? Warum kann Barbara nicht mit ihm ausgehen? Besprechen Sie es mit einer Partnerin / einem Partner.
2. Will Barbara mit Christoph ausgehen oder nicht? Was meint Ihr Partner / Ihre Partnerin dazu?

B. Entschuldigung! Welche Gründe benutzen Sie, wenn Sie mit jemand nicht ausgehen wollen? Machen Sie mit einer Partnerin/einem Partner eine Liste mit Gründen. (*What reasons do you use when you don't want to go out with someone? Discuss these with a partner.*)

MÖGLICHE GRÜNDE

Ich habe Kopfschmerzen.
Ich muß Hausaufgaben machen.
Ich muß meiner Mutter helfen.

Ich muß mir die Haare waschen.
Ich muß mein Zimmer putzen.

Subordinating conjunctions

As you learned in **Kapitel 4**, conjunctions are words that connect individual words, phrases, or entire sentences. While coordinating conjunctions link two equal parts— or independent clauses—subordinating conjunctions link two unequal parts. A subordinating conjunction introduces a dependent clause, which cannot stand alone as a complete sentence; it is *dependent on*, or *subordinate to*, the main clause.

MAIN CLAUSE	DEPENDENT CLAUSE
I'm going shopping	*because I need a new coat.*

Some of the most important subordinating conjunctions are:

als	*when*[1]
daß	*that*
ob	*whether, if*
weil	*because*
wenn	*if, whenever*

Other frequently used subordinating conjunctions are:

bevor	*before*
bis	*until*
damit	*so that*
nachdem	*after*
obwohl	*although, even though*

With coordinating conjunctions, word order does not change. With subordinating conjunctions, the conjugated verb (that is, the verb with the personal ending) moves to the end of the sentence or clause. The dependent clause is always set off from the rest of the sentence by a comma.

COORDINATING CONJUNCTION/NORMAL WORD ORDER
Ich kann nicht, denn ich mache mit einer Freundin einen Spaziergang.

SUBORDINATING CONJUNCTION/DEPENDENT WORD ORDER
Ich kann nicht, **weil** ich mit einer Freundin einen Spaziergang mache.

Note the word order in the following constructions:

1. **Present perfect tense.** The auxiliary **haben** or **sein** moves to the end of the clause, after the past participle.

   Ich weiß, daß sie gestern ausgegangen **ist**.
   Ich kann spazierengehen, nachdem ich die Novelle gelesen **habe**.

2. **Modal verbs.** The modal verb appears at the end of the sentence or clause; it follows the infinitive.

   Leider geht das nicht, weil ich heute abend arbeiten **muß**.
   Bevor ich nach Hause fahren **kann**, muß ich lesen.

3. **Separable-prefix verbs.** The prefix becomes re-attached to the main verb, at the end of the sentence or clause.

   Weißt du, ob sie morgen **mit**kommt?
   Ich muß telefonieren, nachdem ich mich **um**ziehe.

---

[1] **als** is used when referring to the past.

The dependent clause may also begin a sentence. In that case it is considered a single element, and the entire sentence uses inverted word order, with the verb of the main clause still in second position, as always. Note that the two conjugated verbs appear next to each other.

1		2
Jetzt		rufe ich meine Mutter an.

1	2
Wenn meine Mutter Geburtstag hat,	rufe ich sie an.

ALLES KLAR?

A. Wo wollen wir heute einkaufen? Verbinden Sie die Sätze mit **daß**, **ob** oder **weil**. (*Form one sentence out of the two sentences in each section below. Use one of the following conjunctions: **daß**, **ob**, **weil**.*)

1. Wir gehen einkaufen. Peter braucht Shampoo.
2. Peter sagt (es). Die Drogerie Schmidt hat gute Preise.
3. Ich frage. Ist die Drogerie um die Ecke?
4. Peter sagt (es). Es ist neben dem *Hotel zum goldenen Löwen.*
5. Ich frage. Haben Sie auch Vitamintabletten?
6. Peter glaubt (es) nicht. Sie haben dort Vitamintabletten.

B. Was tust du, wenn…? Stellen Sie Fragen an Ihren Partner/Ihre Partnerin. Der Partner/die Partnerin wählt eine passende Antwort. Folgen Sie dem Beispiel. (*Take turns asking questions and providing appropriate answers. Follow the model.*)

BEISPIEL: —Was tust du, wenn du Hunger hast?
—Wenn ich Hunger habe, gehe ich ins Restaurant.

PROBLEM	WAS MACHST DU?
nicht schlafen können (kann)	eine Jacke anziehen — trinke ich
neue Schuhe brauchen	schlafen und viel Orangensaft trinken
einkaufen wollen (will)	ins Kaufhaus gehen
Kopfschmerzen haben (hast)	eine Liste machen
krank sein (bin)	Aspirin nehmen
es ist dir kalt	Schlaftabletten nehmen

(handwritten notes: wenn; st; kan; hor; es mir kalt ist; es min kalt ist; kn.)

C. Was tut er/sie, wenn…? Jetzt berichten Sie. (*Now discuss with another partner what you have learned.*)

—Was tut Dieter, wenn er Hunger hat?
—Wenn Dieter Hunger hat, geht er ins Restaurant.

D. Wann machen wir etwas zusammen? Ergänzen Sie mit **aber**, **weil** oder **wenn**. (Complete the sentences with the correct conjunction, **aber**, **weil**, or **wenn**.)

AXEL: Axel Schneider. Guten Tag!

PETRA: Tag, Axel. Petra hier. Wie geht's denn?

AXEL: Danke, gut. Und dir?

PETRA: Danke, es geht, (1)_____ ich möchte mal etwas unternehmen, vielleicht mit dir zusammen. Möchtest du heute nachmittag mit mir ins Kino gehen?

AXEL: Ich möchte schon, (2)_____ ich muß zu Hause bleiben, (3)_____ meine Mutter krank ist.

PETRA: Ach, das tut mir leid. Möchtest du vielleicht später gehen, (4)_____ dein Vater zu Hause ist?

AXEL: Ich würde gerne, (5)_____ ich habe mich mit Tom verabredet (made plans), (6)_____ wir Tennis spielen wollen.

PETRA: Ach, so. Na, vielleicht morgen? Da können wir zusammen zu Mittag essen.

AXEL: Ach, Petra, ich kann nicht, (7)_____ ich morgen zusammen mit meiner Professorin essen will.

PETRA: Nun, also, du! Wann machen wir denn mal wieder etwas zusammen?

AXEL: Ich weiß es nicht, (8)_____ mach' mal einen Vorschlag!

Question words as subordinating conjunctions

In indirect questions, question words such as **wann**, **warum**, **was**, **wer**, **wie**, **wieviel**, and **wo** may also function as subordinating conjunctions. The verb appears at the end of the sentence or clause.

DIRECT QUESTION	INDIRECT QUESTION
Wieviel kostet das? *How much does that cost?*	Sie möchte wissen, **wieviel** das **kostet**. *She wants to know how much that costs.*
Was willst du kaufen? *What do you want to buy?*	Ich möchte wissen, **was** du kaufen **willst**. *I would like to know what you want to buy.*

Note that in an indirect question or in an indirect statement, the personal pronoun often changes.

DIRECT QUESTION	Helga fragt Karl: "Brauchst **du** einen Hut?" *Helga asks Karl, "Do you need a hat?"*
INDIRECT QUESTION	Helga fragt Karl, ob **er** einen Hut braucht. *Helga asks Karl whether he needs a hat.*
DIRECT STATEMENT	Karl sagt: "**Ich** brauche eine Mütze." *Karl says, "I need a cap."*
INDIRECT STATEMENT	Karl sagt, daß **er** eine Mütze braucht. *Karl says that he needs a cap.*

ALLES KLAR?

Ich bin neugierig (*curious*). Sie haben die folgenden Fragen gestellt, und jetzt habenSie die Antwort. Folgen Sie dem Beispiel. (*You have asked the following questions, and now you know the information. Follow the model.*)

> **BEISPIEL:** "Fritz, wann gehst du einkaufen?"
> —Ich weiß jetzt, wann Fritz einkaufen geht.

1. "Marianne, warum kaufst du dir einen Mantel?"
2. "Susanne und Stefanie, was macht ihr heute abend?"
3. "Herr Schiller, wer ist Ihr Arzt?"
4. "Klaus, wieviel hat deine Jacke gekostet?"
5. "Michael, wie geht es dir?"
6. "Sabine, wann hast du Geburtstag?"

weil / denn

Remember that **weil** is a subordinating conjunction that requires dependent word order, whereas **denn** is a coordinating conjunction that requires normal word order. There is no difference in meaning between the two conjunctions.

> Morgen gehe ich in die Stadt, **weil** ich einkaufen muß.
> Morgen gehe ich in die Stadt, **denn** ich muß einkaufen.
> *Tomorrow I'm going downtown because I have to go shopping.*

ALLES KLAR?

A. Sie tun es, weil/denn…. Bilden Sie neue Sätze. (*Form new sentences, substituting* **weil** *for* **denn** *or* **denn** *for* **weil**.)

1. Wir gehen ins Kino, denn wir wollen einen Film sehen.
2. Sie möchte lieber in die Bibliothek gehen, denn sie hat sehr viel Arbeit.
3. Wir gehen heute schwimmen, weil es so heiß ist.
4. Er macht eine Einkaufsliste, weil er sonst alles vergißt.
5. Morgen haben sie keine Zeit, denn sie müssen zur Universität.
6. Ich möchte nicht tanzen gehen, denn ich habe Kopfschmerzen.
7. Ihr könnt nicht den ganzen Tag Tennis spielen, denn ihr habt zu viel Arbeit.
8. Ich gehe nicht gern mit, weil ich ihn nicht mag.

 B. Ich tue es, weil/denn… Denken Sie an etwas, was Sie gern machen. Ihr Partner/Ihre Partnerin stellt Ihnen Fragen darüber. Sagen Sie, warum Sie es machen. (*Think of something you like to do. Your partner will ask why you do it; answer with a sentence that begins* **Ich tue es, weil…** *or* **Ich tue es, denn…**)

> **BEISPIELE:** —Warum spielst du jeden Tag Tennis?
> —Ich tue es, weil es mir Spaß macht.
>
> —Warum ißt du immer so viel?
> —Ich tue es, denn ich habe immer Hunger.

als / wann / wenn

The words **als**, **wann**, and **wenn** can all be used as subordinating conjunctions meaning *when*; however, they are not interchangeable.

als refers to a single event in the past; it is usually followed by the simple past tense.[1]

> Er hat angerufen, **als** du in der Stadt warst.

wenn is used mainly in the present or future, and may be translated as *when* or *if*.

> Ruf mich bitte an, **wenn** du ankommst.
> *Call me when you arrive.*

> **Wenn** ich eine Telefonnummer haben will, rufe ich die Auskunft an.
> *If I need a telephone number, I call information.*

wann is a question word.

> **Wann** kommt sie nach Hause?
> Ich weiß nicht, **wann** sie nach Hause kommt.

ALLES KLAR?

A. In der Drogerie. Ergänzen Sie mit **als, wenn** oder **wann.** (*Fill in the blanks with* **als,** **wenn** *or* **wann.**)

(1)_____ ich gestern in der Drogerie war, habe ich eine Zahnbürste gekauft. Jetzt habe ich keine Zahnpasta mehr, aber ich weiß nicht, (2)_____ die Drogerie wieder offen ist. (3)_____ sie morgen offen ist, kaufe ich mir auch Seife, denn das letzte Mal, (4)_____ ich auf einer Reise war, habe ich meine Seife verloren. (5)_____ die Drogerie endlich wieder offen, oder soll ich etwa alles im Supermarkt kaufen?

 B. Als ich/wenn ich/wann ich… Besprechen Sie mit einer Partnerin/einem Partner die folgenden Fragen. (*Discuss with a partner the following questions.*)

1. Wo hast du gewohnt, als du 10 Jahre alt warst?
2. Was machst du, wenn du Kopfschmerzen hast?
3. Weißt du, wann das Semester zu Ende ist?
4. Was ziehst du an, wenn es kalt ist?
5. Wie war das Leben, als deine Eltern noch jung waren?

---

[1]You have learned the simple past tense of the verb **sein**; the simple past of other verbs will be presented in **Kapitel 10.**

Schritt 5: Ein R-Gespräch

Gespräch

Worum geht es hier? Judy, eine Austauschstudentin[1] aus New Orleans, geht auf die Post und will ihre Eltern anrufen. Sie hat aber kein Geld. Was macht sie? Warum muß sie warten? Endlich spricht sie mit ihrer Mutter. Warum ist Judy so traurig? Was plant jetzt ihre Mutter?

BEAMTER[2]: Ja, bitte?

JUDY: Ich will Amerika anrufen, New Orleans in Louisiana.

BEAMTER: Sie können selbst durchwählen, wenn Sie in Telefonzelle zwei gehen.

JUDY: Nein, es ist nicht so einfach, denn ich habe kein Geld.

BEAMTER: Na, dann geht es nicht. Der nächste, bitte!

JUDY: Moment mal, bitte. Ich will, daß meine Eltern für den Anruf bezahlen. Kann ich das machen?

BEAMTER: Ach so, ja, natürlich. Das ist ein R-Gespräch. Sie müssen aber warten, denn alle Telefonzellen sind jetzt besetzt. Nehmen Sie bitte Platz. Ich sage Ihnen, wenn eine Telefonzelle frei wird.

JUDY: Danke schön!

BEAMTER: Bitte schön! Der nächste, bitte!

…fünf Minuten später

JUDY: Hallo, Mama!

FRAU SMITH: Ach, Judy, du bist es! Ach, wie schön, daß du anrufst. Wie geht es dir denn?

JUDY: Danke, es geht, aber ich bin so einsam. Ich hoffe, ihr kommt bald zu Besuch!?

FRAU SMITH: Ja, Judy, das ist so eine Sache. Im Frühling können wir nicht kommen, denn die Großmutter ist krank geworden, sehr krank.

JUDY: Was? Ihr kommt nicht? Ich habe mich so gefreut, daß ihr kommt. Ist sie denn wirklich so krank, daß ihr nicht kommen könnt? Du verstehst ja nicht, ich habe kein Geld. Ich habe gehofft, du bringst Geld mit.

FRAU SMITH: Tja, wir schicken dir nächste Woche mit der Post schon etwas Geld, aber im Frühling kommen wir nicht. Wir müssen zwei oder drei Monate bei der Großmutter bleiben, bis sie wieder gesund ist. Verstehst du? Aber vielleicht können wir im Juni kommen. Dann fahren wir eine Woche mit dem Auto nach Italien. Was meinst du dazu?

JUDY: Ja, das ist eine tolle Idee. Bis dann lerne ich jeden Tag fleißig für meine Kurse, damit ich im Juni Zeit habe. Tschüs! Und schönen Dank im voraus fürs Geld.

---

[1] *exchange student*
[2] *official*

ALLES KLAR?

A. Haben Sie verstanden?

1. Wo kommt Judy her?
2. Was will Judy auf der Post machen?
3. Warum gibt es ein Mißverständnis (*misunderstanding*)?
4. Wer soll für den Anruf bezahlen?
5. Warum muß Judy zuerst warten?
6. Was hat Judy von ihren Eltern erwartet (*expected*)?
7. Warum können die Eltern nicht kommen?
8. Welche Pläne hat die Mutter für den Besuch?

B. Am Telefon. Wählen Sie die richtigen Antworten zu den Fragen. (*Choose the word on the right that answers the question on the left.*)

1. Was wählt man?
2. Wo findet man die Telefonnummer für ein Lebensmittelgeschäft?
3. Was sagt man am Ende von einem Gespräch?
4. Wo findet man ein Telefon?
5. Ihr Freund wohnt in einer anderen Stadt. Was wählen Sie zuerst?
6. Was für ein Telefongespräch führt eine Person ohne Geld?

a. ein R-Gespräch
b. in einer Telefonzelle
c. die Vorwahl
d. Auf Wiederhören!
e. in den Gelben Seiten
f. die Telefonnummer

C. Besuch oder Geld? Besprechen Sie es mit einer Partnerin/einem Partner. (*Discuss the following questions with your partner.*)

1. Wie oft besuchen dich deine Eltern?
2. Warum kommen deine Eltern so selten (so oft) zu Besuch?
3. Wie oft möchtest du, daß deine Eltern kommen?
4. Schicken dir deine Eltern Geld? Wie oft?
5. Hast du schon einmal im Ausland (*abroad*) studiert?
6. Hat dich da jemand besucht?

Compound nouns

As you may have noticed, several nouns in the vocabulary of this chapter as well as previous chapters are compound nouns—that is, two or more words connected into one. Such compounds are more common in German than in English. These compounds are written as one word; the noun in the last position determines the gender of the whole compound.

> das Telefon + **die** Zelle = **die** Telefonzelle

Because **Zelle** is feminine, **Telefonzelle** is feminine.

> die Woche + **das** Ende = **das** Wochenende

Since **Ende** is neuter, the compound is neuter as well.

Compounds may include parts of speech other than nouns. Just as English has the words *grandmother* and *grandfather*, in which an adjective is combined with a noun, in German adjectives, verbs, prepositions, and numerals can join with nouns to form compounds. Again, the gender is always determined by the last noun in the grouping.

baden + **das** Zimmer = **das** Badezimmer
groß + **die** Mutter = **die** Großmutter

ALLES KLAR?

A. Der, die oder **das?** Wie ist der Artikel und die Bedeutung der folgenden zusammengesetzten Substantive? (*Give the gender and meaning of the following compound nouns.*)

1. Tischlampe
2. Klassenzimmer
3. Telefonbuch
4. Schreibtisch
5. Wohnungssuche
6. Nachttisch
7. Norddeutschland
8. Deutschlehrerin
9. Hausmann
10. Biergarten
11. Bücherregal
12. Musikfanatiker
13. Tagesarbeit

B. Geschäftsnamen. Sehen Sie sich die folgenden Geschäftsnamen an. Was für Geschäfte sind es? (*Read the compound nouns in the ads below. What kinds of businesses do you think they are?*)

C. **Zusammengesetzte Substantive.** Jede Gruppe (jeweils drei bis vier Personen) versucht, möglichst viele zusammengesetzte Substantive in diesem Buch zu finden. Die Gruppe, die die meisten zusammengesetzten Substantive in fünf Minuten findet, gewinnt das Spiel. (*In groups of three or four, find as many compound nouns as you can in this book. Those in this section don't count. The group that finds the most words within five minutes wins.*)

Word order: time-manner-place

In **Kapitel 4**, you learned about putting the means of transportation before the destination. What happens if there is also an element of time? When there are multiple elements in the sentence, the word order is always: Time-Manner-Place.

	T	**M**	**P**
Wir fahren	eine Woche	mit dem Auto	nach Italien.
Ich lerne	jeden Tag	fleißig	in meinem Zimmer.

All three elements are not always present. In that case, the rule still applies with the missing element simply omitted.

	T	**M**	**P**	
Wir schicken dir	nächste Woche	mit der Post	…	etwas Geld.
Wir müssen	zwei Monate	…	bei der Großmutter	bleiben.

Remember that if there are two or more expressions of time, the general time precedes the specific time:

> Ich trinke **jeden Tag um drei Uhr** einen Kaffee.

A. Wann, wie und wohin gehst du? Wählen Sie Elemente aus jeder Spalte und bilden Sie Sätze. (*Choose an element from each column to form correct sentences.*)

Ich	möchte	heute	nachmittag	mit dem Auto/Bus/Zug	nach Hause	gehen
	muß	morgen	abend	zu Fuß	ins Kino/Museum	fahren
	soll	Dienstag	um 6.00 Uhr	regelmäßig	in die Disco/Bibliothek	
	will	Sonntag	…	langsam	ins Café/Restaurant	
	…	nächste Woche		…	…	

B. Der Besuch bei der Mutter. Bilden Sie Sätze. Achten Sie auf die Wortstellung. (*Create sentences from the elements, paying attention to word order.*)

> **BEISPIEL:** wir / fahren / Sonntag / nach Frankfurt / um 7 Uhr / mit dem Schnellzug
>
> —Wir fahren Sonntag um 7 Uhr mit dem Schnellzug nach Frankfurt.

[handwritten: pronoun close to conjugated verb.]

1. ich / besuchen / meine Mutter / in Toronto / am Mittwoch
2. ich / fahren / mit dem Taxi / zum Flughafen / Dienstag abend
3. ich / ab•fliegen (*depart*) / um 6.40 Uhr / von San Francisco
4. meine Mutter / ab•holen / ich / in Toronto / um 11.50 Uhr / mit dem Auto
5. wir / gehen / in die Stadt / zu Fuß / am Abend

der- and *ein*-words: review and expansion

der-words

As you learned in **Kapitel 4**, the most common **der**-words are:

dieser	*this, that*
jeder	*each, every (singular only)*
welcher	*which*

Declension of the **der**-words:

	SINGULAR			PLURAL
	MASCULINE	**FEMININE**	**NEUTER**	**ALL GENDERS**
NOMINATIVE	welch**er**	welch**e**	welch**es**	welch**e**
ACCUSATIVE	welch**en**	welch**e**	welch**es**	welch**e**
DATIVE	welch**em**	welch**er**	welch**em**	welch**en**

Diese Telefonzelle ist besetzt.
This phone booth is occupied.

Nicht **jeder** Mantel ist so teuer.
Not every coat is so expensive.

Welches Sweatshirt meinen Sie?
Which sweatshirt do you mean?

Note that when a **der**-word appears in place of a noun, it takes the same ending as if the noun were present.

Welches Sweatshirt kostet 50- DM?	—**Jedes.**
Which sweatshirt costs 50 marks?	—*Every one.*
Welche Bluse gefällt dir besser?	—**Diese.**
Which blouse do you like better?	—*This one.*
Ich habe in diesem Zimmer gewohnt.	—**In welchem?**
I lived in this room.	—*In which one?*

ein-words

Remember that the **ein**-words include **kein**, plus all the possessive adjectives: **mein, dein, sein, ihr, unser, euer, Ihr.**

Declension of the **ein**-words:

	SINGULAR			PLURAL
	MASCULINE	**FEMININE**	**NEUTER**	**ALL GENDERS**
NOMINATIVE	mein	mein**e**	mein	mein**e**
ACCUSATIVE	mein**en**	mein**e**	mein	mein**e**
DATIVE	mein**em**	mein**er**	mein**em**	mein**en**

Ein-words may also take the place of a noun. In that case the nominative masculine singular adds -**er** and the nominative and accusative neuter singular add -**(e)s**.

Das ist mein Kamm. Hier ist **deiner**.   *That is my comb. Here is yours.*

Dieses Bild gefällt mir. Aber **sein(e)s**   *I like this picture. But his is nice, too.*
ist auch schön.

Another useful phrase in the **ein**-word category is the expression **was für ein** (*what kind of*). It can be used either as a question or as an exclamation. In this expression the word **für** does not function as an accusative preposition. Instead, the case of the word following **für** is determined by its role in the sentence.

Was für ein Computer ist das?	*What kind of a computer is that?*
In **was für** einer Gegend wohnst du?	*What kind of neighborhood do you live in?*
Mit **was für** Leuten sprichst du?	*What kind of people are you talking to?*
Was für einTag!	*What a day!*

ALLES KLAR?

A. Was hast du gern? Fragen Sie Ihren Partner/Ihre Partnerin, was er/sie schön findet. (*With a partner, take turns asking and answering questions about your preferences. Follow the model.*)

BEISPIEL: —Welche Lampe findest du schön?
—Ich finde diese Lampe schön.
—Warum?
—Sie ist neu und teuer.

1.

3.

2.

4.

B. Neue Kleidung nötig! David Dysert war während der Weihnachtsferien zu Hause. Auf dem Rückweg hat er einen Koffer voll neuer Kleidung verloren. Er ist jetzt wieder an der Uni und ruft seine Eltern an. Ergänzen Sie die Endungen, wo nötig. (*David Dysert was home during Christmas vacation. On the way back he lost a suitcase full of new clothing. He has arrived at the university and calls his parents. Fill in the blanks with the correct endings, as needed.*)

MUTTER: Dysert, guten Tag.

DAVID: Ach, Mutti, bist du das? David hier. Du glaubst nicht, was passiert ist. Ich habe im Zug ein_en_ Koffer (*suitcase*, m.) verloren. Er ist einfach weg (*gone*)! Ich muß sofort neue Sachen kaufen.

MUTTER: Hast du genug Geld? Wir können dir nur hundert Mark schicken. Wie ist das passiert? Welch_e_ Sachen waren in dem Koffer?

DAVID: Hundert Mark helfen schon, aber du weißt, wie teuer es hier ist. Was war im Koffer? Mein_e_ neu_e_ Hosen, mein_e_ neu_en_ Hemden. Jed_e_ Hose kostet etwa DM 70,00, und jed_es_ Hemd mindestens DM 40,00. Ich habe mein_en_ Mantel nicht verloren, mein_e_ Jacke auch nicht. Mein_e_ zwei Pullover sind allerdings auch weg. Was passiert ist, erzähle ich dir später. Es ist alles so schnell geschehen (*happened*).

MUTTER: Wie ist es mit dein_e_ Jeans und dein_em_ neu_en_ Sweatshirt? Hast du sie auch verloren?

DAVID: Ja, alles weg. Und mein_e_ Unterwäsche war auch in dem Koffer. Jed_es_ T-Shirt kostet auch um die DM 20,00.

MUTTER: Ja, ich weiß. Also, ich muß mit dein_en_ Vater sprechen. Vielleicht hat er auf sein_em_ Konto (*bank account*, neut.) noch etwas Geld, aber jetzt, gerade nach der Weihnachtszeit (*Christmas season*)…

DAVID: Ja, ja, ich verstehe, denn ich habe auch wenig Geld im Moment. Soll ich euch heute abend wieder anrufen?

MUTTER: Ja, mach' das, bitte. Bis dann!

DAVID: Tschüs, Mutti.

Die letzten Schritte

Wer macht mit?

Zusammenfassung

A. Wir wollten einkaufen, aber… Ergänzen Sie mit Wörtern von der Liste. (*Complete the sentences with a word chosen from the list below.*)

ob *whether*   weil *b/c*   denn   und *and*

wenn   bis   daß   wo

Am Samstag hat mein Freund Uwe angerufen. Er hat gefragt, (1)_ob_ ich nicht mit ihm einkaufen wollte.

UWE: Ich muß für meinen Großvater ein Geschenk kaufen, (2)_denn_ er hat morgen Geburtstag. Kommst du mit?

ICH: Nein, ich möchte nicht, (3)_weil_ du dich nie entscheiden (*decide*) kannst, (4)_ob_ du etwas kaufen sollst oder nicht.

UWE: Aber ich gehe so ungern allein, (5) _~~und~~ denn_ du bist doch ein sehr guter Freund.

ICH: Also, gut. Ich komme mit. Aber die nächste Frage ist, (6) _wo_ wir uns treffen.

UWE: An der Ecke von der Tannenstraße und der Marktstraße.

ICH: Gut. Aber wir müssen alles schnell erledigen (*take care of*), (7) _~~weil~~ denn_ ich muß um sechs Uhr schon wieder zu Hause sein.

UWE: Na, also so schnell geht es wohl nicht. Es ist ja schon halb drei (8) _und_ das sind nicht einmal vier Stunden.

ICH: (9) _Wenn_ wir uns nicht schnell entscheiden, ist schon wieder eine Stunde vorbei, (10) _bis_ wir uns treffen können.

UWE: Moment. Da ist jemand an der Tür. […] So, das ist meine Freundin, (11) _und_ sie möchte, (12) _daß_ wir zusammen essen gehen. Wir können also heute wohl nicht mehr einkaufen gehen, (13) _denn_ wir haben nicht genug Zeit. Ich muß also allein ein Geschenk für meinen Großvater aussuchen.

B. Bäckerei oder Bibliothek? Ergänzen Sie mit der passenden Konjunktion und schreiben Sie den ganzen Satz. (*Complete the sentences below by inserting an appropriate conjunction; then write out the complete clauses, using correct word order. You will use some words more than once.*)

wenn	und
daß	denn
weil	

1. _Weil_ / wir / haben / kein / Brot, muß ich heute noch zur Bäckerei. _Weil_
2. Ja, mach das, bitte. Ich gehe in die Bibliothek, _weil_ ich / müssen / einige / Bücher / holen. Die brauche ich für morgen.
3. Das heißt also, _daß_ du / mitkommen / zur / Bäckerei / nicht.
4. Das stimmt. Aber würdest du mir ein Brot mitbringen, _weil_ ich / haben / auch / kein Brot?
5. Warum kommst du nicht jetzt mit, _denn_ du / brauchen / Bücher / erst / morgen?
6. Das ist ein guter Vorschlag! Wir machen beides zusammen. Wir gehen zuerst zur Bäckerei _und_ dann / wir / gehen / beide / zur / Bibliothek.

C. Ich bin nicht daran schuld (*guilty*)! Wählen Sie eine Situation auf der Liste und schreiben Sie einen kurzen Brief an die genannte Person. Entschuldigen Sie sich. (*Choose a situation from the list and write a short letter to the person, making your excuses.*)

1. an Ihre Professorin: Sie haben eine Prüfung vergessen.
2. an Ihre Mutter: Sie haben ihren Geburtstag vergessen.
3. an Ihre Eltern: Sie haben Ihr ganzes Geld schon ausgegeben (*spent*).
4. an einen Freund: Sie haben vergessen, daß Sie mit ihm ausgehen sollten.

D. Der Einkaufsbummel. Beschreiben Sie einen Einkaufsbummel. Wer ist mitgegangen? Wo haben Sie eingekauft? Was haben Sie alles gekauft? Wieviel hat es gekostet? Waren Sie mit den Einkäufen zufrieden? (*Describe a recent shopping trip. Who went with you? Where did you shop? What did you buy? Who went with you? What did everything cost? Were you satisfied with your purchases?*)

A. **Bestandaufnahme** (*Inventory*). You and a colleague are taking inventory in a clothing store. Fill in the missing information on your inventory list by asking your colleague questions.

—Wie viele von den schwarzen Hemden haben wir?
—Wir haben 30. Und wieviel kosten sie?
—Sie kosten DM 29,90.

WIEVIELE?	KLEIDERSTÜCK?	FARBE?	PREIS?
20	Sweatshirts		28,90
	Jeans	blau	
35	Pullis	rot	35,-
25	Hemden		
20	Hemden	grün	24,90
	Mäntel	schwarz	75,-
10	Hosen	braun	49,50
	Hosen		55,-
15	Jacken	blau und schwarz	60,-
	Socken	weiß	
10	Kleider	purpur	65,-
	Handtaschen		34,50
50	T-Shirts		
15	Hüte	braun	45,-
	Blusen	weiß	
20	Röcke	grau	39,50
	Paar Schuhe	schwarz	59,90
	Anzüge	dunkelblau	199,50

B. Auskunft. You are the telephone operator and a customer calls you asking for help finding some telephone numbers. Using the information you have, give them what help you can.

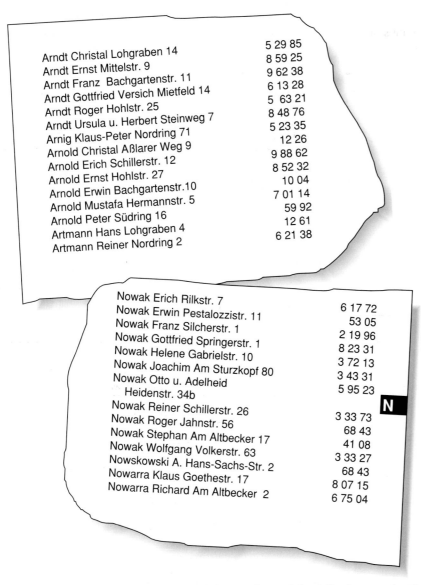

Arndt Christal Lohgraben 14	5 29 85
Arndt Ernst Mittelstr. 9	8 59 25
Arndt Franz Bachgartenstr. 11	9 62 38
Arndt Gottfried Versich Mietfeld 14	6 13 28
Arndt Roger Hohlstr. 25	5 63 21
Arndt Ursula u. Herbert Steinweg 7	8 48 76
Arnig Klaus-Peter Nordring 71	5 23 35
Arnold Christal Aßlarer Weg 9	12 26
Arnold Erich Schillerstr. 12	9 88 62
Arnold Ernst Hohlstr. 27	8 52 32
Arnold Erwin Bachgartenstr.10	10 04
Arnold Mustafa Hermannstr. 5	7 01 14
Arnold Peter Südring 16	59 92
Artmann Hans Lohgraben 4	12 61
Artmann Reiner Nordring 2	6 21 38

Nowak Erich Rilkstr. 7	6 17 72
Nowak Erwin Pestalozzistr. 11	53 05
Nowak Franz Silcherstr. 1	2 19 96
Nowak Gottfried Springerstr. 1	8 23 31
Nowak Helene Gabrielstr. 10	3 72 13
Nowak Joachim Am Sturzkopf 80	3 43 31
Nowak Otto u. Adelheid Heidenstr. 34b	5 95 23
Nowak Reiner Schillerstr. 26	3 33 73
Nowak Roger Jahnstr. 56	68 43
Nowak Stephan Am Altbecker 17	41 08
Nowak Wolfgang Volkerstr. 63	3 33 27
Nowskowski A. Hans-Sachs-Str. 2	68 43
Nowarra Klaus Goethestr. 17	8 07 15
Nowarra Richard Am Altbecker 2	6 75 04

Then switch roles. You call trying to find the numbers of the following people. If you don't have the complete address, get that too.

NAME	ADRESSE	TELEFONNUMMER
Ritter, Sandra	Hutstr. _____	_____
Risch	Jahnstr. ____	_____
Paul, Roland	Krämerstr. _____	_____

Zu zweit: Student 2

A. Bestandaufnahme (*Inventory*). You and a colleague are taking inventory in a clothing store. Fill in the missing information on your inventory list by asking your colleague questions.

BEISPIEL: —Wie viele von den schwarzen Hemden haben wir?
—Wir haben 30. Und wieviel kosten sie?
—Sie kosten DM 29,90.

WIEVIELE?	KLEIDERSTÜCK?	FARBE?	PREIS?
	Sweatshirts	grau	28,90
10	Jeans	blau	40,-
35	Pullis		
25	Hemden	weiß	30,-
	Hemden		24,90
8	Mäntel	schwarz	
	Hosen		49,50
15	Hosen	schwarz	55,-
15	Jacken		60,-
30	Socken	weiß	12,-
	Kleider	purpur	
15	Handtaschen	schwarz	34,50
50	T-Shirts	weiß mit rot	14,90
	Hüte	braun	
15	Blusen	weiß	25,-
	Röcke		39,50
30	Paar Schuhe	schwarz	
5	Anzüge		199,50

B. Auskunft. You call the operator asking for help in finding some telephone numbers. If you don't have the complete address, get that too. You are looking for the following people:

NAME	ADRESSE	TELEFONNUMMER
Arndt, Roger	Hohlstr. _____	_____
Arnold	Bachgartenstr._____	_____
Nowak, Helene	_____	_____

Rippi Hans-Jürgen Wellstr. 14	7 24 43
Rippi Hermann Im Winkel	69 23
Rippschläger Reginald Ludwigstr. 11	3 52 67
Risch Johann Jahnstr. 41	8 45 45
Risch Karl Heinz Ludwigstr. 24	2 65 23
Rischa Marian Weingartenstr. 26	7 58 66
Rischa Sonya Holbeinstr. 22	7 81 33
Rischa Thomas Holbeinstr. 22	7 81 56
Rischer Bernd Hutstr. 22	8 81 09
Rischer Uwe Krämerstr. 7	9 76 30
Rissiling Regina Goethestr. 2	94 14
Ritschanek H. Hansepfad 5	7 44 53
Ritter Bernd Ludwigstr. 7	58 96
Ritter Elfriede Uhlandstr. 25	7 12 67
Ritter Josef Volkerstr. 14	7 18 55
Ritter Karl An der Kirche 6	7 43 47
Ritter Regina Hutstr. 29	7 43 78
Ritter Roland Uhlandstr.17	2 91 04
Ritter Sandra Hutstr. 26	6 41 34
Ritter Stephan Holbeinstr. 22	8 11 41
Rittinger Wolfgang An der Kirche 2	7 22 40

Paul Andreas Hutstr. 7	6 44 00
Paul Anton Uhlandstr. 19	7 42 33
Paul Hermann An der Kirche 3	11 38
Paul Michael Dr. phil. Lampengraben 6	3 70 54
Paul Robert Holbeinstr. 13	8 61 56
Paul Roland Krämerstr.	3 67 20
Paul Sabina Im Winkel	2 65 38
Paul Sandra Volkerstr. 7	7 52 85
Paulaner Thomas Ludwigstr. 23	4 54 21
Pauler Marian Hutstr.19	4 95 32
Pauler Michael Wellstr. 3	5 36 87
Pauler Wolff Im Winkel 7	2 14 02

Then switch roles. You are the operator, trying to to help a customer find some telephone numbers. Using the information you have, give what help you can.

Situationen

 A. Entschuldigung! With a partner, prepare at least two excuses for each of the following situations.

1. A person of the opposite sex wants you to go shopping.
2. A person of the same sex wants you to go to a movie.
3. Your instructor asks you to rewrite a paper (**das Referat**).
4. Someone who has bad table manners asks whether you are on your way to the cafeteria (**die Mensa**).
5. A friend asks you to help with moving (**umziehen**) on Saturday.
6. Your parents don't have much money, but you need $100.00.
7. Your mother (or father) wants you to clean up your room.
8. Someone that you don't like asks you to dance.

B. Die Einladung.

STUDENT 1

You want to go to a concert (**das Konzert**) on Friday evening. Call and invite a friend. You have asked four people already, and are getting desperate for someone to go with you. If your friend is hesitant, suggest doing something before or after (such as dinner or dessert) that you know the friend will enjoy.

STUDENT 2

Your friend calls you and invites you to a concert. Be sure to ask what musicians/kind of music is on the program (**wer spielt/was für Musik spielt man?**). You are not particularly enthusiastic about the music, but you have nothing better to do on Friday night. Try to negotiate doing something additional that you like more.

C. Einkaufen.

STUDENT 1

You are the salesperson in a department store and haven't sold much today. You try to persuade your customer (your partner) to buy the item that she/he is considering. Discuss price (**das kostet nur ____ DM; das ist nicht teuer**), color (**die Farbe steht Ihnen gut** [*looks good on you*]), etc.

STUDENT 2

You are shopping for new clothing. You are not happy with what the salesperson is showing you (**es ist zu klein/groß, es ist zu teuer; die Qualität ist nicht gut; ich brauche kein- ____, die Farbe paßt nicht zu _____**). See whether you can get him/her to show you something in a different color (**Haben Sie etwas in braun?**), price (**Ich möchte nur DM 20,- ausgeben** [*spend*]), or size (**Haben Sie etwas in Größe 36?**).

Tip!

Here are some equivalent German clothing sizes:

WOMEN'S CLOTHING

US	6	8	10
	12	14	16
German	34	36	38
	40	42	44

MEN'S CLOTHING

US	36	38	40
	42	44	46
German	46	48	50
	52	54	56

Themenwortschatz

Substantive / Nouns

Substantive	Nouns
die Apotheke, -n	pharmacy
In der Drogerie	***In the drugstore***
das Deo, -s (das Deodorant)	deodorant
die Drogerie, -n	drugstore
der Kamm, ̈e	comb
die Seife, -n	soap
das Shampoo, -s	shampoo
die Zahnbürste, -n	toothbrush
die Zahnpasta	toothpaste

Kleidung	***Clothing***
der Anzug, ̈e	suit
die Bluse, -n	blouse
die Handtasche, -n	purse, handbag
das Hemd, -en	shirt
die Hose, -n	pants
der Hut, ̈e	hat
die Jacke, -n	jacket
die Jeans (pl.)	jeans
das Kleid, -er	dress
die Kleidung -en	clothing
der Mantel, ̈	coat
die Mütze, -n	cap
der Pullover (der Pulli)	pullover
der Rock, ̈e	skirt
der Schuh, -e	shoe
die Socke, -n	socks
das Sweatshirt, -s	sweatshirt
das T-Shirt, -s	T-shirt
die Unterwäsche (pl.)	underwear

Telefonanruf	***Telephone call***
der Anruf, -e	call
die Auskunft, ̈e	information
die Entschuldigung, -en	excuse
das R-Gespräch, -e	collect call
das Telefonbuch, ̈er	telephone book
das Telefongespräch, -e	telephone conversation
die Telefonzelle, -n	telephone booth
die Vorwahl, -en	area code

Verben / Verbs

Verben	Verbs
an•probieren	to try on
dauern	to take (time), last
durch•wählen	to dial direct
ein•kaufen	to shop
tragen (trägt), getragen	to wear; to carry
treffen (trifft), getroffen	to meet
verschieben, verschoben	to move up (in time), postpone
(etwas) vor•haben	to have (something) planned
vor•schlagen (schlägt vor), vorgeschlagen	to suggest
wählen	to dial; to choose

Adjektive/Adverbien / Adjectives/Adverbs

besetzt	busy, occupied

Nebenordnende Konjunktionen / Subordinating Conjunctions

als	when
bevor	before
bis	until
da-	that
damit	so that
daß	that
nachdem	after
ob	if, whether
obwohl	although, even though
weil	because
wenn	when, whenever

Ausdrücke / Expressions

Auf Wiederhören.	Good-bye. (on the phone)
die gelben Seiten (pl.)	yellow pages
Herzlichen Dank.	Thank you very much.
Sie sind falsch verbunden.	You have the wrong number.
Was für…	What kind of… ? (pl.)
Was für ein…	What kind of a… ? (sg.)
Sonst noch etwas?	Anything else?

Weiterer Wortschatz

Substantive / Nouns

die Einkaufsliste, -n	shopping list
die Einladung, -en	invitation
der Erfolg, -e	success
der Grund, ̈e	reason
der Pfennig, -e	penny
der Spaziergang (̈e)	walk, stroll
der Termin (e)	date, appointment
die Überraschung, -en	surprise
der Wald, ̈er	forest

Verben / Verbs

sich erinnern an (+ acc.)	to remember, recall
sich freuen auf (+acc.)	to look forward to
hoffen *gehofft*	to hope
lassen (läßt), gelassen	to leave; to let
schicken	to send
vergessen (vergißt), vergessen	to forget
versprechen (verspricht), versprochen	to promise
versuchen	to try

Adjektive/Adverbien / Adjectives/Adverbs

einfach	simple
einsam	lonely
erfolgreich	successful
nun	well, well now, well then, (flavoring particle)
sicher	sure
wenig, wenige	little (quantity), few
zuerst	at first

Ausdrücke / Expressions

einen Spaziergang machen	to take a walk
Leider geht das nicht.	Unfortunately that's impossible.
Was gibt's denn?	What's up?

Laß mich in Ruhe – leave me alone

Guten Appetit

Kommunikation

- Purchasing food
- Discussing food and beverage preferences
- Understanding and using the metric system expressions
- Ordering in a restaurant
- Comparing different items to each other

Strukturen

- Comparative and superlative of adjectives and adverbs
- Adjective endings: review/unpreceded adjectives
- Demonstrative pronouns: nominative, accusative, dative

Kultur

- Grocery shopping in Germany
- Restaurant etiquette
- Meals in German-speaking countries
- Traditional and ethnic foods

Kapitel 9

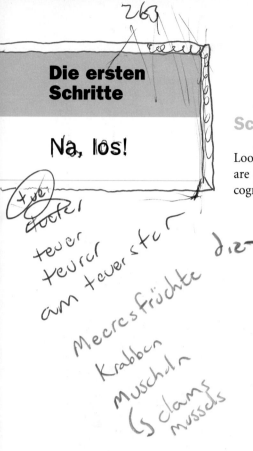

Die ersten Schritte

Na, los!

[handwritten notes:]
teuer
teurer
am teuersten

Meeresfrüchte die
Krabben
Muscheln
(← clams mussels)

- Ich mache das
  lieber als das
- Ich spiele gern Baseball
- Ich spiele lieber Squash
- Ich spiele am liebsten
  Tennis

Schritt 1: Wo kauft man diese Lebensmittel?

Look at the list of items below; some of the words are already familiar to you, while others are cognates that can be easily guessed.

das Bier, -e
die Butter
das Cola, -s
der Fisch, -e
der Joghurt
der Kaffee, -s
die Margarine
das Mineralwasser
der Pfeffer
das Salz
der Tee
der Wein, -e

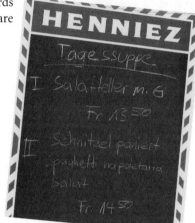

das Brot, -e	*bread*
das Brötchen, -	*roll*
das Ei, -er	*egg*
das Fleisch	*meat*
das Hähnchen	*chicken*
der Käse	*cheese*
der Kuchen, -	*cake*
der Saft, ¨e	*juice*
das Schnitzel	*cutlet*
der Senf	*mustard*
die Wurst, ¨e	*sausage*
das Würstchen,	*hot dog, frankfurter*
der Zucker	*sugar*

ALLES KLAR?

 A. In der Bäckerei, im Lebensmittelgeschäft oder in der Metzgerei? Schauen (*look*) Sie sich die Liste oben an. Fragen Sie Ihre Partnerin/Ihren Partner, wo man die Sachen kaufen kann.

> **BEISPIEL:** —Wo kann man Margarine kaufen?
> —Margarine kann man im Lebensmittelgeschäft kaufen.

B. Kombinationen. Besprechen Sie mit Ihrem Partner/Ihrer Partnerin, welche Kombinationen Sie gern essen oder trinken.

> **BEISPIELE:** —Ich esse gern Brot mit Butter.
> —Ja, ich auch.
>
> —Ich esse gern Wurst mit Senf.
> —Ich esse Wurst lieber ohne Senf.

Schritt 2: **Auf dem Markt**

Germans do their food shopping not only in a **Lebensmittelgeschäft** or a **Supermarkt**, but sometimes in an open-air market (**der Markt**) as well, where they find fresh fruit (**Obst**) and vegetables (**Gemüse**).

1. **der Apfel,** ⸚   apple
2. **die Banane, -n**   banana
3. **die Birne, -n**   pear
4. **der Blumenkohl**   cauliflower
5. **die grüne Bohne, -n**   green bean
6. **die Erbse, -n**   pea
7. **die Erdbeere, -n**   strawberry
8. **die Karotte, -n**   carrot
9. **die Kartoffel, -n**   potato
10. **die Kirsche, -n**   cherry
11. **die Orange, -n**   orange
12. **der Salat**   lettuce, salad
13. **die Tomate, -n**   tomato
14. **die Zwiebel, -n**   onion

south

Erdapfel

Apfelsine

A. Obst und Gemüse. Fragen Sie Ihren Partner/Ihre Partnerin:

—Was für Obst ißt du gern? im Winter? im Sommer?
—Was für Gemüse ißt du (nicht) gern?
—Was hast du als Kind nicht gern gegessen? Ißt du es jetzt gern?

B. Das Grillfest (*barbecue*). Sie haben Freunde zu einem Grillfest eingeladen. Diskutieren Sie mit Ihrem Zimmerkameraden/Ihrer Zimmerkameradin das Essen. Was müssen Sie alles kaufen? Machen Sie eine Einkaufsliste. Auf der Liste steht vielleicht:

Gemüse   Backwaren (*bakery goods*)
Obst   Getränke (*beverages*)
Fleisch

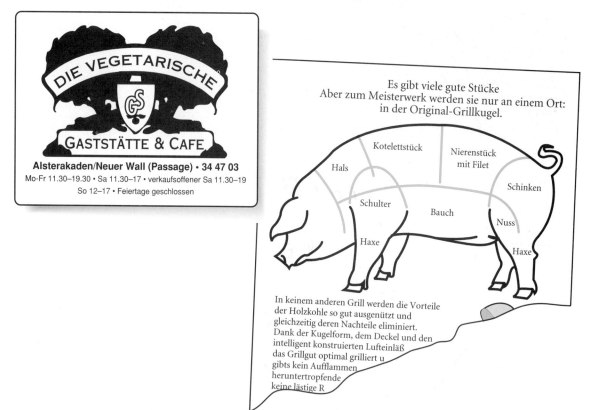

Wer kauft was? Vergessen Sie nicht, manche Freunde sind Vegetarier/ Vegetarierinnen (*vegetarians*)!

BEISPIELE: —Ich meine, wir sollen Würste grillen. Ich kaufe sie bei der Metzgerei.
—Brötchen müssen wir auch haben. Ich gehe zur Bäckerei.

Germans tend to shop more often for fresh foods than do Americans, because there are fewer convenience foods available and because refrigerators are usually small. Frequently a "family" refrigerator is the same size as that of a college student in a dorm room. Until rather recently, there were relatively few supermarkets in Germany — instead, people shopped at the corner-store or the "mom-and-pop" store **(Tante-Emma Laden)** and at specialty shops, i.e., a different one each for canned goods, vegetables, cheese, fresh meat, seafood, etc. People today frequently purchase greater amounts of produce at one time than they did before, in part because they can now select their own fruits and vegetables. (Formerly customers were usually not permitted to handle the produce themselves. This is still the case in some areas.) In addition, residents of German-speaking countries have long been more ecologically conscious than Americans, taking their shopping bags **(Einkaufstüten)** to the grocery store with them each time; if they do not bring their own, customers frequently have to pay for each shopping bag.

Obst & Gemüse

Noch mehr vom Bauern aus der Nachbarschaft!

Deutsche Johannis-beeren	**Deutscher Kohlrabi**	**Deutsche Karotten**
Klasse I, volles Aroma 500 g Schale **2.99**	Klasse I, große Köpfe Stück **-.99**	mit Grün, Klasse I aus der Pfalz Bund **-.99**

Schritt 3: **Wie schmeckt's?**

1. sauer

2. süß

3. salzig

4. scharf

5. lecker

6. saftig

7. bitter

ALLES KLAR?

A. Wie ist...? Beschreiben Sie das Essen und die Getränke von Ihrer Liste in **Aufgabe B, Schritt 2**.

> BEISPIELE: Das Cola ist süß.
> Der Senf ist scharf.

B. Wie schmeckt's? Sie sitzen in der Mensa (*university cafeteria*) mit Freunden. Fragen Sie, was jeder ißt und wie es schmeckt.

> BEISPIELE: —Was ißt du?
> — Ich esse...
> —Und wie ist die Suppe?
> —Sie ist leider zu salzig.

Schritt 4: **Das metrische System**

When shopping anywhere in Europe, you will find that weights and volume are determined by the metric system. It is a simple and useful system to learn.

WEIGHT

das Kilo (gramm) (kg)	= 1000 Gramm (g) (approximately 2.2 lbs.)
ein halbes Kilo (½ kg)	= 500 g (approx. 1.1 lbs)
das Pfund	= 500 g
ein halbes Pfund (½ Pfund)	= 250 g
ein Viertelpfund (¼ Pfund)	= 25 g

VOLUME

der Liter (l)	= 2.1 pints (1.1 quarts)
ein halber Liter (½ l)	= 1.05 pints
ein Viertelliter (¼ l)	= .525 pint (approximately 1 cup)

ALLES KLAR?

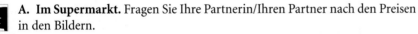

A. Im Supermarkt. Fragen Sie Ihre Partnerin/Ihren Partner nach den Preisen in den Bildern.

BEISPIEL: —Wieviel kostet ein Kilo Nektarinen?
—Ein Kilo Nektarinen kostet...

Südmilch
Joghurt
Original
3.5% 200g
-.59
Joghurt
Original
200g

Frisches Rumpsteak,
zart und mager,
100g
2,28

"Switzerland" Emmentaler,
45% Fett i, Tr. oder "Galbani"
Ital. Gorgonzola 50%
Fett i. Tr., 100g
1,49

Grillweißwurst
10 x 100 g,
SB-verpackt, 1kg
8.90

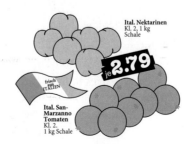

Ital. Nektarinen
Kl. 2, 1 kg
Schale
je 2.79

frisch
aus
ITALIEN

Ital. San-
Marzanno
Tomaten
Kl. 2.
1 kg Schale

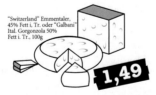

B. Bei der Tankstelle. Fragen Sie nach Benzinpreisen in Deutschland, in Europa, und in den USA.

BEISPIELE: —Was kostet ein Liter Diesel in Deutschland?
—In Deutschland kostet ein Liter Diesel eine Mark acht...
—Was kostet ein Liter Super bleifrei hier?
—Hier kostet ein Liter Super bleifrei ...

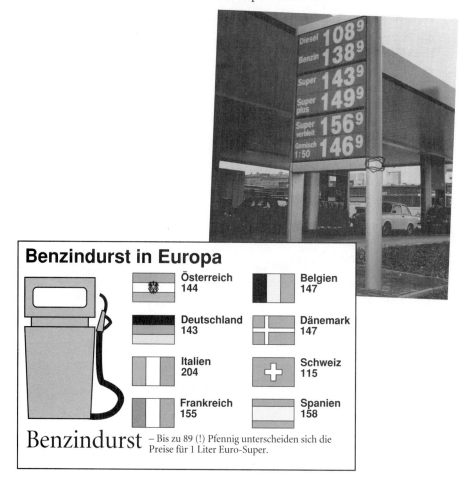

Benzindurst in Europa

	Österreich 144		Belgien 147
	Deutschland 143		Dänemark 147
	Italien 204		Schweiz 115
	Frankreich 155		Spanien 158

Benzindurst – Bis zu 89 (!) Pfennig unterscheiden sich die Preise für 1 Liter Euro-Super.

> *Versuch's mal!* Die *kn-* und *pf-*Laute

Die Speisekarte

Wir empfehlen:

- Pfefferkornsuppe mit Schinkenknochen und Knoblauch
- Pfannkuchen mit frischen Pflaumen
- Hasenpfeffer in der Pfanne
- Kuchen mit feinen Pfirsichen und knusprigen Äpfeln
- Pfefferminz-Tee mit Pfeffernüßen

Schritt 5: **Zum Mittagessen im Restaurant** *Schöne Aussicht*[1]

((🔊)) **Gespräch**

Worum geht es hier? Irina möchte ihren Freund, Jack, aus Amerika, zum Mittagessen einladen. Sie stehen vor dem Restaurant *Schöne Aussicht* und studieren die Speisekarte. Was gibt es? Was sollen sie essen und trinken?

IRINA: Dieses Restaurant ist doch besser als der kleine Imbiß in der Kaiserstraße. Findest du nicht auch?

JACK: Ja, natürlich ist es besser als der Imbiß. Es ist aber auch teurer. Du hast nicht soviel Geld.

IRINA: Aber heute wollen wir einmal wirklich gut essen! Sieh mal, diese schöne Speisekarte. Forelle[2] ist die Spezialität des Hauses[3].

[Sie gehen ins Restaurant.]

IRINA: Geh voraus[4], Jack. In Deutschland geht der Mann immer zuerst ins Restaurant.

JACK: Komisch! Das habe ich nicht gewußt. Andere Länder, andere Sitten[5]!

IRINA: Sieh mal, der Tisch hier auf der Terasse ist noch frei. Den Tisch nehmen wir. Warum sitzt du nicht hier, da ist die Aussicht am schönsten.

JACK: Danke! Was kannst du mir denn empfehlen?

IRINA: Die Spezialität von diesem Restaurant! Hier in Deutschland ißt man sehr oft frische Forelle. Es gibt Forelle *blau* und Forelle *nach Müllerin Art*.

JACK: Was ist denn das? Ich weiß natürlich, was Forellen sind.

IRINA: *Blau* ist gekocht und *nach Müllerin Art* ist gebraten. Ich kann beide empfehlen. Aber vielleicht möchtest du keinen Fisch. Schnitzel ist hier auch nicht schlecht.

JACK: Nein! Forelle mag ich. Was gibt es denn dazu?

IRINA: Gekochte Kartoffeln oder Pommes frites und Salat. Zu den gekochten Kartoffeln und der Forelle *blau* gibt es Butter, zerlassen[6] natürlich.

JACK: Ich möchte Forelle *blau*.

IRINA: Das schmeckt dir bestimmt. Das nehme ich auch. Möchtest du zuerst noch eine Suppe? Die Ochsenschwanzsuppe[7] schmeckt besonders gut.

JACK: Nein, danke! Ich möchte lieber Nachtisch.

IRINA: Herr Ober! Wir möchten gern bestellen.

---

[1]*view*
[2]*trout*
[3]*speciality of the house*

[4]*ahead*
[5]*Other countries, other customs!*
[6]*melted*

[7]*oxtail soup*

ALLES KLAR?

A. Haben Sie verstanden?

1. Wer lädt wen ein?
2. Wie heißt das Restaurant?
3. Was ist besser als der Imbiß?
4. Warum geht Jack vor Irina ins Restaurant?
5. Was sagt Irina zu Jack, nachdem sie einen schönen Tisch gefunden haben?
6. Was ist die Spezialität des Hauses?
7. Was ist Forelle *blau*?
8. Was ist Forelle *nach Müllerin Art*?
9. Was gibt es zu der Forelle?
10. Was gibt es in diesem Restaurant auch?
11. Was möchte Jack lieber *(rather)* als Suppe?
l2. Was sagt Irina zu dem Ober?

B. Persönliche Fragen.

1. Essen Sie gern aus? Wo?
2. Wie oft essen Sie aus?
3. Essen Sie lieber Nachtisch als Suppe?
4. Was bestellen Sie oft in einem Restaurant?
5. Mit wem gehen Sie normalerweise ins Restaurant?

C. "Herr Ober, was empfehlen Sie?" Sie sind der Ober. Ihre zwei Partner oder Partnerinnen sind Gäste in diesem Restaurant. Empfehlen Sie ihnen, was hier gut ist.

BEISPIEL: —Was empfehlen Sie denn heute?
—Was essen Sie gerne? Heute ist besonders gut die Forelle blau. Aber auch das Schnitzel mit Salat kann ich empfehlen.
—Ist die Forelle frisch?...

Table manners in Austria, Germany, and Switzerland are generally more formal than in North America. Before starting to eat, everyone wishes each other **Guten Appetit!**, to which one responds **Danke, gleichfalls**. Tap water is not served with meals, nor found on the table in restaurants; usually juice, mineral water, wine, or beer is offered. If wine or beer is served, people toast each other by saying **Pros(i)t!** or **Zum Wohl!**

In restaurants, people do not hesitate to share a table with strangers if there is no other one available. They ask **Ist hier noch frei?** before sitting down. Diners do not attempt to converse with the person they have joined, however; rather, each person or group maintains its privacy.

One asks for the bill in a restaurant by saying **Zahlen, bitte,** or **Ich möchte zahlen**. In the German-speaking countries the tip (**das Trinkgeld**) is added automatically to the bill. In recent years it has become customary to round up the amount to the next even figure.

```
***************RECHNUNG************

STEAK-RESTAURANT

DATUM : 17.08.96/21:15
KELLNER : GABRIELE KöHLER
L.Nr/RE.Nr. 16/144
PLATZ : 6
    1 Mineralwasser        3,60
    1 Steak (rosa)        16,90
    1 Salat-Beilage        5,00
    1 Folie-Kartoffel      5,00
------------------------------------
Total :                   30,50
====================================
MwSt      15.0%

Rechnungsbetrag               DM

Es bediente Sie
Herr Rumpel

    Bitte, nur den angegebenen
    Betrag zahlen. Zahlen Sie
    bitte an der Kasse.

Baden-Baden ** Hauptstraße 27
```

Comparative and superlative of adjectives and adverbs

Until now you have been using adjectives and adverbs in their basic, or *positive* form; in this chapter you will learn to make comparisons by using the *comparative* and the *superlative*. In English, the comparative and superlative are formed as follows:

POSITIVE:	*big*	*expensive*
COMPARATIVE:	*bigger*	*more expensive*
SUPERLATIVE:	*biggest*	*most expensive*

The comparative

In German, the comparative of adjectives and adverbs is normally formed by adding **-er** to the positive form:

billig	billig**er**
schlecht	schlecht**er**
schnell	schnell**er**

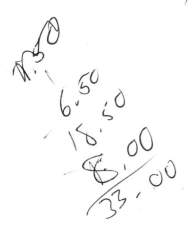

With some one-syllable adjectives and adverbs, an **umlaut** is added. The most common of these are:

alt/jung	älter/jünger
kalt/warm	kälter/wärmer
kurz/lang	kürzer/länger
groß	größer
hart	härter
krank	kränker
oft	öfter

Adjectives that end in **-er** or **-el** usually drop that **-e** in the comparative:

teuer	teurer
sauer	saurer
dunkel	dunkler

Attributive adjectives—that is, adjectives that precede a noun—add the usual adjective endings in the comparative. These endings appear *after* the comparative **-er** ending. Predicate adjectives and adverbs do not take an additional ending after the comparative.

Das billige**r**e Restaurant gefällt mir nicht.
I don't like the cheaper restaurant.

Dieses Restaurant ist billiger.
This restaurant is cheaper.

Eine schöne**r**e Aussicht gibt es nicht!
There couldn't be a more beautiful view!

Die Aussicht gestern war schöner.
The view yesterday was more beautiful.

If unequal items are compared, the comparative + **als** is used:

Der Imbiß ist **billiger als** das Restaurant.
The snack bar is cheaper than the restaurant.

Die Birne ist **süßer als** der Apfel.
The pear is sweeter than the apple.

If equal items are compared, **so** + positive + **wie** is used:

Der Imbiß ist **so teuer wie** das Restaurant.
The snack bar is as expensive as the restaurant.

Gemüse ist nicht **so teuer wie** Fleisch.
Vegetables are not as expensive as meat.

To express a progressive increase, **immer** + comparative is used:

Das Essen in diesem Restaurant wird **immer schlechter**.
The food in this restaurant is getting worse and worse.

ALLES KLAR?

A. Aber dieser ist… Sie kaufen mit Ihrer Zimmerkameradin/Ihrem Zimmerkameraden ein. Alles, was sie/er findet, ist besser. Folgen Sie dem Beispiel.

> **BEISPIEL:** Fleisch — billig
> —Das Fleisch ist billig.
> —Aber dieses Fleisch ist noch billiger.

1. Apfel — reif
2. Brot — frisch
3. Senf — scharf
4. Bier — dunkel
5. Kirschen — saftig
6. Erdbeeren — lecker

B. Wie ist die Beziehung *(relationship)*? Was können Sie über die Beziehung von den Wörtern sagen? Benutzen Sie die Adjektive. Sie können manche mehr als einmal benutzen.

gesund	süß	salzig	teuer	billig
groß	klein	bitter	schnell	

[handwritten: Kaffee ist äu billig als tee]

> **BEISPIEL:** Wasser — Wein
> Wasser ist gesünder[1] als Wein.

1. Butter — Margarine
2. Fisch — Fleisch
3. Kaffee — Tee
4. Cola — Bier
5. Banane — Apfel
6. Würstchen — Schweinebraten
7. Spezialgeschäft — Kaufhaus
8. Bäckerei — Metzgerei
9. Hotel — Motel
10. Restaurant — Imbiß

C. Es ist nicht so… Jetzt erklären Sie die Beziehungen in Aufgabe B im Negativ: nicht so… wie.

> **BEISPIEL:** Wein ist nicht so gesund wie Wasser.

D. Ins Restaurant. Ergänzen Sie mit dem Komparativ.

[handwritten: Immer (+) comparitive is (ers) more + more]

> **BEISPIEL:** Ich nehme die (reif) _____ Äpfel.
> —Ich nehme die reiferen Äpfel.

Wir gehen heute nicht zu dem (klein)_er en_ und (billig)_eren_ Imbiß, sondern in das (groß) _ex et_ und (teuer)_ere_ Restaurant. Das Restaurant hat eine (schön) _ere_ Aussicht, und das Essen ist (lecker) _lecker_

E. Pessimist. Antworten Sie pessimistisch auf die Fragen.

> **BEISPIEL:** Ist das Fleisch teuer?
> —Das Fleisch wird immer teurer!

1. Ist der Joghurt sauer?
2. Ist der Tee bitter?
3. Sind die Portionen klein?
4. Ist der Imbiß billig (teuer)?
5. Sind wir alt?

---

[1]The umlaut on the comparative and superlative of **gesund** is optional. The umlauted form is slightly more common.

The superlative

1. **Adjectives.** The superlative of adjectives is usually formed by adding -**(e)st**- to the positive form:

billig	billig**st**-
schön	schön**st**-
schnell	schnell**st**-

Adjectives ending in -**d**, -**t**, -**ß**, or -**z** add an -**e**- before the -**st**- to facilitate pronunciation:

intelligent	intelligent**est**-

As in the comparative, the stem vowel in most common single-syllable adjectives is umlauted:

alt	**ä**lt**est**-
kalt	**kä**lt**est**-
warm	**wä**rm**st**-

Superlative adjectives that precede a noun add the usual adjective endings.

Wir essen immer in dem billigsten Restaurant.
We always eat in the cheapest restaurant.

Die Imbißstube serviert den frischesten Salat.
The fast-food restaurant serves the freshest salad.

2. **Adverbs.** The superlative of adverbs is formed by using the structure **am ___ -(e)sten.**

Diese Kellnerin arbeitet **am schnellsten.**	*This waitress works the fastest.*
Meine Mutter kocht **am schlechtesten.**	*My mother cooks the worst.*

Note that predicate adjectives may use either the ending -**(st)**-, or the **am ___ -(e)sten** construction.

Dieses Restaurant ist das teuerste.
Dieses Restaurant ist am teuersten. } *This restaurant is the most expensive.*

ALLES KLAR?

A. Nicht das beste Restaurant. Ergänzen Sie mit dem Superlativ.

Wenn wir ausessen, bestellen wir immer das (schön) _____ Essen, aber wir essen immer in den (billig) _____ Restaurants. Wir sitzen immer an dem (schlecht) _____ Tisch. Die (alt) _____ Dame ist immer unsere Kellnerin, und der (langsam) _____ Koch macht unser Essen. Wir bekommen immer den (alt) _____ Fisch und die (klein) _____ Portionen. Nach dem Essen bekommen wir den (bitter) _____ Kaffee. Am Ende sind wir immer die (deprimiert [*depressed*]) _____ Kunden!

B. Wer macht was wie? Wer von Ihrer Familie oder Bekannten macht etwas am schlechtesten/schnellsten/langsamsten, usw.? Wählen Sie ein Wort aus jeder Liste und bilden Sie Sätze im Superlativ.

> **BEISPIELE:** —Mein Bruder fährt am wildesten.
>
> —Meine Freundin kocht am schlechtesten.

fahren	wild
Basketball spielen	schnell
Ski laufen	langsam
kochen	schlecht
Tennis spielen	fleißig
laufen	verrückt
schwimmen	schön
essen	ruhig
sprechen	
...	

Irregular forms

Like English, German has a few very common adjectives and adverbs that are irregular in the comparative and superlative.

gut, besser, am besten	*good, better, best*
hoch, höher, am höchsten	*high, higher, highest*
nah, näher, am nächsten	*near, nearer, nearest*
viel, mehr, am meisten	*much/many, more, most*

Ich habe **viel** Kuchen gegessen, aber du hast noch **mehr** Kuchen gegessen als ich. Peter hat **den meisten** Kuchen gegessen.

I ate a lot of cake, but you ate even more cake than I did.
Peter ate the most cake.

The adverb **gern** is also irregular: **gern, lieber, am liebsten.**

Ich koche gern, aber meine Mutter kocht lieber als ich. Aber mein Vater kocht am liebsten.

I like to cook, but my mother likes to cook more than I.
But my father likes to cook most of all.

ALLES KLAR?

A. Wo sollen wir essen? Schreiben Sie den Absatz noch einmal, aber benutzen Sie den Komparativ für alle Adjektive.

Das Restaurant *Cordon Bleu* ist nah, aber die Preise sind hoch. Das Essen ist aber gut und die große Auswahl (*selection*) von Fisch- und Fleischgerichten (*dishes*) ist fantastisch. Die guten Weine sollen wir auch probieren.

B. Jetzt im Superlativ! Schreiben Sie den Absatz noch einmal, aber benutzen Sie den Superlativ für alle Adjektive.

C. gern/lieber/am liebsten. Fragen Sie Ihre Partnerin/Ihren Partner.

1. Kochst du gern? Kocht deine Mutter lieber? Wer in deiner Familie kocht am liebsten?
2. Wer von deinen Freunden hört am liebsten klassische Musik?
3. Wer ißt am liebsten chinesisch? mexikanisch? italienisch?
4. Putzt dein Zimmerkamerad/deine Zimmerkameradin lieber als du?
5. Was trinkst du lieber — Kaffee oder Tee?
6. Was ißt du am liebsten?

Schritt 6: **Die Einkaufsliste**

Lesestück

Worum geht es hier? Was kochen Sie, wenn Gäste komen? Spielt es eine Rolle, wer die Gäste sind? Andere Studenten? Ihre Eltern? Ihre Professoren? Was tut Frau Ostrowska? Was plant sie? Für wen kocht sie was? Wer soll ihr helfen? Was braucht Frau Ostrowska? Was macht Herr Ostrowski sonst noch in der Stadt?

Frau Ostrowska überlegt sich, was sie braucht. Heute kommt die ganze Familie Zielinski zum Abendessen. Andrei Zielinski ißt gern Fleisch, Elena Zielinska ißt lieber Fisch, die Kinder, Jan und Maria Elida, essen natürlich am liebsten Würstchen und Pommes frites. Frau Ostrowska hat heute keine Zeit zum Einkaufen[1], aber ihr Mann kann das für sie machen. Damit Herr Ostrowski nichts vergißt, macht Frau Ostrowska ihrem Mann eine lange Einkaufsliste:

> Einkaufsliste
>
> vier Brötchen und Brot
> 200 g Wurst, ein Pfund Schweinefleisch
> zwei Pfund frischen Fisch (Hering/Forelle?)
> einen Liter Milch
> 125 g Butter
> ein Stück Schweizer Käse
> sechs Eier
> 250 g Margarine
>
> vier Joghurt
> Obst: Äpfel, Birnen und vielleicht Orangen
> Gemüse: reife Tomaten, Salat und Kartoffeln
> 250 g Zucker
> Pfeffer
> eine Flasche Mineralwasser
> eine Flasche Wein

Um zehn Uhr fährt Herr Ostrowski mit seinem alten Auto in die Stadt. Der Supermarkt ist schon seit acht Uhr geöffnet. Natürlich kann er alles im großen Supermarkt kaufen, aber er geht lieber zuerst zur Bäckerei, dann zur Metzgerei und dann zum Lebensmittelgeschäft. Das macht ihm mehr Spaß. Er hat ja Zeit. Bevor er wieder nach Hause fährt, geht er ins Café und trinkt einen türkischen Kaffee. Ach ja, er muß auch noch tanken; auf dem Weg nach Hause ist eine Tankstelle.

---

[1]**Einkaufen**, here a noun, is derived from the verb **einkaufen** and corresponds to English *shopping*. You will learn about infinitives used as nouns in **Kapital 13**.

Tip!

Masculine and neuter nouns that indicate weight, measure, or number are always used in the singular in German; feminine nouns are plural. There is no preposition *of*, as there is in English.

ein Glas Bier
a glass of beer

zwei Pfund Fisch
two pounds of fish

drei Flaschen Mineralwasser
three bottles of mineral water

In the US, most people have their biggest meal in the evening; in German-speaking countries and most other European countries, the noontime meal is the largest and most substantial. It is the "hot" meal, whereas the evening meal generally consists of sandwiches or other cold foods; for that reason it is called **das Abendbrot.** The noon meal is called **das Mittagessen**, while the first meal is known as **das Frühstück.** Breakfast is not generally the large meal it frequently is in the US (e.g., eggs or cereal and toast), but is frequently a "continental" breakfast, consisting of rolls or bread, juice, and coffee. In many offices, Germans also have a second breakfast (**ein zweites Frühstück**) at around 10:30 or 11:00 a.m., particularly as 1:00 is the general time for the noon meal. These customs, however, frequently reflect the old way of living; in modern times (e.g., the last ten to fifteen years), more and more people have a large meal in the evening, in part because the wife now works and no longer stays home to prepare the noon meal.

ALLES KLAR?

A. Haben Sie verstanden?

1. Warum plant Frau Ostrowska ein Abendessen?
2. Was ist das Problem mit den Gästen?
3. Warum geht Herr Ostrowski einkaufen?
4. Was für Fisch soll Herr Ostrowski kaufen?
5. Warum kauft er nicht im Supermarkt ein?
6. Was muß er auf dem Weg nach Hause machen?

B. Persönliche Fragen!

1. Machen Sie eine Einkaufsliste, bevor Sie einkaufen? Warum?
2. Fahren Sie normalerweise mit dem Bus oder mit Ihrem Wagen in die Stadt?
3. Fahren Sie lieber allein oder mit einem Freund/einer Freundin einkaufen? Warum?
4. Gehen Sie normalerweise zum Supermarkt oder gehen Sie lieber zur Bäckerei, Metzgerei und zum Lebensmittelgeschäft? Warum?
5. Wann und wie oft kaufen Sie ein?
6. Gehen Sie, nachdem sie eingekauft haben, manchmal in ein Café und bestellen Kaffee und Kuchen?
7. Was müssen Sie manchmal auch noch machen?

Adjective endings: review/unpreceded adjectives

In **Kapitel 6,** you were introduced to adjective endings. Following is a brief summary of adjective endings after **der-** words (**dies-, jed-, manch-, welch-**) and **ein-**words (all possessive adjectives [**mein, dein, sein,** etc.], **kein,** and **was für ein**).

Remember that descriptive adjectives always take endings; they must agree with the number, gender, and case of the noun described by the adjective.

Adjective endings following **der-**words:

	MASCULINE	FEMININE	NEUTER	PLURAL
NOMINATIVE	-e	-e	-e	-en
ACCUSATIVE	-en	-e	-e	-en
DATIVE	-en	-en	-en	-en

Adjective endings following **ein-**words:

	MASCULINE	FEMININE	NEUTER	PLURAL
NOMINATIVE	-er	-e	-es	-en
ACCUSATIVE	-en	-e	-es	-en
DATIVE	-en	-en	-en	-en

Unpreceded adjectives

If an attributive adjective is not preceded by a **der-** or **ein-** word (i.e. fresh bread, ripe tomatoes), then the endings on the adjective must demonstrate gender, number, and case. Therefore they are very similar to the **der-** words themselves:

	MASCULINE	FEMININE	NEUTER	PLURAL
NOMINATIVE	-er	-e	-es	-e
ACCUSATIVE	-en	-e	-es	-e
DATIVE	-em	-er	-em	-en

NOMINATIVE MASCULINE:	Frisch**er** Fisch schmeckt am besten.
ACCUSATIVE NEUTER:	Er trinkt nur dunkl**es** Bier.
DATIVE PLURAL:	Sie kocht immer mit reif**en** Tomaten.

As with preceded adjectives, all unpreceded attributive adjectives in a row have the same ending:

Ich esse nur frisch**es**, knuspri**ges**, dunkl**es** Brot.
I only eat fresh, crispy, dark bread.

ALLES KLAR?

A. Herr und Frau Kamarenko. Ergänzen Sie die Adjektivendungen.

Herr und Frau Kamarenko essen oft im Restaurant, aber sie gehen nur in billig**__** Restaurants, denn sie haben nicht viel Geld. Herr Kamarenko bestellt immer gegrillt**__** Fleisch oder gebraten**__** Fisch. Gekocht**__** Gemüse ißt er nicht gern. Frau Kamarenka ist Vegetarierin und ißt nur frisch**__**, roh**__** Gemüse, sauer**__** Joghurt und hausgemacht**__** Brot.

DIE VEGETARISCHE

GS

GASTSTÄTTE & CAFE

Alsterakaden/Neuer Wall (Passage) • 34 47 03
Mo-Fr 11.30–19.30 • Sa 11.30–17 • verkaufsoffener Sa 11.30–19
So 12–17 • Feiertage geschlossen

B. Ich esse/trinke nur ... Wählen Sie ein Adjektiv und ein Substantiv.

BEISPIELE:
—Ich esse nur gegrillten Fisch.
—Ich trinke nur frische Milch.

bitter	Salat
gut	Kaffee
billig	Schokolade
teuer	Milch
frisch	Joghurt
alkoholfrei	Fleisch
gebraten	Brot
gegrillt	Fisch
roh	Gemüse
saftig	Schweinefleisch
salzig	Wein
sauer	Bier
süß	...
scharf	
...	

C. Wieder beim Mittagessen. Sehen Sie sich das Gespräch in **Schritt 5 Zum Mittagessen im Restaurant** *Schöne Aussicht* noch einmal an, und setzen Sie Adjektive ein, wo möglich.

BEISPIEL: Zum guten Mittagessen im teuren Restaurant Schöne Aussicht.

D. Wenn Sie im Restaurant essen... Fragen Sie Ihren Partner/Ihre Partnerin:

1. Bestellst du den gegrillten oder den gebratenen Fisch?
2. Bestellst du einen teuren oder einen billigen Wein? einen süßen oder einen trockenen?
3. Ißt du lieber gekochtes oder rohes Gemüse?
4. Nimmst du den scharfen oder den milden Käse?
5. Ißt du kleine oder große Portionen?

Schritt 7: **Der Imbiß**

Worum geht es hier? Es ist halb zwölf; Boris und Sergei sind zum Einkaufen in der Stadt. Sie sehen eine Imbißstube und Boris sagt, daß er schon wieder Hunger hat. Was sollen sie jetzt essen?

> **BORIS:** Wir haben erst vor drei Stunden gefrühstückt, und ich habe schon wieder großen Hunger.
>
> **SERGEI:** Ja, ich auch. Warum essen wir nicht schnell ein gegrilltes Würstchen?
>
> **BORIS:** Ich habe auch Durst. Sollen wir nicht auch ein schönes kaltes Bier trinken? Würstchen schmecken immer am besten mit einem Bier.

[Sie gehen zu einem Imbiß an der Straßenecke und bestellen.]

> **SERGEI:** Ich nehme ein Würstchen und ein Pils, bitte.
>
> **BORIS:** Das nehme ich auch. [zum Kellner] Für mich dasselbe, bitte.

[einen Moment später]

> **SERGEI:** Hier ist schon unser Bier. Bitte, für dich und für mich. Also, Prost!
>
> **BORIS:** Zum Wohl!
>
> **SERGEI:** Da sind auch schon unsere gegrillten Würstchen. Das hier sieht etwas größer aus; das kannst du haben.
>
> **BORIS:** Danke! Guten Appetit!
>
> **SERGEI:** Gleichfalls! Möchtest du etwas Senf? Den hier mag ich besonders gern, der ist wirklich scharf.
>
> **BORIS:** Ja, bitte. Hier sind auch Servietten[1]. Die ist für dich.
>
> **SERGEI:** Aber am besten beeilen wir uns, denn wir müssen um halb zwei an der Uni sein.

---

[1]*napkins*

Alles klar?

A.. Haben Sie verstanden?

1. Was möchten Sergei und Boris essen und trinken?
2. Was bestellen sie?
3. Wer bekommt die größere Wurst?
4. Warum mag Sergei den Senf?
5. Wann müssen sie wieder an der Uni sein?

B. Persönliche Fragen!

1. Was essen Sie gern zu Mittag/zu Abend?
2. Was trinken Sie lieber, wenn Sie Durst haben? Einen Saft oder ein Bier?
3. Wo essen Sie am liebsten? In einem Restaurant oder zu Hause?
4. Wie ist das Essen in Ihrem Lieblingsrestaurant (*favorite restaurant*)? Ist es billig oder teuer?
5. Was ist die Spezialität des Hauses?
6. Essen Sie gern chinesisch? italienisch? indisch?
7. Wie oft essen Sie in Ihrem Studentenwohnheim/an der Universität? Gibt es dort einen Imbiß? Wie heißt er?
8. Wo ist das Essen besser, in Ihrem Studentenwohnheim, zu Hause oder an der Universität? Was gibt es dort zu essen?

C. Was denkst du? Sprechen Sie mit einer Partnerin/einem Partner über die Restaurants in der Nähe. Vielleicht stimmen Sie überein, vielleicht nicht.

BEISPIEL: —Das neue Restaurant in der Kaiserstraße ist wirklich gut.
               —Nein, ich finde es nicht so gut wie das Restaurant in der Alpenstraße. Es ist zu teuer, und das Essen schmeckt mir nicht.

MÖGLICHE THEMEN

das Restaurant (teuer / billig)
das Essen (zu salzig / nie warm / sehr gut / furchtbar / ...)
die Atmospähre (zu laut / zu dunkel / romantisch / gemütlich *[cozy]* / ...)
Am liebsten esse ich ...

Kulturnotiz: Traditional and ethnic foods

The cuisines of Austria, Germany, and Switzerland have certain characteristic foods that have become famous the world over. For instance, **Sauerbraten** and **Sauerkraut** are immediately associated with Germany, while **Sachertorte** is distinctly Austrian, and **Fondue** is typically eaten in Switzerland. Nevertheless, ethnic foods are becoming more and more popular in the German-speaking countries, many of them introduced by Turkish, Yugoslavian or Italian guest workers.

Demonstrative pronouns: nominative, accusative, dative

As you learned in **Kapitel 2**, demonstrative pronouns are simply the definite articles (forms of **der, die, das**) used with no following noun. They emphasize a person or a thing to which reference has previously been made. Often they occur at the beginning of a sentence. The gender and number of demonstrative pronouns is determined by the noun to which they refer. The case is determined by the way they are used in the sentence.

	NOMINATIVE
MASCULINE	(Möchtest du den Senf?) Nein danke, **der** ist zu scharf.
FEMININE	(Kocht ihre Mutter gut?) Ja, **die** kocht sehr gut.
NEUTER	(Wie ist das Restaurant *Schöne Aussicht*?) **Das** ist wirklich gut.
PLURAL	(Kommen deine Kinder?) Ja, **die** kommen zum Abendessen.

	ACCUSATIVE
MASCULINE	(Möchten Sie den Käse?) Nein, **den** mag ich nicht.
FEMININE	(Haben Sie die Wurst in der Metzgerei gekauft?) Ja, **die** kaufe ich immer dort.
NEUTER	(Wie ist das Restaurant?) **Das** finde ich besonders gut.
PLURAL	(Hast du die zwei Brötchen gegessen?) Natürlich habe ich **die** gegessen.

Dative demonstrative pronouns are less common, but they follow the same pattern:

(Hast du dem neuen Koch geholfen?) Ja, **dem** habe ich geholfen.

ALLES KLAR?

A. Im Imbiß. Sehen Sie sich das Gespräch, **Der Imbiß,** wieder an. Unterstreichen *(underline)* Sie alle Demonstrativpronomen.

 B. Können Sie das empfehlen? Sie arbeiten in einem Supermarkt. Beantworten Sie die Fragen von Ihrem Partner/Ihrer Partnerin.

BEISPIELE: —Wie ist der Käse?
—Der ist heute sehr schön.

1. Wie sind die Würstchen?
2. Wie ist der Salat heute?
3. Können Sie den Hering empfehlen?
4. Wie ist dieses Mineralwasser? Das
5. Empfehlen Sie diesen Wein? Den
6. Wie finden Sie diesen Käse? Den
7. Wie ist das Bier im Sonderangebot *(on sale)*?
8. Mögen Sie dieses Brot? Das
9. Ist die Butter sehr salzig? Die
10. Haben Sie auch billigeren Kaffee? Den
11. Wie ist dieser neue Joghurt? Den

Zusammenfassung

A. Unsere Pläne. Ergänzen Sie.

Morgen gehen wir mit unseren (gut)_en_ Freunden zu dem neu_en_ Imbiß am Adenauerplatz. Der soll (gut)_besser_ sein als das klein_er_ Restaurant "Kaiser." Aber nicht nur (gut)_besser_, sondern auch billig_er_ soll er sein. Die Würstchen mit Brot sind dort natürlich am (gut)_besten_. Sie sind dort nicht _so_ scharf_wie_ im "Kaiser." Aber auch Sauerkraut mit Kartoffeln und Würstchen sollen dort so gut_wie_ im "Kaiser" sein. Es gibt dort auch das (gut)_beste_ Bier in der Stadt. Wir essen am liebsten mit unseren alt_en_ Freunden und Freundinnen zusammen. Die kennen Bier (gut)_besser_ und trinken (viel)_mehr_ als wir. Nachdem wir beim Imbiß gegessen haben, gehen wir ins Kino. Das Kino ist in der Nähe. Wir wollen uns einen amerikanisch_en_ Film ansehen. Ich habe vergessen, wie er heißt. Wir sehen uns (gern)_lieber_ amerikanische Filme an als deutsche, denn deutsch_e_ Filme finden wir nicht so interessant_e_ amerikanisch_e_ Filme. Nach dem Kino gehen wir dann in eine klein_e_ Disco an der Ecke Adenauerplatz und Königstraße, denn wir tanzen alle gern. Dort ist die Musik am (gut)_besten_.

B. Was essen Sie? Schreiben Sie einen kurzen Absatz. Beschreiben Sie, was Sie normalerweise essen und trinken. Sie können die folgenden Fragen benutzen, aber Sie müssen nicht alle beantworten. Benutzen Sie Adjektive, wenn möglich.

> Was essen und trinken Sie zum Frühstück? zum Mittagessen? zum Abendessen?
> Um wieviel Uhr essen Sie normalerweise zu Mittag?/zu Abend?
> Mit wem essen Sie normalerweise?
> Können Sie gut kochen?
> Was kochen Sie gern?
> Was essen Sie gern?
> Was trinken Sie gern?
> Was kaufen Sie jede Woche?
> Wo kaufen Sie Ihre Lebensmittel?
> Wie heißt Ihr Lieblingsrestaurant? Was für Essen gibt es dort?

C. Was haben Sie gegessen? Was haben Sie in den letzten drei Tagen gegessen und getrunken? Machen Sie eine Liste. Dann schreiben Sie einen kurzen Absatz und erklären Sie, was sie gern/am liebsten gegessen oder getrunken haben. Was haben Sie nicht gern gegessen oder getrunken? Warum?

 **Zu zweit: Student 1**

A. In der Mensa. Below is a menu from the student cafeteria in Osnabrück. Compare information with your partner to complete the blank spaces in the menu.

> **BEISPIELE:** —Was serviert man Montag als Hauptspeise (*main dish*)?
> —Man serviert...
> —Wieviel kostet die Suppe am Mittwoch?
> —Die Suppe kostet...

	Suppe	DM	**Hauptspeise**	DM	**Beilagen**	DM	**Nachtisch**	DM
MO	franz. Zwiebelsuppe vegetarisch	0,20	ungarisches Bohnengoulasch vegetarisch Schweinebraten	1,20 1,80	Kartoffel-Püree Blumenkohl mit Sauce Hollandaise	0,20 0,50		0,30 Tages-preis
DI		0,20	Bratkarotten in Pfeffersauce vegetarisch Gegrilltes Forellenfilet mit Sauce Tartar	1,50 1,80	Nudeln gemischter Salat	0,20 0,30	Karamellpudding Obst	0,30 Tages-preis
MI	Erbsensuppe	0,20	Indische Reispfanne vegetarisch Paniertes Schweinekotelett mit Champignonrahmsauce	1,50 1,90	Curry-Reis grüner Salat	0,20 0,30	Kiwiquark Obst	
DO	Hühnersuppe		Rösti vegetarisch Rahmgeschnetzeltes mit Champignons	1,50 1,90		0,20 0,50	Eisbuffet	0,80
FR	Tomatensuppe vegetarisch	0,20	Linseneintopf vegetarisch Putenbrustfilet mit Zwiebelsauce			0,30 0,40		0,30 Tages-preis

Außerdem jeden Tag: Montag–Freitag: GROSSES SALATBUFFET, POMMES FRITES mit Majo/Ketchup

B. Im Eiscafé. You are a new employee in an ice-cream parlour. Ask a colleague how to make the various sundaes and how much you should charge the customers. Make notes on the chart so that you don't forget the information.

> **BEISPIELE:** —Tisch Nummer 3 hat einen Erdbeerbecher (*sundae*) bestellt. Wie mache ich den?
> —Ein Erdbeerbecher hat 3 Kugeln (*scoops*) Erdbeereis, Erdbeersoße und Sahne (*whipped cream*).
> —Und wieviel kostet ein Erdbeerbecher?
> —Der kostet DM 6,00.

TISCH NR.	EISBECHER	BESCHREIBUNG	PREIS
6	Bananensplit		
9	Dama Bianca		
4	Nußknacker		
5	Amarettobecher		
1	Eis-Mohr		

Zu zweit: **Student 2**

A. In der Mensa. Below is a menu from the student cafeteria in Osnabrück. Compare information with your partner to complete the blank spaces in the menu.

BEISPIELE: —Was serviert man Montag als Hauptspeise (*main dish*)?
—Man serviert...
—Wieviel kostet die Suppe am Mittwoch?
—Die Suppe kostet...

	Suppe	DM	Hauptspeise	DM	Beilagen	DM	Nachtisch	DM
MO	franz. Zwiebelsuppe vegetarisch			1,20 1,80		0,20 0,50	Vanillepudding mit Schokoladen-sauce Obst	0,30 Tages-preis
DI	Bohnensuppe vegetarisch	0,20	Bratkarotten in Pfeffersauce vegetarisch Gegrilltes Forellenfilet mit Sauce Tartar		Nudeln gemischter Salat	0,20 0,30	Karamellpudding Obst	
MI	Erbsensuppe	0,20		1,50 1,90		0,20 0,30	Kiwiquark Obst	0,50 Tages-preis
DO	Hühnersuppe	0,20	Rösti vegetarisch Rahmgeschnetzeltes mit Champignons	1,50 1,90	Petersilienkartoffeln Rosenkohl mit Butter	0,20 0,50	Eisbuffet	0,80
FR		0,20	Linseneintopf vegetarisch Putenbrustfilet mit Zwiebelsauce	1,40 1,80	Spätzle grüne Bohnen	0,30 0,40	Schokopudding Obst	0,30 Tages-preis

Außerdem jeden Tag: Montag–Freitag: GROSSES SALATBUFFET, POMMES FRITES mit Majo/Ketchup

B. Im Eiscafé. You are training a new employee in the ice-cream parlour where you work. When asked, tell the trainee what goes into the sundaes and how much they cost.

BEISPIELE: —Tisch Nummer 3 hat einen Erdbeerbecher (*sundae*) bestellt. Wie mache ich den?
—Ein Erdbeerbecher hat 3 Kugeln (*scoops*) Erdbeereis, Erdbeersoße und Sahne (*whipped cream*).
—Und wieviel kostet ein Erdbeerbecher?
—Der kostet DM 6,00.

Eisbecher	Beschreibung	Preis
Erdbeerbecher	3 Kugeln Erdbeereis, Erdbeersoße und Sahne	**6,00**
Bananensplit	2 Kugeln Vanille, Sahne, Schokosoße und Banane	**7,00**
Dama Bianca	3 Kugeln Vanille, Eierlikör (egg liqueur), Mandeln (almonds), Sahne	**8,50**
Amarettobecher	Schokoladeneis, Walnußeis, Vanilleneis, Amaretto, Sahne	**8,50**
Eis-Mohr	3 Kugeln Schoko, Bailey's, Sahne	**8,50**
Nußknacker	2 Kugeln Walnußeis, 1 Schoko, Sahne, Schokosoße	**6,00**

Situationen

A. Möchtest du heute ausessen? Call and invite a friend to dinner. Find out what that friend's favorite restaurant/kind of food is, and make suggestions on where to go.

B. Im türkischen Restaurant. You and a friend are eating in a Turkish restaurant. Look at the menu below and discuss what you would like to eat. Order, thank the server for the food, and comment on your meal. A few of the items are explained below.

die Aubergine	*eggplant*
das Hackfleisch	*ground beef*
der Mürbeteig	*filo dough*
das Fleischklößchen	*meatball*
die Bulette	*hamburger*

Preisliste

DÖNER KEBAP	(Pita-Brot mit gebratenem Fleisch, Salat, Tomaten, Zwiebeln)	**3,50 DM**
PATLICAN KEBAP	(gebratene Aubergine mit Fleisch)	**5,50 DM**
LAHMACUN	(dünne Pizza — aber ohne Tomatensoße — mit Hackfleisch und Zwiebeln)	**2,— DM**
TÜRK. PIZZA	mit SALAT	**2,50 DM**
BÖREK	(Mürbeteig) mit KÄSE oder FLEISCH	**2,00 DM**
1/2 HÄNCHEN		**4,30 DM**
KÖFTE	(Fleischklößchen)	**5,— DM**
TÜRK. BULETTEN	im BROT mit SALAT	**5,50 DM**
KETCHUP • MAJO		**–,30 DM**

C. Unser Restaurant. You and a friend want to open a restaurant. Discuss what you will have on the menu under the following categories: **Salate, Hauptspeisen, Nachtisch, Getränke**. What will be the specialty of the house? How much will you charge for each dish?

D. Alles geht schief. You and a friend are eating in a restaurant and nothing goes right. Enact the situation with your friend and the server.

MÖGLICHE PROBLEME
Der Kellner/die Kellnerin ist zu unfreundlich.
Sie bekommen nicht das, was Sie bestellt haben.
Das Essen ist kalt.
Sie finden ein Haar in Ihrer Suppe.
Sie haben Ihr Geld vergessen.

Überall spricht man Deutsch

German in Eastern Europe

The role of German in eastern Europe is most likely the (indirect) result of an 18th century ruling by Joseph II of the Austro-Hungarian empire that German was to be the official language for all territories under Austrian control. Only after World War II did this change, as Russian replaced German. Since 1989, however, German is reclaiming its former position in Eastern Europe. German represents for these countries a tie to "the West," especially in terms of business and economics, and German culture continues to play a role in Eastern Europe. In addition, many eastern European countries have a large German-speaking minority within their boundaries, e.g. the former Soviet Union, the Czech and Slovak Republics, Hungary, Poland, Romania, and others.

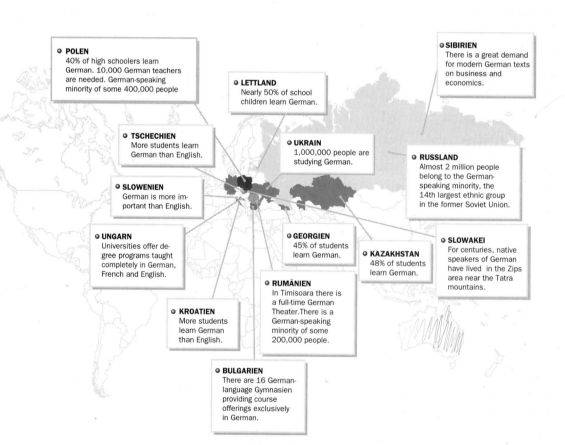

POLEN
40% of high schoolers learn German. 10,000 German teachers are needed. German-speaking minority of some 400,000 people

SIBIRIEN
There is a great demand for modern German texts on business and economics.

LETTLAND
Nearly 50% of school children learn German.

TSCHECHIEN
More students learn German than English.

UKRAIN
1,000,000 people are studying German.

RUSSLAND
Almost 2 million people belong to the German-speaking minority, the 14th largest ethnic group in the former Soviet Union.

SLOWENIEN
German is more important than English.

UNGARN
Universities offer degree programs taught completely in German, French and English.

GEORGIEN
45% of students learn German.

KAZAKHSTAN
48% of students learn German.

SLOWAKEI
For centuries, native speakers of German have lived in the Zips area near the Tatra mountains.

RUMÄNIEN
In Timisoara there is a full-time German Theater. There is a German-speaking minority of some 200,000 people.

KROATIEN
More students learn German than English.

BULGARIEN
There are 16 German-language Gymnasien providing course offerings exclusively in German.

Themenwortschatz

Substantive

Das Essen

die Butter	butter
das Ei, -er	egg
das Eis	ice-cream; ice
das Essen	meal
der Fisch, -e	fish
das Fleisch	meat
das Hähnchen, -	chicken
der Joghurt	yoghurt
der Käse	cheese
die Margarine	margarine
der Pfeffer	pepper
die Pommes frites (pl.)	French fries
das Rindfleisch	beef
der Saft, -̈e	juice
das Salz	salt
das Schnitzel, -	veal or pork cutlet
das Schweinefleisch	pork
der Schweizer Käse	Swiss cheese
der Senf	mustard
die Suppe, -n	soup
die Wurst, -̈e	sausage
das Würstchen, -	hot dog, frankfurter
der Zucker	sugar

Getränke

das Bier	beer
die Cola, -s	coca cola
das Getränk, -e	beverage, drink
der Kaffee	coffee
die Milch	milk
das Mineralwasser, -	mineral water
der Tee, -s	tea
das Wasser	water

Obst und Gemüse

der Apfel, -̈	apple
die Banane, -n	banana
die Birne, -n	pear
der Blumenkohl	cauliflower
die Bohne, -n	bean
die Erbse, -n	pea
die Erdbeere, -n	strawberry
das Gemüse (sg.)	vegetables
die Karotte, -en	carrot
die Kartoffel, -n	potato
die Kirsche, -n	cherry
das Obst (sg.)	fruit
die Orange, -n	orange
der Salat, -e	salad; lettuce
die Zwiebel, -n	onion

Backwaren

das Brot, -e	bread
das Brötchen, -	roll
der Kuchen, -	cake

Beim Einkaufdas

Kilogramm	kilogram [approx.. 2.2 lbs.]
die Lebensmittel (pl.)	groceries
der Liter	liter, quart [approx. 1 quart]
der Markt, -̈e	open-air market
das Pfund, -e	pound [approx. 1.1 lb]
der Supermarkt, -̈e	supermarket
das Stück, -e	piece

Mahlzeiten

das Abendbrot	} evening meal, supper
das Abendessen, -	
das Frühstück	breakfast
das Mittagessen, -	lunch
der Nachtisch	dessert

Im Restaurant

die Imbißstube, -n or der Imbiß, -sse	snack bar
der Ober, -	[male] waiter
die Oberin, -nen	[female] waiter
der Preis, -e	price
die Speisekarte, -n	menu
das Trinkgeld, -er	tip

Verben

aus•essen (ißt), ausgegessen	to eat out
bestellen	to order
ein•laden (lädt ein), eingeladen	to invite

Adjektive/Adverbien

bitter	*bitter*
durstig	*thirsty*
frisch	*fresh*
gar	*done; tender*
gebraten	*fried*
gegrillt	*grilled*
gekocht	*cooked; boiled*
hungrig	*hungry*
lecker	*tasty, delicious*
reif	*ripe*
roh	*raw*
saftig	*juicy*
salzig	*salty*
sauer	*sour*
scharf	*spicy, hot*
süß	*sweet*

Ausdrücke

Guten Appetit! Mahlzeit! }	*Enjoy your meal!*
(Danke,) gleichfalls!	*Thanks, same to you!*
(keinen) großen Hunger haben	*to be (not) very hungry*
(keinen) großen Durst haben	*to be (not) very thirsty*
Pros(i)t!	*Cheers!*
Zum Wohl!	*To your health!*

Weiterer Wortschatz

Substantive

die Tankstelle, -n	*gas station*

Verben

tanken	*to buy gasoline*
sich beeilen	*to hurry*
sich überlegen	*to think about; ponder*

Adjektive/Adverbien

besonders	*especially*
erst	*only, just*
geöffnet	*open*
geschlossen	*closed*
hart (ä)	*hard*
komisch	*funny*
nah (ä)	*close, near*
natürlich	*of course*
oft (ö)	*often*
sonst	*otherwise, besides*
stark (ä)	*strong*

Deutschland und Europa

Germany and Its Neighbors

Der Fall der Berliner Mauer im Jahr 1989, die deutsche Einheit [*unification*], Minderheiten [*minorities*] und die "Europäische Union" (EU) sind die Themen der folgenden Leitseiten.

1. Europa im Internet: EU Leitseiten und Links
Web pages of the "European Union" and its members.
http://www.uni-mannheim.de/users/ddz/edz/net/net.html

2. Ausländer und Minderheiten: Deutsches Archiv
Largest German Internet archive for minority studies.
gopher://pfsparc02.phil15.uni-sb.de/11/gopher-projekt/Aktuelles/courage

See the Prentice Hall home page for related activities and address updates (http://www.prenhall.com/~german).

Unterwegs

Kommunikation

- Talking about other countries
- Discussing travel preparations
- Gathering information about travel services and accommodations
- Narrating past trips and experiences
- Negotiating transactions at the bank and the post office

Strukturen

- Simple past tense
- Infinitives with and without **zu**
  Infinitives without **zu**
  Infinitives with **zu**
  um...zu/ohne...zu/anstatt...zu
- Expressions of time with adverbs

Kultur

- Youth hostels
- Trains and the Eurailpass

Kapitel 10

Die ersten Schritte

Na, los!

Schritt 1: **Wo ist...?**

You have already learned the names of some countries, and you probably know more country names than you think. Look at the map below, then match the names of the countries below with the numbers on the map. Do you know which of these countries are members of the European Union (formerly European Economic Community)?

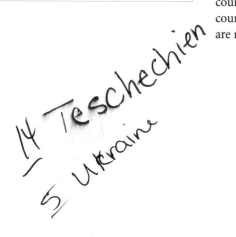

14 Teschechien
5 Ukraine

- 2 England
- 1 Spanien
- 3 Luxemburg
- 6 die Türkei
- 13 Portugal
- 26 Schottland
- 15 Liechtenstein
- 7 Rußland

- 17 Frankreich
- 18 Belgien
- 7 Dänemark
- 4 Italien
- 20 Norwegen
- 18 die Schweiz
- 19 Finnland

- 9 Deutschland
- 10 die Niederlande
- 11 Griechenland
- 12 Schweden
- 25 Irland
- 21 Österreich
- 21 Polen

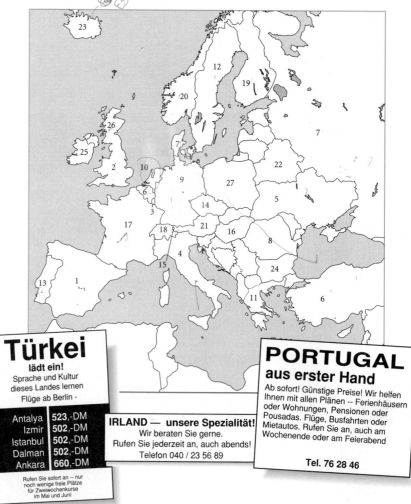

Türkei
lädt ein!
Sprache und Kultur
dieses Landes lernen
Flüge ab Berlin -

Antalya	**523**,-DM
Izmir	**502**,-DM
Istanbul	**502**,-DM
Dalman	**502**,-DM
Ankara	**660**,-DM

Rufen Sie sofort an -- nur
noch wenige freie Plätze
für Zweiwochenkurse
im Mai und Juni

IRLAND — unsere Spezialität!
Wir beraten Sie gerne.
Rufen Sie jederzeit an, auch abends!
Telefon 040 / 23 56 89

PORTUGAL
aus erster Hand
Ab sofort! Günstige Preise! Wir helfen
Ihnen mit allen Plänen -- Ferienhäusern
oder Wohnungen, Pensionen oder
Pousadas. Flüge, Busfahrten oder
Mietautos. Rufen Sie an, auch am
Wochenende oder am Feierabend

Tel. 76 28 46

ALLES KLAR?

A. Wie komme ich dahin? Mit einer Partnerin/einem Partner wählen Sie vier oder fünf Länder. Wie kann man von einem Land ins andere fahren? Denken Sie an so viele Transportmittel wie möglich.

> **BEISPIEL:** von England nach Frankreich
>
> —Wenn man von England nach Frankreich fahren will,
>   kann man…
>   mit einem Schiff fahren.
>   mit einem Auto durch den Tunnel fahren.
>   …

B. Typisches Essen in… Wählen Sie noch vier oder fünf Länder, und sagen Sie, was man in diesem Land ißt oder trinkt.

> **BEISPIELE:** —In Griechenland ißt man viel Lamm und Baklava und trinkt Ouzo.
>   —In der Schweiz ist Fondue typisch.

Schritt 2: **Vor der Reise**

Below is a list of chores you might need to do before starting off on a trip.

zum Reisebüro gehen	*go to the travel agency*
ein Zimmer reservieren	*reserve a room*
zur Bank gehen	*go to the bank*
Reiseschecks kaufen	*buy traveler's checks*
Geld wechseln	*exchange money*
den Paß finden	*find the passport*
den Koffer packen	*pack the suitcase*
den Schlafsack nicht vergessen	*not forget the sleeping bag*
Tickets vom Reisebüro abholen	*pick up tickets from the travel agency*

REISEBÜRO SCHMIDT
Internationale Bus– und Flugreisen
Wolfenbüttel • Braunschweig • Magdeburg • Halberstadt

ALLES KLAR?

Die Reise nach Zürich. Sie fliegen am 19. März nach Zürich. Was machen Sie wann?

> BEISPIELE: —Im Februar gehe ich zum Reisebüro.
> —Am 10. März…
> —Am 18. März…
> —Am 19. März…

Wir haben alles
für die Reise-
Koffer, Zelte,
Schlafsäcke,
Bekleidung,
Rucksäcke, Schuhe
und noch mehr.

Unterwegs Berlin

Auf dem Weg nach . . . ??

Kommen Sie zuert zu uns!

Lichtenberger Str. 10 - 7 83 04 69

Schritt 3: Wo kann man übernachten?

When traveling in Europe or elsewhere, you have the choice of various types of overnight accommodations, depending on your personal preferences and your budget. Consider the following possibilities:

> **das Hotel, -s**
> **die Pension, -en**   *bed-and-breakfast inn or guesthouse*
> **die Jugendherberge, -n**   *youth hostel*
> **das Einzelzimmer, -**
> **das Doppelzimmer, -**
> **mit/ohne Bad**
> **mit/ohne Dusche**

To ask whether something is included in the price, you ask:

> Ist [Frühstück] im Preis enthalten?   OR:
> Ist [Frühstück] auch dabei?

Now read or listen to the following conversation in which Herr Schultz, a businessman, calls to reserve a room at the Gasthaus Waldhorn in Munich. Pay particular attention to the phrases used in making reservations.

🔊 Ein Hotelzimmer reservieren

FRAU SCHWARZ: Gasthaus Waldhorn, guten Tag! Schwarz.

HERR SCHULTZ: Schultz, guten Tag, Frau Schwarz. Ich möchte gern ein Einzelzimmer, aber ein Zimmer, das hinten liegt, bitte.

FRAU SCHWARZ: Für wie viele Nächte, bitte?

HERR SCHULTZ: Für drei Nächte.

FRAU SCHWARZ: Für wann, bitte? Ab heute?

HERR SCHULTZ: Nein, erst ab Sonntag, also für Sonntag bis Mittwoch.

FRAU SCHWARZ: Das können wir Ihnen reservieren, das Zimmer kostet DM 90,—. Mit Bad oder Dusche und mit WC ist klar. Jedes Zimmer hat auch ein Telefon.

HERR SCHULTZ: Schön, und Frühstück ist auch dabei?

FRAU SCHWARZ: Natürlich, inklusive Frühstück. Bei uns gibt es ein tolles Frühstücksbüfett. Soll ich Ihnen das Zimmer reservieren?

HERR SCHULTZ: Ja, bitte, unter dem Namen Schultz, Klaus Schultz. Wohnort: Göttingen.

FRAU SCHWARZ: Schultz mit «teh» oder ohne?

HERR SCHULTZ: Mit einem «teh».

FRAU SCHWARZ: Und wie ist bitte Ihre Telefonnummer?

HERR SCHULTZ: Vorwahl: 0551/ 3 17 60.

FRAU SCHWARZ: 0551/3 17 60, alles klar! Danke schön. Auf Wiederhören!

HERR SCHULTZ: Auf Wiederhören!

ALLES KLAR?

A. Wann hat man was gefragt? Die folgenden Fragen sind aus dem Gespräch. Hören oder lesen Sie das Gespräch noch einmal. Welche Frage kommt zuerst? Nummerieren Sie — 1 für die erste Frage, 6 für die letzte (*last*).

1. _____ Frühstück ist auch dabei?
2. _____ Für wann, bitte? Ab heute?
3. _____ Soll ich Ihnen das Zimmer reservieren?
4. _____ Schultz mit t oder ohne?
5. _____ Wie ist bitte Ihre Telefonnummer?
6. _____ Für wie viele Nächte, bitte?

B. Ein Zimmer reservieren. Benutzen Sie die Fragen von Aufgabe A und spielen Sie mit Ihrem Partner/Ihrer Partnerin ein Rollenspiel, Sie ein Zimmer reservieren. Benutzen Sie Ihren eigenen (*own*) Namen und Ihre Telefonnummer.

Zentral Hotel
Gosestraße 12 • D 38640 Goslar

```
Rechnung:        10068/1                    Datum : 18/08/96
Zimmer : 129                                Anreise : 14/08/96
Gastname : Herrn  Halter                    Abreise : 18/08/96
Anzahl Artikel
                                  Preis      Betrag      Zahlung
    1  Übernachtung          1    60.00      60.00
    3  Übernachtung          1    80.00      240.00
    2  Mineralwasser         1     2.50        5.00
       Telefon Zimmer        1                 5.00
       Visa-Karte            6                           310.40
                          Rechnungstotal     310.40      310.40

Wir danken Ihnen für die Berücksichtigung unseres Hauses und
würden uns freuen, Sie bald wieder begrüßen zu dürfen.
MW-Steuer        Netto       Mwst      Taxe
                                                          Brutto
  1  14.00%      272.28      38.12                        310.40
Seite 1          272.28      38.12               Total    310.40
```

Germany, Austria, and Switzerland, like most other European countries, boast a large number of youth hostels that provide cheap accommodations for young travelers. Hostels were originally used by hikers and bicyclers, but in recent years they are also available for any young people, including those who are traveling by car. The

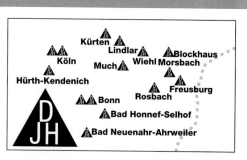

segment of the map here, showing the area around Bonn, gives an idea of just how numerous youth hostels are.

Accommodations are minimal (although standards have improved considerably), but inexpensive. In cities where the cheapest hotel might cost the equivalent of US $35, a bed in a hostel might cost US $7. Generally rooms are dormitory style, with several beds per room. Inexpensive breakfasts are also usually available. Hostels are open only from about 6 pm to 8 am; therefore one cannot lounge around all day. Most also have a curfew, after which the doors are locked.

Hostels are perhaps most important for the possibility they offer "overnighters" to get acquainted with similar-age travelers from around the world. It is not unusual to meet students and other travelers from five to ten other countries in a single overnight stay.

Persons intending to use hostels should be sure to get an international membership card before leaving their home country.

Reisewörter

Weltreise
Reiselust
Dienstreise
Reisewecker
Eisenbahnreise
Reiseprogramm
Gesellschaftsreise
Reisebekanntschaft
Geschäftsreise
Reisevertreter
Ferienreise
Reisegepäck
Luftreise
Reisegeld
Sommerreise
Reiseleiter
Auslandsreise
Reiseandenken
Vergnügungsreise
Reisegesellschaft
Studienreise
Reisebericht
Traumreise
Reisefieber
Autoreise
Reiseweg
Winterreise
Reisedecke
Seniorenreise
Reisebegleiter
Erkundungsreise

Reiseverpflegung
Urlaubsreise
Reiseverkehr
Tagesreise
Reisekoffer
Badereise
Reisezeit
Durchreise
Reiseführer
Hochzeitsreise
Reisegefährte
Entdeckungsreise
Reisebeschreibung
Abenteuerreise
Reisetagebuch
Besuchsreise
Reisewetter
Lustreise
Reisepaß
Schiffsreise
Reisebüro
Vortragsreise
Reisetasche
Forschungsreise
Reiseabenteuer
Erholungsreise
Reiselektüre
Teepreise
Reiseernte
Rundreise
Reiseziel

Schritt 4: Meine erste Europareise

📖 Lesestück

Worum geht es hier? Tony berichtet über seine erste Reise nach Europa. Welche Länder und welche Städte hat er besucht? Finden Sie die Städte auf der Landkarte. Ergänzen Sie die Tabelle.

	STADT	WIE VIELE TAGE?	WARUM WAREN SIE DORT?
1.			
2.			
3.			
4.			
5.			
6.			
7.			
8.			

Tony erzählt:

Vor zehn Jahren reiste ich zum ersten Mal nach Europa. Natürlich flogen wir mit Lufthansa. Aber wer waren "wir"? Ich flog nicht allein, sondern mit zwei Freunden. Wir waren damals gerade zwanzig Jahre alt; das 5. Semester lag schon hinter uns. Weil eine Europareise sehr teuer ist, mußten wir alle jahrelang sparen.

Am ersten Abend waren wir in einem Hotel in Frankfurt, aber sonst übernachteten wir immer in einer Jugendherberge. Dort war es nicht so teuer wie im Hotel, sondern wirklich billig. Da lernten wir Studenten aus vielen anderen Ländern kennen. Wir hatten auch unsere alten Schlafsäcke mit.

Wir waren nur drei Wochen in Deutschland, aber wir haben damals sehr viel gesehen; vor allem sind wir in mehrere Museen gegangen, und wir haben auch viele Kirchen besucht, die alten romanischen[1], gotischen[2] und barocken[3] Kirchen. Ich würde mir diese alten Kirchen gerne noch einmal ansehen.

Also, wo waren wir? Wir fingen unsere Reise in Frankfurt an, aber da waren wir nur zwei Tage. Dann fuhren wir nach Bayern und blieben sechs Tage in München. Wir machten auch Ausflüge[4] in viele kleine Dörfer[5]. Von München fuhren wir über Leipzig (einen Tag) und Halle (einen Tag) nach Berlin, wo wir wieder sechs Tage blieben. Von da gingen wir nach Köln, denn wir wollten die große gotische Kirche, den Kölner Dom[6], sehen. Nach zwei Tagen in Köln fuhren wir nach Bonn, der alten Hauptstadt, wo wir einen Tag blieben. Dann machten wir eine Rheinfahrt und kamen nach Mainz. Am nächsten Tag sind wir von Frankfurt nach Hause geflogen.

---

[1]*romanesque*
[2]*gothic*
[3]*baroque*
[4]*excursions*
[5]*villages*
[6]*cathedral*

Normalerweise fuhren wir von einer Stadt zur anderen mit dem Zug. Aber in den einzelnen[7] Städten gingen wir sehr oft zu Fuß; es war billig und auch gesund. So hatten wir auch viele Möglichkeiten[8], mit Deutschen in Kontakt zu kommen. Mit anderen Menschen zu sprechen und so eine andere Kultur kennenzulernen und immer Deutsch zu sprechen: das hat unsere Europareise interessant gemacht! Als wir zurückkamen, war unsere Deutschlehrerin auf uns und unsere neuen Deutschkenntnisse sehr stolz[9]! Wir allerdings auch!

Kulturnotiz: Trains and the "Eurailpass"

Trains are much more common in Europe than in North America. Large cities like Vienna, Zurich, Berlin, Cologne, Munich, and others have trains arriving or leaving (on average) almost every single minute. There are high speed Inter-City-Express (ICE) trains, Inter-City (IC) and Euro-City (EC) trains, trans-regional trains (Inter-Regio), slower trains stopping at smaller towns, and the really slow trains that stop everywhere. Trains provide the only means of transportation for many Europeans, including thousands of students!

Many North American travelers purchase a "Eurailpass" before leaving for Europe. Such a pass entitles the holder to travel free within western Europe for a given number of days or months. You can travel first or second class, depending on your ticket. The Eurailpass guarantees you rail passage, but not necessarily a seat. A Eurailpass makes sense if you are traveling long distances or, perhaps, if you will be traveling short distances frequently.

There are also many other kinds of pre-paid tickets offered by Europe's national railroads. Any travel agent can offer advice.

---

[7]*individual*   [8]*opportunities*   [9]*proud*

A. Was hat Tony alles gesehen? Erzählen Sie mit Ihrer Partnerin/Ihrem Partner, was diese Studenten alles in Deutschland gesehen haben. Wohin sind sie gefahren? Was haben sie gemacht? Wie lange sind sie in jeder Stadt geblieben?

> **BEISPIELE:** —Sie sind nach Köln gefahren und haben den Kölner Dom gesehen.
> —Sie sind sechs Tage in Berlin geblieben.

B. Persönliche Fragen.

1. Haben Sie dieses Jahr eine Reise gemacht?
2. Wohin sind Sie gereist?
3. Was haben Sie gesehen?
4. Wie lange hat die Reise gedauert?
5. Wo haben Sie übernachtet?
6. Empfehlen Sie diese Stadt/dieses Land?

C. Verbformen. Lesen Sie den Text noch einmal und schreiben Sie alle neuen Verbformen auf. Können Sie die Verbformen gruppieren? Wie? Diskutieren Sie mit einem Partner/einer Partnerin. Wenn Sie fertig sind, fragen Sie Ihre Lehrerin/Ihren Lehrer, ob Sie alle Gruppen gefunden haben.

Simple past tense

German has two past tense forms: the present perfect tense, which you learned in **Kapitel 5**, and the simple past. Except for the verb **sein** (**war**), until now it is the present perfect tense (**ich habe gesehen, ich bin gefahren**) that you have used to discuss events in the past. In normal, conversational German, the present perfect is preferred.

The simple past, however, is frequently found in narration, e.g., in novels, newspapers, and letters that relate a number of sequential events. Also, in conversation the simple past is often used with **sein**, **haben**, and the modal verbs.

As with the present perfect, there are three categories of verbs and their simple past forms: regular verbs, irregular verbs, and mixed verbs.

1. **Regular verbs.** The simple past tense of regular verbs is composed of three parts: stem + **t** + ending.

   Note the simple past endings of the verb **machen**.

MACHEN			
ich	machte	wir	machten
du	machtest	ihr	machtet
er/sie/es	machte	sie	machten
	Sie	machten	

If the stem ends in **-t** or **-d**, an extra **-e-** will be inserted between the stem and the following **-t**.

ÜBERNACHTEN			
ich	übernacht**ete**	wir	übernacht**eten**
du	übernacht**etest**	ihr	übernacht**etet**
er/sie/es	übernacht**ete**	sie	übernacht**eten**
	Sie übernacht**eten**		

Note that with separable-prefix verbs, the prefix still appears at the end of the sentence or clause.

Er **packte** seinen Koffer **aus.**   *He unpacked his suitcase.*

ALLES KLAR?

A. Die Ankunft (*arrival*) **in Frankfurt.** Ergänzen Sie mit dem Imperfekt (*simple past*).

Als ich in Frankfurt (1)_____ (landen), (2)_____ ich mein Gepäck (3)_____ (abholen). Ich (4)_____ (telefonieren) mit einer kleinen Pension und (5)_____ (reservieren) ein Einzelzimmer. Weil ich dort eine Woche (6)_____ (übernachten), (7)_____ ich meinen Koffer (8)_____ (auspacken). Dann (9)_____ (besuchen) ich die Stadt.

B. Vorbereitung (*preparation*) **auf die Reise.** Sie machen Pläne für eine Reise. Aber nicht nur Sie — andere machen das auch. Folgen Sie dem Beispiel.

BEISPIEL: Ich packte meinen Koffer. (du)
            —Du packtest auch deinen Koffer.

1. Ich kaufte Reiseschecks. (wir)
2. Ich wechselte Geld. (Peter)
3. Ich holte die Tickets vom Reisebüro ab. (ihr)
4. Ich reservierte ein Hotelzimmer. (Sabine und Gabi)
5. Ich telefonierte mit dem Tourist Office. (du)
6. Ich kaufte Briefmarken. (wir)

2. Irregular verbs. Irregular verbs in German frequently correspond to irregular verbs in English, e.g., *sing, sang, sung; speak, spoke, spoken;* or *lie, lay, lain.* Such verbs usually have a vowel change in the past tense, and occasionally a consonant change as well. As you learn more and more German, you will see that there are certain patterns of vowel changes, but for now, it is easier to memorize each one.

To the irregular stem of the verb, the following endings will be added:

ich	-	wir	-en
du	-st	ihr	-t
er/sie/es	-	sie	-en
	Sie	-en	

GEBEN: SIMPLE PAST STEM *gab-*			
ich	gab	wir	gab**en**
du	gab**st**	ihr	gab**t**
er/sie/es	gab	sie	gab**en**
	Sie gab**en**		

The simple past stem is the second *principal part* of German verbs. These principal parts are the basis for all verb tenses. While the principal parts of regular verbs are predictable (**reisen**, **reiste**, **gereist**), those of irregular verbs are not, and must be learned. The following list shows the principal parts of some of the irregular verbs you have learned thus far.

Memorize

(1ST PRINCIPLE PART) INFINITIVE	3RD PERS. SG.	(2ND PRINCIPLE PART) SIMPLE PAST	(3RD PRINCIPLE PART) PAST PARTICIPLE
bekommen		bekam	bekommen
bleiben		blieb	ist geblieben
essen	ißt	aß	gegessen
fahren	fährt	fuhr	ist gefahren
finden		fand	gefunden
geben	gibt	gab	gegeben
gehen		ging	ist gegangen
haben	hat	hatte	gehabt *(weak)*
helfen	hilft	half	geholfen
kommen		kam	ist gekommen
lesen	liest	las	gelesen
nehmen	nimmt	nahm	genommen
schreiben		schrieb	geschrieben
sehen	sieht	sah	gesehen
sein	ist	war	ist gewesen
singen		sang	gesungen
sprechen	spricht	sprach	gesprochen
stehen		stand	gestanden
vergessen	vergißt	vergaß	vergessen
verstehen		verstand	verstanden
werden	wird	wurde	ist geworden

Beginning with this chapter, the past tense of irregular verbs will be included in the chapter vocabulary lists. A complete list of irregular verbs is in the **Appendix** at the back of the book.

✓ **A. In die Schweiz.** Ergänzen Sie mit dem Imperfekt.

Vor zwei Jahren (1) _____ (fahren) ich mit meiner Freundin Barbara in die Schweiz. Da (2) _blieb_ (bleiben) wir drei Wochen lang. Zuerst (3) _waren_ (sein) wir in Luzern. Wir (4) _sahen_ (sehen) die Kappelbrücke und das Löwendenkmal. Am Abend (5) _aßen_ (essen) wir in einem typischen schweizerischen Restaurant — wir (6) _bekammen_ (bekommen) Fondue und Raclette. Bald (7) _vergaßen_ (vergessen) wir, daß wir wenig (8) _verstanden_ (verstehen) — weil die Leute alle Schweizerdeutsch (9) _sprachen_ (sprechen) — und wir (10) _hatten_ (haben) einfach Spaß.

✓ **B. Ein Interview mit Herrn Solangen.** Sie haben einen Bekannten (80 Jahre alt) über seine Familiengeschichte interviewt. Sie haben die folgende Geschichte auf Kasette aufgenommen (*recorded*). Schreiben Sie jetzt einen Bericht (*report*) über das Interview. Schreiben Sie die Geschichte noch einmal, aber benutzen Sie das Imperfekt.

BEISPIEL: Herr Solangens Vater kam mit seiner Familie.

Mein Vater ist mit seiner Familie nach Amerika gekommen — er ist damals acht Jahre alt gewesen. Auf der Schiffahrt haben sie ihnen wenig zu essen gegeben und seine Schwester ist krank geworden. Sie sind in New York angekommen und sind in Brooklyn geblieben, weil meine Tante immer noch nicht gesund gewesen ist. Mein Vater ist jeden Tag zum Zeitungsverkäufer gegangen und hat da die Zeitung gelesen, um Englisch zu lernen. Am Ende des Jahres hat er seiner Oma in Deutschland geschrieben: "*I am almost an American now!*"

3. **Mixed verbs and modals.** Mixed verbs form the simple past tense in the same way as regular verbs: stem + **t** + ending.

The difference is that mixed verbs, like irregular verbs, also have an irregular past tense stem.

DENKEN: SIMPLE PAST STEM dach–			
ich	dachte	wir	dachten
du	dachtest	ihr	dachtet
er/sie/es	dachte	sie	dachten
	Sie dachten		

The principal parts of the mixed verbs you have learned thus far are:

(1ST PRINCIPLE PART) INFINITIVE	3RD PERS. SING.	(2ND PRINCIPLE PART) SIMPLE PAST	(3RD PRINCIPLE PART) PAST PARTICIPLE
bringen		brachte	gebracht
denken		dachte	gedacht
kennen		kannte	gekannt
wissen	weiß	wußte	gewußt

The modal verbs are similar to the mixed verbs in the formation of the simple past tense. The principal parts are as follows:

(1ST PRINCIPLE PART) INFINITIVE	3RD PERS. SING.	(2ND PRINCIPLE PART) SIMPLE PAST	(3RD PRINCIPLE PART) PAST PARTICIPLE
dürfen	darf	durfte	gedurft
können	kann	konnte	gekonnt
mögen	mag	mochte	gemocht
müssen	muß	mußte	gemußt
sollen	soll	sollte	gesollt
wollen	will	wollte	gewollt

Note that **sollen** and **wollen** have no vowel change.

ALLES KLAR?

A. Weiter mit Herrn Solangen. Ergänzen Sie mit dem Imperfekt.

Nach zwei Jahren (1) _wollte_ (wollen) mein Großvater New York verlassen. Mein Vater (2) _konnte_ (kennen) die Stadt und viele Leute und er (3) _wollte_ (wollen) nicht gehen. Aber er (4) _mußte_ (müssen) machen, was sein Vater sagte. Der Großvater (5) _dachte_ (denken) nur an das Gold in Kalifornien, wo man sehr reich werden (6) _konnte_ (können). Sie kauften sich einen Planwagen *(covered wagon)* und (7) _nehmten_ (nehmen) viel Essen und wenig Kleidung mit. Sie (8) _wußten_ (wissen) nicht, was vor ihnen lag oder was sie in Kalifornien machen (9) _sollten_ (sollen).

B. Als Kind. Besprechen Sie Ihre Kindheit mit einer Partnerin/einem Partner.

1. Was wolltest du als Kind machen, das du nicht machen durftest?
2. Was wolltest du von Beruf werden, als du fünf Jahre alt warst?
3. Was dachtest du als Kind über deine Eltern?
4. Welches Essen mochtest du nicht als Kind?

Schritt 5: **Reiseschecks**

Gespräch

Worum geht es hier? Cliff ist Austauschstudent[1] in Marburg. Er ist auf Reisen und will einen Reisescheck einlösen. Er spricht mit Frau Feinburg — auch ein Gast im Hotel. Was schlägt sie ihm vor? Hat er Erfolg beim Einlösen?

FRAU FEINBURG: Guten Morgen.

CLIFF: Guten Morgen. Ich möchte einen Reisescheck einlösen. Wissen Sie, ob man das hier im Hotel machen kann?

FRAU FEINBURG: Es ist schon möglich, das hier zu machen. Im Hotel ist der Kurs nicht schlecht, auch nicht in der Wechselstube am Bahnhof. Aber auf der Bank bekommen Sie noch mehr Geld dafür. Gerade links um die Ecke ist eine Sparkasse. Anstatt sie hier einzulösen, würde ich zur Sparkasse gehen.

CLIFF: Ach, so. Danke schön!

[Er geht am Nachmittag zur Sparkasse und spricht mit einem Beamten[2], Herrn Siegbert.]

HERR SIEGBERT: Guten Tag. Bitte schön?

CLIFF: Guten Tag. Ich möchte etwas Geld wechseln, bitte.

HERR SIEGBERT: Kein Problem. Bargeld oder Reiseschecks?

CLIFF: Ich möchte einen amerikanischen Reisescheck einlösen, bitte. Ich möchte natürlich D-Mark.

HERR SIEGBERT: Darf ich mal, bitte, Ihren Paß sehen?

CLIFF: Ach, meinen Paß habe ich vergessen.

HERR SIEGBERT: Ja, also, den Paß müssen wir haben.

CLIFF: Ach so. Da kommt mein Freund. Vielleicht hat er meinen Paß. Filip, hast du vielleicht unsere Pässe? Ich brauche meinen, um einen Reisescheck einzulösen.

FILIP: Nein, deinen habe ich nicht bei mir. Ich habe ihn dir heute morgen zurückgegeben. Anstatt deinen Paß zu benutzen, kannst du nicht meinen benutzen?

HERR SIEGBERT: Nein, ohne Ihren Paß zu haben, kann ich Ihnen Ihre Reiseschecks nicht einlösen.

CLIFF: Das ist wirklich blöd[3], aber dann hole ich jetzt meinen Paß.

---

[1]*exchange student*   [2]*official*   [3]*silly*

ALLES KLAR?

A. Haben Sie verstanden?

1. Warum löste Cliff seinen Reisescheck nicht im Hotel ein?
2. Wo ist die Sparkasse?
3. Was hatte Cliff nicht bei sich?
4. Wer hatte einen Paß?
5. Was mußte Cliff tun, bevor er sein Geld bekam?

USA

Devisenkurse
1. – US$ = DM 1,35   DM 1,– = 0.74 US$

US$	DM	US$	DM	DM	US$
0.05	0,07	30.00	40,50	0,10	0.07
0.10	0,13	40.00	54,00	0,20	0.14
0.15	0,21	50.00	67,50	0,50	0.37
0.25	0,33	75.00	101,25	1,00	0.74
0.50	0,67	100.00	135,00	2,00	1.48
1.00	1,35	125.00	168,75	5,00	3.70
1.50	2,02	150.00	202,50	10,00	7.40
2.00	4,04	200.00	270,00	20,00	14.80
5.00	6,75	250.00	337,50	50,00	37.00
10.00	13,50	500.00	675,00	100,00	74.00
25.00	33,75	1000.00	1350,00	500,00	370.00

Kurse können sich kurzfristig ändern.
Es hilft Ihnen IHRE Bank!

Infinitives with/without *zu*

Infinitives without *zu*

Zu is never used with infinitives after modal verbs.

> Er will mitkommen.
> *He wants to come along.*

> Morgen muß ich ein Zimmer reservieren.
> *Tomorrow I must reserve a room.*

Infinitives with *zu*

Unlike English, German infinitives do not actually include the word to (**zu**): **fahren** = *to go.* Therefore **zu** is necessary in *infinitive phrases* or infinitive clauses. These contain dependent infinitives that appear at the end of the sentence. If the infinitive phrase or clause contains other words in addition to **zu** + infinitive, it is set off from the rest of the sentence by a comma.

> Wir haben versucht **zu sparen.**
> *We tried to save.*

> Wir haben versucht, das Geld für die Reise **zu sparen.**
> *We tried to save the money for the trip.*

In separable-prefix verbs, **zu** appears between the prefix and the main verb.

> Sie hat vergessen, den Scheck ein**zu**lösen.
> *She forgot to cash the check.*

ALLES KLAR?

A. Mein Abenteuer (*adventure*) **in Deutschland.** Ergänzen Sie die Lücken. Manchmal brauchen Sie einen Infinitiv mit **zu,** manchmal ohne **zu.**

sprechen ✓	sehen ✓	besuchen ✓
abholen ✓	verstehen ✓	verlassen
einlösen ✓	beginnen	

Ich flog letztes Jahr nach Deutschland, denn ich wollte meinen Freund Peter

(1) _besuchen_ . Als ich in Frankfurt landete, mußte ich mein Gepäck

(2) _abholen_ . Dann wollte der Beamte meinen Paß (3) _sehen_ .

Ich versuchte mit ihm, Deutsch (4) _zu sprechen_ . Er konnte mich auch

(5) _verstehen_ ! Dann sah ich Peter, aber bevor wir den Flughafen

(6) _verlassen_ durften, ging ich zur Wechselstube, denn ich mußte einen

Reisescheck (7) _einlösen_ . Dann durfte mein Abenteuer in Deutschland

(8) _beginnen_ .

Um...zu, ohne...zu, anstatt...zu

um...zu constructions are the equivalent of *in order to* in English.

> **Um** schnell an**zu**kommen, fliegt man heute.
> *In order to get there quickly, one flies nowadays.*

> Ich brauche meinen Paß, **um** den Reisescheck ein**zu**lösen.
> *I need my passport (in order) to cash the traveler's check.*

> Man reist nicht, um anzukommen,
> sondern, um unterwegs zu sein.
>
> Johann Wolfgang von Goethe
> (1749-1832)

ohne...zu constructions are the equivalent of without plus an **-ing** form in English.

> Sie hat uns besucht, **ohne** ein Geschenk mit**zu**bringen.
> *She came to visit us without bringing a present.*

anstatt...zu constructions are the equivalent of instead of plus an **-ing** form in English.

> **Anstatt** den Reisescheck hier ein**zu**lösen, würde ich zur Sparkasse gehen.
> *Instead of cashing the traveler's check here, I would go to the savings bank.*

ALLES KLAR?

A. Vor der Reise. Besprechen Sie mit einem Partner/einer Partnerin, was Sie vor einer Reise machen müssen. Benutzen Sie **um.... zu**.

> **BEISPIEL:**   Um Informationen zu bekommen, muß man zum Reisebüro gehen.

Zimmer reservieren - anrufen
um mit dem Zug zu fahren - Fahrkarte   muss mann
Reiseschecks einlösen - Paß
fliegen - Ticket
…

B. Was braucht man, wenn man reist? Bilden Sie Sätze mit **um… zu**, **ohne… zu** und **anstatt… zu**.

> **BEISPIELE:**   —Um nach Deutschland zu reisen, braucht man einen Reisepaß.
> —Ohne ein Ticket zu haben, darf man nicht mit dem Zug fahren.
> —Anstatt amerikanisches Geld mitzunehmen, muß man D-Mark haben.

C. Sollen oder möchten. Besprechen Sie mit einer Partnerin/einem Partner, was Sie machen sollen. Was möchten Sie statt dessen (*instead of that*) machen? Folgen Sie dem Beispiel.

> **BEISPIEL:**   —Was sollst du tun?
> —Ich soll lesen.
> —Was möchtest du tun, anstatt zu lesen?
> —Anstatt zu lesen,…

ICH SOLL...	ICH MÖCHTE...
Hausaufgaben machen	Sport treiben
lesen	reisen
putzen	mit Freunden ausgehen
arbeiten	Karten spielen
…	…

D. Probleme mit Baby. Ergänzen Sie mit Hilfe der folgenden Wörter. Manchmal brauchen Sie zu, manchmal nicht.

überlegen	mitnehmen	reisen	schlafen
haben	lassen	nehmen	fahren

Unsere ganze Familie wollte zusammen nach Deutschland _fahren_. Mit einem Kind _zu reisen_, ist es schwierig (*complicated*). Anstatt unser Baby bei den Großeltern _zu lassen_, wollten wir es auch _mitnehmen_! Es genießt (*enjoys*) es auch, meinten wir. Wir waren vier Personen plus Baby. Ohne es uns _überlegt_ haben wir nur vier Tickets gekauft. Das war ein Fehler (*mistake*)! Denn ohne ein Ticket _zu haben_, bekommt man keinen Sitzplatz. Also mußten meine Eltern das Baby auf den Schoß (*lap*) _nehmen_. Normalerweise weint (*cries*) das Baby nach dem Essen anstatt _zu schlafen_, aber im Flugzeug war es ruhig. Also etwas Glück (*luck*) haben wir dennoch gehabt! Aber das nächste Mal _lassen_ wir das Baby zu Hause.

Expressions of time with adverbs

As you learned in **Kapitel 4**, German speakers use am with days or parts of the day to indicate when an event has occurred or will occur.

> Am Montag ist das Restaurant geschlossen.
> *The restaurant is closed on Monday.*

> Am Nachmittag ging Cliff zur Sparkasse.
> *Cliff went to the savings bank in the afternoon.*

These same words can be used as adverbs, with a lower case letter and a final **-s**. As adverbs, they indicate repeated or habitual occurrences. Examples of such words are: **montags, dienstags,** etc.; **morgens, nachmittags, abends, nachts.**

> Das Restaurant ist montags geschlossen.
> *The restaurant is closed on Mondays.*

> Samstags geht die Familie Feinschmidt in die Synagoge.
> *The Feinschmidt family goes to temple on Saturdays.*

The following lists show the sequence of days and the parts of the day in German. As in English, you can create other time expressions by combining a word from the left column with a word from the right one.

vorgestern	*the day before yesterday*
gestern	*yesterday*
heute	*today*
morgen	*tomorrow*
übermorgen	*the day after tomorrow*
früh (morgen)	*early (morning)*
vormittag	*morning, forenoon*
mittag	*noon*
nachmittag	*afternoon*
abend	*evening*
nacht	*night*

Morgen früh gehen wir zur Bank.
Tomorrow morning we're going to the bank.

Gestern abend haben wir in einer Jugendherberge übernachtet.
Last night we stayed in a youth hostel.

To say *tomorrow morning*, use **morgen früh**; *this morning* can be either **heute morgen** or **heute früh**. To express *tonight*, use **heute abend**; this phrase covers the time period before one goes to bed.

Another convenient adverbial time expression is a combination with the suffix **-lang**: **jahrelang**, **tagelang**, **stundenlang**, etc.

Wir mußten jahrelang sparen.
We had to save for years.

Ich habe stundenlang gewartet.
I waited for hours.

ALLES KLAR?

 A. Normalerweise... Besprechen Sie mit einer Partnerin/einem Partner, was Sie wann machen.

BEISPIELE: Morgens stehe ich immer um sieben Uhr auf.
Abends bin ich immer in der Bibliothek.
Donnerstags...
Nachmittags...
...

 B. Pläne fürs Wochenende. Besprechen Sie mit Ihrem Partner/Ihrer Partnerin, was Sie dieses Wochenende machen.

BEISPIELE: Am Freitag abend gehe ich zum Basketball-Spiel.
Samstag früh schlafe ich.
Samstag abend...
Sonntag nachmittag...
...

C. Eine Reise. Erzählen Sie einem Partner/einer Partnerin von einer Reise, die Sie als Kind gemacht haben. Was haben Sie auf der Reise mit Freunden oder Familie gemacht? Morgens? Nachmittags? Abends?

Zusammenfassung *~for Friday~*

A. Per Luftpost in die USA. Ergänzen Sie. Manchmal brauchen Sie das Imperfekt und manchmal den Infinitiv.

sein	mitbringen	sollen
kosten	zurückgeben	weggehen *to leave go away*
wollen	geben	sagen
wissen	kaufen	gehen

Frau Kaiser hat gestern viele Sachen gekauft. Sie _ging_ heute zur Post. Sie ~wollte~ _wollte_ einige Sachen in die USA schicken. Zuerst _gab_ sie dem Beamten einen Brief. Sie _wollte_ ihn per Luftpost schicken. Frau Kaiser _brachte_ auch ein Paket _mit_, aber sie _wußte_ nicht, ob sie es per Luftpost schicken _sollte_. Aber auch per Schiff _kostet_ das schwere Paket DM 64,30. Frau Kaiser _kaufte_ insgesamt 35 Briefmarken. Sie _wollte_ auch Sondermarken (*commemorative stamps*), aber es _gab_ keine. Der Beamte _sagte_ ihr, daß Sondermarken erst übermorgen wieder da sind. Er _sagte_ dann: "So, alles zusammen, DM 91,50." Frau Kaiser _gab_ ihm zwei Geldscheine (*bills*) und er _gab_ ihr DM 8,50 _zurück_. Als sie _ging_, _sah_ sie zu dem Beamten: "Übermorgen komme ich dann noch einmal, um Sondermarken _zu kaufen_." Vielleicht _sollte_ sie sie ihrem Sohn _geben_ _wollte_, denn ihr Sohn sammelt (*collects*) Briefmarken.

brauchte — mit

Redewendung

German **per** means *by* with means of transport. The German preposition **pro** is the equivalent of English *per* when one is dealing with measurable amounts or units. Both prepositions take the accusative.

Ich möchte diesen Brief **per** Luftpost schicken.
I'd like to send this letter by airmail.

Es ist billiger, das Paket **per** Schiff zu schicken.
It's cheaper to send the package by ship.

Das Zimmer kostet DM 60,— **pro** Nacht.
The room costs 60 Marks per night.

Benzin kostet DM 1,46 **pro** Liter.
Gas costs 1 Mark 46 per liter.

B. Eine Geschichte (*story*). Schreiben Sie eine kurze Geschichte und benutzen Sie das Imperfekt. Ihre Geschichte soll 10-12 Sätze lang sein.

> **BEISPIEL:** Es war einmal ein Mädchen aus... Sie war...Ihre Mutter hatte... Ihr Vater war... Eines Tages (*one day*) wollte sie...

C. Die Unterkunft (*accommodations*). Wo übernachten Sie, wenn Sie reisen? Wo übernachten Sie am liebsten? Wo können Sie es sich leisten? Schreiben Sie einen Absatz.

> **BEISPIEL:** —Ich suche immer eine [billige/teure] Pension in der Nähe vom Bahnhof, denn...
> —Das Zimmer muß [dunkel/hell, modern/alt] sein.
> —Es soll [bequeme Betten, eine Sauna, einen Fitneßraum, einen Farbfernseher] haben.
> ...

ATRIUM HOTEL NÜRNBERG

Münchner Str.25 • Hotel in ruhiger Parkanlage, Hallenbad, Sauna, Fitnessraum, Solarien, Kegelbahnen, Bar, Garage
Tel. 09 11 / 4 74 80, Telex 626 167, Fax 474 84 20

300 Betten • EZ ab DM 169,–
DZ ab DM 228,–
inkl. Frühstücksbuffet

D. Letzten Sommer. Schreiben Sie einem Freund/einer Freundin einen Brief. Erzählen Sie, wie Sie letzten Sommer verbracht haben. Benutzen Sie das Imperfekt.

> **BEISPIELE:** —Nachmittags arbeitete ich im Café.
> —Abends ging ich mit Freunden ins Kino.
> —Ende Juli fuhr ich mit meiner Familie nach....

Zu zweit: Student 1

A. Hotels in Hamburg. Below you will find a list of some of the hotels in Hamburg. Your partner has another list. Work together to make a complete chart, so that you have a good overview of the possibilities. You will want to know how many beds each has, with bath, shower, or toilet in the room, radio or TV, bar, breakfast (buffet), price for singles and for doubles and any special features. Then decide where you would like to stay for a week; be prepared to support your choice of hotel.

HOTEL PANORAMA HARBURG
Harburger Ring 8, HH 90
☎ 7 66 95-0, TX 21 64 824
120 Betten, alle Zi. m Bad/Du/WC,
Tel., Radio, TV, Zi.-Bar, 3 Suiten,
5 Konferenzräume bis 150 P.
Ez. 135,00-150,00/Dz.150,00-230,00

AUSSEN ALSTER
Schmilnskystr. 11 Alsternähe
☎ (040)24 25 57, TX 211278
54 Betten, alle Zi. m. Du/Bad, WC,
Kabel-Farb-TV, Radio, Zi.-Tel.,
Frühst.-Buffet, Sauna, Solarium,
Garten
Ez. 130,00-160,00 Dz.180,00-210,00

NOVOTEL HAMBURG NORD
Oldesloer Str. 166, HH 61
☎ (040)55 02 073, TX 21 29 23
248 Betten, Frühstücksbuffet, voll-
klim. Konf.-Räume, alle Zimmer mit
Bad, Farb-TV mit Kabel-Anschl.,
Minibar. Ez. 130,00/Dz. 152,00

SACHSENWALD
CONGRESS HOTEL
2057 Reinbek, Hamburger Str. 4–8
☎ (040)72761-0 TX 2163074
150 Betten, alle Zi. m. Selbst-
w.-Tel., Farb-TV, Minibar, Bad/WC/
Du/WC, Konf.-Räume bis 700 P.,
Sauna, Spez.-Rest., Bar, S-Bahn 20
Min. v. Hbf. Ez. 130,00-155,00
Dz. 150,00/180,00, Suite 260,00

NAME	BETTEN	BAD	DUSCHE	W.C.	RADIO (R) TV?	BAR?	FRÜH-STÜCK?	PREIS FÜR EZ/DZ	ANDERE SACHEN
Panorama	120	x	x	x	R TV	ja	?		
Bellevue									

B. Mit dem Zug.

You go to the train station to get information. You want to travel from Berlin Hauptbahnhof (Hbf) to Halle on a Sunday. You are meeting someone at 3:00 p.m., but you have never been to Halle and would like to see something of the city. Ask about the possibility of arriving earlier; you may have to change trains to do so. Find out when the different trains leave, when they arrive, and whether they have a dining car (**Speisewagen**). Make notes on the different possibilities, decide which train you will take, buy a ticket, and reserve a seat.

MÖGLICHE FRAGEN

—Ich möchte Sonntag von… nach…fahren. Gibt es nachmittags einen Zug?

—Wann fährt der Zug ab?

—Wann komme ich in… an?

—Ich möchte eigentlich früher ankommen. Wann muß ich abfahren, um am späten Morgen anzukommen?

—Hat dieser Zug einen Speisewagen?

—Gut. Ich möchte für den Zug um… eine Fahrkarte kaufen.

—Ich möchte auch einen Platz reservieren, bitte.

Now switch roles. You are the railroad employee. Using the information below, help your customer.

NORDDEICH–BREMEN–HANNOVER

km		E 3113 ⑬	E 3115 ⑬	ICE 783 ⑬	E 3117	IC 755	E 3119	IC 757	IR 2743	E 3129	IC 759	ICE 881
	NorddeichMole	—	—	—	—	—	—	—	—	—	—	—
0	Norddeich	—	0545	—	—	—	0740	—	1109	—	—	—
35	Emden	0516	0622	—	—	—	0742	—	1111	—	—	—
61	Leer	0541	0647	0722	—	—	0813	—	1141	1310	—	—
116	Oldenburg	0625	0728	0747	—	—	0837	—	1205	1335	—	—
161	Bremen	0659	0804	0818	0859	0839	0928	1043	1243	1428	1443	—
						0904		1004	1113	1313	1440	1513
283	Hannover	—	—	0914	1014	—		1214	1411	—	1614	1618
												1714

		E 3133 ⑬◆	IC 851	E 3135	ICE 883	IR 2747	E 3143	E 3145
	NorddeichMole	1431	—	1531	—	—	—	—
	Norddeich	1433	—	1533	—	1742	1944	2100
	Emden	1510	—	1616	—	1748	1946	2102
	Leer	1541	—	1641	—	1826	2016	2142
	Oldenburg	1628	—	1728	—	1851	2041	2207
	Bremen	1704	1718	1804	1818	1935	2128	2300
						2004	2204	2334
	Hannover	—	1814	—	1914	2133	2353	0126

		E 6404 ⑬	E 3104 ⑬	IR 2746	IC 854	IR 2742	ICE 786	E 3124
	Hannover	—	—	0644	0744	1144	1444	—
	Bremen	—	—	0754	0840	1240	1540	—
	Oldenburg	0532	0732	0828	—	1324	—	1632
	Leer	0611	0816	0908	—	1358	—	1711
	Emden	0636	0841	0937	—	1432	—	1744
	Norddeich	—	—	1005	—	1509	—	—
	NorddeichMole	—	—	1008	—	1512	—	—

⑬ = Speisewagen

The trip from Norddeich to Hannover costs DM 70,—. The fee for the seat reservation is DM 3,—.

MÖGLICHE ANTWORTEN

—Dieser Zug fährt um… ab und kommt um… an.

—Nein, der Zug um… fährt nicht am Sonntag.

—Die Fahrkarte kostet… und die Platzkarte (*seat reservation*) kostet… Zusammen macht das…

A. Hotels in Hamburg. Below you will find a list of some of the hotels in Hamburg. Your partner has another list. Work together to make a complete chart, so that you have a good overview of the possibilities. You will want to know how many beds each has, with bath, shower, or toilet in the room, radio or TV, bar, breakfast (buffet), price for singles and for doubles and any special features. Then decide where you would like to stay for a week; be prepared to support your choice of hotel.

HOTEL BELLEVUE
An der Alster 13; A.d. Außenalster
☎ 24 80 11, TX 216 29 29
100 B., a. Zi.m.Bad/Du/WC, Kb.-TV, Rd., M.-bar, Frühst.-Buf. inkl., Ausstell,-u. Konf.-R b. 60 P.
Ez. 120,00-140,00/Dz. 170,00-210,00

MELLINGBURGER SCHLEUSE
Mellingburgredder 1, HH 65
☎ (040) 602 40 01-03
Fax: 040/602 79 12, 70 B; am ruhigen Alsterlauf, Hotel-Rest.
6 Konf.-Räume, Bierstube, Schwimmhalle, Frühst.-Buffet DM 13,- a. Zi.m. Bad o. Du.
Kabel-TV
Ez. 115,00/Dz. 155,00
3-B Zi. 175,00

ALSTER-HOF
Esplanade 12, HH 36
☎ (040)35 00 70, TX 213843
156 Betten, Tel., teilw. Farb-TV, Mini-bar, Frühst-Buffet, Hunde akzeptiert
Ez. 110,00-120,00 Dz. 150,00-190,00

HOTEL FALCK & Restaurant DANMARK
Kieler Str. 33, HH 54
☎ (040)540 20 61, TX 2-12664
150 Betten, erstkl. Komforthotel, Zi. m. Bad/Du/WC, Tel., elektr. Hosenbügler, Frühstücksbuffet DM 15,-, Mini-Bar, Radioweckuhr, Farb-TV Rest. m. orig. dän. Küche
Ez. 110,00-125,00-Dz. 115,00-150,00

NAME	BETTEN?	BAD	DUSCHE	W.C.	RADIO (R) TV?	BAR?	FRÜH-STÜCK?	PREIS FÜR EZ/DZ	ANDERE SACHEN
Panorama	120	x	x	x	R TV	ja	?		
Bellevue									

B. Mit dem Zug. You are an employee of the Deutsche Bahn. A traveler comes to the station and asks for information on train times. With the information below, help your customer. Make sure that the train travels on the day your customer wants to go. The customer may need to change trains. Once the customer has decided, sell the ticket and make the seat reservation.

MÖGLICHE ANTWORTEN
—Dieser Zug fährt um… ab und kommt um… an.

—Nein, der Zug um… fährt nicht am Sonntag.

—Die Fahrkarte kostet… und die Platzkarte (*seat reservation*) kostet…
  Zusammen macht das…

BERLIN – HALLE and LEIPZIG

km		IC 801 🍴	D 2501	D 1603	IC 803 🍴	D 2403	D 2011	IC 705 🍴	D 2503	IC 707 🍴	D 2405
0	Berlin Lichtenberg	—	0635	—	—	0835	0853	—	1035	—	1235
	Berlin Hbf	0628		—	0828			—		—	
	Potsdam Stadt			0720				1028		1228	
19	Berlin Schönefeld	0651	0657		0851	0857	0915	1051	1057	1251	1257
79	Jüterbog		0739	0822		0939	1003		1139		1339
111	Lutherstadt Wittenberg		0807	0853		1007	1038		1207		1407
148	Bitterfeld		0838	0925		1038	1114		1238		1438
178	Halle		0900			1100			1300		
182	Leipzig	0859		0958	1059	—	1148	1259		1459	1500

	D 2112	D 2502	D 1602	IC 802 🍴	D 2110	D 2402	IC 800 🍴
Leipzig	1540	—	1652	1701	1740	—	1901
Halle		1700				1900	
Bitterfeld	1612	1724	1736		1812	1924	
Lutherstadt Wittenberg	1641	1753	1806		1841	1953	
Jüterbog	1707	1819	1835		1907	2019	
Berlin Schönefeld		1748	1900		1906	1948	2100	2106
Potsdam Stadt			1931				
Berlin Hbf				1932			
Berlin Lichtenberg	1812	1924	—	—	2012	2124	2132

🍴 = Speisewagen

The fare from Berlin to Halle is DM 34,—. The fee for a seat reservation is DM 3,—.

Now switch roles. You are the customer. You want to travel from Norddeich to Hannover on a Saturday. You want to arrive in Hannover as early as possible, but you have to work until 11:00 a.m. Your job is 10 minutes from the Norddeich train station. Find out when the different trains leave, when they arrive, and whether they have a dining car (**Speisewagen**). Make notes on the different possibilities, decide which train you will take, buy a ticket and reserve a seat.

MÖGLICHE FRAGEN
—Guten Tag. Ich möchte am… von… nach…. fahren. Gibt es morgens einen Zug?

—So früh kann ich nicht abfahren. Gibt es vielleicht einen Zug am frühen
  Nachmittag?

—Wann fährt der Zug ab?

—Wann komme ich in… an?

—Gut. Ich möchte mit diesem Zug fahren.

—Darf ich bitte einen Platz reservieren?

Situationen

 A. Beim Fremdenverkehrsamt.

STUDENT 1

You are at the travelers' information office in Würzburg, trying to find a hotel room. You need a double room with a toilet and shower. You would like to be in a hotel with a breakfast buffet, because you like to eat a lot in the morning (**ich esse morgens viel**). Your price limit is DM 100,— (**ich kann nur DM 100,— bezahlen**). Arrange to stay for a few days.

STUDENT 2

You work in the traveler's information office in Würzburg. Ask for the customer's requirements (**Einzelzimmer, Doppelzimmer, Bad, Dusche, Preis,** etc.). Use the list below to make suggestions of appropriate hotels (**Das Hotel ____ hat…./Im Hotel _____ gibt es…und es kostet nur…**). Note that the two prices indicate a range from lowest to highest.

Hotels
0688 Würzburg — Vorwahl • Prefix • Indicatif — Tel. + Fax 0931

Plan-Nummer Number Numéro	Hotels	Bettenzahl Beds Lits	Einzel WC	Einzel Bad	Einzel Dusche	Doppel WC	Doppel Bad	Doppel Dusche	P	🚗	↑↓	📷	TV	♿	Sonderangaben
66	**Post Hotel** Mergentheimer Straße Tel. 6 50 05, Tx. 68471	127	79,- 119,-			119,- 169,-			●	●	●	●	●	●	1 Appartement, Frühstücksbuffet Terrasse. K 15/30/50
27	**Hotel Alter Kranen, garni** Kärnergasse 11 Tel. 5 00 30, 5 00 39	26	80,- 90,-			100,- 130,-				●	●	●	●	●	Kabel-TV
16	**Hotel St. Josef, garni** Semmelstraße 28–30 Tel. 5 31 41 (30 86 80)	48	65,- 80,-			110,- 140,-				●		●	●	●	Frühstücksbuffet
72	**Tecknikumhotel** Berner Straße 8, Tel 6 90 61	160	70,-			100,-			●			●	●		Appartements, Tennishalle, Spiel- und Sportraum, Trimm-Pfad, K 40/100/200
35	**Hotel Luitpoldbrücke, garni** Pleichertorstraße 26 Tel. 5 02 44/5	55	85,-	67,-	50,-	140,-	90,-	80,-			●	●		●	Frühstücksbuffet
32	**Hotel Strauß** Juliuspromenade 5 Tel. 3 05 70, Fax 305 75 55	129	70,- 85,-			104,- 115,-			●	●		●	●		Frühstücksbuffet, K 40/70
67	**Gästehaus Brehm** Stengerstraße 18, Tel. 6 40 28, 6 59 01	34	86,- 75,-			108,- 175,-			●		●	●	●		Frühstücksbuffet, Terrasse, K 50
25	**Hotel Zum Winzermännle, garni** Domstraße 32 Tel. 5 41 56, 1 74 56, Fax 5 82 28	43	75,- 90,-	60,- 80,-	35,- 50,-	95,- 150,-	90,- 100,-	70,- 95,- (WC)	●	●	●			●	Frühstücksbuffet, K 25
10	**Hotel Schönleber, garni** Theaterstraße 5 Tel. 1 20 68/9	53	80,- 85,-		48,-	90,- 130,-		75,- 80,-			●	●		●	Behindertengerechte Zimmer
8	**Hotel Babarossa, garni** Theaterstraße 2 Tel. 5 01 44, 5 59 53	25	70,- 75,-	60,- 65,-		100,- 115,-	95,-				●	●	●		Frühstücksbuffet
31	**Hotel Dortmunder Hof, garni** Innerer Graben 22 Tel. 5 61 63	25	70,- 90,-	48,- 70,-	45,- 48,-	120,- 160,-	80,- 100,-	70,- 85,-			●				K 15
36	**Hotel Central, garni** Koellkerstraße 1 Tel. 5 69 52, 5 68 08	36	66,- 70,-		42,-	100,- 115,-		96,- (WC)	●	●	●		●		
30	**Hotel Urlaub** Bronnbachergasse 4 Tel. 5 48 13, 5 31 88	37	60,- 65,-		43,-	100,- 105,-	88,-	68,- 75,-	●	●	●				Frühstücksbuffet, Sauna
64	**Hotel Rosenau** Erthalstraße 1 Tel. 7 12 66, 7 36 86	105	55,- 75,-			89,- 119,-			●	●	●		●	●	Terrasse K 60
13	**Hotel Stift Haug, garni** Textorstraße 16-18 Tel. 5 33 93	30	68,- 75,-		48,- 55,-	100,- 110,-		80,- 85,-				●		●	

B. Eine Weltreise. Sie machen eine Weltreise. Planen Sie die Reise mit einem Partner/einer Partnerin. Sie müssen mindestens zehn Länder besuchen und vier Monate unterwegs sein. Wo wollen Sie hin? Wie lange bleiben Sie? Was nehmen Sie mit?

BEISPIELE: —Ich möchte nach Griechenland fahren.
—Ich möchte lieber zwei Wochen in Italien verbringen.
—Warum können wir nicht beides tun? Für Italien und Griechenland braucht man einen Badeanzug, denn man kann überall schwimmen.
—Gut, dann fahren wir nach…

C. Meine letzte Reise. Beschreiben Sie Ihre letzte Reise. Ihr Partner/Ihre Partnerin fragt…

—wo Sie waren
—wer mitgefahren ist
—was Sie gesehen haben
—was Sie getan haben
—ob Sie gerne wieder hinfahren würden

…

D. Der Besuch. You are studying in Graz, Austria for a year. Your parents are coming to visit and you ask the help of an Austrian friend to plan your tour of Austria. Below are some suggestions of what to see in each city and a map. Once you have discussed your plans, draw your travel route on the map.

BEISPIELE: —Meine Mutter mag klassische Musik. Ich glaube, zuerst müssen wir nach Wien fahren.

—Ja, aber du sollst Salzburg nicht vergessen. Man kann dort das Mozart Haus besuchen.

WIEN
Staatsoper (*state opera*), Spanische Reitschule (*riding school*), Stephansdom (*cathedral*), Kunsthistorisches Museum, Hofburg (*imperial palace*), Sigmund Freud Haus.

SALZBURG
Hohensalzburg (*fortress*), Mozarts Geburtshaus, Sound of Music Tour, Mirabellgarten, Schloß (*castle*) Heilbrunn, Salzbergwerk (*salt mine*), Salzburger Festspiele (*music festival*).

GRAZ
Gotische Domkirche, Schloßberg

INNSBRUCK
Olympiamuseum, Hofburg

BREGENZ
Martinturm (2000 Jahre alt), Bregenzer Festspiele

Jetzt lesen wir!

Worum geht es hier? This story deals with a woman's hotel stay in the port city of Kiel and her problems paying for her room. With a partner, come up with and write down questions you would expect to be answered in such a story.

> BEISPIELE: —Warum ist die Frau in Kiel?
> —Wie lange bleibt sie?
> ...

Fahrkarte, bitte

HELGA M. NOVAK

Kiel sieht neu aus. Es ist dunkel. Ich gehe zum Hafen[1]. Mein Schiff ist nicht da. Es fährt morgen. Es kommt morgen vormittag an und fährt um dreizehn Uhr wieder ab. Ich sehe ein Hotel. Im Eingang[2] steht ein junger Mann. Er trägt einen weinroten Rollkragenpullover[3].

Ich sage, haben Sie ein Einzelzimmer?

Er sagt, ja.

Ich sage, ich habe nur eine Handtasche bei mir, mein ganzes Gepäck[4] ist auf dem Bahnhof in Schließfächern[5].

Er sagt, Zimmer einundvierzig. Wollen Sie gleich bezahlen? Ich sage, ach nein, ich bezahle morgen.

Ich schlafe gut. Ich wache auf. Es regnet in Strömen[6]. Ich gehe hinunter. Der junge Mann hat eine geschwollene[7] Lippe.

Ich sage, darf ich mal telefonieren?

Er sagt, naja.

Ich rufe an.

Ich sage, du, ja, hier bin ich, heute noch, um eins, ja, ich komme gleich[8], doch ich muß, ich habe kein Geld, mein Hotel, ach fein, ich gebe es dir zurück, sofort, schön.

Der junge Mann steht neben mir. Er hat zugehört[9].

Ich sage, jetzt hole ich Geld. Dann bezahle ich.

Er sagt, zuerst bezahlen.

Ich sage, ich habe kein Geld, meine Freundin.

Er sagt, das kann ich mir nicht leisten.

Ich sage, aber ich muß nachher weiter.

Er sagt, da könnte[10] ja jeder kommen.

Ich sage, meine Freundin kann nicht aus dem Geschäft weg.

Er lacht[11].

Ich sage, ich bin gleich wieder da.

Er sagt, so sehen Sie aus[12].

Ich sage, lassen Sie mich doch gehen. Was haben Sie denn von mir[13]?

Er sagt, ich will Sie ja gar nicht.

Ich sage, manch einer wäre froh[14].

Er sagt, den zeigen[15] Sie mir mal.

---

[1] *port*
[2] *entrance*
[3] *turtleneck sweater*
[4] *luggage*
[5] *lockers*
[6] **Es regnet.** . . *it's pouring*

[7] *swollen*
[8] *right way*
[9] *listened*
[10] *could*
[11] *laughs*
[12] IDIOM: *I bet you will*

[13] IDIOM: *What do you want from me?*
[14] **manch**. . . *many a man would be glad*
[15] *show*

Ich sage, Sie kennen mich noch nicht.
Er sagt, abwarten und Tee trinken[16].
Es kommen neue Gäste.
Er sagt, gehen Sie solange[17] in die Gaststube[18].
Er kommt nach.
Ich sage, mein Schiff geht um eins.
Er sagt, zeigen Sir mir bitte Ihre Fahrkarte.
Er verschließt[19] sie in einer Kassette[20].
Ich sitze in der Gaststube und schreibe einen Brief.

Liebe Charlotte, seit einer Woche bin ich im "Weißen Ahornblatt[21]" Servierin. Nähe Hafen. Wenn Du hier vorbeikommst, sieh doch zu mir herein. Sonst geht es mir glänzend[22]. Deine Maria.

"PALISADEN" Erzählungen, 1980

---

[16]IDIOM: **abwarten...** *let's wait and see*
[17]*for the time being*
[18]*lounge*
[19]*locks*
[20]*box*
[21]*acorn leaf* (here: the name of the hotel)
[22]*splendidly*

ALLES KLAR?

A. Haben Sie verstanden?

1. Was soll die Frau morgen um eins machen?
2. Was sucht sie jetzt in Kiel?
3. Wen ruft sie an? Warum?
4. Was ist das Problem? Welche Lösung (*solution*) schlägt die Frau vor?
5. Warum kann sie das nicht machen?
6. Was macht der Mann mit ihrer Fahrkarte?
7. Was macht die Frau eine Woche später?

B. Persönliche Fragen

1. Haben Sie dieses Problem auch schon gehabt? Haben Sie im Restaurant gegessen oder im Hotel übernachtet und kein Geld gehabt? Was haben Sie gemacht?
2. Was würden Sie in dieser Situation machen?
3. Sie haben vorher Fragen zu dieser Geschichte geschrieben. Welche Antworten haben Sie in der Geschichte gefunden? Welche nicht? Warum?

Themenwortschatz

Substantive

Länder

(das) Belgien	*Belgium*
(das) Dänemark	*Denmark*
(das) England	*England*
(das) Finnland	*Finland*
(das) Frankreich	*France*
(das) Griechenland	*Greece*
(das) Irland	*Ireland*
(das) Italien	*Italy*
(das) Liechtenstein	*Liechtenstein*
(das) Luxemburg	*Luxembourg*
die Niederlande	*Netherlands*
(das) Norwegen	*Norway*
(das) Polen	*Poland*
(das) Portugal	*Portugal*
(das) Rußland	*Russia*
(das) Schottland	*Scotland*
(das) Schweden	*Sweden*
(das) Spanien	*Spain*
die Türkei	*Turkey*

Auf Reisen gehen

die Bank, -en	*bank*
das Bargeld	*cash*
die Briefmarke, -n	*stamp*
das Doppelzimmer, -	*double room*
das Einzelzimmer, -	*single room*
das Fremdenverkehrsamt, ⁻er	*traveler's information center*
die Heimat	*homeland, native country*
die Jugendherberge, -n	*youth hostel*
der Koffer, -	*suitcase*
der Kurs, -e	*rate of exchange*
das Paket, -e	*package*

der Paß, ⁻sse	*passport*
die Pension, -en	*bed-and-breakfast inn or guesthouse*
die Postkarte, -n	*postcard*
der Preis, -e	*price*
das Reisebüro, -s	*travel agency*
der Reisescheck, -s	*traveler's check*
der Schlafsack, ⁻e	*sleeping bag*
die Sparkasse, -n	*savings bank*
das Ticket, -s	*ticket*
die Wechselstube, -n	*currency exchange office*

Verben

an•kommen, kam an, ist angekommen	*to arrive*
ein•lösen	*to cash (a check)*
fliegen, flog, ist geflogen	*to fly*
mit•bringen, brachte mit, mitgebracht	*to bring (along)*
packen *(packte)*	*to pack*
reisen *(+)*	*to travel*
reservieren	*to reserve*
übernachten	*to spend the night*
verbringen, verbrachte, verbracht	*to spend (time)*
wechseln	*to exchange*

Ausdrücke

auf Reisen	*on a trip*
bar	*in cash*
Geld wechseln	*to exchange money*
im Preis enthalten	*included in the price*
per Luftpost	*by airmail*
unterwegs	*on the road, underway*

(handwritten: in w/ country w/ article)

Weiterer Wortschatz

Substantive

der Gast, ⸚e	*guest*
die Nacht, ⸚e	*night*

Verben

ab•holen	*to pick up*
an•fangen, (fängt an), fing an, angefangen	*to begin*
holen	*to get*

Adjektive/Adverbien

ab	*as of*
damals	*at that time, back then*
jahrelang	*for many years*
leicht	*light; easy*
mittags	*at noon*
nachmittags	*in the afternoon*
nachts	*at night*
schwer	*heavy; hard, difficult*
vorgestern	*the day before yesterday*
vormittags	*in the morning*

Ausdrücke

anstatt… zu	*instead of*
in Ordnung	*OK, all right*
ohne… zu	*without*
pro Nacht	*per night*
um… zu	*in order to*
vor [zehn] Jahren	*[ten] years ago*
zum [ersten] Mal	*for the [first] time*

An der Uni

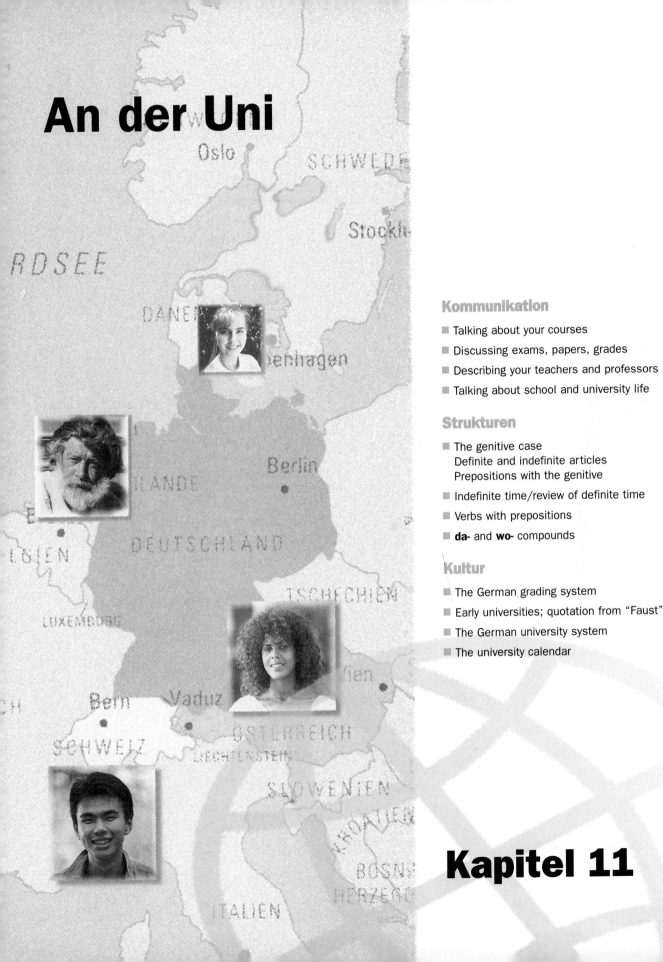

Kommunikation

- Talking about your courses
- Discussing exams, papers, grades
- Describing your teachers and professors
- Talking about school and university life

Strukturen

- The genitive case
  Definite and indefinite articles
  Prepositions with the genitive
- Indefinite time/review of definite time
- Verbs with prepositions
- **da-** and **wo-** compounds

Kultur

- The German grading system
- Early universities; quotation from "Faust"
- The German university system
- The university calendar

Kapitel 11

Na, los!

[handwritten: high school Oberschule]

Schritt 1: Auf der Schule/An der Universität

In German, as in English, the vocabulary used to discuss schools is different from that used to discuss colleges or universities. Below are some terms you will use in talking about your present and past educational experiences. You already know most of them.

DIE SCHULE, -N	DIE UNIVERSITÄT, -EN
der Schüler, -	der Student, -en
die Schülerin, -nen	die Studentin, -nen
der Lehrer, -	der Professor, -en
die Lehrerin, -nen	die Professorin, -nen
das Gymnasium, die Gymnasien	die Hochschule, -n
die Klasse, -n (*grade level*)	

ALLES KLAR?

Als ich Schüler/Schülerin war... Mit einem Partner/einer Partnerin besprechen Sie Ihre Erfahrungen auf der Schule oder an der Universität.

BEISPIELE: —Ich ging auf das Gymnasium in San Francisco.
—Als Schülerin war ich immer sehr fleißig.
—Für mich war die fünfte Klasse die schwerste, weil…
—Mein Englisch lehrer letztes Jahr war sehr…

[handwritten: Man geht auf Gymnasium man besucht ein"]

Schritt 2: Das Studium *[handwritten: (studies)]*

Every school or university system has its milestones (or its trials and tribulations, depending on one's point of view). Below are the German terms for a few of them.

der Aufsatz, ⸚e	*composition*
die Dissertation, -en	*(doctoral) dissertation*
die Klausur, -en	*final exam*
die Zwischenklausur, -en	*mid-term*
die Note, -n	*grade*
das Referat, -e	*oral or written report*
die Prüfung, -en	*exam, test*
die Semesterarbeit, -en	*term paper*

[handwritten: halten (oral)]

Note the following phrases:

eine Prüfung machen/schreiben	*to take a test*
eine Prüfung bestehen *[handwritten: bestanden]*	*to pass a test*
bei einer Prüfung durchfallen *[handwritten: durchgefallen]*	*to fail a test*
ein Referat halten	*to give a report*
ein Referat schreiben	*to write a report*

[handwritten: Ich bin]

Redewendung

Hochschule and **Gymnasium** are false cognates; **Hochschule** does not mean *high school*; rather, it refers to a university-level institution. *High school* is best translated as **Gymnasium**.

Reminder: **Lernen** is usually used for the intial stages of learning and for the task of studying. **Studieren** implies more advanced study; it can sometimes be translated as *to major in.* **Studieren** is not used with respect to elementary or high school.

Ich **lerne** Französisch.
I am learning French.

Wir **lernen** jeden Tag für die Prüfung.
We're studying every day for the test.

Duc **studiert** an der Technischen Universität in Berlin.
Duc is studying at the Technical University in Berlin.

Chia **studiert** Medizin.
Chia is studying (majoring in) medicine.

ALLES KLAR?

 A. Dieses Semester. Besprechen Sie mit einer Partnerin/einem Partner, was Sie dieses Semester in Ihren Kursen machen müssen.

> BEISPIELE: —Dieses Semester habe ich Englisch. Wir müssen eine Klausur und eine Semesterarbeit schreiben.
> —In Mathematik haben wir drei Prüfungen.

B. Prüfungen oder Referate? Besprechen Sie mit einem Partner/einer Partnerin, was Sie lieber in einem Kurs machen.

> BEISPIELE: —Referate sind nicht so schlecht, aber ich schreibe lieber eine Prüfung.
>
> —Ich nicht! Ich habe Angst vor Prüfungen. Ich würde lieber eine lange Semesterarbeit schreiben als eine Prüfung.

Kulturnotiz: The German grading system

The German grading system at the university level might seem like every American student's dream: grades are non-existent! Instead students take courses to prepare them for the mammoth comprehensive exams at the end of each year (for some majors) or at the end of the entire program.

German high schools, however, have a system similar to that of the US, except that the grades are designated by number rather than letter. The rough equivalents are:

GERMAN	AMERICAN
1	A
2	B
3	C
4	D
5	D-
6	F

Therefore, to report that you got an "A" on your last German test, you would say: **Für meine letzte Prüfung in Deutsch habe ich eine Eins bekommen!**

---

2. Seite des Abschlußzeugnisses der Gesamtschule

für _Karin Neumann_

Leistungen im Pflichtbereich

Deutsch	gut
Englisch	gut
Mathematik	befriedigend
Naturwissenschaften	
Chemie	gut
Physik	sehr gut
Gesellschaftslehre	gut
Erdkunde	
Geschichte	
Politik	
Arbeitslehre	
Technik	
Wirtschaft	befriedigend
Religionslehre	
Sport	sehr gut
Kunst	sehr gut

Leistungen in den Wahlpflichtbereichen:

Wahlpflichtbereich I

Naturwissenschaften ———— erteilt ab Klasse 7 _gut_

Wahlpflichtbereich II

Spanisch ———— erteilt ab Klasse _9_ _sehr gut_

Schritt 3: **Studienfächer**

In **Kapitel 4**, **Zu zweit**, you saw a sample high school schedule with some school subjects. The following list contains more subjects that you might study at a university level, either for your major (**das Hauptfach, ¨er**) or your minor (**das Nebenfach, ¨er**).

A course is **der Kurs, -e**; a particular class session is **die Stunde, -n**. To tell someone what subjects you are taking, use the verb **belegen**: Dieses Semester belege ich **Deutsch, Englisch, Psychologie und Geschichte.**

Alle
Bücher
für Studium
und Beruf!

JONSCHER
BUCHHANDLUNG
49074 Osnabrück • Domhof 6
gegenüber dem Theater
Telefon (0541) 2 24 28/2 54 24

die Amerikanistik	*American language and literture*
die Anglistik	*English language and literature*
die Anthropologie	*anthropology*
das Bauingenieurwesen	*civil engineering*
die Betriebswirtschaft, -en	*business administration*
die Biologie	*biology*
die Chemie	*chemistry*
die Fremdsprache, -n	*foreign language*
die Germanistik	*German language and literature*
die Geschichte	*history*
die Informatik	*computer science*
die Kunstgeschichte	*art history*
das Latein	*Latin*
die Mathematik	*mathematics*
die Medizin	*medicine*
die Musikgeschichte	*music history*
die Pädagogik	*pedagogy, education*
die Philosophie	*philosophy*
die Physik	*physics*
die Politologie	*political science*
die Psychologie	*psychology*
die Rechtswissenschaft, -en	*law*
die Soziologie	*sociology*
die Theologie	*theology*
die Wirtschaftswissenschaft	*economics*

ALLES KLAR?

A. Was belegst du? Fragen Sie mindestens fünf Studenten/Studentinnen, was sie dieses Semester belegen und was ihr Lieblingskurs (*favorite course*) ist. Füllen Sie die Tabelle aus und unterstreichen (*underline*) Sie den Lieblingskurs für jede Person. Fragen Sie auch, ob die Person schon ein Hauptfach hat.

NAME	KURSE	HAUPTFACH?
Yi-Ling	Geschichte, English, <u>Deutsch</u>, <u>Mathematik</u>	Mathematik
	3 Politologie, 2 Geschichte <u>Deutsch</u> Tauchen (diving)	

B. Was soll ich belegen? Jetzt besprechen Sie mit den Personen in Ihrer Gruppe die Kurse für nächstes Semester/Quartal.

BEISPIELE: —Ich möchte nächstes Semester Geschichte belegen. Peter, du belegst jetzt Geschichte. Würdest du den Kurs empfehlen?

—Ja, Geschichte 215 ist fantastisch. Frau Professor Lee ist ausgezeichnet!

Kulturnotiz: Early universities; quotation from "Faust"

The earliest German universities had only four divisions or schools: **Theologie, Philosophie, Medizin and Jura.** The first lines of Goethe's *Faust* show this:

> Habe nun, ach! Philosophie,
> Juristerei und Medizin
> Und leider auch Theologie!
> Durchaus studiert, mit heißem Bemühn[1].
> Da steh ich nun, ich armer Tor[2]!
> Und bin so klug[3] als wie zuvor;
> Heiße Magister[4], heiße Doktor gar,
> Und ziehe schon an die zehen Jahr[5]
> Herauf, herab und quer und krumm[6]
> Meine Schüler an der Nase herum[7]—
> Und sehe, daß wir nichts wissen können!
>
> Goethe, "Faust", lines 354-364

---

[1]*effort*
[2]*fool*
[3]*smart*

[4]*schoolmaster*
[5]**an die...** *for almost ten years*
[6]**heraub...**here: *round and round*

[7]**an die Nase...** *to lead around by the nose*

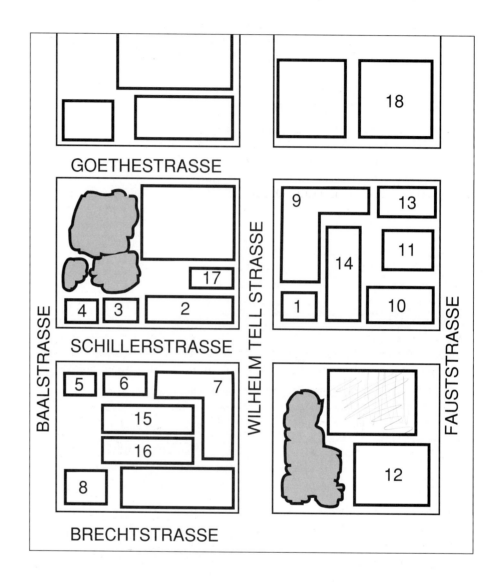

1. Institut für Germanistik
2. Mensa
3. Institut für Anglistik
4. Institut für Geschichte
5. Institut für Kunstgeschichte
6. Institut für Psychologie
7. Studentenwohnheim Dr. Rathenau
8. Institut für Informatik
9. Studenten-Centrum

10. Universitätstheater (Eingang: Fauststraße)
11. Institut für Theaterwissenschaft
12. Labor
13. Institut für Pädagogik
14. Institut für Chemie und Physik
15. Institut für evangelische Theologie
16. Institut für katholische Theologie
17. Institut für Philosophie
18. Bibliothek

Neu an der Uni. Ihre Partnerin/Ihr Partner ist neu an der Uni und fragt, wie man verschiedene Gebäude (*buildings*) findet. Benutzen Sie die Zeichnung links und erklären Sie, wie man dahin kommt.

BEISPIEL: von der Mensa zum Institut für Pädagogik
—Wie komme ich von der Mensa zum Institut für Pädagogik?
—Geh zuerst links in die Schillerstraße. Bieg dann links in die Wilhelm-Tell Straße ein und dann rechts in die Goethestraße. Das Institut für Pädagogik ist dann rechts neben dem Studenten-Centrum.

1. vom Labor zum Institut für Kunstgeschichte
2. vom Studentenwohnheim zum Institut für Theaterwissenschaft
3. vom Institut für Germanistik zum Institut für katholische Theologie
4. vom Institut für Informatik zum Institut für Chemie und Physik
5. von der Bibliothek zum Institut für Psychologie

Kulturnotiz: The German university system

Today the German university system and the American university system are quite different, even though the latter is based on the former. In Germany higher education is, for the most part, free. There are either no tuition costs **(Studiengebühren)** or they are minimal; if they do exist, they are covered by the state. However, parents are required by law to pay for room and board of their student-children, if they can afford it. There are funds available **(BAFög),** often in the form of loans, for those students whose parents are unable to support them.

In some universities, only a limited number of students are accepted in a given discipline **(numerus clausus).** Competition is hence quite keen, especially in medicine. Recently, the federal government in Germany decided that there should be no more "eternal students" **(ewige StudentInnen)** who study for twelve, thirteen, or more years at taxpayer expense; among other reasons cited was that these individuals take up spaces otherwise available to younger students.

Studium — wie lange?
Durchschnittliche Studiendauer an Hochschulen in Jahren

	Erforderliche Dauer des Studiums	Tatsächliche Dauer des Studiums
Italien	4,5 Jahre	7,5 Jahre
Frankreich	über 4	7
Deutschland (alte Länder)	4 bis 5	7
Niederlande	4,1	5,9
Schweden	4	ca.5,5
USA	4, 1 bis 4,2	über 5
Japan	4,1	4,3
Groß-britannien	3,5	unter 4

Quelle: iw
© Globus
9603

Schritt 5: Der Studienplan

(((📼))) Gespräch

Worum geht es hier? Kirsten spricht mit Vang, einem vietnamesischen Austauschstudenten, über seinen Studienplan für das Sommersemester. Was belegt er?

KIRSTEN: So, was belegst du denn im Sommer?

VANG: Ich bin noch nicht ganz sicher. Ich wollte ja Kunstgeschichte belegen, aber Professor Bachmann hält die Vorlesung, und er ist wirklich sehr langweilig. Leider merkt er nicht, wie langweilig er ist!

KIRSTEN: Aber Frau Professor Tashiro hält ein Seminar über die japanische Malerei[1] des 17. Jahrhunderts[2].

VANG: Das habe ich ja vorgehabt, aber gerade zu der selben Zeit trainiert mein Fußballklub. Das interessiert mich doch auch sehr!

KIRSTEN: Wie, bitte? Fußball? Das gibt's doch nicht an der Universität! Frau Professor Tashiro ist weltberühmt[3], und sie ist nur noch dieses Semester hier. Du mußt also wirklich zu ihrem Seminar gehen. Fußball kannst du jeden Tag spielen.

VANG: Also, du hast recht. Ich gehe zu Professor Tashiro. Nun, kannst du mir ein bißchen weiterhelfen? Ich belege auch noch Romantik[4] und ein Seminar über die Frau in der Literatur des 19. Jahrhunderts. Ich muß dann drei Semesterarbeiten schreiben; das reicht!

KIRSTEN: Ja, das reicht. Und mit diesem Studienplan hast du dann freitags immer frei.

VANG: Das habe ich ja von dir gelernt!

KIRSTEN: Dann können wir etwas zusammen unternehmen!

VANG: Wie, bitte? Ich muß auch trainieren!

ALLES KLAR?

A. Haben Sie verstanden?

1. Was ist das Thema dieses Gesprächs?
2. Warum will Vang die Vorlesung von Professor Bachmann nicht belegen?
3. Was schlägt Kirsten vor?
4. Wie ist das Thema des Seminars von Professor Tashiro?
5. Was erfahren wir über Frau Professor Tashiro?
6. Warum will Vang zuerst nicht in ihr Seminar?
7. Welche anderen Vorlesungen oder Seminarc belegt Vang im Sommer?
8. Wie hat Vang sein nächstes Semester geplant?

---

[1]painting   [2]century   [3]world-famous   [4]Romanticism

B. Persönliche Fragen.

1. Wie wichtig ist es für Sie, daß der Professor/die Professorin interessant ist? Belegen Sie nie Kurse mit langweiligen Professoren?
2. Belegen Sie auch Kurse, nur weil die Professorin/der Professor fantastisch sein soll?
3. Beschreiben Sie einen guten Professor/eine gute Professorin. Wie ist er/sie (interessant, lustig [*funny*], berühmt, organisiert, fair, streng [*strict*])?
4. Versuchen Sie ihre Kurse so zu planen, damit Sie einen Tag frei haben? Damit Sie keine Kurse vor 10 Uhr haben? Ist das leicht (*easy*)?

Kulturnotiz: The university calendar

Earlier in this chapter you read about several differences between the German and American university systems. There are others, especially in the academic calendar. German universities have only two semesters: Winter and Summer. The winter semester usually begins around the end of October and continues until February. Of course, an extended vacation does occur around the Christmas and New Year's holidays. The summer semester begins in March and continues until July. Students are then free in the months of August, September, and part of October. Only rarely do university students have exams during a course; most simply study until they are ready for their comprehensive examinations or the exams which allow them to teach in the school system. In fact, many university students stop after taking this test (**das Staatsexamen**) — roughly equivalent to the American master's degree. The next step up is the doctorate. In contrast to American "doctors," Germans frequently pursue non-academic paths, even though they might have a doctoral degree in an academic subject.

The genitive

You have already learned three cases in German: nominative, accusative, and dative. In this chapter you will study the fourth and last case, the **genitive.** The genitive case is used to show *possession*, or a *close relationship between people*, *objects*, or *ideas*. It is widely used in both spoken and written German, where English often uses the apostrophe + **s** or the preposition *of*.

> Die japanische Malerei des 17. Jahrhunderts ist sehr schön.
> *Japanese painting of the 17th century is very beautiful.*

> Ich habe das Buch meiner Professorin gekauft.
> *I bought my professor's book.*

> Die Studenten eines langweiligen Professors lernen oft wenig.
> *The students of a boring professor often learn little.*

You have already learned how to show possession with proper names: **Minhs Vorlesung, Hans' Zimmer**. As the above examples show, however, other genitives follow the noun they modify.

Definite and indefinite articles

The genitive of masculine and neuter nouns is formed by the genitive of a **der**-word **des**, or an **ein**-word, **eines**, and the addition of an **-s** or **-es** to the noun itself. The **-es** is used when the noun is monosyllabic or already ends in an **-s** or **-z**.

> Das Thema **des Aufsatzes** ist das deutsche Schulsystem.
> *The topic of the composition is the German school system.*

> Ich habe den Titel **ihres Buches** vergessen.
> *I've forgotten the title of her book.*

Otherwise, an **-s** is added.

> Ich freue mich auf das Ende **des Semesters**.
> *I'm looking forward to the end of the semester.*

> Die Worte **dieses Professors** sind immer wichtig!
> *The words of this professor are always important!*

With feminine and plural forms, the genitive of **der** is **der,** of **ein, einer**. No ending is added to the noun itself.

> Die Professorin hat nur die erste Seite **meiner Semesterarbeit** gelesen!
> *The professor read only the first page of my term paper!*

> Die Schüler **der beiden Schulen** gaben ein Konzert.
> *The pupils of both schools gave a concert.*

Endings on attributive adjectives which precede nouns in the genitive are usually **-en.**[1]

	MASCULINE	FEMININE	NEUTER	PLURAL
GEN	des jung**en** Schülers	der schlecht**en** Note	des neu**en** Buches	der gut**en** Schulen
	eines jung**en** Schülers	einer schlecht**en** Note	eines neu**en** Buches	keiner gut**en** Schulen.

> Wir belegen nie die Kurse eines langweilig**en** Professors.
> *We never take the courses of a boring professor.*

> Ich habe das Ende der letzt**en** Stunde verpaßt.
> *I missed the end of the last class.*

The genitive form of the interrogative **wer** is **wessen**, meaning *whose*.

> **Wessen** Kurs ist der beste?
> *Whose course is the best?*

> Ich weiß nicht, **wessen** Prüfung das ist — der Name steht nicht darauf.
> *I don't know whose test this is — there's no name on it.*

In colloquial or informal German, many genitive forms are replaced by **von** + dative:

eine Freundin von mir	*a friend of mine*
drei von den Professoren	*three of the professors*
in der Nähe von der Universität	*in the vicinity of the university*

---

[1]The exceptions are feminine and plural unpreceded adjectives, when the adjective takes an **-er** ending (since the genitive article **der** is missing).
> Die Kurse gut**er** Professorinnen sind immer populär.
> *The courses of good professors ar always popular.*

ALLES KLAR?

A. Interessante Themen (*topics*)**.** Ergänzen Sie mit dem Genitiv.

Frau Hun ist Professorin (1)_____ (die moderne Geschichte) an
einer Uni in New York. Im Laufe (2)_____ (das Semester) muß sie viele
Prüfungen und Semesterarbeiten korrigieren. Die Arbeiten (3)_____ (die
besten Studenten) sind immer interessant zu lesen. Die Arbeit
(4)_____ (ein junger Mann) liest sie besonders gern; er
schreibt immer über das Thema (5)_____ (das Kind) im
modernen Leben. Einmal schrieb er über den Effekt (6)_____ (die
moderne Industrialisierung) auf die Familie; ein anderes Referat war über den Beruf
(7)_____ (die Eltern) und seinen Effekt auf Kinder. Die Thesen
(8)_____ (seine Referate) sind immer originell.

 B. Die Familie. Mit einem Partner/einer Partnerin benutzen Sie den Genitiv,
um Familienbeziehungen (*family relationships*) zu erklären.

BEISPIEL: Bruder
—Wer ist dein Bruder?
—Er ist ein Kind meiner Eltern.

1. Großmutter
2. Großvater
3. Tante
4. Onkel

5. Kusine
6. Vetter
7. Schwester

Prepositions with the genitive

Just as some prepositions are always followed by the accusative or dative, a few
prepositions in German are followed by the genitive. These include:

(an)statt	*instead of* **Anstatt** einer Prüfung muß ich eine Semesterarbeit schreiben. *Instead of a test, I have to write a term paper.*
trotz	*despite, in spite of* **Trotz** einer schlechten Klausur bekam ich eine gute Note. *Despite a bad final exam, I received a good grade.*
während	*during* **Während** der Stunde schrieb ich eine Prüfung. *During the class I took a test.*
wegen	*because of* **Wegen** meines guten Referats brauchte ich die Klausur nicht zu schreiben. *Because of my good report, I didn't need to take the final.*

ALLES KLAR?

A. Persönliche Fragen. Antworten Sie in ganzen Sätzen mit dem Genitiv.

1. Was möchten Sie statt Ihrer Hausaufgaben machen?
2. Was machen Sie während der Deutschstunde? während der Englischstunde? Hören Sie gut zu (*listen*), machen Sie Notizen, schlafen Sie?
3. Hatten Sie während der Schulzeit gute Lehrer und Lehrerinnen?
4. Warum sind Sie fleißig? Wegen Noten? Wegen Ihrer Eltern?
5. Hört Ihre Zimmerkameradin/Ihr Zimmerkamerad oft laute Musik? Können Sie trotz lauter Musik lernen?

Indefinite time/review of definite time

The genitive case is also used to express unspecified or indefinite time periods. It is often used in stories or narratives.

> **Eines Tages** entschied ich mich einfach, Deutsch zu lernen.
> *One day I simply decided to learn German.*

> **Eines Abends** ging ich ins Kino, statt für die Prüfung zu lernen.
> *One evening I went to the movies instead of studying for the test.*

As you learned in **Kapitel 4**, specific time is expressed with the accusative.

> **Jeden Tag** muß die Professorin Hausaufgaben korrigieren.
> *Every day the professor has to correct homework.*

> **Letzte Woche** habe ich ein Referat gehalten.
> *Last week I gave a report.*

Following are some additional combinations.

jed-	Sekunde Minute Stunde Tag Woche Wochenende Monat Jahr Jahrhundert Montag, usw. Januar, usw. Winter, usw.	dies- nächst-	Woche Wochenende Monat Jahr Montag, usw. Januar, usw. Winter, usw.

The adjective **ganz** is also used in the accusative with the definite article.

| **den ganzen Tag** | *all day (the whole day)* |
| **die ganze Woche** | *all week long* |

In addition, the following expressions are common. Note that two of them use the genitive.

alle [dreißig Minuten]	*every [thirty minutes]*
alle [zehn Jahre]	*every [ten years]*
während der Woche	*during the week*
im Laufe des Jahres	*in the course of (during) the year*

ALLES KLAR?

A. Übersetzen. Übersetzen (*translate*) Sie die folgenden Sätze ins Englische.

1. Wir schreiben alle zwei Wochen eine Prüfung.
2. Eines Tages vergaß ich, meine Hausaufgaben zu machen.
3. Jeden Montag habe ich Geschichte.
4. Diese U-Bahn fährt alle fünf Minuten.
5. Letzte Woche ging er jeden Tag in die Bibliothek.
6. Als ich eines Abends bei ihm war, wollte er mir eine Geschichte über seine Schulzeit erzählen.
7. Mein Bruder studiert nächstes Jahr an der Universität München.
8. Zwei Jahre lang haben wir jeden Freitag Fußball gespielt.

 B. Was tun Sie regelmäßig (*regularly*)**?** Machen Sie eine Liste von den Dingen, die Sie regelmäßig tun. Wie oft? Mit wem? Warum? Besprechen Sie alles mit Ihrer Partnerin/Ihrem Partner.

> **BEISPIEL:** —Ich mache jeden Tag Hausaufgaben.
> —Fährst du jedes Wochenende nach Hause?

 C. Eines Tages… Ergänzen Sie die Sätze. Dann besprechen Sie kurz Ihre Ideen mit einem Partner/einer Partnerin.

1. Eines Tages möchte ich…
2. Letzte Woche habe ich…
3. Nächstes Jahr fahre ich…

Schritt 6: Frauen bauen auf

📖 Lesestück

Worum geht es? Wie viele Frauen studieren heute Bauingenieurwesen? An welcher Universität studierten Gabriele Masuch und Yiqun Zhuang? Was sind die Themen ihrer Dissertationen?

Frauen bauen auf

In den letzten zehn Jahren haben viel mehr Frauen mit dem Studium des Bauingenieurwesens begonnen. Die Anzahl dieser Frauen ist von vier auf siebzehn Prozent gestiegen[1]. Diesen Trend meldet[2] die Fakultät für Bauingenieurwesen der Ruhr-Universität Bochum. Wann hat dieser Trend begonnen? Als die Fakultät 1986 Umwelttechnik[3] anbot[4], wollten keine Frauen Ingenieure werden. Aber seitdem haben sich nun mehr Frauen für dieses Fach entschieden. Frauen studieren aber nicht nur Bauingenieurwesen, sondern sie interessieren sich auch für andere "Männerberufe". Zwei neue Dissertationen zeigen diesen Trend: Dr.-Ing. Gabriele Masuch hat neulich eine Dissertation über Betontechnologie[5] geschrieben, und Dr.-Ing. Yiqun Zhuang bekam den Doktortitel für eine Dissertation über Naturzugkühltürme[6] ! Als diese Frauen ihr Studium an der Ruhr-Universität in Bochum begannen, waren sie fast die einzigen Frauen. Dies ist nicht mehr der Fall[7]; jetzt studieren viele Frauen "Männerberufe".

Aus: UNI Berufswahl-Magazin

[1] climbed [2] reports [3] environmental technology [4] offered
[5] **Beton**: concrete [6] natural cooling towers [7] case

ALLES KLAR?

A. Besprechen Sie die folgenden Fragen!

1. Was denken Sie: Warum studieren mehr Frauen heutzutage Bauingenieurwesen?
2. Was sind "Männerberufe"? Gibt es immer noch "Männerberufe" und "Frauenberufe"?
3. Was will uns dieser Text zeigen?

B. Meine Meinung. Was sagen Sie zu den folgenden Sätzen?

1. Frauen sollen Ingenieurwesen nicht studieren; Frauen sollen die Kinder zu Hause versorgen (*take care of*) und nicht im Labor arbeiten.
2. Jede Person soll das studieren, was sie studieren will.
3. Es soll "Männerberufe" geben, aber es soll auch "Frauenberufe" geben.

C. Was studieren die Frauen? Hier sehen Sie eine Seite aus "Brigitte", einer deutschen Zeitschrift (*magazine*) für Frauen. Schauen Sie sich die Liste von den populärsten Hauptfächern für Frauen an. Studieren amerikanische Frauen dieselben (*same*) Fächer? Was meinen Sie? Fragen Sie andere Studentinnen. Machen Sie eine Liste von den populärsten Hauptfächern für Studentinnen in den USA. Vergleichen (*compare*) Sie Ihre Liste mit der Liste aus "Brigitte". Wie ist Ihre Reaktion?

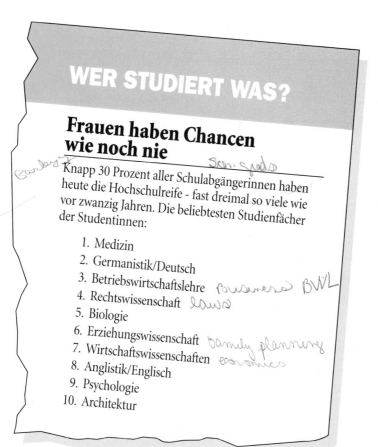

WER STUDIERT WAS?

Frauen haben Chancen wie noch nie

Knapp 30 Prozent aller Schulabgängerinnen haben heute die Hochschulreife - fast dreimal so viele wie vor zwanzig Jahren. Die beliebtesten Studienfächer der Studentinnen:

1. Medizin
2. Germanistik/Deutsch
3. Betriebswirtschaftslehre
4. Rechtswissenschaft
5. Biologie
6. Erziehungswissenschaft
7. Wirtschaftswissenschaften
8. Anglistik/Englisch
9. Psychologie
10. Architektur

Verbs with prepositions

In English, several verbs are almost always used with certain prepositions (*to think of, to be happy about, to wait for*, etc.). German also has special verb-preposition combinations; some are the same as in English, while others are different. These verb and preposition pairs are not the same as separable-prefix verbs. The prepositions do not function as separable prefixes, but simply as prepositions. When they are two-way prepositions, you must learn the case that they require — dative or accusative — as part of the expression. On the next page is a list of some common combinations.

denken an + acc.	*to think of*
	Ich **denke** oft **an** meinen Englischlehrer.
	I often think of my English teacher.
sich entscheiden für + acc.	*to decide on (in favor of)*
	Seitdem haben **sich** mehr Frauen **für** dieses Fach **entschieden.**
	Since then, more women have decided on (in favor of) this subject.
erinnern an + acc.	*to remind (someone) of*
	Ich muß ihn **an** seine Vorlesung **erinnern.**
	I have to remind him about his lecture.
sich erinnern an + acc.	*to remember*
	Er konnte **sich** nicht **an** den Namen des Professors **erinnern.**
	He could not remember the name of the professor.
sich freuen auf + acc.	*to look forward to*
	Wir haben **uns** sehr **auf** das Seminar **gefreut.**
	We were really looking forward to the seminar.
sich freuen über + acc.	*to be happy about*
	Sie hat **sich** sehr **über** ihre Note **gefreut** — eine Eins für ihre Semesterarbeit!
	She was very happy about her grade — an A on her term paper.
sich interessieren für + acc.	*to be interested in*
	Auch Frauen **interessieren sich für** "Männerberufe".
	Women also are interested in "male professions".
schreiben über + acc.	*to write about*
	Sie **schreibt** immer **über** interessante Dinge.
	She always writes about interesting things.
sprechen über + acc.	*to talk about*
	Wir haben gerade **über** dich **gesprochen!**
	We were just talking about you!
sich vorbereiten auf + acc.	*to prepare for*
	Ich **bereite mich auf** die Prüfung **vor.**
	I am preparing for the test.
warten auf + acc.	*to wait for*
	Auf wen **wartest** du denn?
	For whom are you waiting?

The preposition is always listed along with the verb and the case in the vocabularies in this book.

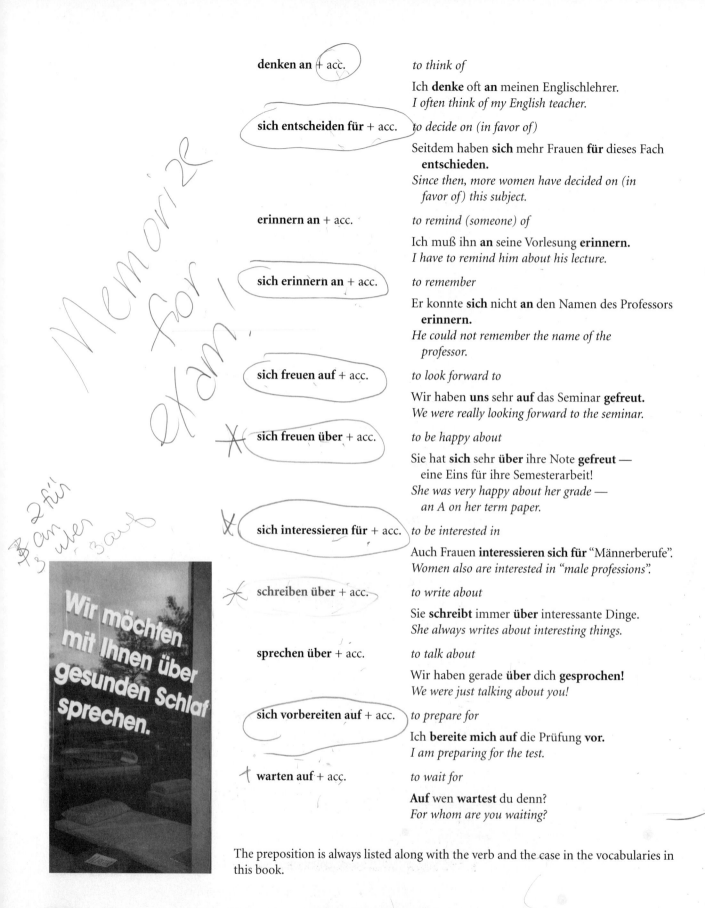

Wir möchten mit Ihnen über gesunden Schlaf sprechen.

ALLES KLAR?

A. Unsere Eltern und unsere Noten. Ergänzen Sie! Wenn es zwei Lücken (*blanks*) gibt, ist die erste Lücke für die Präposition, die zweite für einen Artikel, Adjektiv oder Pronomen.

JIN-HO: An wen denkst du denn?

SANG-SOO: Weißt du, ich denke oft (1) _____ _____ Eltern. Sie interessieren sich doch sehr (2)_____ _____ Studium (nt.). Sie freuen sich so (3)_____ _____ Noten am Ende des Semesters.

JIN-HO: Ja, da haben wir Glück! Auch meine Eltern interessieren sich (4)_____ _____ Noten. Sie freuen sich natürlich besonders (5)_____ jedes "A." Meine Eltern sprechen auch oft (6)_____ _____ Universität, aber sie haben nie studiert.

SANG-SOO: Meine Eltern auch nicht. Aber mein Bruder erinnert sich (7)_____ _____ Studienzeit. Er hat viel Spaß gehabt, aber er hat auch schwer gearbeitet. Jetzt verdient er auch sehr gut.

B. Mußt du... Besprechen Sie die Fragen mit einem Partner/einer Partnerin.

1. Mußt du immer auf deine Freunde warten? auf deine Familie? Oder müssen alle auf dich warten?
2. Freust du dich auf die Sommerferien? auf das neue Semester?
3. Interessierst du dich für Politik? für Theater? für Geschichte?
4. Freust du dich über deine Noten? über deine Kurse?
5. Sprichst du gern über Musik? über Fernsehen? über Politik?

Schritt 7: Unsere Schulsysteme

Gespräch

Worum geht es hier? Klara und Rosa sind Studentinnen. Sie vergleichen[1] ihre Erfahrungen in der Schule. Wer kommt aus welchem Land? Was machen die meisten Deutschen, die meisten Amerikaner in der Schule?

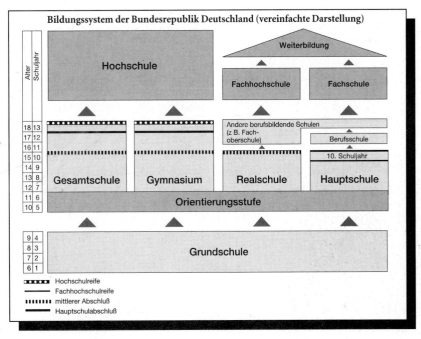

[1]*compare*

	AMERIKANER	DEUTSCHE		
1. Wie lange müssen Schüler zur Schule gehen?	vom 5. -6. Lebensjahr bis 16			
2. Wie viele gehen in welche Schule?	High School - 100% _College Universiti_	Hauptschule - _____% Realschule - _____% Gymnasium - _____%		
3. Was braucht man, um an der Uni zu studieren?	High School Diploma			
4. Wie viele Jahre dauert es bis zum High School Diploma/ Abitur?	12			

ROSA: So, du kommst aus Flensburg? Kannst du mir etwas von dem deutschen Schulsystem erzählen? Ich verstehe nichts davon.

KLARA: Also am besten erzähle ich von Anfang an. In Deutschland muß man vom 6. bis zum 18. Lebensjahr zur Schule gehen.

ROSA: So? Bei uns darf man mit 16 schon aufhören. Bei uns fangen aber viele mit Kindergarten an.

KLARA: Ja, bei uns auch. Der Kindergarten ist allerdings nicht wie die Schule. Ich war auch im Kindergarten. Bei uns kommt dann die Grundschule — sie dauert überall vier Jahre. In der 5. und 6. Klasse überlegt man sich, in welche Schule man nachher gehen will: in die Hauptschule, in die Realschule, in die Gesamtschule oder aufs Gymnasium.

ROSA: Du liebe Zeit! Wer die Wahl hat, hat die Qual[1]. Bei uns gibt es auch die Grundschule, aber sie dauert sechs Jahre. Dann kommt Middle School oder Junior High School und dann endlich die High School.

KLARA: Na, für euch ist es einfacher. Unser System ist etwas strenger[2]. Aber es ist merkwürdig[3], daß etwa 50% der Schüler und Schülerinnen in die Hauptschule gehen. Von da gehen die meisten dann in die Berufsausbildung[4]. Die Realschule steht zwischen Hauptschule und Gymnasium; etwa ein Drittel geht dahin. Diese Leute gehen vor allem in die Wirtschaft[5] oder Verwaltung[6]. Aber ich bin nicht dahin gegangen. Ich war auch nicht in der Gesamtschule; die Gesamtschule ist eine Kombination von allen anderen. Ich ging aufs Gymnasium. Da konnte ich mich auf das Abitur vorbereiten; ich lernte dort Mathematik, Geschichte, Naturwissenschaften, Fremdsprachen, usw. Das Abitur ist die Eintrittskarte[7] zur Universität.

ROSA: Wie? Gehen nur Schüler und Schülerinnen mit Abitur auf die Universität?

KLARA: Eigentlich ja, obwohl es auch den "zweiten Bildungsgang" gibt. Das ist für Leute, die ihre Meinung ändern.

ROSA: Das ist ja sehr streng. Wir müssen natürlich ein "Diploma" haben, aber das bekommt praktisch jeder.

KLARA: Ja, ich habe davon gehört. Ihr geht ja auch nur zwölf Jahre zur Schule, nicht?

ROSA: Ja, natürlich. Ihr nicht?

KLARA: Nein, wir gehen dreizehn Jahre. Es ist eigentlich besser, denn man lernt ja auch mehr. Die anderen gehen allerdings nicht so viele Jahre zur Schule.

ROSA: Das ist sehr viel. Kein Wunder, daß du so viel weißt! Aber unser System hat auch Vorteile[8].

[1]Proverb: The wealth of choices makes it difficult.
[2]more rigid
[3]noteworthy
[4]vocational training
[5]industry, business
[6]administration
[7]admission ticket
[8]advantages

ALLES KLAR?

A. Richtig oder falsch? Verbessern Sie die falschen Sätze!

1. Am Anfang versteht Rosa viel vom deutschen Schulsystem.
2. Die deutschen Kinder müssen vom 6. bis zum 18. Lebensjahr die Schule besuchen.
3. Die amerikanischen Kinder müssen vom 6. bis zum 18. Lebensjahr die Schule besuchen.
4. In Deutschland und in den USA gibt's Kindergärten.
5. Nach der 6. Klasse hat man in Deutschland vier Möglichkeiten (*possibilities*): Hauptschule, Realschule, Gesamtschule und Gymnasium.
6. In den USA hat man dieselben Möglichkeiten wie in Deutschland.
7. Fast die Hälfte der deutschen Schülerinnen gehen auf die Hauptschule.
8. Die Schülerinnen im Gymnasium bereiten sich auf die Uni vor.
9. Personen ohne Abitur haben keine Möglichkeit, die Uni zu besuchen.
10. In den USA und in Deutschland gehen alle Schülerinnen dreizehn Jahre zur Schule.

B. Auf welcher Schule sind die Schüler? Die folgenden Schülerinnen gehen zur Schule in Deutschland. Besprechen Sie mit Ihrer Partnerin/Ihrem Partner, wo man die folgenden Schüler wohl findet. Wo gehen sie in Zukunft hin?

> **BEISPIEL:** Soonwon ist acht Jahre alt, also in der dritten Klasse. Sie kann noch in alle Schulen gehen. Sie muß sich erst in etwa zwei oder drei Jahren entscheiden, auf welche Schule sie gehen will.

1. Soonwon - acht Jahre alt
2. Thang - zwölf Jahre alt - er möchte Tischler (*carpenter*) werden
3. Yi-Shien - sechzehn Jahre alt - sie möchte Sekretärin werden
4. Minh - achtzehn Jahre alt - sie möchte Ärztin werden
5. Sang Soo - fünfzehn Jahre alt - er möchte in der Industrie arbeiten
6. Szu-Hsien - zwölf Jahre alt - er möchte Professor werden

C. Die Vorteile. Was sind wohl die Vorteile des amerikanischen Systems? Gibt es auch Vorteile im deutschen System? Besprechen Sie es mit Ihrem Partner/Ihrer Partnerin.

Gute Schüler verdienen besser
Bruttoverdienst von Arbeitnehmern in DM

■ Schlechte Schüler   ▨ Gute Schüler

	Hauptschüler	Realschüler	Abiturienten
Schlechte Schüler	3.254	4.293	5.147
Gute Schüler	4.056	4.998	5.443

Source: Die Welt, Nr. 156, Tuesday, July 7, 1992, p. 1.

da- and *wo-*compounds

*da-*compounds

In English statements, pronouns often replace nouns in prepositional phrases.

> *I'm thinking about the exam.*
> *I'm thinking about **it**.*

In German, a pronoun used in such a way can refer only to a person. To refer to an inanimate object or a concept, a **da-** compound is used. The prefix **da-** is combined with the preposition; if the preposition begins with a vowel, then **da-** becomes **dar-**. Compare the following sentences:

DA-COMPOUND: OBJECT OR CONCEPT	PREPOSITION + PRONOUN: PERSON
Ich habe von dem amerikanischen "Diploma" gehört.	Ich habe von der berühmten Professorin gehört.
Ich habe **davon** gehört.	Ich habe **von ihr** gehört.
Yuka hat über ihre Ferien geschrieben.	Yuka hat über den Lehrer geschrieben.
Yuka hat **darüber** geschrieben.	Yuka hat **über ihn** geschrieben.
Vang wartet auf den Bus.	Vang wartet auf seinen Freund.
Vang wartet **darauf**.	Vang wartet **auf ihn**.

Da- can be combined with all prepositions except **außer**, **bis**, **ohne**, **seit**, and the prepositions that take the genitive case.

*wo-*compounds

wo- compounds are used in questions, both direct and indirect. They function just like **da-**compounds in that they refer to inanimate objects or to concepts. They can be combined with the same prepositions as the **da-** compounds; when the preposition begins with a vowel, **wo-** becomes **wor-**.

WO-COMPOUND: OBJECT OR CONCEPT	PREPOSITION + INTERROGATIVE: PERSON
Ich habe von dem amerikanischen "Diploma" gehört.	Ich habe von der berühmten Professorin gehört.
Wovon hast du gehört?	**Von wem** hast du gehört?
Yuka hat über ihre Ferien geschrieben.	Yuka hat über den Lehrer geschrieben.
Worüber hat Yuka geschrieben?	**Über wen** hat Yuka geschrieben?
Vang wartet auf den Bus.	Vang wartet auf seinen Freund.
Worauf wartet Vang?	**Auf wen** wartet Vang?

wo-compounds must also be used if the idea or concept being spoken of is not expressly identified:

> Weißt du, **wovon** sie reden?
> *Do you know what they are talking about?*

> **Worüber** haben Sie denn geschrieben?
> *What did you actually write about?*

ALLES KLAR? ☆☆

[handwritten top right: Ihn = him / Sie = Sie]

A. Du auch? Ergänzen Sie mit **da**-Komposita (*compounds*) oder mit der Präposition und dem Pronomen.

1. Ich freue mich auf die Ferien. Freust du dich auch _darauf_ ?
2. Ich erinnere mich gern an unsere Schultage. Erinnerst du dich auch gern _daran_ ?
3. Ich denke oft an unseren Freund Thang. Denkst du auch oft _an ihn_ ?
4. Ich habe mich für Volkswirtschaft entschieden. Hast du dich auch _dafür_ entschieden?
5. Ich muß immer auf Frau Sato warten. Mußt du auch immer _auf sie_ warten?
6. Ich interessiere mich für Kunstgeschichte. Interessierst du dich auch _dafür_ ?

[handwritten margin: Review Pronouns; Thing (pl); Person]

B. Wie bitte? Ihr Zimmerkamerad/Ihre Zimmerkameradin spricht über eine Freundin. Sie machen aber Ihre Hausaufgaben und hören nicht gut zu. Stellen Sie Fragen mit **wo-**.

> BEISPIEL: —Keiko interessiert sich nur für Literatur.
> —Wofür interessiert sie sich?

1. Keiko spricht immer von ihrem Professor.
2. Keiko denkt immer an die Prüfung.
3. Keiko freut sich auf die Ferien.
4. Keiko schreibt über die Kunstgeschichte im 19. Jahrhundert.
5. Keiko wartet auf ihre Noten.
6. Keiko erinnert sich nicht an den Klassenkameraden.

[handwritten answers: Woran denkt sie immer (Prüfung); Worauf – sich; Worüber sie?; Worauf wartet sie; Woran erinnert sie sich / An wen]

Zusammenfassung

A. Schulen in Deutschland. Ergänzen Sie mit dem richtigen Wort.

Realschule	studieren	Job
Schuljahr	Grundschule	sich freuen
vor·bereiten	Abitur	Schulsystem

Das deutsche (1)_____ unterscheidet sich (*differs*) in vielen Aspekten von dem amerikanischen System. In beiden Ländern gehen Kinder, wenn sie sechs Jahre alt sind, zur (2)_____.

Das fünfte und sechste (3)_____ ist in Deutschland ein Jahr der Entscheidung. Geht man danach aufs Gymnasium, so macht man das (4)_____, damit man nachher an der Universität (5)_____ kann. Schülerinnen und Schülern auf der (6)_____ oder Hauptschule jedoch ist das Studium praktisch unmöglich (*impossible*), denn diese Schulen (7)_____ Kinder auf einen Beruf (8)_____.

Viele Schülerinnen und Schüler (9)_____ _____ sehr, daß sie mit der Schule fertig sind. Sie interessieren sich nicht so sehr für das Lernen, sondern viel mehr freuen sie sich auf einen (10)_____, denn so können sie schnell etwas Geld verdienen!

B. Wer ist der beste/die beste? Beschreiben Sie kurz die beste Lehrerin (oder Professorin) oder den besten Lehrer (oder Professor), die/den Sie kennen. Warum ist diese Person so gut und so erfolgreich?

C. Eine lustige Geschichte (*funny story*). Erzählen Sie eine lustige Geschichte aus Ihrer Schulzeit.

> Eines Tages hat mein Lehrer/meine Lehrerin…
> Meine Eltern wollten…

D. Sommerkurse. Sie müssen diesen Sommer nicht arbeiten und möchten einige (*a few*) Sommerkurse belegen. Sehen Sie sich die Anzeigen (*ads*) an. Welche Kurse möchten Sie belegen und warum? Benutzen Sie Verben mit Präpositionen.

> Ich interessiere mich für… Ich bereite mich auf… vor. Ich freue mich auf…

 **Zu zweit: Student 1**

A. Welche Note sollen wir geben? Sie sind Professor/Professorin der Geschichte an der Uni. Sie haben einen Kurs zusammen mit einem anderen Professor/einer anderen Professorin gegeben. Jede Person hat eine Hälfte der Aufgaben korrigiert. Jetzt müssen Sie sich für eine gemeinsame Note entscheiden. Besprechen Sie mit Ihrem Partner/Ihrer Partnerin zuerst, welche Aufgabe am wichtigsten ist. Dann entscheiden Sie zusammen, welche Note jeder Student/jede Studentin bekommt.

BEISPIELE: —Ich finde, die Klausur und die Semesterarbeit sind am wichtigsten.

—Ich finde die Arbeit ein bißchen wichtiger als die Klausur. Die Studenten haben mehr Zeit daran gearbeitet.

—Na, gut. Wie war Rosas Semesterarbeit?

STUDENT/STUDENTIN	REFERAT	SEMESTERARBEIT	KLAUSUR	NOTE
Rosa Lee	interessant, gut organisiert: A		gut: A-	
David Phuong		nicht sehr lang und keine gute These (thesis): B		
Beverly Chung		gut geschrieben, organisiert, aber nicht originell: B+		
Robert Min	Interessant, aber nicht sehr gut organisiert: B+		Sehr gut! A	

B. Die Kandidaten. Sie sind Professor/Professorin und Sie suchen einen neuen Deutschprofessor für Ihre Uni. Sie haben gerade zwei Kandidaten interviewt. Besprechen Sie mit Ihrem Kollegen/Ihrer Kollegin, wer der beste Kandidat/die beste Kandidatin ist. Wenn Sie irgendeine Information über eine Kandidatin/eine Kandidatin nicht haben, fragen Sie den Kollegen/die Kollegin.

	FRAU DOKTOR WEISSMANN	HERR DOKTOR KIM
DOKTORAT	1993: Universität München	
UNTERRICHTSERFAHRUNG	2 Jahre Lektor an der Universität Halle; 3 Jahre Berlitz-Sprachinstitut	
DEUTSCHKENNTNISSE		Sehr gut - hat 5 Jahre in Berlin gelebt und gearbeitet
ENGLISCHKENNTNISSE		Muttersprache
PUBLIKATIONEN	Artikel über Goethe u. Buch über Schiller;	

Zu zweit: Student 2

A. Welche Note sollen wir geben? Sie sind Professor/Professorin der Geschichte an der Uni. Sie haben einen Kurs zusammen mit einem anderen Professor/einer anderen Professorin gegeben. Jede Person hat eine Hälfte der Aufgaben korrigiert. Jetzt müssen Sie sich entscheiden, welche Note Sie geben wollen. Besprechen Sie mit Ihrem Partner/Ihrer Partnerin zuerst welche Aufgabe am wichtigsten ist. Dann entscheiden Sie zusammen welche Note jeder Student/jede Studentin bekommt.

BEISPIELE: —Ich finde, die Klausur und die Semesterarbeit sind am wichtigsten.

—Ich finde die Arbeit ein bißchen wichtiger als die Klausur. Die Studenten haben mehr Zeit daran gearbeitet.

—Na, gut. Wie war Rosas Referat?

STUDENT/STUDENTIN	REFERAT	SEMESTERARBEIT	KLAUSUR	NOTE
Rosa Lee		nicht sehr gut geschrieben und ein bißchen unorganisiert: B		
David Phuong	langweilig, nicht gut vorbereitet: C+		nicht sehr gut: B-	
Beverly Chung	Ausgezeichnet! A		leider fast alles falsch: D+	
Robert Min		Ausgezeichnet! A+		

B. Die Kandidaten. Sie sind Professor/Professorin und Sie suchen einen neuen Deutschprofessor für Ihre Uni. Sie haben gerade zwei Kandidaten interviewt. Besprechen Sie mit Ihrem Kollegen/Ihrer Kollegin, wer der beste Kandidat/die beste Kandidatin ist. Wenn Sie irgendeine Information über einen Kandidaten/eine Kandidatin nicht haben, fragen Sie den Kollegen/die Kollegin.

	FRAU DOKTOR WEISSMANN	HERR DOKTOR KIM
DOKTORAT		1995: Universität von Illinois
UNTERRICHTSERFAHRUNG		4 Jahre High School in Mich. 2 Jahre TA an der U. von Illinois
DEUTSCHKENNTNISSE	Muttersprache	
ENGLISCHKENNTNISSE	Gut – seit 1993 in den USA	
PUBLIKATIONEN		Artikel über Pädagogik Lehrbuch (*textbook*) fürs erste Jahr Deutsch

Situationen

A. Wie ist Professor...? Interview two or three students; find out which classes they are in and ask them how they like the professors at your college or university.

—Hält Professor xxx gute oder langweilige Vorlesungen?
—Schläft man bei seinen Vorlesungen ein?
—Warum meinst du, daß dieser Professor oder diese Professorin gut (oder schlecht) ist?

Report back to the class who the best professors are and why.

B. Das Interview.

STUDENT 1

You are interviewing for a job as a teacher at a private high school. Talk about your own high school experience (**Meine Schulzeit war...**), what you found good and what you would do differently (**Ich fand _____ gut, aber ich würde _____ anders machen**). Answer the principal's questions about your university coursework as well and discuss what has prepared you to teach high school.

STUDENT 2

You are the principal of a private high school interviewing someone for a teaching position. Ask about the candidate's high school experience. What did that person like (**Was gefiel Ihnen während Ihrer Schulzeit?**); what he/she would do differently (**Was würden Sie anders machen?**). Also ask about the candidate's university coursework and why it has prepared him/her for teaching in high school.

C. Die Semesterarbeit.

STUDENT 1

You need an extension on a term paper (**Ich brauche mehr Zeit für die Semesterarbeit**). Explain the reasons to the professor and negotiate a new due date.

STUDENT 2

You are an English professor. A student wants an extension on a paper. You are not pleased with the request. Find out what the student's problem is and negotiate a solution agreeable to both (an extension granted, but a longer paper? a new topic?)

D. Studienberater.

STUDENT 1

You are the peer advisor meeting with one of your advisees. Discuss the student's schedule for next semester. What courses/professors do you (not) recommend? Why?

STUDENT 2

You are talking to your peer advisor about your schedule for next semester. You want to take English, German, history and physics. Find out whether your advisor recommends/does not recommend specific courses or professors.

German in Asia

When most people visualize the inhabitants of a German-speaking city, they normally imagine many blond, blue-eyed people. Some may be darker, but they are clearly of Western European heritage. These days, many foreigners are surprised to see people of different races, often from countries half-way around the world, studying, visiting, and living in Germany. Quite apart from the millions of Asian tourists who flock to the German-speaking countries each year, there is a substantial number of Asians who have, at some point in their lives, lived and worked in Germany.

A vigorous academic exchange with Germany has been part of Asian education for many decades. Hundreds of scholars from Asian countries have studied in Germany as Alexander von Humboldt Foundation Scholars. Acceptance into this program, begun in 1953, requires knowledge of the German language. Many Asian countries have sent their best scholars to Germany on this program, e.g. The People's Republic of China (over 500), Taiwan (over 70), Japan (over 1700), South Korea (over 190). Japan has had more Humboldt recipients than any other country in the world, including the United States, and the People's Republic of China takes fifth place internationally. In Japan, many of these Humboldt scholars go on to have a major impact on the politics and academics in their native country. At least fourteen Japanese university presidents are former Humboldt Foundation Scholars, as is a South Korean Minister of Health.

There are also strong cultural ties between modern Japan and contemporary Germany. Recently, for example, an "exchange concert" of both German and Japanese musical compositions was presented at the German Cultural Center in Tokyo. For several years, such concerts have been held under the aegis of the Goethe Institute, Tokyo. In alternate years, the concerts take place in Germany.

Asians have long been interested in German philosophical and literary scholarship. Native Chinese professors at international conferences often give superb presentations in flawless German. Martin Heidegger's *Sein und Zeit* has been translated six times into Japanese, despite, or perhaps precisely because of, the great difficulty in rendering German philosophy into an Asian language. The Chinese, too, find Heidegger interesting: his concept of "Sein" seems similar to Laotse's concept of Tao. Japanese scholars are rapidly becoming the brightest new stars in the field of German literary research.

A highly respected Japanese journal is devoted solely to German literature and culture **(Doitsu bungaku).** For those who do not read Japanese, German synopses are printed at the end of each issue of the journal.

German instruction in Asian countries has flourished for many years, despite the perception that most Asians learn English as their second language. German has been the most important language for both medicine and law in Japan since the Meiji-era (1868-1912), although English is now slowly taking over in this respect. Still, almost three quarters of a million university-level students in Japan elect to study German. In South Korea and Indonesia, German is frequently taught in the high schools, as well as in colleges and universities.

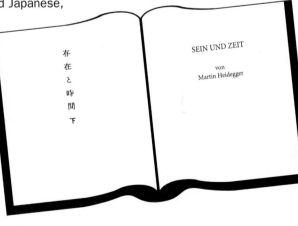

Given the unceasing flow of information and scholars between cultures half a world away, don't be surprised if one day you hear someone in Tokyo say, **"Doitsugo wa tanoshii desu yo."** *(German is fun!)*

Themenwortschatz

Substantive

die Schule

der Aufsatz, -̈e	composition, essay
die Grundschule, -n	elementary school
das Gymnasium, die Gymnasien	high school
die Klasse, -n	class, grade level
die Note, -n	grade
der Schüler, -	[male] pupil
die Schülerin, -nen	[female] pupil
das Schulsystem, -e	school system, educational system

Universität

der Austauschstudent, -en	[male] exchange student
die Austauschstudentin, -nen	[female] exchange student
die Dissertation, -en	(doctoral) dissertation
das Hauptfach, -̈er	major (subject)
die Hochschule, -n	university-level institution
die Klausur, -en	final exam
der Kurs, -e	course, class
das Labor, -s	laboratory
die Mensa, Mensen	student cafeteria
das Nebenfach, -̈er	minor (subject)
die Prüfung, -en	exam, test
das Referat, -e	oral or written report
das Semester, -	semester
die Semesterarbeit, -en	term paper, semester paper
der Studienplan, -̈e	class schedule
die Zwischenklausur, -en	mid-term

Studienfächer   ALL DIE

die Amerikanistik	American language and literature
die Anglistik	English language and literature
die Anthropologie	anthropology
das Bauingenieurwesen	civil engineering
die Betriebswirtschaft, -en	business administration
die Biologie	biology

die Chemie	chemistry
die Fremdsprache, -n	foreign language
die Germanistik	German language and literature
die Geschichte	history
die Informatik	computer science
die Kunstgeschichte	art history
das Latein	Latin
die Mathematik	mathematics
die Musikgeschichte	music history
die Pädagogik	education, pedagogy
die Philosophie	philosophy
die Physik	physics
die Politologie	political science
die Psychologie	psychology
die Rechtswissenschaft, -en OR: Jura	law
die Soziologie	sociology
die Theologie	theology
die Wirtschafts-wissenschaft, -en	economics

Präpositionen mit Genitiv

(an)statt	instead of
trotz	in spite of, despite
während	during
wegen	because

Verben

belegen	to take, register for (a course)
unterrichten	to teach

Adjektive/Adverbien

fällig	due
langweilig	boring

Ausdrücke

eine Prüfung machen/schreiben	to take a test
eine Prüfung bestehen	to pass a test
bei einer Prüfung durch•fallen	to fail a test
ein Referat halten	to give a report
ein Referat schreiben	to write a report

Substantive

die Erfahrung, -en	*experience*
der Fußball, ⸚e	*soccer*
das Jahrhundert, -e	*century*
die Minute, -n	*minute*
die Sekunde, -n	*second*

Verben

denken an (+acc.)	*to think of*
erfahren, (erfährt), erfuhr, erfahren	*to find out, learn*
erinnern an (+acc.)	*to remind (someone) of*
merken	*to notice*
reichen	*to suffice*
schreiben über (+acc.), schrieb, geschrieben	*to write about*
sich entscheiden für (+acc.)	*to decide on (in favor of)*
sich freuen auf (+acc.)	*to look forward to*
sich interessieren für (+acc.)	*to be interested in*
sprechen über (+acc.)	*to talk about*
verdienen	*to earn*
sich vor•bereiten auf (+acc.)	*to prepare for*
warten auf (+acc)	*to wait for*

Adjektive/Adverbien

einzig	*only*
noch nicht	*not yet*
sicher	*certainly, surely*

Ausdrücke

alle [dreißig] Minuten	*every [thirty] minutes*
alle [zehn] Jahre	*every [ten] years*
Du liebe Zeit!	*My goodness!*
Glück haben	*to be lucky*
die Meinung ändern	*to change one's mind*
im Laufe des Jahres	*during the year*
während der Woche	*during the week*

denken an

Sich entschieden für

errinernen an

Schulen und Universitäten

Schooling in Germany

Diese Bibliographie konzentriert sich auf die Jugend- und Studentenkultur. Außer interessanten Netzseiten findet man Links zu virtuellen Zeitungen und Treffpunkten deutschsprachiger StudentInnen.

1. **Freie Universität Berlin**
   Home page of the Free University in Berlin.
   http://www.fu-berlin.de/

2. **Europäische Universitäten: Leitseiten und Links**
   Excellent links to European universities and their home pages.
   http://www.rewi.hu-berlin.de/Internet/uniseu.html

3. **Deutschsprachige Universitätszeitungen**
   German university newspapers and campus publications.
   http://www.cs.tu-berlin.de/~schwartz/studzeit.html

4. **Leitseiten Heidelberger StudentInnen**
   Interesting web pages of students at Heidelberg University.
   http://ix.urz.uni-heidelberg.de/allgemeines/benutzer.html

5. **Digitale Jugendkultur: Infopool und Treffpunkt**
   Virtual meeting places for German speaking youth.
   http://www.wildpark.com/index.html

6. **SchulWeb: Deutschsprachige Schulen im Netz**
   Home pages and links to German schools on the web.
   http://www.educat.hu-berlin.de/schulen/inhalt.html

See the Prentice Hall home page for related activities and address updates (http://www.prenhall.com/~german).

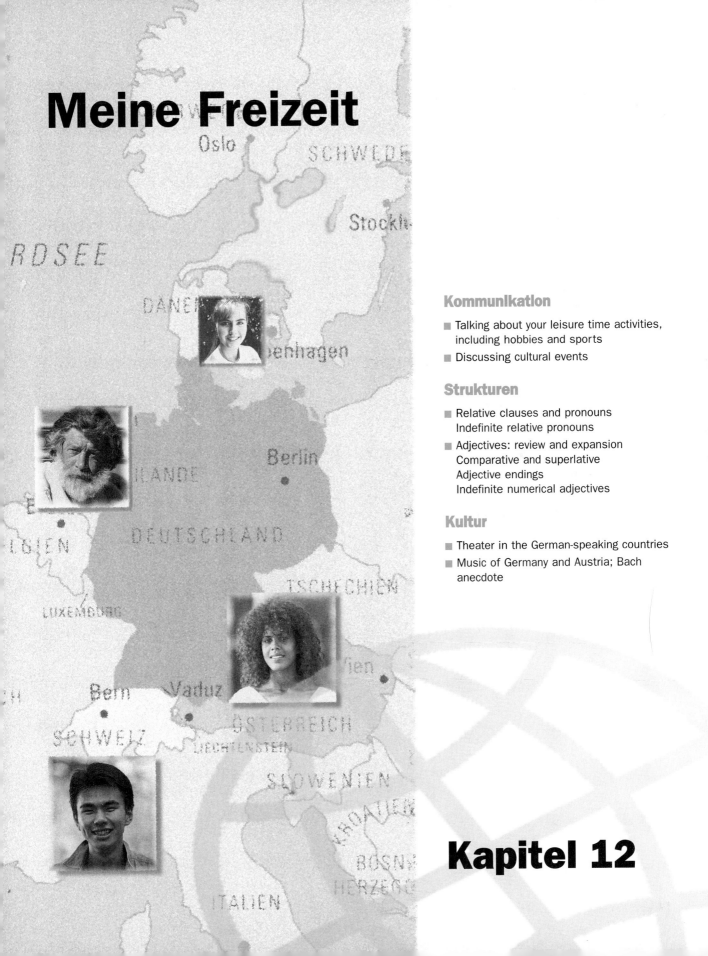

Meine Freizeit

Kommunikation

- Talking about your leisure time activities, including hobbies and sports
- Discussing cultural events

Strukturen

- Relative clauses and pronouns
  Indefinite relative pronouns
- Adjectives: review and expansion
  Comparative and superlative
  Adjective endings
  Indefinite numerical adjectives

Kultur

- Theater in the German-speaking countries
- Music of Germany and Austria; Bach anecdote

Kapitel 12

Na, los!

Schritt 1: Deine Freizeit: aktiv oder passiv?

You have already learned a number of words and phrases to express how you spend your free time. Here are a few new ones:

joggen *verb*	to jog
Tischtennis, Volleyball spielen	to play ping-pong, volleyball
segeln	to go sailing
einen Stadtbummel machen	to stroll through town
einen Spaziergang machen	to take a walk
in den Zoo gehen	to go to the zoo
ein Instrument (Trommel, Klavier) spielen	to play an instrument (the drum, piano)
basteln	to do crafts
etwas sammeln (Briefmarken, Münzen)	to collect something (stamps, coins)
in die Sauna gehen	to go to the sauna
einen Roman lesen	to read a novel
lange schlafen	to sleep late
faulenzen	to lie around, be lazy

Wilhelma
in Stuttgart

Deutschlands einziger
zoologisch-botanischer Garten

Das Erlebnis mit 8000 Tieren und
herrlichen Pflanzen aus aller Welt

ALLES KLAR?

A. In meiner Freizeit. Benutzen Sie die Wörter oben und andere Wörter die Sie kennen, und erklären Sie Ihrer Partnerin/Ihrem Partner, was Sie in Ihrer Freizeit gern machen.

BEISPIELE: —Samstags schlafe ich lange.
—Ich spiele fast jeden Tag Gitarre.

B. In ihrer Freizeit… Besprechen Sie jetzt, was Ihre Familie und Freunde in ihrer Freizeit machen. Wie finden Sie ihre Hobbys?

BEISPIELE: —Meine Schwester macht jedes Wochenende einen Stadtbummel. Ich finde das langweilig.

—Meine Mutter geht zweimal pro Woche in die Sauna. Das finde ich schön; ich gehe oft mit.

meine Schwester	machen	täglich	in die Sauna
mein Bruder	gehen	jede Woche	Tischtennis
mein Vater	sammeln	jedes Wochenende	Volleyball
meine Mutter	segeln	zweimal pro Woche	in den Zoo
meine Großmutter	spielen	alle zwei Wochen	Klavier
mein Großvater	joggen	…	Trommel
mein Freund….	lesen		Briefmarken
meine Freundin…	basteln		Münzen
…	faulenzen		der Roman
	schlafen		die Zeitung
	…		ein Stadtbummel
			ein Spaziergang (einen)
			ins Museum
			…

Handwritten annotations: "Das macht mir nich nich viel Spaß."; "Rad ~~Footbad~~ fahren"

Schritt 2: Freizeit und Kultur

Some leisure-time activities can also be considered "cultural". Here is some of the vocabulary needed to discuss these activities.

das Konzert, -e	*concert* (ins)
das Kunstmuseum, -museen	*art museum*
die Oper, -n	*opera* in die
das Theater, -	*theater*
das Theaterstück, -e	*play*
der Künstler, -	*[male] artist*
die Künstlerin, -nen	*[female] artist*
der Komponist, -en	*[male] composer*
die Komponistin, -nen	*[female] composer*
der Schriftsteller, -	*[male] writer*
die Schriftstellerin, -nen	*[female] writer*
der Schauspieler, -	*actor*
die Schauspielerin, -nen	*actress*

To find out whether someone would like to do something with you, ask **Hast du Lust,… zu…?**

> Hast du Lust, ins Konzert zu gehen?
> Hast du Lust, einen Spaziergang zu machen?

THEATER	erfreut
THEATER	informiert
THEATER	unterhält
THEATER	erschüttert
THEATER	regt an
THEATER	regt auf

Darum besuchen auch Sie Hannovers THEATER!

ALLES KLAR?

 A. Bin ich kultiviert (*cultured*)**?** Besprechen Sie diese Fragen mit Ihrer Partnerin/Ihrem Partner.

1. Interessierst du dich für das Theater? Siehst du lieber Dramen, Komödien oder Musicals? Gehst du oft ins Theater? Was ist dein Lieblingstheaterstück?
2. Interessierst du dich für klassische Musik? Gehst du oft ins Konzert? in die Oper? Wer ist dein Lieblingskomponist/deine Lieblingskomponistin?
3. Gehst du oft ins Kunstmuseum? Wer ist deine Lieblingskünstlerin/dein Lieblingskünstler? Was ist dein Lieblingsstil?
4. Liest du oft zum Spaß (*for fun*)? Wer ist dein Lieblingsschriftsteller/deine Lieblingsschriftstellerin?

B. Kultur-Quiz. Wie kultiviert sind Sie? Geben Sie sich "Kulturpunkte" für die folgenden Antworten.

	FRAGE	PUNKTE
0 = gar nicht 1 = 1-2mal 2 = 3mal 3 = 4mal 4 = mehr als 4mal	1. Wie oft in den letzten zwölf Monaten sind Sie ins Theater gegangen? ins Konzert? ins Museum? in die Oper?	
0 = Ich kenne sie/ ihn nicht. 1 = Ich habe dem Name gehört. 2 = Ich weiß, welchen Beruf (Dramatiker, Komponist, Schriftsteller, Musiker, Künstler) die Person hat(te). 3 = Ich habe einmal etwas von ihm/ihr gesehen, gelesen oder gehört. 4 = Ich habe mehr als einmal etwas von ihr/ ihm gesehen, gelesen oder gehört.	2. Wie gut kennen Sie die folgenden Personen? Richard Strauß Yo-Yo Ma Henrik Ibsen William Shakespeare Mary Cassatt Richard Wagner Christa Wolf Thomas Mann Dorothy Parker Itzhak Perlman Franz Kafka Giacomo Puccini Molière James Baldwin Anton Tschechow Jackson Pollock John Coltrane Toni Morrison Dorothy Sayers Georges Seurat Johann Wolfgang von Goethe Gesamtsumme =	

0-24 Punkte: völlig unkultiviert
25-49 Punkte: mehr oder weniger kultiviert
50-74 Punkte: kultivierter als viele andere
75-100 Punkte: hochkultiviert

Alles klar?

Schritt 3: **Was machen wir in Berlin?**

Lesestück

Worum geht es hier? Letztes Jahr waren Erich und Peter, die in Berlin zu Hause sind, in den USA als Austauschstudenten. Bill schreibt Erich, denn er und sein Zimmerkamerad, José, wollen Erich und Peter in Berlin besuchen. Wie gut kennen sich Erich und Bill? Welche Vorschläge macht Bill? Markieren Sie in der Tabelle, was Bill und José gern machen würden.

✓?	AKTIVITÄT	✓?	AKTIVITÄT
	einen Stadtbummel machen		ins Theater gehen
	in die Oper gehen		einkaufen gehen
	ins Kino gehen		in die Sauna gehen
	schwimmen		Tennis spielen
	segeln		in den Zoo gehen
	tanzen		joggen
	wandern		ins Konzert gehen

Omaha, Nebraska, den 1.12.96

Lieber Erich,

vielen Dank für Deinen Brief vom 25.11, den wir schon heute bekommen haben. Es freut mich, daß Ihr dann zu Hause seid, wenn wir Euch besuchen wollen. Du hast gefragt, was wir gern machen.

In den zwei Wochen, die wir in Berlin verbringen, wollen wir vor allem mit Euch viel unternehmen. Ich hoffe, Du kannst einen Tag fürs Wandern reservieren (am Wochenende?). Wir gehen auch sehr gern schwimmen, wenn es warm genug ist, aber im Hallenbad[1] geht das jedenfalls. Ich selber sitze auch sehr gern in der Sauna, wie Du vielleicht noch weißt. Mein Freund und ich würden auch sehr gern tanzen gehen—wie ist das eigentlich in Deutschland? Tanzt man so gern und so oft wie hier bei uns? Wir interessieren uns beide für den Berliner Zoo, der ja sehr bekannt ist. An einem Nachmittag würde es uns Spaß machen, einen Bummel auf dem Kurfürstendamm[2] zu machen. Abends gibt es vielleicht eine Möglichkeit, in die Oper zu gehen, oder vielleicht ins Theater? Du kennst Dich ja besser aus, vor allem weißt Du, was dann gerade spielt. Du weißt jedenfalls, wie gern wir so etwas machen. Vielleicht erinnerst Du Dich noch daran, daß Wagner mein Lieblingskomponist ist?

Das beste ist wohl[3], Du besprichst das alles mit Peter, dem bestimmt noch andere Dinge einfallen. Wir vier können dann viel Spaß haben. Wir freuen uns nun sehr darauf, Euch Ende Mai in Berlin zu sehen.

Bis dann,

Dein Bill

---

[1] indoor swimming pool
[2] The Kurfürstendamm is Berlin's busiest shopping street.
[3] probably

Kulturnotiz: Theater in the German-speaking countries

Germans, Austrians, and Swiss all love the theater; in each of these German-speaking countries, every town with any claim to culture will have at least one theater; larger towns have ten, twenty, even more. While there is little government support for theater in the US, the opposite is true in Europe, especially in the three countries mentioned. There, subsidies make attendance at almost any performance a possibility for anyone wishing to go. Tickets may cost as little as the equivalent of two or three dollars. The repertoire is extensive: not only original German-language theater, but also many translations of masterpieces from countries around the world, especially the French, American, and English theater. Modern theater in Germany has it roots in the English players who brought Shakespearean drama, as well as other plays, to Germany in the seventeenth century. As you learn more German, perhaps even next semester, you may well read one or more plays by modern Swiss, German or Austrian authors, e.g. Dürrenmatt, Frisch or Handke. When you travel to Europe, you can see dramas by these playwrights as well as by the more "classical" authors like Goethe, Schiller, Brecht, Nestroy, and many others.

A. Ich auch. Besprechen Sie mit Ihrem Partner/Ihrer Partnerin, welche von den Dingen, die Bill vorschlägt, Sie auch gerne machen! Wann? Warum?

BEISPIELE: —Ich gehe immer gerne in die Oper, denn ich mag Musik.

             —Ich gehe auch abends gern tanzen, denn es macht Spaß, mit Freunden zusammen zu sein.

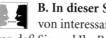 **B. In dieser Stadt.** Mit einer Partnerin/einem Partner machen Sie eine Liste von interessanten Dingen in der Stadt, in der Ihre Universität ist. Schlagen Sie vor, daß Sie und Ihr Partner/Ihre Partnerin einige von den Dingen zusammen machen.

BEISPIELE: —Hier gibt es ein sehr gutes Kunstmuseum. Hast du Lust, ins Museum zu gehen?

             —Ja, sehr gern, denn ich gehe gern ins Museum.

             —Hier in Philadelphia gibt es den ältesten Zoo in den USA. Möchtest du mit mir in den Zoo?

             —Ja, schön! Ich mag die Elefanten am liebsten!

ODER: —Nein, ich gehe nicht gern in den Zoo.

Relative clauses and pronouns

A relative clause is a dependent clause that cannot stand alone, as does an independent clause or sentence. A relative clause provides additional information about a noun or pronoun (called an antecedent) in the main clause or sentence. In English, relative clauses may or may not be introduced by relative pronouns. In German, relative pronouns are never omitted. As with all dependent clauses, the verb appears at the end. The relative clause is always set off from the rest of the sentence by a comma.

      MAIN CLAUSE   RELATIVE CLAUSE

Vielen Dank für deinen Brief, den wir schon heute bekommen haben.
Many thanks for your letter, which we already received today.

      MAIN CLAUSE   RELATIVE CLAUSE

Wir interessieren uns für den Berliner Zoo, der ja sehr bekannt ist.
We are interested in the Berlin zoo, which is very famous.

            MAIN CLAUSE
           RELATIVE CLAUSE

In den zwei Wochen, die wir in Berlin verbringen, wollen wir bestimmt ins Theater gehen.
In the two weeks (that) we are spending in Berlin, we definitely want to go to the theater.

English has the following relative pronouns: *who, whom, whose, which,* and *that.* In German, the relative pronouns are identical to the definite articles, with a few exceptions (the genitive forms and the dative plural form, highlighted below).

	MASCULINE	FEMININE	NEUTER	PLURAL
NOMINATIVE	der	die	das	die
ACCUSATIVE	den	die	das	die
DATIVE	dem	der	dem	**denen**
GENITIVE	**dessen**	**deren**	**dessen**	**deren**

The choice of the relative pronoun depends on three factors: number, gender, and case. The *number* is determined by the noun to which the relative pronoun refers.

> Vielen Dank für deinen Brief, **den** wir heute bekommen haben.

Because **der Brief** is singular, the relative pronoun **den** is also singular.

The *gender* is also determined by the noun to which the relative pronoun refers.

> Wir interessieren uns für den Berliner Zoo, **der** ja sehr bekannt ist.

Because **der Zoo** is masculine, the relative pronoun **der** is also masculine.

The *case* is determined by the function of the relative pronoun in its own clause.

> Das ist der Komponist, **der** sehr berühmt ist.
> Das ist der Komponist, **den** ich gesehen habe.
> Das ist der Komponist, **dem** sie den Preis gegeben haben.
> Das ist der Komponist, **dessen** Oper ich am liebsten höre.

Relative pronouns may also follow a preposition. They then take the case required by that preposition.

> Das ist der Schriftsteller, **an den** ich gedacht habe.
> *That is the writer of whom I was thinking.*

> Kennst du die Frau, **auf die** wir warten?
> *Do you know the woman for whom we are waiting?*

Tip!

Like all relative pronouns, the use of **dessen** or **deren** is determined by the gender of the antecedent, not by the following noun.

Christa Wolf ist die Schriftstellerin, deren Roman ich gelesen habe.
Christa Wolf is the author whose novel I read.

Kennen Sie den Komponisten, dessen Musik mich so beeindruckt hat?
Do you know the composer whose music so impressed me?

ALLES KLAR?

A. Zum letzten Mal. Schauen Sie die folgenden Sätze an. Erklären Sie das Geschlecht (*gender*), den Fall (*case*) und die Zahlform (*number*) von jedem Relativpronomen. Wenn Sie fertig sind, vergleichen (*compare*) und besprechen Sie Ihre Erklärungen mit einer Partnerin/einem Partner.

1. Unser Professor, der Briefmarken sammelt, bekommt fast jeden Tag einen Brief aus dem Ausland.
2. Meine Schwester, die noch sehr jung ist, spielt sehr gut Klavier.
3. Die Frau, mit der ich gesprochen habe, segelt sehr gern.
4. Es sind nicht immer schlechte Studenten, die lange schlafen, sondern manchmal faule Studenten.
5. Die Frau erhielt einen Preis für den Roman, den sie letztes Jahr schrieb.
6. Diese Studentin, deren Schwester ich kenne, geht gern ins Theater.

B. In den Sommerferien. Ergänzen Sie mit dem richtigen Relativpronomen.

San Diego, den 2. 8.96

Liebe Tanja,

Du hast gefragt, was ich in den Sommerferien gemacht habe. Du weißt schon, daß ich in dem Restaurant arbeite, _das_ neben dem Museum steht. Die Freizeit, _____ ich hatte, war ziemlich kurz. Ich bin mit meinem Freund, _der_ zwei Wochen zu Besuch war, ins Theater gegangen. Wir haben Shakespeares «Was ihr wollt» und sein «Viel Lärm um nichts» gesehen – Theaterstücke, _d____ ich nie auf der Bühne (*stage*) gesehen habe. Natürlich sind es Komödien, _die_ ich in der Schule gelesen habe. Am nächsten Tag, _der_ ja Sonntag war, sind wir ins Konzert gegangen. Die Musik, _die_ mir besonders gefiel, war von Schubert. Er ist ein Komponist, _den_ Name ich schon gehört habe, aber _dessen_ Musik ich nicht kannte. Es war ein wunderbares Konzert, an _das_ ich diese Woche oft denke, denn ich soll dieses Wochenende wieder ins Konzert. Hoffentlich spielen sie auch ein Stück von Schubert!

Du erinnerst Dich noch an Susan, mit _der_ wir in den Zoo gegangen sind? Sie arbeitet im selben Restaurant wie ich und wir haben zusammen einen Film gesehen, _der_ wirklich super war! Der wunderbare französische Schauspieler Gerard Depardieu, _den_ Du ja sicher kennst, spielte Cyrano de Bergerac. Auch die Schauspielerin, _die_ Roxanne spielte, war fantastisch!

Also waren meine Ferien, _die_ bald zu Ende sind, sehr interessant. Ich hoffe, daß Deine, _die_ ja erst jetzt beginnen, auch gut sind. Schöne Grüße auch an Deine Eltern, an _die_ ich oft denke.

Deine
Marion

C. Das letzte Ding. Besprechen Sie die Fragen mit einem Partner/einer Partnerin. Benutzen Sie ganze Sätze.

BEISPIEL: —Der letzte Roman, den ich gelesen habe,....

1. Wie heißt der letzte Roman, den du gelesen hast? Hat er dir gefallen? *Killer Kids*
2. Was war die letzte Rockgruppe, zu deren Konzert du gegangen bist? *P Jam*
3. Wie waren die Kurse, die du letztes Semester belegt hast? *Deutsch, 2 Geschichte,*
4. Wer war die letzte Person, mit der du ausgegangen bist? Würdest du mit ihm/ihr wieder ausgehen?

3 Biologie, die ich gegangen bist, war

Die Letze Rockgruppe, die ich gegangen bist, war

die

Kulturnotiz: Music of Germany and Austria

Germany and Austria both have a long tradition of classical music; some of the stars of the world of musical composition are listed below. See how many names from the column on the left you can match with concepts, places, or titles on the right.

Ludwig van Beethoven	Leipzig
Johannes Brahms	waltz king
Franz Schubert	Cosi Fan Tutte
Johann Sebastian Bach	twelve-tone scale
Richard Strauss	Messiah
Johann Strauss	twentieth century
Wolfgang Amadeus Mozart	Lullaby
Paul Hindemith	Unfinished Symphony
Arnold Schönberg	Salome
Georg Friedrich Händel	Choral Symphony

Can you identify which composers are German, which Austrian? Do you know their cities of birth? Which one spent most of his life in England?

Not only are these composers revered for their contribution to musical history, but they are also celebrated in many folk tales and anecdotes. The one below about Bach pokes gentle fun at the composer's dedication to his music:

> Johann Sebastian Bach war ein wunderbarer Komponist, aber seine Frau mußte alle Entscheidungen[1] im Haus treffen. Als die Frau starb, wußte der arme Bach nicht, was er tun sollte. Er saß still und allein in seinem Haus, und versuchte an seine Musik zu denken, denn er wollte zum Gedächtniss an[5] seine Frau etwas Neues und Schönes komponieren. Er setzte sich, nahm die Feder[2] auf, und begann zu schreiben. Bald dachte er nur noch an die Musik. In diesem Moment kam ein Diener[3] ins Zimmer. Am nächsten Tag sollte man Frau Bach zur letzten Ruhe tragen[4], und der Diener wollte wissen, was für Blumen Herr Bach kaufen wollte. Er fragte den Komponisten: "Bitte, Herr Bach, soll ich Rosen kaufen, oder gefällt Ihnen etwas anderes besser?"
>
> Bach schrieb weiter und antwortete: "Ich weiß nicht, frag meine Frau."

---

[1]*decisions*
[2]*quill pen*
[3]*servant*
[4]**zur letzten...** = *to carry her to her final resting place*
[5]*in memory of*

Indefinite relative pronouns

When there is no specific antecedent, German uses the interrogative pronouns as relative pronouns. The pronoun **was** is used only in the nominative and accusative cases, and it is invariable. It often follows words like **alles, nichts, etwas,** and **viel.** The pronoun **wer** can be used in all four cases (**wer, wen, wem, wessen**).

> Er sagt ihr nur das, **was** sie hören möchte.
> *He only tells her what she wants to hear.*

> Das ist etwas, **was** ich nicht verstehe.
> *That's something (that) I don't understand.*

> Weißt du, **wen** er gefragt hat?
> *Do you know whom he asked?*

> Ich weiß nicht, **wer** der Schriftsteller ist.
> *I don't know who the author is.*

ALLES KLAR?

Weißt du? Ergänzen Sie mit dem unbestimmten Relativpronomen.

1. —Alles, _was_ sie sagt, ist falsch!
   —Weißt du, von _wem_ sie das gehört hat?
2. —Weißt du, _was_ sie letztes Wochenende gemacht hat?
   —Nein, ich weiß nur, mit _wem_ sie zusammen war.
3. —Er schreibt nur das, _was_ sein Publikum sehen möchte.
   —Ja, aber sein Publikum weiß auch nicht, _was_ es sehen will!
4. —Weißt du, _wer_ der Autor dieses Romans ist?
   —Nein, ich weiß nur, von _wem_ er nicht ist.

Schritt 4: **Studenten und Studentinnen treiben Sport**

 **Lesestück**

Worum geht es hier? Viele junge Leute treiben Sport; viele davon sind Studenten. Treiben genau so viele Studentinnen wie Studenten Sport? Welche Sportarten treiben Studenten/Studentinnen in Deutschland am liebsten? Werden Studenten und Studentinnen, die keinen Sport treiben, schneller fertig als die, die Sport treiben?

Studenten und Studentinnen treiben Sport

Nur wenige junge deutsche Studenten und Studentinnen sind "Stubenhocker[1]." Vielmehr treiben sie fast alle Sport. Eine Meinungsumfrage[2] zeigte, daß 90 Prozent von 22,000 Studenten sportlich aktiv sind. Das bedeutet, daß 20 Prozent mehr Studenten Sport treiben als Nicht-Studenten, die von demselben Alter sind.

Sportarten wie Schwimmen, Radfahren und Jogging gefallen vielen jungen Studenten besonders gut. Andere junge Leute, besonders die, die in Vereinen Sport treiben, entscheiden sich oft für Tennis, Volleyball und Fußball. Auch Studentinnen treiben Sport, nur sie wählen andere Sportarten als die Männer. Mehrere deutsche Studentinnen entscheiden sich für Gymnastik, während viele deutsche Studenten am liebsten Fußball spielen.

Einige deutsche Studenten, etwa 22 Prozent, treiben auch an der Hochschule Sport. Viele Studenten und Studentinnen wollen, daß die Universitäten mehr Sport anbieten. Studenten, die Sport treiben, studieren nicht nur genauso lang wie Studenten, die keinen Sport treiben, sondern sie sind dazu auch noch viel gesunder.

aus: DAAD, "Hochschule und Ausland", leicht verändert

[1] couch potatoes
[2] opinion poll

ALLES KLAR?

A. Haben Sie verstanden?

1. Was sind "Stubenhocker?" Erklären Sie.
2. Was tun viele Studenten und Studentinnen?
3. Wie viele Studenten und Studentinnen hat man für diesen Aufsatz interviewt?
4. Was für Sportarten treiben Studenten besonders gern?
5. Welche Sportarten treibt man im Verein?
6. Welche Sportarten treiben Studentinnen in Deutschland besonders gern?

 B. Treiben Sie Sport? Treibt Ihr Partner/Ihre Partnerin auch Sport? Allein? Mit einer Mannschaft? Oft? Besprechen Sie das mit Ihrem Partner/Ihrer Partnerin.

1. Welche Sportarten magst du besonders gern?
2. Wie oft treibst du Sport?
3. Gehörst du einer Mannschaft an? Welcher?
4. Gehörst du einem Verein an? Welchem?
5. Treiben deine Eltern Sport? Deine Geschwister? Welche Sportarten?

C. Sport an der Uni. Besprechen Sie dieses Thema mit Ihrer Partnerin/Ihrem Partner.

1. Welche Sportarten sind am populärsten an Ihrer Uni? Sind die Sportarten bei Männern anders als bei Frauen?
2. Welche Sportarten sind am populärsten in der Grundschule? Auf dem Gymnasium?
3. Welche Sportarten sind am populärsten in diesem Land?
4. Sind sie populär, weil viele Personen aktiv daran teilnehmen (*take part*), oder weil viele Personen gern zuschauen?

Adjectives: review and expansion

Comparative and superlative

As you learned in **Kapitel 9**, there are three degrees of adjectives:

POSITIVE:	Wagners *Der Fliegende Holländer* ist sehr schön.
	Wagner's Flying Dutchmann *is very beautiful.*
COMPARATIVE:	Ja, aber *Tristan und Isolde* finde ich schöner.
	Yes, but I find Tristan and Isolde *more beautiful.*
SUPERLATIVE:	Aber *die Meistersinger* ist seine schönste Oper.
	But Die Meistersinger *is his most beautiful opera.*

Let's review the basic rules for the formation of comparatives; fill in the blanks in the following statements.

1. German has only one way of forming the comparative: _er_ is added to the basic form.
   schön — schön**er**
   interessant — interessant**er**

2. Monosyllabic adjectives usually also take an __ller__
   jung — jünger
   kalt — kälter
   groß — größer

3. Adjectives ending in **-el** or **-er** drop the __e__ in the stem before adding the **-er** ending.
   dunk**el** — dunk**ler**
   teu**er** — teu**rer**

4. Adjectives that end in **-e** add only an __r__.
   leise — leis**er**

Now fill in the blanks to review the basic rules for forming the superlatives:

1. German has only one way of forming the superlative: __st__ is added to the basic form.
   schön — schön**st-**
   vorsichtig — vorsichtig**st-**

2. An __est__ is added if the adjective ends in **-t, -d**, an **s** sound, or a vowel.
   interessant — interessant**est-**
   neu — neu**est-**
   süß — süß**est-**

3. Monosyllabic adjectives usually also take an __()__.
   jung — jüng**st-**
   kalt — kält**est-**
   groß — größ**t-**

4. The special forms for predicate adjectives and for adverbs in the superlative combine __am__ along with the adjective ending __sten__.
   schön — **am** schön**sten**
   vorsichtig — **am** vorsichtig**sten**

A few adjectives are irregular in the comparative or in the superlative form. Fill in the blanks to complete the chart.

gut	*besser*	best-	am besten
gern	lieber	liebst-	*am liebsten*
groß	größer	*größt*	am größten
viel	mehr	meist-	*am meisten*
oft	*öfter*	meist-	am meisten
hoch/hoh-[1]	höher	höchst-	*am höchsten*
nah	*näher*	nächst-	am nächsten

Adjective endings

All adjectives, including comparatives and superlatives, take normal adjective endings when they are used attributively, that is, to describe a noun which follows them:

MASCULINE		
NOMINATIVE der frische Salat	ein frischer Salat	frischer Salat
ACCUSATIVE den frischen Salat	einen frischen Salat	frischen Salat
DATIVE dem frischen Salat	einem frischen Salat	frischem Salat
GENITIVE des frischen Salats	eines frischen Salats	frischen Salats

FEMININE		
NOMINATIVE die gute Arbeit	eine gute Arbeit	gute Arbeit
ACCUSATIVE die gute Arbeit	eine gute Arbeit	gute Arbeit
DATIVE der guten Arbeit	einer guten Arbeit	guter Arbeit
GENITIVE der guten Arbeit	einer guten Arbeit	guter Arbeit

NEUTER		
NOMINATIVE das deutsche Bier	ein deutsches Bier	deutsches Bier
ACCUSATIVE das deutsche Bier	ein deutsches Bier	deutsches Bier
DATIVE dem deutschen Bier	einem deutschen Bier	deutschem Bier
GENITIVE des deutschen Bieres	eines deutschen Bieres	deutschen Bieres

PLURAL		
NOMINATIVE die langen Ferien	keine langen Ferien	lange Ferien
ACCUSATIVE die langen Ferien	keine langen Ferien	lange Ferien
DATIVE den langen Ferien	keinen langen Ferien	langen Ferien
GENITIVE der langen Ferien	keiner langen Ferien	langer Ferien

[1]**Hoch** is used adverbially and as a predicate adjective, while **hoh-** is used whenever the word is declined: **Das ist** *hoch* **interessant. Dieses Gebäude ist sehr** *hoch.* **Das ist ein sehr** *hoher* **Berg.**

ALLES KLAR?

 A. Wohin? Wohin möchten Sie gehen? Wohin möchte Ihr Partner/Ihre Partnerin gehen? Vorsicht mit Artikeln und Endungen!

BEISPIEL: —Ich möchte gern ins neue Kino gehen.
—Ich möchte lieber ins alte Kino.
—Vielleicht gehen wir am liebsten ins Museum?
…

Einige Vorschläge: Disco, Disco, Café
Theater, Theater, Oper
Café, Café, Sauna

B. Was finden Sie am besten? Oft gibt es keine "richtige" Antwort. Vergleichen Sie dann Ihre Antworten mit denen anderer Studenten und Studentinnen. Besprechen Sie Ihre Antworten.

1. Das interessanteste Buch, das ich je (*ever*) gelesen habe, ist _One true thing_.
2. Der beste Film, den ich je gesehen habe, ist _Patch Adam_.
3. Den größten Zoo in den USA findet man in _San Deiago_.
4. Die interessanteste Stadt in diesem Land ist _New York_.
5. Der schönste Bundesstaat (*state*) in diesem Land ist _Florida_.
6. Meine schönsten Ferien waren in _Florida_.
7. Die beste Rockgruppe heißt _DMBand_.
8. Das beste Fernsehprogramm heißt _P.E.L_.
9. Das schlechteste Fernsehprogramm heißt _S.P._.

C. Pro Stunde. Ergänzen Sie die folgenden Sätze. Dann besprechen Sie mit Ihrer Partnerin/Ihrem Partner, was billig (billiger, am billigsten) oder teuer (teurer, am teuersten) ist. Erzählen Sie auch, was Sie trotz des Preises am liebsten machen.

BEISPIEL: —Jogging ist am billigsten, das mache ich.
—Ja, aber ins Museum zu gehen kostet auch nicht sehr viel. Es ist fast so billig wie Jogging.
—Schon, aber mit dem Fahrrad fahren ist auch nicht teurer.

1. Wenn man ins Kino geht, kostet es _____, oder _____ pro Stunde.
2. Wenn man schwimmen geht, kostet es _____, oder _____ pro Stunde.
3. Wenn man in die Disco geht, kostet es _____, oder _____ pro Stunde.
4. Wenn man ins Museum geht, kostet es _____, oder _____ pro Stunde.
5. Wenn man ins Café geht, kostet es _____, oder _____ pro Stunde.
6. Wenn man mit dem Fahrrad fährt, kostet es meistens _____.
7. Wenn man Jogging geht, kostet es meistens _____.
8. Wenn man Tischtennis spielt, kostet es meistens _____.

D. Drei Dinge. Schreiben Sie die Namen von drei Büchern, drei Filmen und drei Sportarten auf. Schreiben Sie Sätze, die diese drei Sachen vergleichen. Besprechen Sie dann Ihre Resultate mit Ihrer Partnerin/Ihrem Partner.

BEISPIEL: *Vom Winde verweht; Wem die Stunde schlägt; Rambo III*
Vom Winde verweht war ein sehr guter Film, aber ich fand *Wem die Stunde schlägt* noch besser; am besten war jedoch *Rambo III*.

Patch Adams
You've got mail
Stepmom

Football
Basketball
Tennis

Alice + wonderland
Song Q Solona

E. Wer stimmt überein? Fragen Sie, ob andere Studenten mit Ihren Superlativen aus Aufgabe D übereinstimmen.

BEISPIELE: —Findest du auch, daß *Rambo III* der beste Film ist?
—Findest du auch Volleyball am spannendsten?

Indefinite numerical adjectives

Indefinite numerical adjectives do just what their name suggests: they indicate indefinite amounts. You have already learned many of them as individual vocabulary words; these are words that mean **many, several, a few,** and so on. Indefinite numerical adjectives in German are all plurals.

andere	*other*
wenige	*(a) few*
einige	*some, several*
mehrere	*several*
viele	*many*

When used without a **der-** or **ein-**word, these adjectives take the same endings as other unpreceded plural adjectives.

INDEFINITE NUMERICAL ADJECTIVES			
NOMINATIVE	andere	viele	wenige
ACCUSATIVE	andere	viele	wenige
DATIVE	anderen	vielen	wenigen
GENITIVE	anderer	vieler	weniger

As usual, any additional adjectives that follow these indefinite numerical adjectives take the same endings as they do.

> In Hamburg habe ich **einige neue** Theaterstücke gesehen.
> *In Hamburg I saw several new plays.*

> **Vielen jüngeren** Studentinnen gefällt der neue Film nicht.
> *Many young students do not like the new film.*

> Nur **wenige junge** Leute gehen oft in die Sauna.
> *Only a few young people go often to the sauna.*

If the indefinite numerical adjectives are preceded by a **der**- or **ein**-word, they take the usual plural -**en** ending.

Von den **wenigen** berühmten Schauspielern kannte ich keinen.
I did not know any of the few famous actors.

Keine **anderen** deutschen Filme spielen jetzt.
No other German films are playing now.

Because **alle** and **beide** denote specific amounts, they are **not** indefinite numerical adjectives. Therefore, adjectives following **alle** or **beide** always take an -**en** ending.

Alle ausländischen Studenten dürfen nach Berlin mitfahren.
All foreign students may go along to Berlin.

Beide neuen Filme haben mir gut gefallen.
I liked both new movies.

ALLES KLAR?

A. Die Freizeit. Ergänzen Sie mit Adjektivendungen, wo nötig!

Ihr_e_ Freizeit verbringen die meist_en_ Jugendlichen (*young people*) am liebst_en_ mit Verwandten (*relatives*) und Freunden. Sie unternehmen all_e_ möglich_en_ und unmöglich_en_ Dinge und haben viel_e_ verschieden_e_ Hobbys. Ihr_e_ Lieblingsbeschäftigungen sind: Musik hören, in d_ie_ Disco gehen, sich unterhalten, einem Hobby nachgehen, wandern, spazierengehen, Sport treiben. Sie sagen all_e_, daß sie viel_e_ gut_e_ Freunde oder Freundinnen haben, aber ein_en_ fest_en_ Freund oder ein_e_ fest_e_ Freundin wünschen sich fast all_e_. Nur wenig_e_ jung_e_ Leute lehnen (*reject*) die Gesellschaft ganz ab; sie gehören mit ihr_en_ Freunden und Freundinnen einer Freizeit-"Subkultur" an. Diese "Subkulturen" sind nicht ohne Gefahr, denn da machen viel_e_ jung_e_ Leute ihr_e_ erst_en_ Erfahrungen mit Drogen. Das ist jedoch nur ein_ klein_er_ Prozentsatz (m.).

Aus: *Scala Jugendmagazin*, leicht verändert.

B. Was machen viele? Beantworten Sie die folgenden Fragen. Verlgeichen Sie Ihre Antworten mit denen Ihres Partners/Ihrer Partnerin.

1. Welche Hobbys haben viele junge Leute?
2. Was machen wenige ältere Leute?
3. Gibt es einige neue Bücher oder Filme, die Sie gern haben?
4. Was machen viele Studenten und Studentinnen am Wochenende gern?
5. Was machen viele Studenten und Studentinnen nicht gern?

Schritt 5: **Was machen wir?**

 **Lesestück**

Worum geht es hier? Christoph, Esther und Andreas erzählen uns, was sie in ihrer Freizeit machen. Was tun sie? Haben Sie dieselben Interessen?

Christoph erzählt:

Ich spiele sehr gern in meiner Fußballmannschaft. Ich muß möglichst viele Tore schießen. Am Sonntagvormittag haben wir meistens ein Spiel.[2] Jede Mannschaft in unserer Gruppe spielt zweimal gegen jede andere, einmal zu Hause und einmal auf dem Fußballplatz des Gegners[1]. Im Fußball muß ich noch besser werden. Ich trainiere fast täglich. Ich esse immer kurz nach eins. Danach mache ich meine Hausaufgaben, lerne ein bißchen und lese dann meistens einen interessanten Kriminalroman. Um halb fünf hole ich meinen besten Freund zum Training ab. Nach dem Training gehen wir noch zusammen in den alten Jugendtreff, der in unserer Siedlung[2] ist. Dort spielen wir meistens Karten, manchmal auch Tischtennis. Aber oft sind wir nach dem Training ziemlich müde und unterhalten uns nur noch etwas bei Musik. Aus: Scala Jugendmagazin, leicht verändert

[1] *of the opponent*   [2] *town*

Esther erzählt:

Ich fahre jeden Tag mit der U-Bahn zur Uni. Im Sommer, wenn das Wetter schön und sonnig ist, fahre ich jedoch mit meinem alten Fahrrad. Morgens freue ich mich schon auf den Nachmittag, denn dann habe ich nur selten Vorlesungen. Meistens lege ich mich nach meinem wöchentlichen Seminar ein wenig hin, denn es macht mich sehr müde. In meiner Freizeit treffe ich mich oft mit Freunden und Freundinnen. Wir unterhalten uns oder diskutieren über Dinge, die uns interessieren. Wir haben sehr viel Spaß. Meistens sind wir bei jemand zu Hause oder in einem Pub. Manchmal bin ich zusammen mit einigen Polen, die in Deutschland leben. Sie versuchen, mir Polnisch beizubringen[1]. Das Lernen einer neuen Sprache macht mir Spaß, aber Polnisch ist schwer, besonders die Aussprache[2]. Mein Freund, der erst neunzehn ist, ist einer dieser Polen, aber ich treffe mich nur viermal in der Woche mit ihm, weil er auch gern mit anderen Polen zusammen ist und gern Polnisch spricht. Wenn ich dabei bin, sitze ich nur dumm da, weil ich nichts verstehe. Manchmal gehe ich auch in die Freie Schule (das ist eine Schule, wo es keine Noten gibt) und unterhalte mich, bastle oder mache Unterricht mit den Kindern. Manchmal macht die Freie Schule auch Ausflüge[3]. Da fahre ich meistens mit. Eigentlich möchte ich einen Job haben, damit ich mehr Taschengeld habe, aber einen Job zu finden ist schwer.

Aus: Scala Jugendmagazin, leicht verändert

[1] to teach [2] pronunciation [3] field trips

Andreas erzählt:

Meistens verbringe ich meine Freizeit mit Radfahren oder Fußballspielen. Und wenn ich dazu Lust habe, spiele ich mein Lieblingsinstrument, Schlagzeug[1]. Es steht bei uns zu Hause im Keller. Eigentlich habe ich im Musikverein zuerst nur Trommel gespielt. Dort bin ich durch meinen Vater und meine Schwester hingekommen, die auch Instrumente spielen (Vater: Trompete, Schwester: Saxophon). Ich will jetzt mit vier Freunden eine Band gründen[2], und wir wollen in der Schule üben[3]. Dort können wir uns fast alle Instrumente leihen. Wir wollen erst einmal Tanzmusik machen. Dann wollen wir vielleicht Rock oder Hardrock machen. Wir haben einen Jungen in der Band, der gut Gitarre spielen kann. Auch Fußball spiele ich in einem Verein, das macht mir auch Spaß. Doch leider stehen wir auf dem vorletzten[4] Platz in der Tabelle. Das Training ist hart, aber es macht Spaß. Ich habe noch kein Tor geschossen, bin aber erst drei Monate dabei.

Aus: Scala Jugendmagazin, leicht verändert

[1] percussion, drums [2] start, set up [3] practice   [4] next to last

A. Haben Sie verstanden?

(handwritten annotations in margins)

Jede Mannschaft
Seiner gruppe
Musik hören

1. Wann hat Christoph Fußballspiele? *Sonntagvormittags*
2. Wo spielt seine Mannschaft ihre Spiele? *zweimal*
3. Was liest Christoph gern? *Kriminalroman)* *Spiele* *Tabl* *Karten + Tennis*
4. Was tun Christoph und seine Freunde im Jugendtreff?
5. Wie kommt Esther zur Uni? *U-Bahn*
6. Was tut Esther in ihrer Freizeit? *treffe mit Freund*
→ 7. Was lernt Esther bei den Polen? *Polinisch*
→ 8. Warum trifft Esther ihren Freund so selten? *Sie hat um Deuch leben*
9. Was tut Esther in der Freien Schule? *? Taschengeld*
10. Warum möchte Esther einen Job haben?
11. Warum hat sie keinen Job? *Zu findet es not scherer.*
12. Was tut Andreas in seiner Freizeit? *Radfahren; fußball spielen*
13. Wie kam Andreas in den Musikverein? *Vater & Schwester*
14. Gehört er sonst noch einem Verein an? Welchem? *Fußball*
15. Wie lange spielt Andreas schon Fußball? *3 mts,*

Nur → 16. Spielt seine Mannschaft meistens gut?

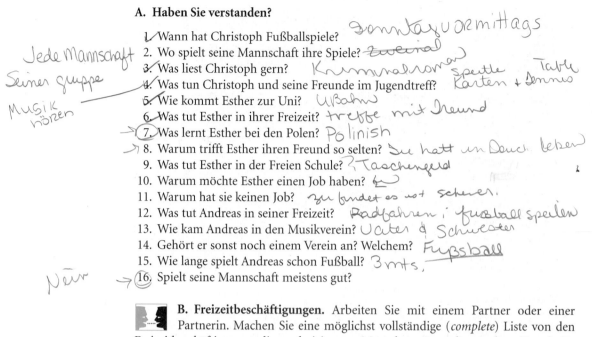

B. Freizeitbeschäftigungen. Arbeiten Sie mit einem Partner oder einer Partnerin. Machen Sie eine möglichst vollständige (*complete*) Liste von den Freizeitbeschäftigungen dieser drei jungen Menschen. Dann besprechen Sie, ob Sie auch so etwas machen. Ihr Partner? Ihre Partnerin? Warum oder warum nicht?

BEISPIEL: —Ich spiele gern Tischtennis. Spielst du auch Tischtennis?
—Nein, Tischtennis spiele ich nicht, denn es ist zu langweilig.
ODER: —Ja, ich spiele auch gern Tischtennis. Wollen wir mal zusammen spielen?

Die letzten Schritte

Wer macht mit?

Zusammenfassung

A. Meine Urlaubswoche. Ergänzen Sie mit Endungen, wo nötig!

Letzt*e* Woche habe ich zu Hause Urlaub gehabt! Ich hatte frei, konnte aber nicht wegfahren. Also, wie verbringt man ein___ Woche zu Hause?

SONNTAG: Heute habe ich mich einfach in die heiß____ Sonne gelegt. Ich wollte braun werden, damit die ander_____ Leute meinten, daß ich am Strand in Italien gewesen bin.

MONTAG: Heute morgen bin ich durch die schön___ Altstadt gegangen. Viele Leute, vor allem viele jung___ Leute, waren unterwegs, denn es war ein sehr schön___, sonnig___ Tag. Am Nachmittag bin ich mit drei Freunden ins neu___ Kino, das bei mir in *der* Nähe ist, gegangen. Am Abend habe ich drei andere Freunde eingeladen, und wir haben bis drei Uhr morgens Skat gespielt. Skat ist ein sehr bekannt___ deutsch___ Kartenspiel.

DIENSTAG: Heute bin ich erst um zwölf aufgestanden und ins Museum gegangen, um mir die wunderschön___ Picasso-Sonderausstellung[1] (f.) anzusehen. Das hat sich sehr gelohnt, denn viel_____ von sein_____ früh_____ Bildern kannte ich noch nicht. Dienstag abend bin ich mit viel___ ander___ jünger___ Studentinnen tanzen gegangen. Erst um zwei Uhr machte der Tanzklub zu; also wieder einmal erst um drei ins Bett.

MITTWOCH: Heute nachmittag habe ich mein___ neu___ Freundin geholfen. Sie hat ein___ gemeinsam___[2] Freund einen Geburtstagskuchen gebacken. Am Abend habe ich meiner Freundin ein besonder___ Essen gekocht; normalerweise habe ich keine Zeit dazu.

DONNERSTAG: Heute haben wir (mein___ Freundin und ich) ein_____ klein___ Ausflug (m.) gemacht. Mit mein___ schön___ neu___ blau___ Wagen sind wir von Philadelphia nach Ephrata gefahren, um uns die alt___ Klostergebäude (pl.) anzusehen. Auf d___ Rückfahrt (f.) haben wir *gegessen* und sind auch einkaufen gegangen. Wir waren so kaputt[3], daß wir sehr früh ins Bett gegangen sind.

FREITAG: Heute bin ich mit zwei Freunden schwimmen gegangen; danach saßen wir in der neu___ Sauna von mein___ Freund Tom. Freitag Abend war wie gewöhnlich Theaterabend. Wir haben ein sehr bekannt___ Stück von Brecht gesehen: Mutter Courage.

SAMSTAG: Heute war mein___ letzt___ frei___ Tag, und ich habe mich entschlossen, so faul wie nur möglich zu sein! Ich habe nichts getan— nur ein bißchen getrunken und gegessen. Ich mußte mich ja von mein___ anstrengend___[4] Urlaubswoche erholen[5]!

---

[1] *special exhibit* [3] here: *worn out* [5] *recover*
[2] *mutual* [4] *strenuous*

B. Das Tagebuch (*journal*). Schreiben Sie jetzt Ihr Tagebuch für eine Woche. Was haben Sie jeden Tag in der Freizeit gemacht? Versuchen Sie, Adjektive wie **viel, wenig,** usw. zu benutzen.

C. Ein Brief. Schreiben Sie an einen Freund/eine Freundin in Österreich. Laden Sie diese Person ein, Sie eine Woche lang an der Uni zu besuchen. Schlagen Sie Dinge vor, die Sie zusammen tun können.

D. Die Broschüre. Sie arbeiten im Fremdenverkehrsamt *(Tourist Office)* in Ihrer Heimatstadt. Schreiben Sie eine Broschüre für deutsche Touristen, in der Sie kulturelle und sportliche Aktivitäten in der Stadt beschreiben.

BEISPIEL: *THEATER:* In Boston gibt es viele gute Theater, wo man Dramen, Komödien oder Musicals sehen kann.

BASKETBALL: Die Basketballmannschaft von Boston, die Boston Celtics, ist eine der besten in den USA. Karten können Sie im Tourist Office bekommen.

A. Ausstellungen (*exhibits*). You and your partner are visiting Darmstadt and have consulted different newspapers for information on current exhibits. Compare information and make a complete list of the possibilities in the table below. Then discuss which exhibit you will see.

BEISPIEL: —In der Kunsthalle am Steubenplatz kann man eine Ausstellung von Papier sehen. Das möchte ich sehen.

—Hmm. Nicht schlecht. Wann ist die Ausstellung geöffnet?

> **Ausstellungshallen auf der Mathildenhöhe:** 10 bis 17 Uhr „Farbe zwischen Fläche und Illusion". **Jugendstilmuseum, Ernst-Ludwig-Haus,** Mathildenhöhe: 10 bis 17 Uhr geöffnet; Atelier des Museums Künstlerkolonie „Meta Memphis" Möbel- und Gebrauchsobjekte aus den Kollektionen 1989 und 1991. **Kunsthalle am Steubenplatz:** 10 bis 18 Uhr „Papier – von der Linie zum Objekt".

NAME DER GALERIE/KUNSTHALLE	ÖFFNUNGSZEITEN	NAME DER AUSSTELLUNG	KÜNSTLER

B. Ins Theater. Exchange information with your partner to complete the schedule of Hannover's cultural presentations.

HANNOVERS THEATER SPIELEN

	Staatsoper	Staatsschauspiel	Theater am Aegi
Samstag 3. November	19.30-22.45 Uhr **Die Zauberflöte** Oper von W. A. Mozart	9.30-21.00 Uhr (keine Pause) **Der Auftrag** von Heiner Müller	20.00 Uhr Besucherring Hannover, H. Zocher **Herbstkonzert** Polizeichor
Sonntag 4. November	19.30-22.00 Uhr **Ariadne auf Naxos** Oper von R. Strauß		16.00 Uhr Berufsfachschule für Bühnentanz **Carmina Burana** Musik von Carl Orff
Montag 5. November	20.00-22.00 Uhr **3. Konzert** Werke von: Alexandr W. Mossolow Sergej Prokofjew Ludwig von Beethoven	keine Vorstellung	keine Vorstellung
Dienstag 6. November		19.30-22.00 Uhr **Theater im Hotel** von John Murray / Allen Boretz	
Mittwoch 7. November		19.30-22.00 Uhr **Der Theatermacher** von Thomas Bernhard	20.00 Uhr - Institut Français **L'Orchestre du Grand Turc**
Donnerstag 8. November	19.30-21.30 Uhr **Der Nußknacker** Ballett von P. I. Tschaikowski	19.30-21.45 Uhr **König Hirsch** von Carol Gozzi	20.00 Uhr Hochschule für Musik und Theater Hannover **Orchesterkonzert**
Freitag 9. November	19.30-22.45 Uhr **Cosi fan tutte** (in ital. Sprache) Oper von W. A. Mozart		20.00 Uhr Eurythmiebühne Den Haag **"Wenn ich einmal groß bin"** von Mauro de Vasconcelos
Samstag 10. November		19.30 Uhr (Premiere) **Der Brand im Opernhaus** von Georg Kaiser	20.00 Uhr Modern-Jazz-Dance-Studio Annette Borsum **New York Dance Show**
Sonntag 11. November	19.30-22.45 Uhr **Don Giovanni** Oper von W. A. Mozart	19.00-22.30 Uhr **Das weite Land** von Arthur Schnitzler	

Zu zweit: **Student 2**

A. Ausstellungen (*exhibits*). You and your partner are visiting Darmstadt and have consulted different newspapers for information on current exhibits. Compare information and make a complete list of the possibilities in the table below. Then discuss which exhibit you will see.

BEISPIEL: —In der Kunsthalle am Steubenplatz kann man eine Ausstellung von Papier sehen. Das möchte ich sehen.

—Hmm. Nicht schlecht. Wann wird die Ausstellung geöffnet?

Hessisches Landesmuseum: 11 bis 17 Uhr geöffnet: Sonderausstellungen: „Dinosaurier aus China". „Rainer Lind – Zeichnungen" und „Farbe zwischen Fläche und Illustration". **Schloßmuseum:** 10 bis 13 Uhr. **Porzellansammlung im Prinz-Georgs-Palais,** im Schloßgarten 7: 10 bis 13 Uhr geöffnet. **Institut für Neue Technische Form.** Eugen-Brach-Weg 6: 10 bis 13 Uhr Braun-Design-Sammlung und „Die Handschrift des Künstlers". **Park der Mathildenhöhe:** „Skulptur gegen Objekt".

NAME DER GALERIE/KUNSTHALLE	ÖFFNUNGSZEITEN	NAME DER AUSSTELLUNG	KÜNSTLER

B. Ins Theater. Exchange information with your partner to complete the schedule of Hannover's cultural presentations.

HANNOVERS THEATER SPIELEN

	Staatsoper	Staatsschauspiel	Theater am Aegi
Samstag 3. November		19.30-21.00 Uhr (keine Pause) **Der Auftrag** von Heiner Müller	20.00 Uhr Besucherring Hannover, H. Zocher **Herbstkonzert** Polizeichor
Sonntag 4. November	19.30-22.00 Uhr **Ariadne auf Naxos** Oper von R. Strauß	19.30-22.15 Uhr **Die Möwe** von Anton Tschechow	16.00 Uhr Berufsfachschule für Bühnentanz **Carmina Burana** Musik von Carl Orff
Montag 5. November	20.00-22.00 Uhr **3. Konzert** Werke von: Alexandr W. Mossolow Sergej Prokofjew Ludwig von Beethoven	keine Vorstellung	keine Vorstellung
Dienstag 6. November		19.30-22.00 Uhr **Theater im Hotel** von John Murray / Allen Boretz	20.00 Uhr **Die Zauberflöte** Staatsoper Polen
Mittwoch 7. November	19.30-22.30 Uhr **Die Fledermaus** Operette von Johann Strauß		20.00 Uhr - Institut Français **L'Orchestre du Grand Turc**
Donnerstag 8. November		19.30-21.45 Uhr **König Hirsch** von Carol Gozzi	
Freitag 9. November	19.30-22.45 Uhr **Cosi fan tutte** (in ital. Sprache) Oper von W. A. Mozart	19.30-21.30 Uhr **Der Parasit** von Friedrich von Schiller	20.00 Uhr Eurythmiebühne Den Haag **"Wenn ich einmal groß bin"** von Mauro de Vasconcelos
Samstag 10. November	19.30-22.00 Uhr **Madame Butterfly** (in ital. Sprache) Oper von G. Puccini	19.30 Uhr (Premiere) **Der Brand im Opernhaus** von Georg Kaiser	
Sonntag 11. November	19.30-22.45 Uhr **Don Giovanni** Oper von W. A. Mozart		17.00 Uhr **Die blaue Stunde** Tucholsky-Programm

Situationen

A. Der Besuch.

STUDENT 1

Next week a friend of yours from your hometown high school is coming to visit you at school. Discuss with your housemate (your partner) how you plan to entertain this friend. You are interested in all types of sports. However, you want to include your housemate and you need to plan activities that all of you will enjoy. After your discussion, make a schedule for the week.

STUDENT 2

Your housemate (your partner) has a high school friend visiting next week and asks your suggestions in planning activities. You enjoy cultural events (plays, museums, concerts). Discuss the possibilities with your housemate, taking into account the visitor's favorite activities as well. Help your housemate make a schedule for the week.

MONTAG	DIENSTAG	MITTWOCH	DONNERSTAG	FREITAG	SAMSTAG

B. Die Fernsehdebatte.

You believe people watch too much TV — no one reads any more; TV is violent (**brutal/gewaltsam**); and it has a bad influence on children (**hat einen schlechten Einfluß auf Kinder**). There are no good programs, and people would be better off reading a newspaper or a good book. Try to convince your partner of the merit of your point of view.

Although some people watch too much TV, you believe it has educational and entertainment value. There are good programs for children (give some examples), news programs and some wonderful comedies and dramas. Try to convince your partner of the merit of your point of view.

NÜTZLICHE WÖRTER:		
	Dokumentarfilme	*documentaries*
	Nachrichten	*news*
	Komödien	*comedies*
	Dramen	*dramas*

C. Sportarten in Freiburg. You and your partner are visiting Freiburg i. Br. and want to take advantage of the region's sport facilities. Look at the directory and then discuss with your partner what you will do with your three days in Freiburg. What can you afford to do? What would you like to do, if only it weren't so expensive (**Ich möchte…, aber es ist zu teuer.**)

Sportplätze/Spielplätze:		**Rollsport**	
Liste der Sportvereine durch das Städt. Sportamt im Rathaus		Schauenberghalle, FT-Sportpark, Schwarzwaldstr. 181	36286/87
Angeln		**Schießsport**	
Auskunft: Zoo- und Angelgeräte Meyer, Ecke Wilhelm- und Erbprinzenstr.	26676	Schützengesellschaft Waldseestr. 86	73282
		Schützenverein St. Georgen, Baldensteinstr. 6	
Flugsport			
Flugplatz, Hermann-Mitsch-Str., Luftaufsichtsstelle	52626	492350	
Flugschule Harter, Flugplatz, Motorflugausbildung	53579	**Squash**	
		7800 Freiburg, Ensisheimer Str. 5	83404
Golf		7802 Merzhausen, Am Rohrgraben 3	40205
Freiburger Golfplatz e.V., Postfach 523,	07661/5569	**Tennis**	
		Bad-Hotel Jägerhäusle, Wintererstr. 89	55101
9 Lochplatz, Freiburg-Kappel, Kirchzartener Str.	+ 0761/515264	Freiburger Tennisclub, Schwarzwaldstr. 179	
Hockey		3367	
Hockey-Abteilung der FT von 1844 Freiburg, Werner Topfer, Oberrieder Str. 45	73576	18 Spielfelder (2 davon unter Traglufthalle) Tennisclub Rot-Weiß, Hammerschmiedstr.7	192
Judo, Karate, Taekwando		9 Spielfelder + Tennishalle m. 2 Pl.	
im FT-Sportpark, Schwarzwaldstr. 181	36286/87	**Tischtennis**	
		Tischtennishalle im FT-Sportpark, Schwarzwaldstr. 181	36286/8
Motorsport		**Trimm-Anlagen und Wanderwege**	
Freiburger Motorsportclub e.V. im ADAC, Günterstalstr. 6	42353	2 Vita-Parcours-Anlagen im Sternwald (Ende der Bürgerwehrstraße) und Mooswald (über die Straße im Wolfswinkel)	
Pferdesport		Wanderwege: Auskunft über die Möglichkeiten beim Verkehrsamt der Stadt Freiburg	
Reitclub Freiburg e.V. + Reitschule, Kappler Str. 29	67034	216-3288/8918	
Eissport		**Wassersport**	
Eissporthalle, Ensisheimer Str.	8314	Seglerkameradschaft Freiburg e.V., Postfach	5444

Source: Freiburg Information, Rotteckring 14, D-79098 Freiburg im Breisgau

D. Auf dem Bauernhof (*on the farm*). Some Germans choose to spend their vacations in the countryside, on a farm. The brochure lists some of their reasons. Read the material, then enact the following situation:

STUDENT 1

You find out that your partner wants to spend her/his vacation on a farm. Ask why: **Warum möchtest du Urlaub auf einem Bauernhof machen?** Listen to his/her reasons, then say whether or not you agree (**Ja, ich glaube dir. Urlaub auf einem Bauernhof ist interessant/schön.** Or: **Nein, ich glaube, Urlaub auf einem Bauernhof ist langweilig.**)

STUDENT 2

Tell your friend why you would like to spend your vacation on a farm (**Urlaub auf einem Bauernhof machen**). You may mention some of the following reasons: **Ich möchte…**

wandern
schwimmen
reiten (*to ride horseback*)
angeln (*to fish*)
Ruhe (*peace and quiet*) haben
Kontakt zur Bauernfamilie haben
Zeit mit meiner Familie haben
mit den Tieren arbeiten/sprechen/spielen
nichts tun

Was glaubst du? Then ask whether your friend agrees.

Erwartungen der Gäste

"Urlaub auf dem Bauernhof" ist eine von vielen Möglichkeiten der Urlaubsgestaltung. Der Bauernhof als Ferienstandort wird oft von Personen und Familien ausgewählt, die ihre Urlaubszeit als Kontrast zum Leben in der Stadt sehen.

Bauernhof-Urlauber haben ganz bestimmte Erwartungen. Sie suchen:

- Naturerlebnis (Tiere, Pflanzen)
- Kontakte mit der Familie
- nette Atmosphäre
- Erholung und Ruhe
- ländliche Stille
- kinderfreundliche Umgebung
- Beschäftigungsmöglichkeiten für Kinder

Viele Urlauber möchten:

- aktiv Sport treiben (z.B. Wandern, Reiten, Radfahren, Angeln, Schwimmen, Skilaufen)
- die Gesundheit durch gesunde Ernährung und Bewegung fördern
- Zeit für die Familie haben
- Hobbys pflegen
- im landwirtschaftlichen Betrieb mithelfen
- die Landschaft, die Kultur, die Menschen und den Hof mit seinen Bewohnern kennenlernen
- ihre Haustiere mitbringen

Gastgeber können diesen unterschiedlichen Ansprüchen gerecht werden, indem sie ihr Angebot schon bei der Planung auf die Zielgruppen (siehe Bild 1) ausrichten.

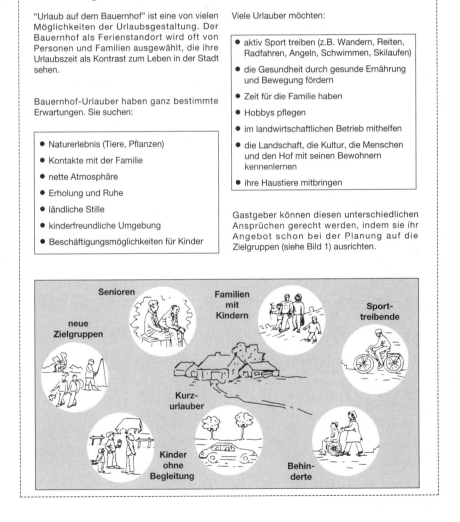

Themenwortschatz

Substantive

Freizeit und Hobbys

die Beschäftigung, -en	activity
die Ferien (pl.)	vacation
die Freizeit, -en	free time
die Gruppe, -n	group
die Gymnastik	gymnastics
das Hobby, -s	hobby
das Instrument, -e	instrument
das Interesse, -n	interest
das Klavier, -e	piano
die Mannschaft, -en	team
die Münze, -n	coin
der Roman, -e	novel
die Sauna, -s	sauna
der Stadtbummel, -	stroll through town
das Tischtennis	ping-pong
die Trommel, -n	drum
der Verein, -e	club
der Zoo, -s	zoo

Unterhaltung

der Komponist, -en	[male] composer
die Komponistin, -nen	[female] composer
das Konzert, -e	concert
die Kunst, ¨e	art
der Künstler, -	[male] artist
die Künstlerin, -nen	[female] artist
das Kunstmuseum, -museen	art museum
der Maler, -	[male] painter
die Malerin, -nen	[female] painter
die Oper, -n	opera
der Schauspieler, -	actor
die Schauspielerin, -nen	actress
der Schriftsteller, -	[male] writer
die Schriftstellerin, -nen	[female] writer
das Theater, -	theater
das Theaterstück, -e	play

Adjektive/Adverbien

alle	all
beide	both
sportlich	athletic

Unbestimmte numerische Adjektive

andere	other
einige	some, several
mehrere	several
viele	many
wenige	(a) few

Verben

aus•wählen	to choose
basteln	to do crafts
faulenzen	to lie around, be lazy
joggen	to jog
sich lohnen	to be worth it
sammeln	to collect something
segeln	to sail

(handwritten notes: "Know s. past", "wählte aus", "T", "sind")

Ausdrücke

ein Tor schießen	to kick or make a goal (soccer)
lange schlafen	to sleep late
Lieblings-	favorite ____
Lust haben + zu	to want to do something

Weiterer Wortschatz

Substantive

das Ding, -e	thing, item
die Gesellschaft, -en	society
das Tier, -e	animal
der Wunsch, ¨e	desire, wish

Verben

an•bieten, bot an, angeboten	to offer
an•gehören	to belong to
besprechen, (bespricht), besprach, besprochen	to discuss
erklären	to explain
planen	to plan
sich unterhalten, (unterhält), unterhielt, unterhalten	to discuss, converse
wünschen	to wish, desire
zeigen	to show

Adjektive/Adverbien

eigentlich	actually
möglich	possible
jedenfalls	in any event
leise	quiet(ly)
verschieden	different, various
ziemlich	quite

Die Welt der Arbeit

Kommunikation

■ Talking about jobs and career plans
■ Interviewing for a job
■ Discussing values important for work
■ Writing an academic and a work history: a **Lebenslauf** (*résumé*)

Strukturen

■ Future tense
Formation and use
Probability with **wohl** and **sicher**
■ Infinitives and adjectives used as nouns
Infinitives used as nouns
Adjectives used as nouns

Kultur

■ Germans at work
■ Guest workers and immigrants

Kapitel 13

Schritt 1: Im Büro oder mit den Händen arbeiten?

ARBEIT IM BÜRO

der Bankkaufmann/die Bankkauffrau	*bank teller*
pl. **die Bankkaufleute**	
der Beamte, -n/die Beamtin, -nen	*official, civil servant*
der Geschäftsmann/die Geschäftsfrau	*businessperson*
pl. **die Geschäftsleute**	
der Informatiker, -/die Informatikerin, -nen	*computer scientist*
der Leiter, -/die Leiterin, -nen	*executive, manager*
(**Geschäftsleiter, Hotelleiterin**, usw.)	

ARBEIT MIT DEN HÄNDEN

der Elektriker, -/die Elektrikerin, -nen

der Klempner, -/die Klempnerin, -nen

der Friseur, -e/die Friseuse, -n

der Koch, ̈-e/die Köchin, -nen

der Mechaniker, -/die Mechanikerin, -nen

ALLES KLAR?

A. Von Beruf sind sie... Sagen Sie, welchen Beruf Ihre Verwandten und Bekannten haben. (Benutzen Sie auch Listen aus **Kapitel 2**, **Schritt 3** und aus dem Zusätzlichen Wortschatz für **Kapitel 2** und **Kapitel 13**.)

BEISPIELE: —Meine Mutter ist Ärztin von Beruf.
—Der Vater meines Zimmerkameraden...
—Meine Schwester will... werden.

B. Über die Berufe. Was wissen Sie über einige der Berufe in Aufgabe A?

1. Welche Berufe lernt man an einer Universität?
2. Welche Berufe sind sehr populär?
3. In welchen Berufen verdient man viel Geld?
4. Welche Berufe sind auch in Zukunft wichtig?
5. Welche Berufe sind in Zukunft weniger wichtig?
6. Welche Berufe finden Sie am interessantesten?

C. Berufe in der Familie. Interviewen Sie 10 StudentInnen. Fragen Sie zuerst, was der Student/die Studentin von Beruf werden möchte. Dann fragen Sie nach den Berufen der Eltern.

BEISPIELE: —Was möchtest du von Beruf werden?
—Ich möchte Lehrerin werden.
—Was ist deine Mutter von Beruf?
—Meine Mutter ist Elektrikerin.

NAME	BERUF		
	DU?	MUTTER?	VATER?

Was sind die Resultate Ihrer Umfrage?

- Arbeiten viele Eltern mit den Händen?
- Wollen viele StudentInnen im Büro arbeiten?
- Wollen viele StudentInnen denselben Beruf wie ihre Eltern lernen?

In **Kapitel 4** you read about the amount of vacation to which workers in Germany are entitled. Still, German workers spend considerable time at the office or at their jobs. Many work an average of 35 hours per week (the typical job), and some workaholics work several more hours at home each week. However, as the accompanying chart shows, many also work formal overtime hours; in fact, almost half of them do some overtime. The second chart shows, however, that overall, Germans are spending fewer hours at work over the course of their "working lives" than did their grandparents. In fact, on the average, persons born in 1967 will work only about 59,500 hours during their lifetimes, whereas their grandparents, born on the average about 1911, worked approximately 99,380 hours during their lifetimes.

This comparison assumes an average life span of about 75 years, contrasted with an average for the grandparents of only 67 years. The current German retirement age is 70; all persons must stop working at official jobs at that age. The USA has a very different policy, at least as of the last few years, since mandatory retirement is no longer in force.

Wir gehen gestärkt in die Zukunft

35 Stunden-Woche

Mehr Geld und das Wochenende bleibt frei

Herzlichen Dank an alle, die das mit uns durchgesetzt haben.

IG Metall
Verwaltungsstelle Osnabrück

Wie oft Überstunden?

Von je 100 Arbeitnehmern in Westdeutschland leisten Überstunden

10	an jedem Arbeitstag
19	mindestens ein-mal pro Woche
10	mindestens ein-mal pro Monat
22	selten
39	nie (einschließlich "keine Angabe")

© Globus 2054

Arbeit ist nicht das ganze Leben
Durchschnittliche Dauer der Lebensabschnitte in Jahren

Die Großeltern (Jahrgang 1911) . . .

...waren Kinder und Schüler
15 Jahre

...haben gearbeitet
47 Jahre

...lebten im Ruhestand
5 Jahre

Ihre Enkel (Jahrgang 1967)...

...waren Kinder und Schüler
19 Jahre

...werden arbeiten müssen
42 Jahre

...haben Aussicht auf Ruhestand
15 Jahre

© Globus 6914

Schritt 2: Arbeiter aus dem Ausland

In addition to the names of professions, the working world also uses many words indicating status or position.

der Angestellte, -n/die Angestellte, -n	*employee, clerk*
der Arbeitgeber, -/die Arbeitgeberin, -nen	*employer*
der Arbeitnehmer, -/die Arbeitnehmerin, -nen	*employee*
der Auszubildende, -n /die Auszubildende, -n;	
der/die Azubi, -s	*apprentice*
der Besitzer, -/die Besitzerin, -nen	*owner*
der Chef, -s/die Chefin, -nen	*boss*
der Kunde, -n/die Kundin, -nen	*customer*
der Selbständige, -n/die Selbständige, -n	*self-employed person, free-lancer*

Herr Pandella ist jetzt selbständig

Lesen Sie jetzt das folgende Gespräch, in dem Frau Nolde einen Bekannten, Herrn Walter, in einem Lebensmittelgeschäft trifft. Füllen Sie danach diese Tabelle aus.

	BERUF?	WO?
Frau Walther		
Herr Pandella	früher:	
	jetzt:	
Frau Pandella		
Katja Nolde		
Enrico Pandella		

FRAU NOLDE: Ach, Guten Tag, Herr Walter.

HERR WALTER: Oh, guten Tag, Frau Nolde. Wie geht es Ihnen?

FRAU NOLDE: Danke, sehr gut. Und Ihnen? Wie geht's Ihrer Frau?

HERR WALTER: Danke gut. Meine Frau arbeitet seit einem Monat bei der Exportfirma Reiter.

FRAU NOLDE: Interessant! Was macht sie denn dort?

HERR WALTER: Ja, wissen Sie, Programmieren ist ihre Spezialität. Wie geht es Ihrer Familie?

FRAU NOLDE: Danke, sehr gut. Mein Mann ist oft weg, aber das Reisen macht ihm Spaß. Und Katja, unsere Tochter, wird langsam eine junge Frau.

HERR WALTER: Sehr schön! Ja, mal sehen, was es hier heute Schönes gibt. Gemüse und Obst sind hier sehr gut.

FRAU NOLDE: Oh, ja. Die haben das beste Gemüse und Obst in der ganzen Stadt.

HERR WALTER: Kommen Sie oft hierher?

FRAU NOLDE: Ja, ich kenne die Besitzer, Herrn Pandella und seine Frau, gut.

HERR WALTER: Woher kennen Sie sie?

FRAU NOLDE: Herr Pandella ist vor etwa zwanzig Jahren als junger Gastarbeiter[1] aus Italien mit seiner deutschen Frau nach München gekommen. Er war damals ein guter und beliebter Koch in unserer Werkskantine[2]. Aber vor ungefähr zehn Jahren hat er sich selbständig gemacht.

HERR WALTER: Natürlich, Kochen ist bestimmt nicht so lukrativ wie dieses Geschäft. Er wird hier wohl viel Geld verdienen.

FRAU NOLDE: Ja, aber zuerst war das Geschäft viel kleiner als jetzt, und er und seine Frau haben alles allein gemacht. Aber nun haben sie drei oder vier Angestellte. Ich bin schon seit Jahren Kundin hier.

HERR WALTER: Ach so, jetzt verstehe ich, warum Sie so viel über die Pandellas wissen.

FRAU NOLDE: Ja, und dann arbeitet meine Tochter Katja mit Enrico Pandella, dem Sohn, im Kaufhaus Hertie.

HERR WALTER: Was macht denn ihre Tochter dort?

FRAU NOLDE: Sie ist zur Zeit Verkäuferin in der Lebensmittelabteilung[3]. Sie wird aber im Herbst anfangen, Zahnmedizin zu studieren.

HERR WALTER: Sie muß sich wohl Geld fürs Studium verdienen?

FRAU NOLDE: Ja, wir haben einfach nicht genug Geld.

HERR WALTER: Ihre Tochter wird das schon schaffen[4].

---

[1]*guest worker*
[2]*factory cafeteria*

[3]*grocery department*
[4]*manage*

ALLES KLAR?

A. Haben Sie verstanden?

1. Wo arbeitet Frau Walter? *Exportfirma Reiter*
2. Was ist Frau Walters Spezialität? *Programmieren*
3. Was erzählt Frau Nolde über ihren Mann? *Er ist weg; das Reisen macht Spaß*
4. Wie beschreibt Frau Nolde ihre Tochter? *sie wird langsam eine junge Frau*
5. Wer sind die Besitzer des Gemüsegeschäfts? *Herr Pandella und seine Frau*
6. Woher kommt Herr Pandella? *nach München*
7. Was hat Herr Pandella früher gemacht?
8. Wie viele Angestellte haben die Pandellas? *3-4*
9. Wie lange ist Frau Nolde schon Kundin in diesem Geschäft? *Katja + Pandella*
10. Wer arbeitet im Kaufhaus Hertie? *dem Sohn*
11. Was wird Frau Noldes Tochter wohl werden?
12. Warum arbeitet Frau Noldes Tochter? *Geld für Studium*

B. Persönliche Fragen.

1. Aus welchem Land sind Ihre Vorfahren (*ancestors*) gekommen? Wissen Sie, welche Berufe sie am Anfang hatten? Haben sie später andere Berufe gehabt?
2. Kennen Sie Leute, die in den letzten zehn Jahren nach Amerika emigriert sind? Welche Berufe hatten sie vorher? Welche Berufe haben sie jetzt?
3. Wieviel Geld fürs Studium verdienen Sie selbst? Wie?
4. Haben Ihre Eltern studiert? Haben sie auch fürs Studiumgeld arbeiten müssen?

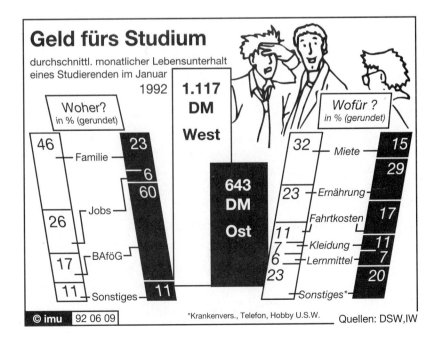

Geld fürs Studium

durchschnittl. monatlicher Lebensunterhalt eines Studierenden im Januar 1992

1.117 DM West

643 DM Ost

Woher? in % (gerundet)

46 — Familie — 23
6
60
26 — Jobs —
17 — BAföG —
11 — Sonstiges — 11

Wofür? in % (gerundet)

32 — Miete — 15
29
23 — Ernährung —
Fahrtkosten — 17
11
7 — Kleidung — 11
6 — Lernmittel — 7
23 — Sonstiges* — 20

© imu   92 06 09   *Krankenvers., Telefon, Hobby U.S.W.   Quellen: DSW, IW

During the decades of the 1950's and the 1960's, Germany sought foreign workers to help build the German post-war economy. These workers, known as **Gastarbeiter**, were imported from several European countries, including Italy, Turkey, Greece, Yugoslavia, and others. Many of these workers have opted to stay in Germany and now reside there permanently; some have married into German families, while others have brought their families from their native countries.

During the decades of the 1980's and 1990's, Germany has had a more or less open door policy with regard to ethnic Germans from other countries, e.g. Russia, Ukraine, Romania, and others. This means that anyone with German heritage (no matter how long ago) is permitted to enter Germany and apply for citizenship. Most of these new immigrants arrive without money and some can scarcely speak German. They are, however, being integrated into the German economic and social life, albeit only gradually.

These two situations — **Gastarbeiter** and ethnic-German immigrants — have resulted in a rather diverse German population, although compared with the USA, Germany is still rather homogeneous. Diversity in Germany has brought problems, including occasional confrontations with neo-Nazi groups (who want no more foreigners in Germany) and many problems with the younger generation of Germans, some of whom think these "foreigners" are taking their jobs and their future. Certainly such thought patterns are not without precedent; one needs only to compare the controversy over recent immigrants to the US.

Schritt 3: **Das Vorstellungsgespräch**

 **Gespräch**

Worum geht es hier? Paola Ramirez bewirbt sich bei dem Personalchef (*personnel director*) der Firma Reiseglück, Herrn Klinker, um eine Stellung. Was erwartet man von der neuen Kollegin?

PERSONALCHEF: Guten Tag, Frau Ramirez.

PAOLA RAMIREZ: Guten Tag, Herr Klinker.

PERSONALCHEF: Ja, ich habe mir Ihren Lebenslauf und Ihre Zeugnisse angesehen und möchte Sie jetzt einmal persönlich kennenlernen. Warum haben Sie sich bei uns beworben?

PAOLA RAMIREZ: Ich habe Ihre Anzeige in der Zeitung gesehen und finde, daß diese Stellung genau das ist, was ich suche.

PERSONALCHEF: Warum finden Sie diese Stellung so interessant?

PAOLA RAMIREZ: Weil ich gerne mit Menschen arbeite und weil ich sehr gern reise. Außerdem bin ich ein ordentlicher, pünktlicher und zuverlässiger Mensch, und ich glaube, ich habe die Persönlichkeit, die zu Ihrem Team paßt.

PERSONALCHEF: Ja, in einem Reisebüro ist natürlich Auslandserfahrung wichtig. Können Sie mal ein bißchen darüber erzählen?

PAOLA RAMIREZ: Ja, wie Sie aus meinem Lebenslauf sehen können, komme ich aus Amerika und spreche natürlich Englisch. Außerdem kann ich gut Spanisch. Ich war auch Austauschstudentin in Kolumbien.

PERSONALCHEF: Das ist genau das, was wir brauchen. Also, ich werde Sie bis nächsten Montag wissen lassen, ob Sie die Stellung bekommen.

PAOLA RAMIREZ: Sehr schön! Sie werden sicher mit mir zufrieden sein. Also, auf Wiedersehen.

PERSONALCHEF: Danke sehr und auf Wiedersehen, Frau Ramirez.

„*Zur Wahl unseres Vorsitzenden möchte ich Ihnen folgenden Vorschlag machen . . .*"

Paolas Lebenslauf

Persönliche Daten
Name: Paola Ramirez
Geburtsdatum und -ort : 8. 12. 1974, San Antonio, Texas, USA
Eltern: José und Maria Ramirez
Wohnort: Hauptstraße 5, 65347 Eltville am Rhein
Famlienstand: ledig
Staatsangehörigkeit: Amerikanerin

Schul- und Universitätsausbildung
Oberschulabschluß: Central High School, San Antonio,
   Texas, 1992
Universitätsabschluß: B.A. University of Massachussetts,
   Amherst, 1996
Hauptfach/-fächer: Deutsch und Spanisch
Nebenfach/-fächer: Wirtschaftswissenschaft
1 Jahr Auslandserfahrung als Austauschstudentin in
   Bogotá, Kolumbien (1994/95)

Arbeitserfahrung
1 Jahr Verkäuferin in einem Kaufhaus, Modeabteilung (1993/94)
1 Jahr Bankkauffrau (1995/96)

Persönliche Interessen
Fremdsprachenkennntnisse: Deutsch, Spanisch
Hobby: Literatur und Musik

Stadt: Eltville

Datum: 22. September 1996

Unterschrift: *Paola Ramirez*

ALLES KLAR?

A. Hat Paola Erfolg? Besprechen Sie mit Ihrem Partner/Ihrer Partnerin, ob
Paola Ramirez die Stellung bekommen wird. Warum?

BEISPIEL: Ich glaube, sie wird die Stellung bekommen, denn sie hat viel
   Auslandserfahrung, die für ein Reisebüro sehr wichtig ist.
   Sie kann auch viele Fremdsprachen.

B. Die Umfrage. Das Institut der deutschen Wirtschaft hat Leiter in Deutschland gefragt, welche Eigenschaften (*qualities, traits*) für eine/-n Azubi am wichtigsten sind. Hier sind zehn Eigenschaften. Mit einem Partner/einer Partnerin besprechen Sie und nummerieren Sie die Eigenschaften. #1 ist das Wichtigste, #10 das Unwichtigste.

___ Ehrlichkeit (*honesty*)
___ Eigeninitiative (*self-initiative*)
___ Fleiß (*diligence*)
___ Leistungsbereitschaft (*willingness to achieve*)
___ Ordnungssinn (*orderliness*)
___ Pflichtbewußtsein (*responsibility*)
___ Pünktlichkeit (*punctuality*)
___ Selbstsicherheit (*self-confidence*)
___ Zielstrebigkeit (*determination*)
___ Zuverlässigkeit (*reliability*)

Weiter unten finden Sie die Resultate der wirklichen Umfrage. Gibt es Unterschiede zwischen Ihrer Meinung und der Meinung der deutschen Leiter? Gibt es Eigenschaften, die gar nicht auf der Liste sind, die Sie wichtig finden?

C. Berufswünsche. Besprechen Sie Ihre Berufswünsche mit einer Gruppe.

- Was für Eigenschaften braucht man für Ihren zukünftigen Beruf?
- Was für persönliche Eigenschaften haben Sie?
- Arbeiten Sie gerne allein oder zusammen mit anderen?
- Besprechen Sie, was Ihnen (un)wichtig ist:

viel Geld   nette Atmosphäre
viel Urlaub   Sicherheit (*security*)
kein Streß   Reisen
eine interessante Arbeit   Ausbildung
viel Verantwortung (*responsibility*)

Aus: *Brigitte, 8/92.*

...RESULTATE DER UMFRAGE:

Zuverlässigkeit	95%
Leistungsbereitschaft	93%
Ehrlichkeit	92%
Fleiß	88%
Eigeninitiative	86%
Pflichtbewußtsein	84%
Zielstrebigkeit	81%
Pünktlichkeit	70%
Ordnungssinn	61%
Selbstsicherheit	46%

The future tense

Formation and use

In **Kapitel 1** you learned that the present tense is used to express all forms of the present, including the progressive and emphatic forms (*I am going, I do go*). You also learned that the present tense can express the future, usually with an adverb of time.

> Morgen fahre ich mit dem Bus zur Arbeit
> *Tomorrow I'll take the bus to work.*
> OR: *Tomorrow I'm going to take the bus to work.*

German also has a regular future tense. It is used to emphasize the conviction that an action will take place, or to make the future context clear, especially when there is no adverb of time.

> Hoffentlich werde ich die Stellung bekommen.
> *I hope I'll get the job.*

The future tense is a compound tense. It consists of the auxiliary verb **werden**, which means *will* or *shall*, plus the infinitive of the main verb.

THE FUTURE TENSE			
ich	**werde arbeiten**	wir	**werden arbeiten**
du	**wirst arbeiten**	ihr	**werdet arbeiten**
er/sie/es	**wird arbeiten**	sie	**werden arbeiten**
	Sie	**werden arbeiten**	

The infinitive is usually placed at the end of the sentence or clause. If the future construction is in a dependent clause, the auxiliary **werden** moves to the end.

> **Werden** wir heute **arbeiten**?
> *Are we going to work today?*

> Sie **wird** wahrscheinlich nicht zur Arbeit **gehen**, weil heute Samstag ist.
> *She probably won't go to work because today is Saturday*

> Ich glaube nicht, daß er heute **kommen wird**.
> *I don't believe that he'll come today.*

If the infinitive is a separable-prefix verb, the separable prefix remains attached to the main verb.

> Sie **wird** nicht **weggehen**.
> *She won't go away.*

ALLES KLAR?

A. In der Zukunft. Schreiben Sie die Sätze im Futur.

werde

1. In einer Stunde habe ich eine Besprechung mit meinem Chef. *haben*
2. Wir besprechen seine Reise nach Amerika. *besprechen*
3. Er besucht dort die Firma Hemingway. *besuchen* *verkaufen*
4. Diese Firma verkauft uns ihre neuen Computer. *verkaufen* *Kommen*
5. Der Kollege bei Hemingway kommt im Januar zu uns, weil er sich unsere
   Verkaufsabteilung (*sales department*) ansehen möchte.
6. Wir verkaufen in diesem Jahr mehr Computer als alle anderen Firmen
   zusammen. *Verkaufen*
7. Ich verdiene dieses Jahr bestimmt sehr gut. *verdienen*
   werde

B. Morgen. Machen Sie eine Liste von den Dingen, die Sie morgen machen werden. Benutzen Sie zuerst das Präsens und dann das Futur.

> **BEISPIELE:** Um sechs Uhr stehe ich auf. Ich werde um sechs Uhr aufstehen.

Probability with *wohl* and *sicher*

In addition to expressing future time, the future tense may indicate probability or likelihood when used with **wohl** or **sicher**.

> Sie werden **sicher** mit mir zufrieden sein.
> *You will definitely be happy with me.*

> Er verdient viel Geld und macht immer Überstunden; er wird **wohl**
> sehr reich sein.
> *He earns a lot of money and always works overtime; he must be very rich.*

ALLES KLAR?

Lotto (*lottery*). Sie haben gerade im Lotto gewonnen. Was werden Sie wohl mit dem Geld machen? Besprechen Sie mit einer Partnerin/einem Partner Ihre Pläne.

> **BEISPIEL:** —Ich werde wohl eine Weltreise machen.

Schritt 4: **Arbeitnehmer und Arbeitgeber**

 **Lesestück**

Redewendung

Official German, like English "officialese", is frequently more difficult to understand than everyday language. The term **der/die Auszubildende**, **-n** literally means *person to be trained*. In everyday speech it is shortened to **der/die Azubi**, **-e**. A less formal term is **Lehrling**.

Worum geht es hier? Es gibt drei Gruppen von Arbeitnehmern: die Arbeiter, die Angestellten und die Beamten. Dann gibt es noch eine Gruppe: die Selbständigen. Der legale Status dieser vier Gruppen ist verschieden, und damit auch ihre sozialen Rechte und Pflichten.

Arbeiterberufe sind z.B. Automechaniker/Automechanikerin, Elektriker/Elektrikerin und Koch/Köchin. Ein Arbeiter oder eine Arbeiterin muß im gewählten Beruf eine Lehre[1] machen. Die Lehre dauert je nach[2] Beruf zwei bis dreieinhalb Jahre. Neben der praktischen Ausbildung in einer kleinen oder großen Firma erhält[3] der Lehrling, offiziell der/die Auszubildende oder Azubi, auch eine theoretische Ausbildung in der Berufsschule, die man jede Woche mehrere Stunden bis man achtzehn Jahre alt ist, besuchen muß. Bei Arbeitern nennt man die Bezahlung **Lohn** (Stunden-, Wochen- oder Monatslohn). Wenn der Arbeiter oder die Arbeiterin sechzig bis fünfundsechzig Jahre alt ist, erhält er/sie eine Rente vom Staat.

> Dieter K., 26 Jahre alt, verheiratet, zwei Kinder. Beruf: Elektriker. Er war ein halbes Jahr Azubi, um Automechaniker zu werden, aber er mochte es nicht, immer dreckige[4] Hände zu haben. Dann war er zwei Jahre lang Azubi bei der Elektroinstallateurfirma Kanzler. Damals mußte er auch auf die Berufsschule gehen. Jetzt ist er selbständig und hat mehr Arbeit, als er will. Bald wird er sich wohl ein Haus bauen[5].

Angestelltenberufe sind z.B. Buchhalter/Buchhälterin[6], Verkäufer/Verkäuferin, Geschäftsleiter/Geschäftsleiterin und Direktor/Direktorin. Die Ausbildung bei diesen Berufen ist sehr verschieden. Die Angestellten sind Arbeitnehmer genau wie Arbeiter. Die Bezahlung von den Angestellten nennt man **Gehalt,** normalerweise ist es ein monatliches Gehalt. Die Angestellten erhalten wie die Arbeiter eine Rente, wenn sie sechzig bis fünfundsechzig Jahre alt sind.

„Mehr Gehalt, mehr Gehalt – ich verdiene mehr als Sie. Bin ich etwa glücklicher?"

[1]*apprenticeship*	[3]*receives*	[5]*build*
[2]*according to*	[4]*filthy*	[6]*bookkeeper*

Ingrid P., 29 Jahre alt, geschieden, ein Kind. Beruf: Geschäftsführerin[7] des Restaurants *Der goldne Löwe*. Abitur und vier Semester Betriebswirtschaftslehre[8] an der Fachhochschule[9] für Wirtschaft in Pforzheim. Bald wird sie sich wohl selbständig machen und ihr eigenes Restaurant in einem kleinen Urlaubsort[10] in Süddeutschland haben. Sie ist auch Expertin für Wein.

Beamtenberufe gibt es nur im öffentlichen Dienst[11]; die Deutsche Post oder die Deutsche Bahn[12] sind Arbeitgeber für die Beamten. Beamtenberufe sind z.B. Briefträger/Briefträgerin[13], Lehrer/Lehrerin, Professor/Professorin und Richter/Richterin[14]. Die Ausbildung bei den Beamten ist natürlich sehr verschieden, und wenn man einmal ein Beamter oder eine Beamtin ist, bleibt man es auf Lebenszeit[15]. Die Bezahlung von den Beamten nennt man auch **Gehalt.** Im Alter[16] erhalten die Beamten vom Staat eine Pension.

Dr. Yvonne L., 34 Jahre alt, ledig. Beamtin im Innenministerium in Bonn. Abitur und Jura-Studium in Kiel. Freut sich, daß in einigen Jahren die Regierung[17] wohl in der internationalen Stadt Berlin sein wird, denn Bonn findet sie zu klein. Ist seit drei Jahren zusammen mit Peter N., und sie möchten bald heiraten, aber sie können nicht übereinstimmen, ob sie Kinder haben sollen.

In der letzten Gruppe, den **Selbständigen,** findet man Berufe wie Arzt/Ärztin, Rechtsanwalt/Rechtsanwältin[18] und Fabrikant/Fabrikantin. Die Ausbildung bei diesen Berufen ist natürlich sehr verschieden. Auch die Bezahlung ist sehr verschieden. Selbständige bekommen einen Teil des Gewinns[19], aber sie erhalten keine Rente oder Pension; sehr oft haben sie eine Altersversicherung[20].

---

[7]*business manager* [10]*vacation spot* [14]*judge* [18]*lawyer*
[8]*business* [11]*public service* [15]*for life* [19]*profit*
administration [12]*national railway* [16]*old–age* [20]*pension insurance*
[9]*business school* [13]*postal carrier* [17]*government*

ALLES KLAR?

A. Richtig oder falsch?

1. Es gibt vier Gruppen von Arbeitnehmern.
2. Die Selbständigen sind auch Arbeitnehmer.
3. Arbeiter müssen eine Lehre machen.
4. Arbeiter erhalten ein Gehalt.
5. Ein Fleischer-Azubi ist ein Angestellter.
6. Die Beamten arbeiten für den Staat.
7. Man ist ein Beamter auf Lebenszeit.
8. Die Selbständigen bekommen eine Rente.

 B. Welche Berufe kennen Sie? Besprechen Sie Berufe mit Ihrem Partner/Ihrer Partnerin.

1. Was für Arbeiterberufe kennen Sie?
2. Was für Angestelltenberufe kennen Sie?
3. Was für Beamtenberufe kennen Sie?
4. Was für Selbständigenberufe kennen Sie?

C. Persönliche Fragen.

1. Was möchten Sie von Beruf werden? *Ich werde Lehrinin von Beruf möchten*
2. Was für eine Ausbildung brauchen Sie für Ihren Beruf?

Ich werde die Universität brechen

3. Wollen Sie lieber ein Angestellter, ein Beamter oder ein Selbständiger werden? Warum? *Ich werde ein Selbständiger wollen.?*
4. Wer von Ihrer Familie, von Ihren Freunden oder Bekannten ist ein Angestellter/eine Angestellte, ein Arbeiter/eine Arbeiterin, ein Beamter/eine Beamtin oder ein Selbständiger/eine Selbständige?

Infinitives and adjectives used as nouns

Infinitives used as nouns

Almost any German verb may be capitalized and used as a neuter noun: **arbeiten - das Arbeiten**. Such nouns have no plural. Often their English equivalents end in *-ing* (*working*). They are frequently used with prepositions, especially the dative preposition **bei** (**beim Arbeiten, beim Lesen**) which is translated, in this case, as *while* (*while working, while reading*).

> **Lesen** ist ihre Lieblingsbeschäftigung.
> *Reading is her favorite pastime.*
>
> **Das Schlafen** bei einem offenen Fenster ist typisch deutsch.
> *Sleeping with a window open is typically German.*
>
> **Beim Essen** kommt der Appetit. (Sprichwort)
> *The appetite grows with eating. (proverb)*

ALLES KLAR?

A. Infinitive als Substantive. Schauen Sie sich die Gespräche und das Lesestück in diesem Kapitel an, und unterstreichen (*underline*) Sie alle Infinitive, die man als Substantive (*nouns*) benutzt.

B. Bilden Sie Sätze. Wählen Sie mit Ihrer Gruppe sieben Infinitive und benutzen Sie diese in Sätzen als Substantive.

> **BEISPIEL:** Lernen macht Spaß.

Adjectives used as nouns

Almost any German adjective can be used as a noun. When an adjective becomes a noun, it is capitalized as usual; *but it takes the same adjective ending as though the missing noun still followed it.* Note the examples below:

> **Die Selbständigen** [Menschen] erhalten keine Rente.
> *The self-employed [people] don't receive any pension.*
>
> **Ein Deutscher** [Mann] wohnt nebenan.
> *A German [man] lives next door.*

Können Sie **dem Kleinen** [Kind] helfen?
Can you help the small child?

Die Alte [Frau] arbeitet noch.
The old woman is still working.

Some commonly used nouns derived from adjectives are:

alt:
der Alte/die Alte; ein Alter/eine Alte (*old man/woman*)

angestellt (*employed*):
der Angestellte/die Angestellte; ein Angestellter/eine Angestellte (*employee*)

arm (*poor*):
der Arme/die Arme; ein Armer, eine Arme (*poor man/woman*)

bekannt (*acquainted*):
der Bekannte/die Bekannte; ein Bekannter/eine Bekannte (*acquaintance*)

deutsch:
der Deutsche/die Deutsche; ein Deutscher/eine Deutsche (*German*)

klein:
der Kleine/die Kleine; ein Kleiner/eine Kleine (*little one*)

selbständig (*self-reliant, independent*):
der Selbständige/die Selbständige; ein Selbständiger/eine Selbständige (*self-employed person*)

verwandt (*related*):
der Verwandte/die Verwandte; ein Verwandter/eine Verwandte (*relative*)

Neuter nouns derived from adjectives usually refer to an abstract or general idea: **das Gute, das Schöne, das Gefährliche, das Neue, das Alte, das Wichtige**, etc.

Das Wichtige am Komputer ist, daß er die Arbeit leichter macht.
The important thing about a computer is that it makes work easier.

Das Neue an dieser Stellung ist die Verantwortung.
The new thing about this position is the responsibility.

Such neuter adjectival nouns occur frequently after **etwas**, **nichts**, **viel**, and **wenig**: **etwas Besonderes, nichts Gutes, viel Interessantes, wenig Schönes**, etc. In those situations the adjective takes the ending **-es** and is always capitalized.

Hast du **etwas Neues** gehört?
Did you hear anything new?

— Nein, **nichts Besonderes.**
— *No, nothing special.*

When an adjectival noun is preceded by **alles**, it take the ending **-e**: **alles Gute, alles Billige**, etc.

Ich wünsche dir **alles Gute**.
I wish you all the best.

ALLES KLAR?

A. Adjektive als Substantive. Sehen Sie sich die Gespräche und das Lesestück in diesem Kapitel an und unterstreichen Sie alle Adjektive, die man als Substantive benutzt.

 B. Im Beruf. Besprechen und beantworten Sie die Fragen mit einer Partnerin/einem Partner.

1. Was ist für dich das Wichtigste am Beruf: viel Geld oder interessante Arbeit?
2. Bei welchem Beruf gibt es nichts Interessantes?
3. Bei welchem Beruf gibt es viel Gefährliches?
4. Möchten Sie in einer Stellung viel oder wenig Neues lernen?

C. Die Firma Hausmann. Ergänzen Sie die Endungen.

Die Außenhandelsfirma (*export firm*) Hausmann hat 21 Arbeiter und Arbeiterinnen. Die meisten Angestellten arbeiten schon lange dort und werden sicher noch lange dort sein. Die Arbeiter und Arbeiterinnen müssen fast alle als Auszubildende oder Azubis dort anfangen. Nur zwei Angestellte haben ihre Lehre bei einer anderen Firma absolviert. Ein Angestellter ist ein Deutscher und eine Angestellte ist eine Deutsche, alle anderen sind Amerikaner. Eine Bekannte von mir hat erzählt, daß man in dieser Firma immer etwas Interessantes erleben (*experience*) kann, denn Hausmann importiert immer das Allerneueste aus der Bundesrepublik. Aber wenn Sie aus Deutschland kommen, werden Sie diese Produkte wohl schon kennen.

D. Was ist gestern passiert? Erzählen Sie! Benutzen Sie Adjective als Substantive zusammen mit **etwas, nichts, viel, wenig,** und **alles,** und beschreiben Sie, was gestern passiert ist.

> BEISPIELE: —Bei der Arbeit ist nichts Interessantes passiert.
> —In der Deutschstunde haben wir viel Neues gelernt.

Schritt 5: **Neue Zeit, alte Lehre**

Worum geht es hier? In **Kapitel 11**, Seite 326, haben Sie gelesen, was die Frauen heute an der Universität studieren: Medizin, Germanistik, Betriebswirtschaftslehre, Rechtswissenschaft, Biologie, usw. Circa 30 % aller Frauen in Deutschland machen heutzutage das Abitur; das sind dreimal so viele wie vor zwanzig Jahren. Aber was für eine Lehre wählen die meisten Frauen in Deutschland, wenn sie kein Abitur gemacht haben und deshalb nicht studieren können? Hier hat sich nicht viel geändert[1]. Die meisten Azubis unter den Frauen wählen dieselben Berufe wie früher. Schauen Sie sich die folgende Tabelle an:

---

[1]*changed*

Die beliebtesten Lehrberufe

Zahl der Lehrlinge Anfang 1994

Junge Männer

81 590	Kfz-Mechaniker
51 750	Elektro-installateur
34 730	Tischler
33 460	Industriemechaniker - Betriebstechnik
32 370	Gas- und Wasserinstallateur
30 770	Maurer
29 350	Maler und Lackierer
29 300	Groß-/ Außenhandels-kaufmann
28 650	Bankkaufmann
27 250	Industriemechaniker - Maschinen- und Systemtechnik

Junge Frauen

51 720	Arzthelferin
47 540	Einzelhandels-kauffrau
41 470	Zahnarzthelferin
40 220	Friseurin
38 140	Bürokauffrau
35 000	Bankkauffrau
34 120	Industriekauffrau
21 270	Steuerberatergehilfin
20 430	Hotelfachfrau
19 930	Lebensmittelverkäuferin

© Globus
2902

Kfz(Kraftfahrzeug)-Mechaniker	*auto mechanic*
Elektroinstallateur	*electrician*
Tischler	*carpenter*
Gas- und Wasserinstallateur	*plumber*
Maurer	*mason*
Maler, Lackierer	*painter*
Großhandel	*wholesale*
Außenhandel	*export*
Einzelhandel	*retail*
Steuerberater	*tax consultant*

ALLES KLAR?

A. Die Lehre. Sehen Sie sich die Tabelle, **Die beliebtesten Lehrberufe**, oben an und notieren Sie sich welche Lehren Jungen und Mädchen heutzutage wählen. Vergleichen Sie das mit den USA.

B. Leiterinnen. Sehen Sie sich jetzt die folgende Tabelle, **Der Chef ist eine Frau**…, an und vergleichen Sie diese Information mit den USA. Kennen Sie viele Frauen, die Leiterinnen einer Firma sind? In was für Geschäften sind die meisten Frauen Leiterinnen?

 C. Männerberufe. Sprechen Sie mit einer Partnerin/einem Partner. An der Universität und in bestimmten (*certain*) Berufen arbeiten jetzt Frauen in traditionellen "Männerberufen". In Deutschland aber findet dieser Trend nicht unter den Arbeiterberufen statt (*take place*). Wie ist es in den USA?

D. Chef oder Chefin? Besprechen Sie mit einer Partnerin/einem Partner, ob Sie lieber einen Chef oder eine Chefin haben. Warum? Warum nicht?

Die letzten Schritte

Wer macht mit?

Zusammenfassung

A. Der Lebenslauf. Beschreiben Sie Ihren Lebenslauf in Stichwörtern (*key words*) oder kurzen Sätzen:

PERSÖNLICHE DATEN

Name: ______________________________

Geburtsdatum und -ort: ______________________________

Eltern: ______________________________

Wohnort: ______________________________

Familienstand: ______________________________

Staatsangehörigkeit: ______________________________

SCHUL- UND UNIVERSITÄTSAUSBILDUNG

Oberschulabschluß: ______________________________

Universitätsabschluß: ______________________________

Hauptfach/-fächer: ______________________________

Nebenfach/-fächer: ______________________________

ARBEITSERFAHRUNG

____

____

PERSÖNLICHE INTERESSEN

____

____

Stadt: ____________________

Datum: ____________________

Unterschrift: ______________________________

B. Die Biographie. Schreiben Sie jetzt Ihren Lebenslauf in einem kurzen Absatz (*paragraph*).

BEISPIEL: Ich bin im Juli 1976 geboren. Als ich vier Jahre alt war, bin ich mit meiner Familie nach Kanada gezogen…

C. In fünf Jahren. Wie sehen Sie Ihr Leben in fünf oder zehn Jahren? Füllen Sie die Tabelle aus.

	BERUF/ STUDIUM?	WOHNORT?	VERHEIRATET? KINDER?	FREIZEIT? HOBBYS?	GELD?
nächstes Jahr					
in 5 Jahren					
in 10 Jahren					

Jetzt wählen Sie eine Reihe (nächstes Jahr, in 5 Jahren oder 10 Jahren) und schreiben Sie einen kurzen Aufsatz (*composition*).

D. Die Anzeige (*advertisement*). Schreiben Sie eine Zeitungsanzeige für eine Stellung als Kellnerin.

VERGESSEN SIE NICHT
Namen des Restaurants/Hotels; Adresse; Telefonnummer; gewünschte Arbeitserfahrung; Stunden-, Wochen- oder Monatslohn…

Friseurin

gesucht, auch Teilzeit

Salon Merkur

Inh. Renate Merkur

Telefon 0 53 09 / 221

Taxifahrer
(auch aushilfsweise)
baldmöglichst gesucht.

Hans Bräkermann
Bramsche Tel. 0 54 61/20 12

Landmaschinen-schlosser

in Dauerstellung gesucht.

Bewerbungen unter
ZH 57526

Zuverlässsige Verkäuferin

für Bäckerei und Lebensmittel gesucht (ganztags). Geboten werden geregelte Arbeitszeit und sehr gutes Gehalt.

ZH 57 551

 **Zu zweit: Student 1**

Die Bewertung (*evaluation*). You and your partner are conducting employee evaluations. Discuss the ratings (on a scale of 1 [low] to 5 [high]) that you have given and the comments you have noted, as well as those made by your partner. Assign a final rating, which both of you can agree upon.

Angestellter: Friderico Palmeros

EIGENSCHAFT	MEINE MEINUNG (1-5)	KOMMENTARE	UNSERE MEINUNG
fleißig	3	arbeitet manchmal sehr schwer; verschwendet (*wastes*) manchmal Zeit	
pünktlich	3	meistens	
ordentlich	4	hat einen guten Ordnungssinn	
zuverlässig	4	man kann sich meistens auf ihn verlassen (*rely*)	
selbstsicher (*self-confident*)	2	nicht sehr selbstbewußt (*self-confident*)	
selbständig	3	kann manchmal allein arbeiten	

Angestellte: Luz Maria Vallejo

EIGENSCHAFT	MEINE MEINUNG (1-5)	KOMMENTARE	UNSERE MEINUNG
fleißig	5	arbeitet sehr schwer	
pünktlich	4	fast immer	
ordentlich	4		
zuverlässig	5	macht immer das, was sie sagt	
selbstsicher	5	will eines Tages Chefin werden	
selbständig	5	kann gut allein arbeiten	

Zu zweit: Student 2

Die Bewertung (*evaluation*). You and your partner are conducting employee evaluations. Discuss the ratings (on a scale of 1 [low] to 5 [high]) that you have given and the comments you have noted, as well as those made by your partner. Assign a final rating, which both of you can agree upon.

Angestellter: Friderico Palmeros

EIGENSCHAFT	MEINE MEINUNG (1-5)	KOMMENTARE	UNSERE MEINUNG
fleißig	5	arbeitet immer sehr schwer	
pünktlich	3	manchmal	
ordentlich	5	sehr!	
zuverlässig	5	macht immer das, was er muß	
selbstsicher	4	sehr selbstbewußt, aber nicht arrogant	
selbständig	5	arbeitet sehr gut ohne Anleitung (*direction*)	

Angestellte: Luz Maria Vallejo

EIGENSCHAFT	MEINE MEINUNG (1-5)	KOMMENTARE	UNSERE MEINUNG
fleißig	3	verschwendet oft Zeit am Telefon	
pünktlich	1	fast nie!	
ordentlich	2	ziemlich unorganisiert	
zuverlässig	4	macht das, was sie soll	
selbstsicher	5	fast arrogant!	
selbständig	3	kann manchmal allein arbeiten	

Situationen

A. Diskussion mit dem Chef. Choose one of the employees who were evaluated in **Zu zweit**. Then, with a partner, enact the following role play, using information from that section.

EMPLOYEE

You are having a meeting with your supervisor to discuss the results of your evaluation. Ask specific questions about the results. (**Warum habe ich nur eine 3 unter «selbständig» bekommen?**) Express your opinion about the evaluation (**Das finde ich (nicht) fair.**) and discuss what you can do in the future to improve your performance. (**Vielleicht kann ich in Zukunft… machen.**)

SUPERVISOR

You are having a meeting with an employee to discuss the results of the employee evaluation. Using the results in **Zu zweit**, give the employee reasons for your ratings (**Sie haben unter «selbständig» eine 3 bekommen, denn Sie arbeiten manchmal gut allein, aber nicht immer.**) Try to give constructive criticism that will help the employee improve his /her performance (**Vielleicht können Sie in Zukunft… machen.**)

B. Nächstes Jahr. Discuss with your partner what you will do differently next year, i.e. what courses you will take, where you will live, how you will spend your free time. Use the future tense.

> **BEISPIELE:** —Nächstes Jahr werde ich keinen Biologiekurs belegen.
> —Nächstes Jahr werde ich allein wohnen.

C. Die Berufsberaterin (*career counselor*).

STUDENT 1

You are someone who has no idea what kind of profession you would like or be good at. Tell the career counselor about yourself (your interests and hobbies); what jobs you have liked and not liked.

STUDENT 2

Your client has no idea what kind of profession he/she would like or be good at. Ask the client about her/his interests, hobbies, work experience, what jobs have been good and not so good. Based on this information, suggest a few possible careers, and explain what qualities are needed and how they fit your client's personality.

D. Das Vorstellungsgespräch. Choose one of the ads below and enact a job interview.

INTERVIEWER

Tell the candidate which qualities are most important for this job (i.e. **fleißig, freundlich, ordentlich, pünktlich, zuverlässig, selbständig**). Ask about the candidate's work experience (**Was für Berufserfahrung haben Sie?**) and education (**Was für eine Ausbildung haben Sie?**)

CANDIDATE

Ask about the qualities that the interviewer considers most important for this job (**Welche Eigenschaften sind für diese Stellung am wichtigsten?**) and try to convince the interviewer that you have these qualities, perhaps giving examples (**In meiner letzten Stellung mußte ich sehr oft allein arbeiten; deshalb bin ich sehr selbständig geworden.**) Tell the interviewer about your work experience and education.

Für unseren Kindergarten
suchen wir zum September 1996
eine

Erzieherin

als Gruppenleiterin, 38,5 Std.
(Mutterschaftsvertretung).
Bewerbungen erbitten wir an
den **Kath. Kindergarten
St. Josef, Stadtmitte**

Sozialarbeiter/Sozialpädagogen für Jugendarbeit

Erwartet wird:
- *Interesse an Jugendarbeit, Planung und Durchführung von Freizeitaktivitäten.*
- *kollegiale Zusammenarbeit im Team*

Schreiben Sie an:
Kirchenkreisvorstand, Krämerstr. 7, 6330 Wetzlar.

Freundliche
Zahnarzthelferin
für Assistenz am Stuhl
gesucht.
Telefon 0 89 07/76 67

Alleinsekretärin für High-Tec-Unternehmen

Ich suche als meine rechte Hand eine perfekte Alleinsekretärin. Sie muß fließend zweisprachig sein (Deutsch/Englisch), fit in allen Sekretariatsarbeiten, selbständig im Denken und Handeln, Interesse für die Technik mitbringen. Idealerweise hat sie bereits Erfahrung mit amerikanischen oder internationalen Firmen.

Es ist also keine Position für eine Anfängerin, ich suche den Profi, eine "Mit"arbeiterin für abwechslungsreiche Aufgaben mit interessanten Zukunftsperspektiven.

Übrigens: Ich brauche Sie bald, spätestens zum 1. Juli. Unser neues Büro wird in zentraler Lage in Darmstadt sein. Schreiben Sie mir also schnell und trotzdem ausführlich, ich antworte gleich.

German in Central and South America

Although more people speak Spanish as their native language than German, more students worldwide learn German as a foreign language than Spanish. Only in North America does Spanish enjoy the position of being the most popular foreign language in the primary and high schools, or in colleges and universities.

There are, however, large numbers of German speakers in many countries of South America, e.g., Brazil, Argentina, Chile, Colombia, Paraguay, and others. Although many Germans emigrated to South America both during and after World War II, some countries can boast of a much longer tradition of German speakers within their borders.

In Brazil, there is a German town called Blumenau, south of Rio de Janeiro, in which German architecture is the norm, and German foods and restauraunts the expected; there German is heard on the street more frequently than Portuguese. Large numbers of German speakers also reside in towns like Porto Alegre in the southern part of Brazil.

In Cali, Colombia, a German-language **Gymnasium** offers a German **Abitur**; this Abitur carries the same privileges as one earned in Munich or Berlin, particularly with regard to entrance to a German university.

In South America, philosophers have long struggled with Heidegger's philosophical work **"Sein und Zeit**." A Mexican translation attempted to render the thoughts by using archaic terms in Spanish (although the translation appeared in 1951), whereas a Chilean translation done shortly after that used the most modern Spanish. It is, after all, Heidegger's work that has been most influential in the "filosofía de la liberacíon" of Central and South America.

Many promising young scholars from South and Central America have spent a post-doctoral research year in Germany as guests of the Alexander von Humboldt Foundation. Their numbers include, among others, citizens of Argentina (over 225), Brazil (over 150), Chile (over 150), and Mexico (over 50).

Themenwortschatz

Substantive

Berufstätige

der Bankkaufmann, die Bankkaufleute (pl.)	*[male] bank teller*
die Bankkauffrau, die Bankkaufleute (pl.)	*[female] bank teller*
der Beamte, -n	*[male] official, public servant*
die Beamtin, -nen	*[female] official, public servant*
der Direktor, -en	*[male] director*
die Direktorin, -nen	*[female] director*
der Elektriker, -	*[male] electrician*
die Elektrikerin, -nen	*[female] electrician*
der Friseur, -e	*[male] hair stylist*
die Friseuse, -n	*[female] hair stylist*
der Geschäftsmann, die Geschäftsleute (pl.)	*businessman*
die Geschäftsfrau, die Geschäftsleute (pl.)	*businesswoman*
der Informatiker, -	*[male] computer scientist*
die Informatikerin, -nen	*[female] computer scientist*
der Klempner, -	*[male] plumber*
die Klempnerin, -nen	*[female] plumber*
der Koch, ¨e	*[male] cook, chef*
die Köchin, -nen	*[female] cook, chef*
der Leiter, -	*[male] executive, manager*
die Leiterin, -nen	*[female] executive, manager*
der Mechaniker, -	*[male] mechanic*
die Mechanikerin, -nen	*[female] mechanic*

Die Arbeitswelt

der Angestellte, -n	*[male] employee*
die Angestellte, -n	*[female] employee*
die Anzeige, -n	*advertisement*
der Arbeiter, -	*[male] worker*
die Arbeiterin, -nen	*[female] worker*
der Arbeitgeber, -	*[male] employer*
die Arbeitgeberin, -nen	*[female] employer*
der Arbeitnehmer, -	*[male] employee*
die Arbeitnehmerin, -nen	*[female] employee*
die Ausbildung	*education, training*
der Auszubildende, - (Azubi, -s)	*[male] apprentice*
die Auszubildende, - (Azubi, -s)	*[female] apprentice*
die Berufsschule, -n	*vocational school*
der Besitzer, -	*[male] owner*
die Besitzerin, -nen	*[female] owner*
die Bezahlung, -en	*pay*
das Büro, -s	*office*
der Chef, -s	*[male] boss*
die Chefin, -nen	*[female] boss*

die Firma, -en	*company*
das Gehalt, ¨er	*salary*
der Kunde, -n	*[male] customer*
die Kundin, -nen	*[female] customer*
der Lebenslauf, ¨e	*résumé*
die Lehre, -n	*apprenticeship*
der Lohn, ¨e	*pay*
die Pension, -en	*pension*
der Selbständige, -n	*[male] self-employed person*
die Selbständige, -n	*[female] self-employed person*
die Stellung, -en	*position*
das Vorstellungsgespräch, -e	*job interview*

Verben

leiten	*to lead*
sich bewerben um (+acc.), (bewirbt), bewarb, beworben	*to apply for*

Adjektive/Adverbien

ordentlich	*tidy, neat*
persönlich	*personal*
pünktlich	*punctual*
selbständig	*self-reliant, independent*
zuverlässig	*reliable*

Weiterer Wortschatz

Substantive

der Dienst, -e	*service*
die Kenntnis, -se	*knowledge*
die Persönlichkeit, -en	*personality*
die Pflicht, -en	*responsibility*
das Recht, -e	*right*
die Spezialität, -en	*specialty*
die Welt, -en	*world*
die Zukunft	*future*

Verben

erwarten	*to expect*
notieren	*to note, write down*

Adjektive/Adverbien

eigen	*own*
heutzutage	*these days, nowadays*

Ausdrücke

sich (dat.) (keine) Sorgen machen	*(not) to be worried*

Der Mensch und die Medien

Kommunikation

- Discussing the influence of the media on our lives
- Talking about various modes of communication
- Expressing wishes
- Making polite requests
- Forming conjectures and hypotheses, expressing contrary-to-fact statements

Strukturen

- Present tense subjunctive
  Indicative vs. subjunctive
  Present subjunctive forms
  würde plus infinitive: review
- Uses of the subjunctive
  Wishes
  Polite requests
  Contrary-to-fact statements
- Past tense subjunctive
- Review of verbs

Kultur

- German television
- TV programming

Kapitel 14

Na, los!

Schritt 1: Die Deutschen und die Medien

The words below relate to various forms of media. You already know most of them. Look over the list, then read the following excerpt from an article entitled "Wie die Deutschen die Medien nutzen."

> **die CD, -s**
> **der Fernseher, -**
> **die Kassette, -n**
> **die Medien** (pl.)
> **das Radio, -s**
> **die Schallplatte, -n** (*record*)
> **das Video, -s**
> **die Zeitschrift, -en** (*magazine*)
> **die Zeitung, -en**

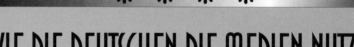

WIE DIE DEUTSCHEN DIE MEDIEN NUTZEN

Seit 1985 hat die Bedeutung[1] der elektronischen Medien erneut zugenommen[2]. 81 Prozent der Westdeutschen sahen 1990 werktags fern, und zwar durchschnittlich[3] zwei Stunden und 15 Minuten. 80 Prozent hörten Radio, durchschnittlich drei Stunden, und 75 Prozent lasen eine Zeitung, durchschnittlich 30 Minuten.

Jeder Fünfte der Westdeutschen hat 1990 täglich ein Buch oder eine Zeitschrift aufgeschlagen[4], 15 Prozent haben Schallplatten oder Kassetten gehört, und vier Prozent haben ein Video angesehen.

In den neuen Bundesländern war die Fernseh- und Rundfunkbeteiligung[5] wie auch die Zeitungsnutzung[6] 1990 höher als im alten Bundesgebiet.

aus: *Deutschland Nachrichten*, leicht verändert

---

[1] *importance*
[2] *increased*
[3] *on average*

[4] *opened*
[5] *radio participation*
[6] *use of newspapers*

Kulturnotiz: German television

Until the advent of cable television, German television was strikingly different from that in North America. There was no programming at all during the day; shows began at the earliest at 5 p.m. The last program was finished by about 1 a.m. There were only three channels available: 1, 2 or 3. Currently, however, a typical household receives 30 or more channels, with some programming available 24 hours per day. In addition to German-speaking channels, cable TV also provides programming in French and Turkish. The initial cable hook-up costs about DM 800,— which can be paid in one lump sum or in installments of DM 10,— per month. In addition, Germans pay a monthly fee of DM 13,— for every TV or radio they own. These fees are collected through the post office and there are fines for those who watch without paying (**schwarzsehen** or **schwarzhören**). The payments help fund programming, as on the three basic channels German TV has far fewer commercials than does US or Canadian television.

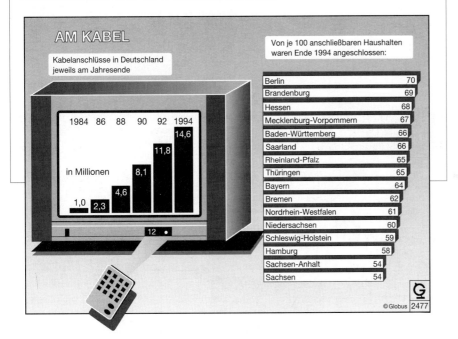

ALLES KLAR?

A. Wie oft sehen die Deutschen fern? Ergänzen Sie die Tabelle mit den Statistiken aus dem Text "Wie die Deutschland die Medien nutzen.".

	PROZENT	ZEITDAUER (length of time)
Fernsehen	81%	
Radio	80%	
Zeitung	76%	
Buch/Zeitschrift		
Schallplatten/Kassetten		
Video		

B. Wie oft sehen Sie fern? Ergänzen sich die Tabelle.

	TÄGLICH	OFT	SELTEN	NIE	STUNDEN PRO TAG/WOCHE
Fernsehen		✓	✓		5 / Woch
Radio	✓				2 / taeglich
Zeitung			✓		1 / woche
Buch/Zeitschrift			✓		30 min / day
Kassetten/CD's		✓	✓		2 / Woche
Video			✓		1 per Wk.

C. Wie oft sehen wir fern? Jetzt vergleichen Sie Ihre Antworten mit denen Ihres Partners/Ihrer Partnerin. Wer sieht öfter fern? hört öfter Kassetten? Vergleichen Sie dann Ihre Resultate mit denen der Deutschen.

D. Elektronische Medien. Besprechen Sie mit einer Partnerin/einem Partner, ob die Bedeutung der elektronischen Medien in Amerika in den letzten Jahren größer geworden oder ob sie zurückgegangen ist? Warum? Warum nicht?

E. Drei Stunden Radio. Der Artikel sagt, daß die Deutschen durchschnittlich 3 Stunden pro Tag Radio hören. Was meinen Sie, wann sie Zeit dazu haben? Hören sie vielleicht Radio im Auto? Bei der Arbeit? Hören Sie Radio, während Sie etwas anderes tun? Was?

Schritt 2: **Fernsehen**

The vocabulary used to talk about TV in German is very similar to English. You already know many of these words, because of their connection with your own language.

der Dokumentarfilm, -e
das Kabelfernsehen, -
der Kriminalfilm, -e
die Nachrichten (pl.) (*news*)
das Programm, -e (*channel*)
die Sendung, -en (*program*)
die Serie, -n
die Quizshow, -s
aktuell (*current, up-to-the-minute*)
aufregend (*exciting*)

die Sportreportage, -n
die Werbung, -n (*advertisement*)
der Bericht, -e (*report*)
die Zeichentrickserie, -n (*cartoon series*)
die Reklame, -n (*commercial*)
der Satellit, -en
der Spielfilm, -e (*feature film*)
lustig (*funny*)
spannend (*thrilling, gripping*)

ARD

8.00 Leichtathletik-WM
Disziplinen: 110 m Hürden Herren Halbfinale · 400 m Hürden Damen Halbfinale · 400 m Hürden Herren Finale · 100 m Damen Finale · 400 m Herren Halbfinale · Diskuswerfen Herren Finale · 200 m Herren Finale · 400 m Damen Finale · 800 m Herren Finale · Siebenkampf: Weitsprung, Speerwurf, 800 m
13.45 Wirtschafts-Telegramm
14.00 Tagesschau
14.02 Das Zaubermädchen vom Titicacasee · Puppenspiel
14.30 D'Artagnan und die drei MuskeTiere · 1. Der Kleine mit dem schnellen Degen · Neue 26teilige Zeichentrickserie
14.55 Philipp · Zuviel des Guten
15.00 Tagesschau
15.03 Spaß am Dienstag
Dangermouse: Big Ben ist weg
15.30 Wenn Körper und Seele streiken . Annelie Keil · Leben zwischen Gesundheit und Krankheit· Film von Heide Nullmeyer
16.00 Tagesschau
16.03 Talk täglich-Termin in Berlin · Thema: Deutsche Einheit - aus der Traum? · Tiefer Graben zwischen Ost- und West Jugendlichen · Moderation: Helga Lensch
16.30 Die Trickfilmschau
Mit Roland and the Ratfink
16.45 Der Doktor und das liebe Vieh (108) . Tierarzt-Serie
17.10 Punktum . Nachmittagsgedanken mit Hanns-Dieter Hüsch
17.15 Tagesschau

ZDF

Vormittagsprogramm
9.00 Tagesschau 9.03 Der Denver-Clan **9.45** Familiengymnastik (10)
10.00 Tagesschau 10.03 ARD-Ratgeber: Heim und Garten **10.35** Mosaik-Ratschläge: 500 Jahre Riesling-Wein · Hobby-Brauer in Bayern · Cocktails - mit und ohne Alkohol
11.00 Tagesschau 11.03 ★ ■
Liebe, Brot und Eifersucht · Ital. Spielfilm, 1954/55 **12.35** Umschau **12.55** Presseschau **13.00** Tagesschau
13.05 ARD-Mittagsmagazin
13.45 Muppet-Babies
Zeichentrickserie
14.05 Kalles-Kleister-Kompanie
Verkehrsspots für Kinder
14.10 Vom Reiz der Sinne
9. Von Genen und Gehirnen Letzter Teil der Sendereihe über die Funktionen menschlicher Sinnesorgane
14.40 Die Welt der dreißiger Jahre
2. Frankreich im verlorenen Frieden Europas - 13teil. Sendereihe von Dieter Franck
15.10 Ich über mich: Fritz Muliar
Ein Porträt des großen Wiener Volksschauspielers
16.00 heute
16.03 Die Biene Maja - Trickserie
16.25 logo · Nachrichten für Kinder
16.35 Supergran-Die Oma aus dem 21. Jahrhundert
Der Marathonlauf · Jugendserie um eine Oma mit Wunderkräften
17.00 heute/Aus den Ländern
17.15 tele-illustrierte
17.50/18.20 Ein Heim für Tiere
Strandgut · Tierarzt-Serie Mit Hans Heinz Moser
19.00 heute

RTL PLUS

6.00 RTL Früh-Magazin **8.35** Show-Laden **9.00** RTL aktuell **9.25** Knight + Daye · Zwei herrliche Chaoten **9.50 ★ ■** Prinzessin Dornröschen Finn. Kinderfilm, 1951 **11.00** Show-Laden **11.30** Die wilde Rose **12.10** Ihr Auftritt Al Mundy **13.00** RTL aktuell **13.10** Der Hammer **13.35** California Clan **14.25** Die Springfield Story **15.10** Der Clan der Wölfe **15.55** Chips **16.45** Riskant! **17.10** Der Preis ist heiß **17.45** Sterntaler **17.55** RTL aktuell **18.00** Ihr Auftritt Al Mundy **oder** Regionales **18.45** RTL aktuell
19.20 Knight Rider
US_Actionserie mit D. Hasselhoff
20.15 ★ Stirb mit einem Lachen
US-Thriller, 1989
Mit Burt Reynolds, Ossie Davies, Dom DeLuise, Dana Ivey u.a. Regie: Burt Reynolds
22.00 Anpfiff - Die Fußball-Show mit Berichten über die Englischen Wochen in der Bundesliga
23.00 Explosiv Magazin mit Olaf Kracht
23.50 RTL aktuell
0.00 ★ ■ Die Frau, von der man spricht · US-Komödie, 1942 Mit Spencer Tracy, Katherine Hepburn, Fay Bainter u.a. Regie: George Stevens
1.50-2.15 Der Hammer (Wh.)

A. Was für eine Sendung ist das? Sehen Sie sich den Ausschnitt aus dem Fernsehprogramm auf Seite 407 an und besprechen Sie ihn mit einer Partnerin/einem Partner:

- Was für eine Sendung können Sie um 16.25 im ZDF sehen?
- Was für eine Sendung können Sie um 8.00 im ARD sehen?
- Was für eine Sendung können Sie um 14.40 im ZDF sehen?
- Was für eine Sendung können Sie um 20.15 im RTL Plus sehen?
- Was für eine Sendung können Sie um 14.30 im ARD sehen?
- Was für eine Sendung können Sie um 17.10 im RTL Plus sehen?

B. Meine Lieblingsserien. Besprechen Sie, welche Sendungen Sie gerne sehen. Welche sehen Sie nicht gern? Welche sehen Sie am liebsten?

BEISPIEL: —Ich sehe Nachrichten gern, aber ich sehe Spielfilme am liebsten.

Kulturnotiz: TV programming

In addition to locally produced programs, most European countries run up-to-date serials and sitcoms from American television. Some countries, for example the Netherlands, do not even dub (**synchronisieren**) the shows, but simply present them in English with local-language subtitles (**Untertitel**). Many American shows and actors are even bigger hits in Europe than they are in the US.

As in the US, Germans are concerned with the amount of violence on TV, and a government committee oversees violence in programming and ensures that certain programs air only after 11:00 p.m. However, this concern does not extend to the issue of sex on TV. Like many other European countries, German programming and advertising is much more risqué than American. In fact, Germany, along with most other European countries, airs a version of the Italian quiz show "Tutti Frutti", in which contestants vie for points (and prizes) by stripping.

Another major difference most Americans notice is the level of news coverage. Although short news shows are broadcast throughout the evening (e.g., **Tagesschau**), serious, lengthy news shows also deal with politics, both domestic and international. Germans, Austrians, and Swiss often know more about individual US Senators and Representatives than do most Americans. The only news show in the US that begins to approach European standards is the Newshour with Jim Lehrer (formerly the McNeil/Lehrer Report).

Schritt 3: An deiner Stelle würde ich einmal zu Hause bleiben

 Gespräch

Worum geht es hier? Tina und ihr Mann Kurt kommen nach Hause. Es ist sechs Uhr abends. Sie sind beide müde. Kurt will schon wieder etwas unternehmen, Tina nicht. Sie versuchen zu entscheiden, was sie zusammen unternehmen wollen.

19.50 Sportschau-Telegramm
20.00 Tagesschau
20.15 Immer Ärger mit
Harry · US-Krimikomödie, 1955 (95 Min.) · Mit Shirley MacLaine, John Forsythe, Edmund Gwenn Regie: Alfred Hitchcock Pechschwarzer Humor, skurrile Charaktere und Shirley MacLaines erste Filmrolle. Hitchcock schuf ein herrliches Krimi-Vergnügen.
21.50 Kulturweltspiegel
Mit Hansjürgen Rosenbauer
22.20 Tagesschau
22.25 Hundert Meisterwerke
Karl Wilhelmson: Kirchgänger im Boot . Von Gisela Hossman
22.35 Wilhelm Zwo - Eine Erinnerungs-Revue von Heiner Herde Kein Kaiser-Porträt, sondern ein unterhaltsamer Rückblick auf eine schwierige und ungeliebte Figur der deutschen Geschichte
23.20 Magnum
Die Dame ist nicht fürs Feuer US-Krimiserie mit Tom Selleck Magnum bekommt Post von einer Toten. Für ihn ist das der Beginn eines sehr persönlichen Falles...
0.05 Tagesschau
0.10 Z.E.N. Andante grazioso

20.15, ARD

Krimi verkehrt, auch das kann Hitchcock. Miss Gravely (Mildred Natwick) und der alte Käpt'n Wiles (Edmund Gwenn) haben **Immer Ärger mit Harry**. Über dessen Leiche ist der kleine Arnie im Wald gestolpert. Arnies Mutter fühlt sich für Harrys Ableben ebenso verantwortlich wie Miss Gravely und der Käpt'n. Grund genug, dem Toten keine Ruhe zu lassen…

TINA: Ich würde mich an deiner Stelle einmal fragen, warum du nie zu Hause bleiben willst.

KURT: Was heißt das, ich will nie zu Hause bleiben? Würdest du lieber den ganzen Abend hier sitzen?

TINA: Manchmal sollte man sich selbst unterhalten. Möchest du nicht etwas lesen? Ein interessantes Buch? Eine Zeitschrift?

KURT: Wenn du nur verstehen könntest, daß nicht jeder so gerne liest wie du.

TINA: Also gut, wie wäre es, wenn wir zusammen fernsehen? Wie wäre es mit einem Spielfilm, einem Dokumentarfilm, einer Sportreportage?

KURT: Das ginge vielleicht. Natürlich keinen Dokumentarfilm, aber auf einen Kriminalfilm oder auf eine Sportreportage hätte ich schon Lust.

TINA: Sieh mal hier im Fernsehmagazin: Um 20.15 Uhr im ARD ein Krimi, ein ganz berühmter Hitchcock, "Immer Ärger[1] mit Harry," mit Shirley MacLaine und John Forsythe.

KURT: Na ja, also wenn es sein muß. Aber morgen unternehmen wir wieder etwas.

[1] *trouble*

ALLES KLAR?

A. Haben Sie verstanden?

1. Was schlägt Tina ihrem Mann vor? *lesen*
2. Warum will Kurt kein Buch oder keine Zeitschrift lesen? *list gern mit Sie*
3. Was schlägt Tina dann vor? *fernsehen*
4. Welche Fernsehprogramme findet Kurt interessant? *Kriminal or Sport*
5. Was für einen Film findet Tina im Fernsehmagazin? *Immer Ärger*
6. Was würden Sie an Tinas Stelle tun?
7. Was für eine Sendung würden Sie an Kurts Stelle wählen? Warum?

An Kurts Stelle würde ich ein Kriminalfilm sehen.

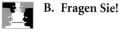 **B. Fragen Sie!**

1. Fragen Sie fünf andere Studentinnen, was sie an einem Abend mit einem guten Freund oder einer guten Freundin am liebsten unternehmen würden.
2. Fragen Sie fünf andere Studentinnen, was sie an einem ruhigen Abend zu Hause unternehmen würden. Würden sie fernsehen? Würden sie ein Buch lesen? Würden sie einen Brief schreiben? Machen Sie eine Liste und schreiben Sie die Resultate an die Tafel.

Present tense subjunctive

Indicative vs. subjunctive

Although you have learned many verb tenses in German, until now you have used primarily the indicative mood. The indicative mood is used to state facts and to ask questions.[1] To express wishes, hypotheses, conjectures, and contrary-to-fact statements, the subjunctive mood is used. Study the following examples:

INDICATIVE
Morgen geht sie ins Kino. (FACT)
Tomorrow she'll go to the movies.

Geht sie morgen ins Kino? (QUESTION)
Will she go to the movies tomorrow?

SUBJUNCTIVE
Ich hätte gerne einen Kassettenrecorder. (WISH)
I would like to have a cassette recorder.

Vielleicht hätte ich mehr Zeit, wenn ich nicht so viel Radio hörte. (CONJECTURE)
Maybe I would have more time if I didn't listen to the radio so much.

Wenn ich mehr Geld hätte, würde ich ins Kino gehen. (CONTRARY-TO-FACT)
If I had more money, I would go to the movies.

---

[1]You have also learned a second mood, the imperative, for commands.

You have already learned the subjunctive forms **möchte** (**Kapitel 3**) and **würde** (**Kapitel 7**).

Ich möchte einen Computer kaufen.
I would like to buy a computer.

Würden Sie lieber einen Macintosh- oder einen IBM- Computer haben?
Would you prefer a Macintosh or an IBM?

The subjunctive forms of **haben**, **sein**, **werden**, **wissen** and the modals are very common in everyday speech. Written German frequently uses the subjunctive forms of other verbs as well.

Present subjunctive forms

The subjunctive in German has only two tenses: the present and the past.

Regular verbs

The present subjunctive forms of regular verbs are identical to their simple past tense forms in the indicative.

INFINITIVE: KAUFEN	SIMPLE PAST: KAUFTE		
ich	kaufte	wir	kauften
du	kauftest	ihr	kauftet
er/sie/es	kaufte	sie	kauften
	Sie	kauften	

Wenn er nur besser **spielte**!
If only he played better!

Wenn wir einen Walkman **kauften**, könnten wir auch unterwegs Musik hören.
If we bought a Walkman, we could also listen to music on the way.

ALLES KLAR?

Reue (*regret*). Schreiben Sie die Sätze in den Konjunktiv (*subjunctive*) um. Folgen Sie dem Beispiel.

BEISPIEL: Er hört keine Nachrichten.
Wenn er nur keine Nachrichten hörte!

1. Wir kaufen keine Videos.
2. Die Eltern schützen die Kinder.
3. Du besprichst die Umwelt nie.
4. Er repariert die Kopfhörer nicht.
5. Sie besucht ihre Tante.

Modal verbs

The present subjunctive forms of the modals are also identical to the simple past indicative, except that they take an umlaut when the infinitive has an umlaut.

INFINITIVE	PRESENT SUBJUNCTIVE
dürfen	ich dürfte
können	ich könnte
mögen	ich möchte
müssen	ich müßte
sollen	ich sollte
wollen	ich wollte

Manchmal **sollte** man sich selbst unterhalten.
Sometimes one ought to entertain oneself.

Wenn du nur verstehen **könntest**, daß nicht jeder so gerne liest wie du.
If only you could understand that not everyone likes to read as much as you.

ALLES KLAR?

Aber... Schreiben Sie die Sätze in den Konjunktiv um. Folgen Sie dem Beispiel.

> **BEISPIEL:** Ich kann nicht gehen.
> Aber wenn ich gehen könnte….

1. Wir müssen zu Hause bleiben. *Aber wenn wir … bleiben müßte*
2. Er will die Sendung nicht sehen. *Aber wenn … wollte*
3. Ich soll die Nachrichten hören. *Aber wenn … sollte*
4. Sie mögen keine Kriminalfilme (sehen). *Aber wenn … möchten*
5. Ich darf keinen Lärm machen. *Aber wenn … dürfte*
6. Sie kann die Politik nicht verstehen. *könnte*

Irregular verbs and mixed verbs

The present subjunctive of irregular verbs and mixed verbs is also based on the simple past tense. The following personal endings are added to the past tense stem:

SUBJUNCTIVE ENDINGS			
ich	-e	wir	-en
du	-est	ihr	-et
er/sie/es	-e	sie	-en
	Sie	-en	

The past tense stem vowel takes an umlaut when possible, i.e., with **a**, **o**, or **u**.

	HABEN[1] (HATTE)	WERDEN[1] (WURDE)	SEIN (WAR)	FAHREN (FUHR)	GEHEN (GING)	BRINGEN[1] (BRACHTE)
ich	hätte	würde	wäre	führe	ginge	brächte
du	hättest	würdest	wärest	führest	gingest	brächtest
er/sie/es	hätte	würde	wäre	führe	ginge	brächte
wir	hätten	würden	wären	führen	gingen	brächten
ihr	hättet	würdet	wäret	führet	ginget	brächtet
sie	hätten	würden	wären	führen	gingen	brächten
Sie	hätten	würden	wären	führen	gingen	brächten

Wie **wäre** es mit einem Spielfilm?
How about a film?

Auf eine Sportreportage **hätte** ich schon Lust.
I would be interested in a sports report.

Wenn ich das **wüßte, könnte** ich euch helfen.
If I knew that, I could help you.

ALLES KLAR?

A. Sophie ist nicht zufrieden. Ergänzen Sie die Geschichte (*story*) mit dem Konjunktiv.

Sophie ist Fernsehfanatiker, aber im Moment hat sie keinen Fernseher. Wenn sie einen Fernseher (1) _____ (haben), (2) _____ (sein) sie froh. Dann (3) _____ (können) sie den ganzen Tag fernsehen. Wenn sie Sportreportagen (4) _____ (sehen), (5) _____ (haben) sie vielleicht mehr Energie. Wenn sie die Nachrichten (6) _____ (hören), (7) _____ (wissen) sie mehr über Politik. Wenn sie einen Dokumentarfilm sehen (8) _____ (dürfen), (9) _____ (denken) sie mehr über die Welt nach. Ohne Information und Unterhaltung zu leben ist sehr langweilig!

---

[1]Note that the -e- in the subjunctive personal endings is already present in the **haben**, **werden**, and the mixed verbs.

B. Medienkritik. Besprechen Sie mit einer Partnerin/einem Partner, wie die Medien besser sein könnten. Wählen Sie Ausdrücke aus der Liste und benutzen Sie den Konjunktiv.

BEISPIEL: —Fernsehen könnte sehr gut sein, wenn es weniger Reklame gäbe.

—Ja, aber wenn es weniger Reklame gäbe, bekämen die Sender nicht so viel Geld, und dann wären die Sendungen auch nicht so gut.

Radio	weniger kosten
Nachrichten	lustiger sein
Seifenoper	interessanter sein
Sportreportagen	es gibt mehr/weniger Reklame
Kabelfernsehen	es gibt mehr/weniger Sex und Horror
Dokumentarfilme	der Schauspieler/die Schauspielerin
die Presse	besser sein
Zeitschriften	aktuell sein
…	spannend sein
	…

würde plus infinitive: review

In **Kapitel 7** you learned to use **würde** plus infinitive to express wishes, hypothetical conditions, or polite requests. In modern spoken German the use of **würde** plus infinitive is much more common than the subjunctive[1]. Their meanings are the same.

Ich **kaufte** mir gern einen besseren Kopfhörer.
Ich **würde** mir gern einen besseren Kopfhörer **kaufen**.
I would like to buy myself better head phones.

Ich **fragte** mich an deiner Stelle, was ich nicht richtig gemacht habe.
Ich **würde** mich an deiner Stelle **fragen**, was ich nicht richtig gemacht habe.
If I were you, I would ask what I didn't do right.

Uses of the subjunctive

Wishes

Wishes are often introduced by an introductory clause with the present subjunctive form of **wünschen**, i.e., **wünschten**.

Wir **wünschten**, es **gäbe** eine Sportreportage um zehn Uhr.
We wish there were a sports show at ten o'clock.

Ich **wünschte**, die Karten für das Konzert **wären** nicht so teuer.
I wish the tickets for the concert weren't so expensive.

---

[1]Exceptions to this are **haben**, **sein**, **wissen**, and the modals.

Often wishes begin with **wenn** and may contain the particles **doch** or **nur** for additional emphasis.

> **Wenn** die Karten für das Konzert **nur** nicht so teuer **wären**!
> *If only the tickets for the concert were not so expensive!*

> **Wenn** ich **doch** den Film noch einmal **sehen könnte**!
> *If I could only see the movie one more time!*

ALLES KLAR?

A. Was wünschen Sie sich? Machen Sie sich eine Wunschliste.

> **BEISPIELE:** Wenn ich nur einen besseren Fernseher hätte!
> Wenn ich nur nicht arbeiten müßte!

handwritten: Wenn ich nur —— / Ich wün̈chte, ich hätte Urlaub / or / daß ich Urlaub hätte

nur Urlaub haben ~~hätte~~ *hätte*	pünktlich sein *wäre*
Geld ~~haben~~ *hätte*	mehr essen können *könnte*
einen CD-Spieler ~~haben~~ *hätte*	zu Hause bleiben dürfen
gesund ~~sein~~ *wäre*	… *dürfte*

 B. Was wünschst du dir? Jetzt fragen Sie Ihre Partnerin/Ihren Partner nach ihren/seinen Wünschen.

handwritten: wäran

Polite requests

The subjunctive is also used to express polite requests, in the form of either statements or questions. Frequently the adverbs **gern, lieber, am liebsten** are added.

handwritten in margin: on ordering / in rest.

> Ich **hätte gern** ein neues Radio.
> *I would like to have a new radio.*

> **Dürfte** ich das neue Buch sehen?
> *Might I see the new book?*

> Heute **bliebe** ich **am liebsten** zu Hause.
> *Today I would like most to stay at home.*

> **Könnten** Sie mir bitte helfen?
> *Could you please help me?*

> **Würden** Sie so freundlich sein und mir helfen?
> *Would you be so kind as to help me?*

ALLES KLAR?

Würdest du bitte…? Stellen Sie höfliche (*polite*) Fragen.

> **BEISPIELE:** Würdest du bitte mitkommen?
> Ich hätte gern noch eine Tasse Kaffee.

würdest du bitte mir helfen	einen Apfel
lauter sprechen	bessere Lautsprecher
nicht rauchen	einen neuen Fernseher
das Video zurückbringen	eine Zeitschrift
keinen Lärm machen	einen Anrufbeantworter
…	…

Contrary-to-fact statements

> Wenn das Wörtchen wenn nicht wär', wär mein
> Vater Millionär.

A contrary-to-fact statement consists of a condition (**wenn**-clause), which is contrary to fact, and a conclusion (**dann**-clause, although the word **dann** itself is optional). Such a statement is expressed in the subjunctive to emphasize its hypothetical nature.

Wenn der Kriminalfilm gut **wäre**, (dann) **würde** ich ihn mir natürlich ansehen.
If the mystery film were good, (then) of course I would watch it.

Wenn wir kein Kabelfernsehen **hätten**, (dann) **gingen** wir öfter ins Kino.
If we didn't have cable TV, (then) we'd go to the movies more often.

Note that the condition introduced by the subordinate conjunction **wenn** is a dependent clause; that is, the verb appears at the end. When the conclusion follows the condition, as in the preceding examples, it takes inverted word order. The condition and the conclusion are separated by a comma.

Wie kann man denken ohne Bücher? Wie **kann** man denken ohne Bücher? Wie kann **man** denken ohne Bücher? Wie kann man **denken** ohne Bücher? Wie kann man denken ohne Bücher? Wie **kann** man denken ohne **Bücher?**
(G.B. Shaw)

Wenn man keine hätte, könnte man denken?

Wenn ich…! Benutzen Sie den Konjunktiv nach **wenn**, und entweder (*either*) den Konjunktiv oder **würde** nach **dann**.

> **BEISPIEL:** Wenn ich Zeit hätte, (dann) ginge ich ins Kino.
> **ODER:** Wenn ich Zeit hätte, (dann) würde ich ins Kino gehen.

(keine) Zeit haben	(keinen) Durst haben
(kein) Geld haben	jünger (älter) sein
(keine) Lust haben	arm (reich) sein
(keinen) Hunger haben	

läse ich ein Buch.

Schritt 4: Der Anrufbeantworter

(((📼))) Gespräch

Worum geht es hier? Franz ruft bei Hilde an, aber sie ist nicht zu Hause. Er muß dem Anrufbeantworter seine Nachricht hinterlassen. Was würden Sie in dieser Situation sagen?

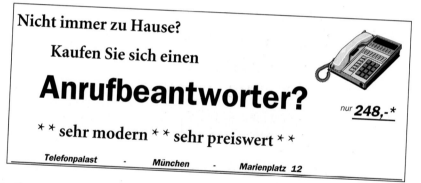

Nicht immer zu Hause?
Kaufen Sie sich einen
Anrufbeantworter?
nur **248,-***
** sehr modern ** sehr preiswert **
Telefonpalast - **München** - **Marienplatz 12**

Anrufbeantworter:
Ja, hier 53 78 09. Leider bin ich nicht zu Hause. Wenn Sie früher angerufen hätten, wäre ich vielleicht noch hier gewesen. Bitte hinterlassen Sie, nach dem Signal, Ihre Nachricht und Ihre Telefonnummer bei meinem unpersönlichen Sekretär. Ich rufe Sie so bald wie möglich zurück. Danke sehr!

Franz: Hilde, guten Tag, hier Franz. Ich bin gerade erst von der Arbeit gekommen. Möchtest du morgen um 20 Uhr mit mir zu einem Bildvortrag[1] über Südkalifornien gehen? Wir könnten nach dem Vortrag noch irgendwo etwas Kleines essen. Ich würde mich sehr freuen. Ich habe über unser Gespräch von gestern lange nachgedacht. Vielleicht sollten wir die Frage ob Kinder oder keine Kinder einmal nicht besprechen. Hoffentlich rufst du mich zurück und nicht dein unpersönlicher Sekretär. Du weißt, ich liebe dich. Tschüs!

---

[1]*visual presentation*

A. Haben Sie verstanden?

1. Wer ruft wen an?
2. Wer ist der unpersönliche Sekretär?
3. Wer hätte vielleicht das Telefon beantwortet, wenn er früher angerufen hätte?
4. Wohin möchte Franz mit Hilde gehen?
5. Was würde er gerne nach dem Vortrag machen?
6. Worüber möchte Franz einmal nicht sprechen?

 B. Was meinen Sie? Besprechen Sie mit einem Partner/einer Partnerin die folgenden Fragen.

1. Würden Sie eine persönliche Nachricht wie die von Franz auf einem Anrufbeantworter hinterlassen? Warum, warum nicht?
2. Was meint Franz, wenn er sagt, daß er nicht über die Frage Kinder oder keine Kinder sprechen möchte? Was für ein Verhältnis *(relationship)* haben Franz und Hilde?

 C. Meine Nachricht. Hinterlassen Sie eine Nachricht auf dem Anrufbeantworter eines Freundes/einer Freundin.

BEISPIEL: —Hier Erika und Gerda. Leider sind wir nicht zu Hause. Aber wenn Sie nach dem Signal Ihre Nachricht und Ihre Telefonnummer hinterlassen, rufen wir Sie so bald wie möglich zurück.

—Guten Tag, Gerda! Hier Peter. Hast du Lust, morgen ins Kino zu gehen? Rufe mich bitte schnell zurück. Du weißt, meine Nummer ist 34 66 22. Tschüs!

Past tense subjunctive

The past tense subjunctive generally indicates a hypothetical or unreal situation that could have happened in the past but did not. The past tense subjunctive consists of the subjunctive form of **haben** (**hätte**) or **sein** (**wäre**) plus the past participle of the verb.

Wenn er nur nicht so schnell **gefahren wäre!**
If only he hadn't driven so fast!

Wenn Sie früher **angerufen hätten, wäre** ich vielleicht noch hier **gewesen.**
If you had called earlier, maybe I would still have been here.

An deiner Stelle **hätte** ich mir dieses Fernsehprogramm **angesehen.**
If I were you I would have watched this TV program.

In the past tense subjunctive, the **würde** plus infinitive construction is not used.

ALLES KLAR?

A. Was habe ich gestern nicht gemacht? Sie sind frustriert, weil Sie gestern so wenig gemacht haben.

> **BEISPIELE:** Wenn ich nur nicht so lange geschlafen hätte!
> Wenn ich doch nur zur Vorlesung gegangen wäre!

so lange schlafen
um 8.00 frühstücken *hätte* *gefrühstückt*
zur Vorlesung gehen
meinen Professor besuchen *hätte*
in die Bibliothek gehen
in der Mensa zu Mittag essen *gegessen* *wäre*
mit meinem Freund ins Café gehen *dahin*
Kein Buch lesen
… *gelesen*

B. Wenn, nur wenn…. Benutzen Sie die Vergangenheitsform des Konjunktivs (*past subjunctive*).

> **BEISPIEL:** Wenn ich keinen Durst gehabt hätte, hätte ich nichts getrunken.

(keinen) Durst haben
(nicht) müde sein
(nicht) krank sein
(nicht) interessant sein
(nicht) teuer sein
…

Schritt 5: **Eine schwerhörige Generation**

📖 Lesestück

Worum geht es hier? Wen spricht der Autor an[1]? Sind unsere Medien noch Kommunikationsmittel, oder hören wir zuviel zu laute Musik?

---

[1] *addresses*

Eine schwerhörige Generation

Vor kurzem verboten die Lehrer eines großen Gymnasiums in Süddeutschland ihren Schülern, in der Schule über Kopfhörer und transportable Kassettenrecorder Musik zu hören. Ihrer Meinung nach isolieren sich sowieso schon zu viele Schüler von ihren Mitschülern und von ihrer Umwelt. Anstatt wenigstens in den Pausen, vor oder nach dem Unterricht[1], miteinander zu sprechen, isolieren sie sich. Kommunikation findet nicht mehr statt. Es ging den Lehrern also nicht so sehr darum[2], die Ohren ihrer Schüler zu schützen. Die Jugendlichen sind oft sowieso uninteressiert, wenn man ihnen sagt, daß Schwerhörigkeit[3] nicht nur eine der häufigsten Berufskrankheiten ist, sondern auch ein Resultat des oft zu lauten Musikkonsums.

Immer mehr Jugendliche brauchen Hörhilfen. In dem Land, wo man den Beat erfunden hat, in Großbritannien, warnen vier staatliche Organisationen vor der neuen Gefahr. Sie kämpfen durch Aufklärung[4] gegen Schwerhörigkeit und sorgen für Schwerhörige und Gehörlose. Jährlich schädigen 200 bis 300 der heute 13- bis 23-jährigen Engländer ihr Gehör so stark, daß sie später nichts mehr hören. Denn sie hören zu lange zu laute Musik.

Nicht so sehr der Lärm einer Tanzparty zuhause ist gefährlich für das Gehör, sondern der Lärm, der über Kopfhörer in das empfindliche[5] Gehörsystem dringt[6].

Besonders heutzutage ist es gefährlich, weil es so viele transportable Kassettenrecorder und Radios in Autos gibt. Wir hören die zu laute Musik also nicht nur zu Hause, sondern auch unterwegs.

aus: Tip – Landeskunde im Deutschunterricht, leicht verändert

[1] *class*   [2] **es ging...**= *The teachers weren't so concerned with...*   [3] *hardness of hearing*
[4] *education*   [5] *sensitive*   [6] *penetrates*

ALLES KLAR?

A. Haben Sie verstanden?

1. Warum hat man an dem Gymnasium in Süddeutschland Kopfhörer und transportable Kassettetenrecorder verboten?
2. Wovor warnen vier staatliche Organisationen in Großbritannien?
3. Warum ist die laute Musik einer Tanzparty für das Gehör weniger gefährlich?
4. Wo hören wir die zu laute Musik?

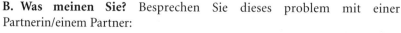 **B. Was meinen Sie?** Besprechen Sie dieses problem mit einer Partnerin/einem Partner:

1. Wie finden Sie das Verbot an dem Gymnasium in Süddeutschland?
2. Ist Gesundheit eine private Sache?
3. Gibt es andere elektronische Kommunkationsmittel, die für den Menschen gefährlich sein könnten? Müssen diese elektronischen Kommunikationsmittel immer gefährlich sein oder können sie auch helfen?

C. Lust auf Sprachen. Sehen Sie sich die Reklame **Lust auf Sprachen an**. Wie lernt man mit diesem System eine Sprache?

Unterbewußtsein	*subconscious*
aufnehmen	*to record*
durchschnittlich	*on average*

Lust auf Sprachen

Mit Lust und Freude lernen Sie leichter und schneller lhre Wunschsprache. Möglich wird das durch SITA LEARNING.

Erfolgreicher durch tiefe Ruhe.

Das SITA LEARNING SYSTEM sorgt durch das integrierte Atem-Biofeedback für die so wichtige tiefe Ruhe und Entspannung. So Kann das Unterbewußtsein den Lernstoff schnell und leicht aufnehmen. Ideal für Menschen, die dann lernen wollen, wenn sie Lust und Zeit haben.

Über 1.100 Vokabeln in eine Woche.

Der Hamburger Prof. Dr. Rainer Dieterich: »In einem Experiment lernten die Testpersonen in nur einer Woche durchschnittlich 1138 neue Vokabeln.«

Das weltweit patentierte SITA LEARNING SYSTEM mit den ausgezeichneten Kassetten-Sprachkursen sollten Sie einfach selbst ausprobieren. Vielleicht gehören Sie dann schon bald zu unseren mehr als 40.000 Kunden.

...erfolgreicher durch Wissen

Erhältlich in Berlin und Dresden bei »Das International Buch«.

Review of verbs

So far you have learned four tenses of the indicative (present , present perfect, simple past and future), the imperative, and two tenses of the subjunctive (present and past). A paradigm for each of these is given below. Complete the explanations and charts to review the verbs.

Present tense

Regular verbs take personal endings depending on the subject. Stem-changing verbs (e→ie, e→i, a→ä, au→äu) change the vowel in the _____ and _____ forms.

REGULAR VERBS (KAUFEN)			
ich	**kaufe**	wir	**kaufen**
du		ihr	
er/sie/es		sie	
	Sie		

STEM-CHANGING VERBS (FAHREN)			
ich	**fahre**	wir	**fahren**
du		ihr	
er/sie/es		sie	
	Sie		

Separable prefixes appear at the end of the sentence or clause: **Wir kaufen heute ein.**

Present perfect (_Perfekt_)

The present perfect consists of an _____ verb and a past _____ that usually begins with **ge-**.

REGULAR VERBS (KAUFEN)			
ich	**habe gekauft**	wir	**haben gekauft**
du		ihr	
er/sie/es		sie	
	Sie		

IRREGULAR VERBS (LESEN)			
ich	**habe gelesen**	wir	**haben gelesen**
du		ihr	
er/sie/es		sie	
	Sie		

CHANGE OF MOTION OR STATE VERBS (FAHREN)			
ich	**bin gefahren**	wir	**sind gefahren**
du		ihr	
er/sie/es		sie	
	Sie		

Separable prefix verbs have the **-ge-** inserted between the prefix and the main verb: **Wir haben gestern eingekauft.** The past participles of inseparable prefix verbs do not begin with **ge-**: **Man hat den Beat in England erfunden.**

Simple past (*Imperfekt*)

The simple past of regular verbs takes the infinitive _____ and adds **t** plus personal endings. The simple past of irregular verbs usually incorporates a vowel _____, and a different set of endings. Mixed verbs have a vowel change like the irregular verbs, but also add a _____ plus the personal endings.

REGULAR VERBS (KAUFEN)			
ich	**kaufte**	wir	**kauften**
du		ihr	
er/sie/es		sie	
	Sie		

IRREGULAR VERBS (SEIN)			
ich	**war**	wir	**waren**
du		ihr	
er/sie/es		sie	
	Sie		

MIXED VERBS (DENKEN)			
ich	**dachte**	wir	**dachten**
du		ihr	
er/sie/es		sie	
	Sie		

Separable prefixes again appear at the end of the sentence or clause: **Wir kauften gestern ein.**

Future tense

The future tense uses a conjugated form of the verb _____ plus the _____ .

ALL VERBS (KAUFEN)			
ich	**werde kaufen**	wir	**werden kaufen**
du		ihr	
er/sie/es		sie	
	Sie		

Imperative

The imperative is formed by using the infinitive _____ and adding endings.

REGULAR VERBS (KAUFEN)		SEIN	
(du)	**kauf(e)!**	(du)	
(wir)		(wir)	**seien wir!**
(ihr)		(ihr)	**seid!**
(Sie)	**kaufen Sie!**	(Sie)	

Separable prefixes appear at the end of the sentence or clause: **Kaufen wir morgen ein**!

Present subjunctive

The present subjunctive of regular verbs is identical with their _____. The subjunctive of irregular and mixed verbs uses the simple past form, adds an _____ and endings.

REGULAR VERBS (KAUFEN)			
ich	**kaufte**	wir	**kauften**
du		ihr	
er/sie/es		sie	
	Sie		

IRREGULAR VERBS (SEIN)			
ich	**wäre**	wir	**wären**
du		ihr	
er/sie/es		sie	
	Sie		

Past subjunctive

In the past subjunctive, the _____ verb is in the subjunctive, and the past participle remains the same.

REGULAR VERBS (KAUFEN)			
ich	**hätte gekauft**	wir	**hätten gekauft**
du		ihr	
er/sie/es		sie	
	Sie		

CHANGE OF STATE OF MOTION VERBS (FAHREN)			
ich	**wäre gefahren**	wir	**wären gefahren**
du		ihr	
er/sie/es		sie	
	Sie		

A. Jürgen ist ein Faulpelz. Ergänzen Sie die Geschichte mit dem Präsens.

Jürgen _bleibe_ (bleiben) jedes Wochenende zu Hause. Da _sehe_ (sehen) er die ganze Zeit fern. Manchmal _machte_ (machen) sie eine Pause und _gehe_ (gehen) zum Kühlschrank (*refrigerator*), aber nur zwischen den Sendungen, denn er _will_ (wollen) keine Minute verpassen. Die Nachrichten _gefallt_ (gefallen) ihm, denn er _könnte_ (können) sich über die Welt informieren – die Welt, die er nur vom Fernsehen _kennen_ (kennen). Seine Lieblingssendungen _sind_ (sein) natürlich Seifenopern, denn die Charaktere _lebe_ (leben) in einer Fantasie-Welt.

B. Jürgen war ein Faulpelz. Schreiben die jetzt dieselbe Geschichte im Imperfekt.

(handwritten margin note:) bleibt / sah / machte / ginge

C. Meine elektronischen Geräte. Besprechen Sie mit einer Partnerin/einem Partner, welche elektronischen Geräte Sie in 10 Jahren haben werden. Wie werden die Geräte aussehen? Wofür wird man sie benutzen? Benutzen Sie das Futur.

> BEISPIEL: —Ich werde in 10 Jahren bestimmt einen Videorecorder haben. Er wird bestimmt teuer sein. Was wirst du haben?
>
> —Ich werde keinen Videorecorder haben, denn ich werde keine Videos ansehen; ich werde nur ins Kino gehen.

D. Machen Sie das nicht! Sagen Sie den folgenden Personen was sie nicht machen sollen.

> BEISPIEL: Brigitte – nicht so viel fernsehen
> → Brigitte, sieh nicht so viel fern!
>
> Herr Schmidt – nicht so oft Radio hören
> → Herr Schmidt, hören Sie nicht so oft Radio!

1. Thomas und Peter – die Zeitung öfter lesen
2. Herr und Frau Otte – nicht so viele Reklame ansehen
3. Frau Martini – einen Anrufbeantworter kaufen
4. Rolf – mich zurückrufen
5. Bettina – nicht so viel Lärm machen

Zusammenfassung

A. Wenn ich…, würde ich…. Bilden Sie 10 Sätze im Konjunktiv. Wählen Sie Ausdrücke aus der Liste.

> BEISPIEL: Wenn ich einen Fernseher hätte, würde ich viel Spaß haben.

k/einen Fernseher	interesssante Bücher lesen
k/einen CD-Spieler	die neuesten Nachrichten
k/eine Zeitung	lesen/hören
k/einen Videorecorder	(keinen) Spaß haben
k/einen Walkman	mir jeden Tag einen Film ansehen
k/ein Radio	nicht so oft fernsehen
…	wissen, was in der Welt passiert
	…

B. Schreiben Sie einen Brief! Sie sind mit Ihrer neuen Wohnung und mit Ihrem Zimmerkameraden/Ihrer Zimmerkameradin nicht zufrieden. Schreiben Sie einen Brief an eine Freundin/einen Freund und beklagen (*complain*) Sie sich. Benutzen Sie manchmal den Konjunktiv.

BEISPIELE: Ich hätte Dir längst schreiben sollen.
Du würdest nicht glauben, was alles passiert ist.
Wenn unsere Nachbarn doch nur nicht so laut wären.
Wenn Robert/Maria nur nicht soviel Geld ausgäbe.

...

Zu zweit: **Student 1**

A. Amerikanische Sendungen in Deutschland. You and your partner want to watch an American TV series. Your partner has a schedule. Ask him/her to check when the shows are on, so that you can complete your chart.

> BEISPIEL: —Wann spielt im West 3 "The Return of Sherlock Holmes"?
> —Das muß "Die Wiederkehr von Sherlock Holmes" sein.
> Es spielt um 23.15 Uhr.

ENGLISCHER NAME	DEUTSCHER NAME	WANN?	IN WELCHEM PROGRAMM?
Sesame Street			Nord 3
Price is Right			RTL Plus
Wheel of Fortune			SAT 1
Dynasty			ZDF

Now switch roles. You have the schedule, and your partner asks you to find the German names and times.

SAT 1

6.00 Guten Morgen **8.35** Nachbarn **9.05** General Hospital **9.50** Teleshop **10.10** Die drei Dorfheiligen Bauernschwank in drei Akten - In der Pause: Börsentelegramm · Anschl.:Zeichentrickfilm **12.05** Glücksrad **12.45** Tele-Börse **13.35** Bingo **14.00** Police Academy **14.25** General Hospital **15.10** Nachbarn **15.35** Teleshop **15.50** Bonanza **16.45** Feste feiern Heute: Oktoberfest **17.40** SAT 1 Blick **17.50** Drei Mädchen und drei Jungen **oder** Regionales **18.15** Bingo **18.45 Guten Abend, Deutschland** Mit Dieter Kronzucker **19.15 Glücksrad** · Gewinnshow **20.00 MacGyver** US-Krimiserie mit R.D. Anderson **20.55 SAT 1 Blick** **21.00 ★ Die Kadetten von Bunker Hill** · US-Spielfilm, 1981 Mit George C. Scott, Timothy Hutton, Ronny Cox, Tom Cruise u.a. Regie: Harold Becker Als die altehrwürdige Militär-Akademie von Bunker Hill geschlossen werden soll, revoltieren die Kadetten.. **23.10 Spiegel TV-Reportage** **23.40 SAT 1Blick** **23.55 Auf der Flucht** Alpträume - US-Krimiserie **0.45 MacGyver** (Wh.v. 20.00) **Ab 1.45 SAT 1 Text für alle**

WEST 3

14.00 Videotext **14.15** aktuell **14.20** FensterPlatz **15.25** Ente Lippens **15.55** aktuell **16.00** Zapp Zarapp (22) **16.30** Die blöden Erwachsenen dürfen alles - Kinderspielfilm **17.45** Objektiv gesehen?**18.00** Akt. Minute **18.01** Lassie **18.30** Du und Dein Tier **19.00 Aktuelle Stunde/Sport** **20.00 Europa-Platz** Eine Straße in... Szczecin und Barcelona · Mit "fremdem Blick" eine unbekannte Straße betrachten und Kultur, Architektur, Essen Straßenleben anders erleben... **20.45 Miami Vice** . Lady Love US-Krimiserie mit Don Johnson **21.30 aktuell** **21.45 Bitte streitet euch nicht** Scheidungskinder zwischen Haß und Liebe · Die Dokumentation verzichtet auf jeden Kommentar - das Wort haben nur drei Kinder, die über ihre Erlebnisse bei immer schlimmeren Streitereien in einer zerbrechlichen Ehe erzählen **22.45 Satirefest mit Hans Lieberg und dem v.e.v. Kabarett** (VPS22.44) **23.15 Die Wiederkehr von Sherlock Holmes** · 6. Der Mann mit dem schiefen Mund 7teilige engl. TV-Serie mit Jeremy Brett, Edward Hardwicke u.a. **0.05 Nachrichten/Zur Nacht**

DFF-LÄNDERKETTE

10.00 Nordmagazin **10.25** Videotext **12.10** Gesehen - gewußt · gewonnen **12.30** Mittagsjournal **13.00** Rückkehr nach Eden (11) **13.45** Die schönsten Feste der Welt **14.10** Vorsicht, Falle! Spezial **14.40** Aus der Rockszene **15.10** Videotext **15.20** Medizin nach Noten **15.30** Aktuell **15.35** Ferdy **16.00** Die geheimnisvollen Städte des Goldes **16.25** Aktuell **16.30** ELF 99 · DasJugendmagazin **18.30** Abendjournal · Dazw.: **18.50** Sandmännchen **19.20** Wetter/ Aktuell **20.00** Das randalierende Rätsel — Berliner Hooligans **20.30 ★** Film Ihrer Wahl · Aus vergangenen Zeiten ca.**22.05** Kripo live ca.**22.15** Spätjournal ca. **22.35** Rücksicht kommt an ca. **22.40** Je t'aime ca. **22.55 ★** Nächte ohne Mond und Sonne · Argent. Krimi,1982 ca.**0.20** Paulus (2) **ca.1.25** Nachrichten

PRO 7

12.20 Der Magier **13.10 ★** Ashant· Schweiz. Abenteuerfilm,1978 **15.10** Trick 7 **16.00** Nachrichten **16.10** Planet der Affen **17.05** Chaos hoch zehn **17.30** Nachrichten **17.45** Tennis, Schläger und Kanonen**18.35** Trick 7 **20.15** Der gnadenlose Ritt US-Western,1966 **21.40 ★** Raffica –Tiger der Wüste · Ital.-span.-ägyp. Abenteuerfilm,1980 **23.05** Einstweilige Vergnügung **23.55** FBI **0.45** Nachrichten **0.55 ★** Die Weibchen Dt.franz.-ital. Krimi, 1970 **2.10** ■ Unwahrscheinliche Geschichten **2.35 ★** Sein gefährlichster Auftrag · US-Krimi,1966 **4.05-5.35 ★** ■ San Francisco Lilly · US-Western,1945

B. Im Elektronikladen. Call up an electronics store for information on their prices for the following products.

BEISPIEL: —Guten Tag, Bonner Musikhaus.
—Guten Tag. Darf ich mal fragen, wieviel Ihre Lautsprecher kosten?
—Wir haben zwei verschiedene. Der SONY kostet….

GERÄT	PREIS
CD's	
Kassettenrecorder	
Kopfhörer	
Lautsprecher	

Now switch roles. Give your customer the prices of the items he/she requests.

GERÄT	PREIS
Videokassette	2 für DM 10,—
Videorecorder	
—Toshiba	DM 349,—
—Samsung	DM 400,—
Walkman	DM 60,—
Anrufbeantworter	DM 50,— bis 70,—

Zu zweit: **Student 2**

A. Amerikanische Sendungen in Deutschland. You and your partner want to watch an American TV series. You have a schedule. Your partner will ask you to find certain shows on certain channels and tell him/her what time they are on.

> **BEISPIEL:** —Wann spielt im West 3 "The Return of Sherlock Holmes"?
> —Das muß "Die Wiederkehr von Sherlock Holmes" sein.
> Es spielt um 23.15 Uhr.

ZDF

Vormittagsprogramm
9.00 Tagesschau **9.03** Der Denver-Clan **9.45** Familiengymnastik (11) **10.00** Tagesschau **10.03** Die Zeugen der Vergangenheit sind unsere Zukunft (4) **11.00** Tagesschau **11.03** ■ Jukebox-Fieber · US-Spielfilm, 1942 **12.30** Vegetarische Sommerküche (kalt) **12.55** Presseschau **13.00** Tagesschau **13.05** ARD-Mittagsmagazin
13.45 Hit-Woch
    Comics, Komik, Kinderfilme
    Heute: Auf dem Rücken der Pferde
    Pingu (VPS13.45)
    Pingu beim Schlittenrennen
    Black Beauty (VPS13.50)
    Das Geheimrezept
    Silas (VPS14.15) Der Zirkusjunge
    Silas erlebt zum ersten Mal Glanz
    und Reichtum einer großen Stadt
    Unser Freund... das Pferd
    (VPS15.45) . Ponys aus aller Wellt
    Schneeflocke (VPS16.15)
    Annettes erster Ausritt
    Film von Jindrich Mann
16.45 logo · Nachrichten für Kinder
17.00 heute/Aus den Ländern
17.15 Der Landarzt (1)
    Alles nochmal von vorn · TV-Serie
    Mit Christian Quadflieg
18.15 Lotto am Mittwoch
    Ziehung A und B
18.30 Der Landarzt (2)
19.00 heute
19.30 Wie würden Sie entschelden?
    Rechtsfälle im Urteil des Bürgers
    Die Sendung befaßt sich diesmal
    mit den rechtlichen Folgen der
    Schwarzarbeit
20.15 Kennzeichen D
21.00 Matlock
    Der Rächer . US-Krimiserie
    Aus einem noch unerfindlichen
    Grund will sich ein junger Mann an
    Strafverteidiger Matlock rächen.
21.45 heute-journal

RTL PLUS

6.00 Rtl Früh-Magazin **8.35** Show-Laden **9.00** RTL aktuell **9.10** Knight + Daye . Zwei herrliche Chaoten **9.35** ★ Der wilde von Montana · US-Western,1963 **11.00** Show-Laden **11.30** Die wilde Rose **12.10** Ihr Auftritt Al Mundy **13.00** RTL aktuell **13.10** Der Hammer **13.35** California Clan **14.25** Die Springfield Story **15.10** Der Clan der Wölfe **15.55** Chips **16.45** Riskant! **17.10** Der Preis ist heiß **17.45** Sterntaler **17.55** RTL aktuell **18.00** Ihr Auftritt Al Mundy **oder** Regionales **18.45** RTL aktuell
19.20 Zurück in die Vergangenheit · US-Abenteuerserie
20.15 ★ **Unter Wasser rund um die Welt** · US-Science-fiction-Film,**1965** . Mit Lloyd Bridges, Shirley Eaton, Brian Kelly u.a. Regie: Andrew Marton
22.00 Anpfiff . Die Fußball-Show mit Berichten über die Englischen Wochen in der Bundesliga
23.00 stern TV
    TV-Magazin mit Günther Jauch
23.35 RTL aktuell
23.45 Powerman I
    Hongkong-Kung-Fu – Film,1986
    Mit Jackie Chan, Samo Hung, Yu-en Biao, Cheung Chung u.a.
    Regie; Samo Hung
1.30-2.05 Catch up

SAT1

6.00 Guten Morgen **8.35** Nachbarn **9.05** General Hospital **9.45** Teleshop **10.05** ★ Die Kadetten von Bunker Hill · US-Spielfilm, '81 · In der Pause: Börsentelegramm**12.05** Glücksrad **12.45** Tele-Börse **13.35** Bingo **14.00** Ollies total verrückte Farm **14.25** General Hospital **15.10** Nachbarn **15.35** Teleshop **15.50** Kung Fu **16.45** Stingray **17.40** SAT1 Blick **17.50** Drei Mädchen und drei Jungen oder Regionales **18.15** Bingo
18.45 Guten Abend, Deutschland
    Mit Dieter Kronzucker
19.15 Glücksrad · Gewinnshow
20.00 Hunter · US-Krimiserie
20.55 SAT1 Blick
21.00 Alles tanzt nach meiner Pfeife . Franz.-ital. Spielfilm, 1969 . Mit Louis de Funès, Olivier de Funès, Noelle Adam u.a. Regie: Serge Korber
22.25 SAT1 Blick/Sport
22.40 Hallo Berlin
    Links und rechts vom Ku'damm
    Unterhaltungsmagazin
23.05 Erben des Fluchs
    US-Gruselserie
23.55 Stunde der Filmemacher
    Filmgeschichte(n)
0.10 Hunter (Wh.v.20.00)
1.00 SAT1 Sport
    Golf . PGA-Tour-Highlights
Ab1.40 SAT1 Text für alle

NORD 3

NDR/RB: 5.00 Flug-Infos **9.00** 7 Weltwunder des Altertums (3) **9.30** Danziger Mission **10.00** Weltwunder der Technik (2)**10.30** Abendschau ● **NDR/RB: 11.00** HH-Journal **11.20** SH-Magazin **11.40** Hallo Niedersachsen **12.00** Buten & Binnen **12.25** - **13.30** Vorschau **15.45** Panorama **16.30** 7 Weltwunder (4) **17.30** Weltwunder der Technik (3) **18.00** Sesamstraße ● **NDR/RB: 18.30** Doppel-Kopf **SFB: 18.30** Berlin Brandenburg **18.56** Wolff u. Rüffel ●**19.00** DAS!
20.00 Tagesschau
20.15 N3 · **direkt** · Treffpunkt
21.00 Sag' die Wahrheit
    Spielshow · Gast: Wolfgang Fierek
21.30 N3 · **international**
    Europa-Magazin
22.00 N3 · **Horizonte** . Werbefeldzug im Osten · Die Dokumentation beschreibt die Situation des Umbruchs · nicht des ökonomischen, sondern des künstlerisch-ästhetischen, psychologischen Wandels
22.45 Zeit für Musik
    15. Jazzfestival Hamburg (2)
    The Very Big Carla Bley Band · Ihr
    Stil, die Begabung zum "doing
    your own thing" ist beeindruckend
23.45 Nachrichten

Now switch roles. Your partner has the schedule, and you need the German name and time to complete your chart.

ENGLISCHER NAME	DEUTSCHER NAME	WANN?	IN WELCHEM PROGRAMM?
Planet of the Apes			Pro 7
Heaven Can Wait			SAT 1
Jungle Book			DFF-Länderkette
Around the World in 80 Days			West 3

B. Im Elektronikladen. You work in an electronics store and a customer calls up for information on the prices of certain products. Answer the customer's questions.

BEISPIEL: —Guten Tag, Bonner Musikhaus.
—Guten Tag. Darf ich mal fragen, wieviel Ihre Lautsprecher kosten?
—Wir haben zwei verschiedene. Der SONY kostet…

GERÄT	PREIS
Lautsprecher	
—SONY	DM 300,— (jeder)
—Yamaha	DM 550,— (Paar)
Kassettenrecorder	von DM 49,90 bis 150,—
Kopfhörer	DM 60,— bis 75,—
CD's	um DM 30,—

Now switch roles. You are the customer calling for the prices of the following items.

GERÄT	PREIS
Anrufbeantworter	
Videokassette	
Videorecorder	
Walkman	

Situationen

A. Die Urlaubsantenne.

STUDENT 1

You are going on vacation with your partner. You must watch TV every day, and you want to buy an "**Urlaubsantenne**" to take with you. Convince your partner that it is a good idea.

STUDENT 2

You are going on vacation with your partner. TV is of little importance to you, and you think the idea of buying an "**Urlaubsantenne**" is stupid. Try to talk your partner out of it.

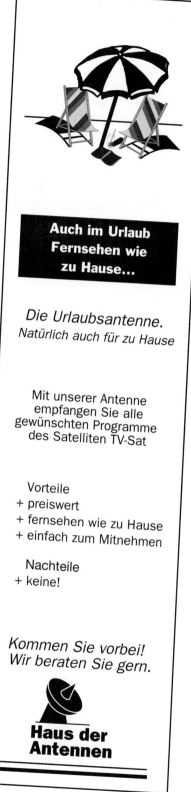

Auch im Urlaub Fernsehen wie zu Hause...

Die Urlaubsantenne.
Natürlich auch für zu Hause

Mit unserer Antenne empfangen Sie alle gewünschten Programme des Satelliten TV-Sat

Vorteile
+ preiswert
+ fernsehen wie zu Hause
+ einfach zum Mitnehmen

Nachteile
+ keine!

Kommen Sie vorbei! Wir beraten Sie gern.

Haus der Antennen

B. Der Computer-Konflikt. In a group of three (1 student, 2 parents) enact the following situation.

STUDENT

Your parents have no computer and have no interest in buying one. You think a computer would facilitate and enhance their lives. Try to convince them what a good idea it is: **für e-mail, Steuer- & Finanzprogramme** (*tax and financial programs*), **Internet, Spiele.**

PARENTS

You have no computer and have no interest in buying one. Convince your child why you don't need one (**es ist teuer, wir telefonieren lieber, wir haben Angst vor der neuen Technik.**)

Apple Computer

Weber

Computersysteme GmbH
Wahmstraße 56
2400 Berlin

Fax (0823) 9 66 47 · Tel. (0273) 6 32 16

 The power to be your best.

Computer Center

Vertrieb von Hard- und Software
Beratung · Schulung · Programmierung

2400 Kiel, Sophienblatt 80
Telefon (06598) 6 52 74

 C. Die Nachrichten.

STUDENT 1

You believe that newspapers give the best news coverage. Tell your partner why (**aktuell, ausführlich** [*comprehensive*], **hat viele Details,**…) and try to convince him/her of your point of view.

STUDENT 2

You prefer to get your news from the radio or television. Tell your partner why (**schnell; man kann hören, während man etwas anderes macht,**…)

D. Sind wir informiert? Sie haben in der Zeitung gelesen, daß wir heutzutage besser informiert sind als früher. Besprechen Sie das mit Ihrer Partnerin/Ihrem Partner. Ist das richtig, oder ist das falsch? Warum? (Es gibt elektronische Medien, Satelliten, CNN, aber wieviele Personen informieren sich? Wieviele sehen sich nur die Nachrichten im Fernsehen oder hören fünf Minuten im Radio?)

E. Beim Einkaufen.

STUDENT 1

You just inherited a lot of money and want to buy many new things (**Stereoanlage, Computer,**…). Go into an electronics store and ask about prices and brands (**Welche Marke ist besser?**) Then decide on five things to buy.

STUDENT 2

You are a clerk in an electronics store. A customer who obviously has a lot of money to spend asks you about prices and brands (**Marken**) of various products. Try to sell them the most expensive items you have. (**Natürlich könnten Sie einen billigen Computer kaufen, aber der teurere Computer ist schneller, intelligenter und einfach viel besser.**)

Themenwortschatz

Substantive

Die Medien

die Kommunikation	communication
das Kommunikations- mittel, -	means of communication
die Medien (pl.)	media

Die Presse

der Bericht, -e	report
die Presse	press
die Zeitschrift, -en	magazine

Das Fernsehen

der Dokumentarfilm, -e	documentary film
das Kabelfernsehen	cable TV
der Kriminalfilm, -e	detective movie
die Nachrichten (pl.)	news
die Politik	politics
das Programm, -e	channel
die Quizshow, -s	game show
die Reklame, -n	advertisement *Commerical*
der Satellit, -en	satellite
die Seifenoper, -n	soap opera
der Sender, -	(Radio/TV) station
die Sendung, -en	program
die Serie, -n	series
der Spielfilm, -e	(feature) film
die Sportreportage, -n	sports show
die Werbung, -en	advertisement
die Zeichentrickserie, -n	cartoon series

Elektronische Geräte

der Anrufbeantworter, -	answering machine
das Gerät, -e	appliance, device, machine
der Kassettenrecorder, -	cassette recorder
der Kopfhörer, -	head phones
der Lautsprecher, -	loudspeaker
die Schallplatte, -n	record
das Video, -s	video
der Videorecorder, -	VCR

Verben

isolieren	to isolate
zurück•rufen, rief zurück, zurückgerufen	to return a call

Adjektive/Adverbien

aktuell	current, up-to-the-minute
aufregend	exciting
elektronisch	electronic
lustig	funny
spannend	thrilling, gripping
transportabel	portable

Weiterer Wortschatz

Substantive

das Gehör	*hearing*
der Lärm	*noise*
die Nachricht, -en	*message; information*
die Schwerhörigkeit	*impaired hearing*
die Umwelt	*environment*
das Verbot, -e	*prohibition*

Verben

beweisen, bewies, bewiesen	*to prove*
erfinden, erfand, erfunden	*to invent*
hinterlassen (hinterläßt), hinterließ, hinterlassen	*to leave behind*
kämpfen	*to fight*
schädigen	*to damage*
schützen	*to protect*
sorgen (für + acc.)	*to care (for)*
statt•finden, fand statt, stattgefunden	*to take place*
sich unterhalten (unterhält), unterhielt, unterhalten	*to entertain oneself, chat*
verbieten, verbot, verboten	*to prohibit, forbid*
warnen	*to warn*

Adjektive/Adverbien

häufig	*often*
schwerhörig	*hard of hearing*
staatlich	*governmental*

Ausdrücke

an [Ihrer] Stelle	*in [your] place*

Mann und Frau in der modernen Gesellschaft

Kommunikation

- Discussing gender issues
- Expressing personal opinions about social issues

Strukturen

- Constructions with **man**, **sich lassen** + infinitive, and **sein** + **zu** + infinitive
- Nouns: review and expansion case and weak nouns noun suffixes and gender
- Review of relative clauses and pronouns

Kultur

- Mother's rights
- Women in the German academic world
- Au-pairs

Kapitel 15

Schritt 1: In der Familie

The following charts describe contemporary trends and attitudes toward the family in Germany. Here are some words that will help you discuss the issues facing today's families.

die Teilzeitarbeit	*part-time work*
die Vollzeitarbeit	*full-time work*
tätig	*active, employed*
schwierig	*difficult, complicated*
traditionell	
das Ehepaar, -e	
(**die Ehe** = *marriage*)	*married couple*
die Kindererziehung	*raising of children*
die Kindertagesstätte, -n	*day-care center*
der Kindergarten, ¨	
unterbrechen	*to interrupt*
aufgeben	*to give up*

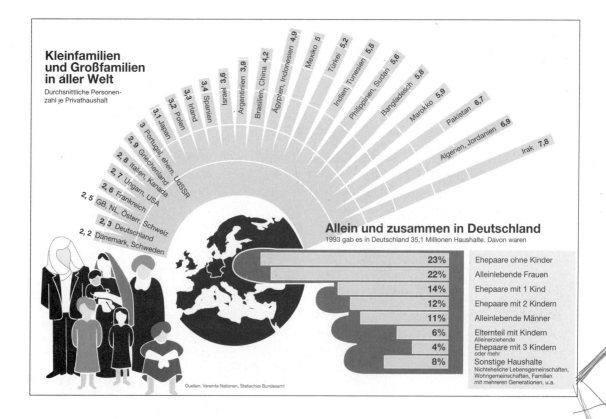

Kleinfamilien und Großfamilien in aller Welt
Durchsnittliche Personenzahl je Privathaushalt

2, 2 Dänemark, Schweden
2, 3 Deutschland
2, 5 GB, NL, Österr. Schweiz
2, 6 Frankreich
2, 7 Ungarn, USA
2, 8 Italien, Kanada
2, 9 Griechenland
3 Portugal, ehem. UdSSR
3,1 Japan
3,2 Irland
3,3 Polen
3,4 Spanien
3,6 Israel
3,9 Argentinien
4,2 Brasilien, China
4,9 Ägypten, Indonesien
5 Mexiko
5,2 Türkei
5,5 Indien, Tunesien
5,6 Philippinen, Sudan
5,8 Bangladesch
5,9 Marokko
6,7 Pakistan
6,9 Algerien, Jordanien
7,8 Irak

Allein und zusammen in Deutschland
1993 gab es in Deutschland 35,1 Millionen Haushalte. Davon waren

23%	Ehepaare ohne Kinder
22%	Alleinlebende Frauen
14%	Ehepaare mit 1 Kind
12%	Ehepaare mit 2 Kindern
11%	Alleinlebende Männer
6%	Elternteil mit Kindern Alleinerziehende
4%	Ehepaare mit 3 Kindern oder mehr
8%	Sonstige Haushalte Nichteheliche Lebensgemeinschaften, Wohngemeinschaften, Familien mit mehreren Generationen, u.a.

Quellen: Vereinte Nationen, Statisches Bundesamt

ALLES KLAR?

act Subject is doing asking

Pass-Subj. being asked.

A. Kleinfamilien oder Großfamilien? Machen Sie in Ihrem Kurs eine Umfrage (*survey*). Fragen Sie jede Studentin/jeden Studenten, wieviele Personen es in ihrem/seinem Haushalt gibt.

PERSONENZAHL IN DEM HAUSHALT	X ZAHL VON HAUSHALTEN IN IHREM KURS	=
2 Personen	x	=
3 Personen	x	=
4 Personen |||	3 x 4	= 12
5 Personen ||	2 . x 5	= 10
6 Personen	x	=
7 Personen		1 x 7	= 7
8 Personen	x	=
	Gesamtsumme a) = 4	Gesamtsumme b) = 29/6
		Durchschnitt = b ÷ a = 4,8

Vergleichen Sie den Durchschnitt in Ihrem Kurs mit dem in der Tabelle. Gibt es mehr Kleinfamilien oder Großfamilien in Ihrem Kurs als in den ganzen USA? Warum? Können Sie einige Hypothesen aufstellen?

B. Wieviele wollen Hausfrau sein? Sehen Sie sich die Statistiken aus Deutschland an. Wie würden die Statistiken aus den USA aussehen? Wollen mehr oder weniger amerikanische Frauen arbeiten? auch nach der Geburt eines Kindes? Warum? Besprechen Sie dieses Thema mit einem Partner/einer Partnerin.

Kulturnotiz: Mother's rights

Most western European countries have a much wider array of social services available to their citizens than does the United States. Germany is a good example, especially in the area of issues related to pregnancy and parenting. A few of its regulations are as follows:

No woman may be terminated from her job during her pregnancy or in the four months following delivery of the child. In addition, no woman may be forced to work during the last six weeks of a pregnancy (although she still receives full pay during that time), and no woman is allowed to work for at least eight weeks after delivery. Many women also take advantage of other provisions in the law; for example, over 90% take an additional leave (after the mandatory eight-week period) of up to four months to care for their newborns. During this leave, the woman receives partial pay. Austria and Switzerland have similar provisions to cover expectant and new mothers.

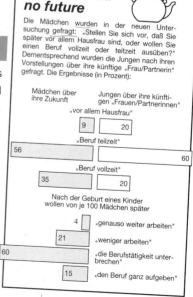

Nur Hausfrau - no future

Die Mädchen wurden in der neuen Untersuchung gefragt: „Stellen Sie sich vor, daß Sie später vor allem Hausfrau sind, oder wollen Sie einen Beruf vollzeit oder teilzeit ausüben?" Dementsprechend wurden die Jungen nach ihren Vorstellungen über ihre künftige „Frau/Partnerin" gefragt. Die Ergebnisse (in Prozent):

Mädchen über ihre Zukunft | Jungen über ihre künftigen „Frauen/Partnerinnen"

„vor allem Hausfrau"
9 | 20

„Beruf teilzeit"
56 | 60

„Beruf vollzeit"
35 | 20

Nach der Geburt eines Kinder wollen von je 100 Mädchen später
4 „genauso weiter arbeiten"
21 „weniger arbeiten"
60 „die Berufstätigkeit unterbrechen"
15 „den Beruf ganz aufgeben"

Schritt 2: "Viel mehr als Geschirrspülen ist bei Männern nicht drin."

Below is a passage from a German newspaper, describing changes in the division of household chores in a typical German household. Before reading it, first look at the new words below. Then study the chart that follows the reading to see which particular chores are mentioned.

der Haushalt, -e	*household*
der Fortschritt, -e	*progress*
sauber	*clean*
schmutzig	*dirty*

Viel mehr als Geschirrspülen ist bei Männern nicht drin

Deutsche Frauen machen immer noch die meiste Arbeit im Haushalt. Nur beim Geschirrspülen und Wäschewaschen helfen deutsche Männer jetzt öfter als vorher.

Beim Geschirrspülen machen jetzt zwölf Prozent der Männer mit[1], 1985 waren es nur sechs Prozent. Noch immer schrubben[2] die meisten Frauen Töpfe und Pfannen[3] - 88 Prozent der Männer machen das nicht.

Auch beim Waschen schmutziger Wäsche haben sich die Männer etwas verbessert. Inzwischen haben schon elf Prozent von ihnen gelernt, die Waschmaschine zu benutzen. Früher waren es sieben Prozent.

Aber das sind nur kleine Fortschritte, denn die Männer machen unangenehmere[4] Arbeiten im Haushalt immer noch wenig. Nur acht Prozent machen das WC sauber. Auch das Bügeln überlassen 95 Prozent der Männer ihren Frauen.

Aber die Frauen können wenigstens auf weitere Fortschritte hoffen: Beim Staubsaugen, Fußbodenwischen, Fensterputzen und Mülleimerleeren machen ein Prozent der Männer mehr mit als früher.

aus: *Berliner Morgenpost*, leicht verändert

---

[1] **mitmachen** = *take part in, join in*
[2] *scour*
[3] *pots and pans*
[4] *uncomfortable, undesirable*

A. Machen Männer Hausarbeit? Ergänzen Sie die Tabelle so wie weit möglich. Dann Besprechen Sie mit Ihrem Partner/Partnerin die Situation in der USA and so weit wie die Situation in Deutschland.

	WO		WIE VIELE MÄNNER				
	IN DEUTSCHLAND	IN DEN USA	1985	JETZT	VIELE	EINIGE	WENIGE
Geschirrspülen							
Wäschewaschen							
WC Saubermachen							
Bügeln							

Geschirspüllen machine

alles vier Woche

		WO		WIE VIELE MÄNNER				
		IN DEUTSCHLAND	IN DEN USA	1985	JETZT	VIELE	EINIGE	WENIGE
Staubsaugen								
Fußbodenwischen								
Fensterputzen								
Mülleimerleeren								

B. Persönliche Fragen. Besprechen Sie die folgenden Fragen mit einer Gruppe. Haben Männer und Frauen andere Meinungen dazu?

1. Wie ist es bei Ihnen zu Hause? Welche von den Arbeiten im Haushalt machen Sie? Ihr Vater? Ihre Mutter? Ihre Geschwister? Ihr Mann? Ihre Frau?
2. Was könnte man tun, um die Rolle der Frau im Haushalt zu verbessern?
3. Glauben Sie, daß die Schule, die Kirche oder der Staat (*government*) der Frau helfen kann/muss, ihre traditionelle Rolle zu ändern? Warum? Warum nicht?
4. Glauben Sie, daß in Zukunft die Männer mehr bei der Haushaltsarbeit helfen werden? Warum? Warum nicht?
5. Glauben Sie, daß Männer schon genug im Haushalt machen? Warum? Warum nicht?
6. Ist die jüngere Generation der Männer und Frauen anders als die ältere? Wie?

Schritt 3: **Männer und Frauen sind gleichberechtigt**

The title of this **Schritt** is taken directly out of the German constitution. Do men and women have equal rights both in theory and in practice? What is the situation in North America?

das Grundgesetz	*official name for German constitution*
rechtlich	*legal*
die Gleichberechtigung	*equal rights*
die Wirklichkeit	*reality*
im Durchschnitt	*on average*
selbstbewußt	*self-confident*
das Vorurteil, -e	*prejudice*
sind ausgesetzt + dat.	*are exposed (to)*

40 Jahre Erfahrung mit dem Artikel 3 des Grundgesetzes haben gezeigt, daß rechtliche Gleichberechtigung von Mann und Frau nicht ausreicht. Frauen und Mädchen brauchen eine aktive Lobby, damit die Gleichberechtigung endlich Wirklichkeit wird.

Denn Frauen...
- sind 52 Prozent der Bevölkerung[1], sind aber im öffentlichen Leben, in Politik und Wirtschaft nicht entsprechend vertreten[2]
- verdienen im Durchschnitt ein Drittel weniger als Männer
- machen immer noch den größten Teil der (unbezahlten) Arbeit im Haushalt und bei der Kindererziehung

- sind öfter arbeitslos als Männer
- sind jeden Tag physischer und emotioneller Erniedrigung[3] ausgesetzt.

Denn Mädchen...
- lernen nicht in der Familie, nicht im Kindergarten, nicht in der Schule und nicht in der Freizeit wie man selbstbewußt wird
- sind in der Schule und im Beruf immer noch Klischees und Vorurteilen ausgesetzt, und haben deshalb weniger berufliche Möglichkeiten
- lernen schon früh ihre "vorgeschriebene[4]" Rolle in der Familie und können sich daher nicht wie Männer frei entwickeln[5]

- sind sehr oft sexuellem Mißbrauch[6] ausgesetzt.

Gleichberechtigung heißt für Frauen und Männer...
- gleiche Chancen und gleiche Rechte im privaten und öffentlichen Leben
- gleiche berufliche Möglichkeiten
- gleiche Bezahlung
- volle soziale Sicherung[7] im Alter.

aus: Gleichstellungsstelle der Landeshauptstadt Stuttgart, stark verändert

[1] *population*   [2] **entsprechend...** *represented accordingly*   [3] *humiliation*   [4] *prescribed*   [5] *develop*   [6] *abuse*   [7] *protection*

ALLES KLAR?

 A. Die wichtigsten Probleme. Interviewen Sie zwei Frauen und zwei Männer und besprechen Sie mit ihnen:

1. Fragen Sie die Frauen, was die drei wichtigsten Probleme in diesem Text sind.
2. Fragen Sie die Männer, was die drei wichtigsten Probleme in diesem Text sind.
3. Welche Probleme haben die Frauen genannt? Welche Probleme haben die Männer genannt? Gibt es Unterschiede? Warum?

 B. Stimmen Sie überein? Besprechen Sie mit Ihrer Partnerin/Ihrem Partner:

1. Womit in diesem Text stimmen Sie überein? Womit nicht? Warum?
2. Welches Problem in dem Text ist am schwierigsten zu lösen? Warum?
3. Ist die Gleichberechtigung von Mann und Frau das wichtigste Problem in unserer Gesellschaft? Oder sind Abstammung (*origin*), Rasse, Sprache, Religion oder sexuelle Orientierung wichtigere Probleme? Warum? Warum nicht?

Kulturnotiz: Women in the German academic world

Although the role of women in German society continues to improve, there is no doubt that more can and will be done. In the business world, for example, women start one of every three new businesses and head one of every four, but the story in the academic world is somewhat different.

In the world of European academia, there is on the one hand greater success, on the other hand less. Female students, for example, can be found with relative ease. They collect degrees at every level, including the doctorate. It is unclear, however, what then becomes of them. Their numbers in academe seem to drop immediately and precipitously once they have attained their desired degree. The further one goes up the academic ladder, the fewer women there are. The following chart shows one example from Berlin:

Student Employees	ca. 55% women
Tutors, part-time instructors	ca. 40%
Five-year teacher contracts	ca. 29%
=(*Wissenschaftliche Mitarbeiterinnen*)	
Professors (lower ranks)	ca. 7%
Professors (upper ranks)	ca. 3.9%

At a recent conference (1995), one participant said that "mechanisms of exclusion are in place and become operative above a certain level in the academic hierarchy." There have been calls for various groups to draw up a specific plan for the promotion of women in academia and to help develop general strategies for the realization of equality between men and women in the academic world.

Schritt 4: Au-pair-Jungen

(((■))) **Gespräch**

Worum geht es hier? Was sucht Frau Scott? Warum ist ein Mann für diesen Job
genau so gut wie eine Frau?

FRAU SCOTT: Ja, guten Tag! Bitte schön?

AYO: Guten Tag! Mein Name ist Ayo Abonja.

FRAU SCOTT: So, Herr Abonja. Was kann ich für Sie tun?

AYO: Ich habe Ihre Anzeige gelesen. Sie suchen doch jemand für Au-pair-
Arbeit, oder?

FRAU SCOTT: Ja, das schon. Ich habe allerdings eher an ein Mädchen gedacht, wissen
Sie. Kommen Sie aber bitte herein.

AYO: Danke.

FRAU SCOTT: Sie wissen wohl, was für Arbeit man hier im Haus machen muß.

AYO: Ja, mehr oder weniger. Das kann auch ein Mann machen.

FRAU SCOTT: So! Können Sie auch Geschirr spülen?

AYO: Klar, das läßt sich ohne weiteres machen.

FRAU SCOTT: Hier muß man auch mit den Kindern helfen, wir haben ja auch ein
neues Baby.

AYO: In Ordnung. Ich habe meinen Eltern mit meinen jüngeren
Geschwistern geholfen, und ich habe auch zwei Gutachten[1] mitgebracht. Möchten Sie sie lesen?

FRAU SCOTT: Gern. (*Sie liest die Briefe.*) Das ist ja erstaunlich! Man lobt[2] Sie ja sehr.
Also, ich sollte doch nicht so viele Vorurteile haben. Wann können Sie
anfangen? Diese Woche schon?

AYO: Ab morgen, wenn es sein muß. Wieviel verdient man bei Ihnen?

FRAU SCOTT: Na, Sie bekommen Unterkunft und Verpflegung[3]. Über Taschengeld
läßt sich noch reden. Ich muß erst mit meinem Mann sprechen, und
morgen sage ich Ihnen Bescheid[4].

AYO: Schon gut. Also bis morgen. Ich komme gegen drei Uhr.

FRAU SCOTT: Schön. Auf Wiedersehen.

---

[1] *references*
[2] *praises*
[3] *room and board*
[4] *notify*

ALLES KLAR?

A. Haben Sie verstanden?

He is a man
Er ist ein man

1. Warum ist Frau Scott überrascht, daß Ayo sich für die Stellung interessiert?
2. Was muß ein Au-pair-Mädchen/-Junge bei den Scotts alles machen? *Sie hat*
3. Welche Erfahrung hatte Ayo mit Kindern? *Geschwister helfen* *eines neues Baby*
4. Was verdient man als Au-pair?
5. Was muß Frau Scott mit ihrem Mann besprechen?
6. Wann könnte Ayo mit dem Job anfangen?
   Ab morgen

Illustration: Olczarek

Kulturnotiz: Au-pairs

Since the end of World War II, young women have been working as au-pairs (a kind of housekeeper-nanny), both in their native countries and abroad. Usually these positions are short-term (1-2 years) and afford young people the opportunity to live and work in an atmosphere different from the one in which they grew up. The salary usually includes room and board, plus a small amount of pocket money. Many au-pairs choose to go abroad to learn a new language; in this way many young German-speakers have come to the US.

Since the early 1980's, young men have been applying for these positions as well. Although many employers still prefer **Au-pair-Mädchen**, especially families with young boys are finding **Au-pair-Jungen** as, if not more, qualified.

These days, many German au-pairs have formal training (**Hauswirtschaftsschule**) and rely on placement agencies, as well as personal connections, to find jobs abroad.

B. Persönliche Fragen.

1. Haben Sie jüngere Geschwister? Haben Sie geholfen, als sie klein waren?
2. Haben Sie, als Sie ein Kind waren, auch manchmal einen Jungen als Babysitter gehabt? Wie fanden Sie das?
3. Glauben Sie, daß Mädchen oder Jungen bessere Babysitter sind? Warum?
4. Wenn Sie Mutter oder Vater wären, würden Sie einen Jungen als Babysitter anstellen? Warum? Warum nicht? Hängt es davon ab (*does it depend*), ob die Kinder Mädchen oder Jungen sind?
5. Möchten Sie mal Au-pair-Mädchen oder -Junge sein? Warum? Warum nicht? Wenn ja, in welchem Land?

Constructions with *man*, *sich lassen* + infinitive, and *sein* + *zu* + infinitive

In both German and English, the emphasis of a sentence is usually on the subject—the person or thing who performs the action.

> *The students discussed the topic.*

Sometimes, however, the person performing the action is less important.

> *The topic was discussed.*
> OR: *They discussed the topic.*

(Precisely who discussed it does not matter.)

German has several different constructions that can shift the emphasis away from the subject of the sentence. All of them focus attention on the action itself rather than on the doer. The most common of these constructions follow.[1]

man

As you learned in **Kapitel 1**, this is usually translated as *one, you, we, they, people,* etc.

> **Man muß** mit den Kindern helfen.
> *You have to help with the children.*

> **Man** kann nicht alles selber machen.
> *You can't do everything yourself.*
> OR: *We can't do everything by ourselves.*
> OR: *One can't do everything oneself.*

Anzeige

MAN(N) SCHÜTZT SICH MIT **KONDOM.**
Schützen Sie sich und andere mit Kondomen vor sexuell übertragbaren Krankheiten—auch vor AIDS.

Bundeszentrale für gesundheitliche Aufklärung
Telefonberatung
0221-892031

---

[1]Reflexive verbs are also used in this manner:
Das versteht sich. (*That is understandable.*)

sich lassen + infinitive

Das **läßt sich** ohne weiteres machen.
That's easily done.

Über Taschengeld **läßt sich** noch reden
We'll have to talk about pocket money. OR: *Pocket money is still up for discussion.*

sein + *zu* + infinitive

Was **ist** sonst noch **zu tun**?
What else is there to be done?

Es **ist** nicht **zu glauben**, daß die Männer so wenig im Haushalt helfen.
It is unbelievable that men help so little in the household.

ALLES KLAR?

 A. Was kann/soll/muß man machen? Was kann, soll oder muß man tun, um eine gute Beziehung zu einem anderen Menschen zu haben? Besprechen Sie das mit einer Partnerin/einem Partner.

> BEISPIELE: —Man kann Geschenke machen, aber ich glaube, man muß auch Probleme zusammen lösen.
>
> —Ja, aber wenn man zusammen Probleme lösen will, sollte man nicht vergessen, daß alle gleichberechtigt sind.

IDEEN

Geschenke geben	zärtlich sein
Unterschiede erlauben	lieben
Spaß haben	keine Vorurteile haben
Fortschritt machen	zusammen träumen
die Wirklichkeit nicht vergessen	Probleme zusammen lösen
manchmal streiten	gleichberechtigt sein

B. Das läßt sich schon machen. Formulieren Sie Fragen und Antworten mit **sich lassen** + Infinitiv. Sie stellen die Frage und Ihr Partner/Ihre Partnerin antwortet.

> BEISPIEL: Kann man die Rolle der Frau in der Gesellschaft ändern?
> —Läßt sich die Rolle der Frau in der Gesellschaft ändern?
> —Ihre Rolle läßt sich nicht leicht ändern.

1. Kann man das Gleichberechtigungsproblem leicht erklären?
2. Kann man dieses Problem lösen?
3. Kann man Vorurteile verbieten?
4. Wie kann man das eigentlich machen?
5. Kann man nichts gegen Vorurteile unternehmen *(undertake)*?

C. Wie läßt sich das auf englisch sagen? Übersetzen Sie die neu formulierten Fragen und die Antworten aus Aufgabe B ins Englische.

> BEISPIEL: —Läßt sich die Rolle der Frau in der Gesellschaft ändern?
> —Ihre Rolle läßt sich nicht leicht ändern.
>
> —*Can a woman's role in society be changed?*
> —*No, the role can not easily be changed.*

D. Ist da was zu machen? Formulieren Sie die Sätze mit **sein** + **zu** + Infinitiv.

> BEISPIEL: Er mußte noch das Problem lösen.
> Das Problem war noch zu lösen.

1. Man kann dreckige (*dirty*) Arbeit auch von Männern erwarten.
2. Man konnte ihn nicht sehen.
3. Das glaube ich nicht.
4. Er muß die Hausarbeit noch machen.
5. Sie muß das Geschirr noch spülen.
6. Wir können Vorurteile nicht erlauben.
7. Man kann die Situation verbessern.
8. Sie kann die Wirklichkeit nicht verstehen.

Schritt 5: Früher gab es Frauenberufe

Lesestück

Worum geht es hier? Dieser Text stammt von dem bekannten Autor Erich Kästner (1899-1974). Seine Erinnerungen, *Als ich ein kleiner Junge war*, hat er 1957 geschrieben. Was hat sich seit 1957 geändert?

Bevor Sie den Text lesen, sehen Sie sich die folgenden Wörter an. Geben Sie die englischen Äquivalente für die deutschen Wörter.

> BEISPIELE:
> **heilen** = *to heal*
> **Gehilfin** = *helper*
> **die Heilgehilfin** = *practical nurse*
>
> **der Zweig** = *branch*
> **die Stelle** = *place*
> **die Zweigstelle** = *branch office*
>
> **altern** = *to age*
> **alternd** = *aging*

der Empfang = *reception*
die Dame = *lady*

die Empfangsdame= reception lady

vertreten = *to represent*

die Vertreterin= representative

das Eis = *ice*
der Schrank = *cabinet, box*

der Eisschrank= ice box

dolmetschen = *to translate*

die Dolmetscherin= translation

der Schuh = *shoe*
die Filiale = *branch, franchise*

die Schuhfiliale= shoe co.

der Dienst = *service*
das Mädchen = *girl*

das Dienstmädchen= service girl

Zeichnung = *signature*
berechtigt = *authorized*

zeichnungsberechtigt= athorize signature

Heutzutage wird ein junges, fleißiges Mädchen, wenn das Geld fürs Studieren nicht reicht, Sekretärin, Empfangsdame, Heilgehilfin, Vertreterin für Eisschränke oder Babykleidung, Bankangestellte, Dolmetscherin, Mannequin[1], Fotomodell, vielleicht sogar, nach Jahren, Leiterin einer Schuhfiliale oder [eine] zeichnungsberechtigte Prokuristin[2] einer Zweigstelle der Commerzbank. Das alles gab es damals noch nicht. Schon gar nicht in einer Kleinstadt. Heute gibt es einhundertfünfundachtzig Frauenberufe, habe ich in der Zeitung gelesen. Damals blieb man ein alterndes Dienstmädchen, oder man heiratete. War es nicht besser, in der eigenen Wohnung für den eigenen Mann als in einem fremden Haushalt für fremde Leute zu waschen, zu nähen[3] und zu kochen?

aus: Erich Kästner, *Als ich ein kleiner Junge war.*

[1]*fashion model*   [2]*clerk*   [3]*sew*

ALLES KLAR?

A. Haben Sie verstanden?

1. Was konnte eine junge Frau werden, als Kästner 1957 seine Erinnerungen schrieb? Wieviele Berufe gab es für Frauen?
2. Welche Möglichkeiten gab es damals für Frauen, die schon viele Jahre bei der Arbeit waren?
3. Was für Berufe gab es für Frauen, als Kästner noch jung war?
4. Was meint Kästner, wenn er schreibt: "Schon gar nicht in einer Kleinstadt"?
5. Was machten viele Frauen damals, wenn sie keine Hausgehilfinnen bleiben wollten?

 B. Frauenberufe heutzutage. Besprechen Sie dieses Thema mit Ihrem Partner/Ihrer Partnerin.

1. Gibt es heute mehr oder weniger Berufe für Frauen als zu Kästners Zeiten? Warum?
2. Glauben Sie, daß es heute auch noch *Frauenberufe* gibt, wie zu Kästners Zeiten? Warum? Warum nicht?
3. Glauben Sie, daß es für Frauen besser ist, im eigenen Haus für den eigenen Mann zu arbeiten, als einen Beruf zu haben? Warum? Warum nicht?
4. Welche Berufe sind bei Frauen zur Zeit sehr beliebt?
5. Stellen Sie sich vor, die Männer bleiben zu Hause und die Frauen verdienen das Geld. Könnten Sie so leben? Warum? Warum nicht?
6. Welche Berufe sind bei Männern zur Zeit sehr beliebt?
7. Die Tabelle unten ist aus dem Jahr 1989. Ist sie immer noch aktuell? Welche anderen Berufe gehören in jede Kategorie? (**Bergmann** = *miner*; **Hebamme** = *midwife*).

in der Regel nur Männer	Männer und Frauen			in der Regel nur Frauen
	häufiger Männer	etwa gleich	häufiger Frauen	
• Soldat	Ingenieur	Lehrer an Sekundar-schulen	Grudschul-lehrer	• Hebamme
• Bergmann	Naturwis-senschaftler		Verkäufer	• Putzfrau
• Regierungs-chef	Politiker		Büroange-stellte	• Kindergärtnerin
• leitender Manager				

Nouns: review and expansion

Case and weak nouns

As you have learned, there are four cases in German: nominative, accusative, dative, and genitive. In most of these cases it is the definite or indefinite article that undergoes certain changes; with a few exceptions (genitive masculine and neuter, dative plural), the noun itself remains the same.[1] Complete the chart to review the cases.

	MASCULINE	FEMININE	NEUTER	PLURAL
NOMINATIVE	der Mann	die Frau	das Kind	_____
ACCUSATIVE	_____	_____	das Kind	die Kinder
DATIVE	dem Mann	_____	_____	den **Kindern**
GENITIVE	des **Mannes**	der Frau	_____	der Kinder

There is, however, one special class of nouns, the so-called *masculine **n**-nouns*, or *weak nouns*. These masculine nouns take an **-en** ending (the "weak" adjective ending) in all cases but the nominative singular.

	SINGULAR	PLURAL
NOMINATIVE	der Student	die Studen**ten**
ACCUSATIVE	den Studen**ten**	die Studen**ten**
DATIVE	dem Studen**ten**	den Studen**ten**
GENITIVE	des Studen**ten**	der Studen**ten**

Wir besuchten unseren Neffe**n** in Österreich.
We visited our nephew in Austria.

Die Ärtzin verbietet dem Patien**ten** zu rauchen.
The doctor forbids the patient to smoke.

Ich kenne die Frau dieses Herr**n**.
I know the wife of this gentleman.

Most weak nouns refer to people and have plurals that end in **-n** or **-en**. A few that you have learned thus far are **der Student, der Junge, der Herr, der Mensch, der Neffe, der Kamerad.** Many other weak nouns are loan-words from other languages. They are usually stressed on the last syllable:

der Präsidént[2]   der Astronáut
der Kommandánt   der Touríst

Weak nouns are usually indicated in dictionaries as follows: **der Student, -en, -en.** The first **-en** is the weak ending, the second the plural form.

---

[1] In the dative, sometimes an optional **-e** is added in certain idiomatic expressions: **nach Hause.** Remember also that in the genitive masculine and neuter, an **-s** or **-es** is added.
[2] The accent marks are shown here only to clarify pronunciation. They are NOT part of the German spelling.

A. Wo ist das schwache Substantiv? Unterstreichen Sie die schwachen Substantive in den Sätzen.

1. Der Professor hat den Studenten nicht verstanden.
2. Der Präsident unterbrach seinen Assistenten.
3. Dieser Mann ist kein guter Mensch.
4. Ich gab meinem Sohn und meinem Neffen Fahrräder zum Geburtstag.
5. Der Beruf eines Astronauten interessiert mich sehr.

B. Substantive identifizieren. Identifizieren Sie alle Substantive in den Sätzen. Fall (*case*)? Geschlecht (*gender*)? Singular oder Plural? Wenn es ein schwaches Substantiv gibt, unterstreichen (*underline*) Sie es.

1. Der Junge, den ich gerade in die Kindertagesstätte gebracht habe, ist mein Sohn.
2. Meine Kusine, die ihren Beruf aufgegeben hat, bleibt den ganzen Tag mit ihren Kindern zu Hause.
3. Die Eltern meines Mannes wollen dieses Jahr in Spanien Urlaub machen.
4. Mit ihrem Lottoticket hat die alte Frau DM 10.000 gewonnen.
5. Wir fragten den Touristen, ob es in seiner Sprache auch solche Probleme gibt.
6. Das Ehepaar glaubte an die Gleichberechtigung von Mann und Frau.

Noun suffixes and gender

When you learn a new noun, you must usually memorize its gender; however, there are some noun suffixes that are gender-specific. The most common ones are:

ALWAYS FEMININE	ALWAYS NEUTER
-ung	-chen
-heit	-lein
-keit	
-schaft	

ALLES KLAR?

**Nachsilben *(suffixes).* ** Welche Substantive, die Sie kennen, passen in diese Kategorien? Machen Sie eine Liste.

-UNG	-HEIT	-KEIT
-SCHAFT	**-CHEN**	**-LEIN**

> **Tip!**
>
> The suffixes -chen and -lein are diminutives; that is, they usually indicate a smaller version of the original noun. Notice that the stem vowel takes an Umlaut whenever possible.
>
> | das **Brot** | bread |
> | das **Brötchen** | roll |
> | das **Buch** | book |
> | das **Büchlein** | booklet. |

Review of relative clauses and pronouns

Kapitel 12 introduced relative pronouns and clauses. As you learned there, relative clauses are dependent clauses that cannot stand by themselves; a relative pronoun joins them to the main clause. Relative pronouns are identical with the definite articles, with the exception of the dative plural form and the rarely used genitive forms.

	MASCULINE	FEMININE	NEUTER	PLURAL
NOMINATIVE	der	die	das	die
ACCUSATIVE	den	die	das	die
DATIVE	dem	der	dem	**denen**
GENITIVE	**dessen**	**deren**	**dessen**	**deren**

The choice of relative pronouns depends on three factors: number, gender, and case. See whether you can remember the rules for each.

1. What determines whether the relative pronoun will be singular or plural?

2. What determines whether the relative pronoun will be masculine, feminine or neuter?

3. What determines the case of the relative pronoun?

4. How is the relative clause separated from the main clause?

The following sentences illustrate the above principles:

Ich habe einen Mann, **der** mir bei der Hausarbeit hilft.
I have a husband who helps me with the housework.

Der Mann, **dem** ich den Brief geschrieben habe, ist mein bester Freund.
The man to whom I wrote this letter is my best friend.

Hier ist die Frau, **die** du gesucht hast.
Here is the woman whom you were seeking.

Die Menschen, **mit denen** wir arbeiten, sind nicht alle verrückt.
The people with whom we work are not all crazy.

ALLES KLAR?

 A. Ehewünsche und Bekanntschaften. Was für einen Menschen suchen Sie? Besprechen Sie Ihre Wünsche mit Ihrer Partnerin/Ihrem Partner.

BEISPIEL: Ich suche eine Partnerin fürs Leben, die humorvoll und sportlich ist.

Ich suche eine Partnerin fürs Leben, die…
Ich wünsche mir einen Bekannten, der…
Ich suche eine Frau, die…
Ich suche Partnerschaft mit einem Mann, der…
Ich wünsche mir eine Freundin, die…
Ich suche einen Mann, der…
…

Er, 27, spontan und reiselustig, sucht nette Sie mit Jeans und Abendkleid für die lauten und die stillen Tage. Bildzuschr. bitte an ZG 9753

„Tell it to my heart, tell me I'm the only one,", Sie , 19, sucht ihn, ab 1,85 + lieb, + . . . ZK 2369

HALLO, HIER BIN ICH
hübsche Bremerin, 22/172, ledig, Abitur, humorvoll und gesellig (kein Discofan), liebevoll, charmant, mit Niveau. Wer paßt zu mir?

Zuschriften bitte u. D 7942

Raum Köln
Sie (Lehrerin, 33) sucht Ihn bis ca. 40, mit Humor, Herz und Verstand. Ich bin vorzeigbar, kulturell interessiert und habe ein paar gute Freunde. Bildzuschriften an ZU 7822

B. Was bedeutet Gleichberechtigung? Ergänzen Sie die Sätze mit den richtigen Relativpronomen.

Wenn man von der Gleichberechtigung im Grundgesetz spricht, meint man, daß Männer und Frauen, ___ in der Bundesrepublik leben, dieselben Rechte haben. Ein Mensch, ___ das nicht versteht, ist altmodisch, oder hat Vorurteile.

Heutzutage hat die Frau, ___ zu Hause bleibt oder ___ zur Arbeit geht, dieselben Rechte wie ein Mann. Dem Mann, ___ das nicht gefällt, kann man nicht helfen. Es gibt nämlich viele Familien, für ___ das kein Problem ist. Leider ist es aber immer noch oft so, daß die Frauen, von ___ man dieselbe Arbeit erwartet, nicht immer dieselbe Bezahlung bekommen.

Das andere Problem, ___ immer wieder aufkommt, ist, wer soll was im Haushalt machen. Die Frauen, von ___ viele täglich arbeiten, müssen das mit den Männern entscheiden. Aber das Problem, ___ eigentlich kein Problem sein sollte, kann man leicht lösen, wenn man nicht immer fragt, wer soll das machen, sondern was soll *ich* machen.

Zusammenfassung

A. Die Gleichberechtigung. Formulieren Sie, wo möglich, die Sätze mit neuen Konstruktionen: entweder mit **man, sich lassen** + Infinitiv, oder **sein** + **zu** + Infinitiv.

> BEISPIEL: …daß man von den Männern nicht viel erwarten kann
> …daß von den Männern nicht viel zu erwarten ist

Einige Männer und Frauen sagen, daß das Problem der Gleichberechtigung der Frauen nicht leicht zu lösen ist; daß man von den Männern nicht viel erwarten kann; daß sie sich von den Frauen nicht gerne helfen lassen; daß man von ihnen keine Hilfe im Haushalt und bei der Kindererziehung erwarten kann. Andere Frauen und Männer meinen, daß man das nicht sagen kann. Da läßt sich schon etwas machen. Das Problem kann man lösen, wenn man das wirklich will. Zuerst muß man mit den Männern sprechen und ihnen zeigen, daß ein Kompromiß zu finden ist; daß man von den Frauen mehr Hilfe bekommt, wenn man ihnen auch hilft; daß man nicht von einer Gesellschaft sprechen kann, wenn nur den Männern erlaubt ist, das zu tun, was sie wollen.

B. Wie läßt sich das auf englisch sagen? Übersetzen Sie den Absatz von Aufgabe A ins Englische.

C. Ich wünsche mir… Fangen Sie jeden Satz mit «Ich wünsche mir" an und benutzen Sie ein Relativpronomen.

> BEISPIEL: Ich wünsche mir einen Mann, der zärtlich ist.
> Ich wünsche mir einen Mann, dem ich helfen kann.

Frau, Partner, Partnerin(nen), Kollege(n), Kollegin(nen), Freund, Freundin…

D. Ein neues Grundgesetz. Schreiben Sie mit 3-4 anderen Studenten ein kurzes Grundgesetz. Schreiben Sie einige Sätze über die Rechte der Menschen. Können Sie etwas zu den Themen Abstammung (*origin*), Rasse, Religion, Politik, Sprache und sexuelle Orientierung sagen?

> BEISPIEL: I. Jede Person (Mann und Frau) soll dieselben Rechte haben.
> II. Man soll keine Vorurteile haben gegen…

E. Zwei Gedichte. Lesen Sie die zwei folgenden Gedichte mehrmals. Dann schreiben Sie einen kurzen Aufsatz (*essay*), in dem Sie die Gedichte vergleichen.

1. Was wollen die Autoren sagen? Erzählen Sie mit Ihren eigenen Worten, worum es in diesen Gedichten geht.
2. Wie ist die Beziehung zwischen den zwei Personen in jedem Gedicht? Sind sie voneinander abhängig (*dependent*)? unabhängig? Was wünschen sie sich?
3. Hat der Unterschied zwischen den zwei Gedichten damit zu tun, daß das eine Gedicht von einem Mann ist und das andere von einer Frau? Erklären Sie!
4. Welches Gedicht gefällt Ihnen besser?

Was kann ich

Was kann ich über
unsere Liebe sagen
eins vielleicht
ich arbeite wieder
gern

Birgit Rabisch
aus: *Nicht mit dir…und nicht ohne mich.*

Du

Du
Du bist
Du bist nicht
Du bist nicht Du

Du bist nur ich
    bist nur durch mich
    bist was ich durch Dich empfinde[1]
Erfreust[2] Du mich dann bist Du gut
Verletzt[3] Du mich dann bist Du böse

Ich liebe Dich
    hasse[4] Dich so wie
ich Dich sehe und
ich weiß nicht
    kenne Dich nicht wie
Du bist

    Bist
Du nicht hier dann bist
Du nirgends[5]
    Ich erkenne[6] Dich an dem was
Du mir tust wie
Du zu mir bist wie
Du riechst[7] schmeckst mich ansiehst

Du bist nur
Du durch
        Mich

Karlhans Frank
aus: *Dimension*

---

[1]*feel, perceive*   [3]*hurt*   [5]*nowhere*   [7]*smell*
[2]*make happy*   [4]*hate*   [6]*recognize*

 **Zu zweit: Student 1**

A. Wir suchen ein Au-pair-Mädchen oder einen Au-pair-Jungen. You and your partner are a husband and wife in the process of hiring an au-pair to look after your five-year-old son and six-month-old daughter. Each of you has interviewed a different candidate. Share your information with each other and decide whom to hire.

	YETUNDE ACHEBE	PAUL FERGUSON
Heimat		Australien
Erfahrung mit Kindern		6 Monate Au-pair in England; hat jüngere Geschwister
Haushaltsarbeit		hat alles während seines Aufenthaltes (*stay*) in England gelernt
Persönlichkeit		selbstbewußt, aktiv, verantwortlich (*responsible*)
Hobbys		Fußball, Schwimmen, Fernsehen

B. Die perfekte Frau für Andrew. You and your partner are trying to arrange a blind date for your friend Andrew; you each have a possible match for him. Look at Andrew's profile and then discuss the two women you have in mind. Decide who would be most compatible with Andrew. Make a suggestion for their first date.

	ANDREW	MAGGIE	JILL
Alter	28	26	
Beruf	Medizinstudent	Sozialarbeiterin	
Körperliche Beschreibung	groß, schlank (*slender*), blondes Haar, blaue Augen	klein, dunkles Haar, braune Augen	
Hobbys	Basketball, Filme, Skifahren, Kochen	Gitarre spielen, Handarbeit, Theater	
Musik	Jazz, Rock	klassische Musik	
Persönlichkeit	lustig, selbstbewußt	freundlich, zärtlich	
Einstellung (*attitude*) zur Ehe und Familie	nicht traditionell aber auch nicht zu liberal (in der Mitte); will 2-3 Kinder	liebt Kinder, will eine große Familie haben; möchte dann nur Teilzeitarbeit machen	

Zu zweit: **Student 2**

A. Wir suchen ein Au-pair-Mädchen oder einen Au-pair-Jungen. You and your partner are a husband and wife in the process of hiring an au-pair to look after your five-year-old son and six-month-old daughter. Each of you has interviewed a different candidate. Share your information with each other and decide whom to hire.

	YETUNDE ACHEBE	PAUL FERGUSON
Heimat	Nigeria	
Erfahrung mit Kindern	2 Jahre Kindergartenlehrerin in Lagos	
Haushaltsarbeit	ihre Mutter ist früh gestorben; mußte den Haushalt für ihre Familie führen	
Persönlichkeit	zärtlich, ruhig, höflich (*polite*), zuverlässig	
Hobbys	Lesen, Theater, Musik	

B. Die perfekte Frau für Andrew. You and your partner are trying to arrange a blind date for your friend Andrew; you each have a possible match for him. Look at Andrew's profile and then discuss the two women you have in mind. Decide who would be most compatible with Andrew. Make a suggestion for their first date.

	ANDREW	MAGGIE	JILL
Alter	28		29
Beruf	Medizinstudent		Personalchefin
Körperliche Beschreibung	groß, schlank (*slender*), blondes Haar, blaue Augen		mittelgroß, schlank, rotes Haar, grüne Augen
Hobbys	Basketball, Filme, Skifahren, kochen		Squash spielen, lesen, backen
Musik	Jazz, Rock		alternative Musik
PersönlichkeIt	lustig, selbstbewußt		selbstbewußt, optimistisch
Einstellung (*attitude*) zur Ehe und Familie	nicht traditionell aber auch nicht zu liberal (in der Mitte); will 2-3 Kinder		Männer und Frauen sollen gleichberechtigt sein (auch in der Ehe); ist nicht sicher, ob sie Kinder will

Situationen

 A. Familienstreit.

STUDENT 1

You are the mother of two small children. You want to go back to your job as a high-school teacher, but your husband doesn't like the idea. Try to convince him of your point of view. (**Ich will nicht nur eine Hausfrau sein. Als Lehrerin kann ich früh nach Hause kommen, um mit den Kindern zu sein. Wir könnten das Geld für unseren Urlaub benutzen…**)

STUDENT 2

You are the father of two small children. Your wife wants to go back to her job as a high-school teacher, but you think she should stay at home with the children. Try to convince her of your point of view. (**Wir brauchen das Geld nicht. Die Kinder brauchen dich. Lehrerin sein ist zu anstrengend für eine Mutter…**)

 B. "Hausmann".

STUDENT 1

You are a husband and father who has made the decision to stay home and take care of the house and children. In the supermarket you run into an old school friend who is the CEO of a large company. Your friend is surprised to discover you aren't working. Explain your reasons. (**Wir haben zwei kleine Kinder. Ich finde es wichtig, daß der Vater viel Zeit mit den Kindern verbringt. Meine Frau verdient mehr, als ich verdient habe…**)

STUDENT 2

You are the (male) CEO of a large company and work means everything to you. In the supermarket, you run into an old school friend who is now a husband and father. You discover that he is staying at home to take care of the children and house, while his wife works. Express your dismay (**Was? Du warst immer der beste Student an der Uni. Der Mann soll seine Familie ernähren** [support]…) and try to convince him to put the children in day-care and come to work for you. (**Ich habe die perfekte Stellung für dich! Wenn du für mich arbeiten würdest, könntest du dreimal so viel wie deine Frau verdienen. Die Kinder brauchen dich nicht. Es gibt wunderbare Kindertagesstätten in dieser Stadt…**).

C. Kleinfamilie oder Großfamilie?

STUDENT 1

You are a woman dedicated to your career, and, although you want children, you prefer a small family. With only two children, day care is not so expensive. Your fiancé wants a big family. Try to dissuade him from this idea. (**Aber eine große Familie kostet so viel. Mit nur zwei Kindern kann man es sich leisten, manchmal in Urlaub zu fahren. Für jedes Kind bin ich 9 Monate schwanger** (pregnant)**! Viele Kinder machen auch viel Arbeit.**)

STUDENT 2

You are a man who grew up in a large family, and you are very close to your six siblings. You would like to have a large family. Try to convince your fiancée of your point of view. (**Wenn man viele Kinder hat, können sie einander unterhalten. Mit einem oder zwei müssen wir sie unterhalten. Mit vielen Kindern hat man eine gute Familienatmosphäre.**)

Jetzt lesen wir!

Worum geht es hier? Wolf Wondratschek is popular both as a poet and as a short-story writer. He was born in 1943 in eastern Germany and has been called a "pop" poet, writing poems in English as well as German.

Aspirin

Sie hat ein schönes Gesicht. Sie hat schöne Haare. Sie hat schöne Hände. Sie möchte schönere Beine haben.

Sie machen Spaziergänge. Sie treten auf Holz[1]. Sie liegt auf dem Rücken. Sie hört Radio. Sie zeigen auf Flugzeuge. Sie schweigen[2]. Sie lachen. Sie lacht gern.

Sie wohnen nicht in der Stadt. Sie wissen, wie tief[3] ein See[4] sein kann. Sie ist mager[5]. Sie schreiben sich Briefe und schreiben, daß sie sich lieben. Sie ändert manchmal ihre Frisur[6].

Sie sprechen zwischen Vorfilm und Hauptfilm nicht miteinander. Sie streiten sich über Kleinigkeiten. Sie umarmen sich. Sie küssen sich. Sie leihen sich Schallplatten aus[7].

Sie lassen sich fotografieren. Sie denkt an Rom. Sie muß im Freibad[8] schwören[9], mehr zu essen.

Sie schwitzen[10]. Sie haben offene Münder. Sie gehen oft in Abenteuerfilme. Sie träumt oft davon. Sie stellt sich die Liebe wie ein großes Geräusch[11] vor. Sie probiert ihre erste Zigarette. Sie erzählen sich alles.

Sie hat Mühe[12], vor der Haustür normal zu bleiben. Sie wäscht sich mit kaltem Wasser. Sie kaufen Seife. Sie haben Geburtstag. Sie riechen an[13] Blumen.

Sie wollen keine Geheimnisse[14] voreinander haben. Sie trägt keine Strümpfe[15]. Sie leiht sich eine Höhensonne[16]. Sie gehen tanzen. Sie übertreiben[17]. Sie spüren[18], daß sie übertreiben. Sie lieben Fotos. Sie sieht auf Fotos etwas älter aus.

Sie sagt nicht, daß sie sich viele Kinder wünscht.

Sie warten den ganzen Tag auf den Abend. Sie antworten gemeinsam[19]. Sie fühlen sich wohl. Sie geben nach[20]. Sie streift[21] den Pullover über den Kopf. Sie öffnet den Rock. Sie denken an Ewigkeit[22].

Sie kauft Tabletten. Der Apotheker sagt, zum Glück gibt es Tabletten.

Wolf Wondratschek
aus: *Früher begann der Tag mit einer Schußwunde*

---

[1] **treten...** *tread on wood*
[2] *are silent*
[3] *deep*
[4] *lake*
[5] *gaunt*
[6] *hairstyle*
[7] **leihen...** *lend each other records*
[8] *outdoor swimming pool*
[9] *swear*
[10] *sweat*
[11] *noise*
[12] *trouble*
[13] *smell*
[14] *secret*
[15] *stockings*
[16] *ultra-violet lamp*
[17] *exaggerate*
[18] *sense*
[19] *together*
[20] *give in*
[21] *slip off*
[22] *eternity*

Interpretation.

1. Beschreiben Sie das Paar. Was für ein Bild haben Sie von ihr und ihm?
2. Wie alt ist das Paar? Woher wissen Sie das?
3. Erklären Sie die Sie-/sie- Formen in diesem Text.
4. Warum sagt sie nicht, daß sie sich viele Kinder wünscht?
5. Was für Tabletten kauft sie?

German in Africa and Australia

*I*n some schools in Australia, German is taught as the first foreign language. Indeed, German is a required subject in about ten percent of the elementary schools in Australia, and there are junior high schools and high schools in both Australia and New Zealand where German is a "must" course.

In Africa, in areas south of the Sahara, German has always been taught in the secondary schools. Although many of these areas were previously occupied by the French, Germany also had colonies in Africa, most of which were formally acquired in 1884-1885. Although Chancellor Otto von Bismarck was most interested in securing the position of Germany in Europe, he also participated in colonial politics; thus Germany took over protective custody of several areas in Africa, in particular Morocco, Togo, the Cameroon, and the areas known at that time as German East Africa and German South West Africa. For a brief period, there was also German interest in Zanzibar (now part of Tanzania). Germany lost all control of these areas subsequent to World War I. During the years of German colonialism and before, German missionaries, doctors, and researchers departed for these areas in Africa. Their influence, and the influence of German in general, is still felt in some areas.

German is still taught in most of these areas, and some German is also taught in Mali. Many schools in Egypt, Algeria, Madagascar, and South Africa (where the related Germanic language Afrikaans is of major importance) regularly offer German at both the high school and the college or university level. In fact, a recent talk at 'Ayn-Shams University in Cairo brought together an audience of about one hundred fifty students and faculty to hear a talk (in German) on language and literature societies of seventeenth-century Germany!

Themenwortschatz

Substantive

Partner und Familie

das Baby, -s	baby
die Bekanntschaft, -en	acquaintance
die Beziehung, -en	relationship
die Ehe, -n	marriage
das Ehepaar, -e	married couple
der Haushalt, -e	household
die Kindererziehung	raising of children
der Kindergarten -	kindergarten
die Kindertagesstätte, -n	day-care center
die Liebe	love

die Gesellschaft

die Gleichberechtigung	equal rights
die Orientierung, -en	orientation
die Rasse, -n	race
die Religion, -en	religion
die Sprache, -n	language
das Vorurteil, -e	prejudice

Andere Substantive

der Fortschritt, -e	progress
das Grundgesetz, -e	official name for German constitution
die Teilzeitarbeit	part-time work
die Verfassung, -en	constitution
die Vollzeitarbeit	full-time work
die Wirklichkeit	reality

Verben

ändern	to change
auf•geben (gibt), gab auf, aufgegeben	to give up
heiraten	to get married
küssen	to kiss
lieben	to love
lösen	to solve
streiten, stritt, gestritten	to fight, argue
umarmen	to embrace
unterbrechen (unterbricht), unterbrach, unterbrochen	to interrupt
verbessern	to improve

Adjektive/Adverbien

beruflich	professionally
gleichberechtigt	equal, having equal rights
rechtlich	legal
schwanger	pregnant
schwierig	difficult, complicated
selbstbewußt	self-confident, self-assertive
sexuell	sexual
sozial	social
tätig	active, employed
traditionell	traditional
zärtlich	tender, gentle

Ausdrücke

(keine) Vorurteile haben	(not) to be prejudiced
(etwas) (dat.) ausgesetzt sein	to be exposed (to something)

Weiterer Wortschatz

Substantive / Nouns

die Anzeige, -n	advertisement
der Teil, -e	part
der Unterschied, -e	difference

Verben

erlauben	to permit
sterben (stirbt), starb, ist gestorben	to die
träumen	to dream
überlassen (überläßt), überließ, überlassen	leave to, entrust to
sich (etwas) vorstellen	to imagine (something)

Adjektive/Adverbien

allerdings	actually, indeed
damals	back then, at that time
dreckig	dirty, filthy
erstaunlich	amazing
fremd	foreign, strange
öffentlich	public
sauber	clean
schmutzig	dirty
sonstig	other

Ausdrücke

klar!	of course!
im Durchschnitt	on average
ohne weiteres	easily, without much ado

Anhang

Pronunciation Guide

das Alphabet

a (ah)	**b** (beh)	**c** (tseh)	**d** (deh)	**e** (eh)
f (eff)	**g** (geh)	**h** (hah)	**i** (ih)	**j** (jot)
k (kah)	**l** (ell)	**m** (emm)	**n** (enn)	**o** (oh)
p (peh)	**q** (kuh)	**r** (err)	**s** (ess)	**t** (teh)
u (uh)	**v** (vau)	**w** (veh)	**x** (iks)	**y** (ypsilon)
z (tsett)				
ß (ess-tsett)	**ä** (äh)	**ö** (öh)	**ü** (üh)	
au (ou)	**ei** (i)	**äu/eu** (oi)		

Aufgaben

1. Practice your pronunciation of the letters of the alphabet. Try to group similar sounds.

   ah   hah   kah

2. Wie schreibt man das Wort? Wie schreiben Sie das Wort **Theater**?

   großes Teh---hah---eh---ah---teh---er---err

Auto	Kaffee	Computer	Haus
Brief	Zoo	Bett	

   Wie schreiben Sie das Wort **alt**?

   kleines ah --- ell---teh

jung	besser	in	elegant	modern

3. Wie schreibt man das? Turn to your neighbor and ask:
   a. Wie heißt du?
   b. Ich heiße ...
   c. Wie schreibt man das?

4. Was ist das Akronym für...
   a. Volkswagen?
   b. Bayrische Motorenwerke?
   c. Die Vereinigten Staaten von Amerika?
   d. Europäische Union?
   e. Gemeinschaft Unabhängiger Staaten?
   f. Christlich Demokratische Union*?
   g. Sozialdemokratische Partei Deutschlands*?
   h. Freie Demokratische Partei*?

Good pronunciation requires a lot of practice; listen closely to your instructor and the tapes provided with this program. In general, the pronunciation of German words is concise and crisp, lacking the glides so common in English. We will now begin a systematic discussion of the sounds heard in German.

---

*German political party

Vowels

The single sound vowels in German are **a, e, i, o, u** and the umlauted vowels **ä, ö, ü**. There are also sounds which contain elements of two vowels (diphthongs) **ei/ai, eu/äu, au**.

The single sound vowels can be long, short, stressed or unstressed. Most often the spelling of the word will give some clue as to the length of the vowel. Whether vowels are long or short can make a difference in the meaning of a word, e.g.:

Staat	*state*	**Stadt**	*city*
rate	*guess*	**Ratte**	*rat*
fühle	*feel*	**fülle**	*fill*

A. Stressed vowels

Stressed vowels are short in the following circumstances:

a. when followed by a double consonant.

   Be**tt**   ne**tt**   Pla**tt**e   a**ll**e   i**mm**er

b. frequently when followed by two or more different consonants, including **ch** and **sch**, but not by **h** itself.

   Ti**sch**   kra**nk**   Ko**ch**   Ab**f**all

c. In many common one-syllable words followed by a single consonant.

   bis   in   ab   es   im   ob   um

Stressed vowels are long in the following circumstances:

a. when doubled.

   H**aa**r   Id**ee**   B**oo**t

   i and **u** cannot be doubled, but **i** can be followed by **e** and is then always long.

   s**ie**   w**ie**   F**ie**ber   w**ie**viel   Sp**ie**gel

b. when followed by an **h**. In such instances, the **h** is always silent and is solely an indication of the length of the vowel.

   Stu**h**l   za**h**len   Ja**h**r   So**h**n   Kü**h**lschrank   se**h**en

c. when the vowel is followed by a single consonant which would belong to the next syllable if the word were separated.

Vater = Va - ter	Bruder = Bru - der	Kino = Ki - no
Möbel = Mö - bel	ledig = le - dig	Türen = Tü - ren

Aufgabe

Practice the following pairs of words to be sure you can distinguish between long and short vowels.

bitte	biete	Stadt	Staat	Hüte	Hütte
Wüste	wüßte	innen	ihnen	im	ihm
still	Stil	denn	den	Betten	beten
offen	Ofen	Wonne	wohne	Anne	ahne

B. Unstressed Vowels

There are two types of unstressed vowels in German. To one group belongs the final **e** and to a second, the final **er**.

Unstressed final **e** is very similar to the short **e** you already learned above. Some examples are:

bitt**e**   biet**e**   Wüst**e**   wüßt**e**   Wonn**e**   wohn**e**

The second group of unstressed vowels is found in those words which end in -er. The sound is like the **u** in butter. Note the following examples:

Vat**er**   Butt**er**   Partn**er**   Met**er**   Schweiz**er**   leid**er**

C. Umlauted Vowels

There are three umlauted letters: **ä, ö, ü**.

Umlaut ä. The long **ä** is similar to the English vowel sound in *made*: später, Väter, zählen. The short **ä** is pronounced like the short German **e**; it resembles the English vowel sound in *rent*: Sprechanlässe, Städte, Männer, häßlich.

Umlaut ö. The **ö** sound is a sound which does not exist in English. In order to produce the long and short **ö**, you position your tongue as for the English *e* and round your lips as for the English *o* (cf. vowels of the alphabet in **Einführung**).

LONG Ö: schön, Österreich, Söhne
SHORT Ö: zwölf, möchte, Wörter, Töchter

Umlaut ü. The **ü** sound is a sound which does not exist in English. In order to produce the long and short **ü**, you position your tongue as for the English vowel sound *e* as in *sea*, and round your lips as for the English *u* sound as in *blue*.

LONG Ü: Übung, grün, Einführung, Stühle
SHORT Ü: müssen, fünf, dürfen, Stück, Mütze, Müll

Consonants

Most consonants in German are pronounced the same as they are in English.

The **b**, **d**, and **g** at the end of a syllable or a word, or when followed by a **t** or **s**, are pronounced like **p**, **t**, and **k**, respectively.

Aben**d**   Ta**g**   schrei**bt**

The letter combination **ch** represents one of two sounds, neither of which exists in English. Ch when preceded by **a**, **o**, **u**, and **au** is produced in the back of the mouth (Na**ch**barschaft, Mittwo**ch**, Bu**ch**, au**ch**). When **ch** is preceded by a letter other than **a**, **o**, **u**, **au**, or **s**, it is produced in the front of the mouth (i**ch**, spre**ch**en, Gesprä**ch**, ri**ch**tig, Bü**ch**erregal, man**ch**mal).

The combination **chs** is pronounced as if it were two separate sounds (**k+s**).

se**chs**   Sa**chs**en   La**chs**   Bü**chs**e

To produce the **l** sound, put the tip of your tongue at the ridge above your upper teeth.

Practice the following words:

Film	ledig	Blatt	viel	links
Lampe	lesen	fallen	alle	Bild

There are two types of **r** sounds in German: the **r** at the beginning of a syllable or within a word and an **r** at the end of a word. To make the sound for an initial or medial **r**, pretend you are gargling without water.

Practice the following words:

Roggenbrot	zurück	richtig	rechts	rot
Frage	Frau	Morgen	schreiben	

An **r** or an **-er** at the end of a word in German corresponds to the *u* sound in the English word *butter*.

Practice the following words:

weniger	Wetter	Bilder	Vater	Bruder	Vetter
Theater	lieber	später	besser	Meter	Dezember

A single **s** at the beginning of a word or syllable and followed by a vowel is voiced, that is, pronounced like English *z* (Fernseher, Sofa, lesen). At the end of a word or stem the **s** is voiceless and is pronounced like an *s* (aus, bisher, Haus). Double **ss** and **ß** are always voiceless (Sessel, wissen, Straße, heißen, weiß).

Note that the letter **ß** is used if the preceding vowel is long (Straße) or before a **-t** (du weißt) and at the end of a word (weiß). There is no difference in pronunciation between **-ss-** and **-ß**. No words ever begin with **ß**.

The combinations **st** and **sp**, when they appear at the beginning of a word or consonant, sound like the English **sh** plus **p** or **t**, respectively. Practice the following examples:

spielen	sprechen	besprechen	Stück
bestellen	Straße	Stunde	Student

If these combinations are located anywhere else in the word, they are then spoken as in English. Practice and compare the following with the words above:

Obst	erst	kosten	Osten	Westen
Herbst	beste			

The letter combination **sch** is pronunced like **sh** as in English *show* (**Sch**rank, **Sch**reibti**sch**).

The letter **v** is usually pronounced like the English *f*:

vier	verstehen	vor

When the word is of foreign origin, the **v** is pronounced like the English *v*:

Adjektive	Adverb

The German letter **w** is pronounced like the English *v*:

wie	Wetter	Woche

The German **y** is similar to the **ü** (**u** with Umlaut). Practice the following words with **y**:

mystisch   Ph**y**siker   Ph**y**sik

The German **z** sounds exactly like the English combination *ts* in the word *nuts*. A **z** at the beginning of a word is pronounced the same as a **z** anywhere else in the word. Note that the combination **tz** has exactly the same sound in German as the **z**.

Practice the following words:

zurück	Schweizer	bezahlen	Zeit	Jahreszeit	
Zimmer	zu	erzählen	Blitz	letzte	zwei

The combination **kn** in German is pronounced as if it were two separate sounds (**k** + **n**), not as in the English word *knee*:

Knie   **Kn**icks   **Kn**eipe

The German combination of **qu** is pronounced like the English combination of *kv*. Practice the following words:

Quantität   **Qu**ecksiber   **Qu**ark   **Qu**atsch   **Qu**äker

The **-ig**, at the end of a word or syllable, is pronounced like the German **ich** (bill**ig**, wicht**ig**, zwanz**ig**).

The combination **-ng** is pronounced like the English *ng* as in *singer*.

The suffix **-tion** includes four sounds: **t**+**si**+long **o** + **n** (Reak**tion**, Na**tion**).

The glottal stop

German syllables or words beginning with a vowel are separated from preceding syllables or words by a short stop, the so-called glottal stop. Many speakers of English will use a glottal stop in words like *co*operate* and *pre*eminent*. Some German examples: **ein*undzwanzig, Sonn*abend, Guten*Abend!, Wieviel*Uhr*ist*es?, Zählen sie von*eins bis*acht!**

Stress

Most two-syllable German words are stressed on the first syllable:

'Abend   'Morgen   'gehen   'kommen   'heute   'gestern

Kapitel 1

Wie geht's? Andere Antworte

ausgezeichnet	*excellent*
fantastisch	*fantastic*
miserabel	*miserable*
prima	*great*
schrecklich	*terrible*
Es geht.	*It's (I'm) OK.*

Kapitel 2

Andere Familienmitglieder und Spitznamen

die Mutti, -s	*nickname for mother; Mom*
die Oma, -s	*nickname for grandmother; Grandma*
der Opa, -s	*nickname for grandfather; Grandpa*
der Schwager, ⸚	*brother-in-law*
die Schwägerin, -nen	*sister-in-law*
der Stammbaum, ⸚ e	*family tree*
der Stiefbruder, ⸚	*stepbrother*
die Stiefmutter, ⸚	*stepmother*
die Stiefschwester, -n	*stepsister*
der Stiefvater, ⸚	*stepfather*
der Vati, -s	*nickname for father; Dad*

Länder[1]

Europa	*Europe*
Rußland	*Russia*
Irland	*Ireland*
Schottland	*Scotland*
Indien	*India*
China	*China*
Japan	*Japan*
Korea	*Korea*
Mexiko	*Mexico*
Kanada	*Canada*
Israel	*Israel*
Großbrittannien	*Great Britain*
Schweden	*Sweden*
Norwegen	*Norway*
Dänemark	*Denmark*
Finnland	*Finland*

Andere Berufe

der/die Angestellte, -n	*[male/female] employee*
der Architekt, -en	*[male] architect*
die Architektin, -nen	*[female] architect*
der Busfahrer, -	*[male] bus driver*
die Busfahrerin, -nen	*[female] bus driver*
der Elektriker,-	*[male] electrician*
die Elektrikerin, -nen	*[female] electrician*
der Friseur, -e	*[male] hair stylist*
die Friseuse, -n	*[female] hair stylist*
der Geschäftsmann, ⸚ er	*businessman*
die Geschäftsfrau, -en	*businesswoman*
der Journalist, -en	*[male] journalist*
die Journalistin, -nen	*[female] journalist*
der Koch, ⸚ e	*[male] cook, chef*
die Köchin, -nen	*[female] cook, chef*
der Krankenpfleger, -	*[male] nurse*
die Krankenschwester, -n	*[female] nurse*
der Maler, -	*[male] painter*
die Malerin, -nen	*[female] painter*
der Mechaniker, -	*[male] mechanic*
die Mechanikerin, -nen	*[female] mechanic*
der Schauspieler, -	*actor*
die Schauspielerin, -nen	*actress*
der Schriftsteller, -	*[male] author*
die Schriftstellerin, -	*[female] author*
der Sozialarbeiter, -	*[male] social worker*
die Sozialarbeiterin, -nen	*[female] social worker*
der Wissenschaftler, -	*[male] scientist*
die Wissenschaftlerin, -nen	*[female] scientist*
der Zahnarzt, ⸚ e	*[male] dentist*
die Zahnärztin, -nen	*[female] dentist*

---

[1]All countries listed here are neuter; however, they are usually used without the article: **Er kommt aus Irland.**

Kapitel 3

Andere Farben

beige	*beige*
bunt	*multi-colored*
dunkel	*dark*
dunkel(grün)	*dark (green)*
geblümt	*flowered*
gepunktet	*polka dotted*
gestreift	*striped*
grasgrün	*green as grass*
grau	*grey*
hell	*light*
hell(blau)	*light (blue)*
himmelblau	*sky blue*
kariert	*checked*
lila	*purple, lilac*
schneeweiß	*snow white*

Eigenschaften

aggressiv	*aggressive*
arrogant	*arrogant*
energisch	*energetic*
enthusiastisch	*enthusiastic*
ernst	*serious, earnest*
intolerant	*intolerant*
(un)kompliziert	*(un)complicated*
modern	*modern*
nervös	*nervous*
optimistisch	*optimistic*
pessimistisch	*pessimistic*
(un)praktisch	*(im)practical*
romantisch	*romantic*
skeptisch	*skeptical*
(un)sympathisch	*(not) likeable*
tolerant	*tolerant*
verrückt	*crazy*

Kapitel 4

Uhren

die Armbanduhr, -en	*wristwatch*
die Bahnhofsuhr, -en	*clock in a train station*
die Digitaluhr, -en	*digital clock/watch*
die Kirchturmuhr, -en	*church tower clock*
die Küchenuhr, -en	*kitchen clock*
die Kuckucksuhr, -en	*cuckoo clock*
die Rathausuhr, -en	*clock on the town hall*
die Standuhr, -en	*grandfather clock*
die Taschenuhr, -en	*pocket watch*
die Wanduhr, -en	*wall clock*
der Wecker, -	*alarm clock*

Andere Geburtstagsgeschenke

die Blume, -n	*flower*
der Blumenstrauß, ̈ e	*bouquet of flowers*
die Flasche Wein	*bottle of wine*
die Halskette, -n	*necklace*
der Hut, ̈ e	*hat*
der Ring, -e	*ring*
der Schal, -e	*scarf*
der Schmuck	*jewelry*
die Schokolade	*chocolate*
die Topfblume, -n	*potted plant*

Andere Substantive

das Gewitter, -	*thunderstorm*
die Temperatur, -en	*temperature*
das Frühjahr, -e	*spring*

Verben

frieren	*to freeze*
turnen	*to do gymnastics*

Adjektive/Adverbien

neblig	*foggy*

Kapitel 5

Wohnen

das Dach, ̈ er	*roof*
der Dachboden, ̈	*attic*
die Dreizimerwohnung, -en	*three-room apartment*
das Erdgeschoß, -sse	*ground floor*
die Garage, -en	*garage*
die Gardine, -n	*curtain*
das Geschirr (sg.)	*dishes*
die Haustür, -en	*front door*
der Keller, -	*basement, cellar*

der Müll	*trash, garbage*
das Stockwerk, -e	*floor, level (of a house)*
die Terrasse, -n	*terrace, patio*
die Treppe, -n	*stairs, staircase*
das WC, -s	*toilet*
das Wochenendhaus, ¨ er	*weekend house*
die Wohnungsnot	*lack of living quarters*
die Wohnungssuche, -n	*search for an apartment*
der Wohnzimmertisch, -e	*coffee table*

Geräte

die Brotschneidemaschine, -n	*bread slicer*
die Kaffeemühle, -n	*coffee grinder*
der Mikrowellenherd, -e	*microwave oven*
der Trockner, -	*dryer*
die Waschmaschine, -n	*washing machine*

Andere Substantive

der Streit, -e	*argument, fight*

Verben

an•hören	*to listen to*
an•sehen (sieht an), angesehen	*to look at*
auf•räumen	*to pick, straighten up*
leeren	*to empty*
liefern	*to deliver*
zerstören	*to destroy*

Adjektive/Adverbien

obdachlos	*homeless*
stabil	*stable, strong*

Ausdrücke

auf Wohnungssuche gehen	*to look for an apartment*
im Garten arbeiten	*to work in the yard*

Kapitel 6

Andere Körperteile

die Augenbraue, -n	*eyebrow*
die Backe, -n	*cheek*
der Blinddarm, ¨ e	*appendix*
der Daumen, -	*thumb*
der Ell(en)bogen, -	*elbow*
die Faust, ¨ e	*fist*
die Ferse, -n	*heel*
der Fingernagel, ¨	*finger nail*
das Gehirn	*brain*
das Gesäß, -e	*behind, bottom*
das Grübchen, -	*dimple*
das Handgelenk, -e	*wrist*
das Kinn, -e	*chin*
der Knöchel, -	*knuckle, ankle*
der Knochen, -	*bone*
die Kehle, -n	*throat*
der kleine Finger, -	*little finger*
die Lippe, -n	*lip*
die Lunge, -n	*lung*
der Mittelfinger, -	*middle finger*
der Muskel, -n	*muscle*
das Ohrläppchen, -	*ear lobe*
der Ringfinger, -	*ring finger*
die Stirn, -en	*forehead*
die Taille, -n	*waist*
die Wange, -n	*cheek*
die Wimper, -n	*eyelash*
der Zeigefinger, -	*index finger*

Andere Krankheiten

das Fieber	*fever*
die Geschlechtskrankheit, -en	*sexually transmitted disease*
die Grippe	*flu*
der Husten	*cough*
der Schnupfen	*runny nose*
der Muskelkater	*sore muscles*

Andere Substantive

der Alkohol	*alcohol*
die Apotheke, -n	*pharmacy*
die Drogerie, -n	*drugstore*
das Krankenhaus, ⁻er	*hospital*
der Unfallwagen, -	*ambulance*
der Krankenwagen, -	*ambulance*
die Kur, -en	*cure*
der Kurort, -e	*spa, place for a cure*
die Meditation	*meditation*
der Patient, -en	*[male] patient*
die Patientin, -nen	*[female] patient*
das Symptom, -e	*symptom*
die Vitaminkapsel, -n	*vitamin capsule*

Verben

sich aus•ruhen	*to rest*
bluten	*to bleed*
sich hin•setzen	*to sit down*
niesen	*to sneeze*
pflegen	*to nurse, tend, take care of*
schwitzen	*to sweat*
sich strecken	*to stretch*
sich verletzen	*to get hurt*
sich etwas verstauchen	*to sprain something*

Ausdrücke

in Ordnung sein	*to be all right*

Kapitel 7

die Autobahn

die Ausfahrt, -en	*exit [from the freeway]*
die Autobahn, -en	*freeway; expressway*
die Einfahrt, -en	*entrance [to the freeway]*
der Fernverkehr	*long-distance traffic*
der Nahverkehr	*local traffic*
die Straßenkarte, -n	*street map*
in der Stadt	*in the city*
die Bank, -en	*bank*
die Buchhandlung, -en	*book store*
der Dom	*cathedral*

die Drogerie, -n	*drugstore*
die Eisenbahn, -en	*train, railroad*
die Fußgängerzone, -n	*pedestrian zone*
das Gebäude, -	*building*
die Hauptstraße, -n	*main street*
der Markt, ⁻e	*market place*
die Oper, -n	*oper*
das Parkhaus, ⁻er	*parking garage*
der Platz, ⁻e	*square*
die Polizei, sg.	*police*
das Rathaus, ⁻er	*town hall*
die Sackgasse, -n	*dead end street*
der Supermarkt, ⁻e	*supermarket*
der Zoo, -s	*zoo*

Universität

das Laboratorium, die Laboratorien	*lab, laboratory*
die Mensa	*cafeteria*
die Sporthalle, -n	*gym*
das Studentenwerk, -e	*student center, student union*
die Studienberatung, -en	*counseling office*

Andere Substantive

der Ort, -e	*location, place*
die Stelle, -n	*place*
das Transportmittel, -	*means of transportation*

Verben

sich aus•kennen, ausgekannt	*to know one's way around*
sich verabreden	*to make a date*
hin•fahren (fährt), ist hingefahren	*to go (to someplace)*
weiter•fahren (fährt), ist weitergefahren	*to keep driving, drive further*

Kapitel 8

In der Drogerie

der Föhn, -s	*blow dryer*
die Haarbürste, -n	*hair brush*
das Haarspray, -s	*hair spray*

der Lippenstift, -e	lipstick
das Make-up	make-up
der Rasierapparat, -e	razor

Andere Kleidung

der Anorak, -s	parka
der Handschuh, -e	glove
das Kostüm, -e	(women's) suit
der Regenmantel, ¨	rain coat
die Sandale, -n	sandal
die Shorts	shorts
der Sportschuh, -e	gym shoe
die Strickjacke, -n	cardigan
die Strumpfhose, -n	panty hose, stockings
der Trainingsanzug, ¨e	warm-up suit
der Turnschuh, -e	gym shoe

die Kommunikation

der Anrufbeantworter, -	answering machine
die Bundespost	German Federal Post office
das Ferngespräch, -e	long distance call
das Fernmeldeamt, ¨er	(German) telephone company
das Ortsgespräch, -e	local call
die Störung, -en	disturbance, interruption
das Telefonsystem, -e	telephone system
das Telegramm, -e	telegram

Verben

läuten	to ring
sich melden	to answer (the telephone)
verbinden, verbunden	to connect

Kapitel 9

Andere Lebensmittel

belegtes Brot	open-faced sandwich
die Brezel, -n	pretzel
die Boulette, -n	hamburger
die Cornflakes (pl.)	cornflakes
das Eis	ice cream
der Hagebüttentee	rosehip tea

der Keks, -e	cookie
die Konfitüre, -n	marmelade
das Leitungswasser	tap water
die Marmelade	jam
das Müsli	muesli
die Nudel, -n	noodle
der Pfefferminztee	peppermint tea
der Pudding	pudding
der Reis	rice
der Schinken	ham
die Spaghetti (pl.)	spaghetti
der Speck	bacon

Obst

die Ananas	pineapple
die Aprikose, -n	apricot
die Johannisbeere, -n	currant
die Pflaume, -n	plum
der Pfirsich, -e	peach
die Weintraube, -n	grape
die Zitrone, -n	lemon

Gemüse

die Brokkoli (pl.)	broccoli
die Gurke, -n	cucumber, pickle
der Mais	corn
die Paprikaschote, -n	pepper
das Radieschen, -	radish
der Rosenkohl	brussel sprouts
der Rotkohl	red cabbage
das Sauerkraut	sauerkraut
der Spargel	asparagus
der Sellerie	celery
der Spinat	spinach
das Weißkraut	cabbage

Kapitel 10

Substantive

Auf Reisen

der Bergsteiger, -	[male] mountain climber
die Bergsteigerin, -nen	[female] mountain climber
die Grenze, -n	border

das Lagerfeuer, -	*camp fire*
der Pfadfinder, -	*boy scout*
die Pfadfinderin, -nen	*girl scout*
der Rucksack, ⏑ e	*back pack*
der Spazierstock, ⏑ e	*walking-stick*
das Zelt, -e	*tent*

Auf der Post
das Päckchen, -	*small package*
das Telegramm, -e	*telegram*

Verben
trampen	*to hike*
zelten	*to camp*

Kapitel 11

An der Uni
das Fachbereich, -e	*discipline*
die Fakultät, -en	*faculty*
der Hörsaal, -säle	*lecture hall*
der Lesesaal, -säle	*reading room*
das Stipendium, -ien	*stipend, scholarship*
die Studiengebühr, -en	*tuition*
pauken	*to cram*

Weitere Studienfächer
das Finanzwesen	*finance*
die Geographie	*geography*
die Romanistik	*Romance languages and literatures*
die Volkswirtschaft	*political economics*

Kapitel 12

Musik und Musikinstrumente
die Blockflöte, -en	*recorder, flute*
das Cello, -s	*cello*
der Chor, ⏑ e	*choir*
die Flöte, -n	*flute*
die Geige, -n	*violin*
die Klarinette, -n	*clarinet*
die Mundharmonika, -s	*harmonica*
die Oboe, -n	*oboe*

die Popmusik	*pop music*
das Saxophon, -e	*saxophone*
der Schlager, -	*hit, pop song*
das Schlagzeug	*drums*
die Trompete, -n	*trumpet*

Sport und Spiel
das Aerobic	*aerobics*
das Eishockey	*ice hockey*
der Fahrradweg, -e	*bicycle path*
der Federball, ⏑ e	*badminton*
der Gewinner, -	*[male]winner*
die Gewinnerin, -nen	*[female] winner*
die Leichtathletik	*track and field*
die Radtour, -en	*bicycle ride*
das Reiten	*horseback riding*
der Sportler, -	*[male] athlete*
die Sportlerin, -nen	*[female] athlete*
der Verlierer, -	*[male] loser*
die Verliererin, -nen	*[female] loser*
das Windsurfen	*windsurfing*
gewinnen, gewann, gewonnen	*to win*
sich trimmen	*to get into shape*
eine Radtour machen	*to go for a bicycle ride*
unentschieden	*a tie (in sports)*

Kapitel 13

Andere Berufe
der Arzthelfer, -	*[male] practical nurse*
die Arzthelferin, -nen	*[female] practical nurse*
der Außenhandels-kaufmann, die Außenhandelskaufleute	*[male] export sales-person*
die Außenhandelskaufrau die Außenhandelskaufleute	*[female] export sales person*
der Berufsberater, -	*[male] career counselor*
die Berufsberaterin, -nen	*[female] career counselor*
der Berufstätige, -n	*working man*
die Berufstätige, -n	*working woman*
der Fabrikant, -en	*[male] company owner*
die Fabrikantin, -nen	*[female] company owner*

der Gas- und
Wasserinstallateur, -e *[male] plumber*
die Gas- und
Wasserinstallateurin,
-nen *[female] plumber*
der Geschäftsleiter, - *[male] business manager*
die Geschäftsleiterin, *[female] business*
-nen *manager*
der Großhandels- *[male] wholesale*
kaufmann *business person*
die Großhandelskaufleute
die Großhandelskauffrau *[female] wholesale*
-en *business person*
die Großhandelskaufleute
der Handwerker, - *craftsman*
die Handwerkerin, -nen *craftswoman*
der Hotelleiter, - *[male] hotel manager*
die Hotelleiterin, -nen *[female] hotel manager*
der Kfz (Kraftfahrzeug)-
Mechaniker, - *[male] auto mechanic*
die Kfz (Kraftfahrzeug)-
Mechanikerin, -nen *[female] auto mechanic*
der Personalchef, -s *[male] personnel*
manager
die Personalchefin, -nen *[female] personnel manager*
der Richter, - *[male] judge*
die Richterin, -nen *[female] judge*
der Schornsteinfeger, - *[male] chimney sweep*
die Schornsteinfegerin,
-nen *[female] chimney sweep*
der Zahnarzthelfer, - *[male] dental hygienist*
die Zahnarzthelferin,
-nen *[femal]e dental hygienist*

Substantive

die Altersversicherung,
-en *old age pension*
die Berufsberatung, -en *career counseling*
der Berufswunsch, -e *dream job*
die Fachhochschule, -n *technical school*
die Gewerkschaft, -en *union*
der Gewinn, -e *profit*
die Praxis, -xen *practice*
das Talent, -e *talent*
die Überstunde, -n *overtime*
die Verantwortlichkeit, -en *responsibility*
die Werbung, -en *advertisement*
(on tv and radio)

Kapitel 14

Substantive

der Ansager, - *[male] announcer*
die Ansagerin, -nen *[female] announcer*
die Antenne, -n *antenna*
die Illustrierte, -n *magazine*
die Kritik, -en *criticism*
der Rundfunk *radio*
die Schlagzeile, -n *headline*
der Standpunkt, -e *point of view*
die Tagesschau, -en *television news*

Verben

aus•schalten *to switch off*
ein•schalten *to switch on*
kritisieren *to criticize*
um•schalten *to switch (channels,*
stations)

Ausdrücke

im Radio *on the radio*
im Fernsehen *on television*
Was gibt's heute? *What's on today?*

Kapitel 15

Hausarbeit

das Bügeln *ironing*
das Fensterputzen *washing windows*
das Fußbodenwischen *scrubbing the floor*
das Mülleimerleeren *taking out the garbage*
das Staubsaugen *vacuuming*
das Wäschewaschen *doing the laundry*

Substantive

das Argument, -e *argument*
die Erniedrigung, -en *humiliation*
die Frauenbewegung, -en *women's liberation*
movement
die Moral *morals*

German - English Vocabulary

This vocabulary includes all the words used in *Alles Klar?* except numbers and words glossed in the margins of the **Lesestücke**. The definitions given are limited to the context in which the words are used in this book. Chapter numbers are given for all words and expressions occurring in the **Themenwortschatz** and in the **Weiterer Wortschatz** sections to indicate where a word or expression is first used. SV indicates that the word is found in the **Supplementary Vocabulary**.

Nouns are listed with their plural forms: **der Abend, -e**. No plural entry is given if the plural is rarely used or nonexistent.

Irregular and mixed verbs are listed with their principal parts. **nehmen (nimmt), nahm, genommen**. Vowel changes in the present tense are noted in parentheses, followed by simple-past and past-participle forms. All verbs take **haben** with the past participle unless indicated with **sein**. For example: **fahren (fährt), fuhr, ist gefahren**. Separable-prefix verbs are indicated with a raised dot: **auf•stehen**.

Adjectives and adverbs that require an umlaut in the comparative and superlative forms are noted as follows: warm (ä).

A

(an)statt (+gen.) instead of 11
    anstatt ... zu instead of 10
ab as of 10
ab•biegen, bog ab, ist abgebogen to turn into (a street, etc.) 7
der Abend, -e evening 1
    am Abend in the evening 1
    Guten Abend! Good Evening! 1
das Abendbrot evening meal, supper 4, 9
das Abendessen, - evening meal, supper 9
aber but, flavoring particle 1, 4
ab•fahren (fährt), fuhr ab, ist abgefahren to drive off, leave 7
ab•holen to pick up 10
die Abkürzung, -en abbreviation
ab•lehnen to reject 12
der Absatz, ̈e paragraph
ab•speichern to store
ach oh, ah 1
das Adjektiv, -e adjective
das Adverb, -ien adverb
das Aerobic aerobics 12 SV
das Afrika Africa
aggressiv aggressive 3 SV
der Akkusativ, -e accusative

aktuell current, up-to-the-minute 14
der Alkohol alcohol 6 SV
alle every, all 11, 12
    alle [dreißig Minuten] every [thirty minutes] 11
    alle [zehn Jahre] every [ten years] 11
allein alone 5
allerdings however, in any event, indeed 10, 15
das Alphabet, -e alphabet
als when 8
also well, so, therefore 5
alt (ä) old 1
    Wie alt bist du (sind Sie)? How old are you? 1
der Altenpfleger, -/die Altenpflegerin, -nen caregiver for the old
das Alter age 1
die Altersversicherung, -en old age pension 13 SV
die Altstadt, ̈e old part of town
das Amerika America 1, 2
der Amerikaner, -/die Amerikanerin,-nen American 1, 2

die Amerikanistik American language and literature 11
die Ampel, -n traffic light 7
an at, at the side of (+dat.) 7
    an Ihrer Stelle in your place 14
an to, toward (+acc.) 7
die Ananas pineapple 9 SV
an•bieten, bot an, angeboten to offer 12
andere other 1, 12
ändern to change 15
der Anfang, ̈e beginning 4
an•fangen (fängt), fing an, angefangen to begin 10
an•gehören to belong 12
angeln to fish 4
angenehm pleasant
der Angestellte, -n, -n/die Angestellte, -n employee 2 SV, 13
die Anglistik English language and literature 11
an•hören to listen to 5 SV
an•kommen, kam an, ist angekommen to arrive 10
der Anorak, -s windbreaker 8 SV; 11
an•probieren to try on 8

der Anruf, -e call 8

der Anrufbeantworter, - telephone answering machine 8 SV; 14

an•rufen, rief an, angerufen to call (on the phone) 6

der Ansager, -/die Ansagerin, -nen announcer 14 SV

an•sehen (sieht) (sich), sah an, angesehen to look at something 5 SV

der Anspruch, ¨e claim

anstatt ... zu instead of 10

anstrengend strenuous

die Antenne, -n antenna 14 SV

die Anthropologie anthropology 11

antworten to answer 4

die Anzeige, -n advertisement 13

an•ziehen (sich), zog an, gezogen to get dressed 6

der Anzug, ¨e suit 8

der Apfel, ¨ apple 4, 9

die Apfelsine, -n orange 9

die Apotheke, -n pharmacy 8

der Appetit appetite

Guten Appetit! Enjoy your meal! 9

die Aprikose, -n apricot 9 SV

der April April 4

die Arbeit, -en work 4

arbeiten to work 1

der Arbeiter, -/die Arbeiterin, -nen worker 13

der Arbeitgeber, -/die Arbeitgeberin, -nen employer 13

der Arbeitnehmer, -/die Arbeitnehmerin employee 13

die Arbeitswelt, -en world of work 13

der Architekt, -en, -en/die Architektin, -nen architect 2

der Ärger annoyance, irritation

das Argument, -e argument 15 SV

der Arm, -e arm 6

die Armbanduhr, -en wrist watch 4 SV

arrogant arrogant 3 SV

der Arzt, ¨e/die Ärztin, -nen physician 2

der Arzthelfer, -/die Arzthelferin, -nen practical nurse 13 SV

das Asien Asia

das Aspirin aspirin 6

der Astronaut, -en, -en/die Astronautin, -nen astronaut

die Atmosphäre, -n atmosphere 13

auch also, too 1

auf on, on top of, onto 7

die Aufgabe, -n activities, exercises

auf•geben (gibt), gab auf, aufgegeben to give up 15

auf•hören to stop 6

auf•nehmen, (nimmt), nahm auf, aufgenommen to take in

auf•passen to watch out 7

auf•räumen to pick up, clean up 5 SV

aufregend exciting 14

der Aufsatz, ¨e composition, essay 11

auf•schlagen, (schlägt), schlug auf, aufgeschlagen to open 14 P

auf•stehen, stand auf, ist aufgestanden to get up 6

Auf Wiederhören Good-bye. (on the phone) 8

Auf Wiedersehen Good-bye 1

das Auge, -n eye 6

die Augenbraue, -n eye brow 6 SV

der August August 4

aus (+dat.) out of, from 1, 4

die Ausbildung education, training 13

der Ausdruck, ¨e expression

aus•essen (ißt), aß aus, ausgegessen to eat out 9

die Ausfahrt, -en exit [from the freeway] 7 SV

der Ausflug, ¨e excursion 10

aus•gehen, ging aus, ist ausgegangen to go out 5

Ausgezeichnet! Excellent 1

aus•kennen (sich), kannte aus, ausgekannt to know one's way around 7

die Auskunft, ¨e information 8

die Auslandserfahrung, -en foreign experience

aus•probieren to try out 5

aus•ruhen (sich) to rest 6 SV

der Außenhandelskaufmann, die Außenhandelskaufleute (pl.) [male] export sales person 13 SV

die Außenhandelskauffrau, die Außenhandelskaufleute (pl.) [female] export sales person 13 SV

außer (+dat.) except for 4

außerdem besides

aus•schalten to switch off

aus•setzen (sich) to be exposed 15

etwas (dat.) **ausgesetzt sein** to be exposed (to something) 15

die Aussicht, -n view 9

die Aussprache, -n pronunciation

aus•steigen, stieg aus, ist ausgestiegen to get off or out 7

die Ausstellung, -en exhibit

aus•suchen to pick out 5

der Austauschstudent, -en, -en/die Austauschstudentin, -nen exchange student 8 SV; 11

das Australien Australia

aus•wählen to choose 12

aus•ziehen (sich), zog aus, ausgezogen to get undressed 6

aus•ziehen, zog aus, ist ausgezogen to move out 5

der Auszubildende, -n, -n/die Auszubildende, -n (Azubi, -s) apprentice 13

das Auto, -s car 3

mit dem Auto by car 4

die Autobahn, -en freeway; expressway 7 SV

der Autor, -en, -en/die Autorin, -nen author 1

B

das Baby, -s baby 15
die Backe, -n cheek 6 SV
die Bäckerei, -en bakery 7
die Backware, -n bakery goods 9
das Bad, ¨er bath 3
der Badeanzug, ¨e bathing suit 4
die Badehose, -n swimming trunks 4
das Badezimmer, - bathroom
die Bahn, -en train 7
der Bahnhof, ¨e train station 7
die Bahnhofsuhr, -en clock in a train station 4 SV
bald soon 2
der Balkon, -s balcony 5
der Ball, ¨e ball 4
die Banane, -n banana 9
die Bank, -en bank 7
der Bankkaufmann, die Bankkaufleute (pl.) [male] bank teller 13
die Bankkauffrau, die Bankkaufleute (pl.) [female] bank teller 13
bar in cash 10
das Bargeld cash 10
barock baroque
Basketball (Gitarre, Karten, Tennis) spielen to play basketball (the guitar, cards, tennis) 2
basteln to do crafts 12
der Bauch, ¨e belly; stomach 6
der Bauernhof, ¨e farm
das Bauingenieurwesen civil engineering 11
der Beamte, -n, -n/ die Beamtin, -nen official, civil servant 7 SV; 13
beantragen to apply
beantworten to answer 5
bedeckt overcast 4
die Bedeutung, -en meaning
beeilen (sich) to hurry 9
begeistern (sich) für (+acc.) to be enthused about something

beginnen, begann, begonnen to begin 4
bei (+dat.) near, at the home of 4
bei•bringen, brachte bei, beigebracht to teach
beide both 12
beige beige 3 SV
das Bein, -e leg 6
das Beispiel, -e example 1
der Bekannte, -n, -n/die Bekannte, -n acquaintance 2
die Bekanntschaft, -en acquaintance 15
bekommen, bekam, bekommen to receive 5
belegen to take, register for (a course) 11
das Belgien Belgium 10
beliebt liked, favored 7
benutzen to use 3
bequem (un)comfortable, (comfortably) 5
der Bergsteiger, -/die Bergsteigerin, -nen mountain climber 10 SV
der Bericht, -e report 14
der Beruf, -e occupation 2
von Beruf by occupation, by profession, by trade 2
beruflich professional(ly) 15
die Berufsausbildung vocational training
der Berufsberater, -/die Berufsberaterin career counselor 13 SV
die Berufsberatung, -en career counseling 13 SV
die Berufsschule, -n vocational school 13
der Berufstätige, -n/die Berufstätige, -n people at work 13 SV
der Berufswunsch, ¨e dream job 13 SV
die Beschäftigung, -en activity 12
beschreiben, beschrieb, beschrieben to describe 6
besetzt busy, occupied 8

der Besitzer, -/die Besitzerin, -nen 13
besonders especially 9
besorgen to arrange for, get
besprechen, (bespricht), besprach, besprochen to discuss 12
die Besprechung, -en discussion 13
besser better 6
Gute Besserung! I hope you feel better soon!
bestehen aus, bestand, bestanden to consist of 6
bestellen to order 9
die Bestimmung, -en rules
der Besuch, -e visit 2
zu Besuch kommen to come to visit 2
besuchen to visit 2
die Betontechnologie cement technology
die Betriebswirtschaft business administration 11
das Bett, -en bed 3
die Bettwäsche (sg.) bed linen 3
bevor before 8
beweisen, bewies, bewiesen to prove 14
bewerben (sich) um (+acc.), (bewirbt), bewarb, beworben to apply for 13
der Bewohner, -/die Bewohnerin, -nen resident
bezahlen/zahlen to pay 5
die Bezahlung, -en pay 13
die Beziehung, -en relationship 15
die Bibliothek, -en library 4
biegen, bog, gebogen to bend 7
das Bier beer 9
das Bild, -er picture 2
der Bildvortrag, ¨e slide presentation
billig cheap(ly) 3
die Biologie biology 11
die Birne, -n pear, light bulb 9
bis zu up to, until 7, 8
bitte please; you are welcome 1

bitter bitter 9

blau blue 3

bleiben, blieb, ist geblieben to remain, to stay 4

der Bleistift, -e pencil 2

der Blinddarm, ¨e appendix 6 SV

die Blockflöte, -en recorder, flute 12 SV

blond blonde, fair 6

die Blume, -n flower 4 SV

der Blumenkohl cauliflower 9

der Blumenladen, ¨ flower shop 7

der Blumenstrauß, ¨e bouquet of flowers 4 SV

die Bluse, -n blouse 8

bluten to bleed 6 SV

die Bohne, -n bean 9

böse angry 3

die Boulette, -n hamburger 9 SV

brauchen to need 3

braun brown 3

brechen (bricht) (sich etwas), brach, gebrochen to break something 6

breit broad; wide 6

die Brezel, -n pretzel 9 SV

der Brief, -e letter 5

die Briefmarke, -n stamp 10

die Brokkoli (pl.) broccoli 9 SV

das Brot, -e bread 9

das Brötchen, - roll 9

die Brotschneidemaschine, -n slicing machine 5 SV

die Brücke, -n bridge 7

der Bruder, ¨ brother 2

die Brust, ¨e chest; breast 6

das Buch, ¨er books 2

das Bücherregal, -e bookcase 3

die Buchhandlung, -en book store 7 SV

die Bude, -n room (slang)

das Bügeln ironing 15 SV

die Bundespost German Federal Post Office 8 SV

bunt multi-colored 3 SV

das Büro, -s office 13

der Bus, -se bus 4

mit dem Bus by bus 4

der Busfahrer, -/die Busfahrerin, -nen bus driver 2

die Bushaltestelle, -n bus stop 7

die Butter butter 9

C

das Café, -s cafe 7

campen to camp, go camping 2

die CD, -s compact disk 4

der CD-Spieler, - CD-player 3

das Cello, -s cello 12 SV

die Charaktereigenschaft, -en character trait

der Chef, -s/die Chefin, -nen boss 4 SV; 13

die Chemie chemistry 11

der Chor, ¨e choir 12 SV

die Cola, -s coca cola 9

der Computer, - computer 3

der Computerprogrammierer, -/die Computerprogrammiererin, -nen computer programmer 2

das Computerspiel, -e computer game 4

die Cornflakes (pl.) cornflakes 9 SV

die Couch, -es couch 3

D

das Dach, ¨er roof 5 SV

der Dachboden, ¨ attic 5 SV

damals at that time, back then 10

damit so that 8

das Dänemark Denmark 10

danke thank you 1

  (Danke,) gleichfalls! Thanks, same to you! 9

  Danke sehr Thank you very much 1

danken to thank 4

Das ist ... That is ... 1

daß that 8

der Dativ, -e dative

dauern to last, to take (time) 8

der Daumen, - thumb 6 SV

die Decke, -n blanket 3

dementsprechend according to that

denken, dachte, gedacht to think 5, 7

denken (an) (+acc.) to think of 11

denn because, for 3, 4

das Deo, - (**das Deodorant**) deodorant 8

der Detektiv, -e detective

das Deutsch German

die Deutsche Mark (DM) German mark 8

das Deutschland Germany 2

der Dezember Dezember 4

dick thick, heavy 6

der Dieb, -e/die Diebin, -nen thief

der Dienst, -e service 13

der Dienstag Tuesday 4

das Dienstmädchen, - female domestic help

dies- this, that 4

die Digitaluhr, -en digital clock 4 SV

das Ding, -e thing, item 12

der Direktor, -en/die Direktorin, -nen director 13

die Disco, -s disco 7

die Dissertation, -en (doctoral) dissertation 11

doch positive response to a negative question 3

der Dokumentarfilm, -e documentary film 14

der Dolmetscher, -/die Dolmetscherin, -nen interpreter

der Dom cathedral 7 SV

der Donnerstag Thursday 4

doof dumb, stupid (slang) 3

das Doppelzimmer, - double room 10

das Dorf, ¨er village

die Dreizimmerwohnung, -en 5 SV

die Droge, -n drug

die Drogerie, -n drug store 6 SV, 8

du you (fam. sg.) 1

    Du liebe Zeit! My goodness! 11

dunkel dark 3 SV, 5

dunkelgrün dark green 3 SV

dünn skinny, thin 6

durch (+acc.) through 3

durch•brechen (bricht), brach durch, durchgebrochen to break through

der Durchschnitt, -e average 15

    im Durchschnitt on average 15

    durchschnittlich on average

durch•wählen to dial direct 8

dürfen (darf), durfte, gedurft may, to be permitted to, may 5

durstig thirsty 9

    (keinen) großen Durst haben to be (not) very thirsty 9

die Dusche, -n shower 3

duschen (sich) to take a shower 3

E

die Ecke, -n corner

    um die Ecke around the corner

die Ehe, -n marriage 15

das Ehepaar, -e married couple 15

die Ehrlichkeit honesty

das Ei, -er egg 9

eigen own 13

die Eigeninitiative self-initiative

die Eigenschaft, -en characteristic, trait

eigentlich actually 12

(es) eilig haben to be in a hurry 7

ein•biegen, bog ein, ist eingebogen to turn into [a street] 7 SV

einfach simple (simply) 8

die Einfahrt, -en entrance [to the freeway] 7 SV

einige some, several 12

ein•kaufen to shop 8

die Einkaufsliste, -n shopping list 8

ein•laden (lädt), lud ein, eingeladen to invite 9

die Einladung -en invitation 8

ein•lösen to cash (a check), to redeem 10

ein•richten to furnish 5

einsam lonely 8

ein•schalten to switch on 14 SV

ein•spielen to add something (subconsciously)

ein•steigen, stieg ein, ist eingestiegen to get in, board 7

die Eintrittskarte, -n entry ticket 11

einzeln single 10

das Einzelzimmer, - single room 10

ein•ziehen, zog ein, ist eingezogen to move in 5

einzig only 11

das Eis ice cream 9 SV

das Eishockey ice hockey 12 SV

der Elektriker, -/die Elektrikerin electician 2 SV; 13

elektronisch electronic 14

der Ell(en)bogen, - elbow 6 SV

die Eltern (pl.) parents 2

die Empfangsdame, -n [female] receptionist

empfehlen (empfiehlt), empfahl, empfohlen to recommend 5

energisch energetic 3 SV

das England England 1, 10

entdecken to discover 5

enthusiastisch enthusiastic 3 SV

entscheiden (sich) für (+ acc.), entschied, entschieden to decide (in favor of) 11

die Entschuldigung, -en excuse 8

    Entschuldigen Sie bitte. Excuse me please. 7

entspannen (sich) to relax 6

entsprechend correspondingly

entweder ... oder either ... or 12

entwickeln (sich) to develop

er he; it 1

die Erbse, -n pea 9

die Erdbeere, -n strawberry 9

das Erdgeschoß, -sse first floor 5 SV

erfahren, (erfährt), erfuhr, erfahren to find out 11

die Erfahrung, -en experience 11

erfinden, erfand, erfunden to invent 14

der Erfolg, -e success 8

erfolgreich successful 8

das Ergebnis, -se result

erhalten (erhält), erhielt, erhalten to receive 12

erholen (sich) to recover 12

die Erholung recovery 12

erinnern (sich) an (+acc.) to remember, recall 8

erinnern an (+acc.) to remind (someone) of 11

erkälten (sich) to catch a cold 6

die Erkältung, -en cold, flu 6

erklären to explain 12

erlauben to permit 15

das Erlebnis, -se experience

erneut again

die Erniedrigung, -en humiliation 15 SV

ernst serious(ly), earnest(ly) 3 SV

erst first, only, recently, just 1, 9

erstaunlich amazing

erwarten to expect 13

die Erwartung expectation

erzählen to tell 5

es it 1

    es eilig haben to be in a hurry 7

    Es freut mich. Happy to meet you. 1

    Es geht mir ... I am ... 1

    es gibt there is, there are 3

    Es tut mir leid. I'm sorry (about that) 1

essen (ißt), aß, gegessen to eat 3

das Essen, - Meal 9

das Eßzimmer, - dining room 5

das Europa Europe

F

der Fabrikant, -en, -en/die Fabrikantin, -nen company owner 13 SV der Fabrikarbeiter, -/die Fabrikarbeiterin, -nen factory worker 2

das Fach, ¨er subject 4

das Fachbereich, -e discipline

die Fachhochschule, -n technical school 13 SV

fahren (fährt), fuhr, ist gefahren to drive, to travel 3

die Fahrkarte, -n ticket [for travelling] 7

das Fahrrad, ¨er bicycle 4

der Fahrradweg, -e bicycle path 12 SV

die Fakultät, -en faculty

der Fall, ¨e, case

fällig due 11

falsch incorrect, wrong 1
   Das ist falsch. That's wrong. 1

die Familie, -n family 2

das Familienmitglied, -er family member 2

der Fan, -s fan

fantastisch fantastic 1 SV

die Farbe, -n color 3
   Welche Farbe hat...? What color is...? 3

fast almost 3

faul lazy(ly) 3

faulenzen to lie around, be lazy 4

die Faust, ¨e fist 6 SV

der Februar February 4

der Federball, ¨e badminton 12 SV

das Fenster, - window 2

das Fensterputzen washing windows 15 SV

die Ferien (pl.) vacation 12

das Ferngespräch, -e long distance call 8 SV

das Fernmeldeamt, ¨er [German] telephone company 8 SV

fern•sehen (sieht), sah fern, ferngesehen to watch TV 5
   im Fernsehen on television 14

der Fernseher, - TV, television set 3

der Fernverkehr long-distance traffic 7 SV

die Ferse, -n heel 6 SV

fertig finished, done 4

das Fieber fever 6 SV

das Finanzwesen 11 SV

finden, fand, gefunden to find, to express an opinion 3
   Wie findest du...? What do you think of...? 5

der Finger, - finger 6

der Fingernagel, ¨ finger nail 6 SV

das Finnland Finland 10

die Firma, -en company 13

der Fisch, -e fish 9

fit fit 3

fit halten (sich), (hält), hielt, gehalten to keep fit, stay in shape 6

das Fitness-Center fitness center

die Flasche, -n bottle 4 SV

das Fleisch meat 9

der Fleiß diligence

fleißig industrious, diligent 3

fliegen, flog, geflogen to fly 8, 10

die Flöte, -n flute 12 SV

der Flughafen, ¨ airport 7

die Flugnummer, -n flight number

das Flugzeug, -e airplane 4

der Flur, -en hall 5 SV

der Föhn, -s blow dryer 8 SV

folgen to follow 4

der Forscher, -/die Forscherin, -nen researcher 11

der Fortschritt, -e progress 15

fotografieren to photograph, take pictures 4

das Fotomodell, -e [female, male] fashion model

die Frage, -n question 1

das Fragewort, ¨er question word 1
   Ich habe eine Frage. I have a question. 1

fragen to ask 7

das Frankreich France 10

die Frau, -en Mrs.; Ms.; woman; wife 1

die Frauenbewegung, -en women's liberation movement 15 SV

das Fräulein, - Miss, Mrs., Ms., unmarried woman 1

frei empty, free 6

der Freitag Friday 4

die Freizeit, -en free time 12

fremd foreign, strange 15

das Fremdenverkehrsamt, ¨er traveler's information center 10

die Fremdsprache, -n foreign language 11

freuen (sich) auf (+acc.) to look forward to 8

freuen (sich) über (+acc.) to be happy about 11

der Freund, -e/die Freundin, -nen friend 2

freundlich friendly 3

frieren, fror, gefroren to freeze 4 SV

frisch fresh 9

der Friseur, -e/die Friseurin, -nen hair dresser 2 SV; 13

froh happy 3

früh early 5

das Frühjahr, -e spring 4 SV

der Frühling Spring 4

das Frühstück breakfast 6, 9

frühstücken to eat breakfast 4

für (+acc.) for 3

der Fuß, ¨e foot 6
   zu Fuß on foot 4

der Fußball, ¨e soccer 11

das Fußbodenwischen scrubbing the floor 15 SV

die Fußgängerzone, -n pedestrial zone 7 SV

G

ganz whole 6
gar done; tender 9
die Garage, -n garage 5 SV
das Gardine, -n curtain 5 SV
der Garten, ⸚ yard, garden 5
  im Garten arbeiten to work
  in the yard 5 SV
der Gas- und Wasserinstallateur,
  -e/die Gas- und
  Wasserinstallateurin, -nen
  plumber 13 SV
das Gast, ⸚e guest 10
der Gastgeber, -/die Gastgeberin,
  -nen host
das Gebäude, - building 7 SV
geben (gibt), gab, gegeben to
  give 1
  es gibt there is, there are 3
  was gibt's heute? what's going
  on today? 14
geblümt flowered 3 SV
gebraten fried 9
der Geburtstag, -e birthday 4
  Wann hast du (haben Sie)
  Geburtstag? When is your
  birthday? 4
die Gedächtniskirche, -n memorial church
das Gedicht, -e poem
die Gefahr, -en danger
gefährlich dangerous(ly) 5
gefallen (gefällt), gefiel, gefallen
  to please 4
das Geflügel (sg.) fowl
gegen against 3
die Gegend, -en area 5
der Gegensatz, ⸚e, opposite
der Gegenstand, ⸚e object
gegenüber across 7
gegrillt grilled 9
das Gehalt, ⸚er salary 13
gehen, ging, ist gegangen to go
  1, 2
das Gehirn brain 6 SV
das Gehör hearing 14
gehören to belong to 4

die Geige, -n violin 12 SV
gekocht cooked; boiled 9
gelb yellow 3
  Gelbe Seiten Yellow Pages 8
das Geld, -er money 7
  Geld wechseln to exchange
  money 10
gemeinsam mutual
das Gemüse (sg.) vegetables 9
der Gemüsesaft, ⸚e vegetable
  juice
genau exactly 7
genug enough 3
genügen to have enough
geöffnet open 9
die Geographie geography 11
  SV
gepunktet polka dotted 3 SV
gerade just 2
geradeaus straight ahead 7
das Gerät, -e utensil, gadget,
  device; appliance 5, 14
die Germanistik German language and literature 11
gern gladly, with pleasure,
  readily 2
die Gesamtschule, -n high
  school
das Gesäß, -e behind, bottom 6
  SV
das Geschäft, -e store 5
der Geschäftsleiter, -/die
  Geschäftsleiterin, -nen business manager 13 SV
der Geschäftsmann,
  Geschäftsleute (pl.) business
  man 13
die Geschäftsfrau,
  Geschäftsleute (pl.) business
  woman 13
das Geschenk, -e present 4
die Geschichte history 11
die Geschichte, -n story
geschieden divorced 2
das Geschirr (sg.) dishes 5 SV
  Geschirr spülen to do the
  dishes 5

der Geschirrspüler, - dishwasher
  5
die Geschwister (pl.) siblings 2
die Gesellschaft, -en society 12
das Gesicht, -er face 6
das Gespräch, -e conversation
das Gesprächsthema, -en conversational theme
die Gestaltung, -en formation,
  organisation
gestern yesterday 4
gestreift striped 3 SV
gesund (ü) healthy 1, 2
die Gesundheit health 6
das Getränk, -e beverage,
  drink 9
getrennt separated 2
die Gewerkschaft, -en union 13
  SV
der Gewinn, -e profit 13 SV
gewinnen, gewann, gewonnen
  to win 12 SV
der Gewinner, -/die Gewinnerin,
  -nen winner 12 SV
das Gewitter, - thunder storm 4
  SV
die Gitarre, -n guitar 2
die Glasdecke, -n glass ceiling
glatt straight, smooth 6
glauben to believe 4
gleichberechtigt having equal
  rights 15
die Gleichberechtigung equal
  rights 15
gleichfalls same to you 9
die Gleichstellung equalization
das Glück luck 3
  Glück haben to be lucky 11
glücklich happy 6
gotisch gothic
der Grad, -e degree 4
grasgrün green as gras 3 SV
gratulieren to congratulate
grau grey 3 SV
die Grenze, -n border 10 SV
das Griechenland Greece 10
die Grippe flu 6 SV
groß (ö) big, great, large 2

die Großeltern (pl.) grandparents 2

der Großhandelskaufmann, die Großhandelskaufleute (pl.) [male] wholesale business person 13 SV

die Großhandelskauffrau, die Großhandelskaufleute (pl.) [female] wholesale business person 13 SV

die Großmutter, ⸚ grandmother 2

der Großvater, ⸚ grandfather 2

das Grübchen, - dimple 6 SV

grün green 3

der Grund, ⸚e reason 8

das Grundgesetz, -e official name for: constitution of the FRG 15

die Grundschule, -n elementary school 11

die Gruppe, -n group 12

grüßen to greet 1

    Grüß dich! Hello! Hi! 1

die Gurke, -n cucumber 9 SV

gut good 1

    Gute Besserung! Hope you feel better! 6

    Guten Abend! Good evening! 1

    Guten Appetit! Enjoy your meal! 9

    Guten Morgen! Good Morning! 1

    Guten Tag! Hello. (lit. Good day.) 1

das Gymnasium, Gymnasien high school 11

die Gymnastik gymnastics 12

H

das Haar, -e hair 6

die Haarbürste, -n hair brush 8

das Haarspray, -s hair spray 8 SV

haben (hat), hatte, gehabt to have 3

    Ich habe ... gern I like 3

Haben Sie eine Frage? (formal) Do you have a question? 1

der Hagebuttentee, -s rosehip tea 9 SV

hageln to hail

das Hähnchen, - chicken 9

halb half 4

    Es ist halb sieben (Uhr). It is 6:30 (o'clock). 4

das Hallenbad, ⸚er inside swimming pool 12 P

hallo! hello! 1

der Hals, ⸚e neck

die Halskette, -n necklace 4 SV

die Halsschmerzen (pl.) sore throat 6

halten (hält), hielt, gehalten to hold, to stop 7

die Hand, ⸚e hand 6

das Handgelenk, -e wrist 6 SV

der Handschuh, -e glove 8

die Handtasche, -n handbag 8

das Handtuch, ⸚er towel 3

der Handwerker, -/die Handwerkerin, -nen craftsman 13 SV

hängen, hängte, gehängt to hang (+acc.) 7

hängen, hing, gehangen to hang (+dat.) 7

hart (ä) hard 9

Hast du eine Frage? (informal) Do you have a question? 1

häßlich ugly 3

häufig often 14

das Hauptfach, ⸚er major 11

die Hauptschule, -n junior high school

die Hauptstraße, -n main street 7 SV

das Haus, ⸚er house 2

    nach Hause gehen to go home 4

    zu Hause to be at home 2

die Hausaufgaben (pl.) homework 3

    Hausaufgaben machen to do homework 3

der Haushalt, -e household 15

das Haustier, -e domesticated animal 12 P

die Haustür, -en front door 5 SV

die Haut, ⸚e skin 6 SV

heben, hob, gehoben to lift 7

das Heft, -e notebook 2

der Heilgehilfe, -n/Heilgehilfin, -nen practical nurse

die Heimat homeland, native country 10

heiraten to get married 15

heiß hot 4

heißen, hieß, geheißen to be called, named 1

    Wie heißt du? (heißen Sie)? What is your name? 1

heiter bright, clear 4

die Heizung heat 4

helfen (hilft), half, geholfen to help 4

hell light 3 SV, 5

hellblau light blue 3 SV

das Hemd, -en shirt 8

heraus•kommen, kam heraus, ist herausgekommen to come out 7

    Heraus! Get out! 7

der Herbst autumn, fall 4

der Herd, -e range, stovetop 5

herein! come in 7

her•kommen, kam her, ist hergekommen to come (from someplace) 7

der Herr, -n, -en Mr.; gentleman; man 1

herunter•kommen, kam herunter, ist heruntergekommen to come down 7

das Herz, -en heart 6

herzlich hearty 8

    Herzlichen Dank. Thank you very much. 8

heute today 2

    Heute haben wir den [5. (fünften) Januar]. Today is [January fifth]. 7

heutzutage in this day and age 13
hier here 1
himmelblau sky blue 3 SV
hinauf•gehen, ging hinauf, ist hinaufgegangen to go up 7
hinein•gehen, ging hinein, ist hineingegangen to go in 7
hin•fahren (fährt), fuhr hin, ist hingefahren to go (to someplace)
hin•legen (sich) to lie down 6
hin•setzen (sich) to sit down 6
hinten in back 7
hinter behind, in back of 7
hinterlassen (hinterläßt), hinterließ, hinterlassen to leave behind 14
das Hobby, -s hobby 12
hoch, höher, höchst- high 6
die Hochschule, -n university level institution 11
hoffen to hope 8
holen to get 10
der Hörsaal,-säle lecture hall
die Hose, -n trousers 8
das Hotel, -s hotel 7
der Hotelleiter, -/die Hotelleiterin, -nen hotel manager 13 SV
der Hund, -e dog
hungrig hungry 9
  (keinen) großen Hunger haben to be (not) very hungry 9
der Husten cough 6 SV
der Hut, ¨e hat 4 SV

I

ich I 1
  Ich auch. I (me) too. 1
ideal ideal(ly) 5 SV
Ihnen to you 1
ihr you (fam. pl.); her; their 1
die Illustrierte, -n magazine 14 SV
der Imbiß, -sse snack bar; snack 9

die Imbißstube, -n snack bar 9
immer always 3
in (+acc./dat.) in; into; 2
die Informatik computer science 11
der Informatiker, -/die Informatikerin, -nen person who works in computer science 13
der Ingenieur, -e/die Ingenieurin, -nen engineer 2
inklusive inclusive(ly) 5
das Inserat, -e newspaper ad 5
das Instrument, -e instrument 12
intelligent intelligent 3
interessant interesting 3
das Interesse, -n interest 12
interessieren (sich) für (+acc.) to be interested in 11
das Interview, -s interview
intolerant intolerant 15 SV
das Irland Ireland 10
isolieren to isolate 14
das Italien Italy 2, 10

J

ja yes, after all, of course, flavoring article 1, 2
die Jacke, -n jacket 8
das Jahr, -e year 1
  alle [zehn Jahre] every [ten years] 11
  Ich bin ... Jahre alt. I am ... years old. 1
  im Laufe des Jahres during the year 11
jahrelang for many years
die Jahreszeit, -en season 4
das Jahrhundert, -e century 11
der Januar January 4
die Jeans (pl.) jeans 8
jedenfalls in any event 12
jed- each, every 4
jetzt now 1
joggen to jog 12

das Joghurt yoghurt 9
die Johannisbeere, -n currant 9 SV
die Jugendherberge, -n youth hostel 10
der Jugendliche, -n, -n/die Jugendliche, -n youth
das Jugendtreff, -s place where youth meet
der Juli July 4
jung (ü) young 3
der Junge, -n, -n boy 2
der Juni June 4
Jura law 11

K

das Kabelfernsehen cable TV 14
die Kabine, -n telephone booth 8
der Kaffee coffee 9
die Kaffeemaschine, -n coffeemaker 3
die Kaffeemühle, -n coffee mill 5 SV
kalt (ä) cold(ly) 4
die Kamera, -s camera 4
der Kamm, ¨e comb 8
kämmen (sich) to comb (one's) hair 6
kämpfen to battle, fight 14
kariert checked 3 SV
die Karotte, -n carrot 9
die Karte, -n card 2
die Kartoffel, -n potato 9
der Käse cheese 9
die Kassette, -n cassette tape 4
der Kassettenrecorder, - cassette recorder 14
kaufen to buy 3
der Käufer, -/die Käuferin, -nen buyer
das Kaufhaus, ¨er department store 7
kein not a; not any 2
der Keks, -e cookie 9 SV

der Keller, - basement, cellar 5 SV

der Kellner, -/die Kellnerin, -nen waiter 2

kennen, kannte, gekannt to know someone 5

kennen•lernen to become acquainted with someone 5, 6

die Kenntnis, -se knowledge 13

der Kfz (Kraftfahrzeug)-Mechaniker, -/die Kfz (Kraftfahrzeug)-Mechanikerin, -nen auto mechanic

das Kilogramm kilogram 9

das Kind, -er child 2

die Kindererziehung raising of children 15

der Kindergarten, ¨ kindergarten 15

die Kindertagesstätte, -n day-care center 15

das Kinderzimmer, - children's room 4

das Kinn, -e chin 6 SV

das Kino, -s movie theatre 7

ins Kino gehen to go to the movies 4

die Kirche, -n church 7

die Kirchturmuhr, -en church clock 4 SV

die Kirsche -n cherry 9

klar! of course! 15

die Klarinette, -n clarinet 12 SV

die Klasse, -n (grade level) class 11

das Klassenzimmer, - classroom 2

die Klausur, -en final exam 11

das Klavier, -e piano 12

das Kleid, -er dress 8

die Kleidung (sg.) clothing 8

klein small 2

der Klempner, -/die Klempnerin, -nen plumber 13

klingen, klang, geklungen to sound

das Knie, - knee 6

der Knöchel, - knuckle, ankle 6 SV

der Knochen, - bone 6 SV

knusprig crunchy 9 SV

der Koch, ¨e/ die Köchin, -nen cook 13

kochen to cook 2

der Koffer, - suitcase 10

der Kollege, -n, -n/die Kollegin, -nen colleague

komisch funny 9

der Kommandant, -en, -en/die Kommandantin, -nen commander

kommen, kam, ist gekommen to come 1

Ich komme /bin aus ... I come/am from ... 1

Wie komme ich zum/zur ...? How do I get to ...? 7

die Kommunikation, -en communication 14

das Kommunikationsmittel, - means of communication 14

kompliziert complicated

der Komponist, -en/die Komponistin, -nen composer 12

die Konfitüre, -n marmelade 9 SV

können (kann), konnte, gekonnt to be able to 3

der Kontakt, -e contact

der Kontinent, -e continent

das Konzert, -e concert 12

der Kopf, ¨e head 6

der Kopfhörer, - head phone 14

die Kopfschmerzen (pl.) headache 6

der Körper, - body 6

der Körperteil, -e body part 6

kosten to cost 5

das Kostüm, -e (women's) suit 8 SV

krank (ä) sick 1

krank sein to be sick 6

das Krankenhaus, ¨er hospital 6 SV

der Krankenwagen, - ambulance 6 SV

die Krankheit, -en sickness, illness 6

die Kreide chalk 2

die Kreuzung, -en crossing, intersection 7

der Kriminalfilm, -e detective movie 14

die Kritik, -en criticism 14 SV

kritisieren to criticize 14 SV

die Küche, -n kitchen 4, 5

der Kuchen, - cake 9

die Küchenuhr, -en kitchen clock 4 SV

die Kuckucksuhr, -en cuckoo clock 4 SV

der Kugelschreiber, - ballpoint pen 2

kühl cool 4

der Kühlschrank, ¨e refrigerator 3

die Kulturnotiz, -en culture note

der Kunde, -n/die Kundin, -nen customer 13

künftig in the future 15 P

die Kunst ¨e, art 12

die Kunstgeschichte art history 11

der Künstler, -/die Künstlerin, -nen artist 12

das Kunstmuseum, -museen art museum 12

die Kur, -en cure 6 SV

der Kurort, - place for a cure 6 SV

der Kurs, -e rate of exchange; course 10, 11

kurz (ü) short 2

der Kurzurlaub short vacation

die Kusine, -n [female] cousin 2

küssen to kiss 15

L

das Labor, -s or -e, laboratory 11

das Laboratorium, -ien lab room 7 SV

der Laden, " store 7
das Lagerfeuer, - camp fire 10 SV
das Land, "er country, land 2
die Landkarte, -n map 2
ländlich rustic
landschaftlich scenically
landwirtschaftlich agricultural
lang (ä) long 6
langsam slow(ly) 7
  Langsamer, bitte! More slowly, please. 1
langweilig boring 11
das Langzeitgedächtnis, -se longterm memory
der Lärm noise 14
lassen (läßt), ließ, gelassen to let, leave 8
  laß uns... let us... 7
das Latein Latin 11
das Laub (sg.) leaves 4
laufen (läuft), lief, ist gelaufen to run 3
laut loud(ly), noisy (noisily) 5
  Lauter, bitte! Louder, please. 1
läuten to ring 8 SV
der Lautsprecher, - loudspeaker 14
leben to live 6
der Lebenslauf, "e résumé
die Lebensmittel (pl.) groceries 9
das Lebensmittelgeschäft, -e grocery store 7
lecker tasty 9
ledig single 2
leeren to empty 5 SV
legen to lay 7
die Lehre, -n apprenticeship 13
der Lehrer, -/die Lehrerin, -nen teacher 2
leicht easy 10
die Leichtathletik track and field 12 SV
leiden, litt, gelitten to suffer 6
Leider geht es nicht. Unfortunately not. 8

leihen, lieh, geliehen to lend 4
leise quiet(ly) 12
leisten (etwas) (sich) to afford 6
die Leistungsbereitschaft willingness to perfom
leiten to lead 13
der Leiter, -/die Leiterin, -nen executive, manager 13
das Leitungswasser tap water 9 SV
lernen to learn; to study (as for an exam) 3
der Lernstoff, -e learning material
das Lernziel, -e learning goals
lesen (liest), las, gelesen to read 3
der Lesesaal, -säle lecture hall
letzt- last 4
die Leute (pl.) people 2
die Liebe love 15
lieben to love 15
lieber rather 12
die Lieblingsjahreszeit, -en favorite season 4
Lieblings - favorite _____ 12
das Liechtenstein Liechtenstein 10
liefern to deliver 5 SV
der Lieferpreis, -e delivery price
liegen, lag, gelegen to lie 4
lila purple, lilac 3 SV
links left 7
die Lippe, -n lip 6 SV
der Lippenstift, -e lipstick 8 SV
der Liter, - liter, quart 9
loben to praise
lockig curly 6
der Lohn, "e pay 13
lohnen (sich) to be worth it 12
lösen to solve 15
das Lottoticket, -s lottery ticket
lukrativ lucrative
die Lunge, -n lung
Lust haben, (hat), hatte, gehabt to want to do something
lustig funny 14
das Luxemburg Luxemburg 10

M

machen to do, to make 1
das Mädchen, - girl 2
der Magen, " stomach 6
die Magenschmerzen (pl.) stomach ache 6
Mahlzeit! Enjoy your meal! 9
der Mai May 4
der Mais corn
das Make-up make-up 8 SV
mal flavoring particle
das Mal time
  zum ersten Mal for the first time 10
der Maler, -/die Malerin, -nen painter 12
die Malerei painting
man one 1
manchmal sometimes 2
der Mann, "er man; husband 2
das Mannequin, -s mannequin
die Mannschaft, -en team 12
der Mantel, " coat 8
die Margarine margarine 9
die Mark German mark 5 SV
der Markt, "e market place; open-air market 7 SV, 9
die Marmelade, -n jam 9 SV
der März March 4
die Mathematik (Mathe) mathematics 11
der Mechaniker,-/die Mechanikerin, -nen mechanic 13
die Medien (pl.) media 14
die Meditation meditation 6 SV
die Medizin medicine 6
mehr more 6, 7
mehrere several 12
mein my 1
meinen to think, to be of the opinion 5
die Meinung, -en opinion
  die Meinung ändern to change one's mind 11
  meiner Meinung nach in my

opinion

die Meinungsumfrage, -n opinion poll

mehr more 6

melden (sich) to answer 8 SV

die Mensa student cafeteria 7 SV; 11

der Mensch, -en, -en human 12

die Menschen (pl.) people 4

merken (sich) to remember 11

merken to notice 11

merkwürdig unusual, strange 11

die Metzgerei, -en meat market 7

mieten to rent 5

der Mikrowellenherd, -e microwave oven 5 SV

die Milch milk 9

das Mineralwasser mineral water 9

minus minus; less

die Minute, -n minute 11

alle [dreißig] Minuten every [thirty] minutes 11

miserabel miserable 1 SV

der Mißbrauch, ⸚ e abuse

das Mißverständnis, -se misunderstanding

mit (+dat.) with, by means of 4

mit•bringen, brachte mit, mitgebracht to bring (along) 10

mit•kommen, kam mit, ist mitgekommen to come along 5

mittag noon 10

das Mittagessen, - lunch 9

der Mittelfinger, - middle finger 6 SV

mittel- middle 13

der Mittwoch Wednesday 4

die Möbel (pl.) furniture 2, 3

möbliert furnished 5

möchte(n) would like (to) 3

modern modern 3 SV

mögen (mag), mochte, gemocht to like 5

möglich possible 12

die Möglichkeit, -en possibility

der Monat, -e month 4

monatlich monthly 5

der Montag Monday 4

die Moral moral 15 SV

morgen tomorrow 1

der Morgen, - morning 1

am Morgen in the morning 1

Guten Morgen! Good Morning! 1

müde tired 1

der Müll trash 5 SV

das Mülleimerleeren taking out the garbage 15 SV

der Mund, ⸚er mouth 6

die Mundharmonika, -s harmonica 12 SV

die Münze, -n coin 12

das Museum, Museen museum 4, 7

die Musik music 4

Musik hören to listen to music 4

die Musikgeschichte music history 11

der Musikverein, -e music club

der Muskel, -n muscle 6

der Muskelkater sore muscles 6 SV

das Müsli muesli 9 SV

müssen (muß), mußte, gemußt must, to have to 3, 5

die Mutter, ⸚ mother 2

die Mutti, -s nickname for mother

die Mütze, -n cap 8

N

nach (+dat.) to, after, past 4

der Nachbar, -n, -n/die Nachbarin, -nen neighbor

die Nachbarschaft, -en neighborhood 5

nachdem after 8

nach•kommen, kam nach, ist nachgekommen to adhere (to one's wishes)

der Nachmittag, -e afternoon 10

die Nachricht, -en message;

information 14

die Nachrichten (pl.) news 14

nächst- next 4

die Nacht night 10

Gute Nacht! Good night! 1

pro Nacht per night 10

der Nachtisch dessert 9

nah (ä) close, near 9

in der Nähe nearby, in the vicinity 7

nähen to sew

der Nahverkehr local traffic 7 SV

der Name, -n name

die Nase, -n nose 6

natürlich of course 9

neben beside, next to 7

nebenan next door 3

das Nebenfach, ⸚er minor 11

neblig foggy 4 SV

der Neffe, -en, -en nephew 12

nehmen (nimmt), nahm, genommen to take 3

Nehmen Sie Platz! Please sit down! 1

nein no 1

nervös nervous 3 SV

nett nice 3

neu new 3

neugierig curious 3

nicht not 1

nicht so gut not so good 1

nicht wahr? isn't that so? 1

nicht nur ... sondern auch not only ... but also 12

nie never 6

die Niederlande Netherlands 10

niemand no one 4

niesen to sneeze 6 SV

noch nicht not yet 4

Noch einmal, bitte! Once more, please. 1

der Nominativ, -e nominative

das Norddeutschland Northern Germany

der Norden north

normalerweise normally, usually

das Norwegen Norway 10

die Note, -n grade 11

notieren to note, write down 13
der November November 4
die Nudel, -n noodle 9 SV
die Nummer, -n number
nun well, well now, well then, (flavoring particle) 8
nur only 3

O

ob if, when, whether 8
obdachlos homeless 5 SV
oben above, upper 6
der Ober, -/die Oberin, -nen waiter 9
die Oberschule, -n high school
die Oboe, -n oboe 12 SV
das Obst (sg.) fruit 4
der Obstsaft, ¨e fruit juice 6
obwohl although, even though 8
oder or 3, 4
der Ofen, ¨ oven 5
öffentlich public 13, 15
offiziell official(ly)
öffnen to open 5
oft (ö) often 3
ohne (+acc.) without 3
ohne weiteres easily, without much ado 15
ohne ... zu without 10
das Ohr, -en ear 6
das Ohrläppchen, - ear lobe 6 SV
der Oktober October 4
die Oma, -s nickname for grandmother
der Onkel, -s uncle 2
der Opa, -s nickname for grandfather
die Oper, -n oper 7 SV; 12
optimistisch optimistic 3 SV
orange orange 3
die Orange, -n orange 9
ordentlich tidy (tidily), neat(ly) 13
die Ordnung order 6
   In Ordnung ok, all right 10
   in Ordnung sein to be all right 6

der Ordnungssinn sense of order
die Orientierung, -en orientation 15
der Ort, -e location, place 7
das Ortsgespräch, -e local call 8 SV
das Österreich Austria 2
oval oval 6

P

das Päckchen, - small package 10 SV
packen to pack 10
die Pädagogik education, pedagogy 11
das Paket, -e package 10
das Papier, -e paper 2
der Papierkorb, ¨e wastebasket 3
die Paprikaschote, -n pepper 9 SV
das Parkhaus, ¨er car park 7 SV
der Partner, -/die Partnerin, -nen partner 2
der Paß, ¨sse passport 10
passieren, ist passiert to happen 5
patentiert patented
pauken to cram 11 SV
der Patient, -en, -en/die Patientin, -nen patient 6 SV
das Pech bad luck
die Pension, -en bed-and-breakfast inn or guesthouse 10
die Pension, -en pension 13
per by means of 10
   per Luftpost by airmail 10
der Personalchef, -s/die Personalchefin, -nen personnel manager 13 SV
das Personalpronomen, - personal pronoun
persönlich personal(ly) 13
die Persönlichkeit, -en personality 13
pessimistisch pessimistic 3 SV

der Pfadfinder, -/die Pfadfinderin, -nen scout 10 SV
die Pfanne, -n frying pan
der Pfeffer pepper 9
der Pfefferminztee, -s peppermint tea 9 SV
der Pfennig, -e penny 8
der Pfirsich, -e peach 9 SV
die Pflanze, -n plant
die Pflaume, -n plum 9 SV
pflegen to nurse, tend, take care of 6 SV
die Pflicht, -en responsibility 13
das Pflichtbewußtsein sense of duty 13
das Pfund, -e pound 9
die Philosophie philosophy 11
die Physik physics 11
die Pizza, -s pizza
planen to plan 12
die Planung planning
der Platz, ¨e place, seat, square 1 SV, 3
plus plus 1
das Polen Poland 10
die Politik politics 14
die Politologie political science 11
die Polizei (sg.) police 7 SV
die Pommes frites (pl.) French fried potatoes 9
die Popmusik pop music 12 SV
das Portugal Portugal 2, 10
die Post post office 7
   per Luftpost by air mail 10
das Poster, - poster 3
die Postkarte, -n postcard 10
praktisch practical(ly) 3 SV
der Präsident, -en, -en/die Präsidentin, -nen president 1
die Praxis, -xen practice 13 SV
der Preis, -e price 9
   im Preis enthalten included in the price 10
preiswert worth the money, of good value 5
die Presse, -n press 14
prima great 1 SV

pro per 10
   pro Nacht per night 10
probieren to try out 5
das Problem, -e problem 5
der Professor, -en/die
   Professorin, -nen professor 2
das Programm, -e program,
   channel 14
Pros(i)t! Cheers! 9
der Prokurist, -en, -en/die
   Prokuristin, -nen attorney
der Prozentsatz, ˫e percentage
die Prüfung, -en exam, test 11
   bei einer Prüfung durchfallen
   to fail a test 11
   eine Prüfung bestehen to
   pass a test 11
   eine Prüfung
   machen/schreiben to take a
   test 11
die Psychologie psychology 11
der Pudding pudding 9 SV
der Pullover, - (der Pulli-s)
   pullover 8
pünktlich punctual 13
die Pünktlichkeit punctuality
purpur purple 3
putzen (sich) to brush 6
putzen to clean, to polish 5

Q

die Quizshow game show 14

R

das R-Gespräch, -e collect call 8
das Radieschen, - radish 9 SV
das Radio, -s radio 3
   im Radio on the radio 14
die Radtour, -en bicycle ride 12 SV
der Rasierapparat, -e razor 8
   SV
rasieren (sich) to shave 6
die Rasse, -n race 15
das Rathaus, ˫er town hall 7 SV
die Rathausuhr, -en clock on the
   town hall 4 SV
rauchen to smoke 6

die Realschule, -n middle school
das Recht, -e right 13
   recht haben to be right 5
rechtlich legal 15
rechts right 7
der Rechtsanwalt, ˫e/die
   Rechtsanwältin, -nen
   lawyer 2
das Referat, -e paper, oral or
   written report 4
   ein Referat halten to give a
   report 11
   ein Referat schreiben to write
   a report 11
regelmäßig regular(ly) 6
der Regen rain 4
der Regenmantel, ˫ rain coat 8 SV
regnen to rain 4
reichen to suffice 11
reif ripe 9
der Reis rice 9 SV
das Reisebüro, -s travel agency 10
der Reiseführer, - travel guide 12
reisen, ist gereist to travel 10
   auf Reisen on a trip 10
der Reisescheck, -s traveler's
   check 10
das Reiten horse riding 12 SV
reiten, ritt, ist geritten to ride
   (an animal) 4
die Reklame, -n advertisement 14
die Religion, -en religion 15
die Rente, -n pension 2
   auf Rente sein to be retired 2
reservieren to reserve 10
das Restaurant, -s restaurant 7
der Richter, -/die Richterin, -nen
   judge 13 SV
richtig correct, right 1
   Das ist richtig. That's right. 1
das Rindfleisch beef 9
der Ring, -e ring 4 SV
der Ringfinger, - ring finger 6 SV
der Rock, ˫e skirt 8
die Rockgruppe, -n rock group
roh raw 9
der Rollschuh, -e roller skate 4
der Roman, -e novel 12

romanisch romanesque
die Romanistik Romance languages and literatures 11 SV
die Romantik romanticism
romantisch romantic 3 SV
rosa pink 3
der Rosenkohl Brussel sprouts 9 SV
rot (ö) red 3
der Rotkohl red cabbage 9 SV
der Rücken, - back 6
die Rückfahrt, -en return trip
der Rucksack, ˫e back pack 10
   SV
die Ruhe rest 7
   Ruhe, bitte! Quiet, please. 1
ruhig quiet(ly) 5
rund round 6
der Rundfunk radio 14 SV
die Rundfunkbeteiligung, -en
   radio participation
das Rußland Russia 1

S

die S-Bahn, -en local [elevated]
   train 7
die Sache, -n thing, object 1, 3
die Sackgasse, -n cul-de-sac 7 SV
der Saft, ˫e juice 9
saftig juicy 9
sagen to say 5
   Wie sagt man ... auf deutsch?
   How does one say ... in
   German? 1
der Salat, -e salad, lettuce 9
das Salz salt 9
salzig salty 9
sammeln to collect 12
der Samstag Saturday 4
die Sandale, -n sandal 8 SV
der Satellit, -en satellite 14
sauber clean 15
sauer sour 9
das Sauerkraut sourkraut 9 SV
die Sauna, -s sauna 12
das Saxophon saxophone 12 SV
schade too bad 7
schädigen to damage 14

der **Schal, -s** scarf 4 SV
die **Schallplatte, -n** record 14
scharf spicy 9
der **Schauspieler, -/die Schauspielerin, -nen** actor 12
scheinen, schien, geschienen to shine 4
schenken to give as a present 4
schicken to send 8
das **Schiff, -e** ship 4
das **Schild, -er** sign 7
der **Schinken** ham 9 SV
schlafen (schläft), schlief, geschlafen to sleep 4
  lange schlafen to sleep late 12
der **Schlafsack, ̈-e** sleeping bag 10
die **Schlaftablette, -n** sleeping pill 6
das **Schlafzimmer, -** bedroom 4, 5
schlagen, (schlägt), schlug, geschlagen to hit 12
der **Schlager, -** hit, pop song 12 SV
die **Schlagzeile, -n** headline 14 SV
schlecht bad 1
schlimm terrible 7
der **Schlittschuh, -e** ice skate 4
Schlittschuh laufen (läuft), lief, ist gelaufen to ice skate 4
schmecken to taste 4
der **Schmerz, -en** pain 6
schminken (sich) to put on make up 6
der **Schmuck (sg.)** jewelry 4 SV
schmutzig dirty 15
der **Schnee** snow 4
schneeweiß snow white 3 SV
schneiden, schnitt, geschnitten to cut 9 SV
schneien to snow 4
schnell quickly, fast 1
  Schnell, bitte! Quickly, please. 1

das **Schnitzel, -** veal or pork cutlet 9
der **Schnupfen** runny nose 6 SV
die **Schokolade** chocolate 4 SV
schon already, (flavoring word) 3, 5
schön beautiful, nice 2, 3
der **Schornsteinfeger, -/die Schornsteinfegerin, -nen** chimney sweep 13 SV
das **Schottland** Scotland 10
der **Schrank, ̈e** wardrobe, closet 3
schrecklich awful(ly), terrible 1 SV, 5
schreiben, schrieb, geschrieben to write 1
  Wie schreibt man...? How do you spell ...? 1
  Schreiben Sie, bitte! Please write. 1
schreiben über (+acc.), schrieb, geschrieben to write about 11
die **Schreibmaschine, -n** typewriter 3
der **Schreibtisch, -e** desk 2
der **Schriftsteller, -/die Schriftstellerin, -nen** writer 12
der **Schritt, -e** step
schrubben to scrub, scour
der **Schuh, -e** shoe 8
die **Schule, -n** school 4
der **Schüler, -/die Schülerin, -nen** pupil 11
das **Schulsystem, -e** school system 11
die **Schulter, -n** shoulder 6
schützen to protect 14
der **Schwager, ̈** brother-in-law 2
die **Schwägerin, -nen** sister-in-law 2
schwanger pregnant 15
schwarz (ä) black 3
das **Schweden** Sweden 10
das **Schweinefleisch** pork 9
die **Schweiz** Switzerland 2

Schweizer Käse Swiss cheese 9
schwer heavy; hard, difficult 10
schwerhörig hard of hearing 14
die **Schwerhörigkeit (sg.)** impaired hearing 14
die **Schwester, -n** sister 2
schwierig difficult, complicated 15
das **Schwimmbad, ̈-er** swimming pool
schwimmen, schwamm, ist geschwommen to swim 2
schwitzen to sweat 6 SV
segeln to sail 12
sehen (sieht), sah, gesehen to see 3
sehr very 1
  Sehr gut! Very good! 1
die **Seife, -n** soap 8
die **Seifenoper, -n** soap opera 14
sein (ist), war, ist gewesen to be 1
seit (+dat.) since 4
die **Seite, -n** page
  die **Gelben Seiten** Yellow Pages 8
der **Sekretär, -e/Sekretärin, -nen** secretary 1
die **Sekunde, -n** second 11
selbständig self-reliant(ly), independentl(ly) 13
der **Selbständige, -n/die Selbständige, -en** self-employed person 13
selbstbewußt self-confident, self-assertive 15
die **Selbstsicherheit** self confidence
der **Sellerie** celerie 9 SV
selten rarely 6
das **Semester, -** semester 11
die **Semesterarbeit, -en** term paper, semester paper 11
der **Sender, -** (Radio/TV) station 14
die **Sendung, -en** program 14
der **Senf** mustard 9
der **Senior, -en** mature adult

der September September 4
die Serie, -n series 14
die Serviette, n napkin
der Sessel, - easy chair 3
setzen (sich) to sit down 7
sexuell sexual 15
das Shampoo, -s shampoo 8
die Shorts (pl.) shorts 8 SV
sicher certain(ly), sure(ly) 8
die Sicherheit, -en assurance
die Sicherung security
Sie you, sg. and pl. formal 1
sie she, they 1
die Siedlung, -en subdivision
die Siegessäule, -n triumphal
column
singen, sang, gesungen to sing 2
sitzen, saß, gesessen to sit 7
das Skat name of a card game
skeptisch skeptical 3 SV
der Ski, -er ski 4
Ski laufen (läuft Ski), lief, ist
gelaufen to ski 4
so...wie as..as 4
die Socke, -n sock 8
das Sofa, -s sofa 5
der Sohn, ⁻e son 2
der Soldat, -en/die Soldatin, -
nen soldier 2
sollen should, to be supposed to 4
der Sommer Summer 4
das Sonderangebot,-e special
offer
die Sonderausstellung, -en special exhibit
die Sondermarke, -n commemorative stamp
sondern but, but rather 4
der Sonnabend Saturday 4 SV
die Sonne, -n sun 4
sonnig sunny 4
der Sonntag Sunday 4
sonst otherwise 9
Sonst noch etwas? Anything
else? 8
sonstig- other 15
sorgen (für + acc.) to care (for) 14
sich (dat.) (keine) Sorgen

machen (not) to be worried 13
sozial social(ly) 13
die Soziologie sociology 11
die Spaghetti (pl.) spaghetti 9
SV
das Spanien Spain 2
spannend exciting, thrilling 14
sparen to save 4
der Spargel asparagus 9 SV
die Sparkasse, -n savings institution 10
Spaß haben to have fun 4
der Spaß, ⁻e fun 4
Spaß haben to have fun 4
spät late 5
Wie spät ist es? What time is
it? 4
der Spaziergang, ⁻e stroll, walk
8
einen Spaziergang machen to
stroll 8
der Spazierstock, ⁻e walking
stick 10 SV
der Speck bacon 9
die Speisekarte, -n menu 9
die Spezialität, -en specialty 13
der Spiegel, - mirror 3
das Spiel, -e game 1
spielen to play 2
Basketball spielen to play
basketball 2
Gitarre spielen to play guitar
2
Tennis spielen to play tennis
2
der Spielfilm, -e (feature) film
14
der Spinat spinach 9 SV
der Spitzname, -n nickname 2
Sport treiben, trieb, getrieben to
engage in sports 6
die Sportart, -en (kind of)
sports 6
die Sporthalle, -n gym 7 SV
der Sportler, - [male] athlete 12
SV
die Sportlerin, -nen [female]
athlete 12 SV

sportlich athletic 12
die Sportreportage, -n sports
show 14
der Sportschuh, -e sport shoe 8
SV
die Sprache, -n language 15
sprechen (spricht), sprach,
gesprochen to speak 3
sprechen über to talk about 11
spülen to rinse 6
staatlich governmental 14
stabil stable, strong 5 SV
die Stadt, ⁻e city 1, 2
der Stadtbummel, - stroll
through town 12
der Stadtplan, ⁻e city map 7
der Stammbaum, ⁻e family tree
der Standpunkt, -e point of view
14 SV
die Standuhr, -en standing clock
4 SV
stark (ä) strong 9
statt•finden, fand statt, stattgefunden to take place 14
das Staubsaugen vacuuming 15
SV
stehen, stand, gestanden to stand
7
steigen , stieg, ist gestiegen to
climb
die Stelle, -n place 7
an Ihrer Stelle in your place
14
stellen to place, to set 7
die Stellung, -en position 13
sterben (stirbt), starb, ist gestorben to die 15
das Stereo, -s stereo 3
der Stiefbruder, ⁻ stepbrother 2
die Stiefmutter, ⁻ stepmother 2
die Stiefschwester, -n stepsister
2
der Stiefvater, ⁻ stepfather 2
das Stipendium, -ien stipend,
scholarship
die Stirn, -en forehead 6 SV
das Stockwerk, -e floor 5 SV
im ersten, zweiten, dritten, ...

Stock on the second, third, fourth ... floor 5

stolz proud

die Störung, -en imposition, interference 8 SV

der Strand, ¨ **e** beach

die Straße, -n street 7

die Straßenbahn, -en streetcar 4

die Straßenkarte, -n street map 7 SV

strecken (sich) to stretch 6 SV

der Streit fight 5 SV

streiten, stritt, gestritten to fight, argue 15

streng strong, severe

der Streß stress 6

   unter Streß leiden to suffer from stress 5

die Strickjacke, -n knit sweater 8 SV

die Strumpfhose, -n panty hose 8 SV

der Stubenhocker home-body, couch-potato

das Stück, -e piece 9

der Student, -en, -en/die Studentin, -nen student 2

das Studentenwohnheim, -e student dorm 5

die Studienberatung, -en counseling office 7 SV

die Studiengebühr, -en, tuition

der Studienplan, ¨ **e** class schedule

das Studentenwerk, -e student center, student union 7 SV

studieren to study 2

der Stuhl, ¨ **e** chair 2

die Stunde, -n hour 4

der Stundenplan, ¨ **e** class schedule 4

das Substantiv, -e noun

suchen to search, to look for 3

das Südamerika South America

das Süddeutschland Southern Germany

der Süden south

der Supermarkt, ¨ **e** supermarket 9

die Suppe, -n soup 9

süß sweet 9

das Sweatshirt, -s sweat shirt 8

sympathisch likeable 3 SV

das Symptom, -e symptom 6 SV

T

das T-shirt, -s T-shirt 8

die Tafel, -n chalkboard 2

der Tag, -e day 1

   am Tag during the day 1

   Guten Tag! Hello! Hi! 1

   Tag! (informal) Hi! 1

   Welcher Tag ist heute? What day is today? 4

tagaus, tagein day after day 4

die Tagesschau, -en television news 14 SV

täglich daily 6

die Taille, -n waist 6 SV

das Talent, -e talent 13 SV

tanken to buy gasoline 9

die Tankstelle, -n gas station 9

die Tante, -n aunt 2

tanzen to dance 2

das Taschengeld, -er pocket money

die Taschenuhr, -en pocket watch 4 SV

tätig active, employed 15

tatsächlich truly, really, surely 1

das Taxi, -s taxi 7

der Tee, -s tea 9

der Teil, -e part 4, 15

teilen to share 5

die Teilzeitarbeit part-time work 15

das Telefon, -e telephone 2, 3

das Telefonbuch, ¨ **er** telephone book 8

das Telefongespräch, -e telephone conversation 8

telefonieren to call 3

die Telefonnummer, -n telephone number 1

   Wie ist deine (Ihre)

Telefonnummer? What is your telephone number? 1

das Telefonsystem, -e telephone system 8 SV

die Telefonzelle, -n telephone booth 8

das Telegramm, -e telegram 8 SV

die Temperatur, -en temperature 4 SV

das Tennis tennis 2

der Tennisschläger, - tennis racket 4

der Tennisspieler, -/die Tennisspielerin, -nen tennis player 1

der Teppich, -e carpet 2, 5

der Termin, -e date, time 8

die Terrasse, -n terrace 5 SV

teuer expensive 3

das Theater, - theater 12

das Theaterstück, -e play 12

das Thema, -en topic 8

der Themenwortschatz, ¨ **e** theme words 1

die Theologie theology 11

theoretisch theoretical(ly)

das Ticket, -s ticket 10

das Tier, -e animal 12

der Tip, -s tip

der Tisch, -e table 2

das Tischtennis ping-pong 12

die Tochter, ¨ daughter 2

die Toilette, -n toilet 3

tolerant tolerant 3 SV

toll great 6

der Topf, ¨ **e** cooking pot

die Topfblume, -n potted plant

das Tor schießen to kick or make a goal (soccer)

tot dead 2

der Tourist, -en, -en/die Touristin, -nen tourist

traditionell traditional 15

tragen (trägt), trug, getragen to wear, carry 8

trainieren to train

der Trainingsanzug, ¨ **e** 12 SV

trampen to hike 10 SV
transportabel transportable 14
das Transportmittel, - means of transportation
träumen to dream 15
traurig sad 3
treffen (sich) (trifft), traf, getroffen to meet 7
der Trend, -s trend
die Treppe, -n stair 5 SV
trimmen (sich) to get into shape 12 SV
trinken, trank, getrunken to drink 3
das Trinkgeld, -er tip 9
der Trockner, - dryer 5 SV
die Trommel, -n 12
die Trompete, -n trumpet 12 SV
trotz (+gen.) in spite of, despite 11
trotzdem nevertheless
tschüs so long, bye 1
tun, tat, getan to do 3
die Tür, -en door 3
die Türkei Turkey 10
turnen to do gymnastics 4 SV
der Turnschuh, -e gym shoe 4 SV

U

die U-Bahn, -en underground train 7
über above, over 7
überein•stimmen to agree 5
überfordern to overdo
überlassen (läßt), überließ, überlassen to leave to, entrust to 15
überlegen (sich) to think about; ponder 9
übermorgen day after tomorrow 6
übernachten to spend the night 10
die Überraschung, -en surprise 8
die Überstunde, -n overtime 13 SV
die Uhr, -en clock, watch 2, 4
   Es ist halb sieben (Uhr). It is 6:30 (o'clock). 4

um (zwei) Uhr at (two) o'clock 4
   Wieviel Uhr ist es? What time is it? 4
um (+acc.) around, at 3
um ... zu in order to 10
umarmen to embrace 15
um•schalten to switch over 14 SV
um•steigen, stieg um, ist umgestiegen to transfer 7
die Umwelt (sg.) environment 14
die Umwelttechnik ecological technology
um•ziehen (sich), zog um, umgezogen to change (one's clothing),
   um•ziehen, zog um, ist umgezogen to move 6
unbequem uncomfortable, uncomfortably 5
und and 1, 4
unentschieden a tie (in sports) 12 SV
der Unfallwagen, - ambulance 6 SV
die Universität, -en university 4
unkompliziert uncomplicated 3 SV
unruhig restless 5
unten lower, below 6
unter beneath, under 7
das Unterbewußtsein subconscious
unterbrechen (unterbricht), unterbrach, unterbrochen to interrupt 15
unterhalten (unterhält), (sich) unterhielt, unterhalten to discuss 12
unterhalten (unterhält), (sich) unterhielt, unterhalten to entertain oneself 14
unternehmen (unternimmt), unternahm, unternommen to do something 7 SV
der Unterricht lesson 4
unterrichten to teach 11
der Unterschied, -e difference 15

unterstreichen, unterstrich, unterstrichen underline
untersuchen to research
die Unterwäsche (sg.) underwear 8
unterwegs on the go, on the road 13
der Urlaub (sg.) vacation 4
die Ursache, -n reason 8

V

der Vater, ⁞ father 2
der Vati, -s nickname for father 2
verabreden (sich) to set or make a date 7 SV
die Verabschiedung, -en saying farewell
die Verantwortlichkeit, -en responsibility 13 SV
das Verb, -en verb
verbessern (sich) to improve 15
verbieten, verbot, verboten to prohibit 14
verbinden, verband, verbunden to connect 8 SV
   Sie sind falsch verbunden. You have the wrong number. 8
das Verbot, -e prohibition 14
der Verbraucher, - consumer
verbringen, verbrachte, verbracht to spend (time) 10
verdienen to earn 11
der Verein, -e club 12
die Verfassung, -en constitution 15
vergessen (vergißt), vergaß, vergessen to forget 8
verheiraten (sich) to get married 5
   verheiratet married 2
verkaufen to sell 2
der Verkäufer, -/die Verkäuferin, -nen salesperson 2
der Verkehr traffic 7
das Verkehrsmittel, - means of transport
verlassen (verläßt), verließ, verlassen to leave 5
verletzen (sich) to get hurt 6 SV

verliebt in love 2

verlieren, verlor, verloren to lose 3

der Verlierer, -/die Verliererin, -nen loser 12 SV]

verlobt engaged 2

vermieten to rent (accomodations to someone) 5

verrückt crazy 3 SV

versalzen to salt too much 9 SV

verschieben, verschob, verschoben to move up (in time) 8

verschieden different, various 12

verschließen (sich), verschloß, verschlossen to exclude (to be excluded from)

versorgen to take care 11

versprechen (verspricht), versprach, versprochen to promise 8

verstauchen (sich etwas) to sprain something 6 SV

verstehen, verstand, verstanden to understand 1

   Verstehen Sie? (formal) Do you understand that? 1

   Verstehst du? (informal) Do you understand that? 1

   Das verstehe ich nicht. I don't understand that. 1

versuchen to try 8

verteidigen (sich) to defend 15 SV

der Vertreter, -/die Vertreterin, -nen sales person

die Verwaltung, -en administration

verwehen to blow away

der Vetter, -n [male] cousin 2

das Video, -s video 14

der Videorecorder, - VCR 14

viel, viele much, many 3, 4

vielleicht perhaps 4

das Viertel quarter 4

   Es ist Viertel vor/nach zehn It is a quarter of/past ten 4

die Vitaminkapsel, -n vitamine capsule 6 SV

die Vitamintablette, -n vitamin tablet 6

die Volkswirtschaft political exonomics 11 SV

vollständig complete

die Vollzeitarbeit full-time work 15

von of, from; by 4

   von Beruf by occupation, by profession, by trade 2

vor in front of 7

   vor [zehn] Jahren [ten] years ago 10

voraus ahead 9

vorbei•kommen, kam vorbei, ist vorbeigekommen to come by 5

vor•bereiten (sich) auf (+acc.) to prepare for 11

vorgeschrieben prescribed

vorgestern the day before yesterday 10

vor•haben, (hat), hatte vor, vorgehabt to have something planned 8

die Vorlesung, -en lecture 4

der Vorlesungssaal, -säle lecture hall 7

der Vormittag late morning 10

vorne up front, in front 7

der Vorschlag, ¨-e suggestion, recommendation

vor•schlagen, (schlägt), schlug vor, vorgeschlagen to suggest 8, 10

vorsichtig careful 7

vorstellen (sich) (etwas) to imagine (something)

die Vorstellung, -en image

das Vorstellungsgespräch, - job interview 13

das Vorurteil, -e prejudice 15

   Vorurteile haben to be prejudiced 15

die Vorwahl, -en area code 8

W

das WC, -s toilet 5 SV

der Wagen, - car, vehicle 6

die Wahl, -en choice, election

wählen to choose; dial 8

während (+gen.) during 11

wahrscheinlich probably 7

der Wald, ¨er forest 8

der Walkman, -s walkman 3

die Wand, ¨e wall 2

wandern, ist gewandert to hike 2

die Wanduhr, -en wall clock 4 SV

die Wange, -n cheek 6 SV

wann when 2

warm (ä) warm 2

warnen to warn 14

warten auf (+acc.) to wait for 11

   Warte mal! (informal) Wait! 1

warten to wait 1

warum why 3

was what 1

   Was für ...? What kind of ...? (pl.) 8

   Was für ein ...? What kind of ...? (sg.) 8

   Was gibt's denn? What's up? 8

   Was ist los? What's going on? What's wrong? 3

das Waschbecken, - wash basin 3

waschen (wäscht) (sich), wusch, gewaschen to wash (one's hands) 6

das Wäschewaschen doing the laundry 15 SV

die Waschmaschine, -n washing machine 5 SV

das Wasser water 5 SV

wechseln (sich) to change

wechseln exchange 10

die Wechselstube, -n currency exchange office 10

der Wecker, - alarm clock 4 SV

weder ... noch neither .. nor 12

weg away 7

wegen (+gen.) because of 11

weh tun, tat, getan to hurt, to ache 6

Was tut Ihnen/dir weh? What hurts? 6

weil because 8

der Wein, -e wine

die Weintraube, -n grape 9 SV

weiß white 3

das Weißkraut cabbage 9 SV

weit far 3

weiter further

weiter•fahren, (fährt), fuhr weiter, ist weitergefahren to keep driving, to drive further 7 SV

weiter•helfen, (hilft), half weiter, weitergeholfen to help along

welch- which 4

die Welt, -en world 13

weltoffen open to the world

wenig, wenige little, few 6

wenige (a) few 12

wenn when, whenever 8

wer who 1

Wer ist das? Who is that? 1

die Werbung, -en advertisement (on TV and radio) 13 SV; 14

werden (wird), wurde, ist geworden to become 2

werktags during workdays

wessen whose

das Wetter weather 2, 4

wichtig important 6

wie as 4

wie how; what 1

Wie bitte? What, please? What did you say? 1

Wie geht es dir?/Wie geht's? How are you? 1

Wie geht es Ihnen? How are you? 1

wieder again 2

wieder•holen to repeat 5

Wiederholen Sie, bitte! Please repeat. 1

wieder•sehen (sieht), sah wieder, wiedergesehen to see again

wieviel, wie viele how much, how many 1

Den wievielten haben wir heute? What is today's date? 7

Wieviel ist...? How much is...? 1

die Wimper, -n eyelash 6 SV

der Wind, -e wind 12

die Windel, -n diaper

windig windy 4

das Windsurfen windsurfing 12 SV

der Winter Winter 4

wir we 1

wirklich honestly, really, truly 2

die Wirklichkeit reality 15

die Wirtschaft economy

die Wirtschaftswissenschaft economics 11

wissen (weiß), wußte, gewußt to know 3

wo where 1

die Woche, -n week 4

am Wochenende on the weekend 4

während der Woche during the week 11

zweimal pro Woche twice a week 6

das Wochenendhaus, -̈er weekend house 5 SV

der Wochentag, -e weekday 4

woher where from 1

Woher kommst du (kommen Sie?) Where do you come from? 1

wohin where to 7

wohl good, well 6

Zum Wohl! To your health! 9

wohl•fühlen (sich) to feel well 6

wohnen to live, to reside 1

die Wohngemeinschaft, -en (WG) group of people sharing an apartment 5

die Wohnung, -en apartment 3

die Wohnungsnot lack of a living quarter 5 SV

die Wohnungssuche, -n search for an apartment 5 SV

auf Wohnungssuche gehen to look for an apartment 5 SV

das Wohnzimmer, - living room 5

der Wohnzimmertisch, -e living room table 5 SV

wolkig cloudy 4

wollen (will), wollte, gewollt to want to, want 3, 5

das Wort, -̈er word

worum what about 4

der Wunsch, -̈e desire, wish 12

wünschen to wish, desire 12

(ich) würde I would 7

die Wurst, -̈e sausage 9

das Würstchen, - wiener, sausage 9

Z

die Zahl, -en number 1

zahlen to pay 7

zählen (zählt) to count 1

der Zahn, -̈e tooth 6

der Zahnarzt, -̈e/die Zahnärztin, -nen dentist 6

der Zahnarzthelfer, -/die Zahnarzthelferin, -nen dental hygienist

die Zahnbürste, -n toothbrush 8

Zähne putzen (sich) to brush one's teeth 6

die Zahnpasta toothpaste 8

die Zahnschmerzen (pl.) toothache 6

zärtlich tender, gentle 15

der Zeh, -en toe 6

die Zeichentrickserie, -n cartoon 14

zeichnungsberechtigt authorized to sign

der Zeigefinger, - index finger 6 SV

zeigen to show 12

die Zeit, -en time 5
  Du liebe Zeit! My goodness!
  11
  (keine) Zeit haben to have
  (no) time 7
die Zeitschrift, -en magazine 14
die Zeitung, -en newspaper 3
die Zeitungsnutzung use of
  newspapers
die Zeitverschwendung waste of
  time
das Zelt, -e tent 10 SV
zelten to camp 10 SV
zerlassen (zerläßt), zerließ, zerlassen to melt (butter)
zerstören to destroy 5 SV
die Zielgruppe, -n groups of
  goals
die Zielstrebigkeit determination
ziemlich quite 12
das Zimmer, - room 3
der Zimmerkamerad, -en, -en/
  Zimmerkameradin, -nen
  roommate 5
die Zitrone, -n lemon 9 SV
der Zoo, -s zoo 7 SV, 12
zu to, too 4
der Zucker sugar 9
zuerst at first 6
zufrieden content, satisfied 3, 13
der Zug, ⁝e train 4
  mit dem Zug by train 4
die Zukunft (sg.) future 13
Zum Wohl! Cheers! 9
zu•nehmen (nimmt), nahm zu,
  zugenommen to add
die Zunge, -n tongue 6
zurück back 5
zurück•gehen, ging zurück, ist
  zurückgegangen to go back 5
zurück•kommen, kam zurück,
  ist zurückgekommen to
  return 5
zurück•rufen, rief zurück,
  zurückgerufen to return a
  call 14
zusammen together 4

die Zusammenfassung, -en
  summary
zusätzlich additional
zuverlässig reliable 13
die Zuverlässigkeit reliability
die Zweigstelle, -n branch
zweimal twice 6
  zweimal pro Woche twice per
  week 6
die Zwiebel, -n onion 9
zwischen between 7
die Zwischenklausur, -en mid-
  term 11

English - German Vocabulary

A

a few wenige 12
abbreviation die Abkürzung, -en
above, over über 7
above, upper oben 6
abuse der Mißbrauch, ¨e 14
according to that
dementsprechend
accusative der Akkusativ, -e
ache weh tun (sich); tat, getan 6
acquaintance der Bekannte, -n, -
1 n/die Bekannte, -n 2
acquaintance die Bekanntschaft,
-en 15
across gegenüber 7
active, employed tätig 15
activities, exercises die Aufgabe,
-n
activity die Beschäftigung, -en
12
actor der Schauspieler, -/die
Schauspielerin, -nen 12
actually eigentlich 12
add something (subconsciously)
ein•spielen
add zu•nehmen, nimmt, nahm
zu, zugenommen
additional zusätzlich
adhere (to one's wishes)
nach•kommen, kam nach,
nachgekommen
adjective das Adjektiv, -e
administration die Verwaltung,
-en
adverb das Adverb, -ien
advertisement (on tv and radio)
die Werbung, -en 13 SV; 14
advertisement die Anzeige, -n
13
advertisement die Reklame, -n
14
aerobics das Aerobic 12 SV
afford leisten (etwas) (sich) 6

Africa das Afrika
after nachdem 8
afternoon nachmittag 10
again wieder 2; erneut
against gegen 3
age das Alter 1
aggressive aggressiv 3 SV
agree überein•stimmen 5
agricultural landwirtschaftlich
ahead voraus 9
airplane das Flugzeug, -e 4
airport der Flughafen, ¨ 7
alarm clock der Wecker, - 4 SV
alcohol der Alkohol 6 SV
all right in Ordnung 10
almost fast 3
alone allein 5
alphabet das Alphabet, -e
already schon 3, 5
also auch 1
although obwohl 8
always immer 3
amazing erstaunlich
ambulance der Krankenwagen, -,
der Unfallwagen, - 6 SV
America das Amerika 1, 2
American der Amerikaner, -/die
Amerikanerin,-nen 1, 2
American language and
literature die Amerikanistik
11
angry böse 3
animal das Tier, -e 12
announcer der Ansager, -/die
Ansagerin, -nen 14 SV
annoyance der Ärger
answer antworten 4;
beantworten 5
answer melden (sich) 8 SV
answering machine der
Anrufbeantworter, - 8 SV; 14
antenna die Antenne, -n 14 SV
anthropology die Anthropologie
11

Anything else? Sonst noch
etwas? 8
apartment die Wohnung, -en 3
appendix der Blinddarm, ¨e 6
SV
appetite der Appetit 9
apple der Apfel, ¨ 4, 9
apply for bewerben (sich) um
(+acc.), (bewirbt), bewarb,
beworben 13
apprentice der Auszubildende,
-n, -n/die Auszubildende, -n
(Azubi, -s) 13
apprenticeship die Lehre, -n 13
apricot die Aprikose, -n 9 SV
April der April 4
architect der Architekt, -en,
-en/die Architektin, -nen 2
area code die Vorwahl, -en 8
area die Gegend, -en 5
argument das Argument, -e 15
SV
arm der Arm, -e 6
around, at um (+acc.) 3
around the corner um die Ecke
arrange for, get besorgen
arrive an•kommen, kam an, ist
angekommen 10
arrogant arrogant 3 SV
art die Kunst ¨e, 12
art history die Kunstgeschichte
11
art museum das Kunstmuseum,
-museen 12
artist der Künstler, -/die
Künstlerin, -nen 12
as wie 4
as..as so...wie 4
Asia das Asien
ask fragen 7
asparagus der Spargel 9 SV
aspirin das Aspirin 6
assurance die Sicherheit, -en
astronaut der Astronaut, -en,
-en/die Astronautin, -nen

at first zuerst 6
at home zu Hause 2
at that time, damals 10
at, at the side of (+dat.) an 7
athlete [male] der Sportler, - 12 SV
athlete [female] die Sportlerin, -nen 12 SV
athletic sportlich 12
atmosphere die Atmosphäre, -n 13
attic der Dachboden, ¨ 5 SV
August der August 4
aunt Tante, -n 2
Australia das Australien
Austria das Österreich 2
author der Autor, -en, -en/die Autorin, -nen 1
authorized to sign zeichnungsberechtigt
auto mechanic der Kfz (Kraftfahrzeug)-Mechaniker, - /die Kfz (Kraftfahrzeug)- Mechanikerin, -nen
autumn der Herbst 4
average der Durchschnitt, -e 15
away weg 7

B

baby das Baby, -s 15
back der Rücken, - 6
back pack der Rucksack, ¨e 10 SV
back zurück 5
bacon der Speck 9
bad schlecht 1
bad luck das Pech
badminton der Federball, ¨e 12 SV
bakery die Bäckerei, -en 7
bakery goods die Backware, -n 9
balcony der Balkon, -s 5
ball der Ball, ¨e 4
ballpoint pen der Kugelschreiber, - 2
banana die Banane, -n 9
bank die Bank, -en 7
bank teller [male] der Bankkaufmann, die Bankkaufleute (pl.) 13

bank teller [female] die Bankkauffrau, die Bankkaufleute (pl.) 13
baroque barock
basement, cellar der Keller, - 5 SV
basketball to play spielen Basketball 2
bath das Bad, ¨er 3
bathing suit der Badeanzug, ¨e 4
bathroom das Badezimmer, -
battle, fight kämpfen 14
be sein (ist), war, ist gewesen 1
be able to können (kann), konnte, gekonnt 3
be all right in Ordnung sein 6
be called, named heißen, hieß, geheißen 1
be enthused about something begeistern (sich) für (+acc.)
be excluded from verschließen (sich), verschloß, verschlossen
be exposed (to something) etwas (dat.) ausgesetzt sein 15
be exposed aus•setzen (sich) 15
be happy about freuen (sich) über (+acc.) 11
be in a hurry (es) eilig haben 7
be interested in interessieren (sich) für (+acc.), interessierte, interessiert 11
be lazy faulenzen 4
be lucky Glück haben 11
be (not) very hungry (keinen) großen Hunger haben 9
be (not) very thirsty (keinen) großen Durst haben 9
be of the opinion (to think) meinen, 5
be permitted to, may dürfen (darf), durfte, gedurft 5
be prejudiced Vorurteile haben 15
be retired auf Rente sein 2
be right recht haben 5
be sick krank sein 6
be supposed to, should sollen 4
be worth it lohnen (sich) 12

beach der Strand, ¨e
bean die Bohne, -n 9
beautiful schön 2,
because of wegen (+gen.) 11
because weil 8
because, for denn 3, 4
become acquainted with someone kennen•lernen 5, 6
become werden (wird), wurde, ist geworden 2
bed das Bett, -en 3
bed linen die Bettwäsche (sg.) 3
bed-and-breakfast inn die Pension, -en 10
bedroom das Schlafzimmer, - 4, 5
beef das Rindfleisch 9
beer das Bier 9
before bevor 8
begin an•fangen (fängt), fing an, angefangen 10
begin beginnen, begann, begonnen 4
beginning der Anfang, ¨e 4
behind, bottom das Gesäß, -e 6 SV
behind hinter 7
beige beige 3 SV
Belgium das Belgien 10
believe glauben 4
belly der Bauch, ¨e 6
belong to gehören 4
belong to angehören 12
bend biegen, bog, gebogen 7
beneath, under unter 7
beside, next to neben 7
besides außerdem
better besser 6
between zwischen 7
beverage das Getränk, -e 9
bicycle das Fahrrad, ¨er 4
bicycle path der Fahrradweg, -e 12 SV
bicycle ride die Radtour, -en 12 SV
big groß (ö) 2
biology die Biologie 11
birthday der Geburtstag, -e 4
bitter bitter 9
black schwarz (ä) 3

blanket die Decke, -n 3
bleed bluten 6 SV
blond blonde 6
blouse die Bluse, -n 8
blow away verwehen
blow dryer der Föhn, -s 8 SV
blue blau 3
body der Körper, - 6
body part der Körperteil, -e 6
bone Knochen, - 6 SV
book das Buch, ̈er 2
bookstore die Buchhandlung,
    -en 7 SV
bookcase das Bücherregal, -e 3
border die Grenze, -n 10 SV
boring langweilig 11
boss der Chef, -s/die Chefin,
    -nen 4 SV; 13
both beide 12
bottle die Flasche, -n 4 SV
bouquet of flowers der
    Blumenstrauß, ̈e 4 SV
boy der Junge, -n, -n 2
brain das Gehirn 6 SV
branch die Zweigstelle, -n
bread das Brot, -e 9
break something brechen
    (bricht) (sich etwas), brach,
    gebrochen 6
breakfast das Frühstück, -e 6, 9
break through durch•brechen
    (bricht), brach durch,
    durchgebrochen
breast die Brust, ̈e
bridge die Brücke, -n 7
bright heiter 4
bring (along) mit•bringen,
    brachte mit, mitgebracht 10
broad breit 6
broccoli die Brokkoli (pl.) 9 SV
brother der Bruder, ̈ 2
brother-in-law der Schwager, ̈
    2
brown braun 3
brush one's teeth Zähne putzen
    (sich) 6
brush putzen (sich) 6
Brussel sprouts der Rosenkohl 9 SV

building das Gebäude, - 7 SV
bus der Bus, -se 4
bus driver der Busfahrer, -/die
    Busfahrerin, -nen 2
bus stop die Bushaltestelle, -n 7
business administration die
    Betriebswirtschaft 11
business man der
    Geschäftsmann, Geschäftsleute
    (pl.) 13
business manager der
    Geschäftsleiter, -/die
    Geschäftsleiterin, -nen 13
    SV
business woman die
    Geschäftsfrau, Geschäftsleute
    (pl.) 13
busy besetzt 8
but, but rather sondern 4
but aber 1, 4
butter die Butter 9
buy kaufen 3
buyer der Käufer, -/die Käuferin,
    -nen
by mit 4; per 10
by occupation, by profession, by
    trade von Beruf 2
by train mit dem Zug 4
bye tschüs

C

cabbage das Weißkraut 9 SV
cable TV das Kabelfernsehen 14
cafe das Café, -s 7
cake der Kuchen, - 9
call (on the phone) an•rufen, rief
    an, angerufen 6
call der Anruf, -e 8
call telefonieren 3
camera die Kamera, -s 4
camp fire das Lagerfeuer, - 10 SV
camp, go camping campen 2
    zelten 10 SV
cap die Mütz, e -n 8
car das Auto, -s 3
car park das Parkhaus, ̈e 7 SV
car, vehicle der Wagen, - 6

card die Karte, -n 2
care (for) sorgen (für + acc.) 14
career counseling die
    Berufsberatung, -en 13 SV
career counselor der
    Berufsberater, -/die
    Berufsberaterin, -nen 13 SV
careful vorsichtig 7
caregiver for the old der
    Altenpfleger, -/die
    Altenpflegerin, -nen
carpet der Teppich, -e 2, 5
carrot die Karotte, -n 9
carry tragen (trägt), trug, getragen 8
cartoon die Zeichentrickserie, -n 14
case der Fall, ̈e,
cash das Bargeld 10
cassette recorder der
    Kassettenrecorder, - 14
cassette tape die Kassette, -n 4
catch a cold erkälten (sich) 6
cathedral der Dom, -e 7 SV
cauliflower der Blumenkohl 9
CD die CD, -s 4
CD-player der CD-Spieler, - 3
celerie der Sellerie 9 SV
cello das Cello, -s 12 SV
cement technology die
    Betontechnologie
century das Jahrhundert, -e 11
certainly, surely sicher 11
chair der Stuhl, ̈e 2
chalk die Kreide 2
chalkboard die Tafel, -n 2
change (one's clothing), to move
    um•ziehen (sich), zog um,
    umgezogen 6
change ändern 15
change one's mind die Meinung
    ändern 11
change wechseln
character trait die
    Charaktereigenschaft, -en
cheap(ly) billig 3
checked kariert 3 SV
cheek die Backe, -n; die Wange,
    -n 6 SV
Cheers! Pros(i)t! Zum Wohl! 9

cheese der Käse 9
chemistry die Chemie 11
cherry die Kirsche -n 9
chest die Brust, ⸚e 6
chicken das Hähnchen, - 9
child das Kind, -er 2
children's room das
    Kinderzimmer, - 4
chimney sweep der
    Schornsteinfeger, -/die
    Schornsteinfegerin, -nen 13
    SV
chin das Kinn 6 SV
chocolate die Schokolade 4 SV
choice die Wahl, -en
choir der Chor, ⸚e 12 SV
choose aus·wählen 12
choose wählen 8
church clock die Kirchturmuhr,
    -en 4 SV
church die Kirche, -n 7
city die Stadt, ⸚e 1, 2
city map der Stadtplan, ⸚e 7
civil engineering das
    Bauingenieurwesen 11
claim der Anspruch, ⸚e
clarinet die Klarinette, -n 12 SV
class (grade level) die Klasse, -n 11
class schedule der Studienplan,
    ⸚e;der Stundenplan, ⸚e 4
classroom das Klassenzimmer, - 2
clean sauber 15
clean putzen 5
clean up aufräumen SV 5
clear heiter 4
climb steigen , stieg, ist gestiegen
clock, watch die Uhr, -en 2, 4
close, near nah (ä) 9
clothing die Kleidung (sg.) 8
cloudy wolkig 4
club der Verein, -e 12
coat der Mantel, ⸚ 8
coca cola die Cola, -s 9
coffee der Kaffee 9
coffee mill die Kaffeemühle, -n
    5 SV
coffeemaker die Kaffeemaschine,
    -n 3

coin die Münze, -n 12
cold kalt (ä) 4
cold die Erkältung, -en 6
colleague der Kollege, -n, -n/die
    Kollegin, -nen
collect call das R-Gespräch, -e
    8
collect something sammeln 12
color die Farbe, -n 3
comb der Kamm, ⸚e 8
comb one's hair kämmen (sich) 6
come kommen, kam, ist
    gekommen 1
come (from someplace)
    her·kommen, kam her, ist
    hergekommen 7
come down herunter·kommen,
    kam herunter, ist
    heruntergekommen 7
come along mit·kommen, kam
    mit, ist mitgekommen 5
come by vorbei·kommen, kam
    vorbei, ist vorbeigekommen 5
come in herein! 7
come out heraus·kommen, kam
    heraus, ist herausgekommen 7
come to visit zu Besuch
    kommen 2
comfortable, (comfortably)
    bequem 5
commander der Kommandant,
    -en, -en/die Kommandantin,
    -nen
commemorative stamp die
    Sondermarke, -n
communication die
    Kommunikation, -en 14
compact disk die CD, -s 4
company die Firma, -en 13
company owner der Fabrikant,
    -en, -en/die Fabrikantin, -nen
    13 SV
complete vollständig
complicated kompliziert
composer der Komponist,
    -en/die Komponistin, -nen 12
composition, essay der Aufsatz,
    ⸚e 11

computer der Computer, - 3
computer game das
    Computerspiel, -e 4
computer programmer der
    Computerprogrammierer, -
    /die Computer-
    programmiererin, -nen 2
computer science die Informatik
    11
computer science worker,
    programmer der
    Informatiker, -/die
    Informatikerin, -nen 13
concert das Konzert, -e 12
congratulate gratulieren
connect verbinden, verband,
    verbunden 8 SV
consist of bestehen aus, bestand,
    bestanden 6
constitution die Verfassung, -en 15
consumer der Verbraucher, -
contact der Kontakt, -e
content zufrieden 3
continent der Kontinent, -e
conversation das Gespräch, -e
conversational theme das
    Gesprächsthema, -en
cook der Koch, ⸚e/ die Köchin,
    -nen 13
cook kochen 2
cooked; boiled gekocht 9
cookie der Keks, -e 9 SV
cooking pot der Topf, ⸚e
cool kühl 4
corn der Mais 9 SV
corner die Ecke, -n
cornflakes die Cornflakes (pl.) 9
    SV
correspondingly entsprechend
cost kosten 5
couch die Couch, -es 3
cough der Husten 6 SV
counseling office die
    Studienberatung, -en 7 SV
count zählen 1
country das Land, ⸚er 2
course der Kurs 11
cousin [male] der Vetter, -n 2

cousin [female] die Kusine, -n 2
crafts basteln 12
craftsman der Handwerker, -/die Handwerkerin, -nen 13 SV
cram pauken 11 SV
crazy verrückt 3 SV
criticism die Kritik, -en 14 SV
criticize kritisieren 14 SV
crossing die Kreuzung, -en 7
crunchy knusprig 9 SV
cuckoo clock die Kuckucksuhr, -en 4 SV
cucumber die Gurke, -n 9 SV
cul-de-sac die Sackgasse, -n 7 SV
culture note die Kulturnotiz, -en
cure die Kur, -en 6 SV
curious neugierig 3
curly lockig 6
currant die Johannisbeere, -n 9 SV
currency exchange office die Wechselstube, -n 10
current aktuell 14
curtain die Gardine, -n 5 SV
customer der Kunde, -n/die Kundin, -nen 13
cut schneiden, schnitt, geschnitten 9 SV

D

daily täglich 6
damage schädigen 14
dance tanzen 2
danger die Gefahr, -en
dangerous(ly) gefährlich 5
dark dunkel 3 SV, 5
dark green dunkelgrün 3 SV
dative der Dativ, -e
day before yesterday vorgestern 10
day-care center die Kindertagesstätte, -n 15
December der Dezember 4
decide entscheiden (sich) für (+ acc.), entschied, entschieden 11
defend verteidigen (sich) 15 SV
degree der Grad, -e 4
deliver liefern 5 SV

delivery price der Lieferpreis, -e
Denmark das Dänemark 10
dental hygienist der Zahnarzthelfer, -/die Zahnarzthelferin, -nen
dentist der Zahnarzt, ¨e/die Zahnärztin, -nen 6
deodorant das Deo, - (das Deodorant) 8
department store das Kaufhaus, ¨er 7
describe beschreiben, beschrieb, beschrieben 6
desire wünschen
desire der Wunsch, ¨e 12
dessert der Nachtisch 9
destroy zerstören 5 SV
detective der Detektiv, -e
detective movie der Kriminalfilm, -e 14
determination die Zielstrebigkeit
develop entwickeln (sich)
device das Gerät, -e 5, 14
dial wählen 8
dial direct durch·wählen 8
diaper die Windel, -n
different verschieden 12
digital clock die Digitaluhr, -en 4 SV
diligence der Fleiß
diligent fleißig 3
dimple das Grübchen, - 6 SV
dining room das Eßzimmer, - 5
director der Direktor, -en/die Direktorin, -nen 13
discipline das Fachbereich, -e
disco die Disco, -s 7
discover entdecken 5
discuss besprechen, (bespricht), besprach, besprochen 12
discussion die Besprechung, -en 13
dishes das Geschirr (sg.) 5 SV
dishwasher der Geschirrspüler, - 5
dissertation die Dissertation, -en (doctoral) 11

divorced geschieden 2
do, to make machen 1
documentary film der Dokumentarfilm, -e 14
dog der Hund, -e
done; tender gar 9
done fertig 4
double room das Doppelzimmer, - 10
dream job der Berufswunsch, ¨e 13 SV
dress das Kleid, -er 8
dress an·ziehen (sich) , zog an, gezogen 6
drink das Getränk, -e 9
drive off, leave ab·fahren (fährt), fuhr ab, ist abgefahren 7
drive fahren (fährt), fuhr, ist gefahren 3
drug die Droge, -n
drug store die Drogerie, -n 6 SV, 8
due fällig 11
dumb doof 3
during während (+gen.) 11

E

each, every jed- 4
ear das Ohr, -en 6
ear lobe das Ohrläppchen, - 6 SV
early früh 5
earn verdienen 11
easily ohne weiteres 15
easy chair der Sessel, - 3
easy leicht 10
eat breakfast frühstücken 4
eat essen (ißt), aß, gegessen 3
eat out aus·essen (ißt), aß aus, ausgegessen 9
ecological technology die Umwelttechnik
economics die Wirtschaftswissenschaft 11
economy die Wirtschaft
education, pedagogy die Pädagogik 11

education, training die Ausbildung 13

egg das Ei, -er 9

either ... or entweder ... oder 12

elbow der Ell(en)bogen, - 6 SV

election die Wahl, -en

electrician der Elektriker, -/die Elektrikerin, -nen 2 SV; 13

electronic elektronisch 14

elementary school die Grundschule, -n 11

embrace umarmen 15

employee der Angestellte, -n, -n/ die Angestellte, -n 2 SV, 13

employee der Arbeitnehmer, - /die Arbeitnehmerin, -nen 13

employer der Arbeitgeber, -/die Arbeitgeberin, -nen 13

empty leeren 5 SV

empty, free frei 6

energetic energisch 3 SV

engage in sports Sport treiben, trieb, getrieben 6

engaged verlobt 2

engineer der Ingenieur, -e/die Ingenieurin, -nen 2

England das England 1, 10

English language and literature die Anglistik 11

Enjoy your meal! Mahlzeit!; Guten Appetit 9

enough genug 3

entertain oneself unterhalten (sich) (unterhält), unterhielt, unterhalten 14

enthusiastic enthusiastisch 3 SV

entrance [to the freeway] die Einfahrt, -en 7 SV

entry ticket die Eintrittskarte, -n 11

entrust to überlassen (überläßt) überließ, überlassen 15

environment die Umwelt (sg.) 14

equal rights die Gleichberechtigung 15

equalization die Gleichstellung

especially besonders 9

Europe das Europa

even though obwohl 8

evening der Abend, -e 1

evening meal das Abendbrot 4, das Abendessen, - 9

every, all alle 11, 12

every [ten years] alle [zehn Jahre] 11

every [thirty minutes] alle [dreißig Minuten] 11

exactly genau 7

exam die Prüfung, -en 11

example das Beispiel, -e 1

excellent! ausgezeichnet! 1

except for außer (+dat.) 4

exchange wechseln 10

exchange money Geld wechseln 10

exchange student der Austauschstudent, -en, -en/die Austauschstudentin-nen 8 SV; 11

exciting aufregend, spannend 14

excursion der Ausflug, ̈e 10

Excuse me please. Entschuldigen Sie bitte. 7

excuse die Entschuldigung, -en 8

executive, manager der Leiter, - /die Leiterin, -nen 13

exhibit die Ausstellung, -en

exit [from the freeway] die Ausfahrt, -en 7 SV

expect erwarten 13

expectation die Erwartung, -en

expensive teuer 3

experience das Erlebnis, -se

experience die Erfahrung, -en 11

explain erklären 12

export sales person[male] der Außenhandelskaufmann, die Außenhandelskaufleute (pl.) 13 SV

export sales person[female] die Außenhandelskauffrau, die Außenhandelskaufleute (pl.) 13 SV

expression der Ausdruck, ̈e

expressway die Autobahn, -en 7 SV

eye das Auge, -n 6

eye brow die Augenbraue, -n 6 SV

eyelash die Wimper, -n 6 SV

F

face das Gesicht, -er 6

factory worker der Fabrikarbeiter, -/die Fabrikarbeiterin, -nen 2

faculty die Fakultät, -en

fail a test bei einer Prüfung durchfallen 11

fair blonde, 6

fall der Herbst 4

family die Familie, -n 2

family member das Familienmitglied, -er 2

family tree der Stammbaum, ̈e

fan der Fan, -s

fantastic fantastisch 1 SV

far weit 3

farm der Bauernhof, ̈e

fashion model das Fotomodell, -e [female, male]

father der Vater, ̈ 2

favored beliebt 7

favorite season die Lieblingsjahreszeit, -en 4

favorite _____ Lieblings - 12

feature film der Spielfilm, -e 14

February der Februar 4

feel well wohl•fühlen (sich) 6

fever das Fieber 6 SV

fight der Streit 5 SV

fight streiten, stritt, gestritten 15

final exam die Klausur, -en 11

finances das Finanzwesen 11 SV

find finden, fand, gefunden 3

find out erfahren, (erfährt), erfuhr, erfahren 11

finger der Finger, - 6

finger nail der Fingernagel, ̈ 6 SV

finished fertig 4

Finland das Finnland 10

first floor das Erdgeschoß, -sse 5 SV

first erst 1, 9

fish angeln 4
fish der Fisch, -e 9
fist die Faust, ⸚e 6 SV
fit fit 3
fitness center das Fitness-Center
flight number die Flugnummer, -n
floor das Stockwerk, -e 5 SV
flower die Blume, -n 4 SV
flower shop der Blumenladen, ⸚ 7
flowered geblümt 3 SV
flu die Erkältung, -en 6; die Grippe 6 SV
flute die Flöte, -n 12 SV
fly fliegen, flog, ist geflogen 8, 10
foggy neblig 4 SV
follow folgen 4
foot der Fuß, ⸚e 6
for für (+acc.) 3
for many years jahrelang
for the first time zum ersten Mal 10
forehead die Stirn, -en 6 SV
foreign fremd 15
foreign experience die Auslandserfahrung, -en
foreign language die Fremdsprache, -n 11
forest der Wald, ⸚er 8
forget vergessen (vergißt), vergaß, vergessen 8
formation, organization die Gestaltung, -en
fowl das Geflügel (sg.)
France das Frankreich 10
free time die Freizeit, -en 12
freeway die Autobahn, -en 7 SV
freeze frieren, fror, gefroren 4 SV
French fried potatoes die Pommes frites (pl.) 9
fresh frisch 9
Friday der Freitag 4
fried gebraten 9
friend der Freund, -e/die Freundin, -nen 2
friendly freundlich 3
front door die Haustür, -en 5 SV
fruit das Obst (sg.) 4
fruit juice der Obstsaft, ⸚e 6

frying pan die Pfanne, -n
full-time vollzeitig 15
fun der Spaß, ⸚e 4
funny komisch 9; lustig 14
furnish ein•richten 5
furnished möbliert 5
furniture die Möbel (pl.) 2, 3
further weiter
future die Zukunft (sg.) 13

G

gadget das Gerät, -e 5, 14
game das Spiel, -e 1
game show die Quizshow 14
garage die Garage, -n 5 SV
gas station die Tankstelle, -n 9
gender das Geschlecht, -er
geography die Geographie 11 SV
German das Deutsch
German Federal Post Office die Bundespost 8 SV
German language and literature die Germanistik 11
German mark die Deutsche Mark (DM) 5 SV, 8
Germany das Deutschland 2
Get out! Heraus! 7
get holen 10
get hurt verletzen (sich) 6 SV
get in, board ein•steigen, stieg ein, ist eingestiegen 7
get into shape trimmen (sich) 12 SV
get married verheiraten (sich) 5; heiraten 15
get off or out aus•steigen, stieg aus, ist ausgestiegen 7
get undressed aus•ziehen (sich), zog aus, ausgezogen 6
get up auf•stehen, stand auf, ist aufgestanden 6
girl das Mädchen, - 2
give a report ein Referat halten 11
give as a present schenken 4
give geben (gibt), gab, gegeben 1
give up auf•geben (gibt), gab auf, aufgegeben 15
gladly gern 2

glass ceiling die Glasdecke, -n
glove der Handschuh, -e 8
go gehen, ging, ist gegangen 1, 2
go (to someplace) hin•fahren (fährt), fuhr hin, ist hingefahren
go back zurück•gehen, ging zurück, ist zurückgegangen 5
go home nach Hause gehen 4
go in hinein•gehen, ging hinein, ist hineingegangen 7
go out aus•gehen, ging, ist gegangen 5
go to the movies ins Kino gehen 4
go up hinauf•gehen, ging hinauf, ist hinaufgegangen 7
Good evening! Guten Abend! 1
Good morning! Guten Morgen! 1
Good night! Gute Nacht! 1
good gut 1; wohl 6
Good-bye. (on the phone) Auf Wiederhören 8
Good-bye. Auf Wiedersehen 1
gothic gotisch
governmental staatlich 14
grade die Note, -n 11
grandfather der Großvater, ⸚ 2
grandmother die Großmutter, ⸚ 2
grandparents die Großeltern (pl.) 2
grape die Weintraube, -n 9 SV
great prima 1 SV; groß (ö) 2; toll 6
Greece das Griechenland 10
green grün 3
green as grass grasgrün 3 SV
greet grüßen 1
grey grau 3 SV
grilled gegrillt 9
groceries die Lebensmittel (pl.) 9
grocery store das Lebensmittelgeschäft, -e 7
group die Gruppe, -n 12
guest der Gast, ⸚e 10
guest house die Pension, -en 10

guitar die Gitarre, -n 2
gym die Sporthalle, -n 7 SV
gym shoe der Turnschuh, -e 4
SV
gymnastics die Gymnastik 12

H

hail hageln 4
hair das Haar, -e 6
hair brush die Haarbürste, -n 8
hair dresser der Friseur, -e/die
Friseurin 2 SV; 13
hair spray das Haarspray, -s 8
SV
half halb 4
hall der Flur, -en 5 SV
ham der Schinken 9 SV
hamburger die Boulette, -n 9
SV
hand die Hand, ̈e 6
handbag die Handtasche, -n 8
hang hängen, hängte, gehängt
(+acc.) 7
hang hängen, hing, gehangen
(+dat.) 7
happen passieren, ist passiert 5
happy froh 3; glücklich 6
hard hart (ä) 9
hard or difficult schwer 10
hard of hearing schwerhörig
14
harmonica die Mundharmonika,
-s 12 SV
hat der Hut, ̈e 4 SV
have haben (hat), hatte, gehabt 3
have (no) time (keine) Zeit
haben 7
have enough genügen
have fun Spaß haben 4
have something planned
vor•haben, (hat), hatte vor,
vorgehabt 8
having equal rights
gleichberechtigt sein 15
he er 1
head der Kopf, ̈e 6
headphone der Kopfhörer, - 14
headache die Kopfschmerzen

(pl.) 6
headline die Schlagzeile, -n 14 SV
health die Gesundheit 6
healthy gesund (ü) 1, 2
hearing das Gehör 14
heart das Herz, -en 6
hearty herzlich 8
heat die Heizung 4
heavy schwer 10; dick 6
heel die Ferse, -n 6
Hello! Guten Tag! (lit. Good
day.) 1
hello! hallo! 1
help helfen (i), half, geholfen 4
help along weiter•helfen, (hilft),
half weiter, weitergeholfen
here hier 1
high hoch, höher, höchst 6
high school das Gymnasium,
Gymnasien 11
high school die Gesamtschule,
-n; die Oberschule, -n
hike wandern, ist gewandert 2;
trampen 10 SV
history die Geschichte 11
hit schlagen, (schlägt), schlug,
geschlagen 12
hit song der Schlager, - 12 SV
hobby das Hobby, -s 12
hold halten (hält), hielt, gehalten
7
homeless obdachlos 5 SV
homework die Hausaufgaben
(pl.) 3
honestly wirklich 2
honesty die Ehrlichkeit
Hope you feel better! Gute
Besserung! 6
hope hoffen 8
horseback riding das Reiten 12
SV
hospital das Krankenhaus, ̈er 6 SV
host der Gastgeber, -/die
Gastgeberin, -nen
hot heiß 4
hotel das Hotel, -s 7
hotel manager der Hotelleiter, -
/die Hotelleiterin, -nen 13 SV
hour die Stunde, -n 4

house das Haus, ̈er 2
household der Haushalt, -e 15
how; what wie 1
How are you? Wie geht es
dir?/Wie geht's? 1; Wie geht es
Ihnen?
How do I get to ...? Wie komme
ich zum/zur ...? 7
How do you spell ...? Wie
schreibt man...? 1
How does one say ... in German?
Wie sagt man ... auf deutsch? 1
how much, how many wieviel,
wie viele 1
however allerdings 10, 15
human being der Mensch, -en, -
en , 12
humiliation die Erniedrigung,
-en 15 SV
hungry hungrig 9
hurry beeilen (sich) 9
hurt weh tun (sich), tat, getan 6
husband der Mann, ̈er 2

I

I ich 1
I'm sorry (about that) Es tut mir
leid. 1
ice cream das Eis 9 SV
ice hockey das Eishockey 12 SV
ice skate Schlittschuh laufen
(läuft), lief, ist gelaufen 4
ice skate der Schlittschuh, -e 4
ideal(ly) ideal 5 SV
if ob 8
image die Vorstellung, -en
imagine (something) vorstellen
(sich) (etwas)
impaired hearing die
Schwerhörigkeit (sg.) 14
important wichtig 6
imposition die Störung, -en 8
SV
improve verbessern (sich) 15
in; into in (+acc./dat.) 2
in any event jedenfalls 12
in back hinten 7
in cash bar 10

in front of vor 7
in love verliebt 2
in my opinion meiner Meinung nach
in order to um ... zu 10
in spite of, despite trotz (+gen.) 11
in the evening am Abend 1
in the future künftig 15
in the morning am Morgen 1
in your place an Ihrer Stelle 14
included in the price im Preis enthalten 10
inclusive(ly) inklusive 5
incorrect falsch 1
index finger der Zeigefinger, - 6 SV
industrious fleißig 3
information die Auskunft, ⸗e 8; die Nachricht, -en 14
inside swimming pool das Hallenbad, ⸗er 12 P
instead of (an)statt (+gen.) 11
instead of anstatt ... zu 10
instrument das Instrument, -e 12
intelligent intelligent 3
interest das Interesse, -n 12
interesting interessant 3
interpreter der Dolmetscher, -/die Dolmetscherin, -nen
interrupt unterbrechen (unterbricht), unterbrach, unterbrochen 15
intersection die Kreuzung, -en 7
interview das Interview, -s
intolerant intolerant 15 SV
invent erfinden, erfand, erfunden 14
invitation die Einladung -en 8
invite ein•laden (lädt), lud ein, eingeladen 9
Ireland das Irland 10
ironing das Bügeln 15 SV
irritation der Ärger
isn't that so? nicht wahr? 1
isolate isolieren 14
it er; sie; es 1

Italy das Italien 2, 10

J

jacket die Jacke, -n 8
jam die Marmelade, -n 9 SV
January der Januar 4
jeans die Jeans (pl.) 8
jewelry der Schmuck (sg.) 4 SV
job interview das Vorstellungsgespräch, - 13
jog joggen 12
judge der Richter, -/die Richterin, -nen 13 SV
juice der Saft, ⸗e 9
juicy saftig 9
July der Juli 4
June der Juni 4
junior high school die Hauptschule, -n
just gerade 2; erst 1,9

K

keep driving, drive further weiter•fahren, (fährt), fuhr weiter, ist weitergefahren 7 SV
keep fit, stay in shape fit halten (sich), hielt, gehalten 6
kick or make a goal (soccer) das Tor schießen
kilogram das Kilogramm 9
kindergarten der Kindergarten, ⸗ 15
kiss küssen 15
kitchen die Küche, -n 4, 5
kitchen clock die Küchenuhr, -en 4 SV
knee das Knie, - 6
knit sweater die Strickjacke, -n 8 SV
know wissen (weiß), wußte, gewußt 3
know one's way around aus•kennen (sich), kannte, gekannt 7

know someone kennen, kannte, gekannt 5
knowledge die Kenntnis, -se 13
knuckle, ankle der Knöchel, - 6 SV

L

laboratory das Labor, -s or -e, 11
land das Land, ⸗er 2
language die Sprache, -n 15
large groß (ö) 2
last letzt- 4
late morning vormittag 10
late spät 5
Latin das Latein 11
law Jura 11
lawyer der Rechtsanwalt, ⸗e/die Rechtsanwältin, -nen 2
lay legen 7
lazy faul 3
lead leiten 13
learn; study (as for an exam) lernen 3
learning goals das Lernziel, -e
learning material der Lernstoff, -e
leave behind hinterlassen (hinterläßt), hinterließ, hinterlassen 14
leave to überlassen (läßt), überließ, überlassen 15
leave verlassen (verläßt), verließ, verlassen 5
leaves das Laub (sg.) 4
lecture die Vorlesung, -en 4
lecture hall der Hörsaal, -säle; der Lesesaal, -säle; der Vorlesungssaal, -säle 7
left links 7
leg das Bein, -e 6
legal rechtlich 15
lemon die Zitrone, -n 9 SV
lend leihen, lieh, geliehen 4
less minus
lesson der Unterricht 4
let us... laß uns... 7
let lassen (läßt), ließ, gelassen 8

letter der Brief, -e 5
lettuce der Salat, -e 9
library die Bibliothek, -en 4
lie around faulenzen 4
lie down hin•legen (sich) 6
lie liegen, lag, gelegen 4
Liechtenstein das Liechtenstein 10
lift heben, hob, gehoben 7
light blue hellblau 3 SV
light hell 3 SV, 5
like mögen (mag), mochte, gemocht 5
likeable sympatisch 3 SV
liked beliebt 7
lilac lila 3 SV
lip die Lippe, -n 6 SV
lipstick der Lippenstift, -e 8 SV
listen to an•hören 5 SV
listen to music Musik hören 4
liter der Liter, - 9
little, few wenig, wenige 6
live leben 6
live wohnen 1
living room das Wohnzimmer, - 5
living room table der Wohnzimmertisch, -e 5 SV
local call das Ortsgespräch, -e 8 SV
local traffic der Nahverkehr 7 SV
local [elevated] train die S-Bahn, -en 7
location der Ort, -e 7
lonely einsam 8
long lang (ä) 6
long distance call das Ferngespräch, -e 8 SV
long-distance traffic der Fernverkehr 7 SV
longterm memory das Langzeitgedächtnis, -se
look at an•sehen (sieht), sah an, gesehen 5 SV

look at something an•sehen (sieht) (sich), sah an, gesehen 6
look for an apartment auf Wohnungssuche gehen 5 SV
look forward to freuen (sich) auf (+acc.) 8
lose verlieren, verlor, verloren 3
loser der Verlierer, -/die Verliererin, -nen 12 SV
lottery ticket das Lottoticket, -s
loud(ly), noisy (noisily) laut 5
Louder, please. Lauter, bitte! 1
loudspeaker der Lautsprecher, - 14
love die Liebe 15
love lieben 15
lower, below unten 6
luck das Glück 3
lucrative lukrativ
lunch das Mittagessen, - 9
lung die Lunge, -n
Luxemburg das Luxemburg 10

M

magazine die Illustrierte, -n 14 SV; die Zeitschrift, -en 14
main street die Hauptstraße, -n 7 SV
major das Hauptfach, ¨er 11
make a date verabreden (sich) 7 SV
make-up das Make-up 8 SV
man der Mann, ¨er 2
mannequin das Mannequin
many viel, viele 3, 4
map die Landkarte, -n 2
March der März 4
margarine die Margarine 9
market place der Markt, ¨e 7 SV, 9
marmelade die Konfitüre, -n 9 SV
marriage die Ehe, -n 15
married couple das Ehepaar, -e 15
married verheiratet 2
mathematics die Mathematik 11

May der Mai 4
meal das Essen, - 9
meaning die Bedeutung, -en
means of communication das Kommunikationsmittel, - 14
means of transport das Verkehrsmittel, -
means of transportation das Transportmittel, - 14
meat das Fleisch 9
meat market die Metzgerei, -en 7
mechanic der Mechaniker,-/die Mechanikerin, -nen 13
media die Medien (pl.) 14
medicine die Medizin 6
meditation die Meditation 6 SV
meet treffen (sich) (trifft), traf, getroffen 7
melt (butter) zerlassen (zerläßt), zerließ, zerlassen
memorial church die Gedächtniskirche, -n
menu die Speisekarte, -n 9
message die Nachricht, -en 14
microwave oven der Mikrowellenherd, -e 5 SV
mid-term die Zwischenklausur, -en 11
middle mittel- 13
middle finger der Mittelfinger, - 6 SV
middle school die Realschule, -n
milk die Milch 9
mineral water das Mineralwasser 9
minor das Nebenfach, ¨er 11
minus minus
minute die Minute, -n 11
mirror der Spiegel, - 3
miserable miserabel 1 SV
Miss, Mrs., Ms., unmarried woman das Fräulein, - 1
misunderstanding das Mißverständnis, -se
modern modern 3 SV
Monday der Montag 4
money das Geld, -er 7

month der Monat, -e 4
monthly monatlich 5
moral die Moral 15 SV
more mehr 6, 7
More slowly, please. Langsamer, bitte! 1
morning der Morgen, - 1
mother die Mutter, ⸚ 2
mountain climber der Bergsteiger, -/die Bergsteigerin, -nen 10 SV
mouth der Mund, ⸚er 6
move in ein•ziehen, zog, ist eingezogen 5
move out aus•ziehen, zog aus, ist ausgezogen 5
move up (in time) verschieben, verschob, verschoben 8
movie theatre das Kino, -s 7
Mr. der Herr, -n, -en 1
Mrs.; Ms.; woman; wife die Frau, -en 1
much viel, viele 3, 4
muesli das Müsli 9 SV
multi-colored bunt 3 SV
muscle der Muskel, -n 6
museum das Museum, Museen 4, 7
music club der Musikverein, -e
music die Musik 4
music history die Musikgeschichte 11
must, have to müssen (muß), mußte, gemußt 3, 5
mustard der Senf 9
mutual gemeinsam
My goodness! Du liebe Zeit! 11
my mein 1

N

name der Name, -n
napkin die Serviette, -n
native country die Heimat 10
near, at the home of bei (+dat.) 4
nearby, in the vicinity in der Nähe 7

neck der Hals, ⸚e 6
necklace die Halskette, -n 4 SV
need brauchen 3
neighbor der Nachbar, -n, -n/die Nachbarin, -nen
neighborhood die Nachbarschaft, -en 5
neither .. nor weder ... noch 12
nephew der Neffe, -en, -en 12
nervous nervös 3 SV
Netherlands die Niederlande 10
never nie 6
nevertheless trotzdem
new neu 3
news die Nachrichten (pl.) 14
newspaper ad das Inserat, -e 5
newspaper die Zeitung, -en 3
next door nebenan 3
next nächst- 4
nice nett 3; schön 3
night die Nacht, ⸚e 10
no nein 1
no one niemand 4
noise der Lärm 14
nominative der Nominativ, -e
noodle die Nudel, -n 9 SV
noon mittag 10
normally normalerweise
north der Norden
Northern Germany das Norddeutschland
Norway das Norwegen 10
nose die Nase, -n 6
not a kein 2
not any kein 2
not nicht 1
not only ... but also nicht nur ... sondern auch 12
not so good nicht so gut 1
not yet noch nicht 4
note, write down notieren 13
notebook das Heft, -e 2
notice merken 11
noun das Substantiv, -
novel der Roman, -e 12
November der November 4
now jetzt 1

number die Zahl, -en 1; die Nummer, -n
nurse pflegen 6 SV.

O

object der Gegenstand, ⸚e
oboe die Oboe, -n 12 SV
occupation der Beruf, -e 2
occupied besetzt 8
October der Oktober 4
of course natürlich 9; klar! 15
of, from; by von 4
offer an•bieten, bot an, angeboten 12
office das Büro, -s 13
official(ly) offiziell
official, civil servant der Beamte, -n, -n/die Beamtin, -nen 7 SV; 13
often häufig 14; oft (ö) 3
oh, ah ach 1
ok, all right in Ordnung 10
old age pension die Altersversicherung, -en 13 SV
old alt (ä) 1
old part of town die Altstadt, ⸚e
on a trip auf Reisen 10
on average durchschnittlich
on average im Durchschnitt 15
on foot zu Fuß 4
on television im Fernsehen 14
on the go, on the road unterwegs 13
on the radio im Radio 14
on the second, third, fourth ... floor im ersten, zweiten, dritten, ... Stock 5
on the weekend am Wochenende 4
on, on top of, onto auf 7
Once more, please. Noch einmal, bitte! 1
one man 1
onion die Zwiebel, -n 9
only einzig 11
only nur 3; erst 1, 9
open auf•schlagen, schlägt, schlug auf, aufgeschlagen 14
open geöffnet 9

open öffnen 5

open-air market der Markt, ⸚e 7 SV, 9

open to the world weltoffen

opera die Oper, -n 7 SV; 12

opinion die Meinung, -en

opinion poll die Meinungsumfrage, -n

opposite der Gegensatz, ⸚e,

optimistic optimistisch 3 SV

or oder 3, 4

orange die Apfelsine, -n

orange die Orange, -n 9

orange orange 3

order bestellen 9

order die Ordnung 6

orientation die Orientierung, -en 15

other andere 1, 12

other sonstig 15

otherwise sonst 9

out of, from aus (+dat.) 1, 4

oval oval 6

oven der Ofen, ⸚ 5

overcast bedeckt 4

overdo überfordern

overtime die Überstunde, -n 13 SV

own eigen 13

owner der Besitzer, -/die Besitzerin, -nen 13

P

pack packen 10

package das Paket, -e 10

page die Seite, -n

pain der Schmerz, -en 6

painter der Maler, -/die Malerin, -nen 12

painting die Malerei

panty hose die Strumpfhose, -n 8 SV

paper das Papier, -e 2

paper das Referat, -e 4

parents die Eltern, (pl.) 2

part der Teil, -e 4, 15

part-time teilzeit 15

partner der Partner, -/die Partnerin, -nen 2

pass a test eine Prüfung bestehen 11

passport der Paß, ⸚sse 10

patented patentiert

patient der Patient, -en, -en/die Patientin, -nen 6 SV

pay bezahlen/zahlen 5

pay der Lohn, ⸚e 13

pay die Bezahlung, -en 13

pay zahlen 7

pea die Erbse, -n 9

peach der Pfirsich, -e 9 SV

pear die Birne, -n 9

pedestrial zone die Fußgängerzone, -n 7 SV

pencil der Bleistift, -e 2

penny der Pfennig, -e 8

pension die Pension, -en 13

pension die Rente, -n 2

people die Leute (pl.) 2

people die Menschen (pl.) 4

pepper der Pfeffer 9

pepper die Paprikaschote, -n 9 SV

peppermint tea der Pfefferminztee, -s 9 SV

per night pro Nacht 10

per pro 10

percentage der Prozentsatz, ⸚e

perhaps vielleicht 4

permit erlauben 15

personal pronoun das Personalpronomen, -

personal(ly) persönlich 13

personality die Persönlichkeit, -en 13

personnel manager der Personalchef, -s/die Personalchefin, -nen 13 SV

pessimistic pessimistisch 3 SV

pet das Haustier, -e 12 P

pharmacy die Apotheke, -n 8

philosophy die Philosophie 11

photograph fotografieren 4

physician der Arzt, ⸚e/die Ärztin, -nen 2

physics die Physik 11

piano das Klavier, -e 12

pick out aus•suchen 5

pick up ab•holen 10

pick up, clean up auf•räumen 5 SV

picture das Bild, -er 2

piece das Stück, -e 9

pineapple die Ananas 9 SV

ping-pong das Tischtennis 12

pink rosa 3

pizza die Pizza, -s

place die Stelle, -n 7; der Ort, -e 7

place for a cure der Kurort, -e 6 SV

place, der Platz, ⸚e 1 SV, 3

place stellen 7

plan planen 12

planning die Planung

plant die Pflanze, -n

play spielen 2

play das Theaterstück, -e 12

pleasant angenehm

please; you are welcome bitte 1

Please repeat. Wiederholen Sie, bitte! 1

Please sit down! Nehmen Sie Platz! 1

Please write. Schreiben Sie, bitte! 1

please gefallen (gefällt), gefiel, gefallen 4

pleasure (with) gern 2

plum die Pflaume, -n 9 SV

plumber der Klempner, -/die Klempnerin, -nen 13; der Gas- und Wasserinstallateur, -e/die Gas- und Wasserinstallateurin, -nen 13 SV

plus plus 1

pocket money das Taschengeld, -er

pocket watch die Taschenuhr, -en 4 SV

poem das Gedicht, -e

point of view der Standpunkt, -e 14 SV

Poland das Polen 10

police die Polizei (sg.) 7 SV

polish putzen 5

political economics die Volkswirtschaft 11 SV

political science die Politologie 11

politics die Politik 14

polka dotted gepunktet 3 SV

pop music die Popmusik 12 SV

pork das Schweinefleisch 9

Portugal das Portugal 2, 10

position die Stellung, -en 13

possibility die Möglichkeit, -en

possible möglich 12

post office die Post 7

postcard die Postkarte, -n 10

poster das Poster, - 3

potato die Kartoffel, -n 9

potted plant die Topfblume, -n

pound das Pfund, -e 9

practical nurse der Arzthelfer, - /die Arzthelferin, -nen 13 SV

practical nurse der Heilgehilfe, -n/Heilgehilfin, -nen

practical(ly) praktisch 3 SV

practice die Praxis, -xen 13 SV

praise loben

pregnant schwanger 15

prejudice das Vorurteil, -e 15

prepare for vor•bereiten (sich) auf (+acc.) 11

prescribed vorgeschrieben 15 P

present das Geschenk, -e 4

president der Präsident, -en, -en/die Präsidentin, -nen 1

press die Presse, -n 14

pretzel die Brezel, -n 9 SV

price der Preis, -e 9

probably wahrscheinlich 7

problem das Problem, -e 5

professional(ly) beruflich 15

professor der Professor, -en/die Professorin, -nen 2

profit der Gewinn, -e 13 SV

program die Sendung, -en 14

program, channel das Programm, -e 14

progress der Fortschritt, -e 15

prohibit verbieten, verbot, verboten 14

prohibition das Verbot, -e 14

promise versprechen (verspricht), versprach, versprochen 8

pronunciation die Aussprache, -n

protect schützen 14

proud stolz

prove beweisen, bewies, bewiesen 14

psychology die Psychologie 11

public öffentlich 13, 15

pudding der Pudding 9 SV

pullover der Pullover, - (der Pulli, -s) 8

punctual pünktlich 13

punctuality die Pünktlichkeit

pupil der Schüler, -/die Schülerin, -nen 11

purple purpur 3

purple lila 3 SV

put on make up schminken (sich) 6

Q

quarter das Viertel, - 4

question die Frage, -n 1

question word das Fragewort, -̈er 1

quickly, fast schnell 1

Quickly, please. Schnell, bitte. 1

quiet leise 12

quiet ruhig 5

Quiet, please. Ruhe, bitte! 1

quite ziemlich 12

R

race die Rasse, -n 15

radio der Rundfunk 14 SV

Radio/TV station der Sender, - 14

radish das Radieschen, - 9 SV

rain der Regen 4

rain regnen 4

raincoat der Regenmantel, -̈ 8 SV

raising of children die Kindererziehung 15

range der Herd, -e 5

rarely selten 6

rate of exchange der Kurs, -e 10, 11

rather lieber 12

raw roh 9

razor der Rasierapparat, -e 8 SV

read lesen (liest), las, gelesen 3

reality die Wirklichkeit 15

really tatsächlich 1; wirklich 2

reason der Grund, -̈e 8

reason die Ursache, -n 8

receive bekommen, bekam, bekommen 5

receive erhalten (erhält), erhielt, erhalten 12

receptionist die Empfangsdame, -n [female]

recommend empfehlen (empfiehlt), empfahl, empfohlen 5

record die Schallplatte, -n 14

recorder die Blockflöte, -en 12 SV

recover erholen (sich) 12

recovery die Erholung 12

red cabbage der Rotkohl 9 SV

red rot (ö) 3

redeem ein•lösen to cash (a check), 10

refrigerator der Kühlschrank, -̈e 3

regular(ly) regelmäßig 6

reject ab•lehnen 12

relationship die Beziehung, -en 15

relax entspannen (sich) 6

reliability die Zuverlässigkeit

reliable zuverlässig 13

religion die Religion, -en 15

remain bleiben, blieb, ist geblieben 4

remember merken (sich) 11

remember erinnern (sich) an (+acc.) 8

remind (someone) of erinnern an (+acc.) 11

rent (accomodations to someone) vermieten 5

rent mieten 5

repeat wieder•holen 5

report der Bericht, -e 14; in academic circles das Referat, -e 4

research untersuchen

researcher der Forscher, -/die Forscherin, -nen 11

reserve reservieren 10

reside wohnen 1

resident der Bewohner, -/die Bewohnerin, -nen

responsibility die Pflicht, -en 13; die Verantwortlichkeit, -en 13 SV

rest ausruhen (sich) 6 SV

rest die Ruhe 7

restaurant das Restaurant, -s 7

restless unruhig 5

result das Ergebnis, -se

resume der Lebenslauf, ̈e

return a call zurück•rufen, rief zurück, zurückgerufen 14

return trip die Rückfahrt, -en

return zurück•kommen, kam zurück, ist zurückgekommen 5

rice der Reis 9 SV

ride (an animal) reiten, ritt, ist geritten 4

right das Recht, -e 13

right rechts 7

ring der Ring, -e 4 SV

ring finger der Ringfinger, - 6 SV

ring läuten 8 SV

rinse spülen 6

ripe reif 9

rock group die Rockgruppe, -n

roll das Brötchen, - 9

roller skate der Rollschuh, -e 4

romanesque romanisch

Romance languages and literatures die Romanistik 11 SV

romantic romantisch 3 SV

romanticism die Romantik

roof das Dach, ̈er 5 SV

room das Zimmer, - 3; (slang) ̅ die Bude, -n

roommate der Zimmerkamerad, -en, -en/Zimmerkameradin, -nen 5

rosehip tea der Hagebuttentee, -s SV 9

round rund 6

rules die Bestimmung, -en

run laufen (läuft), lief, ist gelaufen 3

runny nose der Schnupfen 6 SV

Russia das Rußland 1

rustic ländlich

S

sad traurig 3

sail segeln 12

salad der Salat, -e 9

salary das Gehalt, ̈er 13

sales person der Vertreter, -/die Vertreterin, -nen

sales person der Verkäufer, -/die Verkäuferin, -nen 2

salt das Salz 9

salt too much versalzen 9 SV

salty salzig 9

same to you gleichfalls 9

sandal die Sandale, -n 8 SV

satellite der Satellit, -en 14

satisfied zufrieden 3

Saturday der Samstag 4; der Sonnabend 4 SV

sauerkraut das Sauerkraut 9 SV

sauna die Sauna, -s 12

sausage die Wurst, ̈e 9

save sparen 4

savings institution die Sparkasse, -n 10

saxophone das Saxophon 12 SV

say sagen 5

scarf der Schal, -s 4 SV

scenically landschaftlich

scholarship das Stipendium, ien

school die Schule, -n 4

school system das Schulsystem, -e 11

Scotland das Schottland 10

scour schrubben

scout der Pfadfinder, -/die Pfadfinderin, -nen 10 SV

scrub schrubben

scrubbing the floor das Fußbodenwischen 15 SV

search, look for suchen 3

search for an apartment die Wohnungssuche, -n 5 SV

season die Jahreszeit, -en 4

seat der Platz, ̈e SV **3**

second die Sekunde, -n 11

secretary der Sekretär, -e/Sekretärin, -nen 1

security die Sicherung

see sehen (sieht), sah, gesehen 3

see again wieder•sehen (sieht), sah, gesehen

self confidence die Selbstsicherheit

self-confident, self-assertive selbstbewußt 15

self-employed person der Selbständige, -n/die Selbständige, -en 13

self-initiative die Eigeninitiative, -en

self-reliant, independentl selbständig 13

sell verkaufen 2

semester das Semester, - 11

send schicken 8

sense of duty das Pflichtbewußtsein 13

sense of order der Ordnungssinn

separated getrennt 2

September der September 4

series die Serie, -n 14

serious(ly), earnest(ly) ernst 3 SV

service der Dienst, -e 13

set (put) stellen 7

set a date verabreden (sich) 7 SV

several mehrere 12; einige 12

sew nähen

sexual sexuell 15

shampoo das Shampoo, -s 8

share teilen 5

shave rasieren (sich) 6

she sie 1

shine scheinen, schien, geschienen 4

ship das Schiff, -e 4

shirt das Hemd, -en 8

shoe der Schuh, -e 8

shop ein•kaufen 8

shopping list die Einkaufsliste, -n 8

short kurz (ü) 2

shorts die Shorts (pl.) 8 SV

should sollen 4

shoulder die Schulter, -n 6

show zeigen 12

shower die Dusche, -n 3

siblings die Geschwister (pl.) 2

sick krank (ä) 1

sickness, illness die Krankheit, -en 6

sign das Schild, -er 7

simple (simply) einfach 8

since seit (+dat.) 4

sing singen, sang, gesungen 2

single einzeln 10

single ledig 2

single room das Einzelzimmer, - 10

sister die Schwester, -n 2

sister-in-law die Schwägerin, -nen 2

sit down hin•setzen (sich) 6

sit down setzen (sich) 7

sit sitzen (sitzt), saß, gesessen 7

skeptical skeptisch 3 SV

ski das Ski laufen (läuft Ski) 4

ski der Ski, -er 4

skin die Haut, ¨e 6 SV

skinny, thin dünn 6

skirt der Rock, ¨e 8

sky blue himmelblau 3 SV

sleep schlafen (schläft), schlief, geschlafen 4

sleep late lange schlafen 12

sleeping bag der Schlafsack, ¨e 10

sleeping pill die Schlaftablette, -n 6

slicing machine die Brotschneidemaschine, -n 5 SV

slide presentation der Bildvortrag, ¨e

slow(ly) langsam 7

small klein 2

small package das Päckchen, - 10 SV

smoke rauchen 6

smooth glatt 6

snack der Imbiß, -sse 9

snack bar die Imbißstube, -n 9

snack bar der Imbiß, -sse 9

sneeze niesen 6 SV

snow der Schnee 4

snow schneien 4

snow white schneeweiß 3 SV

so long tschüs 1

so that damit 8

soap die Seife, -n 8

soap opera die Seifenoper, -n 14

soccerball der Fußball, ¨e 11

social(ly) sozial 13

society die Gesellschaft, -en 12

sociology die Soziologie 11

sock die Socke, -n 8

sofa das Sofa, -s 5

soldier der Soldat, -en/die Soldatin, -nen 2

solve lösen 15

some einige 12

sometimes manchmal 2

son der Sohn, ¨e 2

soon bald 2

sore muscles der Muskelkater 6 SV

sore throat die Halsschmerzen (pl.) 6

sound klingen, klang, geklungen

soup die Suppe, -n 9

sour sour 9

South America das Südamerika

south der Süden

Southern Germany das Süddeutschland

spaghetti die Spaghetti (pl.) 9 SV

Spain das Spanien 2

speak sprechen (spricht), sprach, gesprochen 3

special exhibit die Sonderausstellung, -en

special offer das Sonderangebot,-e

specialty die Spezialität, -en 13

spend (time) verbringen, verbrachte, verbracht 10

spend the night übernachten 10

spicy scharf 9

spinach der Spinat 9 SV

sport shoe der Sportschuh, -e 8 SV

sport suit der Trainingsanzug, ¨e 12 SV

sports show die Sportreportage, -n 14

sprain something verstauchen (sich etwas) 6 SV

Spring der Frühling 4; das Frühjahr, -e 4 SV

square (as in location) der Platz, ¨e SV 3

stable stabil 5 SV

stair die Treppe, -n 5 SV

stamp die Briefmarke, -n 10

stand stehen, stand, gestanden 7

standing clock die Standuhr, -en 4 SV

stay bleiben, blieb, ist geblieben 4

stay-at-home body der Stubenhocker

step der Schritt, -e

stepbrother der Stiefbruder, ¨ 2

stepfather der Stiefvater, ¨ 2

stepmother die Stiefmutter, ¨ 2

stepsister die Stiefschwester, -n 2

stereo das Stereo, -s 3

stipend das Stipendium, -ien

stomach der Bauch, ¨e 6; der Magen, ¨ 6

stomach ache die Magenschmerzen (pl.) 6

stop auf•hören 6; halten (hält) hielt, gehalten 7

store ab•speichern
store das Geschäft, -e 5
store der Laden, ¨ 7
stovetop der Herd, -e 5
straight ahead geradeaus 7
straight glatt 6
strange merkwürdig 11
strange fremd 15
strawberry die Erdbeere, -n 9
street die Straße, -n 7
street map die Straßenkarte, -n 7 SV
streetcar die Straßenbahn, -en 4
strenuous anstrengend
stress der Streß 6
suffer from stress unter Streß leiden 5
stretch strecken (sich) 6 SV
striped gestreift 3 SV
stroll einen Spaziergang machen 8
stroll through town der Stadtbummel, - 12
stroll der Spaziergang, ¨e 8
strong stark (ä) 9; stabil 5 SV
strong, severe streng
student cafeteria die Mensa 7 SV; 11
student center, student union das Studienwerk, -e 7 SV
student der Student, -en, -en/die Studentin, -nen 2
student dorm das Studentenwohnheim, -e 5
study studieren 2
stupid (slang) doof 3
subconscious das Unterbewußtsein
subdivision die Siedlung, -en
subject das Fach, ¨er 4
success der Erfolg, -e 8
successful erfolgreich 8
suffer leiden, litt, gelitten 6
suffice reichen 11
sugar der Zucker 9
suggest vor•schlagen, (schlägt), schlug vor, vorgeschlagen 8, 10
suggestion der Vorschlag, ¨e

suit (women's) das Kostüm, -e 8 SV
suit (men's) der Anzug, ¨e 8
suitcase der Koffer, - 10
summary die Zusammenfassung, -en
summer der Sommer 4
sun die Sonne, -n 4
Sunday der Sonntag 4
sunny sonnig 4
supermarket der Supermarkt, ¨e 9
be supposed to sollen 4
supper das Abendbrot 4; das Abendessen 9
sure sicher 8
surely tatsächlich 1
surprise die Überraschung, -en 8
sweat schwitzen 6 SV
sweat shirt das Sweatshirt, -s 8
Sweden das Schweden 10
sweet süß 9
swim schwimmen, schwamm, ist geschwommen 2
swimming pool das Schwimmbad, ¨er
swimming trunks die Badehose, -n 4
Swiss cheese Schweizer Käse 9
switch off aus•schalten
switch on ein•schalten 14 SV
switch over um•schalten 14 SV
Switzerland die Schweiz 2
symptom das Symptom 6 SV

T

T-shirt das T-shirt, -s 8
table der Tisch, -e 2
take nehmen (nimmt), nahm, genommen 3
take (time) dauern 8
take a shower duschen (sich) 3
take a test eine Prüfung machen/schreiben 11
take in auf•nehmen, nimmt, nahm auf, aufgenommen

take care of pflegen SV 6, versorgen 11
take place statt•finden, fand statt, stattgefunden 14
take, register for (a course) belegen 11
taking out the garbage das Mülleimerleeren 15 SV
talent das Talent, -e 13 SV
talk about sprechen über 11
tap water das Leitungswasser 9 SV
taste schmecken 4
tasty lecker 9
taxi das Taxi, -s 7
tea der Tee, -s 9
teach unterrichten 11; bei•bringen, brachte bei, beigebracht
teacher der Lehrer, -/die Lehrerin, -nen 2
team die Mannschaft, -en 12
technical school die Fachhochschule, -n 13 SV
telegram das Telegramm, -e 8 SV
telephone das Telefon, -e 2, 3
telephone book das Telefonbuch, ¨er 8
telephone booth die Telefonzelle, -n 8
telephone company das Fernmeldeamt, ¨er 8 SV
telephone conversation das Telefongespräch, -e 8
telephone number die Telefonnummer, -n 1
telephone system das Telefonsystem, -e 8 SV
television news die Tagesschau, -en 14 SV
tell erzählen 5
temperature die Temperatur, -en 4 SV
ten years ago vor [zehn] Jahren 10
tender, gentle zärtlich 15
tennis das Tennis 2
tennis player der Tennisspieler, -/die Tennisspielerin, -nen 1

tennis racket der Tennisschläger, - 4

tent das Zelt, -e 10 SV

term paper die Semesterarbeit, -en 11

terrace die Terrasse, -n 5 SV

terrible schlimm 7

test die Prüfung, -en 11

Thank you very much. Danke sehr! 1

Thank you very much. Herzlichen Dank! 8

thank danken 4

thank you! danke! 1

Thanks, same to you! (Danke,) gleichfalls! 9

that daß 8

that jen- 4

theater das Theater, - 12

theme words der Themenwortschatz, ⁻e 1

theology die Theologie 11

theoretical(ly) theoretisch

there is, there are es gibt 3

therefore also 5

they sie 1

thick dick 6

thief der Dieb, -e/die Diebin, -nen

thing, object die Sache, -n 1, 3; **item** das Ding, -e 12

think about überlegen (sich) 9

think denken, dachte, gedacht 5, 7

think of denken (an) (+acc.) 11

thirsty durstig 9

this dies- 4

three-room apartment die Dreizimmerwohnung, -en 5 SV

thrilling aufregend, spannend **14**

through durch (+acc.) 3

thumb der Daumen, - 6 SV

thunderstorm das Gewitter, - 4 SV

Thursday der Donnerstag 4

ticket das Ticket, -s 10

ticket [for travelling] die Fahrkarte, -n 7

tidy (tidily), neat(ly) ordentlich 13

tie (in sports) unentschieden 12 SV

time das Mal

time die Zeit, -en 5

tip das Trinkgeld, -er 9

tip der Tip, -s

tired müde 1

To your health! Zum Wohl! 9

to, after, past nach (+dat.) 4

to, too zu 4

to, toward (+acc.) an 7

Today is [January fifth]. Heute haben wir den [5. (fünften) Januar]. 7

today heute 2

toe der Zeh, -en 6

together zusammen 4

toilet die Toilette, -n 3; das WC, -s 5 SV

tolerant tolerant 3 SV

tomorrow morgen 1

tongue die Zunge, -n 6

too auch

too bad schade 7

tooth der Zahn, ⁻e 6

toothache die Zahnschmerzen (pl.) 6

toothbrush die Zahnbürste, -n 8

toothpaste die Zahnpasta 8

topic das Thema, -en 8

tourist der Tourist, -en, -en/die Touristin, -nen

towel das Handtuch, ⁻er 3

town hall das Rathaus, ⁻er 7 SV

track and field die Leichtathletik 12 SV

traditional traditionell 15

traffic der Verkehr 7

traffic light die Ampel, -n 7

train der Zug, ⁻e 4

train die Bahn, -en 7

train station der Bahnhof, ⁻e 7

train trainieren

transfer um•steigen, stieg um, ist umgestiegen 7

transportable transportabel 14

trash der Müll 5 SV

travel fahren (fährt), fuhr, ist gefahren 3; reisen 10

travel agency das Reisebüro, -s 10

travel guide der Reiseführer, - 12

traveler's check der Reisescheck, -s 10

traveler's information center das Fremdenverkehrsamt, ⁻er 10

trend der Trend, -s

trousers die Hose, -n 8

truly tatsächlich 1; wirklich 2

trumpet die Trompete, -n 12 SV

try versuchen 8

try on an•probieren 8

try out aus•probieren 5

try out probieren 5

Tuesday der Dienstag 4

tuition die Studiengebühr, -en

Turkey die Türkei 10

turn into (a street, etc.) ab•biegen, bog ab, ist abgebogen 7

turn into [a street] ein•biegen 7 SV

TV, television set der Fernseher, - 3

twice a week zweimal pro Woche 6

twice zweimal 6

typewriter die Schreibmaschine 3

U

ugly häßlich 3

uncle der Onkel, -s 2

uncomfortable, uncomfortably unbequem 5

uncomplicated unkompliziert 3 SV

underground train die U-Bahn, -en 7

understand verstehen, verstand, verstanden 1

underwear die Unterwäsche (sg.) 8

Unfortunately not. Leider geht es nicht. 8

union die Gewerkschaft, -en 13 SV

university die Universität, -en 4

university level institution die Hochschule, -n 11

unusual merkwürdig 11

up front, in front vorne 7

up to, until bis zu 7, 8

use benutzen 3

usually normalerweise

utensil das Gerät, -e 5, 14

V

vacation der Urlaub (sg.) 4

vacation die Ferien (pl.) 12

vacuuming das Staubsaugen 15 SV

various verschieden 12

VCR der Videorecorder, - 14

veal or pork cutlet das Schnitzel, - 9

vegetable juice der Gemüsesaft, -̈e

vegetables das Gemüse (sg.) 9

verb das Verb, -en

Very good! Sehr gut! 1

very sehr 1

video das Video, -s 14

view die Aussicht, -n 9

village das Dorf, -̈er

violin die Geige, -n 12 SV

visit besuchen 2

visit der Besuch, -e 2

vitamin capsule die Vitaminkapsel, -n 6 SV

vitamin tablet die Vitamintablette, -n 6

vocational school die Berufsschule, -n 13

vocational training die Berufsausbildung, -en 13

W

waist die Taille, -n 6 SV

wait warten 1

wait for warten auf (+acc.) 11

Wait! Warte mal! (informal) 1

waiter der Kellner, -/die Kellnerin, -nen 2

waiter der Ober, -/die Oberin, -nen 9

walk der Spaziergang, -̈e 6

walking stick der Spazierstock, -̈e 10 SV

walkman der Walkman, -s 3

wall die Wand, -̈e 2

wall clock die Wanduhr, -en 4 SV

want to do something Lust haben, (hat), hatte, gehabt

want to, want wollen (will), wollte, gewollt 3, 5

wardrobe, closet der Schrank, -̈e 3

warm warm (ä) 2

warn warnen 14

wash (one's hands) waschen (wäscht) (sich), wusch, gewaschen 6

wash basin das Waschbecken, - 3

washing machine die Waschmaschine, -n 5 SV

washing windows das Fensterputzen 15 SV

waste of time die Zeitverschwendung

wastebasket der Papierkorb, -̈e 3

watch out auf•passen 7

watch TV fern•sehen (sieht), sah, gesehen 5

water das Wasser 5 SV

we wir 1

wear tragen (trägt), trug, getragen 8

weather das Wetter 2, 4

Wednesday der Mittwoch 4

week die Woche, -n 4

weekday der Wochentag, -e 4

weekend house das Wochenendhaus, -̈er 5 SV

well wohl 6

well also 5

well, well now, well then, (flavoring particle) nun 8

what was 1

What color is...? Welche Farbe hat...? 3

What day is today? Welcher Tag ist heute? 4

What do you think of...? Wie findest du...? 5

What hurts? Was tut Ihnen/dir weh? 6

What is today's date? Den wievielten haben wir heute? 7

What is your name? Wie heißt du/heißen Sie? 1

What is your telephone number? Wie ist deine/Ihre Telefonnummer? 1

What kind of ...? (sg.) Was für ein ...? 8; **(pl.)** Was für ...? 8

What time is it? Wie spät ist es? 4

What time is it? Wieviel Uhr ist es? 4

what about worum 4

What's going on? What's wrong? Was ist los? 3

What's up? Was gibt's denn? 8

What's going on today? Was gibts heute? 14

Pardon me, what did you say? Wie bitte? 1

When is your birthday? Wann hast du/haben Sie Geburtstag? 4

when (past time) als 8; (in questions) wann 2; (in sense of whenever) wenn 8

where wo 1

where from woher 1

where to wohin 7

whether ob 8

which welch- 4

white weiß 3

who wer 1

whole ganz 6

wholesale business person [male] der Großhandelskaufmann, die Großhandelskaufleute (pl.) 13 SV

wholesale business person [female] die Großhandelskauffrau, die Großhandelskaufleute (pl.) 13 SV

whose wessen

why warum 3

wide breit 6

wiener das Würstchen, - 9

win gewinnen, gewann, gewonnen 12 SV

wind der Wind, -e 12

windbreaker der Anorak, -s 8 SV; 11

window das Fenster, - 2

windsurfing das Windsurfen 12 SV

windy windig 4

wine der Wein, -e

winner der Gewinner, -/die Gewinnerin 12 SV

Winter der Winter 4

wish, desire wünschen 12

wish der Wunsch, ¨e 12

with, by means of mit (+dat.) 4

without ohne (+acc.) 3

without ohne ... zu 10

women's liberation movement die Frauenbewegung, -en 15 SV

word das Wort, ¨er

work arbeiten 1

work die Arbeit, -en 4

work in the yard im Garten arbeiten 5 SV

worker der Arbeiter, -/die Arbeiterin, -nen 13

world die Welt, -en 13

worth the money, of good value preiswert 5

would like möchte(n) 3

wrist das Handgelenk, -e 6 SV

wrist watch die Armbanduhr, -en 4 SV

write schreiben, schrieb, geschrieben 1

write a report ein Referat schreiben 11

write about schreiben über (+acc.), schrieb, geschrieben 11

writer der Schriftsteller, -/die Schriftstellerin, -nen 12

wrong falsch 1

Y

yard, garden der Garten, ¨en 5

year das Jahr, -e 1

yellow gelb 3

Yellow Pages die Gelben Seiten 8

yes, after all, of course, (flavoring article) ja 1, 2

yesterday gestern 4

yoghurt das Joghurt 9

You have the wrong number. Sie sind falsch verbunden 8

you (fam. pl.); her; their ihr 1

you (fam. sg.) du 1

you, sg. and pl. formal Sie 1

young jung (ü) 3

youth der Jugendliche, -n, -n/die Jugendliche, -n

youth hostel die Jugendherberge, -n 10

place where youth meet das Jugendtreff, -s

Z

zoo der Zoo, -s 7 SV, 12

INDEX

This index contains all grammar points, vocabulary sets, pronunciation material, cultural notes, *Überall spricht man Deutsch* sections, and most *Tip!s* and *Redewendungen* contained in **Alles klar?**

CREDITS

Text Materials

25 Excerpt from Die Weber by Gerhart Hauptmann and Dat Stunnenglas and Weg un Ümweg covers reprinted with the kind permission of Verlag der Fehrs-Gilde, Neumünster; 47 courtesy of Lintracht, Inc. and America Woche; 66 reprinted with the permission of Möbel-Kiste;106 Luise; 118 Michel + Co.; 144 adapted from Bild-Zeitung; 151 American Association of Teachers of German, Modern Language Association; 158 Reprinted with the permission of Lady Gym; 172 Prof. Dr. Hans Harald Bräutigam, Die Zeit (Hamburg); 194 Göttingen; 208 CMDA Bonn; 209 Red Cross; 217 Osnabrück; 228 DeTeMedien: München; 254 Die Vegetarische Gaststatte & Cafe; 256 Jugendscala, March 1988; 260 Hildebrandts Fisch Restaurant; 269 Die Vegetarische Gaststatte & Cafe; 272 El Greco, Schwejk, La Luna; 283 Reisebüro Schmidt; 286 (DJH logo) Deutscher Wanderverlag, Dr. Mair & Schnalbel & Co., (Reisewörter) Tilde Michels, in: Der fliegende Robert, Viertes Jahrbuch der Kinderliteratur; 288 Skandinavisches Reisebüro; 301 Atrium Hotel Nürnberg; 302 Hotel Guide; 303 Train Schedule; 304 Hotel Guide; 305 Train Schedule; 306 Würzburg Hotels;309 Helga Novak/Palisaden; 316 Jonscher Buchhandlung; 319 Globus-Kartendienst; 326 UNI Berufswahl-Magazin; 327 Brigitte Dossier - Berufswahl '92; 329 TIP; 331 W. Lorenz and J. Wagner, Universität Hannover printed in Die Welt, Nr. 156; 334 Didactica, Die Neue Schule, Typisten-Studio, Direkt Computerschulung; 344 Deutschlands einziger zoologisch-botanischer Garten; 355 DAAD, "Hochschule und Ausland," leicht verändert; 362-363 Scala Jugendmagazin, leicht verändert; 366 Verkehrsamt der Stadt Freiburg; 368 and 370 Hannovers Theater; 371 Pferdessport Muskelkater, Hallorenmuseum, Carl-Zeiss-Planetarium; 373 AID 1991: Auswertungs- und Informationsdienst für Ernährung, Landwirtschaft und Forsten; 378 Globus-Kartendienst, IG Metall; 381 Quellen: DSW, IW printed in Mitteldeutsche Zeitung; 382 HARB Trading and Contracting; 383 Welt am Sonntag, Sonntag, 11. November 1990; 385 Brigitte '92; 388 Welt am Sonntag, Sonntag, 11. November 1990; 393-394 Globus-Kartendienst; 404 Deutschland Nachrichten, leicht verändert; 405 Globus-Kartendienst; 406 (left) Frankfurter Algemeine, (right) Studentenpresse, Pressevertriebs; 416 Reprinted with permission of the Wissenschafsliche Buchgesellschaft; 420 Text by Prüfungen zum deutschen Sprachdiplom der Kulturministerkonferenz (KMK), Stufe II and illustration by Ofczarek printed in TIP; 421 SITA; 426 Hallo, Hermann! by Jim Unger printed in TIP; 436 Quellen: Vereinte Nationen, Statistisches Bundesamt and graphic by Christoph Blumrich printed in Zeitschrift Deutschland; 437 Der Spiegel 39; 438 Berliner Morgenpost; 444 Illustration by Ofczarek; 445 Bundeszentrale für gesundheitliche Aufklärung;448 TIP; 454 (top) Birgit Rabisch/Nicht mit dir … und nicht ohne mich, (bottom) Karlhans Frank/Dimension; 458 Wolf Wondratschek

Photographs

Photographs are by the authors except for the following:

Cover and chapter openers (far left) Bernard Regent/Diaf (left center) T. Borredon/Explorer (right center) Robert Frerck/Odyssey Productions (far right) Frank Siteman/Monkmeyer Press; 25 Charlotte Kahler; 52 Robert Frerck/Odyssey Productions; 105 Charlotte Kahler; 183 (top) H. Gyssels/Diaf, (bottom) Fabricius-Taylor/Jerrican; 360 Muriel Raoux, Kani Alavi/East Side Gallery3